monsoonbooks

THE DEFENCE AND FALL OF SINGAPORE

Brian P. Farrell is Professor of History at National University of Singapore, where he has been teaching Military History since 1993. He is an authority on British Empire military history and in particular the fall of Singapore in 1942. His other books include *The Basis and Making of British Grand Strategy 1940-1943: Was There a Plan?*, *Between Two Oceans: A Military History of Singapore From First Settlement to Final British Withdrawal* (co-authored), *Sixty Years On: The Fall of Singapore Revisited* (co-edited) and *Leadership and Responsibility in the Second World War* (edited).

PRAISE FOR *THE DEFENCE AND FALL OF SINGAPORE*

'An exhaustive account of the clash between Japanese
and British Empire forces ... A multi-pronged attack on those
who made the defence of Malaya and Singapore their duty'
BBC History Magazine

'A complete and authoritative account ... a compelling read'
The British Army Review

'Startling ... reveals the real reason why the daring attack failed'
The Daily Express

'Excellent ... fills a yawning gap in the historical record'
Times Literary Supplement

T0159432

THE DEFENCE AND FALL

OF SINGAPORE

1940–1942

BRIAN P. FARRELL

monsoonbooks

Published in 2021
by Monsoon Books Ltd
www.monsoonbooks.co.uk

No.1 The Lodge, Burrough Court, Burrough on the Hill,
Melton Mowbray LE14 2QS, UK

ISBN (paperback): 9789814423885
ISBN (ebook): 9789814423892

First published in 2005 by Tempus Publishing Limited, UK.
Updated edition published in 2015 by Monsoon Books, Singapore.

Cover design by Cover Kitchen.
Front: Following the surrender of Singapore by the British in 1942, Japanese
soldiers march through the streets, in front of the General Post Office building.
Frontcover photograph©Robert Hunt Library/Mary Evans.
Back: Japanese troops celebrating atop a British gun, Singapore 1942.
Backcover photograph©Mainichi Shinbun.

National Library Board, Singapore Cataloguing-in-Publication Data
Farrell, Brian P. (Brian Padair), 1960- author.
The defence and fall of Singapore 1940-1942 / Brian P. Farrell. – Updated
edition – Singapore : Monsoon Books Pte Ltd, 2015.
pages cm
"First published in 2005 by Tempus Publishing Limited."
Includes bibliographical references and index.
ISBN : 978-981-4423-88-5 (paperback)
1.   World War, 1939-1945 - Campaigns - Singapore. I. Title.
D767.55
940.5425957 -- dc23   OCN913498128

Printed and bound in Great Britain by Clays Ltd, Elcograf S.p.A.
23 22 21   4 5 6

Contents

Note on Citations

Readers wishing to consult full and detailed endnote citations
may find them online at:
www.monsoonbooks.co.uk/citations/the-defence-and-fall-of-singapore

Introduction

When this book was first published ten years ago, I wrote that it was difficult to find anyone personally involved in the defence and fall of Singapore, now more than 70 years ago. That is even more so today. But anyone wanting to know more about it can easily find something to read. The literature devoted to this historical event ranges from the useless to the enduring. The latter includes studies of the campaign as a whole, or aspects of it, or institutions or groups involved in it. Personal memoirs provide accounts of events from different vantage points and points of view, enough to give a pretty reasonable cross-section of personal experience. So the first question any historian writing about the defence and fall of Singapore in the Second World War must answer is "why do we need another book on this?"

The idea that a topic has been "done," that there is nothing more to be said, is based on misunderstanding how we engage history. Every generation reconsiders the past, often with new questions to ask, new interests to pursue, new prejudices to probe. But you need something more specific to persuade readers to travel down a beaten trail. You need to answer yes to at least one of the following questions. Is there new information that must be considered? Are there previously unavailable primary sources that must be explored? Is there some serious gap in our knowledge that must be filled? Are there defining myths that need to be debunked? Important dimensions that need to be reassessed? Regarding the defence and fall of Singapore in the Second World War, the answer to all those questions is yes.

The most common description from the British point of view is that the fall of Singapore in 1942 was the largest and most humiliating surrender of a British army in the Second World War, if not in the history of the British Empire. One study, *Singapore: The Battle that Changed the World*,[1] described the defeat as the death blow of the British Empire itself. The fall of Singapore involved several member states of the Empire, so it provoked international recriminations and finger-pointing. Such trauma affected the release of official records to the archives for scholarly research. In the 1960s the British government changed its policy regarding official records, allowing most to be released to researchers after 30 rather than the previous 50 years of retention. That led to a decision to release all declassified records from the Second World War in 1972, in one fell swoop. One of the more notable classified exceptions was a significant amount of material relating to the defence and fall of Singapore. Many documents relating to that disaster were held over for a full 50 years. Australia, the principal independent partner in the failed defence of Singapore, followed suit with its records. We were always bound to know less about this campaign than any other the British Empire fought during the war, because it ended in total defeat and mass surrender. Many contemporary records were destroyed in Singapore to prevent their falling into Japanese hands. The British and Australian decisions to hold on to many surviving documents, mainly because most were so full of finger-pointing, left us relying too heavily on constricted "official" histories and incomplete or unreliable memories.

Starting in 1992, British and Australian authorities bit the bullet and began to release their remaining relevant official records.[2] While this provoked yet another round in the endless argument between the two over who to blame for defeat and disaster, it also made available to researchers war diaries, reports, telegrams, and other records read up to then only by the tightly constrained "official" historians–who did not cite their sources. It is now possible to explore with authority such questions as why commanders in Malaya and Singapore made the decisions they did, how the troops actually fought, what the air force did, what impact intelligence had, and what happened in the final battle on Singapore island. Some of these records were cited in previous works, one by this author.[3] But this study is the first to draw on all previously retained British and Australian primary sources, plus translated Japanese records, to explain why Malaya and Singapore fell as easily as they did. This allows it to add new information and correct old misconceptions about this touchstone of imperial military history.

What about serious gaps in our knowledge? Four stand out: why the defence of Malaya became so badly disconnected from grand strategy for the war as a whole; why the army lost battles so easily in Malaya; what happened on Singapore island in the last battle; and how the Japanese did what they did, from planning to conquest. In the Japanese case, our knowledge was always circumscribed because many Japanese documents were destroyed by Allied bombing attacks in 1945. A trickle of memoirs over the years did a bit to redress this, but a more important source is the collection of postmortem narratives written shortly after the war by Japanese officers, prompted by Allied military intelligence. All the narratives related to the Malayan campaign, written by officers involved in directing it, are now available in English. That allows this study to explain with more authority how the Japanese won so easily, why the mistakes they made were not decisive, and why this was not a "close run thing" at the end–as has too often been believed.

That leads to the next question. Beyond the Japanese situation in the last battle on Singapore island, there is a long list of myths that can now be debunked with authority. They include the following untenable but long-standing claims: the prewar strategy to defend Singapore was abandoned in 1940; the air force did no serious fighting at all; local resources were so badly misused the army was crippled; decisions in Singapore, not London, turned defeat into disaster; the Australians cut and ran in the final battle, destroying the defence. The most famous myth of all is the claim Singapore fell because the great guns of its coastal defences pointed the wrong way. On one level this study can only repeat what others have argued—the problem was neither that simple nor decisive. But on another level, it makes a more original contribution. It explains why the condition of Singapore's fixed defences provides vital insight into how the British Empire planned to defend these colonies.

The final question is whether new dimensions in the story are significant enough to justify a reassessment. The answer is yes. Individuals and circumstances have understandably been the central focus of serious studies about the fall of Singapore. What needs to be better understood is the military system by which the British Empire tried to defend itself. Personalities will always matter in warfare. One theatre commander will behave differently from another in the same position. The British Empire armed forces that defended Malaya and Singapore were however the product of a military system shaped by the Great War. The army in particular could not cope with the return of mobility to land warfare in France in 1940. That shock did not spark change rapidly enough to affect how it defended Singapore. This left the army exceptionally vulnerable when it was forced to fight a campaign for which it was simply not equipped, either mentally or physically.

The fall of Singapore, simple defeat, was a consequence of two things: the fact no one resolved a fundamental dilemma at the heart of imperial defence after the Great War, and the course of war in Europe from spring 1940. Circumstances forced the British to fight for sheer survival against a much stronger enemy, leaving very little to spare for other duties. They also brought the putative enemy within easy striking distance of the colonies the British were now least able to protect. Finally, circumstances left the defenders of Singapore facing an enemy with no serious distractions at hand and time to strike. But defeat is one thing—disaster another. How did defeat become disaster?

The argument that the fall of Singapore was caused by a chain reaction of mistakes stretching over two decades is not original. But the most popular version is that defeat became full scale disaster not because of what happened before the Japanese attacked but rather *solely* because incompetent commanders mishandled the campaign.[4] This is not tenable. There was no disconnection between the decisions that left Singapore vulnerable in the first place and the campaign in which it was lost. The same military system directed both. The weakest link was the intersection between different levels of command and responsibility. Plans to defend the Empire in a war against Japan were based on a grand strategy that never made military sense. Never. That compromised theatre strategy for defending the Far East against a Japanese attack. That theatre strategy compromised the army's campaign strategy to defend Malaya. That strategy compelled it to fight at the wrong places and times with the wrong tactics. The system produced the plans, men and means. It, not they, invited disaster. This study reconnects things which should never have been separated: the politics of imperial defence, the plans they produced, and how they shaped what happened on the spot. From 1921 to 1942 the British Empire's military system tried to defend Singapore by insisting the situation must fit the plan, at all levels. This was the reverse of sound military practice, at any level. This book explains why it was made, why it persisted, and how it turned defeat into disaster.

Acknowledgements

This book really began to come to life in 1995, when I joined a team writing a general military history of Singapore. That project was led by Malcolm Murfett, whose deep knowledge, commitment to scholarship and great energy made it work–and inspires me still. While working on that book, my research convinced me the story of the most dramatic moment in Singapore's military history badly needed serious reassessment. My chance to do just that came from Hew Strachan. When he heard I was working on the defence and fall of Singapore in the Second World War he invited me to approach Tempus, on whose behalf he was General Editor of the series Battles and Campaigns. This launched a partnership with Tempus and my very patient and understanding publisher, Jonathan Reeve. I thank them both for all their support. My employer, the Department of History, National University of Singapore, generously supported my work with both time and money. I am especially grateful to the Department Head, Tan Tai Yong, and the Dean of the Faculty of Arts, Lily Kong, for their confidence. A memorable conference we hosted at the National University of Singapore, on the 60th anniversary of the surrender of the island, gave me the chance to share ideas with, and learn from, the finest scholars working on the Pacific War and the defence of the British Empire. My friends and colleagues Karl Hack and Paul Kratoska generously shared references and ideas. I came away the wiser from exchanges with Joan Beaumont, Chris Bell, Peter Dennis, Alec Douglas, Kent Fedorowich, John Ferris, the late Henry Frei, Jeffrey Grey, Greg Kennedy, Vincent Orange, Peter Stanley and Martin Thomas. Three friends who have done very fine work on the defence and fall of Singapore taught me a great deal about it: Raymond Callahan, Clifford Kinvig and Alan Warren. Archivists in London, Cambridge, Oxford, Canberra, Ottawa and Singapore were most helpful. Alexander Farrell and Dan Crosswell read early drafts and gave me most welcome and necessary hard headed criticism. Several cohorts of my students at NUS worked on the subject in their honours seminar in various years and thought I was teaching them; when they read this book they will realize it was the other way around. Three particular friends walked through this story over and over again with me, on the ground and on paper. I hope they are satisfied with how I tell the tale, because I dedicate this book to Dan Crosswell, Sandy Hunter, and Jeyathurai A.

The Singapore Strategy

In 1919 the British government and its military advisers made four major decisions. Military spending must be drastically reduced, to help rebuild an economy drained by a war of unprecedented severity. But British power, prosperity and influence rested on maintaining control of a worldwide Empire, so the United Kingdom (U.K.) must hold what it had. To do that it must persuade its Dominions and colonies to offer their support without claiming a larger voice in policy in return. Finally, its only ally in the Far East was now openly identified as the only likely future enemy in the region. There was no way to reconcile these conflicting imperatives without paying an unwelcome political, economic or military price. Something had to give. When it reviewed the defence of the Empire, the British government decided its first priority was to preserve British authority in directing that defence. It concluded the only way to cut costs and still maintain control of imperial defence was to adopt plans to defend the Empire in the Far East that were not militarily realistic. This decision was justified by assuming the Empire could improvise if and when it ever became necessary.

The British Empire was a satisfied power, with a vested interest to prevent changes to the international order by force. But the world does not stand still. Whatever policy the British adopted had to be one they could adjust to meet changing circumstances. Because they did not have the muscle to defend the Far East, the British replaced it by pretence. This did not matter in circumstances in which the mere existence of a plan could deter any threat and reassure the Empire. But it became fatal when circumstances changed and the British found they could not improvise without paying too high a price somewhere else. In for a penny in for a pound. The British decided to increase the stakes rather than call off the gamble and change the plan. The defence of Singapore rested on a promise never meant to be kept. Unfortunately, because the policy was not realistic, none of the military plans could be either.

1

The Naval Key to the Far East

The defence of the British Empire was a responsibility assumed by the British government. But from the First World War, if not before, British power was no longer strong enough to protect the Empire in Asia if it was already engaging a great power in Europe. The Empire that spanned the globe, recklessly increased soon after 1918, was largely built in an earlier period, when the relative strength of British power was greater–and threats not so serious. The loose concept that came to be known as "imperial defence" was based on three cornerstones. The U.K. would take the lead to confront any grave challenge by a first class power to the survival of the Empire itself. Two such potential challenges were a general European war and a Russian invasion of India. The second cornerstone was that the Royal Navy (RN) would guarantee the security of the maritime lines of communication that bound the far flung Empire together. However, the Admiralty always insisted that rather than parcel out warships in small packets to defend every position, it would concentrate its strength to fight and win a decisive battle, to maintain "command of the sea." This led directly to the final cornerstone: the maxim, agreed in principle, that each section of the Empire would be primarily responsible for its own local defence.[1]

For some parts of the Empire this was no real problem. The small fragments in the South Atlantic and South America faced no serious foe. Canada sat to the north of the American colossus. British governments at the turn into the twentieth century laid down what became a permanent maxim: the Empire must never again find itself fighting the U.S.A.[2] But for the Dominions, colonies and protectorates of Africa, Asia and the Pacific, no such pragmatic solution was available. Only the large Indian Army could even try to defend its area without extra help from the mother country. Other colonies and Dominions remained utterly dependent on British help to face anything beyond a pin prick attack or local unrest. The RN, with some assistance from the British Army where necessary, seemed more than capable of coming to the rescue. But from the very beginning of the twentieth century, unexpected problems undermined this whole concept.

When the drive for empire provoked war in Southern Africa in 1899, instead of the mother country coming to the aid of outlying territories, she called them for help. The RN made this relatively easy to do, but the weakness of the British Army raised disturbing questions. These forebodings were justified by the much sterner test of the Great War. Provoked into war to check a perceived German threat to the balance of power in Europe, the British again found themselves in a struggle much more serious than first envisaged. The drift into total war again forced the mother country to rely heavily on direct military assistance from the Empire. The combined efforts of the Allied Powers won victory and the armies of the British Empire played a very major role indeed. But if ever there was a pyrrhic victory ....

By 1919 the following points stood out. First, the most dangerous threat to the survival of the Empire was another general European war, which would threaten the survival of the U.K. as a great power. Should any power emerge triumphant as hegemon, it would be a colossus parked on the doorstep of the mother country–strong enough to challenge its command of the seas, divert its trade, threaten its territory. The Empire would obviously collapse if the metropolis could no longer project power overseas. So the British could not, in their own interest, stand aside in a major European war. But nor could they wage one without military assistance from the Empire. This stood the very basis of imperial defence on its head. Second, the economic power of the Empire was gravely compromised by the cost of the war. It seemed unlikely the British could afford to deploy forces strong enough to police such a huge empire and at the same time contain the always most dangerous threat on the doorstep. Finally, if the U.K. had to fight another general European war, the rest of the Empire might again face, simultaneously, a local threat and a call for help from the British. The British Empire risked being overstretched should it face any serious challenge close to home.[3]

This made the problem of remoteness, as measured from the mother country, more acute. Only the U.K. had any real strength, when measured against other major powers. The other parts of Empire were too weak to provide a serious independent contribution. Even the large Indian Army was no exception. By now it was treated as an imperial strategic reserve. But it depended on the U.K. for leaders, weapons and equipment needed to wage war outside its Northwest Frontier.[4] The British insisted on remaining the principal author of policy for imperial defence, on the grounds only they had the strength, experience and perspective to manage the problem as a whole. This guaranteed that whatever threats they saw as most urgent would be first priority. Remoteness need not necessarily have been geographic. Should there be only one challenge, with no threats arising elsewhere, there seemed no reason to doubt British willingness and ability to meet it. But the South African and Great Wars raised a prospect the rest of the Empire could only see as ominous: what if the threat of the moment pulled the main forces away from their region? What would be left to face trouble elsewhere?

Neither the British government nor its military advisers were blind to this potential dilemma, but there were real limits on what they could do about it. Indeed, economic and political pressures compelled them to take steps that made it worse. To keep spending under control and make scarce resources available to rebuild the economy, the so-called "Ten Year Rule" was introduced in August 1919. This stated that all defence spending must be based on the assumption the Empire would not be involved in another major war for at least ten years. The Treasury used this leverage to clamp down tight control on budgets for the armed forces.[5] Now more than ever creative solutions would be needed to tackle the problem of imperial defence. This seemed especially the case regarding the Asia-Pacific region.

There was no serious threat to the Pacific Dominions and Asian colonies during the Great War. The minor German forces in the area were easily swept up–but mainly by the Japanese. At the time this meant British policy worked according to plan. Since 1902 the U.K. and Japan had been military allies, an alliance that marked the first step by the British away from the "splendid isolation" of their zenith. Japan charged dutifully into a war that did not concern it, coming to the aid of its ally–and seizing the chance to scoop up German colonies. Eventually, the demands of total war in Europe forced the British to rely extensively on Japanese help. The Imperial Japanese Navy (IJN) secured the Pacific Ocean, convoyed British Empire shipping through the Indian Ocean, even helped in the Mediterranean. This all eased the burden on the RN, allowing it to concentrate on the main threat. But it also raised three concerns. The threat was so serious the navy *had* to concentrate its full strength to meet it. That left the Far East territories depending on outside help for security. And there were question marks about this outside help.

The Japanese alliance provided an obvious strategic benefit to the British Empire. But not the least gain was that it assured British territories they would not be coveted by the Japanese. Japanese intentions no longer seemed benevolent. Japan tried during the war to establish a position of dominance in China. This seemed to reflect a dangerous ambition in some circles to expand Japanese empire and power, to reach beyond their crowded home islands. This ambition focused on areas of great interest to the Western powers, most of whom had important economic assets in and around China and wished to keep China open and weak. That was certainly true for the British. By itself this would have posed problem enough, given that imperial defence now depended on the Japanese being a friend, or at least not a foe. What made the problem far worse was that Japanese behaviour provoked a chilly response from the Americans.

It was by no means inevitable there would ever be war between Japan and the U.S.A. But from 1919 responsible British authorities could not safely assume they would never clash. Long standing frictions became focused on the question of Japanese ambitions in China and what they represented for the future international order in East Asia. The U.S.A. was now the wealthiest and strongest power in the world and looked forward to using that strength to its own advantage. The "Open Door" policy indicated the Americans would object to any attempt by any power to become preeminent in China. Japanese behaviour raised American hackles, not least because for more than a decade these two rising powers had already identified each other as their principal potential enemy in any contest over the future direction of Asia and the Pacific.[6] This raised for the British a nightmare scenario: a possible clash between the friend they needed in Asia, and the friend they needed most in all the world.

U.S. intervention tipped the balance in the Great War, economically and to a lesser extent militarily. The Germans won the war in the east, and only lost it in the west because American backing made the Allies strong enough to prevail. The British knew this. And of course they were determined to stay on the good side of the Americans. This suggested that if events forced the British to choose between the Japanese and the Americans, there would be no choice. But it was not quite that simple.

On the one hand, taking steps to avoid annoying the Americans would not necessarily produce a British-American military alliance. Such an alliance was not likely to emerge before a direct attack on either power. American governments were constrained by widespread public mistrust of, as well as constitutional obstacles to, alliances and entanglements that might lead to commitments. The British might well find they turned away from one ally but did not gain another to take its place. On the other hand, if the Japanese ever decided they needed to challenge Western power and interests in Asia, that would make the alliance with the British obsolete. Some argued prolonging the alliance would give the British the leverage to cultivate better relations with Japan. Voices in Australia and New Zealand joined that chorus, underlining their sense of menace from a power so much closer to home than the mother country. Others replied that the risks of antagonizing the Americans were greater than the chances of diplomacy keeping the Japanese friendly. Canadian leaders supported that point, which only reminded everyone how geography complicated matters of imperial defence.[7]

British policy makers faced a tall order. Nothing could be done that might annoy the Americans. Yet Japan was the only real military threat to the

Empire in Asia, and placing it at arms length might bring that threat closer without gaining any compensating gratitude from the Americans. American-Japanese friction made standing still on the status quo impossible. Nor could commitments be reduced. Despite less money and smaller forces, no British government seriously considered abandoning territories on the grounds they could no longer be protected. British policy makers simply did not believe the U.K. could maintain its standard of living, and preserve its place in the world, without the Empire. And they assumed potential foes would see any voluntary reduction of commitments as a sign of weakness.[8] A new policy was therefore required. It must identify clear priorities, find a credible way to meet increased commitments with decreased resources, and command support at home and in the Dominions.

Any external attack on the Empire in the Far East could only come, at least at first, from the sea. This kept the navy front and centre in imperial defence. When the Imperial War Cabinet asked the Admiralty in March 1917 to advise Empire governments on "the most effective scheme of naval defence of the Empire" after the war, the Admiralty answered in May 1918: "The whole naval force of the Empire to form one Navy, all effective units being under the control of an Imperial Naval Authority, both in peace and war. Ships to be available to serve in any waters, and officers and men in any ship." The Dominion governments rejected this proposal as "impracticable." All agreed the Empire's navies should be able to work as one, but none felt they would have any real voice in directing a single imperial navy. That raised two dangers. The first was constitutional. Most Dominions, especially Canada and Australia, had been pushing for some years for a greater voice in defence and foreign policy. They felt their war effort entitled them to such–and public expectations made it politically almost imperative. Folding their own small navies back into an imperial service would be regressing. The second was strategic. Most Dominions were not confident an imperial navy in which they had little say would always be available if they needed its protection. The Dominions suggested that a "highly qualified representative of the Admiralty" be sent on tour to advise them how best to develop separate naval forces that could nevertheless work together as a coherent imperial coalition. The Admiralty went out of its way to restate for the record its "declared views" on how best to defend the Empire, but duly assigned Lord Jellicoe, wartime commander of the Grand Fleet, to make a grand tour. He set out in February 1919, sailing, appropriately, on the battlecruiser HMS *New Zealand*. His orders were to advise Dominion governments, in light of war experience, as to how well suited their naval services were to both local needs and "ensuring the greatest possible homogeneity and cooperation between all the Naval forces of the Empire."[9] Jellicoe interpreted his orders as a nod and wink to use his mission as a platform to promote an ambitious policy for imperial defence.

On 16 August 1919, the day after the British government adopted the "Ten Year Rule," Jellicoe exploited an Australian request for a review of the naval situation in the Pacific to submit a report that, if followed, would have voided that policy from the start. Jellicoe argued the only real threat to the Empire in the Pacific was Japan, and to face that threat properly the Empire must permanently maintain a major battlefleet in the Far East. Major battlefleet meant eight battleships, eight battlecruisers, and a full complement of smaller warships in support. In order to maintain such a fleet, it must build a major naval base in the region. The obvious site was Singapore, "the naval key to the Far East." Positioned between India, Japan and Australia, a fleet based in Singapore could protect all the Empire's possessions and trade routes, drawing on the base facilities to engage and defeat the Japanese fleet.[10] Given a free hand the Admiralty would have supported all these arguments. Its planners had already identified Japan as the only serious threat to imperial security in Asia, a majority favoured Singapore as a main theatre base, and all agreed the RN should always be as large as possible. Jellicoe's proposal was strategically logical. Japan was a perceived threat. An empire needing to be strong in two or more oceans should maintain its navy accordingly. Such a fleet would need a proper base. Unfortunately, the nation simply could no longer afford such a large navy. There was never any chance Jellicoe's "Pacific Fleet" would materialize.[11]

Nevertheless, the core of Jellicoe's program became the focal point in the search for a revamped imperial defence policy. The government could not be persuaded to deploy a fleet to protect the Empire in Asia, but would not leave it defenceless either. If the navy could not station a battlefleet in the region, it could at least send the main fleet to meet any emergency that might arise. For that fleet to operate, it would need a proper base. Arguments about the best location for that base continued for some time, Hong Kong and Sydney both attracting support. But that issue was settled in June 1921 when the government agreed in principle a base large enough to maintain the main fleet must be built in Singapore. The "Singapore strategy" was already taking shape. A fleet capable of defeating the next strongest naval power, the "one power standard" fleet, would base its battle-line closer to home. But in an emergency, the entire fleet, or such strength as was necessary to meet the threat, would be despatched to the Far East, operate from a major regional base, and defeat the enemy.[12]

At an Imperial Conference in London later that summer, Dominion leaders were briefed about the new strategy and the decision to build the base, then informed that the British government nevertheless leaned towards renewing the Anglo-Japanese Alliance.[13] But fate, in the person of the American government, had already taken a hand. All these decisions were made pending a meeting of the leading naval powers later that year, arranged by American invitation. The conference met in Washington from November 1921 to discuss reductions in navy size and naval spending, and new security arrangements for Asia and the Pacific. The Americans decided to take the initiative, using their great economic and industrial power as leverage. Catching everyone off guard, they made bold proposals for a comprehensive disarmament and security agreement. These included truly sweeping cuts in the size of navies and general international guarantees to replace bilateral alliances. For the British and the Japanese the message was not subtle. Accept this new international security order, allow your alliance to lapse, and determine the size of your navy by agreement, rather than by a unilateral calculation of security needs–or the U.S.A. will go its own way, build a navy far stronger than anyone else could match, and pursue its own interests accordingly. Fume as they might, the British delegation ultimately had no real choice. The government would not fall out with the Americans, and the nation simply could not afford a naval race.[14]

The ensuing Washington Agreements of 1922 marked a turning point in imperial defence, but not one the government of the day could have done anything rational to prevent. Three agreements were concluded that together laid the basis for a new international order in the Far East. A Five-Power Naval Limitation Agreement, good for 10 years, established a "holiday" on new capital ship building during that time, and restricted the powers to ceilings on the total tonnage of capital ships they could maintain and on how large each ship could be. This was usually expressed as a ratio, and for the three most important powers the ratio was U.S.A. 5, U.K. 5, Japan 3. Future naval conferences would explore even more ambitious limitations. A Nine-Power Agreement bound the signatories to respect the sovereignty and territorial integrity of China and the status quo regarding enclaves and interests. And a Four-Power Agreement, adding France to the three major powers, pledged the signatories not to build any new fortifications and naval bases in the "Pacific region," defined as an area including Hong Kong but excluding Hawaii and Singapore.[15]

These agreements have been criticized as a historic blunder by the British government. They supposedly erred by shifting the basis of imperial defence from the tangible fact of naval power to the unreliable quicksand of international agreements. The British gave away both the freedom to maintain the RN at whatever strength imperial defence required, and the Japanese alliance that was the best hope of keeping the only real threat in the Far East under control.[16] These criticisms are unfair. Economic exhaustion had already made it seem impossible to maintain the largest navy in the world. As for replacing the alliance with the new American order, the fact was that however much of a rival the U.S.A. often appeared to be, especially in world trade, it was not seen as a military threat or a putative enemy. At the broadest level, British and American interests were not incompatible. Neither wanted to see any major change in the international order in Asia brought about by aggression, and neither wanted any other power to dominate the region. Fundamental harmony of interest brought the British Empire into an American alignment aimed very clearly at containing any future Japanese threat to the status quo in the Far East. What mattered most about the new "Washington system" was indeed how Japan would respond, and the British had already identified Japan as the threat by adopting the "Singapore strategy" before the agreements were made. The real issue was not whether an ally was needlessly spurned and power abdicated, but whether these agreements still allowed for a viable basis for imperial defence, if a threat ever did materialize.

Prospects for a viable imperial defence under the new "Washington system" rested on three things: circumstances, intentions and capabilities. Measuring all three at the time of the Washington Agreements, it can not be said British strategy was anything worse than a calculated risk. The unavoidable element of risk was that if a general European war erupted the British would ask for help from the Empire, and might not be able to send out the fleet–so if a threat then arose in the Far East the situation could be very difficult indeed. But a general European war was nowhere in sight at the time. Germany was prostrate; the new Soviet Union was hostile but not capable of starting a general war; France was not a likely enemy. The U.S.A. did not seem likely to offer any kind of security alliance, but was not going to attack the Empire. Nor, at the time, was Japan. The Japanese accepted the Washington Agreements as part of a new approach expressed by the term "Taisho democracy," identifying relatively liberal civilian-dominated governments with the imperial reign of the time. Japan would seek prosperity and power by international trade and co-operation.[17] As long as this national direction prevailed, the inherent risk in the "Singapore strategy" was not immediately dangerous. And even that danger was reduced as long as there was no trouble in Europe. With the IJN restricted by agreement to 60% of the battle-line strength of the RN, the British felt that as long as the navy was free to concentrate its forces it could send out a battlefleet strong enough to prevail. But what would happen if circumstances deteriorated and Japanese intentions changed? Would British capabilities still suffice to meet the challenge?

This need to realign circumstances, intentions and capabilities, to respond effectively to changes, was the real challenge to the new "Singapore strategy"–indeed to imperial defence as a whole. The problem can be divided into things over which the British had little or no control, and decisions only they could make. The most dangerous factor the British could not control was Japanese intentions, and here there were grounds for caution from the start. Powerful forces in Japan which supported imperial expansion and regional dominance as the best national policy were provoked by the Washington Agreements and remained a dangerous opponent of Taisho democracy.[18] If the climate of opinion shifted enough to jeopardize the policy of international co-operation, British and Japanese interests were almost bound to clash. The British Empire was after all the paramount status quo power enjoying the fruits of the very system Japanese imperialists wanted to challenge. Another factor the British could not control was American policy. If Japan turned its back on the "Washington system," the British could only hope its principal author would defend it by something more than protests. Here was the nub of the problem: if the Washington system broke down, would the "Singapore strategy" really work?

The real danger was the fact the British now had an empire bigger than they could afford to defend if international order really began to collapse. No government after 1922 could really do anything about that. The few voices, usually from the Treasury, that called for reducing the burdens the armed forces were asked to bear never weakened the consensus that power and prosperity rested on empire.[19] But every Cabinet refused to maintain armed forces large enough to wage general war until the very eve of another such war, for three reasons. First, it was natural to hope such a war would never come and therefore to want to avoid the expense involved. Second, every interwar Cabinet believed it could prevent another such war by effective diplomacy, albeit with different agendas for different governments. Finally, public opinion rejected such a policy outright and would have removed any government that pursued it before general war was clearly imminent. That moment did not come before 1939. So the only alternatives were to use diplomacy to limit the threats the Empire faced, and to make the best use of available resources to face the most likely threats. Both alternatives shaped the development of the "Singapore strategy" and plans for imperial defence against Japan. But the most important element was the system by which decisions on imperial defence were made.

On paper at least, the British system for making decisions on defence policy and grand strategy was the best organized in the world. The Cabinet took collective responsibility for the defence of the nation and Empire and therefore for all policy and strategy decisions at the highest level. The Cabinet was advised by the Committee of Imperial Defence (CID), a typically British instrument marrying flexibility with organization. Chaired by the Prime Minister, the CID consisted of the service ministers and whomever else the Prime Minister felt should be there, including, when it seemed relevant, representatives of Dominion governments. It met when he felt it should meet, or when problems were referred to it. A secretariat kept records of discussions and decisions and ensured the latter were followed up. The system was further strengthened in 1923 by the establishment of the Chiefs of Staff Committee (COS). This body brought together the professional heads of the three armed services, meeting regularly to discuss common problems, collate information, prepare plans, and profer advice to the Prime Minister, CID and Cabinet, as required. In due course the COS presided over an infrastructure of triservice sub-committees that brought the services together to work on intelligence, plans, logistics, and other matters. The CID also from time to time established sub-committees to assist its deliberations, a notable one being the Oversea Defence Committee (ODC).

The premise of this system was collective responsibility for a collective decision taken after collective deliberations. The idea was that before any decision relating to defence and grand strategy was made, there would be a thorough review of all relevant factors involving all interested parties, British and imperial. What should emerge was a consensus that might lean one way as opposed to another but would be based on considered and rounded advice. That should produce a policy which could be implemented, and monitored, in the same coherent fashion. Despite Jellicoe's insubordination at the start, the decision to adopt the "Singapore strategy" was made by just such a process, as indeed were the decisions to accept the Washington Agreements and abandon the Japanese alliance. Those decisions were logically fulfilled in February 1923 when the British government confirmed the earlier decision to build a fleet base at Singapore, and accepted the related strategy as the basis of imperial defence in the Far East.[20]

Whether or not this system for decision-making could provide effective imperial defence through the "Singapore strategy" depended on one thing: how successfully it could respond to change. Three questions needed answers. First, what was the best way to relate diplomacy and defence policy to each other? Second, what was the most dangerous threat, and the best strategy to meet it? Third, what must be done to make sure that best strategy could be applied if the need arose? The inherent weakness in the system was exposed during the 1920s, before any real threat arose, by the way it approached these constant questions. The first was answered at best erratically, at worst by wishful thinking. The second was exposed as unanswerable–but that revelation was ignored. Answers to the third rested on complacency and faith. Here was the rub: good organization could not overcome political reluctance to confront difficult military problems. Collective responsibility in fact only entrenched a tendency to compromise and hope for the best, rather than cold-bloodedly prepare for the worst. Everyone could and did hide behind everyone else. Root problems could not be tackled without exposing weakness, and rupturing the united front presented to public opinion and the world. This military system accentuated the political caution of a satisfied and overstretched power. Its very nature produced decisions that made a difficult problem intractable.

Too much attention has been paid to the first question, the connection between diplomacy and defence policy. This is largely because the "Singapore strategy" became a political football from 1923. From 1923 to mid-1931 two Conservative and two minority Labour governments alternated between launching work on the base, stopping it altogether, reviving it, then slowing it down again. This undoubtedly delayed completion of the base by a number of years, annoyed the Dominions, and frustrated the services.[21] But in the end it did not prevent the base from being completed before war finally came, so what does it matter? A common answer is that the attitudes responsible for this stop and go influenced policies that did do much damage. A popular target is Ramsay MacDonald's decision to rely on international disarmament as the best policy for imperial defence, and to sacrifice the Singapore base to aid that policy. While subsequent events certainly made MacDonald look naive, his inherently foolish policy was only pursued in 1924 and from summer 1929 to summer 1931. The Admiralty was beside itself when MacDonald offered to hobble the navy in order to bring about world peace–but never at any time before 1939 was the fleet even built up to the levels authorized by government policy. Non-partisan retrenchment and economic depression did much more than idealism to keep the RN below the strength it really needed should push came to shove.[22] A more serious failure was the policy of the Conservative government from 1924 to 1929. It tangled the problems of diplomacy with the second question–how to face the most dangerous threat–in a knot that could never be untied.

When Stanley Baldwin led the Conservatives back into government in October 1924, the damage was already done. Unfortunately, Baldwin's administration made it irreparable. The central issue was cost. Financial constraints dogged every aspect of the "Singapore strategy" from start to finish. The Admiralty ultimately chose to develop a site at Sembawang on the north coast of Singapore island, on the Straits of Johore, barely two kilometres from the mainland of the Malay peninsula, rather than a site next to the commercial harbour on the south coast of the island, in the Straits of Singapore, because the cost of building harbour defences seemed prohibitive. The purse strings tightened further to rule out the base the sailors really had in mind. The so-called "Green Scheme" envisaged a truly massive facility with a floating dock, two sealed inner basins, at least 10 docks, and large enough wharfage, maintenance and repair, supply, ancillary and above all petrol storage capacity to handle the main fleet itself: at least a dozen capital ships with a full complement of escorts. This was more than the government could stomach, so in March 1923 the Admiralty submitted a revised proposal, known as the "Red Scheme." This reduced facility would retain the floating dock and one graving dock, but cut the sealed basins, all other docks, and some 40% of the wharfage and other capacity. Such a base would only be able to handle the needs of any "peacetime fleet" sent out to the Far East–no more than 20% of the main fleet. This was the plan accepted by the government. As it was, with air, ground and harbour defences plus petrol storage, the cost still ran to £ 25 million.[23] Even had it stood unchanged, this would not have been enough. But it did not so stand.

Back in office, the Conservative government reviewed the Singapore base project in light of imperial defence and foreign policy as a whole. Leading the charge was Winston Churchill, now Chancellor of the Exchequer. In December 1924 Churchill complained the base project was much larger and more expensive than required, arguing "he did not believe there was the slightest chance of war with Japan in our lifetime." The only reason for such a war would be a Japanese invasion of Australia, which idea was "an absolute absurdity."[24] Churchill was not alone in thinking so, but the stubborn defence of Admiralty plans mounted by the COS stiffened his determination to pare the plans down. By late 1926 the base was further reduced in a "truncated Red Scheme." The plan which finally resulted in a contract in November 1926 maintained the docking and petrol storage of the Red Scheme but excised all repair capacity. Warships needing serious maintenance would have to rely on the facilities of the commercial harbour. Nor did the government press work on the base with any great energy. When Labour returned to office in June 1929, they inherited nothing more than drained swamps and road work. The floating dock had arrived and large petrol stocks were accumulated. But without a base they were worse than useless, a target to tempt any attacker.[25] But the Conservatives did at least make sure Labour could not cancel the base outright by writing in penalty clauses for cancelling contracts. This was due in no small measure to pressure from the Dominions. In March 1929 Australian Prime Minister Stanley Bruce delivered a categorical warning: without the base "Australia ... can only regard herself as deserted by the Empire." This forced the Labour government, at the Imperial Conference of October 1930, to promise the base would eventually be completed, in return for agreement to suspend work not yet contracted for another five years.[26] But all that now meant was that a useless base would be built as the basis of an improbable strategy.

The long argument in the 1920s produced a formula for the "Singapore strategy": to develop a base able to support a battlefleet "superior in strength, or at least equal to" the battlefleet of the IJN–a fleet that could win a decisive battle in the Far East. This was already problematic in one sense, if general war threatened in Europe. Now that unavoidable risk was compounded to the point of folly: not so much by the Washington treaty limits but rather by reduction to the "truncated Red Scheme." Now, even if the situation did allow the RN to despatch a battlefleet strong enough to beat the IJN, the Singapore base would not be able to support it! Admiralty planners estimated that at least seven capital ships, plus a full complement of escorts, would be required to take on the IJN–under any circumstances. The facility to be completed at Sembawang would simply not be able to handle such a fleet. This was indeed the "strategic illusion." However varied Admiralty plans may have been regarding how the fleet might wage war against Japan once it arrived in the Far East, all plans depended on the main base at Singapore.[27] This was the choke point. The answer to the second question was that a major war against Japan was the worst threat–but because the government would not pay for a base large enough to support a fleet strong enough to handle that threat, there was no answer.

Critics of the "Singapore strategy" did not at the time concentrate on this fundamental flaw in it. There are several reasons for this. At the time the threat of war with Japan did indeed seem, to many, distant enough for other answers to be pursued. Few within the decision making loop were ready to argue the money should be found no matter what else must be sacrificed. The Dominions made substantial contributions to the cost of the base, to encourage its completion, but faced their own limits, as Bruce made clear: "... Australia's economic circumstances impel her to devote all her energy and resources to reproductive works rather than to armaments."[28] Most important, many British and Dominion officials were convinced that to maintain imperial unity and public confidence they must have a plan, however rough, for imperial defence. The Singapore plan was the only card in play.

Nevertheless there was criticism, and it did expose the impracticality of the whole strategy. But what mattered most was how the critics were kept at bay. The two most celebrated were Jan Smuts, in 1923 as Prime Minister of South Africa, and Admiral Sir Herbert Richmond, in 1925 as C-in-C East Indies Station. At the Imperial Conference of 1923, Smuts criticized the most obvious flaw: if there was a major crisis in Europe it seemed at least doubtful the British government would send the fleet, especially after the reductions accepted at Washington; but the only scenario in which Japan might attack the Empire was if the British were engaged in Europe. The simultaneous wars problem was the worst threat, this strategy could not handle it, therefore it would not suffice. Smuts was a renowned figure, commander of imperial forces in African campaigns in the First World War, member of the Imperial War Cabinet, author of a seminal report that led to the creation of the Royal Air Force (RAF). An imperial statesman of such stature had to be answered. In reply Leo Amery, First Lord of the Admiralty, doubted that a crisis large enough to pin down the fleet would again erupt in Europe, then doubted Japan would in any case dare to confront British power–but finally insisted that even if worst did come to worst this would mean an attack on the whole international order in Asia, and that would surely lead to American intervention. In other words, if the gap in their strategy was ever exposed the British proposed to rely on American support.[29] This argument was frank but reckless. It was probably fair and even more probably necessary to assume that in any real international meltdown the U.S.A. would be at least sympathetic and certainly not hostile. But there is a large jump from sympathy to alliance, and the British had no guarantee they would enjoy the latter if push come to shove.

Richmond's critique was less public but more penetrating, yet led to no more positive result. Naval war plans for the Far East were updated frequently in Admiralty War Memoranda (Eastern), circulated to commanders-in-chief. The 1924 version provoked a response from Richmond in 1925. A renowned student of naval history and strategy, his voice commanded respect. Richmond criticized virtually every aspect of the plan. He argued that naval strategy did not seem to be aligned with foreign policy, it assumed war with Japan would be exclusively naval and did not allow for interservice co-operation, and the operational strategy by which Japan could supposedly be defeated did not make sense. His fundamental point came in a much quoted paragraph:

> To my mind, since our forces are not adequate for a war in the East at the same time as one calling for the use of naval force in Europe, there is a great deal of unreality in a plan for such a condition of affairs: and wholly wrong to convey the impression that our strength is sufficient to enable us to do so. It is better frankly to acknowledge our inability than to continue to live in a fool's paradise.

Richmond's main concern was to persuade the Admiralty to prepare a more realistic second plan for war against Japan, one that assumed the main fleet might not be available to take the offensive. The argument revolved around Phase I, defined by Admiralty planners as The Period Before Relief: the time that must elapse between the onset of crisis or war and the arrival of the main fleet in the Far East. Phase II was the Period of Consolidation, Phase III the Period of Advance, when the fleet would either find and destroy the IJN or strangle Japan. But if the fleet could not be sent in enough strength then no later phase could be pursued, by whatever plan. This was indeed the crux of the matter. The Admiralty agreed an offensive strategy was desirable and diplomacy should be pursued to reduce the risk of simultaneous challenges. But it did not want to plan for a defensive strategy, because that could not win a war. It also felt that doubts about what might be done beyond Phase I could only be answered by circumstances at the time, but meanwhile some basis for strategic planning was required. And time did not seem to be pressing. So while they appreciated Richmond's critique, it prompted no reassessment.[30]

The "Singapore strategy" was not in fact a realistic grand strategy for war against Japan. It was an optimistic plan to shift the main fleet to the Far East if war approached, followed by a collection of vague ideas about how it might wage war if it arrived intact. All overlooked the fatal flaw: the base would not be large enough to support a fleet strong enough to pursue any plans for a Phase II and III, even if one was sent. The critics could not be answered convincingly. Grand strategy could only be altered by truly radical change. But that prospect was too daunting, because imperial unity now seemed to rest on this plan. The Empire was not going to be left defenceless but could not afford either a Pacific Fleet or a true fleet base. So improvisation was the order of the day. Awkward critiques and intractable problems were left to mature—perhaps in the hope time would evaporate rather than rot them. Unfortunately, that also tended to entrench one plan as the only strategy available. Avoiding consideration of awkward alternatives was just that: avoiding the problem, not tackling it. The one aspect of the whole problem that did seem relatively concrete was the connection between how to move the fleet and meanwhile how to hold its base: the period before relief. Because this was the only pressing issue, the fine tuning of the "Singapore strategy" came into focus here. This raises our third question: how to make sure the best strategy could be applied if war did break out.

By its very nature this question called for flexible thinking and planning. The central issue was never in dispute and was identified by the Admiralty in October 1919:

It is unlikely ... in view of the days of economy ahead of us and the rapidly increasing strength of Japan ... that we shall be able to maintain a Fleet equal to hers in the Far East in peace time. It follows therefore, that at the commencement of a war with Japan, we should find ourselves in Naval inferiority for a time ... Taking the worst situation ... it is possible that a period of three months might elapse before our Naval supremacy in the Far East could be established. During this period, Japan would have had practically a free hand at sea.

This problem was noted as a main reason why Singapore was ultimately selected as the main base site: "This port may be considered sufficiently far from any Japanese possessions to make an attack upon it in force improbable during the period available before the Fleet arrives." Yet when Singapore was recommended in June 1921 geography alone was not enough. The CID warned the Cabinet: "... unless the defences of Singapore are strengthened, there would, under existing conditions, be every inducement to a Japanese commander in the early stages of a war to attack the fortress, with a view to denying its use to the British fleet in subsequent operations ..."[31] The British Empire would not start a war; it would be attacked and have to respond. There would be no fleet in the Far East when trouble began, but there would be a base. Grand strategy for war against Japan rested on whatever fleet was despatched being able to use that base. The base would have to be held before the fleet could arrive–Phase I, the Period Before Relief. Planners expected this period to last 42 days. In response to the Washington Agreements the Admiralty called for Singapore's defences to be built up to withstand the maximum scale of seaborne attack–fleet bombardment and invasion–and made the following categorical warning:

Should Japan at any time declare war on the British Empire, the position of Australia, New Zealand, India, and our Eastern colonies will be one of grave danger until the arrival of the Main Fleet in the East. For a rapid concentration of the Fleet in the East it is essential that a secure base at Singapore can be counted on.[32]

The services agreed on the challenge, but not on how best to meet it. For one thing, geography was neutral. Singapore was close enough to both Japanese and friendly waters to be useful, far enough to be difficult for the Japanese to attack. Japan was some 4000 km from Singapore. To launch a seaborne invasion at such a distance would be a massive undertaking, but the British could not rule it out. The U.K. was nearly four times as distant. Should the Japanese decide to attack the British Empire, they would win any race to reach the theatre first. Another problem was the island itself. Singapore is a small island shaped like a rough diamond, measuring some 40 km wide by 24 km high, similar in size and shape to the Isle of Wight. The island is mainly flat, with no strong natural defensive features, and before the Second World War consisted mainly of mangrove swamp, jungle, and plantations, with urban development restricted to the south central area. Again similar to the Isle of Wight it lies in the very shadow of the mainland, barely a kilometre off the southern coast of the Malay peninsula. It also sits in the Straits of Singapore, the shortest sea route between the South China Sea and the Indian Ocean, like a cork in a bottleneck. From January 1923 it was connected to the mainland by a fixed link causeway, in the centre of the north shore. In principle an attacker could come at Singapore either from the south, directly from the sea, or the north, overland. All this made the defence of Singapore a problem for all three services. The army must repel any attackers that managed to land either on the mainland or directly on the island; the air force must deny control of the air to any attacker.

For a time the War Office (WO) did take seriously the threat of an invader taking the long way around, landing in Malaya and advancing on the island from the north. But by 1925 the general consensus was that this was not a practicable operation of war. British Malaya was a peninsula approximately the size of England, stretching nearly 800 km from the Thai border in the north to the town of Johore Bahru opposite Singapore. It is shaped like a carrot, narrow at the top, bulging out in the middle, narrowing again in the south. A range of mountains rising to over 2000 metres ran down most of the spine, overgrown by jungle which spilled out to dominate much of the country. There were few good roads and only one trunk railway. The east coast, the one facing Japan, was as yet nearly undeveloped. It seemed unlikely a large modern army with heavy weapons and equipment could make any strategic advance through such countryside. While it stipulated that for the naval base to be usable any hostile force must be kept at least 50 km to the north on land, out of artillery range, the Army therefore shifted its focus to the problem of a direct attack from the sea.[33]

The Army and the RN argued the defence of the base should rest with batteries of heavy guns, emplaced permanently as coastal artillery. These fixed defences would always be there, to face anything from surprise raid to full-scale invasion. An infantry garrison could protect the batteries by dealing with any invaders reaching shore. The RAF argued that a mixed force of fighter, dive and torpedo bomber aircraft should play at least an equal role in the defences. Using the loophole provided by an Army requirement for spotter aircraft for the guns, the Chief of the Air Staff (CAS), Air Chief Marshal Sir Hugh Trenchard, insisted fighters would be needed to protect them. He went on to argue bombers could attack a hostile fleet some 240 km out to sea, a much greater range than the 40 km the biggest guns could manage, and damage it enough to prevent any invasion. The argument went round and round for years on pretty much the same points, in part because each side had valid concerns. Guns were a proven method of coast defence but aircraft had never yet done in war what Trenchard claimed they could do. On the other hand everyone agreed the farther away an invader was attacked the better and sooner or later technology would provide aircraft that could live up to Trenchard's promise. Trenchard made an attractive point when he argued that providing a strong force of aircraft would be cheaper than building up fixed defences with the largest calibre guns. But he undercut it by claiming mobility would make such a force even more attractive. The RAF was certainly in vogue with the government at that time. It demonstrated its usefulness as a cheap alternative to expensive ground forces by successfully patrolling large areas of unrest for a fraction of the price, notably in Iraq. Trenchard argued that provided the necessary airbases were in place, squadrons could be usefully employed in a variety of areas but shifted quickly into Singapore to face any emergency. This did not impress the First Sea Lord, Admiral of the Fleet Lord David Beatty. He insisted such a crucial base required reliable defences permanently available on the spot. It was too risky to rest Singapore's protection on forces as yet unproven in war and which might not even arrive in time if the call came.[34]

The undercurrents of this argument are more interesting than its main points. Neither the WO nor the Admiralty were pleased when the RAF was established as an independent service in 1918. Their hostility increased in the strained financial climate after the war. Both resented this new competitor for scarce funds, as well as sincerely believing the airpower required for their own operations would be more effective under their control. The RAF on the other hand struggled to survive as an independent service and developed a tendency to exaggerate the strategic merits of anything it could do on its own. Regarding the "Singapore strategy," if the RAF could persuade the government to rely on it as the main defence force for the all-important Phase I, it would score an important coup that must help it survive.[35] Driven by such ulterior motives, the argument became erratic. The soldiers and sailors were right to point out air defence was as yet unproven and the security of the base could not be compromised. For that very reason it is less clear how everyone missed the obvious parallel in Beatty's rebuttal to the "Singapore strategy" itself. If squadrons of aircraft might be prevented from moving to the base by trouble elsewhere, why did that same problem not apply to the fleet?

That problem was simply too fundamental to tackle without being forced to admit the whole strategy was impractical. The service chiefs were no more willing to do that than their political masters. It might have led to a major policy and budget defeat for one of them. What ensued instead were compromises based on three points. First, Singapore must be defended at all times as strongly as possible, especially after work began on the base and large reserves of petrol began to accumulate. Second, guns and aircraft were both required. Third, costs must be kept down. The result by 1930 was a growing hole in the ground on the north coast with increasing stocks of petrol nearby, protected by some old coastal defence batteries with aging guns, two airfields with a handful of obsolete bombers, and a garrison of two infantry battalions to help repel an attack from the sea.[36] These were paltry results a decade after the conception of the "Singapore strategy." Why was so little achieved?

The challenge identified in 1919 was to find a policy for imperial defence in the Far East that identified clear priorities and possible threats, found a credible way to meet commitments with less resources, and commanded general support. The threat was clear: a Japanese seaborne attack on the British Empire. The priority seemed clear: only a general war in Europe was more dangerous than a determined Japanese attack on the Empire. What did not seem at all clear was what could be done if the two coincided. That undermined the credibility of the strategy designed to meet the threat. More important, that strategy was rendered void from the start by the decision not to build a base large enough to support the fleet required. The "Singapore strategy" was simply not credible. Despite that, by 1930 it was the only British Empire grand strategy for any war against Japan.

There was no realistic clear-cut solution. The British Empire would not be left defenceless. To nearly everyone involved that was unthinkable. A battlefleet would not be stationed in the Far East. To everyone but the Admiralty that was too expensive. Something else must be done. This was something. Yet while Japan might one day be the enemy, for now it was only the threat, an apparently distant threat. As yet there did not seem to be any great turmoil in Asia. China was again embroiled in massive internal strife, but this was nothing new nor yet menacing. From October 1929 economic turbulence spreading out from the stock market crash in the U.S.A. seemed worrying, especially for what it might do to Japan. But at first this only seemed to underline that all important dynamic of British policy: keep defence spending down to the barest minimum, in order not to jeopardize efforts to strengthen the economy. There might have been a danger, but it was not yet clear and present. So first things came first.

Personalities are often seen as crucial and they certainly mattered. The vigour with which MacDonald pursued his vision of disarmament, the energy

Churchill put into his drive for retrenchment, and the monumental clash of egos that fuelled the debate between Trenchard and Beatty all did damage. But they were not decisive. A Chancellor other than Churchill would also have opposed the full Green Scheme base, if perhaps less acrimoniously. A First Sea Lord other than Beatty would also have contested Trenchard's plans and overlooked the flaws of those of his own service, again perhaps more quietly. What mattered more was the combination of personalities with circumstances, and the system by which defence policy was made. The Conservatives did not pursue disarmament with MacDonald's naive passion nor try to cancel the naval base, but did adopt the Ten Year Rule, sign the Washington Agreements, cut defence spending, and pare the base down to pointlessness. Politicians operating in an open democratic system are forced to balance conflicting interests and weigh multiple risks. These men preferred to wait on events, especially when they saw reason to hope problems might solve themselves if left alone.

This was underlined in 1928 when Churchill persuaded the Cabinet to reset the Ten Year Rule on an ongoing basis, renewed daily until decided otherwise. Service chiefs forced to fight for every penny in tight budgets not surprisingly chose to compromise on plans and strategies rather than force a showdown that might go against them, especially when the menace seemed distant.[37] A system that brought together all interested parties to tackle a problem, but held them all collectively responsible for the policy to deal with it, was all but certain, in the atmosphere of the 1920s, to produce a compromise. The real problem was that it produced an unrealistic one. That is not to say another system must have done better. Rule by decree for example carried its own obvious risks, if the dictator was less than infallible. At any rate, in the U.K. the system of collective responsibility was long evolved, deeply entrenched, the only machinery at hand. Under the circumstances calculated risks could not be avoided. But making decisions only after a searching review of all relevant factors by all interested parties, working supposedly in a common interest, was supposed to make it impossible to settle on a plan that could simply never work in the real world–no matter what happened. Instead it made things even worse.

Acknowledging the "Singapore strategy" could never work after the "truncated Red Scheme" was adopted would have meant admitting the British Empire had no realistic military plan to defend itself against Japan–even in the best of circumstances. This would have forced the British government to make a categorical choice: relax the policy of retrenchment and build the necessary base; ask Australia to take the lead in defending the region; or admit the problem was insoluble and write off the Empire east of India as indefensible in a general war. None of these choices was seriously considered. British officials believed that once it became clear they were not prepared to defend the Empire in the Far East their authority there would surely be challenged, from within and without. Asking Australia to take the lead would also have been seen as a sign of weakness, and in any case the Australians were not then either ready or willing to take on the challenge. As for retrenchment, in retrospect the dozens of millions of pounds required would not have shattered the British economy–so this fudge seems like a catastrophic failure of government. Building a proper base may not have changed the course of history; after all, the prospect of sending out the fleet remained problematic. But it would have shown clarity on the main point, a sober and realistic focus on the bare necessities for credible defence. Few saw the fatal flaw so clearly, but many saw how dire the alternatives were. Waiting for better economic times, when more might be done, seemed more attractive than making a choice that might never in the end be put to the test. This was the path of least resistance. A system of collective decision making took that path for one reason. It was easier to try to make the situation fit the plan than admit there was no plan.

Circumstances, intentions and capabilities remained the test. The "Singapore strategy" seemed like a necessary risk to take in the 1920s, for political and economic reasons. Circumstances were not pressing, intentions were not hostile, capabilities seemed not beyond redemption. This latter point was wrong, fatally wrong, after the strategy was voided by the system. All the Admiralty's ambitious plans to defeat Japan were useless, because the fleet needed to execute them would not have been able to operate in the Far East even if it was sent out. War plans were like a chain, stretching from grand strategy for the central direction of imperial defence at the highest level, through theatre strategy for operations in an area of the world, to operational strategy in a particular campaign, right down to battlefield tactics. For the last link in the chain to be effective the connections between every link must be realistic, and well aligned with each other. The right forces must be in the right place, with the right means, at the right time. The mission must be clear and realistic at all levels to be accomplished at any level. This was manifestly not the case here. The "Singapore strategy" could never have worked even in the unlikely event the fleet actually deployed. That left plans to hold the base before it arrived, let alone plans to take the war to Japan, pointless and resting on thin air. The chain was never properly linked.

The ostensible purpose of the "Singapore strategy" was to provide a viable basis for defending the Empire against Japan. When searching examination revealed that the only realistic plan would cost more than the government was willing to pay, the system of collective responsibility found reasons not to adopt a policy based on first principles and concrete military imperatives. The best that can be said is that its authors thought this strategy was better than none at all, and hoped it might yet be made effective if the need ever arose. It made no sense to base grand strategy on the arrival of a main fleet that could not then be sustained. The real reason this strategy became British policy was because it allowed the British government to deny the obvious. Unless and until an enemy attack proved otherwise, they could insist the Empire was still prepared to defend itself come what may.

2

The Roads to War

In April 1930 the British government hailed the just completed London Conference on naval disarmament as a success for international cooperation. It looked forward to a further round of naval diplomacy and to the general conference on disarmament being organized by the League of Nations the following year. But the ensuing decade dashed all hopes to build a stable new international order. By autumn 1939 the British Empire was again at war in Europe, to prevent a resurgent Germany from destroying the balance of power. Italy was an unfriendly neutral, which complicated the situation greatly in the Mediterranean and North Africa. And Japan was now a real threat, pursuing an expanding war in China, bullying British nationals there and threatening British interests in the whole region. On the surface this sea change in affairs did not seem to affect plans for imperial defence. When British officials met Dominion counterparts in November to request help for the war in Europe, Australian representatives asked about the Japanese threat. Winston Churchill, back in office as First Lord of the Admiralty, categorically assured the Australians the "Singapore strategy" still stood: "We could, however, subscribe to two principles, namely that we should never allow Singapore to fall, nor permit a serious attack on either Australia or New Zealand."[1]

These were brave words, but by now they were nothing more than a gamble on the course of the war. The truth is that events in the 1930s forced the British to face in 1939 something perilously close to their worst case scenario. Their response made it even harder to defend the Empire in Asia. Grand strategy depended on there being no serious trouble in Europe; there was general war in Europe. Theatre strategy depended on the arrival of the main fleet in Singapore. The fact the Australians demanded assurances the fleet would still be dispatched speaks for itself. Operational strategy focused on holding the base during the period before relief. The immediate defences of the island were more or less complete, but developments in the 1930s made the defence of Singapore much more complicated. This was aggravated by pursuing theatre defence plans that were neither realistic nor sensibly connected to the other links in the chain. Even the hidden link was not in place.

The Americans were well disposed but there were as yet no plans for effective military cooperation. All this was topped off by complacency about Japanese fighting power that was an integral part of all plans and preparations–and should by now have been looking at least a bit casual.

The acid test of the "Singapore strategy" was always going to be whether it could work if circumstances, intentions and capabilities changed. That test was always going to be daunting after the decision to settle for a base too small to handle the fleet necessary to make it work. Unfortunately, the problems of the 1930s made the 1920s seem serene by comparison. While on the one hand the clear threat of war provoked a gradual revival of defence spending and preparations, on the other hand this revival was erratic and uneven. Until very late in the day deterrence took pride of place over readiness, not always in ways that made the two compatible. From 1933 on British decision makers were challenged by so many serious problems, many pulling in different directions, that they could not bring foreign and defence policy together coherently. By autumn 1939, the only real chance for an effective defence against Japan rested on the war in Europe going exactly as the Allies hoped or on the Japanese being as feeble as many thought they were.

Our three central questions remained constant. First, how could diplomacy and defence policy best be related to each other? Second, what was the most dangerous threat, and the best strategy to meet it? Finally, what must be done to apply that strategy? This time, the answer to the first question was clear in principle, and a reasonable consensus arose between ministers and advisers: diplomacy must find a way to reduce the threats facing the Empire, if it could not avert war altogether. This policy foundered on several rocks; regarding Japan, a fundamental clash of interests from 1931 was the real problem. The answer to the second question remained constant in one respect: the worst threat was a fullscale assault by Japan. But as to the best strategy, while it came under direct challenge at least twice, and was increasingly undermined by events, the "Singapore strategy" remained operative. This led to more dramatic change in the third key question: how to hold the naval base in the period before relief. On this level, the problem became insoluble.

The optimism of 1930 was never warranted. The economic upheaval generated by the crash of the New York stock exchange in autumn 1929 spread across the globe, ruining currencies, banks, and companies, escalating to the Great Depression that destroyed first national confidence and then the international order itself. Tariff walls and economic nationalism became the order of the day in all the principal industrial economies. The U.K. was hit hard. Many of its already suffering older industries, notably shipbuilding, were driven near to the wall. But the effect on two nations in particular was catastrophic. The German economy was virtually paralyzed and unemployment soared out of control. Fear and anger proved fertile breeding grounds for extremism. The fragile Weimar Republic collapsed in the rise to power of Adolf Hitler and the Nazi Party. From January 1933 Germany was led by a man who made no bones about his desire to restore Germany as a great power, renounce the peace settlement of 1919, and bring about a new order in Europe. In Japan, national politics had already taken a turn towards more assertive nationalism in 1927 with the accession of an administration led by Baron Tanaka. Tanaka was far more sympathetic to the imperial course than his predecessor and pressed for a more aggressive foreign policy, especially towards China. In this atmosphere the impact of economic turmoil on Japan was explosive. American loans and supplies of raw cotton declined sharply, banks failed, and crucial primary export industries, such as silk, were devastated. This spread severe hardship through regions of the country closely associated with the army, source of much of its manpower.[2] The repercussions proved fatal to democracy and internationalism in Japan.

While there was nothing like the coherence of either leadership or program that emerged in Germany, the critical mass in Japanese decision making shifted steadily towards imperial expansion and hegemony in China as a new national policy. This resurgence of support for imperial expansion overwhelmed a political system always vulnerable to military domination. No government could be formed without the consent of the Imperial Japanese Army (IJA) and IJN, who had the prerogatives of appointing the War and Navy Ministers and direct access to Emperor Hirohito. While it is true the miserable state of interservice cooperation in Japan made the British situation look solid by comparison, a growing number of officers at all levels in both services increasingly favoured an imperial policy, and became more willing to take direct action. This was particularly true of the IJA, which was riven by factional feuding. The high command proved unable to prevent extremist officers from unleashing a campaign of intimidation and even assassination against politicians and officers who opposed a new course. The Kwantung Army, deployed to protect Japanese interests in Manchuria, became a concentration point for those eager to force Japan to pursue a more forward policy. Civilian and military imperialists focused on Manchuria, with its abundant land and raw materials, as an essential area of interest in any policy seeking outlets for expansion. Most came to see it as a first step towards the ultimate goal: dominance of China proper.[3]

In September 1931 the Kwantung Army staged an incident that gave it an excuse to launch an allout conquest of Manchuria.[4] Control of Manchuria would put the Japanese in a position to expand their own power, threaten the Soviet Union to the north, and leave them poised to dominate China. That would not only jeopardize the large British interests in China, it would shake the very basis of the international system in Asia, on which the Empire's security really rested. Yet the British could not respond to this Japanese adventure because they were too hard pressed by problems at home.

That same month, the Labour government broke under the pressure of economic troubles that sparked an outright mutiny at the RN base at Invergordon, in response to wage cuts, and forced the nation to abandon the gold standard. MacDonald formed a new National government but could only retain a few of his party colleagues, and found himself leading an administration dominated by the Conservatives. Under the circumstances there was no chance whatever of any British military response to events in Manchuria. The COS wanted no part of the matter in any case, arguing there were no concrete national interests directly threatened by the Japanese move and the last thing the Empire needed was trouble with Japan.[5] Unfortunately, there were two complicating factors. The Americans were not willing to make a direct response either, but were very angry about the Japanese move and pressed for strong diplomatic action. And the League of Nations became involved, when China complained to that body and appealed for help under the provisions of its Covenant. This put the new British government in a dangerous position.

Public opinion strongly supported the League of Nations as the principal bulwark of international order. The idea that a global organization of states would act together to resist acts of aggression or violations of international law was seen as morally superior to the discredited "old diplomacy" based on bilateral alliances, balance of power, and the amoral pursuit of national interests. But for the British, this new approach of collective security actually threatened them with unlimited liability. While the small member states of the League might condemn an aggressor, there was little they could do if conflict ensued. The burden would fall on the great powers, and the abdication of the U.S.A. left the U.K. and France carrying the load. This meant in theory the British were now obliged to risk war to defend anyone anywhere when League rules were broken, rather than only defend their own direct interests and territories. The COS and Colonel Maurice Hankey, the influential Secretary of the CID, warned successive governments not to place too much emphasis on the League as a force in international affairs. Their voices were trumped by the appeal of pleasing public opinion and posing to the world as a moral leader. Successive governments stated repeatedly the U.K. would lead the way to establish collective security.[6] Now they paid the price.

The National government found to its dismay it had to respond to the

Manchurian Crisis. This was a tall order. Something must be done that would satisfy public opinion, not anger the Americans, and not provoke the Japanese. But anything likely to satisfy the public was almost bound to anger the Japanese. British leaders were themselves divided. As for the Americans, neither party really trusted the other to pursue joint action without leaving the other in the lurch if the situation became tense.[7] To appease public opinion a British aristocrat was sent to China as leader of a League Commission of Inquiry. Lord Lytton moved slowly, to allow events to settle the issue themselves. The Kwantung Army duly overran Manchuria, exciting widespread admiration and pride in Japan. Fighting spread to Shanghai, a focal point for Western interests in China, in the spring of 1932. This prompted the American government to announce a new policy: nonrecognition of any changes made by force in the status quo in China. This hollow denunciation proved to be the only response by the author of the "Washington system" to its demise. Lytton finally had no choice but to report. He informed the League in October that chronic internal strife in China was not irrelevant, but had to admit the Japanese had instigated a war of conquest. The Japanese stormed out of the room, and out of the League itself in March 1933.[8]

These 18 months were the turning point in international relations in the Far East. Japan went from ostensible partner in the League of Nations and "Washington system" to a hungry imperial power, absorbing the fruits of conquest, but smarting over chastisement strong enough to annoy but too weak to deter. The British and Americans blamed each other for failing to "solve" the crisis, and this mistrust affected how they saw each other for the rest of the decade.[9] As for the League, it was exposed as a failure but in a manner that made the British look weak. Circumstances had indeed changed, drastically and rapidly. It now had to be assumed intentions would change also. In their *Annual Review* for 1932, the COS remarked "The above events prompt inquiry as to our own readiness to face aggression by Japan. The situation is about as bad as it could be." They noted that only light naval forces were deployed in the Far East, the Singapore base and its defences remained far from complete, the Japanese moved in Manchuria with little or no warning and great speed, and for all intents and purposes the Empire was in no position to defend itself against Japan. The COS concluded bluntly "We have no hesitation in ascribing this highly dangerous weakness mainly to the assumption that at any given date there will be no major war for ten years." On 23 March 1932 Cabinet in effect terminated the Ten Year Rule.[10]

Unfortunately, the government moved at a snail's pace away from pursuing disarmament towards rebuilding a position of strength. Fundamental differences between France and Germany ruined the disarmament conference on which so much emphasis was placed; the talks collapsed in 1933 and Hitler pulled Germany out of the League that same year. The COS *Annual Review* for 1933 made an even more forceful case. The emergence of an unpredictable Germany was a potential disaster. Grand strategy depended on the RN providing a fleet strong enough to face the IJN while at the same time maintaining superiority in home waters. Should Germany embark on a large expansion of its forces, as now seemed likely, this would be problematic. Worse, the Admiralty claimed to have intelligence of Japanese plans for a seaborne invasion to take Singapore by a coup de main, nearly activated at the height of the trouble in Shanghai, that would take only 10 days to mount. Cabinet took up the issue in November and finally, 21 months after abandoning the 10 Year Rule, took the next halting step towards preparedness. A Defence Requirements Committee (DRC), chaired by Hankey, was established to investigate requirements for imperial defence, and prepare a program to meet the worst deficiencies.[11]

Now that a clear danger was emerging, the system was responding. The problem was identified. But it was obvious how difficult it would be to reach a consensus on what must be done, for the same old reason: the cost, economic and political, of facing a still not present danger. The DRC was instructed only to itemize the worst deficiencies, and required to "take full account of the financial position of the country." Nor was it clear how Japan could be mollified, even if this could be done without annoying the Americans. After all, Japanese expansion by force caused the problem in the first place, and it would not be in the Empire's interest to stand aside if Japan tried to become hegemon in China. But what could it be offered to cease and desist? For the next three and a half years, diplomacy was hesitant and erratic, in a policy that can only be characterized as drift. A weak and divided government, led by Prime Ministers who tried to avoid trouble abroad at almost any cost– MacDonald until 1935, then Baldwin–twisted from one ad hoc approach to another. Given that defence policy must be related to foreign policy, it suffered accordingly.

The DRC investigations quickly complicated the problem. The COS, led by the First Sea Lord, Admiral Sir Ernle Chatfield, regarded the Far East as the immediate priority.

They argued that once Singapore was secure and the RN strong enough to cover its responsibilities the overall position would be much healthier. The Treasury, represented by Warren Fisher, insisted the U.K. could not possibly afford to face two firstclass enemies in separate theatres at the same time. The compromise report that went to the Cabinet implanted what became a permanent tilt to British policy. The DRC envisaged an ultimate accommodation with Japan, but for the moment it was necessary to "show a tooth" to regain credibility in the Far East; however, "… we take Germany as the ultimate potential enemy against whom our 'long range' defence policy has to be directed." Cabinet referred the report to a Ministerial Committee, which took nearly six months to argue it out. It finally recommended a program onethird smaller than what the DRC identified as the bare minimum to restore the services to acceptable readiness.[12]

The British voice that spoke with the greatest strength and consistency for the rest of the decade shaped the debate from the start: Neville Chamberlain. The Chancellor accepted the premise Germany was "the ultimate enemy" and home defence came first. At the same time, he hoped to find a diplomatic way to resolve differences and preempt another major war, in both Europe and the Far East. Defence spending must be regarded first as a step to restore credibility to British power and therefore diplomacy and second as insurance in case diplomacy failed–but rearmament must not jeopardize diplomacy. It must also be based on what the economy could afford, rather than on what the services required, if the two clashed. A strong economy was indeed the "fourth arm" of defence, the basis from which all else must flow, so rearmament without financial limits would be counterproductive. The catastrophe of another land war in Europe should be avoided at almost any cost. The best way to meet all these requirements was to build up an air force that could deter any attack on the U.K. itself, threaten Germany with direct assault, but not entangle the British in a continental commitment, with the risk of massive casualties on the ground. Many decision makers in London shared some or even all these assumptions, which is not surprising. The British Empire was a satisfied power. It did not want to fight anyone, and any major war anywhere could only jeopardize its interests. And concentrating on the air force promised to produce rapid, relatively cheap and publicly impressive increases in power that, if worst came to worst, would be poised for home defence. This all seemed persuasive, and Chamberlain led the way in pulling together what policy there was in the middle 1930s.[13] But while building up the air force might in the last resort protect the U.K., it would not secure the Far East. There, Chamberlain had other ideas.

The Chancellor mounted a protracted lobby to pursue a rapprochement with Japan. This engaged time and energy for no good result, foundering on Japanese behaviour. In 1934 the Japanese made public statements on the need to dominate China proper, and at the end of the year gave the required notice to terminate the naval agreements.[14] Chamberlain was meanwhile persuaded that whatever happened it was necessary to complete the base and defences at Singapore, both to reassure the Dominions and colonies, and to have any hope to impress the Japanese. During 1933 and 1934 previous obstacles were swept aside and the government committed itself to complete the "truncated Red scheme" with coastal and air defences. But as part of his drive to preserve the "fourth arm," and rely on diplomacy to reduce threats, in mid1934 the Chancellor launched a major assault on the "Singapore strategy."

Chamberlain hoped to scuttle the whole policy to send out the main fleet to face the IJN. He based his argument squarely on the premise the nation could not afford two major wars at the same time, so it made more sense to reach an accommodation with Japan in order to be ready to face the ultimate enemy, Germany. When completed the Singapore base should be used only by light units and submarines, which by their presence could cover the Empire's interests without provoking a clash or overstretching the fleet. This also promised substantial savings, shipbuilding being the most expensive and timeconsuming capital equipment in rearmament. This amounted to the very gamble with the security of the Empire east of India the Treasury first suggested in 1921. The Admiralty categorically refused even to consider such a gamble. Chatfield threatened not very subtly to lead the Board in a mass resignation. What really aroused the sailors was the sense the Chancellor wished to prevent any serious expansion of the fleet itself, a fear shared by Hankey. They insisted the fleet must be expanded as a general requirement of imperial defence period, not just to support the "Singapore strategy." The end result was a standoff brokered by Baldwin in July 1934. The base would be completed. The strategy would stand. But while DRC proposals to expand the fleet would be considered, they too would be reduced by at least one third and the navy would stand behind the air force in priority. Meanwhile, diplomatic efforts to woo Japan would continue.[15]

In retrospect, this was a fateful decision. It meant completing the base before expanding the fleet enough to give it a realistic chance to use it. Given how long it took to build and commission major warships, this further self-imposed delay in ending the "naval holiday" and launching new capital units added an uncertain number of years to the danger time in which the RN might well not be able to take the lead against Japan if trouble erupted. It also guaranteed that if Japan did attack the British Empire it would indeed go for Singapore, to knock out the base on which its enemy's strategy would depend. Sadly, diplomacy found no solution.

In 1935 Hitler renounced the Treaty of Versailles and announced fullscale rearmament. In response the British concluded with him an AngloGerman Naval Agreement, which recognized this *fait accompli* by allowing Germany to build a navy up to 35% of the strength of the RN. This angered the French and shattered the 1919 settlement, but, making the best of something they could not stop anyway, the British regarded it as a worthwhile bargain, containing Germany in the one area that threatened them most. No such rationalizing could conceal the repercussions of the dispute that broke out over Italian aggression against Ethiopia that autumn. Once again the existence of the League forced the government to intervene in a matter it really wanted to ignore, especially as in the midst of the "crisis" Baldwin won an election by promising to uphold collective security. And once again the result was disaster, because the British were caught trying to make it look as if they were taking serious action against Italy while privately working to avoid any such thing. The Italians were not stopped but rather driven towards Hitler, who used the distraction to dismantle more pieces of the old settlement. This left the League in complete ruin, and also wrecked British hopes to entice Italy into a front to contain Germany. That added to the strategic worries facing the Empire, especially the RN, now contemplating possible trouble in the Mediterranean as well as home waters and the Far East. Meanwhile, an attempted coup in Tokyo in February 1936, launched by middle ranking army officers demanding a more assertive imperial policy, signalled further trouble in the Far East. This was compounded by ongoing strife in China and renewed Japanese naval building. British rearmament did increase, but the emphasis remained on the air force, the Treasury remained stubborn, and consensus remained elusive.

By 1937, five years after the Ten Year Rule was terminated, British policy was more disjointed than ever. And there were worrying signs German rearmament was moving ahead rapidly, as German policy became more menacing. But in the spring things changed dramatically. The British government was compelled to thrash out its policy for imperial defence in a comprehensive review for an Imperial Conference of Prime Ministers in London. Taking charge was Neville Chamberlain, who replaced Baldwin in May. Chamberlain could now impose his personality and views on British policy far more deeply. A forceful and confident man, he did just that.

The drift in British policy rapidly came to an end. It was replaced by a determined effort to reach a lasting settlement of outstanding difficulties, first with Germany, ultimately with Japan. Chamberlain also hoped either to lure Italy back into a bloc to contain Germany or find an agreement with it also, perhaps as part of an overall European settlement. This marked the beginning of coherent appeasement, a determined attempt by the leading satisfied power to preempt another general war through diplomacy. Chamberlain was anything but a weak leader. He feared general war, not defeat, believing that even a victorious war would destroy the social order and therefore British power and prosperity. The new Prime Minister regarded the Americans with suspicion, fearing they would talk tough but act little, leaving others to face the consequences. He loathed the Soviet Union, seeing it as perhaps the most implacable threat to British civilization in the longest run. He believed by instinct that Hitler was an uncouth but rational statesman with whom an acceptable revision could be reached. And he regarded rearmament as he had from the start: a necessary corollary to diplomacy but one that must be controlled by economic means and guided by diplomatic ends.[16] While the "Singapore strategy" proved irreversible even to him, in all other respects Chamberlain's voice nearly always proved decisive for the next three years. The system at last had firm leadership. Unfortunately, the leader made an incorrect diagnosis.

In July the IJA provoked what became a full scale war in China –and as it turned out the prologue to a world war. The British government did not welcome the military confrontation in China. Given a recent change in government in Tokyo, with a broad coalition under Prince Konoye taking office, they saw reason to hope the more aggressive militarists would be reined in. Failing that, disagreements about policy and priorities remained loud and acrimonious amongst leading Japanese. Some saw the Soviet Union as the ultimate enemy and favoured concentrating for a showdown with it, whilst moving slowly in China. But there were countervailing signs. The Japanese not only terminated the naval agreements and walked out of the 1935 London Naval Conference, they then embarked on an ambitious naval expansion program. More Japanese leaders, including the new Prime Minister, came to favour direct action in China. This ambivalence in Japanese policy made it more difficult for the British to reach any sort of accommodation with Tokyo. Just about the only thing on which there was wide agreement amongst the Japanese was that once fighting in China started it must be prosecuted until Japanese dominance was secure.[17] But Japanese dominance in China was the one thing that in the end the British, and more important the Americans, could not accept.

A "turning point that failed to turn" came at the end of 1937 when the war took a turn for the worse. Japanese forces advancing up the Yangtze valley, in the very heart of the area of greatest economic interest to the U.K., put the old imperial city of Nanking to the sword in a brutal sack and pillage. During the fighting Japanese aircraft "accidentally" bombed American and British gunboats, causing casualties. Public opinion was aroused and tensions ran high.[18] The two Western governments were provoked enough to arrange staff discussions on possible naval cooperation. But neither Chamberlain nor President Roosevelt believed their publics were aroused enough to be ready for war in Asia. Nor did they, especially Chamberlain, believe the other was ready to stand firm in solidarity if a confrontation loomed. The staff talks were kept secret and nothing substantial came of them. The Japanese apologized and offered compensation, and the crisis diminished. But the Japanese were now clearly on a collision course with Western interests in China.[19]

The harder the Japanese tried to conclude their war in China, the deeper they bogged down in it. The IJA found to its dismay that while it won battle after battle, China was simply too large to subdue by military means. Japanese supply lines were stretched to the limit in the interior. Japanese forces moved along the coast, taking Hainan island and the southern regions in 1939, but found themselves restricted mainly to large towns and major arteries when they advanced inland. China was also too divided politically to find someone who could offer a surrender that would truly end the war with Japan in firm control.[20] The British offered the Japanese trade concessions, loans, sympathetic help in discussions with the Chinese and the Americans, and other bits and pieces. The Prime Minister, the FO and the Embassy in Tokyo pursued such initiatives tirelessly, to no avail. All they really had to offer was good will and minor bribery. That was worth much less to the squabbling cabal of imperialists in Tokyo than success in China.[21]

The problem peaked in 1939 with a crisis over the British concession in the northern city of Tientsin. The Chinese attitude towards extraterritorial enclaves had changed dramatically. No longer humiliations to be exorcised, they were now contact points to seek help in fighting the most dangerous enemy. The more the war bogged down, the more upset the Japanese became over these foreign loopholes. When a Japanese offical was assassinated within the British concession in April, tensions exploded. British officials argued over how to proceed. Some felt the suspects should be handed over to the Japanese, to avert confrontation. Others argued this would only whet Japanese appetites and provoke more pressure. The Japanese made the argument moot in June by subjecting the concession to a virtual siege.[22] But when Cabinet asked what could be done to retaliate, the answer was grim. The COS reported that the minimum force required for any effective deployment to the Far East was eight capital ships. That would leave only three operational capital ships available for home waters and the Mediterranean. But this was now totally unacceptable with Germany rearmed and the European situation very tense. So the most that could be spared for the Far East was two. If the Japanese took up the challenge, such a small squadron could only withdraw and leave Singapore open or be destroyed. They concluded "... that, without the active cooperation of the United States of America, it would not be justifiable, from the military point of view, having regard to the existing international situation, to take any avoidable action which might lead to hostilities with Japan."[23]

How had matters come to such a sorry state? While the main reason was of course the policies of aggression pursued by Germany and Japan, on the British side the key factor was Chamberlain's policy of determined appeasement. The Prime Minister focused on Germany, culminating in the controversial Munich Pact of September 1938, by which war over Czechoslovakia was averted. But for Chamberlain the real point was a written promise from Hitler to resolve future problems by negotiation, not by force. He regarded this as the basis of the final political settlement that was his real goal, to prevent changes in the international order by war; this was the famous paper waved in the air to laud "peace in our time." Not until 1939 was it clear the Prime Minister fatally misread Hitler, who wanted to destroy the old order and replace it by one fashioned on radically different lines. Such a war would shatter the balance of power in Europe. British policy finally changed when the British nation determined correctly in the first half of 1939 that Hitler was bent on doing just that. Now at last the U.K. began seriously to prepare for war.[24] It was, for the Far East at least, much too late. There was indeed an impressive rise in defence spending, but the focus remained on the air force, with its dual roles of home defence and the strategic bombing deterrent. The government did not accept a renewed continental commitment until spring 1939, and only then introduced conscription to build up the mass army required for such a campaign. The navy, despite a large increase in its programs from 1936, found itself worse off now that it faced three possible foes in three different theatres. It would take time to complete new ships laid down from 1936, and some older vessels were undergoing modernization refits that rendered them unavailable until 1940. The Prime Minister placed so much emphasis on appeasement the government failed to adjust rearmament to the changing situation, and found itself too far behind to catch up when the moment of truth arrived in Tientsin. [25]

Chamberlain did not do this by himself. From 1935 the COS supported the policy to use diplomacy to reduce the number of possible threats. Chamberlain was also on solid ground when he argued that only after there was clearly no other choice would public opinion and the Dominions accept the need to risk another major war–a situation that did not develop before 1939. It is also fair to say the U.S. government made no great effort to resist German and Japanese actions either; President Roosevelt slowly led public opinion towards the distant point where it might be ready to join an antiaggression bloc.[26] But the Prime Minister should be held accountable for allowing rearmament, and therefore defence policy, to become so detached from diplomacy. He was simply too certain of his own judgement, too convinced his diplomacy would produce a lasting settlement, to make sure the insurance policy received enough attention to prepare the nation for war if he failed. As he found out starkly over Tientsin, Chamberlain was negotiating from a position that in Europe was at best uncertain, and in the Far East was simply weak. The bare minimum was indeed secured. The air force was in a position to defend the home islands and the navy could dominate home waters. But beyond that the position of strength, and therefore the initiative, now lay with the powers who rearmed more aggressively. The failure of appeasement in Europe meant that if it failed in Asia there was little the British could do about it until they threw caution to the winds and seriously prepared to fight a general war. That would take time.

Fate sometimes arranges things in ironic harmony. June 1939 was one such occasion. The gathering clouds of war at least prodded the British and Americans to renew secret talks on possible naval and other cooperation. But in the midst of the Tienstin crisis the British could only tell the Americans that as the risk of war in Europe now seemed so high it was doubtful whether within the next year they would be able to send a strong fleet to the Far East. The Americans, who were now prepared to discuss naval cooperation in the Pacific, including possibly even operating from Singapore, absorbed this news the RN was too overstretched to do anything but bluff against Japan.[27] Both parties allowed the ambivalence of their relationship, and mutual suspicions between governments, to impede efforts to work together to protect vital interests that in Asia were fundamentally aligned. Now they, and the world, had to pay the price. Tension over Tientsin was reduced by a tortuously worded diplomatic agreement, the British recognizing Japan's "special interest" in north China. This fooled no one. Chamberlain felt obliged to personally reassure a new and worried Australian government, now led by Robert Menzies, that promises to Canberra made in March still stood. Tientsin pulled the veil away. British policy failed to deflect any threats, much less appease anyone conclusively. American assistance had not been secured, and the effort put into rearmament had not been directed into the means needed to stand up to Japan. Circumstances and intentions had outpaced capabilities.[28]

Fate is however fickle, and almost immediately stepped in to buy the British some time. When war broke out in Europe on 3 September, Japan did not jump into the fight. Chamberlain's last card to deter Germany was an effort to bring the Soviet Union into an antiGerman front. Hating and mistrusting the Soviets as he did, the Prime Minister did not press the talks hard enough. In late August Hitler outbid him, buying the Soviets off with a promise to share a carveup in Eastern Europe. But in July the "strike north" bloc in Japan, hoping to exploit European distractions and confident of Japanese military prowess, instigated the Kwantung Army to launch a probe into Siberia. There the Japanese discovered the difference between dealing with a power that put appeasement first and a power that prepared seriously for war. The Red Army sent the Japanese forces reeling back in heavy defeat. The IJA was not ready to take on a modern mechanized army prepared for a major campaign on the open plain. While this disaster could be concealed from the public the Nazi-Soviet Pact could not, and the government fell. Tokyo, in confusion, stayed its hand.[29] The British government, for the moment, did not face a war in the Far East. Nevertheless the climb-down over Tientsin made it clear this might be only a stay of execution.

It is noteworthy that even Chamberlain at his most determined could not overturn the "Singapore strategy." Besides his attempt to discard it in 1934, the plan faced one more bid to replace it by something quite different before war finally broke out in Europe. But it remained official policy, despite dramatic changes in circumstances and intentions that outpaced changes in capabilities. This needs to be explained, not least because of the negative effect it had on plans at the theatre level. The COS remained convinced any attack by Japan on the British Empire in the Far East would focus on a campaign to conquer Singapore as fast as possible. As the decade advanced, British planners found it harder to estimate just what circumstances might obtain if and when this main threat materialized. Changes were made, but they made an already problematic strategy all but impossible. The main reason for this was the real wellspring of the "Singapore strategy": the politics of imperial defence.

When the COS successfully pressed the government to abandon the Ten Year Rule in spring 1932, they commented in detail on the poor state of Singapore's defences, but did not question the prevailing war plan. If Singapore were lost and the fleet could not deploy, "The whole of our territory in the Far East, as well as the coastlines of India and the Dominions and our vast trade and shipping, lies open to attack."[30] On 23 March 1934 the Admiralty and the FO prepared a joint memorandum to influence government policy at the illfated naval conference scheduled for 1935. To underline the damage done by naval reductions and restrictions they asked: "If we have to send out to the Far East an adequate fleet, how is our security in Home Waters to be obtained, and what is the minimum strength of our naval forces in those waters that can be accepted?" This of course had always been an inherent problem, but events now pushed it forward. The proposed solution was based on this definition of the "minimum strategical requirement for security":

We should be able to send to the Far East a fleet sufficient to provide 'cover' against the Japanese fleet; we should have sufficient additional forces behind this shield for the protection of our territories and mercantile marine against Japanese attack; at the same time we should be able to retain in European waters a force sufficient to act as a deterrent and to prevent the strongest European naval Power from obtaining control of our vital home terminal areas while we can make the necessary redispositions.[31]

The solution was of course a rapid and substantial increase in naval strength. This was the lobby that provoked Chamberlain, two months later, to try to scrap the "Singapore strategy" altogether. The COS rebutted this challenge. But this success would mean very little if the grand strategy was not viable, or could not be made so. The problem could not be compartmentalized: without rearmament, the RN would be too small to meet its obligations; if it could not do so the strategy to fend off a Japanese attack could not be implemented; without a strongly defended base it could not even hope to try.

From early 1933 the COS, strongly supported by Hankey and some Dominion and colonial governments, pressed the government to complete the naval base and its defences as fast as possible. Cabinet had already decided in June 1932 to complete the "truncated Red Scheme," but refused to announce the decision or set a deadline. Some ministers insisted the U.K. must not give any other power an excuse to abandon the ongoing Disarmament Conference in Geneva; others wanted the Treasury to review the project again. By spring 1933 these objections faded. In April Cabinet agreed to complete the first stage of the defences by 1938, and approved additional funds for another airbase and other facilities.[32] But it made no comment on proposals by Chatfield to station an advance force of battlecruisers at Singapore. This was a long standing Admiralty idea which could have breathed some life into the whole "Singapore strategy" by deploying capital ships in the Far East in peacetime. Such a vested interest would have sparked pressure from its own commander, let alone public and Dominion opinion, for reinforcement in an emergency. Perhaps for that very reason, Chatfield was overborne. A year later he hinted the idea was rejected off the record for "political reasons." While such a deployment would not have made the base large enough for the fleet, nor the fleet large enough for war, it might well have provoked more public attention to these problems, with unpredictable results. Given that it would also threaten the policy to seek reconciliation with Japan, as well as the desire to concentrate the fleet closer to home, Chatfield's comment seems credible. Instead the government decided in 1934 to deploy the ships in the Mediterranean, from where they might be shifted west or east as events might require. While they did this, Hankey toured the Empire to "consult" Dominion governments on defence problems; one of his most important tasks was to reassure the Australians the "Singapore strategy" remained sound.

The obvious wobble in the whole strategy was underlined at the end of the year when the government ruled that on completion the Singapore base would be placed on a "care and maintenance" basis: only to be brought up to full operation as much as six months after the onset of an emergency.[33] Chamberlain's hand is not hard to detect in this; nor is the influence of identifying Germany as "the ultimate enemy."

The different proposals made by Chamberlain and Chatfield represented polar opposite suggestions regarding the "Singapore strategy": abandon it, versus take a concrete step to implement it. Pursuing either one might have forced British decision makers to accept the fact their strategy for war against Japan was not viable and something drastic must be done before it was too late. Instead they opted to muddle along, maintaining a strategy never plausible to begin with, then undermined by financial pressures, now rapidly being overtaken by geopolitics. What they lost in 1934 was the chance to restore clarity and realism to the search for a policy that might offer credible protection against Japan. This would have meant going back to first principles and establishing priorities. If Germany was the ultimate enemy but Japan could not be appeased, then how much would the Empire sacrifice in order to defend itself in the Far East–or how great a risk was it willing to take that it could not? No such overhaul took place before the European situation took its fatal turn for the worse. Chatfield dominated the COS and although he could not win more of the rearmament pie he could and did preserve the RN's dominance of war plans against Japan. With nothing to replace the "Singapore strategy" the Admiralty clung to it. They hoped that completing the base and upgrading the defences would make it look to public opinion at home and abroad as if real progress was being made building a credible defence against Japan. And even if a threat emerged in less than optimal conditions, something might still be done to keep the Japanese at bay long enough to find countermeasures to repel them. There was no review, while conditions were still fluid, of how the strategy might be altered or even replaced, or how the three services might combine their resources. It was still the navy's plan. The sailors kept control and continued to hope events would fall into line with that plan.

In March 1936 events in Europe exposed the risk run by this approach. The COS were asked to report on how ready the services were to wage war on Germany. They admitted that if hostilities erupted in Europe before much greater progress was made in rearmament, it would be "very difficult" to move a battlefleet to the Far East within six weeks. But when pressed by the Australians, Chatfield insisted the "Singapore strategy" remained the only possible basis for defence against Japan–and argued current conditions were exceptionally bad and likely to improve. It is hard to see on what basis he made that last argument. Chatfield knew full well it was more likely events would deteriorate faster than the RN could be strengthened.[34] It might be reasonable to hope appeasement would work in Europe, but by that time it was imprudent not to consider what must be done if it did not. Here was the dilemma. What would it cost the British to admit to the Australians that if the situation got any worse the Empire might be in very deep trouble indeed, but they had no idea what could be done about it?

When the COS began to prepare for the Imperial Conference scheduled for spring 1937, they came under sustained pressure from civilian and military authorities in the Far East regarding the "period before relief." The chiefs were forced to admit that because the deterioration of the situation in Europe had so outpaced British rearmament, the six week timetable was no longer credible. Chatfield argued the most sensible strategic move would be to extend the period to six months, to cover all possible delays that might be caused by events in Europe. That would make it possible to increase stocks in the region, and rewrite local plans on the basis of a prolonged defence. But this most sensible strategic move would certainly shock and alarm the Australians. That might gravely upset imperial cooperation and even affect public confidence. So on balance it looked better to extend the period to 70 days, a figure that allowed for some change in related plans without causing too much political uproar. The issue bogged down in the CID until March 1938, when the change was finally and quietly approved.[35] Meanwhile the review of imperial defence went ahead at the Imperial Conference.

The conference met in May and June: just before the Japanese sparked the war in China that would grow to engulf all of Asia; just as the vigorous new Prime Minister took charge of British policy; at the last moment it might still have been possible to accelerate rearmament, and make changes in grand strategy, in time for them to take effect when they turned out to be needed in 1940. The British nevertheless offered reassurances that, based on what they knew, can only be described as wilfully optimistic. Chatfield assured Dominion leaders that even if the U.K. was at war in Europe, any attack by Japan would still be met by deploying a fleet strong enough to contain it. If necessary, in the last resort the Eastern Mediterranean would be denuded in order to redeploy the fleet. Even before the fleet began to receive new vessels, and while its older ones underwent refits, at its anticipated nadir in 1939 the RN still expected to find eight capital ships to send east. But just weeks before, on 26 April, the Admiralty Board submitted to Cabinet a Memorandum on the New Standard of Naval Strength that made a starkly different statement:

With the rise of modern navies in Europe our present standard of naval strength would not only be insufficient for the defence of our position in the Far East if we were already at war in Europe, but it would preclude at any time the despatch of a sufficient fleet to the Far East to deter Japan from aggression.

The only solution was the most rapid possible expansion of the RN to the necessary level, defined by the Admiralty as 20 capital ships, 15 aircraft carriers, 100 cruisers, and appropriate supporting vessels. Given that the order of battle then included 15 capital ships, seven aircraft carriers and 62 cruisers, and that the Admiralty surely did not expect Cabinet to fund their entire request, what can we make of this?[36]

It is true the Admiralty noted they could trim this list if an agreement was reached with Japan, but the figure they offered was a cut of £3 million, in a shopping list of some £104 million. This fraction was offset anyway when other Dominions rejected Australia's call to forge a rapprochement with Japan. Canada in particular balked at making the conference a forum for setting a common imperial foreign policy.[37] It was the worst of all possible worlds, and it was shaping up fast. The U.K. had the responsibility to defend the Empire as a whole without any guarantee the Dominions would assist other than in their own local defence. It could not possibly do so without their help in a general war, but the Dominions were divided. Strategically it was impossible to make advance commitments. Politically it seemed necessary to do so. And the spectre of real trouble in more than one area at the same time loomed ever larger. Under the circumstances, the British offered their assurances for the same reason Chatfield did the year before. They decided that to admit it might be impossible to send out the fleet, before events gave them absolutely no choice but to make such a confession, would do more harm than good. Such a confession would encourage Japan, infuriate the Australians, and discourage the Far Eastern colonies, perhaps even rebound on public opinion at home and other powers in Europe.

Technically this was not lying to the Australians. The British still insisted they could not know just what the situation might be at any moment of crisis. But it was at best a dangerous promise. The Australians in particular made plans assuming the grand strategy on which they were based was at least credible. It was not. But if there was deception it was self-deception, and the Australians can fairly be charged with sharing in it. The "Singapore strategy" eroded before their eyes, but they never insisted on concrete assurances. They preferred to accept vaguer promises that allowed them to hide behind British pledges and avoid increasing their own spending. This promise to maintain a strategy that was never viable kept the Dominions in line behind British policy, in return for assurances the policy would not be overwhelmed even by a turn for the worse.[38] To call this a calculated risk would be generous, because the strategy itself was so defective. This was a reckless gamble with the solidarity the Empire would need desperately if it ever needed it at all. If there was no way to cut the Gordian Knot, such as a rapprochement with Japan, or a huge naval expansion overnight, then both governments preferred to play for time rather than cancel the existing policy and start afresh.

The base was ceremonially opened in February 1938, well before it was completely finished. Predictably, this did not settle Dominion jitters. When the brief glow of the Munich Agreement faded,the Australians pressed the British to renew their promise they would send a fleet to use the base. The Admiralty promised on 1 November that it still regarded the "Singapore strategy" as the basis for imperial defence against Japan, and still intended to send seven capital ships east if necessary–but did not say why it was sure this could be done. And things were now finally beginning to change inside the Admiralty. A new First Sea Lord, Admiral Sir Roger Backhouse, felt the strategy no longer made sense. He decided it was time to reconsider grand strategy for war in the worst case: in Europe against two enemies as well as against Japan. Fobbing off the Australians irked him enough to press his planners to get on with just such a review.[39]

On 9 January Backhouse informed the Australian Naval Board he now wondered how the commitment to send seven capital ships to the Far East could be met if war came sooner rather than later. This candour was underlined by a pivotal appreciation of the situation in Europe submitted by the COS on 20 February. For the first time, the COS advised it was necessary to assume the worst case was the most likely and was imminent:

> The British Empire would be threatened simultaneously in Europe, the Mediterranean and the Far East by an immense aggregate of armed force, which neither our present nor our projected strength is designed to meet, with France as our only major ally.

This report marked the point at which the service chiefs argued British grand strategy must now be changed. The Empire now faced a major war likely to overstretch its resources. Despite this clear warning Chatfield, promoted to the Cabinet as Minister for Coordination of Defence, held out for the prevailing strategy. That provoked a lively debate, revolving around an ever clearer difference in appreciation between the former and the present First Sea Lord.[40]

Chatfield continued to insist any fleet sent out must be strong enough to face the Japanese in a fleet engagement. Backhouse felt circumstances had changed too drastically to do this. The two principals became caught up in a broader debate over whether the Mediterranean must now take precedence over the Far East. Such arguments provoked Australian Prime Minister Joseph Lyons on 10 March to warn Chamberlain that speeches hinting the Far East would be reduced in priority prompted the Australian press to infer "that in the event of war Great Britain may not be able to defend her overseas possessions." But all Lyons asked for was "some supplementary and reassuring statement for use here." While the British pondered their reply, German forces moved into the rump of the Czech state. This violated the Munich understanding, dooming Chamberlain's policy of appeasement. On 20 March Chamberlain nevertheless provided the necessary reassurance: even if the British found themselves fighting all three aggressive powers at once "it would still be His Majesty's Government's full intention to despatch a fleet to Singapore." That fleet would have three objects: to prevent any invasion of the Dominions or India, keep open the sea lanes, and "prevent the fall of Singapore." But these promises were cut off at the knees by this warning:

If we were fighting against such a combination never envisaged in our earlier plans, the size of that fleet would necessarily be dependent on a) the moment when Japan entered the war and b) what losses if any our opponents or ourselves had previously sustained.

Lyons did not dwell on the caveats. What mattered to him was the promise. This was unwise, because Chamberlain's caution signaled something vital: the Admiralty was moving away from its long held position.[41]

The Plans Division supported Chatfield, assuming the Japanese would wait for the British to assemble a fleet before they attacked, and the Eastern Mediterranean would be abandoned to allow the fleet to redeploy. But Backhouse tilted the other way, asking for a second opinion from Admiral Sir Reginald Plunkett Ernle Erle Drax. Defying the comic opera image of his name, Drax was a firebrand whose criticisms of the lack of realism and offensive spirit in naval war plans earned him in 1937 a rebuke from Chatfield and early retirement. Pointedly recalled by Backhouse to review the plans, Drax sparked the second and final prewar challenge to the "Singapore strategy." His challenge provoked a crucial change: the strategy was shelved in practice, but remained official policy on paper.

Drax argued that in a war against all three likely enemies, the best grand strategy was to concentrate the fleet against the weakest link–Italy. The fleet could not knock out Germany. But it could quickly "crumple" Italy, whereas it would take time to even assemble against Japan, let alone deliver a rapid knockout blow. Meanwhile, a "flying squadron" of two capital ships would reinforce the small forces in Singapore. This should deter any Japanese move into the Indian Ocean or invasion of Australia, and if aggressively handled could keep the Japanese off balance enough to prevent them doing irreparable harm before the main fleet could arrive. Drax was too optimistic about his time-frame for war against Italy, but this was the first truly different proposal regarding imperial defence against Japan to come from the Admiralty since the inception of the "Singapore strategy." It showed a healthy willingness to confront changing circumstances and search for a new formula.[42] Unfortunately, while this did provoke change, vested interests kept it from going far enough.

The Admiral resisted pressure from the British Ambassador in Tokyo for a show of strength in the Far East on the grounds it now made more sense to stand firm against Italy, which was lining up solidly with Germany. On 5 April the Deputy Chief of the Naval Staff (DCNS), Rear Admiral A.B. Cunningham, underlined the Admiralty's change of heart in a memorandum on the *Dispatch of a Fleet to the Far East*:

> The conclusion which emerges from the foregoing considerations is that there are so many variable factors which cannot at present be assessed, that it is not possible to state definitely how soon after Japanese intervention a Fleet could be dispatched to the Far East. Neither is it possible to enumerate precisely the size of the Fleet that we could afford to send.

Cunningham's comment captured how much and how little had changed. The Admiralty was now planning to concentrate in the Mediterranean, which reversed standing priorities. But the war plan for defence against Japan remained to send out a fleet to engage the main force of the enemy as soon as possible, not a squadron to distract and delay the enemy until something else could be done. The too careful phrasing indicated the Admiralty knew it could no longer promise the fleet would be sent out at any given time, but could not bring itself to drop the "Singapore strategy" entirely and replace it by the "flying squadron" idea. What remained was the worst of both: the promise to send out the fleet was not retracted but the commitment to do so at a fixed time was. The CID accepted Cunningham's paper on 17 April, noting the COS must now reconsider what was required to hold Singapore in Phase I. Australia and New Zealand were not impressed. This time their complaint, on 28 April, was more pointed: while they might not doubt the British intention to race to the rescue, they did doubt "the ability of Great Britain to despatch a fleet of capital ships to the East in time to prevent the fall of Singapore, and the security of Singapore itself before the arrival of the fleet." To no avail. The

"Singapore strategy" was now officially contingent on events, rather than a timetable to be implemented no matter what.[43]

The only thing that ever made the "Singapore strategy" look even remotely realistic as a war plan was the official priority it had in grand strategy: "if trouble does start, we will come whatever the risk." The Admiralty now advised the government to reduce that priority, in favour of an offensive in the Mediterranean. But it would not abandon the commitment in principle to send the fleet out, nor replace the plan by something else. The hollowness of this gamble became clear in June when the Tientsin crisis forced the Admiralty, for the first time, to answer a concrete question: what exactly could be done right now? The European situation reduced the fleet of seven or eight capital ships to two–Drax's "flying squadron." Without a guarantee of American help, the main fleet of the IJN, some 10 capital ships and six aircraft carriers, could only be met in battle if the Mediterranean was almost abandoned. The Admiralty no longer wanted to do this, but nor did it want to adopt any alternative. It embraced Drax' suggestion on grand strategy, but not the plan he suggested for the Far East. Backhouse could not force the issue; exhaustion, which killed him shortly after, forced him to step down in July. The Prime Minister agreed to stand firm in Europe and appease Japan. On 6 July the CID duly raised the "period before relief" yet again, from 70 to 90 days.[44]

That was how matters stood when war broke out in Europe in September. Not only did the Japanese sit quiet for the moment, even announcing their intention to do so, the Italians also sat on the sidelines, going no farther than verbal support for Germany. This allowed the new First Sea Lord, Admiral Sir Dudley Pound, to press for another review of grand strategy. Pound, coming from the post of CinC Mediterranean Fleet, was no great advocate of the "Singapore strategy." He persuaded the COS to raise the "period before relief" yet again, this time to a full 180 days. This meant that even though the British were at war only with Germany, over whom the RN had crushing superiority, the defenders of the naval base were now expected to hold on for *six months* before the main fleet could arrive to take over any war against Japan. Pound's focus was underlined when he appointed the forceful Cunningham to replace him in the Mediterranean, where Italy had to be watched.[45] The Allies moved slowly and deliberately, intending to wear Germany down in a long war with their superior resources. They envisaged steadily mobilizing their imperial war machines behind a defensive shield erected on a western front in France, which would pin the German Army down. In due course Allied economic, air and sea power would tip the balance. Full assistance from the Empire was absolutely necessary, and the British were gratified to see rapid declarations of war by Canada, Australia and New Zealand.[46] But what about the threat from Japan?

In September the government considered whether or not to offer to mediate between China and Japan. On the COS advice they decided it was now in the interests of the British Empire for that war to continue, to keep the Japanese occupied.[47] The COS went on to review the strategic situation in the Far East in light of the war with Germany. On 31 October they advised that while Japan did not seem to pose an immediate threat, it must be expected to exploit any development in Europe to its own advantage, and could not be counted on to sit still for long. This was the situation when Dominion representatives met the British in London in November. In return for sending help in Europe, the Dominions wanted reassurance in the Far East. Churchill's promise came in a memorandum on 17 November, in which he argued Singapore was now a powerful and well-defended fortress, which would take an army of 50,000 four to five months to subdue. Given the great distance involved, the time required, their own prudence, and their preoccupation elsewhere, the Japanese were unlikely to try it, even less likely to go after Australia. On that basis the promise was restated: if it was really necessary the fleet would and still could drop all else and come to the rescue.[48]

It could be argued Churchill was on reasonable ground regarding an invasion of Australia or New Zealand, but by now Singapore was surely another matter. Changes in circumstances, intentions and capabilities since 1931 left the "Singapore strategy" in tatters, and the British knew this. They were more candid with the Americans about prospects in the Far East than they were with their own Dominions. The "Singapore strategy" rested on sending out a force that could handle the main fleet of the IJN in a fleet engagement. War with Germany, the souring of relations with Italy, the failure of appeasement to detach or deflect any threat, the lower priority accorded the RN in rearmament, and the long time it took to expand a navy left the Admiralty quietly admitting by summer 1939 that in *any* circumstances it would now be six months before it could send help. The original premise was six weeks. Confessing such difficulties to the Americans was seen, wrongly, as the most likely way to persuade them to line up with the British Empire to contain Japan. Confessing them to the Dominions was seen as sure to undermine imperial solidarity, threaten public confidence, and above all inhibit the Dominions, especially Australia, from sending help for the war in Europe.[49] It might be fair to say it was not unreasonable to gamble before 1931 that the Empire would not face three enemies, or three threats, at the same time. But it is also fair to argue that from 1932 the British failed to adapt their grand strategy for imperial defence; instead, they carried on trying to make the situation fit the plan. Imperial solidarity now rested on little more than a gamble on the war in Europe.

Our third and final question was what must be done to make sure the best strategy could be implemented. That amounted to the problem of Phase I, the "period before relief." The links were spelt out bluntly in the complaints made by Australia and New Zealand in April 1939. The crux of the matter was also identified by Churchill in that memorandum of November. Leave aside for the moment the fact the base was too small period. If Singapore was now truly a well defended fortress, able to hold out for six months before the main fleet arrived, then much might yet be salvaged. Even if British forces were hard pressed elsewhere when Japan attacked, a stout six month defence could stop the Japanese doing irreparable harm in the Far East before a counterattack could be mounted. If Singapore was now indeed a well defended fortress ....

The mere presence of five 15" guns and a garrison of 20,000 men did not however make Singapore a fortress capable of holding off a full scale invasion for six months. That depended on basing theatre plans for defence on a realistic grand strategy, and on those plans being themselves realistic. They would then shape campaign strategy. That would determine what was tactically possible. The longer the "period before relief" became, the more important it was to reassess plans–in unison. When the COS decided to retain the "Singapore strategy" in principle but void it in practice by exponentially increasing the "period before relief," this put the critical burden of defence on the forces stationed in the theatre.

Defending the British Empire in the Far East became a more daunting challenge in the 1930s. Economic development in Malaya, fuelled by expansion in the rubber and tin markets, steadily opened up much of the peninsula, especially on the west coast. Railroads and a trunk road were eventually brought from Singapore right up to the border with Thailand. For their part, the Thais extended those connections to their southern ports of Singora and Patani, on the east coast of the Kra Isthmus. Bush and swamp were cleared for plantations. Lateral roads were built in the centre and the south. Roads connected the east coast ports of Kuantan to Kuala Lumpur and Endau to Singapore. Advances in aircraft technology gave a new generation of combat planes greater range, more striking power, and promise of more to come. The Japanese pressed ahead with large expansion programs for all their forces. In China, they developed and tried out purpose built equipment, and new techniques, for amphibious operations. And in 1938 and 1939 they seized areas of southern China, including Hainan island, that brought them to the doorstep of Hong Kong and significantly closer to Malaya and Singapore. All these developments, added to the massive increase in the period before relief, pushed aside the consensus of the 1920s that distance and rough terrain ruled out a major threat from the north and forced any attacker to come directly at Singapore from the sea.[50] Unfortunately, it was replaced by plans that did not fit with each other, nor with a grand strategy now itself dislocated. This dangerous result was produced by service rivalries, cumbersome decision making, and especially the tendency to fit the situation to the plan.

The problem of how to hold the naval base was by no means ignored. It was reviewed by the COS on several occasions, the Joint Planning Staff (JPS) at least twice, other CID subcommittees, staff colleges in the U.K. and India, and at least half a dozen times by theatre commanders–especially Malaya Command, the army formation responsible for the defence of Malaya and Singapore.[51] Theatre commanders naturally wanted to be told categorically what their mission was, and what they would be given to accomplish it. Their superiors could not tell them because grand strategy was always contingent in fact if not on paper, and because they would not admit this before events gave them no choice. This was the kind of problem the system was designed to tackle. It required everyone to address difficulties faced by someone else, to see the problem as one that could only be solved by all working together, at all levels. Unfortunately too few did. Too few even saw the need to try. Service tunnel vision prevailed. In spite of all this activity the services found themselves working at crosspurposes regarding Phase I. There is more than enough blame to go around, but the most serious failure to think beyond one's own requirements came from the RAF.

In autumn 1933 the Admiralty tried for the first time to pull together the problems of sending the fleet to the east and facing an attack before the fleet arrived. The 1933 War Memorandum (Eastern) was sent to Admiral F.C. Dreyer, CinC China Station, for comment. The acerbic Dreyer made the same critique offered by Richmond nearly a decade before. The assurance the fleet would be sent no matter what seemed a bit shaky. Ideas about how it would actually engage the Japanese were so vague it hardly seemed there was a plan at all, beyond sending out the fleet. In January 1934 Dreyer, the GOC (General Officer Commanding) Malaya Command, and AOC (Air Officer Commanding) Far East, joined by Australian and New Zealand staff officers, met in Singapore to discuss how to hold the base before the fleet arrived. They agreed it still seemed unlikely a major attack could be mounted from the north. But with their forces so small and the base defences still far from completed, a determined invasion of the island was a real threat.[52] This fear that a half completed facility would tempt Japan to attack was addressed by the decision to complete the base and defences once and for all. But before this could bear fruit, theatre authorities concluded the defence of the island now depended on defending a much larger area. Unfortunately, they did not move in step.

The first sign the services were moving out of step came in spring 1932. The RAF persuaded the CID to "partly accept" the claim it could take the lead in defending both Malaya and Singapore. This led to a 1934 decision to establish an RAF base on the mainland.[53] In principle there was nothing wrong with either of these moves. Advances in technology made it ever more likely an attacker would bring greater force to bear from the air from longer range; it also made the idea of using defending air forces to keep the enemy at arms length more attractive. This made it logical to look to the mainland, especially the east coast and the north, for forward bases to enable the RAF to protect Singapore by dominating the South China Sea and all approaches to Malaya. Unfortunately, the way RAF Far East went ahead with these plans was anything but logical.

It all started to go wrong in 1936. In the autumn the Air Ministry sent out Squadron Leader Lawrence Darvall of its Directorate of Operations and Intelligence to tour the overseas commands. Darvall conducted an intensive tour of Far East Command in November. After meeting the Governor, the AOC Far East, the GOC Malaya Command, and the CinC China Station, Darvall reported they were all coming to see the arrival of the fleet in an emergency as problematic, which made all defence schemes "at present false," and coming around to the view that "the only force which may be able to come to their assistance and which may be counted upon is the Royal Air Force." This impression of coherence was misleading. Despite complaining there was "no clearcut common interservice defence plan for the whole of the South China Sea quadrilateral," RAF Far East unilaterally began to construct airbases on the mainland. And it did not coordinate this fundamental change of plans with the other services.[54]

The GOC Malaya Command, Maj.Gen. William Dobbie, only uncovered this initiative after "close questioning" of the AOC. Dobbie and the WO were both concerned by this development, as well they might be. These bases were being sited without any army input. The RAF was locating them as close to the east coast as possible, to increase their striking range over the sea. But that made them more vulnerable to being seized by an invader. This was bound to transform the whole problem of defending Singapore. If the Japanese seized airbases virtually on its doorstep, they would be able to isolate it before strong reinforcements could arrive by sea or air. That gave the army no choice but to defend such bases on the ground. But that could mean dispersing its forces in small groups over a widespread area, defending bases located without any attention paid to ground defence. Despite these problems, the WO and Dobbie both accepted there was no turning back. The RAF would spread out and its bases would have to be defended.[55] Yet when the vital issue of the future deployment of air reinforcements arose, Darvall and the new AOC, Air Commodore Arthur Tedder, sorted out recommendations to London in consultation with the Governor, Sir Shenton Thomas–but not with Dobbie.

Darvall told the Air Ministry that RAF Far East required substantial reinforcements to play the larger role now likely to be required of it, and these reinforcements should spread out on the mainland. Tengah, Seletar and Sembawang bases should be completed in Singapore, bringing the total number of airstrips on the island to four, but most squadrons sent to the Far East should be deployed on mainland bases. This advice rested on two arguments. First, concentrating all aircraft in one small area on the island would make it easier for an enemy to destroy them by sabotage on the ground; dispersing them over a wider area would reduce this risk. Second, wider deployment would make it harder to tie down aircraft in "restricted operations for the immediate defence of the naval base." The Air Ministry agreed. This was unfortunate because the advice rested on weak premises, grounded in interservice rivalry and suspicion. Tedder and Darvall saw the wartime role of airpower as being to exploit its tactical mobility by defending the Far East theatre as a whole, responding flexibly to whatever threat emerged and smashing the enemy at sea. They both complained that what the army and navy really wanted was "executive control" of airpower, which they would misuse in restricted operations around Singapore and its immediate approaches. Darvall insisted airbases outside Singapore could be secured against sabotage by minimal local defence because there were few Japanese in the area, so there was no need to concentrate aircraft inside the army defended zone on the island. A dispersed RAF would be harder to knock out and could strike back more effectively. Despite apparently getting along well with Lt.Col. Arthur Percival, Dobbie's GSO1, and despite his own complaints about the lack of common plans, Tedder sited mainland airbases without any real consultation about how this would affect other services plans. By the time he realized it would take more than "a few extra aircrafthands" to defend the bases, the damage was done.[56]

The airmen believed the other services remained too narrowly focused on Singapore island itself. They felt Dobbie and Admiral Sir Charles Little, CinC China Station, tended to regard RAF squadrons as being at their disposal. Major combined service exercises in February 1937 and 1938 did narrowly focus on defending the island against invasion launched directly from the sea.[57] But a change was in fact already developing in Malaya Command thinking, one that escaped the airmen long enough to be compromising. Having accepted the fact there would be airbases on the mainland, Dobbie and Percival comprehensively reconsidered the defence of Singapore. They noted several changes: the threat from the air was much greater as technology advanced; infrastructure development in much of Malaya made the peninsula easier to move through; Japanese amphibious capabilities were much greater, including the ability to deploy armoured vehicles. This led them to a seminal conclusion: the only way to defend Singapore was to defend the whole Malayan peninsula.[58]

Here were two services facing a common problem, both concluding their defence horizons must expand to meet a changing threat, but neither finding a way to pull their efforts together coherently. Both had to cope with the fact that the "Singapore strategy" was clearly eroding but London would not cancel it. Both had some reason to be wary of the other. Dobbie did sometimes behave as if he was the de facto commander of all forces in the area, and Malaya Command did continue to study the threat of a direct attack on Singapore itself. But the greater fault lay with the RAF. It did not take long for Tedder to realize the problems of defending the airbases could be quite serious, but he made no great effort to tackle the issue. Indeed, in 1938 the RAF continued to build airbases on the mainland, especially in the north near the Thai border. It intended to replace the navy in the lead role in theatre defence.[59] That seemed very possible, but meanwhile the army was being compromised. Dobbie pushed hard for reinforcements to enable Malaya Command to face its much expanded defence problem, but his change in plans far outstripped the strength of his command. On top of everything else he now had to protect widely dispersed airbases. Had RAF Far East been strong enough to devastate an invasion force at sea this might not have been so serious. Plans called for 11 combat squadrons to be stationed in the theatre in wartime. But that was only a distant prospect, not a reality. By 1939 there were still only four operational squadrons in the theatre, all based in Singapore.[60] Malaya Command might well fall between two stools if war came before major reinforcements. To protect airbases it must disperse, but if those airbases remained nearly empty an enemy invasion would succeed. The advancing force could then pick off a dispersed defending army one group at a time. The dangerous questions remained open. Would reinforcements arrive in time? If not, could the army recover and concentrate to fight the main battle on the ground?

Ultimately this misconnection was rooted in the RAF belief the next war could be won by independent air action. On the grand scale, this meant a strategic bombing offensive against the enemy homeland. In the Far East, it translated into replacing the navy as the service that would inflict the strategic blow against the enemy main force, at sea. In principle this had some attractions. But it was also driven by continuing determination to remain an independent service, with full control over its own striking power. That produced a very dangerous situation when the RAF went ahead with its own change of plans long before it had the capability to make them realistic, without considering how this would affect the army. Even given any indication the army might still be "thinking small" about Singapore, that should have prompted the airmen to push harder for a synchronized reorganization of theatre defences, instead of going ahead on their own. London was so caught up in the naval "Singapore strategy" it failed to make sure overseas commands worked together coherently. Because there was no unified command in Singapore to compel the services to stay in step, in the end it came down to their own attitudes. The airmen were so determined to keep their hands free to exploit their instrument to the full, as they saw best, that they resorted to establishing a *fait accompli* for the others. Apparently to them a common defence plan meant making the others conform to the air plan. Given the shift in thinking at Malaya Command such unilateralism was worse than unnecessary.

Malaya Command never wrote off the possibility of a direct attack on Singapore, but the change in its thinking from 1936 was fundamental. It can best be traced through Percival's experience as GSO1. Even before he arrived in Singapore, briefing notes on the current state of its defences, given to him in January 1936, zeroed in on what was changing:

> Singapore can be attacked in two ways:
> a) By a coup de main directed on the island.
> b) By a siege commencing with a landing in Malaya and the reduction of the fortress by military action from the North and by starvation ... or, of course, by a combination of the two.

> The defensive organization designed to meet the former method of attack has been carefully prepared and will within the next 18 months be completed. These preparations, although they offer certain loopholes ... are such that they will probably deter the possible enemy from attempting a coup de main, unless of course he loses his head. In fact they may result in forcing him, should he decide at any time, to attack Singapore by the "slow but more sure" method. It is therefore of importance to ensure that the defensive organization is adequate to deal with this latter form of attack.

The notes went on to complain about the drive to develop infrastructure on the peninsula, to exploit its natural wealth. Natural defences would need to be bolstered, but for any fight on the mainland "the size of the garrison of Singapore and Malaya would appear to be insufficient to provide the necessary general mobile reserve ... to back up the mobile columns without leaving the fortress too weak." All in all, "it appears therefore that the Back Door is at present being left unlocked."[61]

The big issues in the notes were reinforcements and the relationship between island and mainland defence. Percival spent 20 months as GSO1 helping Dobbie press relentlessly for the former and rethink the latter. They reoriented Malaya Command's defence plans quite drastically. Unfortunately their new plans were not synchronized with the erosion in practice of the "Singapore strategy," but rather with its now implausible continuity on paper. Nor did they manage to stay in step with RAF Far East.

The new movement in Malaya Command thinking ironically spurred the airmen's desire to disperse their forces. Percival's briefing notes acknowledged the need for strong airpower, even suggesting "steps which result in the maintenance of an intact air force under any conditions of attack should be accelerated." Given this encouragement plus cordial personal relations between Percival and Tedder, it is possible to see why the airmen decided they could take the path of least resistance to avoid Dobbie. But Percival also pointed out to Tedder the need to take military concerns into account when siting airbases, and pressed for better coordination.[62] It is harder to grasp just how plans finally became disconnected between headquarters, considering the vision Dobbie and Percival sketched out in 1937-38. Malaya Command concluded their task now required them to defend all of Malaya: "Operations on Mainland become more probable in proportion as strength of Fortress [Singapore] increases. Therefore defence of Mainland is assuming increasing importance." Dobbie and Percival drafted a scenario that envisaged a "deliberate attack" by Japanese forces, making a slow but methodical advance from the north down to Singapore. On the other hand there remained the possibility of a direct attack to seize the island by a coup de main. Therefore:

> The plan of defence to meet either form of attack is much the same, although as the coup de main attack may be expected to develop very much quicker than the deliberate form of attack the defence must be organized in such a way that it will be capable of dealing with the former. Later, if it becomes clear that the enemy intends to embark on a different form of operation, the necessary adjustments can be made in the defence organization to deal with the new conditions.[63]

That should have been clear enough, especially when reinforced by an exposition of the combined picture from the army point of view. The "fortress" could only be taken after its defences were worn down, particularly by enemy air attacks. Therefore:

> The primary responsibility, apart from diplomacy, for preventing an enemy from establishing shore based aircraft within striking distance of Malaya

rests with our Naval and Air Forces. It is essential, therefore, that sufficient Air Forces should be immediately available in this area should such a threat develop. The Army is, however, responsible for providing ground protection, as far as its resources will admit, for aerodromes and landing grounds. This is a task for which, in Malaya, Infantry [sic] alone is suitable.[64]

There is some evidence the army staff in Singapore continued to believe it would be difficult for an enemy to move a large army through Malaya's terrain against "even moderate opposition." On the other hand they acknowledged the development of new amphibious assault equipment by the Japanese made their problem worse. Finally, Percival argued the Japanese were likely to occupy Thailand in order to move up air forces to support an advance on Malaya. This meant Malaya Command must be ready to fight a battle in northern Malaya, for which it needed more troops.[65]

This does not indicate a theatre headquarters groping in the dark–quite the reverse. Malaya Command remained clear on its mission: "the principal object of the defence of Singapore is to protect the Naval Base here against attack until the arrival of the British Main Fleet and to afford security to our forces subsequent to its arrival." It recognized this mission was in danger of being compromised by global developments, knew it had to expand its own plans, and realized it must try to back up the air forces as best it could.[66] Yet Dobbie, Percival and Tedder, who were all gone by autumn 1939, needlessly made the situation worse than the one they found. Dobbie and Percival spelt out the need to defend all of Malaya, pressed slowly ahead to develop fixed defences in Johore which they hoped would become a strong cordon to protect the naval base from the north,[67] and made the case for prior reinforcement. But they did not question the increase in the period before relief, nor stop Tedder from building airfields in locations very hard to protect from ground attack, without any firm promise there would be aircraft to use them when the need arose. The result by autumn 1939 was the following. The navy was still supposed to bear the burden of any war against Japan, but it would be at least six months before it could deploy, no matter what. That in practice shifted the point man role to the air force, which responded by building facilities even though it had no idea when it would be able to use them effectively. The army now had to hold the naval base for six months instead of six weeks, could only do so by defending the whole Malay peninsula, but could not choose its own ground on which to fight.

There is no convincing reason this disarray was allowed to become as bad as it did. Granted the world situation changed very much for the worse from 1931 and the starting point was not strong, given the inherent flaws in the "Singapore strategy." Nevertheless, the challenge to realign capabilities to meet changing circumstances and intentions was badly mishandled. The reluctance of the British government and COS to make painful decisions about imperial defence in order to make it militarily realistic can only be deplored. Gambling on appeasement, and/or the assumption the Americans would and could save the Empire in the Far East, amounted to hoping something would happen somewhere else to extract the British from an intractable mess they would not face up to. The same can be said for the tepid way the Australians pressed for "guarantees" on the "Singapore strategy," avoiding uncomfortable answers that might force them to make changes. Shifting priorities to a possible offensive against Italy only compounded the risk being run in the Far East. By expanding the "period before relief" to six months, then allowing RAF Far East to build airbases on its own, the central direction of imperial defence passed the whole buck to Malaya Command, gambling it would not have to face the consequences. Yet inadequate guidance and support from London can not excuse the authorities in Singapore, especially the air force, for falling out of step with each other, and doing so little about it.

What surely should have happened was a complete overhaul of the mission assigned to the services in Singapore after the drastic increases in the "period before relief." It should have focused on the most likely way available forces could at least deny Singapore to the Japanese, and thus keep them at bay, should they attack before things improved elsewhere. Instead each service went ahead on its own with plans almost bound to fail if anything untoward did occur–and responsibility starts with the COS. They extended Phase I exponentially, which made the "Singapore strategy" ridiculous, but clung to that strategy anyway. This made it difficult for theatre commanders to reorient their own plans. And nobody made sure those plans stayed in step. The British government and its military advisers are not the main reason war broke out in Europe in 1939, and that war was the greatest cause of the danger looming over Singapore. But they did fail to produce realistic defence plans in response. The Empire's military system simply could not produce viable plans, because that would provoke too many political dangers. Instead it stubbornly tried to make the situation fit the plan, which only postponed those dangers.

Preparing for War

In June 1921 the British government made Singapore the focal point of imperial defence in the Far East by deciding to build a principal naval base there. In June 1940 another British government faced the ruin of that policy after the military disaster of the fall of France. This unexpected and catastrophic reversal changed the Empire's strategic position dramatically for the worse. As a policy to defend a distant region in a global empire, the "Singapore strategy" always depended on the situation in Europe being under control. Now the United Kingdom found itself fighting total war against a stronger enemy on its very doorstep, without any strong allies. The government supposedly admitted the "Singapore strategy" was now unworkable, for the moment at least, and rolled up its sleeves to fight for the U.K.'s very survival. The fall of France, more than any other single event, compromised Singapore. But the French surrendered a full 18 months before the Japanese finally attacked the Western Powers and ignited the Pacific War. So what happened in between? Was nothing done to make Singapore more defensible? Could anything decisive have been done? This section will address those questions.

The course of the war from spring 1940 forced the British to take calculated risks in grand strategy. But even this was not enough. To win an expanding war the British needed to find stronger allies. Unfortunately, while defeat finally brought some hard-headed clarity into the making of grand strategy, it did not ripple down the chain of decision-making. Not even defeat could persuade the British to set aside broader concerns in order to defend the Far East with concrete plans based on strategic realities. The Japanese on the other hand adopted a criminally irresponsible national policy, but devised a professionally sound grand strategy to attack the Western Powers. The combination doomed Singapore to defeat and opened the door to possible disaster.

3

The Bottom Falls Out

It is important to remember just how shocking the fall of France in 1940 was. The Allies fully expected the formidable French Army, with British help, to pin the Germans down on a defensive front, as happened a generation before. Behind that shield, the superior economic strength of the two empires would be patiently mobilized, for a long war of attrition.[1] That was the context in which the British called for and received Dominion pledges of assistance. In that November 1939 discussion R.G. Casey made the Australian position crystal clear: "If Australia were to put in the full war effort of which she was capable, his Government would require a most comprehensive undertaking regarding the security of Singapore." In return for Dominion forces to help fight the war in Europe, the British had to give Churchill's assurance on the "Singapore strategy." They did so assuming the war in Europe would go so well Japan would not dare challenge the Western Powers in Asia.[2] That comfortable assumption was shattered by the German armed forces, who in six startling weeks overran the Low Countries, drove the British Army off the continent, and forced France to surrender and accept a new status as a German protectorate. This defeat had dire and direct consequences for the Far East, for three reasons.

First, the British now found themselves the only major power facing both a rampant Germany and an opportunistic Italy, Mussolini having entered the war to share the spoils. The army lost nearly all its heavy weapons and equipment. The air force was now pinned down defending the homeland against a much larger foe, to ward off possible invasion. And the navy was now forced to defend against that threat as well as protect widespread imperial interests and lines of communication, without French help. Frustration with the lack of progress in the war provoked a change of government on the very day the German assault began, bringing Winston Churchill into office as Prime Minister. Churchill inherited the policy of gradual mobilization, which meant the economy was far from ready to wage total war. That plus the weakness of the armed forces left the British with their backs truly against the wall. In one of the most dramatic examples of leadership in history, Churchill inspired the nation to face a desperate emergency. But girding up for total war would take time, and meanwhile the enemy looked poised to deliver a *coup de grace*.

Churchill's first success was to put together a coalition government pledged to reject any compromise with Hitler and fight total war. But when he asked the COS how ultimate victory could still be won their reply was chilling. In the long run Germany could be defeated by "economic pressure, by a combination of air attack on economic objectives in Germany and on German morale and the creation of widespread revolt in her conquered territories."[3] Meanwhile the homeland must repel an invasion. That could only be done by winning control of the air. The RAF was outnumbered almost four to one but the COS believed its well prepared air defence network could prevail by day. However, facing an almost certain massive German bomber offensive by night, the COS could only conclude:

> prima facie Germany has most of the cards; but the real test is whether the morale of our fighting personnel and civil population will counter balance the numerical and material advantages which Germany enjoys. We believe it will.[4]

This confession of weakness could not have been more stark. Home defence was always first priority in imperial defence, but this was worse than anything ever imagined. The situation was now so grave nearly every resource must be concentrated around the home islands, to ward off total defeat. Every overseas command would pay the price.

The second problem was the holes left by the French and Dutch collapse. With France now neutral at best and possibly hostile, the French fleet was a threat rather than an ally in the Mediterranean. The British had to control the Mediterranean sea lanes in order to secure the oil resources of the Middle East, plus the lines of communication to India, the Far East and the Pacific Dominions. The navy now had to face a large Italian fleet to protect these vital interests, and the army was heavily outnumbered by Italian forces in colonies in Africa. A small proportion of the French armed forces rallied to an obscure officer named Charles De Gaulle, who escaped to England and appealed to the French to fight on. But the majority in government and the armed forces followed the lead given by the new administration at Vichy, led by Marshal Petain. Petain assumed the Axis Powers would now win the war, and opted to collaborate with Germany in order to preserve as much of France as possible. Nearly all France's overseas colonies followed his lead. That included the large territory of French Indochina, comprising modern day Vietnam, Laos and Cambodia.

The French colonial authorities were never very impressed by the British

"Singapore strategy", but always assumed there was a strong connection between Singapore's security and their own. The empires shared a common interest in maintaining western ascendancy in the region. That feeling persisted in the summer of 1940, but the surrender of the homeland left the Indochina administration with no hope of support from home should trouble arise.[5] British appeals fell on deaf ears when French officials in Indochina opted instead to obey the orders of the legitimate government. The Dutch government on the other hand escaped to England and defiantly carried on the struggle in exile. But with the homeland overrun, the colonial authorities and military forces in the Netherlands East Indies also had no hope of any support from home. Dutch forces were hopelessly inadequate to defend such a large area. Instead of enjoying the protection of allied colonies acting as buffers between Singapore and Japanese held areas, British colonies now found themselves in the midst of a region suddenly wide open to attack.

The third consequence of the fall of France was the impact it had on Japan. The Axis victories in Europe seemed to many Japanese to open a historic window of opportunity. The war in China was gridlocked, and Japan depended so much on imports of vital raw materials, imports that came from supplies controlled by the Western powers, that a determined policy of economic pressure might well bring the Japanese economy to its knees. But if the Japanese could gain control over the large supplies of raw materials in Southeast Asia, especially the oil fields of the Dutch colonies, that could make Japan strong enough to finish its war in China and defy any American pressure. The first move came even before the French surrender. The French colonial authorities in Indochina agreed on 20 June to a Japanese "request" to stop all further transit of supplies to China through French territory and host Japanese "inspectors" who would monitor the situation. More Japanese pressure induced the British on 17 July to close the so-called Burma Road for three months, stemming another flow.[6] But the crux of the matter was whether Japan should take advantage of this new situation by changing its national war policy.

The Yonai government was cautious. Any move south risked overloading an army taxed by the war in China, tempting the Soviet Union to take advantage by causing trouble in the north, and above all provoking a direct confrontation with the Americans. Critics, especially in the Army, insisted Germany was winning the war, its goals fit well with the Japanese agenda, closer ties with it could deter the Americans, and its victories must be exploited. The West was weak, now was the time to strike. Yonai was forced to resign, Konoye returned to office, and a seminal decision was made in late July. On the 26th, the new Cabinet settled a new "Basic National Policy." The following day it agreed, in a Liaison Conference with Imperial General Headquarters, to adopt "Principles to Cope with the Changing World Situation." The latter document was the more important, and the driving force behind it was the Army. The new policy was spelt out as follows:

> The Japanese Empire will strive for the immediate settlement of the China Incident by improving internal and external conditions in keeping with the changes in the world situation and, at the same time, will solve the southern area problem by taking advantage of opportunities. Changes in policies, with emphasis placed on measures for the southern area, will be decided in consideration of various conditions, internal and external. Various preparations for the matters described in the above items will be undertaken as soon as possible.

The Navy agreed Japan must gain control over the area's raw materials, yet wanted this done without hostilities if at all possible. The Army agreed every effort must be made to avoid war, but insisted on forging closer ties with the Axis and pursuing the southern advance. The British were the primary target, but the real danger was American intervention. All parties agreed four conditions would require Japan to fight: an all-out American economic blockade; a rift between the British and Americans; should there be any significant increase in the strength of British or American forces in the region; and any American deployment from British bases, especially Singapore. The tilt in policy was pronounced:

> As the settlement of the China Incident is generally completed, armed strength will be used where necessary insofar as various internal and external conditions permit, to solve the problem of the southward advance ... In employing armed strength, efforts will be made to limit the war adversary to Great Britain insofar as possible. However, thorough preparations for the commencement of hostilities against the United States will be made as it may prove impossible to avoid war with that country.[7]

This decision set Japan on a course for war against the Western Powers. Japanese troops duly moved into northern French Indochina. The Americans responded quickly. On 27 September they embargoed the export of scrap iron to Japan. But that same day Japan, Germany and Italy concluded the Tripartite Pact. This alliance called on the parties to assist each other if any were attacked by a power not currently involved in either the "European War" or the "China Incident." In effect Germany and Japan were using each other to deter American intervention against either.[8] Taken together these steps amounted to a fundamental shift in Japanese policy. Japan was now going to take advantage of the war in Europe to establish control over Southeast Asia, even if that meant war with the United States.

On one level this reveals the shocking irresponsibility that characterized decision making in Tokyo. The Navy supported the southern advance but opposed war with the Americans. All attempts to establish whether or not Japan could survive a protracted war against the U.S.A. indicated the answer was no. Yet the Navy folded under the threat of losing a share of national resources or even facing civil war, blaming the Army for pushing ahead with a policy it called "a complete bluff."[9] But on another level this shift spelt potential disaster for Singapore. Singapore's fate now rested on a three way race: between Japanese preparations to advance south, British efforts to reverse the fortunes of war in Europe and find something to spare for the Far East, and American preparations for war. The ultimate consequences of any Japanese advance looked reckless even then. But they were definitely in pole position when this race started.

There was little the Churchill government could do to ease Singapore's predicament. What it did amounted to the opposite of the Japanese course: the most fundamental decision was sound, but the immediate situation in the Far East was not taken in hand. The new Prime Minister was every bit as strong willed as Chamberlain but far better suited to lead the nation and empire in total war. Churchill had long experience in government, a strong sense and deep knowledge of history, boundless energy, charisma, and unshakeable determination to fight and win total war against an enemy he recognized as a mortal threat to British civilization. Trumpeting "action this day" he took advantage of the clear and present danger that now allowed the government to assume draconian powers to prosecute total war, and took firm control of the central direction of the war. The Prime Minister named himself Minister of Defence, with no department but with a small secretariat, through which he supervised the network of committees working under the COS. Two Cabinet level Defence Committees were set up, to connect the coalition Cabinet to the most important decisions regarding the direction of the war; but in fairly short order the day to day making of grand strategy settled into the hands of the Prime Minister and the COS.[10] This reorganization meant strategic decisions could now be pushed forward faster and more vigorously. It did not guarantee these decisions would be effective, because by itself it did nothing to address the root problem: the tendency to try to fit the situation into the plan.

Churchill started well in the summer of 1940 by adopting two fundamental policies: nothing could be done that would jeopardize home defence; in order to win the war the British must bring the Americans in on their side as soon as possible, by any means necessary.[11] The Prime Minister steered through decisions that by October transformed British war policy. The U.K. and its allies would fight to the death to destroy the Axis, especially Nazi Germany. The nation would commit itself to providing whatever the armed forces needed to win the war. If this required mobilizing the economy beyond its means, at the risk of becoming dependent on American economic support, so be it. According to British calculations in September, the German war economy was seven times stronger than the British. The COS agreed the German Army was too formidable to face in another continental campaign. Given all that, after a lengthy review the COS produced in September a new grand strategy for total war, one based on the assumption the enemy was stronger. The home islands and their supply lines must be defended at all costs. Vital overseas deposits of natural resources must be denied to the enemy, which meant the Empire must fight to hold what it had. All-out mobilization would generate enough power to wear down the enemy by a grand strategy of attrition without confronting his main force on the ground. If all went well a strategic offensive would then finish him off, but it could not be launched before spring 1942 at the earliest. It would be launched only "when numerically inferior forces can be employed with good chance of success, to reestablish a striking force on the Continent with which we can enter Germany and impose our terms."[12]

This "backs to the wall" situation forced Churchill and the COS to reassess the problem of defending the Far East. The shock of the fall of France was so great it even provoked one insider to suggest the British now had no choice but to give way on the policy they cherished the most. To preserve the Empire, it might be necessary to delegate real authority for defending much of it to the Dominions. On 17 June the Director of Military Operations and Plans at the WO urged his department to face hard facts. Under the circumstances:

> ... we have all got to fight with what we can have and not with what we would like to have. Rather than send further forces far overseas to England to help in the defence of the British Isles, the Dominions would ensure a more economical and strategically sounder employment of our resources if they undertook the defence of important areas in their own vicinity.

The logical result would be to ask Australia to assume responsibility "for Singapore and Malaya, British North Borneo." The DMO & P argued this was not a new idea; at the Imperial Conference of 1930 the CIGS urged governments to breathe life into the principle of "regional responsibility for the defence of the Empire." Then, the suggestion was shelved. But now, with invasion imminent, it might be time to drop the desirable and concentrate on the truly essential. The British could either simply ask the Dominions to provide the necessary troops or go so far as to ask them to "assume full responsibility for defence." But "if control from home is likely to break down, this latter course would be preferable." Australia could not have taken on such a burden even if asked. But the point is the suggestion was made. June 1940 was so tense there were other dire "emergency" suggestions: promise the Americans the RN would sail to Canada rather than surrender; abandon the Eastern Mediterranean; even, in some circles, sue for peace. None were pursued. Probably only an invasion of the U.K. itself would have persuaded the government to delegate control of the overseas Empire. But the central direction of the war could not pretend things did not need to change at all. On 19 June it bluntly admitted to the Australians that for the foreseeable future the "Singapore strategy" could not be implemented: "We see no hope of being able to despatch a fleet to Singapore." Then on 28 June the British admitted that as there was little hope the naval situation would soon improve, it was necessary to improve the air and ground defences of Malaya.[13] This connection between the "Singapore strategy" and theatre defence plans, the familiar Phase I problem, was the crux of the matter. If one changed, must not the other also?

The Australians were livid, but that did not change the fact the RN was now so overstretched it had nothing to spare to help the Far East. The COS confirmed this in their September review: the RN would only run risks elsewhere to sortie to the Far East if the Dominions themselves were invaded. The message was clear: the Mediterranean was a higher priority than the Far East in grand strategy, and the promise to send a fleet to relieve Singapore was suspended until further notice.[14] Yet that apparent clarity was already being confused by the closer attention now finally being paid in London to theatre defence plans. The Prime Minister and COS remained convinced the Japanese would not invade the Dominions as long as Singapore remained available as a base for a British fleet that might be sent out. The COS review confirmed the earlier decision to shift primary responsibility for defending the Far East from the navy to the air force. They stipulated however that the mission remained the same: to hold the naval base, to preserve it as either a deterrent against attack or a staging point for a counterattack. This decision was influenced by developments in Singapore itself.

Prospects for effective co-operation at the theatre level faded alarmingly from autumn 1939, after a change of command. Lt.-Gen. L.V. Bond took over as GOC Malaya Command while Air Vice-Marshal J.T. Babington became AOC Far East Command. Bond and Babington inherited the problem created by indiscriminate construction of airbases on the peninsula, but soon aggravated it. From the beginning Bond insisted it was dangerous to try to hold all Malaya with a garrison as small as his command. When war broke out in Europe Malaya Command was reinforced according to a prearranged plan. GHQ India dispatched Emu Force, later renamed 12th Indian Brigade. This increased Bond's force to seven regular infantry battalions, plus coastal artillery and the various Volunteer Forces of Malaya and the Straits Settlements.[15] In April 1940, shortly before all hell broke loose in Europe, Bond warned the COS that while he agreed it was necessary to defend all Malaya to hold the naval base, given the current weakness of RAF Far East he needed from 39 to 42 regular infantry battalions; at that point he had nine. Drawing an obvious conclusion, Bond proposed to rewrite his plans: to do what he could with what he had.[16] This provoked such an intense dispute with Babington that on 25 June it was referred to the COS for resolution.

Babington argued that absent the fleet the lead role belonged to the air force. It could only pummel an invader at sea from the mainland airbases, but could only use them if they were protected on the ground by infantry. Bond replied he had to base his plans on his mission–which remained to hold the naval base "on the possibility of the arrival of the fleet"–and his capabilities. Despite the fact Singapore island's fixed defences were now quite strong, Malaya Command was so understrength it could only spare one regular battalion outside Singapore and Johore. Bond insisted that until he was greatly reinforced the only safe thing he could do was concentrate in Johore and Singapore. This was the most difficult type of dispute, because both parties were absolutely right. If an enemy seized the mainland airbases Singapore would quickly be isolated. But spreading the army out would doom it to defeat if the air force did not repel the invader, which it was nowhere near strong enough to do.[17] This was the same problem first raised by Dobbie and Percival three years before. Now, finally, Bond's common sense forced the COS to pay attention.

The COS could not provide what Bond and Babington needed most, reinforcements, but they had a duty to provide clear direction. The fact they told the Australians the fleet was now not available, but did not consider changing Bond's mission, was not a good omen. Their reply to Singapore made the problem even worse. On 15 August the COS circulated a memorandum entitled The Situation in the Far East in the Event of Japanese Intervention Against Us. The document, which quickly became known as "the Far East Appreciation," spelt out the strategy by which Malaya and Singapore were in fact defended when war broke out 16 months later. The key point was the statement of the "defence problem":

Primarily the security of India, Malaya and Australasia depends on our ability to control the sea communications leading to them. The foundation of our strategy in the Far East must, therefore, remain the basing of an adequate fleet on Singapore. Until we have defeated Germany and Italy however, or drastically reduced their naval strength, we are faced with the problem of defending our interests in the Far East without an adequate fleet. In the absence of a fleet, we cannot prevent damage to our interests in the Far East. Our object must, therefore, be to limit the extent of the damage and in the last resort to retain a footing from which we could eventually retrieve the position when stronger forces become available.

The COS expected any Japanese attack to be methodical, moving towards Singapore step by step. They reaffirmed their view Japan would not attack the Dominions while Singapore remained available, acknowledged that to hold Singapore it was necessary to hold all Malaya, especially to prevent the enemy from basing powerful air forces within striking range of Singapore, and agreed this would require ground and air reinforcements. While they described Singapore's defences as "formidable," the COS agreed Japan would realize the "Singapore strategy" was now stymied by the war in Europe, but argued the prospect of war with the U.S.A. would keep it cautious. They concluded British policy should be to build up defence forces in the Far East as steadily as possible and seek Dutch co-operation, because their territories must be secured to guard Singapore against attack from the south and east. The devil, as always, was in the detail. The crucial error came right here. The COS contradicted their warning the "Singapore strategy" was suspended until further notice by supporting theatre defence plans that only made sense if it was still assumed any Japanese attack would automatically trigger that strategy.

RAF Far East must defend the South China Sea and all of Malaya to defend Singapore. To do that it needed 22 squadrons, some 336 first-line aircraft. This strength should be achieved by the end of 1941. There were at that point eight squadrons with some 88 aircraft, none of them fighters. The COS set an intermediate target for the end of the year: to deploy two fighter squadrons and reinforce existing squadrons to full strength. Meanwhile Malaya Command must be reinforced. Nothing could be spared from home or the Middle East, nor as yet India, but Australia should be asked to provide a division, and Malaya Command should prepare to receive a further division as soon as possible. This would raise Bond's infantry strength from nine to 27 battalions, the equivalent of three divisions. As the air force grew, that number might be trimmed to two. Until then, the army must defend all Malaya: "It is also clearly essential to ensure that the aerodromes required for the operation of our own air forces are rendered safe from capture."[18]

This was a big step towards the disaster that overtook the defenders of Singapore in 1942. The COS compelled Malaya Command to spread out to protect an air force that existed only on paper. This was to hold a naval base for a fleet that would not come unless matters improved dramatically elsewhere. With the Battle of Britain raging and invasion looming, what real prospect was there that sufficient reinforcements could be sent any time soon? Even with their backs to the wall, the central direction of imperial defence still could not reconcile the old contradiction: how best to stand and fight now while still making it possible to adopt the optimal strategy next year. What else might they have done? There was one practical alternative. If the brunt of any early battle was going to fall on the army, the army commander could have been given a free hand to fight as he saw fit. This would not have made matters on the ground any worse than they already were, because Bond did not have enough troops to hold the whole peninsula. It would have freed Malaya Command from the order to hold an intact naval base for six months, by now an absurd proposition, and allowed it to make the most of whatever possibilities it could find to fight a prolonged battle. Unfortunately, this alternative was brushed aside. Why?

London still could not bring itself to cancel the "Singapore strategy" outright. Unleashing the army amounted to doing just that. It meant accepting a close investment of Singapore, ending very likely in its fall. When the COS talked about "in the last resort to retain a footing" they wanted the Dominions and Allies to assume this meant Singapore. In fact it did not. By now the RN plan should Malaya and Singapore be attacked was to send a covering force to Ceylon to protect the Indian Ocean, not to Singapore to effect its relief.[19] But admitting this outside the inner circle meant upsetting the promises on which everyone's plans rested.

Changing the theatre defence plan meant changing imperial defence policy. Siding with Bond meant withdrawing the "Singapore strategy," on the grounds that if the Japanese attacked before the war in Europe improved dramatically the British would not be able to send adequate reinforcements. Therefore, there was no sense basing defence plans on the need to hold the naval base because it was useless. The best that could be hoped for was that the army would make the Japanese pay a high price in time and men, if allowed to concentrate in defence. But this meant confessing to the Americans and the Dominions that as things stood Singapore could not be held. This vital connection between grand strategy–serving notice the fleet could not come for the foreseeable future–and theatre strategy–planning to fight on the assumption it might not come at all–was too much for London to make. They feared the Americans would doubt the British even could co-operate in defence against Japan, so would make no plans to do so. As for the Dominions, they would insist that if Singapore was vulnerable so were they, so they could spare no forces for the war in Europe. Siding with Babington on the other hand allowed the COS to argue that while the situation was indeed grim, and Malaya must be reinforced, Singapore would still be held. The "Singapore strategy" was only interrupted, not terminated. Plans and deployments must proceed on the basis all would yet be well.

Churchill and the COS correctly assumed the Allies could still win the war even if they suffered heavy defeats in the Far East, provided the home islands remained secure. But when it came to connecting their new grand strategy to a sensible plan to defend the Far East these decisions made matters worse. The navy did not plan to come until things improved in Europe. But the army and air force would continue to base their theatre plans on the assumption it would come as soon as possible, no matter the circumstances. This contradiction made the warning given to the Australians in June merely an appeal for help in Malaya, not a realignment of strategy. There was no easy answer to this dilemma, but there is a difference between a calculated risk and a gamble. A calculated risk is a decision that takes into account the possibility things might go badly wrong, but leaves open a chance to survive if they do. The decision to fight total war was a calculated risk. Coexistence with Nazi Germany was intolerable, total war was necessary, but nothing must jeopardize home defence and enticing the Americans. But the decision to retain the air plan to defend Singapore, in order to preserve the "Singapore strategy," was a gamble. If it went wrong, the battle would be lost so quickly the British would be unable to save Singapore. The consequences they hoped to avoid by not renouncing the strategy would then be suffered anyway– probably aggravated. Siding with Bond would have been a calculated political risk with possible consequences for the coalition. Siding with Babington was a military gamble very likely to compromise the defence of Singapore, with definite consequences.

It does not seem unfair to think that if even the spur of dire emergency was not enough to clear away these contradictions in imperial defence, nothing would. But the men who made these decisions had their reasons. Foremost were the Mediterranean situation and the Americans. Churchill and the COS agreed the most promising way to relieve the Far East was to secure the Mediterranean. The COS made the point bluntly in the "Far East Appreciation": "Our best hope of being able to supply naval forces for the Far East in the near future lies in the possibility of early and successful action against Italian naval forces in the Mediterranean."[20] This connection dated back to the shift in naval thinking in 1939. It was now strengthened by three other factors: the need to deny raw materials to the enemy, the need to protect allied lines of communication, and the fact there was already a war going on in the theatre.

The Prime Minister pressed for more offensive action, and the ensuing discussions produced two important points of consensus. First, the real threat was German intervention. The British erroneously believed the German economy was already fully mobilized for war. As a result they assumed the German petrol position was far worse than it really was. A German move into the theatre would threaten both to cut the imperial lines of communication and seize the oil fields of the Middle East. So the British should take the war to Italy, to knock it out now before the Germans intervened.[21] Second, theatre commanders should be left as much latitude as possible to accomplish their missions. This stemmed from pressure from Churchill for an early and bold offensive against the Italians in North Africa. The COS sheltered the theatre commanders, especially General A.P. Wavell, GOC Middle East Command, by arguing the heavily outnumbered British forces must first stop Italian attacks, then build up for their own. The price they paid was to agree the theatre stood behind only the U.K. itself for priority in grand strategy, and the largest possible offensive would be mounted as soon as possible. London directed Wavell to concentrate on holding Egypt as his top priority, then clearing North Africa as soon as he could.[22]

Developments in the autumn only strengthened Churchill's focus on the Mediterranean. Feeble Italian offensives in Africa soon bogged down. German pressure on Spain and Vichy France suggested a larger threat might soon appear. Italy attacked Greece, but soon found its forces pinned down by an energetic defence. This opened up both the prospect of a new front on the continent, and the danger of German intervention in the area. On 11 November the Mediterranean Fleet scored a dramatic victory by knocking out three Italian battleships and damaging several smaller craft, in a raid by carrier-borne aircraft on the anchorage at Taranto. Wavell meanwhile launched a campaign in East Africa, and a probe in early December into Italian lines in western Egypt which unexpectedly turned into a major advance against much larger forces. The effects on the Far East were important. The fleet remained very heavily committed. More than twice as many ground and air forces were already scheduled to be sent to the Mediterranean as to the Far East. And the Prime Minister was now fully absorbed by the war at hand.[23]

Notwithstanding the Mediterranean connection, the really decisive issue for the defence of Singapore was the question of American support. Churchill correctly decided that his most urgent task in the summer of 1940 was to convince the Americans the survival of the U.K. and its empire was now a vital American interest. From the earliest days of his premiership he spent more time cultivating relations with President Roosevelt, and building the coalition that alone could lead to victory, than on anything else.[24] It was time well spent, but it took time to convince the American government and public this was their war as well, and the British could not win it by themselves. Unfortunately, not all questions involving the Americans were sensibly handled. Some unforced errors surfaced over the Far East.

The British outlined their new grand strategy in secret talks with American officers in London in August and September. These talks were part of a flurry of diplomatic activity that summer, as Roosevelt moved cautiously, in an election year, to build a consensus that the British must not be defeated. The American grand strategy plans, the "Rainbow" series, were based on the premise the U.S. would wage coalition warfare, likely in alliance with the British Empire. The British assured their American counterparts American economic aid was "fundamental to our whole strategy."[25] The fall of France had an impact on American opinion as well, but there was also powerful opposition to military involvement overseas. This multi-faceted sentiment, often wrongly seen as simple "isolationism," was however stronger regarding Europe than Asia. While the two parties still found it difficult to establish a common position regarding security in the Far East, American domestic politics suggested that might be done before any American intervention in Europe.

Churchill, his Cabinet, and the COS agreed war to the death would require more power than the Empire could generate. Their resulting mobilization plans and grand strategy took shape by December as a calculated risk of the highest stakes: to fight coalition warfare with a coalition strategy, and coalition resources, before they had a coalition! Given the immensity of that decision, it is not surprising the idea to rely on the Americans to fill the gaps was built into many British plans. One of the most important plans so affected was the "Singapore strategy." In his first important telegram to Roosevelt after taking charge as Prime Minister, Churchill noted on 15 May "I am looking to you to keep the Japanese dog quiet in the Pacific, using Singapore in any way convenient." At first there seemed some grounds for optimism. After its annual exercises in May, the bulk of the US Pacific Fleet was retained in Hawaii rather than returned to the mainland, as was normal practice.[26] This forward deployment certainly encouraged the British, but in response the Admiralty overplayed its hand.

The Admiralty now looked to the Americans to provide the fleet to make the "Singapore strategy" viable. In November they went so far as to propose that nine of the USN's 14 battleships redeploy to Singapore. But while both navies agreed they must contain Japan, they disagreed on how important it was to retain Singapore.[27] Even the re-election of President Roosevelt did not make it politically possible to deploy a large American fleet so far from its main support facilities, let alone run the strategic risk of dangling long supply lines across Japanese held areas. That same month the Chief of Naval Operations (CNO) of the USN, Admiral Harold Stark, submitted a plan that took shape as a new American grand strategy: Plan Dog. The plan stipulated that if and when the U.S. intervened on the Allied side, the coalition should concentrate first on the European war, containing Japan with the minimum essential forces. Stark ruled out deploying from Singapore, arguing the Pacific Fleet could better help Allied forces hold Southeast Asia by threatening any Japanese advance from its base in Hawaii. The Americans warned the British public opinion would see pressure to take responsibility for Singapore as an appeal to "pull British chestnuts out of the fire."[28]

The Prime Minister took heed, but the Admiralty did not. Roosevelt's re-election in November cleared the way for full scale staff talks on grand strategy and joint plans. Most conversations to this point had been confined to technical co-operation and loose exploratory discussions on strategy, so the British readily agreed to such talks.[29] By now there was a sharper focus in British grand strategy. The threat of invasion was postponed at least through the winter; the Battle of Britain had been won; German night bombing attacks were heavy but did not seem likely to be fatal after all; things seemed at least promising in the Mediterranean. On the other hand the German threat remained ominous and shipping losses were now becoming a problem. Above all, it was crystal clear the military power required to win the war could only be produced by a fully integrated total war effort, in which the main burden would be carried by the Americans. The COS were now a settled team, Pound being joined by General Sir John Dill as CIGS and Air Chief Marshal Sir Charles Portal as CAS. Churchill and his new team made two cardinal decisions that December. First they made a direct appeal to Roosevelt, warning him that unless the U.S. threw its full weight into the war soon then civilization itself would be at risk.[30] Second, they decided to proceed with all their plans even before the Americans intervened. They would assume that blessed day would come early enough to make all plans viable. The Admiralty took this literally regarding plans for war against Japan. Churchill wanted the COS to acknowledge the Americans must take the lead to contain Japan and not press them to use Singapore. The Admiralty, supported by the FO, carried on lobbying for a large American deployment there.[31]

This disagreement was not the only dispute over detail in grand strategy, but it was the most significant for imperial defence in Asia and it says much about the British military system. Pound agreed as a member of the COS that above all else the Americans must be brought into the war. But as First Sea Lord he carried on pressing them to do something they saw as unwise. When he argued "Allied priorities in Asia" they heard "selfish British interests." This is understandable. In fact, it reflected the basis of British grand strategy. Arguments over the priority of different theaters and different campaigns, such as whether protecting shipping in the Atlantic was more urgent than preparing a major bombing offensive against Germany, could not easily be resolved. The way forward turned out to be the fact everyone's plans required far more power than the Empire could generate. Hence the agreed solution to look to the Americans to make all plans possible–make the situation fit the plan.[32] The Americans were now to bail out the "Singapore strategy," so theatre commanders could carry on planning as if it was still operative. Churchill was too preoccupied trying to secure American intervention at the highest level, and too distracted by active operations, to end the argument. The "Singapore strategy" was neither replaced nor sensibly reoriented to a new grand strategy because the British military system still found it easier to make circumstances fit delicately balanced plans. Progress in the Mediterranean, and persuading the Americans, would make it possible to preserve the "Singapore strategy." Meanwhile, the Far East could be managed by some fine tuning.

That fine tuning started with a COS request to theatre commanders to report how they proposed to implement the new "Far East Appreciation." On 16 October, Bond, Babington, and the C-in-C China Station, now Vice-Admiral Geoffrey Layton, produced a Tactical Appreciation of Defence Situation in Malaya. The theatre commanders clearly understood their problem:

> Our problem therefore in the absence of a capital ship fleet is to make the best dispositions possible to secure most important of our (Far East) interests without cover which capital ship fleet would provide.

The commanders assumed the U.S. would be benevolently neutral, Japan would have strong enough land, sea and air forces–up to 10 divisions and some 700 aircraft–to launch any scale of invasion it wished, would establish a position in Thailand before striking, and would have the initiative. They argued that even if an attack did not come before RAF Far East reached its target strength of 336 aircraft at the end of 1941, at no time, even if reinforced according to plan, would Malaya Command be strong enough to repel invading forces that reached Malaya. Reasons included the need to cover all Malaya and protect airbases but still maintain a field force for mobile operations, the weakness of local volunteer forces, but especially the air strength of the enemy and the problem of Thailand. Because British policy was to avoid an early clash with

Japan a Japanese move into Thailand was not to be regarded as a *casus belli*. The Japanese could establish a strong base there without any interference from naval or air forces. Spread out as it must to guard airbases, Malaya Command would not be able to hold those in the north against such a proximate threat; a potential position at Jitra, covering the airbase at Alor Star, was singled out as unsatisfactory. Theatre commanders felt that RAF Far East required not 336 but rather 566 first line aircraft to carry out both its missions: to maintain air supremacy and devastate an invasion force at sea. Even with that many, the threat from Thailand now must be considered. Theatre commanders saw a possible answer. If the British responded to any Japanese move into Thailand by seizing part of the border area in self-defence, that could provide cover to the northern airbases and guard against a Japanese approach overland.[33]

This was very much an air plan appreciation rather than an integrated ground-air defence plan. There were only two points that addressed combined tactical problems. One was the warning the defensive position at Jitra, chosen solely because it was in the right place to protect airbases, was unsuitable for a land battle. The other, much more important, was the call for a pre-emptive strike into southern Thailand. This was seen as a way out of the interservice dispute. It could be. But it was also clear recognition of yet another threat to which there was as yet no answer, other than on paper. Not only could Bond and Babington not work together, they now felt the problem was even greater than hitherto realized and the only answers were even greater reinforcement and a more ambitious plan.

Even as this appreciation went forward, the COS response was already brewing. The impulse came from Layton. Taking up his post in Singapore in September, the new man soon found out how bitter interservice rivalry had become and drew his own conclusions. Layton told the Admiralty that Babington was being unreasonable, insisting that because the defence of Malaya was an air problem "first, last and all the time," he should "have the first and last word in what was to be done and not to be done," even though he had no air force. He was encouraged in this unilateralism by the Secretary for Defence, C.A. Vlieland, who objected to any steps to prepare for war that would disrupt economic activity in the colonies. Layton called for changes, starting by replacing Babington. The COS realized this deadlock could not continue, because it made it impossible to settle a comprehensive defence plan to protect the Far East without the fleet. But their response was less than decisive. On 17 October the Prime Minister agreed to create a new intermediate military authority in the region, to improve co-operation in plans and preparations. Air Chief Marshal Sir Robert Brooke-Popham was appointed C-in-C Far East Command.[34]

Everything about this new command suggests that what might have been a productive experiment in unified command was seen by the COS as an ad hoc measure to buy time. Brooke-Popham was 62 years old, had actually retired in 1937 and was not up to date on many professional matters. His most recent job had been Governor of Kenya, where he earned a reputation for being patient and conciliatory. And as an airman he was hardly likely to challenge the primacy of the air plan. Brooke-Popham was made responsible for co-ordinating defence plans, operations and training of ground and air forces in Burma, Malaya, Singapore, Borneo and Hong Kong. However he was not given control over the adminstration, finance and training of the two services, both of which continued to report to their home departments. With a headquarters staff of only seven the new command could not have exercised such detailed supervision in any case. Worst of all, the navy was entirely excluded from his purview, on the grounds its responsibilities covered a larger area, the war at sea was global and indivisible, and therefore it must be controlled directly from the Admiralty, through its own commanders. Adding final insult to injury the new GHQ Far East would rely on the Far East Combined Bureau (FECB), an interservice organ controlled by the navy, for intelligence. The absurd result was that an out of date airman, not known to be the type to rock the boat, was made responsible to defend the base of a service that did not answer to him, which was not now planning to use the base anyway, but on whom he must rely for intelligence, in order to supervise the operations of two services who were at daggers drawn, and who could go over his head.[35] It is hard to resist the conclusion the COS expected Brooke-Popham to replace whichever service commander was more disposable with someone more affable, and settle a defence plan that did not challenge London's desire to keep the "Singapore strategy" alive.

Before he left London Brooke-Popham met individually with Portal, Dill and Ismay, but not with the COS collectively, and he did not meet either the Prime Minister or the First Sea Lord. Considering that his job was to pull together imperial defence east of India, revolving still around the navy, this was strange to say the least. When the new GHQ Far East opened in Singapore on 18 November, two instructions rang in his ears: avoid any clash with Japan, and do the best you can with what you have and what we can send you.[36] Brooke-Popham wasted little time getting acquainted with the problems of his new command and soon drew definite conclusions. Regarding relations between the services, he hit the nail right on the head:

Every operation should have been looked upon as a combined operation of two, or very often the three, services; for a long time there was a tendency for one of the services to work out a plan on its own and then see how one or both the other services could come in.

Unfortunately he was less clear sighted on which service was the worst sinner:

Personal relations with the Army Headquarters were good, but I felt in the early months a reluctance at times to accept advice, and a suspicion that GHQ, with a Royal Air Force officer as C-in-C, were dealing with matters which were properly the function of the GOC.

Perhaps the new C-in-C did not notice that when GHQ Far East ran a readiness exercise in December, Babington left Malaya on tour and only returned for the final review.[37]

When it came to co-ordination at the highest level, the new C-in-C soon agreed with Layton that the War Committee in Singapore was ineffective and the main reason was Vlieland's obstructive attitude. The idea to have a civilian official chair this committee, whose task was to coordinate defence activities involving the civil government and all three services, dated back to Tedder, who successfully lobbied to have Vlieland take the post. The experiment went sour when an argument erupted over the colony's priorities in contributing to the war effort, sparked by calls for increased training call outs for European volunteers. The British government, asked to settle the matter, decreed the colony must concentrate on maximizing tin and rubber production, to earn vital dollars. Vlieland took this literally enough to insist the first principle in defence preparations must be:

... to keep the whole of Malaya intact as far as may be found possible, to minimize disturbance of normal life and activity within the country and avoid anything in the nature of precautionary havoc.

By applying this policy rigidly Vlieland was bound to annoy the services, but he aggravated the problem by jumping into the dispute over defence plans and strategy, despite denying any intention to do so. Firmly convinced any close defence of Singapore and its approaches was a folly he called the "Singraltar" error, Vlieland backed the air force when it emphasized the defence of the whole peninsula. When the Governor unwisely took eight months home leave in 1940 and refused to accelerate his return, Vlieland exploited this to manipulate the War Committee. Brooke-Popham found the committee kept no systematic records, which made it difficult to trace what had been agreed and what was being done about it. He also discovered the army and navy wanted Vlieland out and soon concluded they were right.[38]

The most important problem facing the new command was of course the state of defence plans and preparations. Here, early returns were mixed. Soon after theatre commanders submitted their tactical appreciation, a conference in Singapore, chaired by Layton and attended by Dominion officers and an American observer, called for more ground and air reinforcements. Brooke-Popham and Layton warned London they needed to make firm plans for co-operation with the Dutch, which meant accepting as policy the need to help the Dutch resist any Japanese attack; Layton called for a clear declaration of what Japanese moves would be seen as cause for war. Given that any Japanese attack on the Dutch colonies would pose a mortal threat to Singapore, this was indeed an unavoidable liability that needed attention. The Prime Minister demurred, insisting the Americans take the lead in the region and fearing concrete steps in advance might complicate things politically for President Roosevelt. Notwithstanding this vagueness, talks with Dutch officers in late November laid useful groundwork for practical co-operation.[39] But the big challenge was to convince the home governments the defence of Southeast Asia was one indivisible problem, which required the combined and co-ordinated efforts of the British Empire, the Dutch and the Americans. This was a matter of national policy, so all Far East Command could do was report and recommend.

In December, Brooke-Popham did just that. His approach to London reflected some recent movement. That autumn Malaya Command finally received some sizable reinforcement: two British battalions withdrawn from enclaves in China, two Indian brigades, the 6th and 8th, and the headquarters of 11th Indian Division. This increased the force to some 17 battalions; that same month the Australians offered to lend a brigade pending further Indian reinforcements, which the COS indicated would be forthcoming. The COS also decided to send American fighter aircraft, ordered as part of the British mobilization for total war.[40] On 7 December Brooke-Popham received an FECB intelligence summary on "Japan's next move." It repeated the familiar arguments: the Japanese were unlikely to risk a direct attack on Singapore or Malaya, or even the Dutch colonies, because that might provoke war with the Americans. What they might do was move into Thailand, which would put them on Malaya's doorstep. That same day the C-in-C Far East sent a full appreciation to the COS. He called for a much firmer policy to contain Japan, on the grounds that weakness would only encourage the Japanese and American policy was hardening. Finally, he noted he was closely considering the proposal to launch a pre-emptive strike into southern Thailand, to ward off the most likely threat. Whatever unfolded, he would need much larger forces.[41]

Brooke-Popham was right about the need to prepare a common defence in Southeast Asia. But his proposals ran afoul both of the government's reluctance to make political commitments that might annoy the Americans and of the Prime Minister's determination to focus on the war at hand. In September Dill lobbied the Prime Minister to ask the Australians to divert their 7th Division, slated for the Middle East, to Malaya. Churchill refused, arguing the risk in the Far East was acceptable. The Prime Minster soon turned this into a policy. Churchill argued that as long as the "garrison" was strong enough to hold the "fortress," and the Americans could intervene, there was no need to hold all Malaya. He preferred to build up forces for the offensive in the Mediterranean; a strong defence of "the approaches to Singapore" should still make it possible for the fleet to intervene. Thanking the Australians in December for offering to lend their brigade to Malaya, he argued it would be "unwise to spare aircraft to lay idle in Malaya on the remote chance of an attack by Japan when they should be playing their part in Europe."[42]

Matters came to a head in early January 1941, when the COS responded to the appeals from Singapore. They agreed the Far East needed larger forces, but argued European experience showed that the RAF could be outnumbered and still prevail–so their figure of 336 aircraft should suffice. They would try to accelerate reinforcements, especially of fighters, "taking into account the demands of theatres already the scene of war." This caveat reflected the Prime Minister's blunt comment on 13 January:

> I do not remember to have given my approval to these very large diversions of force. On the contrary, if my minutes are collected they will be seen to have an opposite tendency. The political situation in the Far East does not seem to require, and the strength of our Air Force by no means warrants, the maintenance of such large forces in the Far East at this time.[43]

The dissonance could not have been more dangerous. London called on theatre commanders to work to a strategy that could only succeed if the war in Europe took a spectacular turn for the better overnight, or if a friendly neutral could be persuaded to "pull British chestnuts out of the fire." The response in Singapore was to sidestep the dispute over plans by proposing an even more ambitious plan. That provoked the Prime Minister to declare the war at hand must come first. Most ominous was the fact that Churchill and the COS clearly disagreed over the connection between grand strategy and the defence plan for Malaya and Singapore, but did not resolve the matter.

Churchill saw the problem as one that could be solved by concentrating available forces to defend Singapore itself, especially because the threat of American intervention would deter the Japanese. This of course flew in the face of the reassessment accepted in 1938. The central problem was whether or not all Malaya must be defended; this should have been argued out to a firm conclusion there and then. Failing to do so, especially failing to make clear to Churchill that Singapore was not a "fortress" in anything but name, was careless to say the least on the part of all concerned.[44] Churchill, the COS, and Brooke-Popham all failed to grasp the nettles raised by the fall of France and the open dispute between Bond and Babington. Defence plans for the Far East were compromised at every level by two decisions: to gamble on the Americans and thus to ignore the contradictions between circumstances and plans. If things did not go just as the British hoped, they now ran the very real risk of losing "a footing from which we could eventually retrieve the position ...."

4

Great Expectations

In 1941 the Axis Powers transformed the war by attacking the two strongest powers in the world. This virtually guaranteed their ultimate defeat. But at the time the struggle seemed to hang in the balance, because the U.S.A. and U.S.S.R. were not as prepared for war as their enemies. The correlation of forces shifted very much in the Allies favour, but it would take time to generate their full power. For the British Empire, this meant one price of final victory would be defeat in the Far East. But while that defeat may be traced to larger forces it could no longer control, the Empire's preparations to defend the Far East determined just how heavy it must be. The British military system not only failed to reconnect grand strategy and defence plans, it broke the chain beyond repair. The main reason was the fact decision makers in London and Singapore badly misread the short-term correlation of forces. This created a climate of unjustified optimism. That climate persuaded them to take liberties that left the Empire in the Far East wide open to disaster.

In spring 1941 the Americans made three moves that set them on course for war. Staff talks with the British and Canadians, held in Washington, produced in March a basis for a coalition grand strategy. The agreement, known as ABC-1, established that if–read when–the U.S. entered the war, the coalition would concentrate on defeating Germany first, and contain Japan by a defensive stand in the Pacific. That same month President Roosevelt answered British appeals by steering through Congress what became known as the Lend-Lease policy, allowing the U.S. government to supply massive quantities of assistance to the Allies. And in May, Roosevelt declared an Unlimited National Emergency and directed the USN to protect shipping carrying supplies to the U.K. The ABC-1 agreement made it possible to pursue joint war plans; Lend-Lease not only underwrote British mobilization but also amounted to the start of true American mobilization, as it provoked a large increase in American war production; and naval assertion put the Americans on a collision course with Germany.

Things did not look so promising at the front. German bombing attacks on the home islands remained heavy until late in May. The British bomber offensive began to absorb a massive slice of British resources, but did little damage to Germany. German pressure on the vital supply lines increased to the point where Churchill was forced to declare the Battle of the Atlantic. A serious dispute erupted in the COS over the priority this struggle should have in grand strategy. Much of the RN's attention was devoted to this campaign yet merchant shipping losses rose alarmingly. Italian forces were overcome in East Africa, but Allied victories in North Africa provoked the feared German intervention, there and in the Balkans. Heavy casualties were suffered in Greece and Crete as both were lost. A grim struggle erupted when Axis forces in North Africa were stiffened by German armour, which forced the Allies back onto the defensive in Egypt. British Empire forces also struggled to hold on to the Middle East, and suffered heavy air and naval losses in the Mediterranean. German combat power seemed more daunting than ever.

Then, on 22 June, the war changed fundamentally. Hitler launched operation *Barbarossa*, a campaign to destroy the Soviet armed forces and break the Soviet state. More than three million German and Axis troops attacked more than five million Soviets. This clash, the largest land war in history, became the fulcrum of the global war. It would certainly determine the result of that war. Churchill immediately allied the U.K. with the Soviet Union, rightly seeing the German move as a godsend. The Soviets could now replace the beaten French Army as the land power that would grind down the main force of the main enemy; more than two-thirds of the German Army and Air Force were engaged in the assault. This brought immediate relief to the U.K. from the threat of invasion, and made it difficult for the Germans to escalate their commitment in the Mediterranean. The Prime Minister insisted it must be British policy to do whatever could be done to keep the Soviets in the war.[1] The Soviet Union was also of course an Asian power, so the attack had a direct and fundamental impact on the Asian situation. The most important consequence was that it forced the Japanese to decide once and for all whether or not to go to war against the Western Powers.

Retracing the deliberations in Tokyo in 1941 is like watching someone finally realize they have painted themselves into a corner. The Japanese watched with concern as the Western Powers took halting steps to co-ordinate their defences in Asia and the U.S. moved towards war, while their own efforts to "resolve the China Incident" made little progress. They responded by opening direct talks with the American government, strengthening relations with the Axis Powers, concluding a Neutrality Pact with the Soviet Union in April, and pressing Dutch colonial authorities to allow Japan unhindered access to the vital raw materials of the East Indies, especially oil. All these efforts exploded when the Germans attacked the U.S.S.R. and the Dutch flatly refused to submit to Japanese pressure. The Japanese response was the opposite of the British experience–practical operational plans were made for war, but they were connected to a national war policy and grand strategy almost criminally irresponsible.

Events in June provoked a debate in Tokyo, culminating in an Imperial Conference on 2 July. The conference agreed on an "Outline of the Empire's National Policy to Cope with the Changing World Situation." The new policy rested on two tracks: negotiations with the United States to avert hostilities, and preparations for war. The majority clearly wanted the first track pressed with all possible effort, but also agreed war must be faced:

> Regardless of whatever changes may occur in the world situation, Japan will adhere to the established policy of creating a Greater East Asia Co-prosperity Sphere and thereby contribute to the establishment of world peace. As before, Japan will strive for the settlement of the China Incident, advance toward the Southern Area in order to lay the foundation for her self-support and self-defence, and, depending upon the situation, settle the northern issues. Japan will overcome all obstacles in order to attain the above-mentioned goal.

If it became necessary in order to prosecute the advance south, "... Japan will not hesitate to declare war against Britain and the United States." As a first step the Japanese decided to force the French to allow them to occupy bases in southern Indochina. This would make it easier to intimidate the Dutch into reconsidering the oil question, and put Thailand under pressure should that be desirable.[2] The French-Japanese "Mutual Defence Agreement" was announced on 21 July. The American response was swift and fateful. Roosevelt announced on 26 July what amounted to an economic blockade of Japan: embargoing all supplies of strategic raw materials, especially oil, and freezing all Japanese assets, measures quickly echoed by the British and Dutch.

For the rest of the year Japanese government and military leaders engaged in what seems like almost constant debate. But the quantity of these discussions far outweighed their quality. The Japanese were shocked by the American response, which itself is revealing.[3] On the most important question, what must Japan do to preserve its most vital interests, the rigidity of Japanese thinking was suicidal. The "negotiations" with the Americans in Washington, on which so much emphasis was placed until very late in the day, are the clearest evidence. Ambassador Nomura had strict instructions which amounted to an order to persuade the U.S. government to stand aside and let Japan do whatever it wanted:

> 1. Japan would strive for a settlement of the China Incident. 2. Diplomatic affairs would be conducted on the basis of the Tripartite Alliance. 3. Japan

was sincerely enthusiastic about the adjustment of diplomatic relations with the United States.

The Japanese had thrown their lot in with the Axis Powers and would not abandon their policy of imperial hegemony in China. But those decisions provoked an American response that threatened to break the Japanese economy. As seen from Tokyo this gave them a choice: "surrender" to American economic strangulation and give up their dreams of hegemony, or fight.[4] On the surface this does not seem dissimilar to the existential dilemma the British faced after the fall of France. What differed was how the Japanese handled the problem.

Whereas the British responded by wooing the strongest power in the world, and reacted pragmatically when fate dropped a surly but powerful ally in their lap, the Japanese decided to fight a war they were not strong enough to survive. They had four reasons. First, they did not believe their social structure would survive failure in China. Second, they hoped Germany would win its war and thus make their problem easier. Third, they thought they could grab and exploit enough natural resources in Southeast Asia to make it possible to stand up to an economy nearly ten times the size of their own in a protracted war. Finally, they convinced themselves their main antagonist did not have the moral fibre to fight total war to the finish, whereas their disciplined warrior society would face any sacrifice required. Regarding German assistance, the Japanese acknowledged the most they could expect was German success in Europe, which could also divert American forces. But rather than join their ally in a joint attack to finish off the Soviets, the Japanese decided to use that war as a giant diversion and start their own in the south.[5] The direct comparison is of course the Allied decision to concentrate on Germany first. As for economic strength, experts all agreed the economic blockade of Japan would deplete stocks of strategic raw materials, especially oil, within a year–unless operations in China were curtailed. The Army and Navy flatly refused to do that, which left only one alternative:

> Under such circumstances, even the minimum demands of a materials mobilization plan could not be met unless Japan seized the southern area, rich in natural resources, at the outset of war and gained command of the sea and air by swiftly destroying the military strength of the United States, Great Britain and the Netherlands in that area.

Economic officials acknowledged Japanese production would at first dip alarmingly, but assumed that if all went well the southern resources could be harnessed within two years. Responding to the American embargo, the President of the Planning Board:

... felt it necessary to submit to the Government and to Imperial General Headquarters a report of the resources it would be necessary for Japan to mobilize in the event of war, and urged them to execute a war aimed at the acquisition of resources in line with these demands.[6]

Japanese leaders, especially in the Navy, clung to the hope the Americans might yet agree to let them have all the Dutch oil they needed, in order to crush China. This only underlined their bankruptcy in national policy. The Americans shut that door on 3 September by calling for all further negotiations to be based on four principles: respect for the territorial integrity and sovereignty of all nations; non-interference in the internal affairs of other countries; equal opportunity for trade; maintenance of the status quo in the Pacific. Given that this would have required Japan to stop bullying the Dutch, pull out of the French colonies, and give up their war in China, this meant war. Both principals kept negotiating until the very day war broke out. But Japan would not give up its demand for access to raw materials in order to fight on in China, so the outcome was predictable.[7] Further discussions in Tokyo led on 6 September to an Imperial Conference that ratified an "Outline for the Execution of the Empire's National Policy." The Navy later described these decisions as marking a "Shift in Emphasis in National Policy from Political to Military Strategy." Despite further twisting and turning to keep alive the search for a "diplomatic solution," Japanese policy was now driven by strategic concerns. Preparations for war were propelled by two considerations: the longer Japan waited the stronger those it would attack became, and the worse the weather would turn. Imperial General Headquarters insisted on setting a deadline for the success of negotiations, after which Japan must go to war. Prince Konoye resigned on 16 October and the Emperor intervened to direct the new administration to review the whole situation again. But the new government that took office two days later was led by General Tojo Hideki as Prime Minister. The momentum for war was now unstoppable.[8]

The decisive shift came when the services, especially the Army, concluded correctly the Americans were stalling to buy time to prepare for war. When the new government met in late October, the question was now how and when to attack. It is true two plans were discussed, but as both relied on the Americans dropping all their demands even the most optimistic Japanese leader surely saw the writing on the wall. A Naval Operations Plan submitted on 20 October became the basis for decision. An Imperial Conference on 5 November finally drew the bottom line–either an agreement by 1 December, or Japan must go to war against the Western Powers before it became too weak to do so. The war plan called for conquering the southern area within five months, after which "… by use of war materials in stock and of resources in the southern area after the commencement of hostilities, there was an excellent prospect that the material power of the Japanese Empire would be sufficient to carry out a protracted war."[9]

Was this decision rational? Applying the test of circumstances, intentions and capabilities, the answer is no. True, the Germans were at that point knocking at the gates of Moscow, but the Japanese made no serious plans to fight any kind of concerted war with their allies. Indeed, discussions in Tokyo about national policy were themselves so awkward they resembled coalition bargaining more than policy making in one nation. And yes, the Americans were giving Japan no choice–if, that is, definitive military victory in China was essential for the very survival of Japan. But it depends on how one defines survival. These Japanese deliberations were littered with warnings about protracted war and American strength, and they also expected the British to fight hard. The Japanese admitted there was no way they could force an American surrender, and they could only look to the intangibles. The only way Japan could survive a war against the Americans was if everything went exactly as they planned and the Americans were as effete as they hoped. Did Japanese leaders ask themselves this question: what would be more difficult, coping with failure in China or coping with an American invasion of Japan? This is even less impressive than the wishful thinking behind the "Singapore strategy," because the stakes, national existence, were higher. But what about Japanese grand strategy, their plan to attack the Western Powers? Was it any more sensible? Yes and no.

Japanese military planning moved forward from late 1940 on the assumption the advance south might lead to war, but only shifted into high gear in summer 1941 and only became direct preparation for war in the autumn. As in all other respects the German attack on the Soviet Union was decisive. It finally forced the Japanese to settle on a concrete grand strategy. Planners faced three imperatives. First, Japan must take on the Americans, British and Dutch at the same time. Navy planners were especially adamant it would be far too risky to attack the Europeans alone, because that would leave the powerful US Pacific Fleet poised to strike from the flank against any Japanese advance. It was simply assumed the Western Powers would stand together. Second, the offensive must be relentless and fast. Western positions must be taken and their forces destroyed before powerful reinforcements could arrive. Finally, victory must be won cheaply. The entire IJN was available, but it had to deal with the US Pacific Fleet as well as launch and support all attacks in Southeast Asia. Due to its commitments in China, Manchuria, and at home, the IJA could only spare 11 divisions for the whole campaign, one-fifth of its strength. Several formations would have to participate in more than one offensive.[10] The decision to go to war might have been unwise, but the operational plan it spawned was not. Its most revealing feature was also its most impressive: for all that Japan had been thinking about war with Western Powers for decades it had no concrete plan to fight them, so had to make one in haste from scratch.

Japanese plans to fight the U.S.A. dated back to 1909, but the Japanese only began to prepare vague contingency plans to fight the British from 1937. "An extremely rough study of war strategy" for fighting both major Western Powers was completed by the Navy General Staff in March 1941.[11] Two developments then intersected to influence further planning. First, from January, the C-in-C of the Combined Fleet, Admiral Yamamoto Isoroku, directed his staff to study the idea of knocking out the main body of the US Pacific Fleet by a surprise attack by carrier-borne aircraft. Second, influenced by German lobbying, the Army General Staff became interested in attacking Singapore. Taking Singapore would, it was argued, be a "decisive factor in the downfall of Great Britain," and allow the Japanese to put unbearable pressure on the Dutch colonies. This consideration was a factor in putting pressure on Thailand and French Indochina from early 1941. Planners felt British naval and air forces in Malaya and Singapore would make a direct attack too risky, so staging bases would be required. These ideas came together in the summer when events forced the Japanese to turn broad scenarios into co-ordinated attack plans. Several options were considered, but in August a consensus developed. Initial attacks would be made against Malaya, starting with the seizure of ports and airbases in southern Thailand, and the Philippines. Once Allied forces there were destroyed, the advance would continue along those two lines until the Dutch colonies and oilfields were secured. Meanwhile, the Combined Fleet would attack and neutralize the US Pacific Fleet.[12]

The plan to attack Hawaii created a problem when Yamamoto concluded he would need all six of the navy's fast fleet carriers. This would deprive the expeditionary forces in the Southern Area of the airpower they needed to prevail. Command exercises in September clarified the issue and a solution was found. Yamamoto would have all he required, so the vital strike on the main enemy force could succeed. But the attack on Malaya and Singapore must also rapidly succeed, to preclude outside reinforcement, so the IJA would transfer some of its air corps from Manchuria, to ensure three to one superiority in the air. The resulting Naval Operations Plan of 20 October became informal orders on 29 October to fleets and forces already moving into their assembly areas. The momentum this generated was decisive in the Imperial Conference of 5 November, which confirmed the operational plan. The Army General Staff expected to take the Philippines in 53 days, Malaya and Singapore within 100 days, and the Dutch colonies within 150 days. Regarding the attack on the British, one complication was already anticipated: a British pre-emptive move into Thailand. This would be dealt with in two ways. If no British advance was made before the invasion force sailed, it would invade southern Thailand. The Thais, already being put under pressure, would be given a very late demand for full co-operation, followed quickly by the entry of Japanese forces from French Indochina, to secure Bangkok and move south. If the British advanced before the invasion forces put to sea, Japanese forces would land further north, then advance rapidly overland to seize the bases needed to support the assault on Malaya. Once they had the initiative, the Japanese would advance down the peninsula to take Singapore.[13]

A Liaison Conference on 13 November approved the "Plan to Speedily Conclude Hostilities against the United States, Great Britain, the Netherlands and the Chiang regime." The Japanese expected conquering Burma would be enough to provoke rebellion in India, Australia could be isolated from the British and the Americans, and the latter could be fought to a standstill by stubbornly defending the conquered areas–assuming swift and successful exploitation of captured resources. Meanwhile, Japan's oil supply would "barely suffice" to maintain the war effort.[14] If the Germans failed to crush Soviet power, if Japan could not quickly and fully exploit captured oil, if any of the assumptions about the Americans were wrong, this grand strategy could not succeed.

On the other hand, as a campaign plan to overrun Southeast Asia this strategy was very likely to succeed. The Japanese forces assembled by early November were certainly strong enough for the job. It is interesting to note the Japanese were indeed going to mount an indirect attack on Singapore, as the British expected, and that both sides were aware how important bases in southern Thailand were for any force attacking Malaya. But once the IJA agreed to provide the necessary airpower, the operational problem became manageable. The Japanese had the advantages of being prepared for war, with experienced and powerful forces on hand, and knowing where and when they would attack. They could expect to concentrate stronger forces against the widely separated groups of Allied forces, and defeat them in detail. Singapore was in their sights.

Two problems undermined British plans in the first half of 1941: setbacks in the field, especially in the Mediterranean, and shortfalls in production. This concentrated minds in London even more on the war at hand. The ABC-1 agreement actually made the immediate problem more acute. While the

Americans accepted British grand strategy in principle, they made it clear they did not agree it should always be based on relative military weakness. The world was divided into spheres of operations for purposes of strategic direction. The Far East would be shared. While the future Allies would stand on the defensive in the Pacific, it was unclear what the US Pacific Fleet planned to do, but clear the Americans expected the British to strengthen their forces in the area as soon as possible. Most problematic was the warning "… the details of the deployment of the forces of the Associated Powers at any one time will be decided with regard to the military situation in all theatres." This was nothing more than common sense, but it also indicated the British had work to do to pin the Americans down to their grand strategy.[15]

Churchill's objection to reinforcing the Far East prompted the COS, on 23 January, to give ground in order to keep the idea in play. They assured the Prime Minister they would pursue this without interfering with active operations elsewhere.[16] Unfortunately those operations ran into many problems. The bomber offensive against Germany made little headway, but the Air Staff became more determined than ever to prosecute it. The Battle of the Atlantic and setbacks in the Mediterranean put the RN under more pressure than ever, while uncertainty about German intentions kept Prime Minister and COS focused on home defence. Matters came to something of a head when Australian Prime Minister Menzies visited London to press the case for reinforcing the Far East.

On 9 April Churchill and the COS reviewed the situation. They agreed they could not promise to deploy a fleet until the overall situation improved, the Mediterranean would be stood down only if the Dominions were attacked, but such an attack would provoke American intervention anyway. The Prime Minister objected to any guarantee to the Dutch and categorically spelt out his views on defence in the Far East:

> All our action must be judged from its effect on our power to win the war against Germany … The Prime Minister said that he was prepared to enter into any declaration, or into any commitment, provided the Americans were in it with us.

Dill, provoked by the shift of the burden of defending Singapore onto the ground forces, argued alone for higher priority in grand strategy for the Far East. On 29 April the CIGS admitted the Army could spare no forces from the U.K. but insisted nevertheless: "Whatever happened, events in the Middle East could not lose us the war, provided we maintained our position in this country and at Singapore." The Prime Minister would have none of it. At the Defence Committee that day, Churchill spelt out to Menzies the gist of a directive he circulated the day before: only an invasion of the U.K. would really tempt the Japanese to attack, the loss of Egypt and the Middle East would be a disaster second only to a successful invasion, and above all:

> ... it may be taken as almost certain that the entry of Japan into the war would be followed by the immediate entry of the United States on our side. These conditions are to be accepted by the Service Departments as a guide for all plans and actions. Should they cease to hold good, it will be the responsibility of Ministers to notify the Service Staffs in good time.[17]

The policy was set: in the Far East, the British would stay in step with the Americans, rely on them, and send only what they could spare.

This decision starkly reflected the British dilemma as the war became a clash of titans. In Europe they could do little more but wait to see what the Germans did next. In Asia, they could lobby the Americans but not push them. By now London's focus was on Eastern Europe. The German invasion of the Soviet Union provoked a reassessment of British grand strategy, but to no positive effect for the Far East. The Soviets called for a so-called "Second Front," a major invasion of Western Europe to draw off German forces. The COS insisted on taking advantage of the German move east to build up British strength and press existing campaigns forward. They argued this could be no more than a breathing space ending in Soviet defeat before the end of the year. An occasionally bitter debate raged in London until the end of October, when the Prime Minister agreed no new campaigns should be undertaken.[18] There were quid pro quos, and most affected the Far East. The campaign to clear North Africa and regain control of the Mediterranean remained front and centre. And if the British could not send forces to help the Soviets, they must send what they could. That led to an agreement, concluded in three way talks with the Americans and Soviets in September, to supply large amounts of materiel to assist the Soviet war effort. Not only did this place further strain on the RN to escort the supply convoys, it also cut into plans to supply weapons to overseas commands. Both British production, and equipment ordered from the U.S. originally intended for British Empire forces, had to be drawn on for this imperative in alliance politics.[19]

In spite of all that, when Roosevelt responded to the Japanese move into Indochina by imposing a virtual economic blockade on Japan the British moved along with him. Churchill and Roosevelt met to discuss the war at a shipboard conference off Newfoundland in August. One area in which there was less than full agreement was the Far East. The British nightmare was a Japanese attack on the Western Powers other than the U.S.; confident as Churchill was that this would provoke the Americans, much damage might be done before they could intervene. More to the point, Churchill's attitude amounted to "in for a penny in for a pound": if the Americans were going to try to deter the Japanese so must the British, and that deterrence would be more effective if it were public and united. But the American staffs remained reluctant to concentrate forces in Singapore. Worse, the State Department watered down a joint public warning to the Japanese.[20] Being in step with the Americans meant going neither faster than they did, nor in any different direction.

Further calls for reinforcements underlined the fact there was no avoiding those restrictions. On 14 September Portal not only rejected Far East Command's urgent calls to complete the reinforcement program that year but also set back the end of 1941 target to the end of 1942. An overall shortage of resources and the urgent need to accelerate the expansion of RAF Middle East were cited as the main problems–but to them must be added the emphasis on the bomber offensive, and the redirection of supplies to the Soviets.[21] The connection to the Mediterranean also surfaced when the British became annoyed by Australian demands to relieve their 9th Division, besieged in Tobruk, by exchanging it for another formation. This operation not only cost ships, lives and money, it even provoked Churchill to direct the COS to examine whether the three Australian divisions in the Middle East and North Africa could be traded for two Indian divisions in Malaya, which would then become an Australian responsibility. Such delegation of responsibility to defend Singapore was already too late even when the WO briefly considered it in June 1940. The fact Churchill suggested it now indicated how badly the war was straining imperial relations. The COS objected on military grounds. Such a move would strain already overstretched troop shipping and naval escorts. A straight swap of combat divisions would cause serious logistical problems, because the two armies needed different service units and supplies. Most interesting, the COS argued the Indian units were not yet ready to fight Germans–which indicated they considered the Japanese a less daunting foe.[22]

British grand strategy by September 1941 was to take advantage of the German attack in the east by going on the offensive in the Mediterranean, while bombing Germany, protecting the Atlantic, and guarding against invasion. Those tasks required more than 40 divisions, nearly 250 squadrons, and all the navy's capital ships and aircraft carriers. By comparison there were now the equivalent of three plus divisions and 14 squadrons in Malaya and Singapore–but Far East Command remained well below the strength everyone agreed it needed, in all areas. The military authorities in Singapore must be given credit for clear and timely warnings they needed more forces. But when it came to rethinking war plans, aligning them with grand strategy, and testing them against circumstances, intentions, and capabilities, the verdict can not be so positive. Singapore and London failed to break the habit to make the situation fit the plans. The authorities in Singapore had to grope in the dark because of the political difficulties in organizing an anti-Japanese coalition– but made this worse by their own decisions.

Brooke-Popham's first task was to put his own house in order. He enjoyed some success but could not solve the most serious problems: inadequate resources and disjointed plans. GHQ Far East was relocated to the naval base, but this did not increase the C-in-C's leverage over that service. Vlieland was forced out after the Governor agreed to sacrifice him–possibly because he was told in London there would be no early completion of the air reinforcement program, therefore harmony was essential. Babington left on the completion of his tour, Bond was relieved at the C-in-C's request. They were replaced in April and May by Air Vice-Marshal C.W.H. Pulford and by Percival, now promoted to Lt.-General. Percival and Pulford restored friendly personal relations between the two service headquarters. But Brooke-Popham admitted in July that despite their good working relationship the services were still not "thinking instinctively as integral partners"[23]–yet did nothing to change that.

Far East Command tried actively but no more successfully to align grand strategy with theatre defence plans. One problem stands out: a climate of optimism settled in early in the year, prodding it to take a fateful path. This did not come from confusion about the mission. Brooke-Popham bore always in mind that it was British policy to avoid a clash with Japan while at the same time trying to deter it, and rightly tried to emphasize closer co-operation with the Dominions and potential allies.[24] But the air of complacency that settled in around his headquarters undid both efforts.

In February, just as the 22nd Australian Brigade arrived in Singapore, Brooke-Popham convened a conference with the Dutch and Australians, plus American observers, to discuss common strategic problems. Far East Command had three objectives: to promote the closest possible co-ordination with the Americans, convince the other parties to accept their analysis of the situation, and persuade the Australians to keep their brigade in Malaya, rather than send it on to the Middle East. On 18 February an FECB appreciation suggested that if Japan did attack the British Empire it would "mobilize its maximum effort" for a "life and death struggle" and use seven divisions to attack Malaya. A debate arose when the Australians tabled an appreciation by their Chiefs of Staff claiming the Japanese could concentrate rapidly and simultaneously against any two of the three key areas: Malaya, the Dutch colonies, and Australia. The Australians suggested they would be willing to retain their 8th Division in the theatre but warned it needed equipment they could not supply, and emphasized the need to deploy a strong naval force at Singapore as soon as possible.[25]

Brooke-Popham and Layton encouraged the Australians to retain the 8th Division but change their minds about the strategic situation. Arguments were provided as ammunition to "help" their Australian colleagues restore the focus on Singapore. Far East Command prevailed when the conference report of 25 February matched an earlier British draft. It was agreed an attack on the British, Dutch or the Dominions was of "vital importance for the others." It was accepted Japan would find it "very hazardous" to attack the Dominions as long as Singapore remained available for any Allied fleet to use, the Japanese would have to attack the Dutch colonies before they could strike Australia, but could not securely hold those colonies as long as the British could threaten them from Singapore. The Dominions were therefore not likely to be invaded "initially," and the Japanese probably could not launch simultaneous major attacks against the British and Dutch. The main conclusion was:

> At the moment the more probable course, and one in conformity with Japanese traditional step by step policy, is the development of their hold on Indochina and Thailand and attack on Malaya with the object of capturing Singapore.

Overriding even that however was the importance of the U.S.A., "a governing factor." On this point Far East Command was emphatic, and its growing optimism emerged. Japan was surely aware of the danger of American intervention, and in the best case: "If U.S.A. intervenes actively on our side, Japan would have no other course but to adopt a defensive strategy and abandon her major expeditions to the south."[26]

Far East Command felt encouraged by such success, especially when Canberra said it would not only retain 8th Australian Division but also deploy the whole formation north of Australia.[27] On the other hand the most serious problem remained unsolved: concrete plans for Allied co-operation could not be made without firm commitments from London about reinforcements, and an American commitment to join a common defence. This was addressed by the Foreword to the conference report:

> The members of the Conference wish to emphasize the importance of all the Governments concerned making a definite agreement to co-operate fully in the event of any one of them being forced to take military action to counter

Japanese aggression. Such agreement need not be made public.[28]

To reinforce the point Brooke-Popham sent a telegram to the COS on 7 March, warning: "There are in my view only two moves which might have powerful influence in final Japanese decision to seek war: 1) Declaration of America's immediate intention to intervene 2) Belief that substantial British reinforcements are on the way." The telegram proposed something suggested by Darvall, now back in Malaya as Brooke-Popham's principal air staff officer: the British Ambassador should tell the Japanese that a British fleet led by seven capital ships and three aircraft carriers, as well as four heavy bomber squadrons, was on the move to the Far East:

> Realize that the bluff might soon be called, but situation could hardly be worsened by positive action on our part. Belief that we had moved strong mobile forces from West would at once undermine Japanese confidence in swift military success in this theatre, strengthen hand of moderates counseling caution and cast doubts upon German reports of their prospects of quick successes in West.[29]

This was arrant nonsense. As soon as the Japanese realized it was only a bluff they would be even more assertive; what price "positive action on our part"? But it underlines a crucial fact: despite real concerns over reinforcements and American indecision, Far East Command was becoming more optimistic.

This optimism resurfaced during another conference held in Singapore, the ADB talks, from 21 through 27 April, "to prepare plan for conduct of military operations in Far East on basis of report of Washington conversations." The appreciation of why Japan might attack south was based on precisely the same considerations being discussed in Tokyo. The delegates all agreed on what Japanese moves their governments should see as cause for war. Beyond a direct attack, the list included any move into central Thailand, or any Japanese advance below 6 degrees north clearly aimed at one of their territories. Despite the policy to concentrate on Germany first they nevertheless considered offensive action against Japan. The US Pacific Fleet was singled out as the main battle force, especially "before the arrival of the British fleet." Ground forces would protect the naval and air bases on which the vital lines of communication rested. On the "Singapore strategy," the Admiralty's wavering emerged. While "the immediate object" was to deploy to the base as planned:

> In the unlikely event of its proving impossible for the British Fleet to operate from Singapore, it will operate from bases in the Indian Ocean ... So many developments must precede the arrival of the British Far Eastern Fleet that it

is not profitable to examine in greater detail the operations that would then be possible.[30]

The point could not have been put more clearly. The Allied position in Southeast Asia now rested entirely on the Americans. The conviction that a firm American stand would either deter the Japanese or divert their blow was certainly the prime mover in Far East Command's new optimism. It was not much reduced by failure to follow through on what mattered most: the political will to implement agreements by concrete measures to prepare a common defence. Some technical progress was made in the following months. But it all rested on the home governments agreeing to combine to defend the region as a whole. The COS largely accepted the report, but rejected the idea of planning offensive operations from Hong Kong and refused to press the Americans to strengthen the Philippines if it detracted from their buildup in the Atlantic. The Americans however rejected any prior commitments and directed theatre commanders to reconsider the ADB agreement. But that decision only reached Far East Command on 25 November. Apart therefore from the technical agreements, the alliance faced war without a common defence plan in Southeast Asia. This left them vulnerable to defeat in detail. This was due entirely to the home governments. The Americans would not jeopardize their domestic political situation by moving towards common defence before public opinion was ready; the British had little choice but to accept this, and hope the US Pacific Fleet would indeed be potent.[31] Their own stress on the need to prepare in common thus makes Far East Command's optimism harder to understand.

One possible explanation was the growing strength of British Empire forces in the region–but the reinforcement situation also gave grounds for concern. Malaya Command grew steadily in absolute terms. 8th Australian Division, commanded by Maj.-Gen. H. Gordon Bennett, was reinforced by 27th Australian Brigade in August. But its third brigade was deployed in the Dutch colonies. This left Bennett, much to his disgust, commanding an understrength formation. 15th Indian Brigade arrived in March, followed by 22nd Indian Brigade and the headquarters of 9th Indian Division in April. 28th Indian Brigade arrived in September. Following in the autumn were a reconnaissance battalion, anti-aircraft artillery, one anti-tank and three field artillery regiments–some arriving only weeks before war broke out. The growth of the Command prompted Brooke-Popham to press for a corps headquarters. III Indian Corps was accordingly formed in May. Lt.-Gen. Sir Lewis Heath, fresh from leading 4th Indian Division to victory in East Africa, was appointed to command. By late autumn Percival's field forces amounted to ten regular brigades, organized in three divisions of two brigades each–8th Australian, 9th and 11th Indian–plus two brigades deployed in Singapore Fortress, 28th Indian Brigade as corps reserve and 12th Indian Brigade command reserve. These were supported by second-line Indian battalions deployed as airbase defence forces, plus various Volunteer Forces. The whole amounted to some 32 regular infantry battalions plus artillery and engineers–a far cry from the seven battalion force Bond found so constraining the year before.[32]

Despite Churchill's attitude, RAF Far East also grew. By February it had 10 squadrons in Malaya and Singapore. But there were still no fighter units, only half the squadrons had relatively modern aircraft, there were only a handful of reconnaissance aircraft, the torpedo-bombers were obsolete, and most aircrew were not battle experienced. The staff was so small and inexperienced Brooke-Popham told London "Am satisfied that the immediate supply of six or eight experienced officers from U.K. or Middle East would improve air force in the Far East by more than reinforcement of two modern fully equipped squadrons plus reserves." The staff officers were not sent, but other assets were: the Brewster Buffalo, an American-made fighter aircraft, and enough personnel to double the command in size in the second half of 1941. This allowed Pulford to establish a dedicated air defence command in Singapore in July, boasting fighter squadrons and anti-aircraft batteries, under the command of a Group Captain with Battle of Britain experience. Better still, the construction of a network of six early warning radar stations, from Mersing to Singapore, made good progress. By August RAF Far East boasted 12 squadrons, including two fighter squadrons with two more forming, one reconnaissance and one night-fighter unit. With promised Dutch reinforcements it could expect to deploy 215 aircraft, including some 75 fighters.[33]

Unfortunately this reinforcement looked better on paper than it was in practice. The staff was not adequately bolstered. The torpedo-bombers were not replaced. Reserves were inadequate in all categories. Brooke-Popham warned the Air Ministry about the weakness of this critical command time and again. His staff argued on 3 September that the Japanese would establish themselves in southern Thailand and northern Malaya and deploy 600 aircraft there. They would then wear down the defenders first, before striking for Singapore. Brooke-Popham spelt out his own forebodings to the COS, in an important telegram sent on 20 August. Without at least seven fighter squadrons, more modern bombers, and stronger reserves of all types, he doubted his air force could contain such a Japanese offensive:

This means bluntly that at present not only is our ability to attack shipping deplorably weak but we have not the staying power to sustain even what we could now do. As our air effort dwindles (as it would if war came now) so will enemy chances of landing increase. Long stretches of beach cannot be strongly defended everywhere and fighting inland is therefore certain to occur. In these conditions our troops might expect to receive little support from the air.

This accurate forecast spelt out the dire prospect awaiting the defenders of Singapore. The enemy could not be repelled while at sea because the air force was too weak. That same air force would not be able to fight for long because it was too shallow. That would leave the ground forces to fight the main battle on their own.[34]

Yet Brooke-Popham did not let this gloomy prospect seriously affect his general optimism. His telegram was prompted by an appreciation from Percival arguing he needed stronger ground forces to compensate for the lack of airpower. The C-in-C left London in no doubt of his priority:

It is the power to strike at shipping that matters most here ... I have no doubt what our first requirement here is. We want to increase our hitting power against ships and our capacity to go on hitting. In this way we shall make it difficult for the enemy to land and equally difficult for him to nourish any initial successes.[35]

By "first" Brooke-Popham meant ultimate rather than immediate priority. He already knew the authorized strength would not be reached until at least mid-1942, something confirmed by the Air Ministry that same month.[36] An effective anti-shipping capability certainly was important, as the initial battles in December would show. But surely the "first" priority was to deploy an effective fighter force, with enough reserves to sustain a fight and maintain control of the air–first in both senses of the word? Clearly, neither the COS nor GHQ Far East as yet sensed how close real danger was.

This hard judgement is borne out by the development of theatre plans and their connection to grand strategy. Three problems were decisive: the connection between the "air plan" and the deployment of Malaya Command; the idea of a pre-emptive strike into Thailand; and the role of the navy. The "air plan" remained the basis for defending Malaya and Singapore, despite the serious weaknesses in RAF Far East that GHQ knew would not soon be remedied. RAF Far East saw its role as to repel any invasion force at sea.[37] Brooke-Popham was candid: "The number and location of aerodromes in Malaya was based on the principle of relying mainly on air power for defence." Six bases were already operational on the mainland by February. But because it took time to build airbases, and the air force was expected to grow to 22 squadrons requiring 27 bases, construction had to proceed before squadrons were on hand to use them. By the autumn 11 bases were available: three in the northwest, three around Kota Bharu, one at Kuantan, four others near Kuala Lumpur and in Johore. This continued to outstrip the resources on hand–only nine were occupied by the eve of war.[38]

The airmen later admitted unilateral construction did produce bases "tactically weak to defend," but argued that problem was solved in 1941. Joint army-air force Aerodrome Defence Boards were set up to make sure ground defence was fully considered before construction began. Unfortunately this innovation only began in July, and the damage was already done. Excuses abound–the terrain, topography, the mission, the need to intercept far out to sea, etc. The truth is that the services, the air force especially, still were not in the habit of working in tandem at all levels.[39] Two concrete examples stand out. The airbase at Alor Star forced Malaya Command to select the unsuitable defensive position at Jitra to protect it, when there was a far better location for a defensive stand not far south, near Gurun. The airbases around Kota Bharu were right on the east coast, and would be attacked on the first morning of any amphibious invasion. On 26 July GHQ Far East, reacting to the Japanese move into southern Indochina, discussed the need to reconsider the directives to air and ground forces. Darvall suggested "… perhaps it would be far better to get the GOC and AOC, with their staffs, to sit round a table and discuss this problem, so that a clear picture can be given to both Commanders of what threat they are being asked to counter." One can only wonder why this was not already standard operating procedure![40]

The airmen believed the only way to defend Malaya was to repel an invasion far out to sea, and to do that they must attack an oncoming force several times. Hence they must be as close to it as possible. Malaya Command's dispositions were dictated by this requirement, and by the promise the air force would inflict 40% casualties on any invasion force before it hit the beach. Percival worked on that basis–on the understanding his job would be to repel, even "mop up," those who ran the gauntlet.[41] Given the Order of Battle of RAF Far East, and how long it would now take to raise it to the required strength, this can hardly be seen as prudent. Yet even as events overtook it, theatre commanders kept working to the plan–and nobody in London moved to stop them.

Far East and Malaya Commands spent most of 1941 developing the idea of a pre-emptive strike into southern Thailand. The concept of "forward defence" was first considered in 1937. By 1940, the fact it would not force anyone to abandon any existing policy or plan made it more attractive. What came to be known as operation *Matador* emerged by August as the focal point of planning in Singapore.[42] The impetus came from the COS, who indicated they were willing to consider the military advantages of a pre-emptive advance. On 8 February the C-in-C sent London the first outline plan. The premise was simple: any Japanese occupation of the border areas of southern Thailand would so jeopardize the defence of Malaya it must be seen as a cause of war. Recent improvements to roads, bridges, ports and airbases in the area meant the Japanese could use this infrastructure to build up strong air forces, shift their ground forces to outflank the defences of northern Malaya, and concentrate to defeat them in detail. The British could prevent this by advancing before the Japanese landed, to one of three lines: as far north as Chumpon, which would allow them to deny all six airfields in southern Thailand (plus the important offshore British airbase at Victoria Point); up to Bandon, which would deny five bases; or at least to the major port of Singora on the southeast coast. Any advance would depend on whether Malaya Command had enough formations to conduct this operation and still protect other areas that might be invaded, including Singapore itself—and especially on beating the Japanese to the punch.[43] Those problems became the focus of discussion for the next nine months; the plan even forced the central direction of the war to reconsider the connection between grand strategy and plans to defend Singapore.

That connection was spelt out by the theatre commanders as often as possible, starting with the report on the February staff talks. Layton emphasized its value to the common defence: "Given prompt reactions by ourselves on any sign of Japanese occupation of southern Thailand, e.g. by forestalling action in the Kra Isthmus, it is not going to be too easy for the Japanese to deploy and maintain superior forces for an attack on this front."[44] This ran into London's deep reluctance to stipulate what actions might be taken as cause for war before the British government could be certain of American support. Far East Command, with reason to believe the COS were interested at least in an advance to Singora, pressed ahead. On 24 March Brooke-Popham sent the COS a telegram outlining the military advantages to denying the area from Singora to the border, but stressing the need to beat the Japanese to the port.[45] This meant the government either had to stipulate in advance certain actions as cause for war that would automatically trigger the operation, or be willing to authorize it very rapidly indeed if a crisis arose. This was the heart of the matter. GHQ Far East now felt the operation was the best available military strategy to prolong the defence of the naval base. But the whole plan depended on beating the Japanese to the beaches in order to repel them. Did the military advantages outweigh the political risks of violating Thai neutrality first?

This question could only be resolved in London, but posing it widened the rift between Churchill and Dill. The COS failure to sort out the argument with the Prime Minister over whether to defend all Malaya, or merely the immediate approaches to Singapore, backfired when the discussions with Menzies provoked Churchill to insist the war in Europe came first–and the government would stipulate if and when priorities would change. The forward defence proposal forced the COS to raise the issue again. They suggested it would take three months to deploy effective reinforcements, so Far East Command would require that long a warning to be able to face any onslaught. But Churchill only grudgingly agreed to allow Far East Command to study ideas for a pre-emptive advance, grumbling:

> ... we must not tie up a lot of troops in these regions which we can so readily and rapidly reinforce from India. We are not now attempting to defend Singapore at Singapore, but from nearly 500 miles away. I view with great reluctance the continued diversion of troops, aircraft and supplies to a theatre which it is improbable will be lighted up unless we are heavily beaten elsewhere.

The COS answered back this time, arguing the Far East was being left dangerously weak when relatively small reinforcements could help it more than mere numbers might suggest. Churchill did not relent: concentrate on the war at hand and stay in step with the Americans in the Far East. So there would be no advance political commitments or major reinforcements for the Far East. The COS told Brooke-Popham they agreed it would be militarily desirable to launch a pre-emptive advance in the event a Japanese invasion appeared imminent, and authorized him to continue plans and preparations, but had to add three warnings. First, all activity must be unobtrusive. Second, the government would not stipulate any automatic triggers in advance and would decide at the time whether to authorize the operation. Finally, he could not count on receiving any "extra" forces in order to make the plan viable.[46]

To draft a viable plan for any pre-emptive advance Far East Command had to face up squarely to such political and operational difficulties. They failed, for a familiar reason: the plan seemed so much the optimal answer to everyone's problems they preferred to assume its loopholes could somehow be made right on the day, rather than abandon it as impractical. One draft proposal dated 9 May was especially revealing. Malaya Command could not win an encounter battle in Thailand against a Japanese force operating from an established beachhead. It must forestall the Japanese. This meant violating Thai neutrality first, the very political complication that concerned London. But this might not be so difficult. The most likely scenario would be that Japan had already provoked war with the Western Powers but not yet moved into southern Thailand. That would make any British advance a minor matter, "more than covered by the general disturbance caused by the outbreak of war." On the other hand, "The risk to Malaya is only great if the Singora area is not in our hands. From the military point of view therefore we should gain more than we should lose by such a move."[47] This was classic folly: assume your enemy will oblige you, so you can choose your favourite plan.

The planners were forced to spell out the details when the German invasion of the Soviet Union and the Japanese move into southern Indochina raised the temperature. On the one hand the government's decision to assist the Soviets only further constrained Far East Command. On the other hand the COS persuaded the Prime Minister to agree to bolster Malaya Command up to 32 regular battalions. That reinforcement entrenched the plan for a pre-emptive advance in Far East Command headquarters. Their first reaction to the Japanese move was to argue it made an advance more important than ever. The Japanese were expected to move against Russia before moving south, which meant there was still time to prepare. But their new position gave them the chance to strike at Thailand and Malaya much faster than previously estimated. Moving into Thailand would actually shorten the line to be defended. The Japanese could concentrate much stronger forces on the border, if allowed to build up there, than if they were forced to advance from further north or assault a defended coast. On 2 August, Percival sent London his appreciation of the strength he required while the air force remained understrength. One of his key requirements was the need to assign nine to 15 battalions, with tank support, to the pre-emptive advance.[48]

On 5 August the COS reported to the War Cabinet it would be strategically advantageous to pre-empt the Japanese by an advance into southern Thailand, and Far East Command had been asked to report on the plan, the forces required, and how long in advance they needed authorization to move for the advance to succeed. The answers brought the issue to a head. Far East Command spelt out its new plan, *Matador*, in an exchange of telegrams between Brooke-Popham and the COS during August. Brooke-Popham argued an advance to Singora would not overstretch the supply lines of his forces, and would produce the following advantages: deny the Japanese the only good port in the area; force them either to assault a defended beach or land further north and advance along a narrow axis; deny them several important airbases and landing strips; screen the lines of communication and airbases in northern Malaya. The operation would require four brigade groups, plus 76 aircraft in support. Three points were crucial. First, the whole plan was based on facing the Japanese on the ground "allowing proportion of casualties from air action before and during landing." Second, Malaya Command was two brigades short of the strength it needed to mount the operation and cover its other tasks. Finally, everything depended on taking Singora 24 hours before the Japanese could land, which meant the advance must begin well before their invasion force hit the coast.[49]

Brooke-Popham's notice that he needed more forces to do *Matador*, plus the argument in London over whether or not to accept the political risks, left the COS reconsidering the whole matter. Their ambivalence surfaced in a telegram on 1 September: "Can you say if operation *Matador* is a practicable proposition ... We understand that you consider advance to Line C [Chumpon, furthest north] to be impossible with forces at present available. Does this also apply to Line B?" The replies from Far East Command upped the ante. Line C was out of the question, Line B too risky to be worth the effort. But reconnaissance on the ground suggested that in the rainy season, from November to March, the Japanese could not use tanks off the roads. This meant that in the wet season the operation could be launched with three brigades. For the dry season four were needed. Unless more reinforcements were sent that would mean using the command reserve brigade, and there would not be adequate anti-tank and artillery support. But given the recent arrival of reinforcements, Far East Command felt it could now launch the operation any time after 15 September.[50]

The presumption that swayed Far East Command to opt for *Matador* was expressed therein: the Japanese are not likely to strike before March 1942; if the Allies stand firm that makes an early attack even less likely; so we have time to develop this optimal theatre defence plan. The general optimism was undiminished, indeed spelt out in a briefing paper on the Possibilities of the Japanese Attacking in the South on 8 September: the Japanese will operate as the Germans do, which means concentrating great strength, especially in the air, before launching a major operation; they will have learned from watching the European war to take British sea and airpower seriously; they are concentrating first on the Soviets in the north; they can not neglect home defence and the American threat. The Japanese would feel they needed some 500 to 700 aircraft to take on the British in Malaya, but could probably only deploy around 300. Given that they could only mount one major operation at a time:

> Until the commitment in the North has been liquidated, or it is certain that the United States will be definitely neutral, Japan could not make available the air organization which she would think adequate to support an attack against our territories. So long, therefore, as we maintain an adequate air

force, some 250 in strength, and will clearly react to a threat to the Singora area, the risk of a Japanese move to the South is small.

In the unlikely event the Japanese threw caution to the winds and took risks elsewhere to amass enough force to attack Malaya, the problems of maintaining such large forces so far from the home base would still defeat them: "It is clear that we could not do it and it is extremely doubtful if the Germans could."[51]

Such special pleading helps explain why Far East Command was now sold on *Matador*, despite the huge uncertainties they could not resolve: authorization to launch, and the need to reach the beaches first. The one of course determined the other. A telegram sent by the COS on 17 September should have made Far East Command reconsider, because it sounded a death knoll for *Matador*: "Our policy in the Far East is still to avoid war with Japan. We do not therefore intend in present circumstances to operate in Thailand before its violation by the Japanese." That reflected an intense debate in the War Cabinet which ended where it began, with the Prime Minister refusing to accept any risk that might complicate American intervention. This meant that unless the Japanese were indeed obliging enough to move into northern Thailand well before they invaded the south, the whole plan was null and void. Even if intelligence warnings that a Japanese force was setting to sea were received immediately, believed immediately, and sent to London immediately with the proper emphasis, that would still require at least 12 hours, to be very generous. Such an invasion fleet could now leave from southern Indochina, which meant a mere four day voyage. Add at least another 12 hours for London to reply, again being optimistic. One day gone. The COS asked what minimum warning time was needed to authorize the operation. On 21 September Brooke-Popham replied that the advance could begin 36 hours after the green light was received. If everything went exactly to plan, the Thais offered no resistance at all and there were no delays of any kind, it would take a day to reach Singora. By that optimistic dead reckoning, the force would have at most 12 hours to dig in there. Yet this did not deter either London or Singapore. The COS accepted an advance to Singora as "most desirable as a defensive measure," but noted authorization could only be given at the time.[52] Whatever the pros and cons of *Matador* on the operational level, strategically it was already a plan that could not work.

Nevertheless, by October *Matador* became one of Far East Command's two plans for the defence of Singapore. 11th Indian Division was assigned to execute it. The Prime Minister and COS did not reconsider the restriction that made it futile: "We cannot lay down in advance what action by Japanese should be regarded as constituting an act of war and therefore automatically bringing appropriate countermeasures into force."[53] As a result the ground and air forces of Malaya and Singapore prepared to go to war with yet another plan bound to fail. Why did neither the COS nor Far East Command decide that if the government was not prepared to accept the only condition on which the operation had a chance then the whole idea must be reconsidered? There was no lack of pressure to do this from Malaya Command and III Indian Corps. Brooke-Popham kept pushing for prior approval, but that does not explain the COS position.[54] What did influence both London and Singapore were expectations the Japanese would not soon attack, could be deterred, and would have trouble concentrating forces.

The prime consideration in all these strategic calculations was the American factor. Concern about American reactions crippled the plan for forward defence. That same concern was just as important in shaping the final major decision involving Singapore before war broke out: the role of the navy. Bothered by the bickering between civil and military authorities in the Far East, the British government sent out Duff Cooper, a junior minister and political ally of the Prime Minister, to study how to improve regional administration. On 29 September Cooper met in Singapore with Brooke-Popham, Layton, Governor Shenton Thomas, the British Ambassadors to Thailand and China, and the Australian Special Representative to the U.K., en route to London. Brooke-Popham reported the sentiments of this high-powered meeting to the COS. It was generally agreed there was no serious danger of a Japanese attack in the south for some months, because they were preparing to strike the Soviets in the north. Indeed, strengthening British defences might put some useful pressure on the Japanese in Indochina. Because the absence of a British fleet allowed the Japanese to strike where they chose, it was more important than ever to deploy a fleet to Singapore as soon as possible. In a pregnant phrase, the report argued that the propaganda and deterrent value of deploying even a small squadron of one or two capital ships was bound to be great.[55]

Nothing could have more clearly underlined the unreasonable optimism prevailing at the top in the Far East than this report. The Japanese were moving into southern Indochina. The Soviets were being hammered in Europe. Japanese-American talks were going badly. To assume on the basis of nothing stronger than guesswork and wishful thinking that the Japanese would not go south was reckless; to fail to act on the basis they could go south, any time they wished, was cavalier. There was however one powerful authority very receptive to both the optimistic mood expressed by the report and the specific suggestion for naval deterrence: the Prime Minister.

Among the papers the American delegation passed to the British at the summit conference in August was a formal response to the ADB conference report calling for a combined defence in the Far East. The Americans rejected the report on two grounds. First, it called for advance political commitments they were not yet ready to make. Second, it made an ambiguous British pledge to send only a small naval force to Singapore.[56] Such comments sparked Churchill's interest, to the chagrin of the Naval Staff. The Prime Minister considered it imperative to convince the Americans the British would carry their weight. The appeal from Singapore, and the political upheaval in Tokyo in mid-October, prompted the Prime Minister to make a proposal: why not send a "flying squadron," one fast modern capital ship and one aircraft carrier, to Singapore? This would encourage the Empire, impress the neutrals, reassure the United States, and deter the Japanese. The Admiralty strongly dissented. This ignited an argument that marked the true climax of the "Singapore strategy."

For months the Naval Staff had been working on plans to create an Eastern Fleet. By August the idea was to assemble in the Indian Ocean triangle between South Africa, Aden and Singapore a force of some seven older capital ships, an aircraft carrier, 10 cruisers and 24 destroyers–hopefully by March 1942, if not the end of 1941. There were three obstacles to this design. First, it depended on all going well in the Atlantic and the Mediterranean; but in the autumn the RN suffered heavy losses in the latter, including a battleship and an aircraft carrier, and damage to two other capital ships. Second, all the nominated vessels needed refitting with modern equipment, especially radar. The third obstacle was Churchill. Naval planners felt a larger force, even one composed of older slower battleships, would be more likely to deter the Japanese, because it would force them to accept the risk of an American counterattack if they decided to concentrate against it. For the Prime Minister this was too cautious and would take too long. He preferred a smaller force of faster newer vessels that could be sent out earlier, and pose more of a threat to carry the war to the Japanese. There the discussion stood until events in October forced it onto the agenda of the Defence Committee.

In a truly blazing row, both the First Sea Lord, Pound, and his Vice-Chief of Naval Staff, Vice-Admiral Sir Tom Phillips, argued strenuously against a "flying squadron." The Prime Minister was strongly supported by Deputy Prime Minister Clement Attlee and Foreign Secretary Anthony Eden. The ministers were keenly aware of pressure from the Dominions for a naval buildup, and attracted by the publicity value of an early deployment. The main issue was not operational. It did not really matter whether or not this small force could act as an effective fleet-in-being, or whether the Japanese could destroy it by taking moderate countermeasures. What mattered is that it would arrive sooner rather than later, and, boasting at least one of the newest ships in the RN battleline, could be trumpeted as a serious demonstration of British resolve. Irritated by arguments over preparations for the offensive in North Africa, over what could be done to assist the Soviets, and over the priority of the bomber offensive, the Prime Minister ran out of patience. The Defence Committee decided on 20 October to dispatch the battleship HMS *Prince of Wales* and the aircraft carrier HMS *Indomitable* to South Africa. Ostensibly the decision whether or not to send them on to Singapore, joining the battlecruiser HMS *Repulse* in the Indian Ocean en route, would be taken after they arrived. In fact it had already been made. That was made clear by comments to that effect while the force was at sea, and by the prior nomination of Phillips himself as C-in-C Designate Eastern Fleet.[57]

The "Singapore strategy" was thus revived after all, but in a very modified form. The navy was coming, but not with the Main Fleet, nor with Pound's obsolescent fleet–rather with Force Z, something akin to the Drax idea of a "flying squadron." The Admiralty was forced against its will to send out a small squadron; left to its own devices it would not have sent anything to Singapore. In the tense atmosphere of autumn 1941, the Prime Minister needed something there. Churchill was admittedly influenced by implausible ideas of offensive possibilities for his "fleet-in-being," but this was not his main motive for insisting on Force Z. Early and dramatic action offered some chance to reassure the most vital ally, mollify others, and perhaps give the adversary pause. This was an overdetermined political decision in grand strategy. It did not of course deter the Japanese. On the contrary, they took resolute steps to counter it. The land-based 22nd Naval Air Flotilla, specially trained and equipped to destroy enemy surface vessels, was deployed to southern Indochina. The Japanese decision to go to war was driven by such desperation that only the arrival of the main fleet itself might have deterred them. On the other hand Force Z did encourage all friendlies in the region, particularly Far East Command.

Despite the fact the political situation was deteriorating, Japanese forces were assembling, and their own forces remained critically short of requirements, the mood in GHQ Far East responded to the naval decision like a war horse rising to the trumpet. An internal memorandum dated 30 October, Strategy in the Far East in the Presence of a British Fleet, sums up the feeling. Anticipating the deployment of a strong British fleet "in the comparatively near future," the draft assumed the Japanese had already been deterred by inadequate forces, so the arrival of a battlefleet in Singapore "would almost certainly prevent war breaking out in the Far East." This would allow theatre commanders to redeploy "a large proportion" of their air and ground forces, especially to assist China. The forces left in Malaya would be those required to "assist the fleet." This would not strain the air force too much as apparently "air striking forces to deal with Japanese surface forces are not likely to be required."[58] Weeks away from war, Far East Command was convinced the arrival of two British capital ships would keep the Japanese at bay. It also believed the "Singapore strategy" could still be implemented in its original form: the navy leading the way by itself, the other services acting only as auxiliaries. Brooke-Popham complained when his services failed to work together as integral partners–but examples are set from above and this one was stark. After the experiences of combined arms fighting in Norway, Dunkirk, Greece, and Crete, this concept of a surface naval force dominating the operations area by itself was hopelessly out of date. The contrast to the integrated battle plans being finalized by the Japanese was painful. Japanese plans brought together land-based and carrier-borne airpower, surface forces and ground troops in one combined operation. It is obvious whose battle plans better combined strategic imperatives with tactical capabilities.

Eighteen months after ostensibly being set aside, the "Singapore strategy" remained alive and well in the minds of those responsible for the defence of Singapore. The fleet was not coming, but ground and air forces must hold its base and plan all their operations accordingly. A "flying squadron" was coming, but no one in Singapore was thinking about what it could actually do when it arrived; they focused instead on reviving the original strategy wholesale, sometime in 1942. Force Z provoked false hopes among those it was sent out to help without intimidating those it was supposed to deter. The air force would not reach the necessary strength for another year. But its plans, and those of the army, remained based on the assumption it would deal a body blow to any invading force. The plan to launch a pre-emptive advance just assumed the defenders could construct coastal defences strong enough to repel an invader in less than a day, because that invader would be decimated by the air forces. But the air forces had no effective anti-shipping strike capability, and the restrictions on launching the advance made it impossible for the ground forces to win a race to the Thai coast. The only alternative was to fall back to defend a line dictated by the need to protect airbases, forcing the ground troops to fight in vulnerable positions. And even the optimistic C-in-C acknowledged that if the fight dragged on he would need strong reinforcements very rapidly, or his weak air forces would soon be whittled away. The COS agreed neither air nor ground forces were strong enough, but could not remedy this before spring 1942 at the earliest. Approving *Matador* without delegating the authority to launch it was sheer folly. Failing to resolve the dispute over whether or not to defend all Malaya was irresponsible. The central direction of the war not only failed in 1941 to make sure defence plans for Singapore were realistic, it made them weaker still.

On the eve of war, it is hard to see how matters could have been much worse–but easy to see the impact of the military system. By November 1941 the British were indeed part of what became a war-winning coalition. But American reluctance to commit in advance left British Far East defences standing on their own until at least spring 1942. The emphasis on staying in step with the Americans yet maintaining full authority over imperial defence determined plans for the Far East. Looking at the war as a whole, the British were right to take a calculated risk on the Far East.[59] But carelessness turned that risk into an outright gamble. The COS could not make RAF Far East strong enough to do its job, but were not therefore obliged to approve an operation that could not succeed! Neither London nor Singapore clearly understood what they had done. Both became so optimistic about the situation that they were able to rationalize and justify what they preferred to do anyway: make the situation fit the most appealing plan. The British military system, driven by unreasonable optimism, produced war plans that compromised the defence of Singapore before a shot was fired.

5

Conceiving Defeat

Lt.-Gen. Arthur E. Percival arrived in Singapore to take responsibility for its defence on 16 May 1941. Lt.-Gen. Yamashita Tomoyuki assumed command of the army that would attack Singapore on 6 November 1941. The fortunes of war gave the Briton six and a half months to prepare for the challenge, while the Japanese had only one. Yet Yamashita had the more manageable assignment, not just because he knew when the test would come. The combination of circumstances, intentions and capabilities gave Yamashita and his forces a difficult but realistic mission–but left Percival and his an all but impossible one.

The decision to appoint Percival GOC Malaya Command indicated that the Imperial General Staff wanted to strengthen the defence of Singapore. Dill's lonely battle to raise the priority of the Far East led him to bypass more senior candidates to appoint his protege to the job, based on Percival's prior experience in Malaya, the glowing reports he received there, and Dill's own confidence in him. Percival had one of the sharpest minds in the British Army, wide-ranging experience, was courageous and diligent–but not imposing in appearance, nor assertive in manner.[1] Five weeks elapsed between nomination and departure, time he used to become fully briefed on the current situation in the Far East and how the central direction of the war saw it. The influence this had on him would become obvious. That included the relations he established with those with whom he had to work. The most significant were Brooke-Popham, Shenton Thomas, Pulford, Heath, Bennett, and his own staff.

Percival shared two common views about Brooke-Popham: he was past his prime, and his staff meddled too much in issues properly left to service headquarters. This did not interfere with their working together, but this was due in no small part to Percival's willingness to accept the primacy of the air force in the defence of Malaya, despite knowing how badly this overstretched his army. This no doubt smoothed relations with Pulford, albeit a genuine friendship also sprang up. Percival claimed these good relations trickled down to the staff and unit levels. While soldiers and airmen hardly became an integrated team in 1941, the situation did improve after the change of commanders. Some effort was now made to work together to press London for reinforcements, defend airbases and prepare the advance into Thailand–a far cry from the earlier paralysis.[2] Percival did not establish similar strong relations with the Governor. Indeed, the GOC soon accepted the prevailing view in the services: the reluctance of the civil government to take strong measures to prepare for war was a major obstacle to strengthening the defences of Malaya and Singapore. The service commanders made little progress against London's directive that priority was to maximize production and exports. Civil-military relations were not in good shape by autumn 1941 in Singapore.[3]

Percival could not establish good working relations with either of his key subordinates. Percival was junior to Heath on the Army List, had less experience in high command in the field, but was now his boss. Percival was appointed by London, Heath by Delhi. Percival valued staff training and experience, having had the unusual number of four staff college postings as well as five staff appointments in his career–whereas Heath turned down all offers for staff college training. Percival never served in India, did not know the Indian Army, and had a less than open mind about it. Given that it made up most of Malaya Command, and he was a career Indian Army man, Heath resented that attitude. Worse, given that he already had a military victory and knighthood to his credit, Heath also resented being placed under someone with neither.[4]

Percival would have been a miracle worker to establish smooth relations with Bennett. The only point which the GOC should undoubtedly have clarified was the authority Bennett enjoyed as the commander of a national contingent. The template for instructions to Dominion commanders operating within a British-led force was clear enough by this time and could have been ascertained without much trouble.[5] Apart from that, Percival joined a long list of officers who found Bennett more than a handful. Bennett was everything Percival was not: prickly, obnoxious, demonstrative, suspicious. There is no doubt the Australian was a fighter; unfortunately, he included many of his own comrades among the enemy. Bennett was a leading figure in a long-running Australian dispute over the proper military system for Australia. He had a blind prejudice against regular force officers. The reason he insisted on bringing his headquarters to look over the shoulder of one brigade in Malaya was fear he would be shuffled out of his command by rivals on the General Staff. Unfortunately most of his own staff were regulars, which produced a nearly dysfunctional headquarters. That general quarrelsomeness spilled over into relations with Percival. Percival was not ruthless. Given an opportunity to ask for Bennett to be replaced, he demurred.[6] The end result was that Malaya Command did not work smoothly with either of its main field formations. There is plenty of cause to explain effect here; appointing Bennett was a serious

Australian error. But it all mattered, because the weakness of the defending forces hardly allowed the luxury of bickering between commanders.

Percival's staff could not do much to improve matters. It was too small and inexperienced. Malaya Command struggled to cope with the responsibilities of a field army, plus those of an overseas administrative command, with the manpower of a corps headquarters. Percival never had more than four senior staff officers, including his Brigadier General Staff, K.S. Torrance, and constantly had to raid field battalions for qualified appointees. That was a two-edged sword, jeopardizing the combat readiness of the field force while giving the impression the GOC only really rated officers with staff training. While at least some had such training, compared to only one on Pulford's staff, Percival made two unfortunate judgements. One was to rely too much on Torrance, who seems to have been almost a caricature of the pedantic staff officer so lampooned by critics of the British Army. The other was to get off on the wrong foot with his new Chief Engineer, Brig. Ivan Simson, who arrived to assume his duties in August. Mystery will always surround Simson. He claimed he was sent out with orders, to be confirmed by the CIGS, to revamp the entire system of field and fixed defences for Malaya and Singapore, incorporating the latest ideas and techniques from England–but arrived without any such written instructions. No such orders were ever sent to Percival, he never pressed for them, and Simson received no reply to his own appeal for confirmation. Simson and Percival should have sorted this issue out, because it hampered their effort to work together when that became very necessary.[7]

Sadly, nothing done in autumn 1941 improved the command and control situation in Singapore. Cooper stirred things up by concluding Thomas and Brooke-Popham should both be replaced by a new structure, headed by a Commissioner-General for the Far East in Singapore, who could pull together the civil-military direction of policy. Cooper's report did not reach London until 24 November; meanwhile such lobbying did not improve the direction of affairs in Singapore. The COS did decide on 1 November to replace Brooke-Popham by someone younger and more up-to-date, but the changeover was delayed for two reasons. First, Churchill wanted their first choice, Lt.-Gen. Sir Bernard Paget, to take over the more important Home Forces Command. That incumbent, General Sir Alan Brooke, was appointed to replace Dill as CIGS. Second, due to naval objections, the COS did not agree until 25 November to make the appointment a Commander-in-Chief directing all three services. Brooke-Popham did not find out he would be replaced by Lt.-Gen. Sir Henry Pownall until 29 November. But from 1 November he was a lame duck, which did not sharpen the work of GHQ Far East. Finally, Layton knew since April he would be replaced when and if a fleet deployment took place, and by November Phillips was on the way.[8] Not all was gloom and doom at the top in Singapore. But with both Cs-in-C on the way out, strife in civil-military relations, and discord within the army, there was certainly no firm grip on the rudder.

Yamashita had his own problems, but they did not add up to as great a weight as those facing Percival. To begin with, he had more recent command experience in combat. Percival came from a divisional command in England, but had not commanded any formation larger than a brigade in combat, and that in 1918. His appointment was two steps up. Yamashita came from an appointment as head of a military mission to Germany but had combat experience as a division commander in China, where he gained a reputation for inspirational leadership from the front. He was even briefly nominated to command Japanese forces defending Manchuria against a possible Soviet attack, so his appointment to command Twenty-Fifth Army was no acceleration. Regarding those with whom he must work, Yamashita faced greater potential danger than Percival, but enjoyed greater immediate support.

Yamashita's immediate superior was General Count Terauchi Hisaichi, Commander Southern Army. Terauchi nominated Yamashita to command the assault on Malaya and Singapore, and made sure he received what were rated the best divisions in the army. Their naval counterparts were Vice-Admiral Kondo Nobutake, whose Southern Force covered all operations in Southeast Asia, and Vice-Admiral Ozawa Jisaburo, commanding Malaya Force, protecting the convoys assaulting Thailand and Malaya. They had no real problem establishing a rapport and agreeing on plans. Two of his divisional commanders were solid professionals: Lt.-Gen. Matsui Takuro, commanding the 5th Division, and Lt.-Gen. Mutaguchi Renya, commanding 18th Division. But Yamashita did have a problem on his staff, with his other division commander, and at the summit. Yamashita was badly compromised by his involvement in factional feuding, especially the aborted coup of February 1936. His equivocal attitude at that time angered the Emperor himself. Yamashita took this so much to heart that he threw himself into battle seeking expiation by death on the field of honour. That plus charisma and assertiveness established his reputation as a hard charger, but did not regain the Imperial blessing nor assuage his enemies. Yamashita then crossed Tojo after he returned from Germany in autumn 1941. His report infuriated Tojo and his faction by casting doubt on the value of the Axis alliance, and urging the Army to follow the lead of the Foreign Ministry in foreign policy. Yamashita only escaped being sidelined in Manchuria because Terauchi persuaded rivals to annoy Tojo by appointing Yamashita to the combat command. But the commander charged with the conquest of Singapore now had an enemy in the Prime Minister, waiting to pounce on any blunder. Allied with Tojo were Lt.-Gen. Nishimura Takuro, commanding the Imperial Guards Division, and Lt.-Col. Tsuji Masanobu, Chief Operations Officer at Twenty-Fifth Army headquarters. Nishimura led the most prestigious formation in the army and was well connected, but without the skill and experience to back it up. Tsuji was more sinister. He was one of the authors of the training, doctrine and battle plan the army was about to use to conquer Malaya and Singapore, but was widely seen as Tojo's plant and expected to cause trouble.[9] Malaya and Singapore faced an attack led by a general with some worries, but also with strong personal motivation to smash its defenders as rapidly as possible.

Percival's latitude to make battle plans was constrained by five factors. First was his mission. That remained unchanging: "The main reason for the defence of Malaya was to preserve the facilities of the Naval Base at Singapore." Second was the policy to rely on the air force to take the lead, which required the army to defend its bases. Third was the decision to plan an advance into southern Thailand to pre-empt the Japanese, which would further strain the ground forces. Fourth was the policy to maximize production and exports, which meant minimal interference with the economy. Finally, the delay in building up air and ground forces to their authorized strength both complicated Percival's planning task and meant any early attack must be faced with resources the COS accepted were inadequate.[10]

London's decision not to change the mission left the authorities in Singapore little choice. If the task remained not only to hold the naval base but also "to retain use of its facilities up to six months without relief ..." then it was indeed "necessary to hold enemy air forces out of effective range of Singapore and the Malacca Strait for as long as possible."[11] This plus the decision to rely on airpower to interdict an invasion forced Percival to spread out his army to protect the airbases. Another complication imposed on him was a Far East Command directive to defend against invasion by close defence of the vulnerable beaches themselves. This risked spreading the defenders out in long linear positions that could be breeched by concentrated attack; the alternative was to prepare tighter defensive positions on the roads further inland, concentrating to block any advance. Brooke-Popham opted to defend the beaches on two grounds: the enemy would be most vulnerable when actually landing, and it was on the coast that air and ground forces could best be combined to resist attack. This was expressed in a typical instruction to brigades in April 1941:

In view of the increasing strength of the RAF in Malaya and of the extent of disorganization which air attack may be expected to inflict on an attempt to effect a landing on an open beach the policy of the defence [of Johore and in general] has been modified ... The enemy will be defeated on the Mersing beaches, any who land will be killed or driven into the sea ...[12]

The primacy of the air force was reiterated in June by GHQ Far East, which admitted "... we may have been underestimating the number of troops necessary for the defence of aerodromes in the North and on the East coast." The defence plan rested on concentrating at least two-thirds of the available squadrons in bases within range of an invasion force still at sea, which meant northern and central Malaya. It was not modified despite the decision to delay building up RAF Far East–which meant the plan would fall between two imperatives if the Japanese attacked first. On the one hand the air force was still too weak to be sure it could pummel an invader. On the other hand, as the airmen themselves accepted "... the field army on the west coast, down which the main enemy thrust on land was expected to develop, had to make large detachments to protect aerodromes on the east coast." Plans remained well ahead of capabilities. In July Pulford organized Norgroup, a subcommand to assist army operations in northern Malaya. But after one exercise he stood it down, because he did not yet have enough squadrons to keep it active.[13]

Malaya Command's responsibility was to translate broad directives from London and GHQ Far East into specific battle plans. Percival had to accept a degree of uncertainty due to the global situation, and live with a gap between what his command was expected to do and what it could actually do at any given moment. His real task was to make sure both uncertainty and gap were handled as sensibly as possible. By mid-1941 the AIF was designated command reserve. 12th Indian Brigade, under command of Singapore Fortress, defended Johore. With a second Australian brigade en route to Singapore, Percival wanted to give Bennett's two-brigade division the concrete mission to defend Johore. This sensible move would reduce friction over what the Australians could be asked to do by keeping them together under their own commander, free his best trained brigade to become command reserve, and relieve Singapore Fortress of a mainland distraction, allowing it to concentrate on the island. But when the Japanese moved into southern Indochina Darvall objected. He argued that as the Indian brigade was training to defend Johore it should stay there, because while defence plans assumed the Japanese would move through Thailand "... until they go into Thailand, it is essential that our dispositions should be the best that can be made to meet an attack solely based on Indochina." This abrupt concern for the needs of the moment cut against the grain of all other directions from GHQ Far East requiring Percival to work to the master plan![14] Percival got his way, but such erratic direction did not help much.

Brooke-Popham did at least support Percival's estimate, submitted on 2 August, of the forces he needed while RAF Far East remained understrength. Percival asked for the equivalent of five full strength divisions plus two tank regiments–some 48 infantry battalions, as opposed to the 32 now in or en route to Malaya. That would give III Indian Corps two divisions at the full strength of three brigades each and Malaya Command one full division in reserve. It was this estimate the COS accepted as reasonable but warned could not be met before well into 1942. This underlined how the focus on the air force determined all plans. Percival insisted his plans were based on the assurance the *existing* air force would reduce any invading force by some 40%. The reinforcements he did receive nevertheless enabled Percival to reorganize his army at the end of August. These were, as it turned out, the arrangements by which Malaya Command went to war. III Indian Corps, with five brigades instead of the optimal nine, was assigned to defend northern and central Malaya, which included any advance into Thailand. 8th Australian Division took over the defence of Johore. Singapore Fortress retained two brigades for the defence of the island, made up mainly of the four regular battalions of the prewar garrison. 12th Indian Brigade went into command reserve. The regulars were supported by the Volunteer Forces of the various districts. Penang was designated a Fortress Command and a Lines of Communication Area was set up in central Malaya.[15] But except for Singapore Fortress, none of these commands were strong enough to handle their task.

Singapore island was the area least likely to be attacked and partly because of that the most defensible. By autumn 1941 its fixed defences were formidable. Fortress Command, opened in October 1940, controlled two Fire Commands of coastal artillery which boasted five 15", six 9.2" and eighteen 6" guns, primarily designed and equipped to repel attack from the sea. They were supported by smaller quick-firing guns, a network of machine-gun pillboxes stretching along the south coast from southwest to northeast, and field defences the garrison had been working on since September 1939. There were now four operational airbases on the island, most of the available fighter aircraft were deployed there, and the radar early warning network was nearing completion. On top of all that, Force Z was closing Singapore, set to arrive in early December. Barring an attack by the entire IJN Combined Fleet, Percival could regard Singapore as well defended.[16]

There was only one area in Johore that seemed vulnerable: the towns of Endau and Mersing on the east coast, connected by a good road to Singapore. Bennett's task was complicated by the fact his third brigade was not sent to Malaya. The need to hold one brigade in reserve left only one forward, not enough to hold both Endau and Mersing. But the plans the Australians made addressed the situation pretty well. They left a small force in Endau and concentrated at Mersing and along the road the Japanese must use to advance–and spared some thought to how to cope with an enemy advance from the north. Given that an early attack did not seem likely, the approaches to Singapore were being taken in hand by late 1941.[17]

The real dilemma was faced by the hopelessly overstretched III Indian Corps. Singapore and Johore were strongly defended in order to force the Japanese to take the long way around, through the north. This meant that even if he released his command reserve brigade to help in the north, Percival could only allow III Indian Corps to engage the enemy with at most 60% of his field force–whereas they could throw everything they had against it. Worse, geography forced the Corps to disperse its two divisions to the point where neither could help the other in the initial battles. Heath later identified this failure to concentrate the ground forces as a crucial error, which in principle was correct.[18] But Percival had little choice, short of being insubordinate, but to spread his army out. The undeveloped coastline of eastern Malaya was a potential advantage neutralized by the decision to build airbases near Kuantan and Kota Bharu. These lay right in the path of any invasion from the South China Sea and thus had to be defended. Both brigades of the 9th Indian Division were pinned down to that task. 22nd Indian Brigade deployed around Kuantan in late May. The beaches it had to defend were nearly 30 km long and bisected by the Kuantan River. This would both stretch out and divide any force trying to hold them. But the airbase was barely 15 km inland, the road from Kuantan connected the east coast to the trunk road in the west– and the orders were to hold the coast. The brigade deployed one battalion to defend the beaches and one to cover the airbase, leaving only one in reserve. This was not enough to resist any major invasion–unless the air force did indeed rip it up beforehand.[19]

Maj.-Gen. A.E. Barstow, GOC 9th Indian Division, headquartered in Kuala Lumpur, had to direct both that formation and the even more distant 8th Indian Brigade. It deployed late in 1940 around Kota Bharu in the northeast corner of Malaya, connected to the interior by only a railway line. Its commander, the dynamic Brigadier "Billy" Key, used the time to get acquainted with its daunting mission. Kota Bharu boasted three airbases near the coast–one barely three kilometres inland–and was a mere 20 km south of the Thai border, astride the railway. It was certain to be attacked right away. The airbases formed a triangle, with Bachang at the tip almost on the beaches, some 50 km north of Gong Kedah and Machang. The Kelantan River separated the more than 50 km of beaches from the railway and the border.

These were the airfields the RAF would rely on most to assault any invasion fleet, so their defence was Key's priority. But his brigade was also too weak to hold such a large area unless the air force wore down the enemy on the way in. Sensibly anticipating his dilemma, Key had his engineers make extensive preparations to demolish the airbases and the railway, especially the many bridges along its course through the jungle interior of Kelantan.[20]

11th Indian Division had to cover the relatively open country of the northwest, including the trunk road and railway the Japanese were expected to use as their main axis of advance. It was directed to defend the border and the northern state of Kedah–which meant above all covering the important airbases, especially Alor Star. This was asking for trouble. On 24 July III Indian Corps gave orders that underlined the problem:

> The vital necessity however, of preventing the enemy establishing himself on aerodromes in North Malaya renders the denial of those at Kepala Batas and at Jabi [Alor Star] of first importance. In addition, political and economic reasons render it undesirable to evacuate extensive territory. The enemy will, therefore, be opposed NORTH and EAST of these important places.

That required the division to stand on "the Jitra position." But there was another consideration. A road running from Patani across the border would allow the enemy to outflank the position at Alor Star. So this road through Kroh had to be denied, no matter what, in order to hold Kedah. Corps staff had a suggestion:

> It is for consideration whether this task cannot best be carried out by the occupation of a position as far forward as "The Ledge," 20 to 28 miles beyond the frontier [ie. in Thailand, on the road from Patani] and if this course is decided on preparations to occupy it at short notice will be made.[21]

This was not the first suggestion to modify the plan, but it did throw a vital point into the discussion: whether *Matador* was executed or not the back road must be blocked, and tactically the best place to do it was in Thailand, at "The Ledge." What followed is best explained by noting that five different levels of command–the COS in London, GHQ Far East, Malaya Command, III Indian Corps, and 11th Indian Division–were now all required to try to perfect the same plan, one central to all their concerns, but each brought a different agenda to the task. Throw in the air force for good measure and the challenge was daunting: everyone had to be brutally honest about whether they could do what was most required of them in order for all to succeed. This is exactly the kind of challenge the British military system was most likely to fumble, because it called for categorical decisions in advance. The COS could not compel the government to delegate the authority that alone offered any chance to win the race to the Thai coast. But they did not order GHQ Far East to set the plan aside, because they were too attracted by the hope it could cover the northern airbases. GHQ Far East lobbied hard for authorization to order the advance, but did not grasp the tactical problems. Neither Brooke-Popham nor the COS ever understood that a blocking advance into Thailand to "The Ledge" was tactically imperative regardless of all other considerations. Malaya Command did not drive this point home to its superiors, but at least took it on board. Percival and Heath adjusted *Matador* by reducing the advance to Patani to an advance to "The Ledge" by a mobile column, to block the road. This was tactically realistic, but still useless if the political hurdle of moving into Thailand was not cleared–and neither they nor Brooke-Popham put that point across in an argument that could not be ignored.

Maj.-Gen. D.M. Murray-Lyon, GOC 11th Indian Division, decided *Matador* was the only realistic way to defend the airbases, so he threw himself behind the plan and focused his division's time and energy on it. Unfortunately, he seems to have concluded the decision to advance was therefore a given, whereas Malaya Command regarded *Matador* as an option that might or might not be triggered when the time came. Finally there was the air force. Brought into the planning in July, it was told the plan relied heavily on airpower to interdict the railway and roads along which a Japanese counterattack was expected, and pressed to commit enough squadrons to make it viable. But Pulford could not promise more than a single flying boat to carry a demolition party to a spot where it could cut the railway! Even if concentrated in the north, the air force could only offer to assist "with such units as the situation at the time permitted."[22]

Everything depended on the Thais offering no more than token resistance, but the Thais warned all and sundry they would resist any incursion. The British tried to persuade the Thais to stand up to the Japanese, but also prepared covert operations in southern Thailand to either assist a British advance or delay a Japanese one. Both were heavily obstructed by Josiah Crosby, British Ambassador in Bangkok. Crosby was convinced only he knew how to approach the Thais: if "properly handled" they would rebuff the Japanese but if annoyed or feeling compromised they would give way. Crosby was kept out of the *Matador* loop because GHQ Far East rightly concluded he was in practice an advocate for the Thais, but he guessed something was in the works. No amount of lobbying the Thais could change the fact Crosby was wrong: the Japanese were on their border in strength and there was nothing the British could do that would stiffen the Thais to rebuff a Japanese ultimatum.

The plan called for leaflets to be distributed to the Thais by the advancing forces, appealing to them not to resist. But to keep the plan secret, including from Crosby, they were not to be printed until the last possible minute–for a plan which relied on blinding speed at a moments notice to succeed.[23]

The evolution of *Matador* clearly exposed the weakness of the British military system. The COS and Brooke-Popham never understood how all plans relied on blocking "The Ledge." Murray-Lyon never grasped the fact *Matador* was not a given. Percival later complained about this, but at the time either did not discover his subordinate's hasty assumption or did nothing to correct it. Murray-Lyon's division found itself caught between planning to move forward and working on a defensive position, without clear guidance on what its first priority should be. Divisional headquarters tilted towards *Matador*, the plan much less likely to be implemented, at the expense of the Jitra plan–but nevertheless put much time and energy into both, thereby diluting both.[24]

11th Indian Division was not responsible for the decision to defend north of the airbases, but did select the Jitra position. The position was not well suited for a defensive battle but it was the best ground north of the airbase. It was set up as a linear defence, some 22 km long. The left flank stretched through open rice paddy to the sea. The main position straddled the road and railway in mixed paddy and rubber plantation, broken up by two copses of woods near the road. The right flank ran through rubber plantation until it reached steeply rising hills covered by dense jungle. The division trained as early as June to defend against an advance down the road in brigade strength by an enemy designated the "6th Slit Regiment." Lessons learnt included the need to delay the enemy by an outpost stand north of the main position to allow the main forces to organize, the danger of a tank-led attack coming along the main road, and the difficulty of holding the left flank in dry weather. To stop tanks it was decided to dig a long and deep anti-tank ditch in the centre of the main position. But that would not help outpost forces to inflict delay without being overrun by tanks–and the danger posed by the copses near the road seems to have been overlooked. No one took these problems in hand. Murray-Lyon felt *Matador* made the weakness of the position moot. III Indian Corps did not have much confidence in the Jitra position either; as early as July it suggested the division prepare a rear position at much stronger ground around Gurun to the south, to be occupied "as circumstances dictate." An exercise to practice a withdrawal through Kedah was actually scheduled for early 1942. Meanwhile though, the only alternative to *Matador* was this very unfinished plan to stand and fight at Jitra–for as long as three months.[25]

On 29 October the COS sent what all should have seen as a clear signal to concentrate on Jitra. They reminded Far East Command British policy was still to avoid war, and until the Americans agreed to support any advance into Thailand there would be no prior approval. Brooke-Popham's increasingly desperate pleas produced more warnings on 25 and 29 November that the government was still not prepared to delegate authority–and might require as much as 36 hours to authorize the move after hearing the Japanese were at sea. Yet Far East Command kept pressing for *Matador*.[26] Given that by now there was abundant evidence the Japanese were preparing to attack, this begs an explanation. There is one: Far East Command was now so committed to *Matador* as the best way out of its dilemma that it convinced itself events would unfold as it desired. On 15 November Darvall commented on reports the Japanese were about to move into Thailand:

> It is certain that the weather in southern Thailand, particularly in the Singora area, will be anything but suitable for landing operations until the end of January. It seems that if the Japanese decide to move before January they must risk a counter-occupation of the southern area by ourselves.

London still refused to authorize any such "counteroccupation," but Far East Command now relied on it. Brooke-Popham assured the COS on 27 November that while Japanese activity seemed ominous they were not about to strike. The terrain in southern Thailand was now so wet it was unlikely the Japanese were preparing to move through it to attack Malaya. Giving him the authority to launch *Matador* remained the best way to tackle the problem.[27]

Far East Command may have been the prime mover, but it remained in good company. It was irresponsible of everyone not to ensure the Jitra plan was properly in hand until *Matador* became viable, but Murray-Lyon was surely the most duty bound. He continued to focus on the advance. The plan as finalized gave him three brigades for the main advance to Singora–which included the corps reserve–plus a two battalion battle-group to block the interior road at "The Ledge," and of course no tanks. Yet still no one suggested it might be best to set it aside for the time being. RAF Far East always considered its prospects for success "remote," yet went along. Percival's staff had no confidence in it. But Malaya Command let it settle in, to the detriment of the only alternative.[28]

The last detailed outline of *Matador* sent to the COS arrived on 2 December, six days before war broke out. It assumed at worst a "slight delay" from Thai resistance, estimated the main forces could be concentrating on the Thai coast "within 48 hours" of being ordered to advance, anticipated seizing "The Ledge" within three hours, noted it would take another 24 hours to dig in at the Thai coast, and a full month to prepare for a major attack from further north in Thailand after the monsoon. No one asked what would happen if 11th Indian Division lost the race to the coast and met the Japanese in an encounter battle. The RAF was now prepared to support the advance with two bomber and two fighter squadrons, but it did not matter. The Japanese needed only four days to sail from southern Indochina to the Thai coast. Singapore needed 12 hours to detect a Japanese sortie and request the green light, London 36 hours to give it, Malaya Command at least six hours to order the advance, and 11th Indian Division now required 72 hours to be dug in at Singora–nearly six days.[29] The whole project was an irresponsible fantasy. Yet it was now the main plan to defend Singapore. It is hard to see how defence plans could have become more disjointed. The fatal combination is familiar. Lulled by the conclusion the enemy was not yet ready to strike, or could not do so with real force, the military system carried on trying to make the situation fit the plan. This allowed it to keep the "Singapore strategy" promise alive. Unfortunately for the defenders, the Japanese had other ideas.

It is sometimes still stated that the Japanese prepared to attack Malaya for many years before they struck, but this is incorrect. Vague contingency outlines, amounting to little more than broad principles for an attack in the south, only began to take shape as concrete operational plans from July 1941.[30] The Japanese did enjoy the advantage of knowing when and where they would strike. That advantage was diluted by the very late decision to go to war, which gave the formations that would do the fighting less than a month to finalize their plans. But staff planning proceeded on the assumption war would begin in 1941, and developed along two tracks. One was to draft the overall plan of attack on Thailand and Malaya by air, naval and ground forces. The other was to prepare a doctrine for ground operations in Malaya.

The attack plan went through three stages. First, General Staff Headquarters drafted a broad outline. This was reviewed, along with IJN battle plans, in the discussions in September and October, resulting in a Basic Agreement. This was the plan that assigned the crucial mission of conquering Singapore to the Twenty-Fifth Army, hitherto operating in southern China, and allocated its formations. It culminated on 10 November in an Army-Navy Agreement for the assault on Malaya. Meanwhile, Twenty-Fifth Army staff drew up a draft Operational Outline, completed on 3 November. At this stage Yamashita inherited the plans. He was brought in, according to standard IJA practice, to finalize and implement a battle plan already largely sketched out. Yamashita spent six days discussing matters in Tokyo, then flew to Saigon for six more days of detailed discussions with his staff, the staff of the 3rd Air Group assigned to support him, and Vice-Admiral Ozawa and his staff.

Southern Army formally directed Yamashita on 15 November to execute Plan E as soon as Imperial General Headquarters confirmed the decision to go to war and designated X-Day. The very next day Yamashita issued the penultimate Operational Plan. Finally, on 23 November the war plan was issued as Fushu Op Ord Ko-No. 1:

> The mission of the Army is to speedily occupy Singapore and topple the bastion of the British aggression to the Far East; the Army will have operational co-operation provided by the Southern Fleet, the 3rd Air Group and the Fifteenth Army. The Army, in collaboration with the navy, will make a surprise landing at dawn on X-Day to southern Thailand and northern British Malaya; the main force should immediately rush to the left bank of River [Perak] and occupy crossing points and airfields, to prepare for further operations.[31]

The advance was already spelt out in some detail thanks to three crucial changes in the outline plan, two made by the commanders preparing to execute it. First, an argument between navy and army staffs over whether to attack Kota Bharu at the same time as the main attack on Thailand was resolved on 18 November by Yamashita and Ozawa. Attacking Kota Bharu right away would both protect the main landing from air attacks by defenders based there and allow the Japanese to seize those airbases and accelerate their own buildup. The two commanders agreed the potential gains of the simultaneous attack outweighed the risks, the navy would provide additional air support, and the operation would last two nights, transports withdrawing to safety during daytime. Second, Yamashita decided to forego his reserve, the 56th Division. Transport shipping was stretched to the breaking point, so the army commander decided he would need supplies to keep his advance moving ahead more than additional troops. This left him only two and three-quarter divisions for his attack on Malaya; the remainder of 18th Division was assigned to attack Borneo.[32] That meant his main fighting force, the infantry, would be outnumbered. Several factors influenced this bold decision, but a crucial one was the third change in the initial plan. The first draft envisaged a buildup in southern Thailand and at Kota Bharu for five weeks after the beachheads were established, followed by a methodical advance into central Malaya. After the northern airbases were captured and pressed into use, the final bound would be the advance to Singapore.[33] This would have suited the defenders very well, given their own need to rely on rapid reinforcement from other theatres. Unfortunately for them the Japanese dropped this idea. They decided instead to press the main attack as quickly as possible.

This change stemmed mainly from the other planning track: perfecting a doctrine for operations in Malaya. In December 1940 Imperial General

Headquarters established a unit in Taiwan to gather information about jungle warfare and the region. It was given the cover name Taiwan Army Research Section. Comprising some 30 officers and men, they threw themselves into their work, paying special attention to Malaya. By the autumn they concluded the attack plan should be changed for three reasons: the growing strength of the defences and the threat of reinforcements; shipping constraints; and superior Japanese fighting power, on the ground and in the air. Their lobbying helped persuade the General Staff, and Twenty-Fifth Army, to adopt a strategy based on a calculated risk. Taking chances with its supply lines, the army would seize the initiative and drive the enemy back without pause, never giving him a chance to regroup and dig in. Yamashita called it a "driving charge" or Kirimomi Sakusen.[34] This became the new battle plan, and it fit well with Japanese intentions in general. Their grand strategy was to rapidly destroy Western forces in Southeast Asia and the Western Pacific, pre-empting outside intervention–but they had to economize their overstretched ground forces at the same time. This strategy also better suited Yamashita's personal style of command. The plan took final shape by the last days of November. Elements of 5th Division would launch the main attacks in southern Thailand, adjusting to any British advance if necessary. A regimental battlegroup of 18th Division would invade Kota Bharu. A second wave would follow in six days, once the Thai ports were ready. Meanwhile both forces would advance as rapidly as possible to the Perak River and central Malaya, 5[th]Division's attack in the west being the main advance. The Imperial GuardsDivision would drive into Thailand from French Indochina, cement Japanese control in Bangkok, then advance down the peninsula from the north, joining the attack as soon as possible. As the advance moved south, another battlegroup from 18th Division would prepare to launch a follow-up invasion on the east coast, probably at Mersing. The army would then conquer Singapore, having destroyed its foe on the mainland.[35]

This is an excellent example of a campaign plan well tailored to circumstances, intentions and capabilities. The need for speed and economy of force, plus the plans and dispositions of the defenders, spread out as they were, made the "driving charge" the best choice. The fact Yamashita's infantry was outnumbered was reasonably expected to be offset by the nearly 600 first-rate combat aircraft assigned to support his campaign. It took a bit of haggling but in the end the air plan was focused: naval air would support the invasions, cover the seas, pressure Singapore, assist the land battle if possible; army air would win control of the air, then assist the land battle. At the operational level, the plan called for air and ground forces to fight an integrated battle. A tank corps and extra field artillery were attached to give the advance more punch, plus extra engineer units to keep it moving. Fifteenth Army would rapidly overrun British air bases in southern Burma, helping to interdict outside reinforcements. The naval support was a powerful balanced fleet led by a covering squadron with two battleships, strong air support, cruisers, destroyers, and submarines. The Japanese could expect to dominate the sea as well as the air, allowing them to launch outflanking amphibious attacks if need be.[36]

The contrast between attack and defence plans was stark. Political complications did not stymie Japanese plans and preparations; the Thais would be told to cooperate but whatever their attitude they would be invaded. The invasion forces would assemble in Hainan and southern Indochina as late as possible, to prolong Allied uncertainty.[37] This campaign strategy was neither disjointed nor unworkable. The main force, the army, had the means at hand to accomplish its mission, with the necessary supporting arms tailored to its requirements. Compare that to the RAF situation! And the most dangerous possible enemy moves were anticipated and addressed. The defenders also anticipated several things correctly. The Japanese were going into southern Thailand, they did stress the need to move air support forward, they would threaten the east coast, and they would make their main advance in the west. What the British did not anticipate was the strategy of the "driving charge"– nor, properly, the basis on which it rested. The Japanese expected to be better fighters than their enemies. They were right and they planned accordingly.

6

Men and Arms

Plans are concepts by which instruments will be used. Armed forces are instruments. Their ability to execute plans and accomplish their mission depends heavily on how well prepared they are to fight. In Malaya and Singapore in 1941, that rested on five factors. One, command and leadership, has been explored. The other four now must be: training, equipment, support, and intelligence. In the abstract the two sides seemed roughly even. The Japanese had more combat experience, but the defenders had been on the ground for many years. But beyond that a real gap opened up. The Japanese combat forces enjoyed stronger support, were better equipped, better trained, and made better use of intelligence. There is an underlying reason common to all four: the Japanese prepared to fight in Malaya, whereas the British Empire forces prepared to fight period.

Percival's efforts to train his troops for war were complicated by several factors. Too little was done before he arrived. The piecemeal manner by which his command was reinforced made it difficult to conduct formation training. It also meant many units needed time to acclimatize and adjust to the country. And it made his army something of a patchwork. Its imperial commonality did not compare very well to the homogeneity of the Japanese. The inexperience of many personnel made it necessary to conduct quite basic training. Shortages in equipment complicated training at all levels. Orders to defend on the beaches combined with unreasonably tight control of expenditure to interfere with the training of many units, because this required them to spend a lot of time working on defences. This was aggravated by the civil government's reluctance to interfere with normal routine. This made it harder to obtain labour for defence-related works, stifled the training of volunteer units and interfered with preparations, such as clearing fields of fire, that commanders wished to take. These complications were all inflicted on Percival and his commanders by external factors. There were others generated from within. The most important was the general approach taken by British Empire armed forces to training for war and the system by which they defined and instilled battle doctrine–their own ideas about how to fight. It all added up to a dangerous outcome. The defenders were not well prepared to fight in Malaya–especially not beyond the initial battles against invasion.

Notwithstanding all the above, the main cause was familiar: they tried too often to apply a general approach to each particular situation.

There is general agreement the pace and spirit of training improved in Malaya Command after Percival assumed command–and that it needed to.. The peacetime mentality that surrounded the prewar garrison was undoubtedly a serious impediment. Kirby summed it up in 1935: "The training of infantry units for normal mobile warfare is not easy in Singapore owing to the difficulties of the terrain and the climate. All Bns. stationed in Singapore therefore suffer and their standard of training falls during their tour of duty in the garrison."[1] The first serious critic of the training of Malaya Command was the commanding officer of one of its few battalions to emerge from the campaign having added to its regimental reputation: Ian Stewart of 2nd Battalion Argyll and Sutherland Highlanders [2nd Argylls]. Stewart's postmortem was blunt:

All contests are in great measure decided in the training period, and war, particularly jungle warfare, is no exception. In the lack of realistic, ruthless training from General to Private, in all spheres, psychological, tactical and physical, lies the whole secret of our failure in Malaya.

The GSO1 Staff Duties and Training at Malaya Command saw it a bit differently:

There is no doubt whatever that the Garrison of Malaya was NOT trained for the campaign and the responsibility for this fact must be accepted as the fault of the higher command. There are, however, in my humble opinion, a number of factors which mitigated against complete and proper training of the forces.

But Major Ashmore then listed 10 different reasons that made his acceptance of responsibility seem theoretical.[2] This question of training has been discussed by every memoir and study of the campaign, but as nearly all neither read nor used the surviving war diaries of the units involved there has been more heat than light. The diaries indicate training did indeed fall short–but system, circumstances and attitudes were all culpable.

One of the most serious impediments to training was the need to build defence works. The decision to defend on the beaches led to a directive from GHQ Far East to complete a comprehensive network of coastal defences as quickly as possible. Some effort had already been invested building defences in Singapore and northwest Malaya, but now the demands on time rose considerably. Percival later argued privately that this was unavoidable, especially on the east coast where little had been done. In his published despatch he explained his training policy:

> A balance, therefore, had to be struck between the employment of troops on defence works and their field training. I decided that the proper course was to build up a foundation of good individual and sub-unit training, which could be done concurrently with the construction of defences. If hostilities did not break out in the autumn I hoped that we might then expect a period of three months (December/February) during which we could concentrate on higher training ... Towards the end of September, the defences having made good progress, I directed that an increased proportion of time should be allotted to training.[3]

But the war diaries indicate things were not so clear-cut. 22nd Indian Brigade, defending Kuantan, recorded the following in October and November: "Work continued throughout the month on beach, river and field defences." 8th Indian Brigade, watching Kota Bharu, recorded extensive work on beach defences into November. 2nd Argylls and 4/19 Hyderabadis worked so intensively on beach defences at Mersing, in May, that they did no training at all that month. Yet when 22nd Australian Brigade took over the sector in September, having been told they would "have a rest, as the position had already been completed," they were so unhappy with the defences that "Until the outbreak of war and during the first few weeks the men worked like slaves preparing the positions."[4] As for the all important Jitra position, working harder on both training and defence works diluted each for all units involved. 2nd Battalion The East Surrey Regiment [2nd East Surreys] conducted no less than seven battalion or larger exercises from August to November, but only one lasted longer than a day and "preparation of defensive posns continued throughout this period." These tasks were recorded on 22 October in the diary of 2/9 The Jat Regiment [2/9 Jats]: "During the month there has been very little work done on the defensive posts at Jitra, as working parties of 250 men daily were supplied to build roads in the position." In at least one battalion, 3/16 Punjabi Regiment [3/16 Punjabi], this policy of having some companies digging and some training had been going on since April. 11th Indian division's history admitted that apart from a "weekly battalion exercise"–rarely overnight–and a monthly brigade or division exercise–apparently one of the latter–only one company per battalion was field training at any given time.[5]

This all supports Percival's rather plaintive explanation: "What was lacking was the ability to drop the construction of defences and take a formation, complete with all its arms, off into the country and carry out intensive training."[6] Sadly, the result was both disrupted training and incomplete defences. Even in Singapore one battalion, 1st Battalion The Manchester Regiment [1st Manchesters], a machine-gun battalion responsible for beach defences, reported that only one-third of the defences in its sector were completed when war broke out. 11th Indian Division engineer headquarters was on the ground at Alor Star from November 1940, 9th Indian Division engineers worked on their sectors from May 1941. When Simson toured the Jitra position days before war broke out, he found work progressing on one unfinished anti-tank ditch. Murray-Lyon was unwilling to address the problem because he was busy with *Matador* preparations, and on returning to Malaya Command Simson found "no concern there."[7]

Simson wasted little time addressing these problems. He travelled all over Malaya in August and September, taking copious notes in order to plan a comprehensive network of defensive positions. As late as mid-October the only works he found actually underway were the uncompleted position at Jitra and the defences on the south coast of Singapore island. This prompted him to present Percival a plan for a country-wide system of fixed defences in depth. Simson wanted to prepare anti-tank and machine-gun positions covering defiles on all passable roads, bolstered by the wiring of all bridges, with minefields on the flanks to channel the attackers onto the defences. In addition he wanted to complete the network of defences in northern Johore which Dobbie began in 1938-39, and prepare coastal defences on the northern shore of Singapore island. Percival did not accept the plan and did not explain why. He did allow Simson to approach battalion commanders with it but they gave him no support either–no surprise, given Percival's attitude. But this was all according to Simson's memoirs. Percival made no mention of such a discussion–and in interviews and correspondence in the 1950s Kirby told Simson bluntly that he overstated his case and weakened his credibility.[8] The war diaries shed only indirect light on this controversy–but there is some corroboration for Simson, in addition to documenting work on defences. As early as 19 August 9th Indian Division engineers mentioned the new CRE, noting he was sending material for obstacles and design blueprints. Two weeks later it was descriptions of anti-tank obstacles and ditches. The next week approval for a long-desired floating bridge came through, the following week orders to lay depth charges in rivermouths. As late as 2 November Simson sent drawings of another new type of anti-tank obstacle.[9] Whatever the truth of Simson's story, there is no doubting he tried to galvanize defence works. On the other hand, the explanation Percival later offered rested on the most controversial impediment to both defence works and training: the constraints placed on him by governments in London and Singapore.

Civil-military relations feature prominently in all analyses of the fall of

Singapore, but their impact is usually exaggerated. Nothing Shenton Thomas and his officials did or did not do before the war either doomed Singapore or could have saved it. But there is no doubt they did more harm than good. After the war Percival and Thomas pointed the finger at each other. Thomas insisted his hands were tied by London's order to maximize production. The civil government did all it could especially given–a claim that irked Percival– the fact that "never once prior to the Japanese invasion was any warning given of the great danger in which we were placed. On the contrary." The GOC argued that everything he did was affected by some consideration from which government help was required; its officials were hamstrung by a bureaucracy wedded to cumbersome procedure and a framework of administration "less suited to war conditions than any other part of the Empire." Percival had a point. Thomas was Governor of the Straits Settlements but only High Commissioner to the Malayan states, whose legal status was protectorate rather than colony. The whole country was in fact administered by a British civil service that answered to the Colonial Office, but preserving Malayan sensitivities entailed working through layers of administration. Any measure that required government assistance or approval might have to go through as many as 11 different offices if it were country wide–the Straits Settlements plus the mainland states and federal government. A typical list of addressees for an 11th Indian Division request for help included British Advisers in Kedah and Kelantan, the Resident Councillor in Penang, and the Resident in Perak, Selangor, and Pahang. Percival put it well: "It should be realized that the GOC Malaya did not have a free hand in developing the defences of Malaya."[10]

Indeed he did not. Percival went on to raise a crucial issue: money. The armed forces were not released from peacetime restraints on expenditure until 11 December 1941, three days after war broke out. Up to then, spending was strictly controlled by the WO, and the CO pressed similar restraint on the government. By 1941 the annual cost of the authorized defence plan for Malaya and Singapore neared £5 million. More than £4 million was spent by April. All expansions to the scheme, including the beach defences on the mainland and the Jitra position, had to be submitted to the WO and Treasury for approval. Percival's ceiling for write-offs on his own authority would be raised, if active operations began, to the ridiculously low sum of £500! A typical example of how these constraints worked was a notice from the State Engineer in Pahang to the CRE 9th Indian Division on 19 October that work would begin on pillboxes needed for airbase defences "as soon as deposit of $5000 has been made."[11]

The controls on spending were enough to void Simson's ambitious plans for country-wide defences even had Percival embraced them. They hurt most on an issue that did real damage: manpower and labour. There was not enough money to train and equip more volunteers than were already available. An outbreak of violent strikes in April and May made the government reluctant to press for more. Thomas was convinced the strikes occurred because European managers were called up for volunteer training. He forced the army to cut short the exercise. This interrupted training schedules, hurt relations with the Governor, and even aggravated Percival's relations with Bennett, when the Australians refused to help suppress the strikes.[12] Greater damage was done by the effect of parsimony on the labour supply. The WO refused to increase pay rates above Indian scales, as it expected most labour to be obtained there. The CO, worried about a backlash to any such influx, obstructed the local government's effort to do just that. All appeals for conscription of labour were rejected for a similar reason: fear it would provoke internal unrest or doubts about British power. Local civilian workers naturally preferred to work on the economy as the wages were higher. Percival's labour companies and field engineers were hopelessly overworked, as the unit diaries attest. Those from India needed time to adjust to local conditions. Finally, exasperated, Percival declared in November he would unilaterally increase wages.[13] It was too late. Much of the defence engineering work was done by private contractors supervised by the Public Works Department, including pillboxes and the anti-tank ditch at Jitra. Many were not completed by the time war broke out; the excavator at Jitra dug less than 20 metres a day and the ditch was still incomplete when it was needed.[14]

Another policy that ate up labour was the priority given to the construction of airbases, which the GOC accepted. Heath put it crudely: "We could have done with tens of thousands of coolies."[15] The root problem was the policy of peacetime governance, the perception Malaya and Singapore were contributing to a distant war but not involved in one themselves. From July 1941 at the latest this was unwise. It was driven partly by London's failure to see the problem, partly by the policy to maximize production, but certainly also by concern that British control over the multiracial society of the colonies was shaky enough that any sign of weakness might be dangerous. The key question was which was the greater danger: internal unrest or Japanese invasion? The civil government did not settle on the latter till very late in the day, and the home government did not press the issue. So apparently all the services could do was complain, pester, and improvise–but there was more to this.

Percival criticized the government, and European civilians in general, for the "air of unreality" he felt pervaded the colonies. This sense of being a safe area supposedly crippled war preparations, famous examples being refusal to allow army exercises to damage rubber trees or golf courses. The bureaucracy was cumbersome but most problems, including civil defence, denial or demolition of resources, stockpiling, and possible evacuation of civilians were at least discussed with the services. At one point in June the Governor even talked about making plans to "scorch the earth" if an enemy advanced into British territory. Scratch below the surface though, and it was rhetoric. The Governor only talked tough when it came to war preparations. He was in fact determined to disrupt the normal routine as little as possible, and his main reason was fear of internal unrest.[16]

New evidence, however, indicates that Percival agreed with this fear, and thus shared responsibility for this "air of unreality." Attempts to raise irregular units for covert operations ran afoul of both bureaucratic suspicion and internal security concerns. Thomas flatly refused to allow Asian civilians to be recruited. Percival agreed in writing on 3 October, listing as one objection "The suggestion to Asiatics that there is any chance of the enemy entering the country may have serious psychological effects." After meeting the Governor and the GOC on 24 October, the director of the organization trying to develop covert operations minuted that personal pique or bureaucratic intrigue might be at work but also noted "They appear to be scared stiff of Asiatic reactions." To confirm this view he bluntly challenged Percival on 20 November "We believe that for psychological reasons both H.E.[Thomas] and yourself are averse to training and using Asiatics." Percival admitted this point two days later, barely two weeks before war broke out.[17] These revelations make it clear that finger-pointing at the civil government for obstructing war preparations must now be qualified. The military also felt it was in a politically delicate colony, and did not quite throw caution to the winds either.

The problems of running a heterogenous empire also surfaced when it came to training Malaya Command's large Indian and Australian contingents. For the Indians, the two worst were "milking" and disaffection. 5/11 Sikhs war diary noted a common example of the former: "The Bn arrived in Malaya in August having been throughly milked, 450 recruits and 6 BOs [British officers] unable to speak Urdu having joined a few weeks prior to embarkation." The problem was caused by the rapid ten-fold expansion of the Indian Army after the fall of France. The only way to form the new units required without unacceptable delay was to take large cadres from units that were almost trained and transfer them to form the nucleus of a new unit, replacing them by raw recruits. Few Indian battalions sent to Malaya escaped such milking.[18] This dilution of units contributed to the other problem: disaffection.

The political situation in India was fragile, the nationalist movement strong and active, and this was reflected in the army. The problem attracted attention from Churchill himself, concerned about the "loyalty" of this indispensable pool of imperial manpower. Many British officers were inclined to blame weak and inexperienced leaders unable to handle young and frustrated troops. But in some cases there were political forces at work as well. The entry in the 1st Kapurthala Infantry war diary for 18 September 1941 noting "six NCOs sentenced to six months rigorous imprisonment, dismissed from service reduced to ranks for disobeying lawful commands of superior officer ..." may be frustratingly ambiguous–but the number involved and severity of punishment sparks curiosity. This unit was a "princely state battalion," quasi-regular forces affiliated with the Indian Army, donated by their potentate as an act of solidarity. There were five in Malaya, most assigned to airbase defence, and their "steadiness" was often questioned.[19] But the war diaries also record a good deal of trouble among the regular contingent: 5/11 Sikhs, 2nd Frontier Force Regiment, 9th Indian Division engineers and even the division provost unit.[20] The cause of these problems was unclear, but there is no doubt about the problem that erupted in 4/19 Hyderabadis in May 1940.

Two companies of the battalion refused to obey orders from the 7th to the 9th of May. The unit was stood down and the neighbouring British unit, 2nd Argylls, discreetly placed on alert. The battalion dealt with the trouble itself, identifying the cause as the decision to return an Indian officer to India for discipline because he "expressed views which were considered to be highly objectionable in an officer holding a commission in the service." The war diary records that the battalion rapidly "settled down," but there was more to it. Higher command found it necessary to intervene. Bond convened an inquiry into the affair, and the brigade commander personally briefed all officers of 5/2 and 5/14 Punjabi on the "facts of the case."[21] There was a distinct unease here, and it had deeper roots.

On 5 October 1939, two months after the battalion arrived in Singapore, the war diary recorded the following: "It appears that certain interested parties in Singapore are spreading false rumours, engineered by them, with the object of creating discontent among Indian soldiers." To counter this, visits to the camp by influential Indian civilians were arranged, followed in January 1940 by a bolder initiative: "Note tour by journalists of camp and unit, paid off days later with articles in local press 'strongly condemned the prevailing false rumours amongst certain circles in Malaya, that the Indian troops were not being well looked after and were discontented.'"[22] This was the underlying fear: Indian nationalists in Singapore and Malaya would exploit the influx of Indian troops by playing on both petty grievances and political feelings, to provoke trouble. This fear of subversion did not abate.

9th Indian Division blamed the Klang strike in May 1941, which it had to help suppress, on Congress party manipulators among Tamil plantation workers. GHQ Far East warned the War Office in June that while it did need another Indian brigade to replace one diverted to Iraq, the current schedule of reinforcements raised a danger, particularly if Bennett's Australian troops were not retained: there could be too many Indian as compared to "white" troops in Malaya by the autumn.[23] This was not just an operational concern. The Empire in India and the Far East was, with reason, regarded as politically fragile. And there is no doubt British attitudes were the main cause. The British brought India into the war without asking Indians, then sent them to Malaya where too often they were treated disrespectfully. The imperial colour bar was very strong in Malaya and Singapore. This was a familiar grievance among local Asian civilians, but a nasty shock to incoming Indian troops, especially Indian officers. Giving someone a commission, sending him overseas and asking him to defend you with his life, then banning him from your swimming club because he was black was hardly the best way to pull an imperial force together–but it happened in Malaya and Singapore time and again. This made it even harder to defend a multi-racial empire in which some were more equal than others.[24] Malaya Command never forgot that in February 1915 an Indian battalion stationed in Singapore mutinied, and had to be suppressed by force.

Imperial problems with the Australians were different but also not trivial. Bennett was in the country from February to August 1941 with only one brigade to supervise. The commander of 22nd Australian Brigade, Brig. H.B. Taylor, thus found himself under the microscope of an egotistical superior with not enough to distract his attention. Predictably their relationship soon soured, and training suffered. Percival, wary of provoking a status argument, did not intervene, as he might have with a British formation. There is no doubt both Australian brigades worked hard and learnt much in the time available.[25] But Bennett's conclusion that Taylor was not good enough did come to matter.

There is a good deal of exaggeration surrounding relations in 1941 between the Australians and everyone else in Malaya. Yet there is enough evidence to suggest there was more than minor friction. Australians seemed to get along better with Asian civilians than European residents did, and better with those residents in Malaya than they did in Singapore. The Aussies attributed this to snobbery from European civilians, and there are enough examples to indicate this was not just a chip on the shoulder. Boys will be boys and troops sometimes fight when they go drinking in pubs, but friction between Australian and British troops was serious enough to occupy a fair bit of Bennett's time, at least once provoking a heated discussion with Heath and Percival. This was a hastily assembled polyglot imperial army carrying baggage that made it harder to unite. Australian frustration was blamed on long months of training while Australians elsewhere were in action, which seems fair. Keeping an army on short notice for war month after month was bound to provoke frustration. But the Australians matched British condescension with their own far from reticent attitude about what they would do to the Japanese if they ever had a chance, how much higher their pay was, how much larger their meat ration.[26] To put this in perspective: the different national components would fight the Japanese and not each other if war came to Malaya, but they were not as smooth a team as an all-Australian or all-British force would have been.

The most important issue relating to training was of course quality–not just how much training, but what kind and how effective. The constraints facing Malaya Command have been established and must be taken into consideration. Having said that, it was responsible for the most serious error of all: failure to instill in its combat formations an effective doctrine for fighting in Malaya. But even here, this was the result not just of actions in theatre but of the imperial military system itself.

Brooke-Popham reported on 3 July 1941: "... a fine lot of munitions is coming along now, and papers on lessons learnt during operations are arriving much quicker and in greater numbers."[27] This was five months before a shot was fired–ample time, if the necessary equipment was indeed coming in, and the right lessons being taught and practiced on the ground, to make some difference. Unfortunately he was too optimistic on both points. All Indian and Australian units sent to Malaya left with very low issues of equipment, to accelerate their arrival. This plus the fact they had to spread out in Malaya affected training, especially larger formation training. Most combat units did not receive full war scales until November. A common example was 1/13th Frontier Force Rifles, deployed at Kota Bharu. They only received Bren guns–the standard issue light automatic weapon, the main firepower of all infantry platoons–that month. Most artillery units did not receive their main weapon, the 25 pounder field gun, until then either. That plus the late arrival of some units also hampered brigade and division training. That influenced Percival's decision to start with lower level training. At one point Malaya Command offered this helpful advice to commanders short of important weapons parts: "[they] must constantly agitate until they get them."[28] Then there was the problem of what equipment was issued and how was it used. The army followed too closely equipment scales laid down in England. It would have been better to experiment and adjust to local conditions, as the AIF did to an extent. The army became too dependent on roads and vehicles yet carried too much unnecessary gear on the man. This was an imperial army organized, equipped, and trained along generic lines shaped by conditions near the metropolitan centre. But one size did not fit all, and the necessary adjustments could only have been made on the spot.

The Indian brigades that arrived in 1941 were all originally intended to fight in the Middle East, so their training focused on open desert conditions. Most of the gunners had never worked with infantry. Nearly all the infantry had never seen a tank. And the armies of the British Empire had not fought a modern war in terrain dominated by jungle.[29] Unavoidably there was much to do. Unfortunately there was little help at hand. Units of the prewar Singapore garrison very rarely trained in the bush, leaving little in the way of accumulated practical experience for newcomers to draw on. This was summed up by Kirby's 1935 statement: "The training of infantry units for normal mobile warfare is not easy in Singapore owing to the difficulties of the terrain and the climate."[30] Apparently, "normal" mobile warfare was not possible in Malaya. This was not one man's opinion. This very much reflected institutional bias. The Empire's armies were shaped by the British Army. In 1941 it was focused on the last major war it had to fight–on the plains of northern Europe–and the one it was fighting–in North Africa. This influenced its doctrine in all respects. The best Malaya Command could have done would be to modify this; being a product of this system, it could not escape it entirely. So how then did it prepare troops for something other than "normal" mobile warfare?

Stewart of the Argylls believed it did not, that "What was achieved was in spite of and not with the assistance of the General Staff." He acknowledged the difficulties that impeded training in 1941 but probed beyond them:

> [Malaya Command] had to break away from the preconceived and conventional Army ideas, a far easier thing to state than to achieve, for orthodoxy had been taught as a religion ... But the greatest weakness was that an adequate training organization was lacking. There was no DMT [Director of Military Training] of a high rank backed by the necessary schools for evolving and teaching the new techniques that were so urgently required ... In practice there was no co-ordination of ideas, or formulation of a common tactical doctrine for jungle.

Malaya Command staff disagreed:

> The suggestion that more training of troops should have been carried out is an old one and originated, I think, from Ian Stewart who commanded the

Argylls. From the angle of the purely regimental officer … this is an attractive theory but bears no relation to the realities of the situation. 12 Indian Brigade was able to carry out realistic training because they were the Theatre Reserve and so were not committed to construct any defence works nor were they tied to any specific operation.[31]

The debate rests on two points: was there a more realistic battle doctrine at hand than the one the army adopted? If not, why not? But if so, did the army practice it in training–and if not why not?

Stewart sketched out the most effective battle doctrine used in Malaya. The jungle favoured the attacker. The restricted visibility of dense bush negated the advantage of firepower and made it harder to control larger bodies of men. This made it impossible to fight a static defence based on holding a specific line of ground in jungle country, because it was too easy to infiltrate between positions or go around them. Worse, men not accustomed to the jungle could too easily become intimidated by it, especially if they sat passively awaiting attack. The main tactical feature was the road, essential for strategic movements of large formations over long distances. So battle revolved around control of the road. But because "to lose the initiative in jungle is death" the defence must emphasize mobility and aggressiveness. And that often meant fighting for the road off the road, fighting to inflict losses on the enemy rather than hold a specific location. If the defence must focus on the road then the position must be deep, infantry companies lining up behind each other to absorb the blow, counterattacking on the flanks. If it could be off the road then it should spread out. Regardless, the emphasis must be counterattack. There were two effective methods. One was to fix the enemy by attacking him frontally with a small force, then with the main force outflank or encircle him, making him either give way or be destroyed. The other was called "filleting": attacking a defile along the road by frontal assault with concentrated force, blasting through in great depth, dispersing the enemy into the bush on either flank. In almost every situation, the best tactical formation was to rely on the smallest groups possible. The battle could be orchestrated by senior officers, but should be fought at the lowest possible level of command.[32]

These tactics were almost as unsuitable as could be imagined to the prevailing battle doctrine favoured by the British Army, conditioned as it was by recent experience, ancient customs and entrenched attitudes. Colonels, not section commanders, made the crucial decisions in battle. The orthodox defensive battle was to hold a line of fixed positions in a static defence, relying on the firepower of dug in troops and their heavy machine guns. They would fix the enemy, who would then be killed or driven off by the firepower of the supporting artillery. The gunners were the battle winners in a "textbook" battle. Counterattack was a standard tactic, but to repel an incursion and restore a line. Control meant senior officers directing the battle and holding the line, not sergeants playing hide and seek with the enemy in the bush. It also meant preserving lines of communication and supply from being cut by flanking or encirclement. In 1941, before it became possible to resupply by air on a large scale, this meant either giving up a compromised position or restoring it.[33]

Malaya was however a battlefield with more than just jungle, and the army would face different problems in battle. How then did it train to fight, as an army? Percival argued it did all it could, drafting and circulating manuals and directives on tactics and issuing instructions on training "as and when required." The obstacle was not direction: "But doctrine had not only to be disseminated but practiced and it was for this that opportunity was lacking."[34] Manuals and instructions there were, aplenty. The Australians brought *Notes on Jungle Lore (Compiled by an officer who has served with the Malay Regiment)*. The Indian Army brought *Tactical Handling of Anti-Tank Rifles* and *Effects of Air Bombing*, as well as a manual on jungle warfare. Malaya Command circulated its own *Training Instructions on Tank Hunting* in April 1941, as well as *Tactical Notes on Malaya* in 1940, among others.[35] But the question is whether such instructions were absorbed by the troops. The answer is largely not; the main reason was Malaya Command.

Percival decided to solve the problem by leaving tactical training to the units themselves. Command schools were restricted to officer training, intelligence, camouflage, chemical warfare and physical training, subjects requiring "technical knowledge." How to fight a battle was apparently something units could sort out themselves. The direction of training was assigned to a major on the Command staff without a directorate in support.[36] The result was predictable. The war diaries and memoirs now make it possible to assess the extent to which a battle doctrine focused on local conditions was absorbed: units were in practice left largely to their own devices. Hard pressed by other distractions, most fell back on standard British Army thinking about how to fight on the defensive.

One junior officer who went through the Malaya Command Officer Training Unit remembers a training syllabus based on doctrine laid down in England, with no lessons about conditions specific to Malaya. As for the manual *Tactical Notes on Malaya*:

> Everything in it was sound, but there was so little of it. Once a soldier had read that, knew his weapons and had done some manoeuvres in open country, he was regarded as trained for the defence of Malaya.

There was actually very little information on dense jungle country, seen as impenetrable, so training plans all but disregarded it.[37] At the opposite end of the training scale was 12th Indian Brigade. It is not true the brigade was free to train realistically because it was command reserve. It only took on that role in September 1941, and its diaries show that the previous two years were marred by the same distractions other formations faced.[38] But this formation, commanded by an experienced brigadier and three hard-driving battalion commanders, pushed hard to train in conditions that were as realistic as possible–and along the way stumbled on the idea that conventional static defence was asking for trouble in Malaya.

12th Indian Brigade trained with an intensity and initiative that stood out in Malaya Command. It learnt the differences between open country, rubber plantations and jungle, and how best to move and fight in all three. While the rest of the garrison took afternoons off on the quiet days of October 1939, 4/19 Hyderabadis spent two nights a week in the jungle, and 2nd Argylls made their transfer to Mersing an opportunity to practice air attack and ambush along the road. The brigade discovered how penetrable the jungle could be, how easy it was to turn the flank of a fixed position in close or mixed country, and how important it was to move and fight off the road when in contact. Their fieldcraft was good enough by February 1941 that a two-brigade exercise with air force participation produced a complaint from "enemy" airmen that "this bde could not be seen because they don't use the roads." That same month, 2nd Argylls outflanked a defence line on Singapore island by making a river crossing Fortress Command said was "not possible." The battalion made a route march along the east coast from Mersing to Singapore, some 200 km, from 16 to 23 July 1941. 5/2 Punjabi made a similar route march to Labis in October. What stands out was the decision to modify instructions on paper by applying lessons drawn from training in the field. But instead of being seen as a role model by Malaya Command, its staff dismissed the brigade, Stewart in particular, as overzealous. Simson praised the brigade's training to Percival, but Torrance called Stewart a "crank," and the GOC made no comment.[39]

This was the crux of the problem. The staff of Malaya Command did not follow up its circulation of paper to make sure the army did all it could to apply it in practice. Percival could not do this himself, but should have made sure Torrance did. Instead he allowed him to deride one of the few commanders who showed real initiative. The danger signs were all discovered in time to be acted on–had anyone been alert enough to do so. 1/8 Punjabi trained to fight a delaying action north of Jitra as early as February 1941. 15th Indian Brigade noted one prominent lesson: "it is well nigh impossible to stop the enemy small parties getting round your flanks in the rubber and jungle."

2/9 Jat discovered that for short moves near the enemy it was better to march than jump on and off trucks, taking time assembling and dispersing. Malaya Command was well aware that many units were bound far too closely to the large number of vehicles they brought into the field. Trucks were necessary for strategic movement, but near contact they produced two bad distractions: a too narrow focus on the road and too much concern with the security of vehicles behind the "line."[40]

Tanks were a special problem. *Tactical Notes on Malaya* dismissed the country as not suitable for tanks. Nevertheless Percival asked for two regiments, to counter enemy armour. This followed conventional British thinking at the time: the best way to stop a tank was with another tank. For some time it looked as if the British would send light tanks–larger types were believed to be too heavy for many bridges–and the Australians would supply crews. But neither men nor vehicles became available before war broke out.[41] The army had to make do with armoured cars, of which it had perhaps three dozen, and Universal or Bren carriers, a tracked open-topped armoured infantry carrier available in ample numbers. Neither could defeat tanks, but other means were available: anti-tank guns, mines, obstacles covered by guns, even improvised explosives. The war diaries have many references to tank-hunting training. Malay Command issued a detailed instruction in April which spoke sensibly of combining gunners, obstacles, and hunting teams to work together, and warned "All officers must be tank-minded. Against an enemy equipped with tanks movement must be from anti-tank obstacle to anti-tank obstacle." But there is no record of this advice being followed up below divisional headquarters. Percival noted that Heath was not very co-operative on training matters. No war diaries record combined arms anti-tank exercises; most only refer to improvised explosives, "Molotov cocktails." 11th Indian Division first decided to train infantry to use guns in the anti-tank role at Jitra, then changed its mind and assigned the role to gunners–but did not work the two together. Finally, there was the bizarre episode of the anti-tank manual. In late November Simson found "stacks" of WO pamphlets on fighting tanks sitting unused at Command headquarters. Why they were not circulated remains unclear. Simson persuaded Percival to allow him to rewrite the manual with reference to local conditions, and circulate it to unit commanders. The Japanese beat him to it.[42]

The AIF trained with a more open mind and more initiative than most of the rest of Malaya Command.[43] Percival singled out their two brigades and the 12th and 28th Indian as well trained for war. The latter was certainly not. Arriving in late September, it hardly had time to send three officers forward to Jitra for a week to learn about "jungle" tactics, let alone acclimatize the whole formation.[44] But the other three brigades were in decent shape where it mattered most: doctrine and attitude. The rest of the army was not.

The brunt of the coming battle was going to be borne by III Indian Corps. Its units trained either to advance into Thailand–into a tactical void– or hold a fixed line by static defence, with methodical counterattacks to maintain the line. This was the doctrine of the set-piece battle. It reflected the tendency to use European-based doctrine, emphasizing firepower, and the directives to hold beaches and airbases, which focused Malaya Command on positional fighting. Jitra was the worst case. 11th Indian Division trained to fight that defensive battle as if it was going to fight on the Western Front in 1916. Command and field officers expected to hold a "line," with a front and a rear, and a supply connection between the two that must be maintained. Their mental map was static defence warfare. There were only three places in northwest Malaya where such tactics might work: Gurun, Kampar and Tanjong Malim. The rest of the area called for more flexible tactics. It was not enough to know that relying too much on the road and on vehicles was unwise, or that flanks could be turned. What mattered was training to do something about it. Instead the army trained to fight the way it knew best– whether it suited the terrain and circumstances or not.

The air force faced similar problems. As its role was more important its problems were more damaging. RAF Far East needed adequate numbers of first-rate aircraft, flown by well trained aircrew, to accomplish its mission. The most important aircraft for the defence plan was the torpedo bomber, the most potent ship-killer. The two available squadrons had well-trained and experienced aircrew but were equipped with the Vildebeeste, a biplane so obsolete it is not even mentioned in the authoritative *Jane's Aircraft of the Second World War*. It was being replaced by the more modern Beaufort. But the replacements were to come from Australia, and technical problems delayed them so much that only six arrived before war broke out. The medium bombers, the Blenheim and the Hudson, were not only too few in number–six squadrons–but crewed largely by newly arrived and only half trained aircrew. The doubling of the command in size obscured a shuffle. Many personnel whose tour expired were rotated, replaced by personnel from the U.K. or the Dominions who had no grasp of local conditions. This was most damaging in the four fighter squadrons. Their aircraft, the American-supplied Buffalo, was ruled obsolete for European conditions. It was heavy, underpowered and slow to climb. The pilots, many of them New Zealanders fresh from flying school, badly needed training and local experience. All training programs were hampered by shortages of spare parts, equipment, funds, personnel, and obstruction from London. The Air Ministry refused to authorize an Operational Training Unit, prompting Pulford to set up his own at the expense of his squadrons resources. Training had to focus on the basics. That left little time for training with the army; 12th Indian Brigade worked with aircraft twice in two years.[45]

One of the most tenacious impressions about the fall of Singapore is that comprehensive Japanese preparations gave them a tremendous advantage. This needs to be corrected. For years the IJA's equipment, training and doctrine focused on fighting the Soviet Red Army in North Asia. Operations in China brought valuable combat experience, but not in tropical terrain or conditions. The Imperial Guards Division arrived first in southern Indochina, but had not fought as a formation since 1905. Its supposedly elite troops were not regarded as well trained, and Twenty-Fifth Army staff considered its officers arrogant and unco-operative. 5th Division was on semi-active service in the Shanghai area. 18th Division operated near Canton until late October. 3rd Air Group Headquarters only arrived in mid-October, and delays in transporting equipment and supplies meant it only "barely succeeded in deploying all the unit by the beginning of December" and accumulated "barely enough" supplies to go to war.[46] On the other hand, the foundations were very strong.

The army preparing to conquer Singapore enjoyed three important advantages over its opponent. Its standard peacetime training was very intense. Its formations were deliberately assembled for this campaign rather than coming together haphazardly. And it had a lot of combat experience. Life for the private soldier in the prewar IJA was an experience matched in harshness and intensity by only the French Foreign Legion or the German Waffen SS in Western armies at that time. Leave was rare, discipline strict, training constant and calibrated, in conditions where casualties were common. Imbued with the cult of imperialism and empire worship, Japanese soldiers were taught from their school days to prepare for war and expect to die for the imperial cause. Social pressures in Japanese culture reinforced both the message and the harshness. Whatever the case with the Guards, front line combat units in the IJA were truly combat ready in 1941.[47] The 5th Division was a specialist formation, concentrating on amphibious operations for two decades. From 1937 it conducted them in battle in China, helping develop equipment and techniques which made the IJA a world leader in this area. It would lead the assault on Thailand and began to train for the campaign before it moved south. The 18th was a veteran light infantry division, equipped to move quickly and fight in difficult terrain. They were reinforced by extra allotments of light artillery, also suited for difficult terrain, combat engineers, including bridging units, and light and medium tank companies, to dominate the roads.[48] What brought them all together was the toughness, combat experience and battle-readiness of the IJA in general.

This good foundation was bolstered by what one analyst saw as the most important Japanese advantage in this campaign: "mental readiness and adaptability." The most vital work of the Taiwan Army Research Section was to establish the battle doctrine by which the army would fight in Malaya. The army needed to learn quickly how to fight in the tropics and the unit did not let it down. The unit drew on a wide variety of sources, including a thorough personal reconnaissance on the ground in Malaya by Capt. Kunitake Terito, moving in mufti from January through March 1941. It compiled a corpus of knowledge from which it distilled a doctrine for jungle warfare. Then it persuaded the General Staff to accept this doctrine, and organize, equip and train accordingly. Most important, the doctrine was tested and refined by 10 major exercises. They ranged from a full scale dress rehearsal involving two regiments to battalion-sized experiments. This was realistic combat training, focused on a specific operation. To discover how to transport men, equipment and horses over long distances by sea with as few ships as possible, then assault without punitive losses, the unit conducted a week-long exercise at sea. To test ideas about jungle combat, a battle group of infantry, artillery and engineers, using bicycles, carried out a strategic advance through jungle areas in Taiwan, in an area roughly 1000 km wide–similar to the distance from the Thai border to Singapore. These exercises were carried out by test units, but the lessons drawn were accepted as the basis for battle doctrine in Malaya. On 12 August the General Staff directed Twenty-Fifth Army to concentrate on training for operations in Malaya. In October it appointed Tsuji its Chief Operations Officer.[49]

The doctrine was laid down in a long manual published by the unit. 400,000 copies were printed and issued to all officers and men assigned to invade Southeast Asia. Some 70 pages long, Read This Alone-And the War Can Be Won was carefully studied by Yamashita's whole army. Much of the document focused on intangibles such as motivation and morale. The mixture of races in Malaya Command was singled out as a weakness that could be exploited; the Japanese held Indian troops in near contempt. There were also detailed instructions about conditions in Malaya, ranging from advice on how to treat the natives, to comments on wild animals, to how to move in battle in extreme heat, to this instructive comment on dense jungle:

> ... it will be necessary to form special operation units for the task. This type of terrain is regarded by the weak-spirited Westerners as impenetrable, and for this reason–in order to outmaneuvre them–we must from time to time force our way through it. With proper preparation and determination it can be done.[50]

What mattered was applying such advice in battle. Once the General Staff decided to adopt the doctrine, the professional readiness of the IJA did the rest. Divisions were streamlined for light infantry operations, replacing vehicles with bicycles for tactical movement in advance to contact. Rifle companies focused on infiltration and flanking movements off the road. Tanks and air support would blast through prepared defences that could not be readily outflanked. Equipment was sensibly chosen: light rather than heavy artillery, fighting kit of minimal weight for each rifleman, grenade dischargers–often called knee mortars–for organic fire support for small fighting units. The Japanese Medium Tank Type 97 would have been slaughtered by a British unit equipped with Valentine tanks–but was not going to face one. The IJN's Zero fighter was faster and more maneuverable than the Buffalo, could operate at very long range, and was flown by combat experienced pilots; the IJA's K-43 or Oscar fighter was also better than anything Pulford had available. The Japanese would control the sky. This would allow their efficient modern bombers to throw their weight around. That edge in the air was a fail-safe element in their whole plan.[51]

Not everything went just as Tsuji and Yamashita wished. The invading units, army and navy, were only able to practice assault loading and unloading together once, with mixed results.[52] Nevertheless, by December this was a well-balanced expeditionary force prepared to carry out a specific operation. All its combat units had absorbed a common doctrine tailored to fighting in the country they would invade. Considering how quickly it all came together, this testifies to the general combat readiness of Japan's armed forces. Japanese preparations did not have to be perfect, just better than those of their enemy. They were.

The final aspect of preparing for war was perhaps the most important: intelligence. The collection, collation and appreciation of information about the enemy was essential to success in battle. It was another activity that connected the entire chain of command, from central direction of the war to battlefield commanders. It also had great influence on policies, plans, and preparations. There were five ways to gather intelligence about an enemy during the Second World War. First, it could be openly collected by public access, ranging from reading newspapers, to tracking shipping movements and stock markets, to using embassies, military attaches and observers to cultivate contacts. Second, it could be covertly collected by human intelligence, by espionage. This could range from military officers posing as tourists taking notes and photos, to agents hidden inside an enemy organization, to traitors. Third, it could be gleaned from friendly powers. Fourth, it could be extracted from prisoners of war. Finally, it could be acquired by intercepting and analyzing radio traffic, and decyphering coded messages–signals intelligence. Everyone did all these things routinely. How successfully intelligence was applied depended on three things: how accurate it was, the system by which it was disseminated, and the extent to which it was believed and acted upon. This was a complex process, ranging from reactions to a single event to slowly developing an overall impression of an enemy–how he was organized, how he operated. Good information could get lost in a poor system, or be rejected by someone who preferred to believe something else.

By 1941 the central direction of the war in London had a well organized system for collecting and applying intelligence. The FO carried out its traditional role to appreciate the intentions of other powers. The intelligence directorates of the armed services collected information in their respective spheres, coming together in the Joint Intelligence Committee (JIC). They had access to all sources of intelligence gathering, including the Secret Intelligence Service or MI6, and a very important signals intelligence organization for deciphering intercepted messages, run by the Government Code and Cypher School (GC & CS) under FO oversight. Commanders in the Far East were served by regional branches of these organizations, including signals intelligence; there was an interception station at Kranji, on the north coast of Singapore island. But the intelligence network in the Far East was handicapped by scarce resources, rivalries and attitudes. Regional organizations were at first based in Hong Kong, but until 1938 Singapore was the only station with permanent intelligence officers. The budget for air intelligence in 1938 was £100. Signals intelligence in 1934 indicated that the Japanese had agents listening in to the conference chaired by Admiral Dreyer, but the commanders in Singapore dismissed the idea an agent could betray their meetings, as "only officers were present." And priorities shifted slowly from concerns about internal security, especially communist agitation, to the Japanese. The FECB only moved to Singapore in August 1939, the same year Special Branch–the security arm of the police–began to take serious interest in Japanese activities. As one expert put it, British intelligence in the Far East was "heavily reorganized but only marginally improved" by 1940. Nevertheless, by the time Far East Command began operating, there was a network in place. Information circulated around the Empire, especially back and forth between London and Singapore. Progressively tighter Japanese security, the withdrawal of British garrisons from China, and Western economic pressure on Japan combined to reduce the flow of intelligence– but it never dried up completely.[53] The problem was how it was appreciated and applied.

Despite the fact that a good deal of accurate information was available to London and Singapore regarding Japanese capabilities and intentions, it did not prompt the military system to change any plans or policies. Two seminal points have already been discussed. In London, the Prime Minister was the most important advocate of the point of view that the Japanese were cautious, would surely be deterred by the threat of American intervention, and in any case could not do irreparable damage even if they did strike—not least because of the weight the Americans would throw against them. In Singapore, Far East Command became very optimistic in autumn 1941 regarding Japanese intentions and capabilities. Brooke-Popham, convinced himself the Japanese would not attack Malaya before the end of the monsoon in February 1942. Two questions need answers here. Why did such attitudes take hold? And what effect did they have on readiness for war in Malaya and Singapore?

Too many saw for too long a simple explanation for what turned out to be some very wrong assumptions: notions of racial superiority. The problem was more complex. Three more nuanced factors had greater effect: mirror imaging, ethnocentrism, and policy concerns. Mirror imaging was the tendency to evaluate what an enemy could, would or should do based on your own situation. An example was Brooke-Popham's argument that among indications the Japanese would not attack in autumn 1941 was the fact "they would have been more likely to have done so in 1940, when our forces were far weaker than they were at the end of 1941." This ignored Japanese capabilities and intentions in 1940. Ethnocentrism is evaluating an enemy by measuring him in every respect against yourself. The British armed services held themselves up as the standard by which all others, American, German, Italian, Japanese, were measured. An example was the important GHQ Far East appreciation of 8 September 1941 titled Possibilities of the Japanese Attacking in the South. It argued that as the Germans and British could not stock enough resources to maintain airforces capable of offensive action in more than one overseas theatre the Japanese could not either. Mirror imaging and ethnocentrism were influenced by, but went beyond, racial feelings. Policy concerns amounted to the instinct that it would be safer to "put up a brave front." The desire to impress the Americans with British resolve to defend Singapore, such as by sending out Force Z, was one example. Another involved one of the relatively few British professional experts on the Japanese. Col. G.T.Wards, who spoke Japanese fluently and served for a number of years as an attache in Tokyo, gave a lecture in Singapore in April 1941 to senior commanders and staff officers. Concentrating on the IJA, Wards warned them it was a first class fighting machine in every respect. Several officers strongly challenged his views and Bond publicly dismissed them as "far from the truth as I know from my information, which I receive from all sorts of sources. What Major Wards has told you is merely his own opinion and is not in any way a correct appreciation of the situation." Wards took this up privately with Bond, who replied "… we must not discourage the chaps; we must keep their spirits up."[54] Mirror-imaging, ethnocentrism, and policy concerns shaped the application of intelligence in Malaya and Singapore by creating a set of fixed assumptions, against which information was evaluated.

The best way to demonstrate this is to identify what accurate intelligence about the Japanese was available at the time–which means indulging in a bit of hindsight–and explain why it did not prevail when it mattered. One of the most widely circulated appraisals of the IJA was the Military Intelligence Directorate's annual *Handbook of the Japanese Army*, supplemented by *Periodical Notes*. The 1939 edition made the following warning:

> They are very well led, have excellent spirit, as an Army are well knit together, confident, and have exceptional powers of endurance. As a result they are very mobile. The weakness of the Japanese Army in the past has lain in lack of material, and in the means, experience and ability to improve material. This weakness is fast disappearing and with the completion of the 1935-1940 rearmament scheme, the Japanese Army should in all respects be a well equipped and modern fighting machine and almost up to the highest standards.

Who, one wonders, set "the highest standards"? Such ambivalence, set against a detailed evaluation of the IJA's organization, tactics, training, and weaponry, surely threatened to dilute any warning. This manual was issued down to battalion officers. The "General Staff HM Naval Base Singapore" adapted and reprinted it in 1941, issuing 1500 copies titled *Japanese Army Memorandum*. They incorporated additions and modifications made in March by the General Staff India, expressly to "give regimental officers a general idea of the characteristics, organization, armament, tactics and training of the Japanese Army." In 56 detailed pages the manual emphasized the Japanese tendency to use envelopment tactics in battle from the largest formation to the smallest unit, their expertise at minor tactics, their readiness to fight at night, and improvements made in such items as tanks and landing craft. But it undermined any warning value on page 38:

> These notes are based on the tactics employed during the Sino-Japanese hostilities which broke out in 1937, but it must be remembered that in these operations Japan was engaged against an inferior enemy, that she enjoyed almost complete air superiority, that her artillery was seldom engaged by enemy counterbattery fire or her infantry by the action of hostile AFV's [armoured fighting vehicles], and that she was able to take risks with her communications in the field which would have proved fatal against a more enterprising enemy. The conclusions that may be drawn from these

operations should therefore be treated with some reserve. The exaggerated idea of their prowess, gained as a result of their victorious advance through China may lead the Japanese officers and men to feel that similar tactics to those employed on that occasion may succeed against other enemies. This may lead to large initial losses in a future war. There is evidence, however, that such a danger is well realized by senior commanders and staff officers.[55]

Such ambivalence invited field officers to conclude the Japanese could be dangerous but were hardly as good as their own army. It also indicated why this view developed: the war in China. British appreciations of Japanese efficiency changed for the worse from 1937. Many assumed Japanese problems in China indicated they were hardly a force to be reckoned with. Experts in Tokyo and London continued to rate the IJA highly but only a few, such as Wards, did not dilute their warnings. British observers around Shanghai became convinced the Japanese were overrated–at the same time the Japanese tightened security, drastically reducing the access foreign observers had to their newest weapons and best formations. And the buildup of Malaya Command concentrated "optimistic" officers, from China and India, in Singapore. The Australians arrived in Malaya with appreciations influenced by Wards, warning the Japanese must be taken very seriously. They and he found a wall of skepticism, later encountered by Simson, which suggests the most comforting view of Japanese capabilities took hold in Malaya and Singapore. Even the more cautious view of the Japanese that prevailed before 1937, noting that the IJA was well tailored to operations in Asian conditions, assumed the Japanese would find things much harder against an enemy "which held its nerve and its fire." The British decided they were such an enemy. In that atmosphere, information that did not fit this consensus was too often weeded out in favour of intelligence or assumptions that did.[56]

Malaya Command was clearly swayed by this "weeding" tendency. This drowned important warnings or accurate appraisals in a pool of more comforting assumptions. In August 1940 12th Indian Brigade was given a "valuable lecture" by a naval expert on Japanese landing methods. The "chief lesson" was seen as "the Jap is a real expert at landing ops but if he is surprised so as to upset his very detailed plans he takes a long time to recover as he can't think quickly." The first many troops heard about the Japanese was either en route or upon arrival, and many briefings reflected the sort of objections senior officers threw at Wards: the Japanese were not mechanically inclined, they could not see well in the dark, they floundered without a fixed plan or senior leaders, on and on. For every soldier that dismissed this as a "load of rubbish," several others lapped it all up. The army did not expect to be fighting an opponent more efficient than itself.[57]

Far East Command went even further. In a note to Brooke-Popham in June, Darvall evaluated the threat of Japanese air attacks. His calculations of their range and bomb load were much too low. He did not realize the range of their combat aircraft made it possible to attack southern Thailand and Kota Bharu from bases in southern Indochina. When Percival submitted a draft of his appreciation of what he needed to defend Malaya, Far East Command argued it was too pessimistic. The Japanese could not maintain a heavier scale of air attack than the Germans or British. It was wrong to assume the threat of American intervention would not seriously distract them. The Soviets would pose enough of a threat to contain Japanese forces even if "Germany succeeds in knocking out Russia quickly," and most incredibly of all "the Japanese must expect that we shall manage to produce a number of heavy ships in the Singapore area within sixty to ninety days, and so cause a serious deterrent to the Far East position. They must also expect that we shall find a means of reinforcing the air force, particularly bombers."[58] Anyone who could seriously argue by this time that the Japanese would be deterred by the prospect of reinforcements–knowing full well they were not on the way and there might be serious consequences if the Japanese attacked first–can only be seen as complacent at best.

Nothing shook that complacency. On 18 August an FECB appreciation on the warning time to be expected before any attack argued that as the most the Japanese could spare was three divisions "Japan would scarcely contemplate an attack on Malaya with so small a force." But that is exactly what it prepared to do. The report concluded the situation would need to be reconsidered if "Japanese forces in Indochina should reach the proportion required for the invasion of Malaya" and "If aerodromes in Southern French Indochina should be lavishly stocked with bombs and petrol." This did provoke a response. Brooke-Popham told his intelligence chief "I consider that the most valuable information of a Japanese intention to attack Malaya would be the establishment of modern long range aircraft particularly fighters on the aerodromes which they have taken over in southern Indochina." Long-range fighters and bombers were the most obvious indication of a possible attack, because they were the units that could most rapidly be concentrated when they were needed.[59] Yet the alarm bell remained silent. The shortage of British sources in the area plus careful Japanese security did have an effect– but the now deeply entrenched assumptions had even more.

The evaluation of Possibilities of the Japanese Attacking in the South on 8 September summed up the strength of ethnocentrism and mirror-imaging at Far East Command. Assuming "Japanese military teaching is based very largely on German instruction" and student would behave as did teacher, but not as effectively, the paper estimated the most the Japanese could deploy to support an attack on Malaya was 250 to 300 aircraft–and given the respect they must have for the RAF "they would all have to be the best."[60] The actual figure turned out to be twice as high–and they were. The conclusive signal was sent by the high-level meeting in Singapore on 29 September, advising the Prime Minister the Japanese were more likely to strike north than south, and not likely to attack at all before the monsoon ended in early 1942. That was such a fantastic misreading of Japanese intentions and capabilities that it can only be seen as negligence. For Malaya Command it translated into the expectation there would be no attack before February–and when they did come the Japanese would advance methodically, by the book. Such calculations influenced everything: training schedules, intensity, plans, and above all expectations. On 21 October Percival chaired a meeting at which FECB and GHQ Far East representatives briefed Malaya Command senior officers. The FECB representative gave an indecisive and ambiguous briefing on recent Japanese moves. To "clarify" the situation, the GHQ representative gave a far more confident presentation pretending to be a Japanese staff officer brieing the Emperor, one which left the impression "the Japanese were in no position to attack Malaya at this time or in the near future." Ashmore was certain this had a profound effect on the officers listening–the day after Japanese naval attack plans received first approval.[61]

It is easy to cite examples of British mistakes about the Japanese or sound warnings not heeded. The point is to explain why intelligence failed so badly, why as one expert put it the Japanese achieved "surprise despite warning."[62] Structural problems did have some effect. Despite FECB's status as the apex of the intelligence network it still remained very largely a naval organization; as a result it did not pay enough attention to the problems of other services. Brooke-Popham asked for but never received a trained air intelligence officer. SIS was especially weak, never having enough agents, especially in Indochina, to meet requirements to watch airbases and ports.[63] But these things paled in comparison to the weight of the great consensus that infected London and dominated Singapore: the Japanese were not likely to move, at least not soon; even if they did the American threat would divide their forces enough to salvage the situation; and anyway they were not formidable enough to annihilate the forces on hand before help could arrive. This can all be brought out in sharper relief now that we know a good deal more about the last component: signals intelligence.

By 1941 the GC &CS network in England that read intercepted German messages–codenamed Ultra, the word for copies of decrypted messages circulated to those on a very small list–was doing so well its product became an integral part of the central direction of the war. But signals intelligence had advantages and disadvantages. Its greatest advantage was that one could tap into the unguarded conversations of an enemy unaware his traffic was compromised. The disadvantages included the danger of relying too heavily on access to traffic you might suddenly be shut out of, and the difficulty of circulating information to all who might need to know without compromising the source and therefore turning off the tap. Not surprisingly security was emphasized and circulation severely restricted. This sometimes caused skepticism about warnings derived from signals intelligence disguised as something else. That excuse does not hold for GHQ Far East, which was in the loop. By 1941 interception units in England, Australia and Singapore were working on Japanese signals, and there was growing co-operation with the Americans. As a result a good deal of Japanese naval and diplomatic traffic was being read, enough to make it the most reliable source of intelligence by the time the real crisis began in July.[64]

Intercepted traffic gave the British some insight into the shift of Japanese attention to the south and the ongoing debate in Tokyo. A message to Japanese diplomats in Singapore in April was the first signal of close interest, followed by one in May directing the Consul-General to escalate subversive activity. It was known as early as 23 June that the Japanese "intend in the near future to occupy Indochina," thanks to "most secret and reliable information" taken from the Germans. An intercept on 4 July spelt out in some detail the decision to move south, including the resolve to go to war if necessary. Such information certainly had some effect on the JIC in London. In April they correctly identified the shift in Japanese attention, in May they accurately forecast Japanese operational intentions. Everybody wavered a bit in August and September, possibly due to events on the Eastern Front, the possibility the Japanese would decide to exploit them by stabbing the Russians in the back, and the conviction with which GHQ Far East pressed that argument.[65] But the flow of signals intelligence soon became so grim there was no reason for those in the loop to remain unmoved.

In October two vital messages were intercepted: orders to recall the Combined Fleet two months early from its maneuvers at sea and orders to all Japanese consuls to provide immediate detailed information on all Western naval and air movements. By now FECB received intercepts from the Japanese Consul in Singapore, regarding subversion and local defences, on an almost daily basis. Unambiguous warnings were soon received. First, there were intercepts of two messages to the Japanese Consul in Singapore—on 7 November, warning that the last Japanese merchant vessel to visit Singapore would leave on the 16th, and on 11 November, telling him to return to Japan without relief. They were reinforced by a report on 13 November by the British Consul in Saigon that some 50, 000 Japanese troops had moved through the area within the month. Finally, interception units in the region warned that the IJN was changing all its call signs after only three weeks instead of the usual six months.[66] This convinced FECB to warn that war was imminent on 18 November. The JIC and the British Embassy in Tokyo had already drawn that conclusion. But Brooke-Popham still insisted, on 10 November, that the Japanese would only enter Thailand if they thought it would not provoke war with the West. He then sent what must now be seen as that inexplicable message to the COS on 27 November, deprecating any early attack on Malaya–and both Malaya Command and Churchill still thought war would not come before February 1942.[67]

These revelations only emphasize the point, but do so dramatically: the British military system, in both London and Singapore, completely failed in 1941 to appreciate Japanese capabilities, and failed to appreciate Japanese intentions until it was far too late–in spite of having enough information to at least warrant some reconsideration. After reading the intercept about the Imperial Conference of July, and after the Japanese move south that same month, anyone who believed they could still safely assume the Japanese would not attack in 1941 was not being prudent. The most dramatic example of this general failure was the case of the Zero fighter. Reports were received in Singapore in May and September, based on tests of Zeros captured in China, which gave clear warning of its impressive performance. Senior officers in Singapore were also aware of the limitations of their own Buffalo and their half-trained pilots. And the Zero was identified by Brooke-Popham himself as the weapon to watch for any indication of a Japanese attack. Yet days before war broke out the C-in-C assured journalists his fighters were "good enough for Malaya." The message did not get through. Darvall has been identified as the villain, but this is too simple. The hard truth is that the British military system from the Prime Minister on down believed what it wanted–what it needed–to believe.[68]

The contribution the Japanese made to this self-delusion brings out its most important cause. The Japanese did not concentrate their forces for an attack south until the very last moment. This helped fool the British because the British were looking for the Japanese to behave the same way they would– moving methodically, making full logistic preparations, taking care of the flanks first, taking no serious risks. Reinforcing this was the almost desperate desire to avoid war with the Japanese. The effect was to justify the tendency to play for time: we are not ready for them yet, so they will not come yet, and we will interpret our intelligence accordingly. This did far more damage than the lack of intelligence officers, or the shortcomings of those on station. On 24 November the Director of Military Intelligence (DMI) at the WO criticized Brooke-Popham's appraisal on the grounds "he discusses what Japan *ought* to do, while we, in addition, considered what she *may* do." But he then argued it was still only possible Japan might be "forced into war," a "mad dog act." The DMI sent Far East Command weekly intelligence summaries all through this period. The summary for the week ending 10 December appraised the Value for War of the Japanese Army. Five pages of detail included many warning notes about Japanese strengths, but also suggested it was weak in minor tactics–where in fact it excelled–could be careless on the flanks–which might cost it against "a more virile opponent"–and reached the following conclusion:

> The Japanese Army is a formidable fighting machine but probably has not yet reached the efficiency of the major western armies. It is, however, trained for and will probably only be required to fight in Eastern Asia where it will have inherent advantages over an opponent.[69]

With a few exceptions, the British simply could not bring themselves to believe the Japanese would dare attack the Western Powers. More than underestimating the Japanese, the British badly overestimated themselves. The armed forces defending Singapore prepared for war on the assumption they had a margin of both time and quality in which to work. They were wrong.

The main reason the Japanese escaped similar intelligence failures was because they were better prepared for war, especially in Malaya. The Japanese operated a formal intelligence system similar to other powers. Japanese signals intelligence was not as effective as their adversaries, although they did receive useful information from both the Italians and the Germans. They also made up for this by other means, especially by tapping into the large pool of Japanese citizens living and working abroad. From at least 1936 Japanese regular and irregular intelligence operatives were directed to gather as much general information as possible about the "Southern Area," including Malaya and Singapore.[70] But they were also hampered by assumptions ranging from racial to ethnocentric and by rivalries, especially between the intelligence brances of the armed services. A reasonably accurate picture of enemy intentions and capabilities was developed by late 1941. But this had more to do with good luck, timely moves and an ability to work effectively under pressure than with any deeply entrenched, smoothly organized espionage machine.

The first really important product of timely moves and good luck stemmed from an October 1940 decision to share intelligence with the Axis partners.

That same month a fast merchant vessel sailed alone for Singapore carrying important secret documents. Italian signals intelligence detected the departure of the SS *Automedon* and passed the word to the Germans. A German surface raider sank her in the Indian Ocean on 11 November; a lucky shot knocked out her bridge crew before they could destroy their most important cargo, allowing the Germans to seize the pouches. They passed the windfall on to the Japanese. Included in it was the defining paper on grand strategy and the defence of the Far East, the Far East Appreciation. This confirmed Japanese suspicions about gaps in British defences in the Far East, and was soon reinforced by reports from Japanese agents in London indicating how low the region had sunk in British grand strategy.[71] Knowing the RN was in no position to sortie east, and the RAF would be hard pressed to replace it, underpinned all subsequent Japanese decisions.

The idea the Japanese intelligence machine in Malaya and Singapore was omnipresent, flawless and subverted better behaved democracies needs to be re-evaluated, for three reasons. First, it did not provide the armed forces with all they required when the need arose. Second, it enjoyed an advantage caused by British policy, not by its own ability. Finally, it was not the only player in the "great game." Those who lived through the fall of Singapore on the losing side believed forever that the Japanese planned the attack down to the last detail over many years. The Japanese military disagreed. They complained about going to war badly short of accurate maps, felt British counterintelligence made it difficult for Japanese operatives to do their job, felt they knew very little about conditions in Johore and not enough about defences in Singapore, and later claimed "The best sources of information for Malaya and Singapore were British and Australian newspapers and magazines, far better than any loose talk sources." The big problem here was how rapidly the Japanese moved from being generally interested in the area to preparing earnestly to attack it. Without a serious war plan there was no incentive to collect all this miscellaneous data on roads, bridges, railways, climate, etc. in an organized fashion useful for staff planners. Before the end of 1940, nobody in Tokyo tried to pull this activity together. Much ground was then made up, but some gaps were left unfilled. Twenty-Fifth Army did not know the ground as comprehensively as the defenders later thought it did.[72]

A very valuable advantage handed to the Japanese was the appeasement policy practiced by the authorities in Singapore. British officers would have been surprised to hear the Japanese felt impeded by their security because the military was by 1941 beside itself at the Governor's refusal to take strong action against ever more provocative Japanese behaviour. The police Special Branch began in 1939 to get a decent grasp of the extent of Japanese espionage emanating from Singapore, but ran into immediate obstacles. The colonial government took British policy to avoid war as licence to prevent any friction with the Japanese. A feud between Major K.S. Morgan, running the Japanese section of Special Branch, and Col. Hayley Bell, station chief of MI5, the military head of security and counterintelligence in Singapore, interfered so much with counterintelligence work that Bell was ordered home in May 1939, probably due to a lobby by the Governor. A lot of potentially useful intelligence did not circulate, and the Japanese were not impeded as they might have been. In November 1940 FECB saw a golden opportunity to steal a cipher machine being sent to the Japanese Consulate and copy it before it could be missed. The Colonial Secretary vetoed the operation. Such misguided policy allowed nearly 300 Japanese agents in the region, 62 in Singapore alone, to ferret away. By November 1941, 163 of them were on a "Black List" of known Japanese agents and sympathizers, set up by FECB at least a year earlier. Nearly all were merely watched; the government would not move unless London took the gloves off.[73]

It is now also possible to strip away the sanctimony surrounding Japanese espionage and subversion. The prevailing impression is that Japanese tin mines, pineapple plantations, photo studios, barber shops and bordellos all over Malaya and Singapore were organized in a strategic conspiracy to keep an eye on all military installations and sensitive areas, and every Japanese was part of a well prepared spy ring. This is wrong, but only because it is exaggerated. The Japanese certainly did make extensive use of expatriates and there were cases of barbers turning out to be majors, but it was not as systematic as the British thought. That helped the Japanese, because the less formal structure of their covert activities partly fooled British counterintelligence—which, mirror imaging, was looking for something more like itself.[74] It also entangled the Japanese with British organizations trying to do the same thing, for the same reasons.

In July 1940 the British government established the Special Operations Executive (SOE), a covert organization hidden in the Ministry of Economic Warfare. Its mandate was to carry the war to the enemy by conducting sabotage and subversion, and organizing, equipping and leading underground resistance groups. After months of discussion it agreed on 1 March 1941 to establish a branch in Singapore. Instructed to work "in close co-operation with" GHQ Far East and the local government, the new Oriental Mission (OM), led by Valentine St. John Killery, was ordered to prepare covert activities, including operations in Japanese occupied territories and "stay behind" parties in British areas that might be overrun. Killery, who soon gained the splendid cover name 0.100, went out in April with a budget of £50,000 and the good will of the Prime Minister. He ran into a wall of skepticism, rivalry, bureaucracy, and obstruction from Singapore to Shanghai. Along the way, as the paper trail now makes clear, the British were every bit as active as the Japanese in using expatriates, including other Europeans, for covert operations. Killery himself had formerly been Chief Representative in the Far East of Imperial Chemical Industries. His mission was scouted in advance by A.E. Jones, travelling under the cover of his regular job with the Asiatic Petroleum Company. By autumn 1941 the "great game" was in full play in Southeast and East Asia, and it is doubtful there was a major corporate or merchant office not involved one way or another.[75]

The real action settled on Thailand and Malaya. The Japanese cultivated contacts with Malay nationalists and infiltrated agents across the border. But they put stronger emphasis on cultivating Indian nationalists, especially in Thailand. In October Major Fujiwara Iwaichi was sent to Bangkok to set up F.Kikan, an organization ordered to use nationalist contacts to subvert Indian troops in Malaya. Fujiwara did not have much time but had abundant energy, good contacts and a well chosen target.[76] The Thai government concluded the Japanese were more dangerous but still clung to neutrality. This led to such confusion that no one, including the Japanese, could be sure whether the Thais would fold or not, and as war approached they stepped up pressure on the Thais to co-operate. Japanese officers working undercover were allowed to wander all over Thailand gathering information without official hindrance. They frequently ran into British officers doing the same thing in preparation for *Matador*.[77] On top of Crosby's obstruction, Killery failed to win the confidence of Percival, Brooke-Popham and Layton, which further weakened SOE efforts. In July Killery asked Percival to support preparations for irregular operations. Percival finally refused in October. Many in the high command felt the covert operations program contradicted the policy to avoid war with Japan and threatened their own resources. Lt.-Col. A.G. Warren, Royal Marines, went out with Killery to help develop special operations. He visited many regular units and laid the groundwork for training for irregular operations, including No. 101 Special Training School at Jurong, on Singapore island. But Warren could not overturn Brooke-Popham's veto on organizing "left behind" parties in Malaya. SOE battled against the tide. By November it was barely ready to assist *Matador* and could do little in Malaya, let alone Indochina. Warren, with some foresight, was organizing an escape route that would later prove useful. The ultimate responsibility lay in London, which did not clarify how covert operations should be reconciled with avoiding war. Indeed, the only time Foreign Secretary Eden gave any direction was to support Crosby against SOE.[78] The only beneficiary of this confusion was the Japanese. Having clarified their national policy, they were able to prepare covert operations to assist their landing in Thailand and advance on Malaya much more effectively than such British operations could threaten them.

The final gift handed the Japanese was the reluctance to interfere with their "tourist" activities, including blatant overflights, in Malaya. Darvall did once suggest shooting down overflyers, but the policy to avoid war intervened. Tsuji exploited this to make personal reconnaissance flights over northern and central Malaya. The Japanese might have thought they would face one squadron each of Hurricane and Spitfire fighters in Malaya, and that a large battlefleet was assembling in the Indian Ocean. But their overall estimate of the size and composition of Malaya Command and RAF Far East was pretty accurate, and the arrival of Force Z was deliberately advertised. The Japanese had a decent idea of what their enemy had ready, and were not impressed:

> The ground forces in these territories are essentially native armies formed around a nucleus of white troops, which constitute about 30 per cent of the forces. They are not well trained and their combat ability is generally below standard. However they are inured to tropical weather and climate. We must also remember that their planes perform well and their pilots are quite good.[79]

This was more accurate than the British appraisal of the Japanese. In intelligence, as in training, the Japanese rapidly parlayed a starting position not focused on Malaya, but rather sound in general, into an effective appreciation of the enemy, the theatre, and the intangibles. It would pay off.

There is no doubt the war in Europe was the most important reason Singapore was so vulnerable by December 1941. But this is not enough to explain the problem. Nor was the fact the Japanese knew where and when they were going to strike decisive, given how late they made their final decision, how rushed their detailed preparations were, how much warning the defenders had available. The British got the most important policy decision right and the Japanese got it wrong: what kind of war to fight against whom, and with whom. But the British military system was the main factor that turned probable defeat towards possible disaster. This reduces the importance of individuals to a more realistic level. Churchill did not untie the defence of Singapore knot with the same ruthlessness he showed to keep the nation fighting against Germany–but he had good company. Percival did not challenge the mission or the directives that compromised his army. But had he done so he would just have been replaced. Yamashita may be likened to the driver of a racing car climbing into an already prepared vehicle, to steer the machine to victory. The most crucial difference lay right there. For all its fatal blindness in national policy, the Japanese military system was about to do something the British could not then envisage, let alone cope with.

The British suffered "surprise despite warning" because they did not anticipate the kind of war their enemy was ready to fight. Even when it became obvious the Japanese were about to invade Thailand, the high command in Singapore still believed they would not charge into Malaya because the wet ground of the monsoon season would make it too difficult to consolidate lines of supply. Reinforcing that view was the estimate that airbases in southern Indochina could only hold some 250 aircraft–in fact correct–not enough to support an advance into Malaya. Surely no one would launch a distant offensive before their supply lines were secure and their air support was fully concentrated in forward bases? But that is exactly what the Japanese were about to do: bounce right through southern Thailand and move their air support up at the same time the spearhead pierced into Malaya. They were going to take calculated risks from grand strategy to minor tactics and fight at maximum tempo, the "driving charge," until they swept into Singapore. The gamble of taking on the Americans made this one seem small change by comparison.

British unreadiness to cope with that kind of warfare was more than an intelligence failure. It was an indictment of a system that could only wage war by predictable grand strategy, methodical strategy, and set-piece tactics. That approach was already discredited in France, the Balkans and Africa. The Far East was only part of a larger pattern. This was the last British Empire force to go to war using the prewar military system–an echo, if you will, of an approach to war already being reconsidered at home. It is tempting therefore to see the problem as the system being overwhelmed by the pace of events. This would mislead. The British Empire had been thinking about the defence of Singapore for two decades. When the test came its defences were, relatively speaking, weaker than ever. This can not be written off as the misfortune of having to face the worst possible scenario. Because the military system could not respond effectively to changing circumstances, intentions and capabilities, Singapore was always vulnerable.

The fate of Singapore now rested almost entirely on the Japanese. This was not inevitable. Nothing in war is. What combatants do face however are margins of victory and error. The Japanese were criminally reckless to think they could prevail against the Americans. But their preparations for war gave them a very large margin of error in Malaya. On the other side, the British turned their decision to rely on the Americans from the calculated risk Churchill saw it as to the gamble it was in the Far East. They could not steel themselves to make ruthless political choices, such as invading Thailand as a tactical imperative, or freeing the army to fight its own battle. But it took such ruthlessness to give the British any real chance to hold Singapore, as things now stood. The real issue was now how long it would take the Japanese to conquer Singapore, and at what price. The root cause was the military system that tried to make the situation fit the plan and the battle fit the doctrine.

The Four Crippling Blows

On 1 December 1941 Malaya Command went on full alert and volunteer forces were mobilized. But the next afternoon Force Z steamed into the naval base at Sembawang, welcomed by a blaze of publicity. The arrival of capital ships provoked general delight. Even as they berthed however, 12 Japanese submarines took up patrol stations in the South China Sea, to screen their invasion forces. Those forces reached the coast off Kota Bharu shortly before midnight on 7 December, and off Singora about three hours later. Almost exactly a month later, in the early morning of 7 January 1942, a 5th Division battlegroup charged down the trunk road to assault 11th Indian Division at Slim River. Their attack exploded into a rampage that tore two brigades apart, dispersing their remnants into the jungle. This cleared the road to Kuala Lumpur and open country, barely 70 km to the south. That left the defenders no choice but to break contact and make a strategic retreat to the southern state of Johore, guarding the approaches to Singapore. The Japanese "driving charge" won the race, placing Singapore under the gun before reinforcements strong enough to keep them at bay could arrive.

The damage was done by four crippling blows. The first blow was the failure of all prepared defence plans. Within a week the Japanese won control of the sea, dominance in the air, overran the border and beach defences and seized the initiative on the ground. The second blow was the relentless Japanese "driving charge" in the northwest, pressing so hard they hustled the defenders into headlong retreat without being able to regroup. The third blow was failing to devise a new strategy to stop the onslaught. The final blow was failing to handle the Japanese in battle, which undermined everything else. The root cause of these blows was identical. The Japanese fought by taking calculated risks at every level, advancing at maximum tempo; the defenders simply could not adjust to the tempo, at any level. The Japanese advance exposed the terrible dilemma inflicted on Malaya Command by the contradiction between its role in grand strategy and the realities on the ground. If it retreated to regroup, the Japanese would cut Singapore off. If it stood and fought, it would be defeated in detail. Left to fight alone, it floundered indecisively while the chain of command tried to resolve the clash between an obsolete mission and a compromised army. They failed. This guaranteed Singapore would fall.

7

Plans Up in Smoke

Both attacker and defender showed some boldness in the first battle, the invasion of Thailand and Malaya. But while the Japanese acted decisively, British moves were erratic and indecisive. Japanese forces assembled off the southern tip of Cambodia as late as possible under the cover of bad weather, changing course to steer towards their targets at the last moment. It worked. The main force went undetected until 1300hrs on 6 December, when a Hudson flying out of Kota Bharu spotted it steaming towards Malaya, less than 300 km away.[1] London and Singapore now realized war was imminent. Signals intelligence intercepts indicated Japanese forces were preparing to move, and the breakdown of talks in Washington was ominous. Coming to the same conclusion, President Roosevelt finally on 2 December assured the British that if the Japanese attacked them or the Dutch "we should obviously all be together." This typically offhand comment by the President was rightly regarded as the long sought guarantee of American support. The COS duly authorized Brooke-Popham on 5 December to launch *Matador* on his own authority, if the Japanese attacked any part of Thailand or Allied territory or he was certain they were en route to do so.[2]

Despite the signals intelligence pointing to invasion, Phillips obeyed an earlier order to fly to Manila to confer with his American opposite number. *Prince of Wales* was immobilized for a boiler repair, and *Repulse* left on 5 December to visit Australia. This dispersal meant the new Eastern Fleet could not respond instantly to the Japanese approach even if ordered to. As for Brooke-Popham, the sudden authorization he sought for so long instantly transformed itself in his eyes into a hot potato. Brooke-Popham found it convenient to be swayed by panicky telegrams from Crosby urging him not to be first to violate Thai neutrality because this would provoke stiff resistance, and by warnings from his staff the COS "have now made you responsible for declaring war." Given the situation Phillips behaviour was inexplicable. Brooke-Popham has even less excuse. His whole plan depended on the very authority he now enjoyed–and tactical imperatives forced the British to risk Thai resistance if they wanted to pre-empt invasion. The lame duck C-in-C would not respond decisively even though he should have known Crosby's concerns were irrelevant. On the other hand London's behaviour was just as remarkable. The JIC concluded on 5 December the Japanese fleet was at sea, and the Admiralty had already urged Phillips to make sure his squadron was not caught in Singapore by a sudden attack. But no one gave him a direct order to return and prepare it for war forthwith.[3] The British were still waiting to be forced into war, even though they had Roosevelt's assurance and their own plans rested on pre-empting invasion.

We will never know what would have happened had Brooke-Popham responded to the first sighting report by acting decisively: ordering an immediate all-out air attack on the Japanese troop transports, urging Phillips to intercept the enemy, and ordering 11th Indian Division to launch *Matador* immediately. There is absolutely no chance he would or could have. There were two reasons: his own confusion and caution, and the sluggish and uncoordinated manner by which the British war machine adjusted from expecting months of warning to dealing with hours. Phillips could not respond because his fleet was dispersed. Brooke-Popham did not move because he decided the Japanese were trying to bait him by feinting an attack towards Thailand. By now the risk they would actually invade and thus ruin all his plans was far greater than whatever consequences there still might be from moving first, but the C-in-C was paralyzed with indecision. He found it "pertinent to record that, until the Japanese had committed some definite act of hostility against the United States, the Dutch or ourselves, permission had not been given to attack a Japanese expedition at sea." This was absurd, but still no orders came from London demanding instant action. Brooke-Popham sat tight, ordering Pulford to keep contact with the Japanese. But his aircraft lost them in more bad weather, which allowed the Japanese to get close enough to be confident they could no longer be intercepted. At 0900hrs on 7 December they separated, to make simultaneous attacks on southern Thailand and Kota Bharu. British aircraft regained contact in the afternoon; one Catalina was shot down, making its crew the first casualties of the war. But the sighting report did not reach Brooke-Popham until 2100hrs. By then it was too late to reach Singora first. But that made it even more vital to block The Ledge, and an attack on Kota Bharu had to be expected. Brooke-Popham informed London shortly before midnight "have decided not to operate *Matador*" because he still felt this might be a feint, but if not the plan was now redundant anyway. Yet incredibly he only ordered Malaya Command to postpone *Matador* until further notice, leaving 11th Indian Division in limbo, and made no move to prepare an air strike or press the navy. This all guaranteed the Japanese would not be resisted until they actually hit the shores. That meant the air plan was already dead, the navy could only intervene after the fact if at all, and *Matador* was out of the question. That left Brooke-Popham only one sane option: scrub *Matador*, advance on The Ledge immediately, and get ready to fight at Jitra. Instead he went to sleep, having passed on the hot potato.[4]

The Japanese landed at Patani virtually unopposed, but the landings at Singora and Kota Bharu suggest the defenders missed a priceless opportunity to do what their plans envisaged: exploit the confusion of amphibious landings to hit the enemy hard. Yamashita's main force off Singora expected to be guided by signal lights flashed by comrades at the Japanese Consulate. But those officers started a party to celebrate the outbreak of war, fell drunk and slept through their mission. It took more than three hours to load the assault troops into landing craft, nearly half those craft ran aground or foundered in very choppy water—one platoon actually turned tail and deserted out to sea—and the landing dragged on well into the afternoon before a beachhead was secure. Thai troops resisted sporadically until mid-afternoon. Their government gave deliberately vague orders, trying to deflect the Japanese as much as possible. But it gave in to pressure and accepted de facto Japanese occupation that same day. Sporadic local resistance petered out pretty quickly. The rough weather did impede Japanese air support, but its prompt arrival would have been very necessary to secure the landing had there been any Allied resistance. As it was air units were setting up at the airfield even before the Thais gave in. 5th Division untangled itself without serious interference and organized a battlegroup to advance towards the Malayan border.[5]

The supporting landing at Kota Bharu, the first significant battle of the campaign, was a different story. The Japanese prevailed but paid a serious price; the battle suggests why the defence plans failed immediately, and why that was so important. Always worried about this assault, the Japanese made one final modification by deciding to concentrate their initial landing in one sector: along the Sabak beach just east of the key airbase at Badang, closest to the coast. This proved decisive. The choppy water delayed and disrupted the assault loading from "the finest liners in Japan" into the landing craft long enough to sicken many Japanese troops and give the defenders ample warning.[6] 8th Indian Brigade spotted the threat at 1145hrs, began to engage with 18 pounder beach defence guns soon after, asked for air support shortly after 0100hrs, and by 0200hrs five Hudson bombers of No. 1 Squadron RAAF at Badang were in the air.[7]

The Japanese first wave was pushed off course by rough seas. But an officer in the van recognized town lights and the streams of the estuary breaking up the beaches, where Badang met Sabak, and opted to press straight in. The Takumi Detachment numbered some 5500 troops. Reinforced by one battalion loaned from 22nd Indian Brigade, plus two static battalions guarding airbases, Key had nearly that many himself. But the long coast to defend, with airbases so near, forced him to leave two battalions in reserve and spread the other two out to the breaking point. The defences consisted of a chain of concrete pillboxes strung along the beach every several hundred metres, with a second line of machine-gun foxholes some distance behind covering the gaps in between, protected by mines and barbed wire entanglements. The Japanese described them as "extremely strong." The battle erupted around the pillboxes, especially two held by A and B Companies of 3/17 Dogra Regiment [3/17 Dogra]. Each company held a sector five kilometres long. Fighting was intense but the Japanese concentrated in numbers to overwhelm the defenders and establish a foothold. The Australian airmen threw everything they had at the invaders, with some success. One transport was so badly damaged it eventually sank, two others were damaged, and the Japanese were hard pressed to land their second wave before retiring out of danger as planned, after dawn. This retreat by the supporting vessels, plus the prolonged close quarter fighting around the beach, persuaded Key the situation was not yet perilous. He passed this up the chain of command at 0725hrs, describing a counterattack to retake a pillbox "... hell of a scrap but anticipate recapture."[8] Bad weather, dispersal, airpower and confusion were already combining to prove him wrong.

Heavy rainfall after daybreak made it harder for Allied airmen to find their targets offshore and, crucially, delayed counterattacks to restore the situation behind the beaches. Key tried to concentrate a strong two battalion attack once he was confident the beaches to the south would not be hit, but due to swollen creeks and dense undergrowth only two companies arrived in time to intervene. Only one of Kota Bharu's airbases was fully manned so at dawn Pulford had to send in five squadrons from Singapore, Kuantan and Alor Star to reinforce the attacks made by the bombers on station. One unit failed to find the enemy; others, especially the torpedo bombers, arrived too late to hit worthwhile targets and found themselves very hard pressed by Japanese fighters. Seven heavy Japanese air attacks made matters worse. The air force, despite heroic efforts by No. 1 Squadron RAAF which flew itself into exhaustion, was simply too dispersed and outgunned to accomplish its most vital mission: find and hit the transports while they were still full of troops. The torpedo bombers, most feared by the Japanese, could not even attack at night. Percival sent 4/19 Hyderabad from the command reserve to help but it did not arrive until early the next day. Because Key could not rapidly concentrate a strong counterattack the Japanese grew too strong to repel; his attacks appeared to them to be platoon sized pin pricks.[9] By late afternoon, the fog of battle set in. There is a persisting story: someone told Pulford that Badang was under attack by enemy infantry, the AOC duly ordered all aircraft flown away, but the base was abandoned in panic when an unknown officer ordered it evacuated. All agree the ground crew left without completing the vital task of denial, leaving runways usable and large stocks of petrol and bombs intact. And Key, Station Commander C.H. Noble and Wing Commander R.H. Davis, commanding No. 1 Squadron RAAF, confirmed by personal reconnaissance that enemy infantry were not yet attacking the base. But the war diaries tell a rather different story. Noble reported to Pulford around 1600hrs that Badang was under attack. Half an hour later RAF Far East ordered the denial and evacuation of all three bases. There was in fact no ground attack until nearly six hours later. 1st Hyderabads then had to fight for their lives, mounting at least two bayonet charges before being driven into the jungle by superior force. Along the way their commanding officer and adjutant went missing, probably murdered by their own men when they tried to stop the retreat.[10] The Japanese completed their landing the night of 8/9 December. Key was authorized at 2045hrs to withdraw his brigade when he deemed necessary, rather than see it destroyed at Kota Bharu. With the airbases lost, there was no reason to stand fast. 8th Indian Brigade moved south to regroup on 9 December, conceding the coast and bases to the enemy.[11]

Kota Bharu was a serious setback for the defenders of Singapore. The Japanese suffered some 800 casualties, many while trying to land, one of their heaviest tolls of the campaign. The dedication of the aircrews shows what might have been achieved had the air plan had the muscle it needed. But the rest of the air force was simply too far away to intervene when needed. When it did arrive it was outnumbered by superior Japanese fighters. Worse, concentrating on Kota Bharu diverted most of RAF Far East away from the main force that really should have been its prime target, at Singora.[12] Key was well placed to conduct a stubborn fighting retreat through a long stretch of difficult country; had the bases at Kota Bharu been properly destroyed, its loss need not have been disastrous. But they were not, which allowed the enemy to press them rapidly into service. The losses the Takumi Detachment suffered did not shatter it, while the distraction it provided helped the main force settle in. Key fought an energetic battle and had the right idea trying to concentrate for a counterattack with real punch. But terrain, weather and distance all hampered his efforts to respond, just as they compromised his force to begin with. Malaya Command could not help in the short time in which the battle was decided, even had Key told them immediately he was in trouble, because the position was simply too distant. Noble was not responsible for the panic evacuation but could not prevent it. That plus the murder of the Hyderabad officers raised doubts about discipline under pressure. Defeat at Kota Bharu was caused by several problems, but they all surfaced in a hard fought battle ending in a controlled retreat. This was a clear warning of the consequences of relying on the air plan. If such problems undid the defence here, their effect in more difficult conditions was bound to be worse.

Those more difficult conditions were already at hand. RAF Far East not only failed to cripple the invaders before they landed, it was defeated in less than 100 hours. This was not due to any reluctance by the aircrew to engage. Four things did the damage: the power of the enemy, the tempo and relentlessness of his assault, the dispersal of the defenders, and their general unreadiness for war. Pulford had 181 serviceable aircraft the day war broke out, 79 of them Buffalo fighters. The Japanese had nearly 600, more than 200 of them first-class fighters. Rapid seizure of the Thai airfields allowed them to bring some aircraft forward immediately, while those striking from Indochina assembled en masse long before they reached the target. Japanese bombers attacked in numbers, ranging from nine to swarms of more than 60. They hit Singapore three hours after the landing at Kota Bharu began, catching it unprepared despite at least half an hours warning provided by the radar network.[13] But nearly all their initial effort was concentrated on the airbases in the north, to win control of the air. Using over 200 aircraft the Japanese hammered the northern airbases repeatedly for the first three days. Bombers were reinforced by fighters strafing at low level, both careful not to target runways they hoped soon to use. Norgroup was blasted from one base after another. An eyewitness summed up its ordeal on 10 December:

> The following day found Butterworth Aerodrome a graveyard of burnt out and damaged aircraft, comprising Blenheim Mk. I and IVs, Buffaloes, of the following squadrons Nos. 34, 62, 27 and 21. No. 34 Squadron had no maintenance crews at Butterworth, and aircrews were responsible for refuelling, bombing up, dispersal, and affecting temporary repairs to their own aircraft, and in some instances other units aircraft. This was carried out by the flying crews amongst whom were several ex-tradesmen. It was decided to evacuate aircraft from Butterworth at 11 o'clock, and 33 flying crews of the unit returned to Tengah in the six aircraft that could fly.[14]

Pulford's command simply was not ready for war at this tempo against an enemy this tough. Buffalo pilots found themselves fighting a more experienced enemy–flying faster and more maneuverable aircraft able to operate at long range–and fared badly. Aircraft were so scarce the 68 serviceable bombers, as well as some fighters, were pressed into reconnaissance service as well. Not once in these first crucial days did RAF Far East manage to press home an attack by more than 10 bombers.[15] Pulford had to remind units to concentrate on troopships, something that should have been self-evident. Singora was not finally singled out as the priority target until reconnaissance confirmed that a force of more than 20 ships was unloading there, early on the morning of 9 December. The order that was already too late went out at 1010hrs:

> Confirmed maximum striking force Blenheim bombers load with G.P.s [general purpose bombs] to leave Butterworth and to proceed up West Coast out of sight Mainland and then cut straight across to Singora. Attack military target Singora. Return by any best route. If attack really successful repeat best dose quickly.

They would be joined by six bombers flying up from Tengah. But after a full day of being roughed up in the air and on the ground, Norgroup could only promise to send up six Blenheims "with fighter escort if possible." The disarray was indicated by a signal from the Station Commander at Alor Star:

> Situation appears to warrant evacuation in near future. Where do we go and what armament etc. will be available. Propose sending serviceable aircraft to Butterworth as soon as runway is serviceable. Do we demolish or is Station and aircraft and equipment left behind in the event of evacuation.

No one expected to be forced into retreat by air attack alone. Few had any idea when the full denial of a base was necessary or how to go about it. Pulford could only reply "When situation warrants it demolish all you can and get away with all you can to Butterworth."[16] Meanwhile the "maximum striking force" came to grief. There were no fighters available so the bombers went in alone. The six from Tengah attacked the target where "lots of aircraft" were already deployed and ecountered perhaps 40 fighters, who shot down three of them. The six from Butterworth were caught preparing to take off and shot up. Only one survived. Squadron Leader Alan Scarf pressed on and attacked Singora. Japanese fighters shot him up repeatedly, forcing Scarf to make an emergency landing at Alor Star. Rushed to the hospital where his wife was working as a nurse, he died before she could donate her blood to try to save him. Such suicidal bravery earned Scarf a posthumous Victoria Cross, but gallantry alone could not even up such bad odds.[17]

The other end of the spectrum came out under pressure when airbases were evacuated, especially at Kuantan and Alor Star. Kuantan was simply abandoned by all but a small demolition party, in an evacuation senior officers "did not consider it necessary that the general movement from the Station should have been made." From then on it could only be used as a forward staging point. Alor Star was blown up literally behind 11th Indian Division, preparing to defend it at Jitra. This shook the troops so badly Percival persuaded Pulford to order on 11 December:

On account of disastrous affect on morale when demolition of aerodrome is ordered, buildings and petrol are not repeat not to be fired. Buildings should be broken up as much as possible and petrol allowed to run to waste.

This of course made it impossible to deny facilities properly. As a result at least four bases were left as valuable gifts to the enemy when evacuated in haste.[18] Nothing went right for RAF Far East in this first battle, and it never recovered. Norgroup was reduced from 110 operational aircraft to 55 in one day, many destroyed on the ground. Some of those losses were connected to treason at Alor Star, helping the Japanese catch the defenders when they were most vulnerable, loading aircraft with ammunition and fuel.[19] Bases further south were safer, but from there it was harder to attack a fleeting target such as invasion shipping. Pin prick attacks had no chance in daylight to avoid crippling losses, especially when fighter escort could not be arranged. With the Buffalo force reduced to 43 serviceable aircraft in three days, this was unavoidable. FECB reported as many as 100 Japanese fighters already moved up into Thailand on 10 December. By the end of 11 December Pulford was forced to restrict his bomber force to night attacks and pull his squadrons south to regroup. The Japanese could hit hard in great numbers covered by their strong fighter forces, but he had to conserve his command—or there would be no protection for the crucial bases at Singapore and future reinforcement convoys.[20] Within four days the air force lost its main battle without ever being able to engage in strength. Inferiority in numbers was one reason, lack of training and preparedness another, flawed intelligence a third. But pulling them all together was the tempo and ferocity of the Japanese onslaught. RAF Far East sagged under such pressure. That left the army more compromised than ever. Now it had to fight its crucial first battles without air support, from positions dictated by the need to protect the very bases the air force had just abandoned.

An even more spectacular defeat ended the sortie by the senior service to attack the enemy invasion forces. After the initial sightings of the Japanese fleet, HMS *Repulse* and Phillips both rushed back to Singapore and the crew of *Prince of Wales* hurried to complete repairs. But the fleet could not be made ready for sea before the afternoon of 8 December, too late to intercept the Japanese. This certainly came as a relief to the enemy: "The whereabouts and movements of the battleships *Prince of Wales* and *Repulse* ... were of grave concern to all forces engaged in the initial landing operations in Malaya." Japanese aircraft overflew Singapore; submarines rearranged their patrol line to keep watch.[21] Meeting Brooke-Popham and the Governor on the morning of 8 December, Phillips found himself in a tight spot. It was too late to pre-empt invasion, but his force could do great damage to Japanese efforts to build up ground forces if it attacked transports unloading offshore. On the other hand if it were caught by superior surface forces, or attacked by strong enemy air forces without fighter cover to keep them at bay, it could be destroyed. That would give the Japanese uncontested control of the South China Sea, allowing them to launch more invasions anytime they liked. This was ominous given the news coming in from Hawaii. The attack by the Combined Fleet on the US Pacific Fleet at Pearl Harbor was a major defeat for the Allies. The Americans lost eight battleships sunk or badly damaged and suffered over 4000 casualties. The full extent of the battle was not then clear to authorities in Singapore, but they were aware the most important assumption of all plans for imperial defence against Japan might already be ruled out: the Americans might not be able to absorb or deflect Japanese power. The most sensible strategic move would have been for the Eastern Fleet to sail to safer waters around Java. There it might combine with other Allied naval forces, out of range of Japanese air attacks, to pose a threat as a "fleet in being," menacing the Japanese by its proximity. This was the very course of action Churchill and Pound were considering in London. But tradition tipped the balance. The reputation of the navy, hard won over centuries, made it unthinkable to leave the army and air force to fight in Malaya without trying to help, just as it went against the grain to avoid an engagement at sea. Such a move could really only come after a direct order from London, as an act of grand strategy. The Governor did suggest consulting London first, but time pressed. Phillips decided the fleet must intervene before the Japanese progressed too far. Hearing no veto from London, Phillips took his capital ships and four destroyers to sea late in the afternoon of 8 December, aiming to attack Japanese transports in the early morning hours of 10 December.[22]

Deciding to intervene was one thing, how Phillips did so quite another. Phillips is still sometimes criticized for being blind to the menace posed by airpower to surface ships, because of some controversial arguments he made before the war. This is not entirely fair. The hard lessons of Norway, Greece, Crete, and the RN's own success at Taranto had had their effect. Phillips was aware it would be difficult to survive attacks by strong air forces without fighter cover, being rightly especially worried about torpedo bombers. He decided to attack only if he could catch the enemy by surprise, asked for reconnaissance ahead of the fleet as it moved north, and for fighter cover off Singora on the morning of 10 December. Unfortunately he sailed before Pulford could fully respond; that led to avoidable problems. One thing Phillips did lack was recent command experience at sea, indeed sea time period. He was unreasonably committed to total radio silence at sea, unaware this would do his fleet more harm than good. The Japanese were not very good at detecting positions by intercepting signals, and he would be unable to work out problems in co-operating with the air force, or responding to sudden developments, if he remained silent. Both these situations did arise. Because of the hammering it was taking in the north, RAF Far East could not promise fighter cover for the intended attack. Only one squadron was designated to support the fleet. It should have gone up to Kuantan if not Kota Bharu, but the attacks on those bases forced it to stay in Singapore. Phillips was of course informed of all this but carried on anyway, without reply. This left both Pulford and his own chief of staff, Rear Admiral A.F.E. Palliser, left behind in Singapore, unsure where he was or what his intentions were. This meant they might not be able to help the fleet if it suddenly ran into trouble. The fleet was spotted by Japanese aircraft in late afternoon. Knowing he was compromised Phillips carried on until after dark, then changed course and headed back towards Singapore.[23] But a few hours later a sudden development changed everything.

Units of 22nd Indian Brigade defending the beaches at Kuantan were in a jittery mood that night. They were rattled by the heavy air attacks on, and panicky evacuation of, the nearby airbase, plus air reconnaissance reports of barges and a large vessel approaching from the north. Around the same time Phillips was changing course, Indian gunners spotted what they thought was a Japanese force attempting to land and started firing. The contagion spread, and soon several artillery and machine gun positions were firing at suspected contacts. These reports, tending to confirm each other, went up the chain of command, reaching Malaya Command and RAF Far East around 2200hrs. Some officers on the spot began to doubt there was in fact any attack, but without anything to gainsay the reports authorities in Singapore assumed an invasion was underway. Pulford dispatched nine bombers to engage; two crashed into each other on takeoff, the other seven found no Japanese and returned. Two fighters sent at dawn to reconnoiter confirmed there was no enemy force attacking Kuantan. Unfortunately however, while the original report of an invasion in progress was sent to the fleet around midnight, the subsequent reports were not. Phillips not surprisingly decided to change course to intercept the apparent invasion.[24] The fog of war then set in.

Phillips believed Japanese torpedo bombers were no more effective and had no greater range than their British equivalents. He assumed that off Kuantan he would be safely out of range. He was wrong. The Japanese torpedo bomber, the Nell, was the finest in the world. Its range allowed it to go all the way to Singapore if necessary and its weapon was the best then in use. The squadrons of 22nd Naval Air Flotilla were among the best trained in the IJN and were on his trail. Unknown to the British fleet, it was first spotted in the early afternoon by a patrolling Japanese submarine, whose report ignited an all-out response:

> The entire naval force, which was returning towards Camranh Bay, was ordered to intercept these battleships ... Steps were taken to retire transports and other vessels which might hinder a naval engagement in the Gulf of Thailand. The plan of battle ordered by the Commander-in-Chief of the Malay Force and confirmed by the Commander-in-Chief of the Southern Force, was to maintain contact with enemy battleships by aircraft and submarines throughout the night and, at dawn, to attack the enemy fleet with the entire strength of the naval air force. Surface units were to coordinate their actions with the air force attack.

The British narrowly missed bumping into the force of cruisers and destroyers covering the unloading at Kota Bharu. Shortly before that, another Japanese submarine spotted the British force moving towards Kuantan, made a failed torpedo attack the British never even detected, and shadowed it. Kondo concluded his fleet could not catch the enemy before they came under air cover from Singapore and broke off that pursuit–but also ordered his submarines and the entire 22nd Naval Air Flotilla to destroy the British capital ships. Phillips played into their hands by dawdling off Kuantan after dawn, then turning north to investigate the reported transport and small barges, a mission one destroyer could have dealt with. This proved fatal. The Japanese aircraft missed him on their sweep south, but one scout plane spotted the British around 1015hrs, just as they were completing their search of the empty barges. Ten squadrons, with 52 torpedo and 33 medium bombers, moved in to attack just after 1100hrs.[25]

Phillips drove the final nails in his own coffin by observing radio silence. No one in Singapore knew where he was. The C-in-C probably assumed Palliser would anticipate the fleet to respond to the reports from Kuantan– not an unreasonable assumption. But that meant Phillips would have been expecting fighter cover off Kuantan when he arrived. He should have been told no invasion was detected, but he should also have realized something was wrong when he saw neither enemy force nor friendly fighters. Then Phillips made things worse by maintaining radio silence even after the Japanese air attack began. That made no sense whatsoever, and doomed his fleet. The capital ships and three destroyers fought hard, and *Repulse* fought well. But their anti-aircraft guns alone were no match for such a heavy attack. Both battlewagons were badly damaged by torpedoes within an hour, finally provoking an exasperated Capt. W. Tennant of *Repulse* to radio for help at 1158hrs. Pulford received the message at 1219hrs and immediately ordered his fighters aloft. No. 453 Squadron had all 11 Buffaloes in the air within six minutes. It was too late. *Repulse* sank at 1233hrs, *Prince of Wales* at 1320hrs. Japanese aircraft did not interfere with efforts by the destroyers to rescue survivors and flew off when British fighters approached just as *Prince of Wales* was going down, taking Phillips and the last remnants of the "Singapore strategy" with her. At a cost of three aircraft, the Japanese won total control of the South China Sea.[26]

This was a catastrophe for the defenders, immediately recognized as such. Churchill wrote "In all the war I never received a more direct shock" and reflected with horror there were now no Allied capital ships between India and Hawaii: "Over all this vast expanse of waters, Japan was supreme and we were everywhere weak and naked."[27] Layton resumed command of an Eastern Fleet that was again reduced to three vulnerable old cruisers and some destroyers, knowing full well there was little he could now do to defend his base. The impact on Singapore and Malaya was devastating. Percival became more concerned than ever about possible invasions at Kuantan, Mersing, even Singapore, which made him unwilling to redeploy forces from those positions. The Governor called it "a grim day." Tan Kah Kee, a leading local businessman who organized activities supporting Chinese resistance to Japanese operations in China, "could not sleep a wink all night" and was even warned he should leave Singapore while he could. George Rocker, Veterinary Officer for the state of Selangor, vividly expressed the reaction of the general public:

> Over the wireless to Ipoh and to Kuala Lumpur, to London and to New York, and belting the whole world, came the outrageous shock from Singapore. Christ! The *Prince of Wales* and *Repulse*, both sunk by Japanese airmen! Both? Incredible! The clubs and the hotel bars were silent that night. Our complacency was sunk too; vanished as completely as our proud ships.[28]

The causes of this defeat remain controversial. It was the first time in history capital ships at sea were sunk by air attack alone, which added to the shock. Churchill and Pound were extremely busy, reacting to the attack on Hawaii, trying to arrange an early conference on grand strategy with the Americans, watching a Soviet counteroffensive in Moscow and the ongoing battle in North Africa. They did not get around to dealing with this problem—as clearly they should have. The Buffaloes may not have saved the fleet—or they might have interfered with the lethal torpedo attacks, which had to be made by straight runs at low level, enough to do some good. In any case there was no excuse for not doing everything possible. The Japanese were determined to destroy the two ships and certainly would have hunted them down, but why make it easy for them? Phillips made the cardinal mistakes, and his conduct during the battle was inexplicable. But this was also another example of the failure of a military system–a failure produced by poor intelligence plus the inability of London, Singapore and the commander at sea to respond effectively to the tempo of the enemy onslaught. The Admiralty reverted to its plan to build up a larger force of older ships to cover India, and began to abandon the defenders of Singapore to their fate.[29] Yet incredibly no one raised the question of whether Percival's mission to hold the naval base–hold, not deny– should be reconsidered. Meanwhile Percival's army, deprived of naval and air support, was still compelled to protect bases that could not be effectively used. Suddenly it was now saddled with full responsibility for stopping the enemy before he could isolate Singapore. But even as the capital ships sank, Malaya Command was already engaged in the battle that would destroy its slim chance to accomplish that mission.

It all started with Brooke-Popham's monumental mishandling of *Matador* and went downhill from there. The C-in-C simply was not prepared to make a command decision. By telling London late on 7 December the operation was impossible, but keeping 11th Indian Division in a holding pattern, he clearly sought to be supported or overruled. GHQ Far East then asked whether they were authorized to advance if Kota Bharu was attacked but Thailand was not. This underlined how completely Brooke-Popham failed to grasp the tactical imperative to at least block The Ledge, and how intimidated he still was by the idea of making the first move. As late as 1040hrs on the 8th Percival was told to be careful about sending scouting forces into Thailand because Thai intentions remained unclear–but *Matador* might still be done, in which case caution could be set aside. But GHQ Far East already knew there were Japanese forces at Singora unloading from at least six large transports, having been so informed by air reconnaissance at 0915hrs. Brooke-Popham never in fact terminated *Matador* at all. Percival was briefing the legislative council on the outbreak of war and only returned to headquarters around 1100hrs, when he finally took the initiative to issue orders that reached 11th Indian Division around 1330hrs: stand down from *Matador* and move into the defensive position at Jitra. Yet this still did not end the confusion. At 2000hrs Percival "told General Heath that *Matador* Operation was NOT definitely off. He was to try to hold on in the forward area for a day or two if possible." The definitive statement came only at 1015hrs on the morning of the 9th when Percival finally told Heath he "could regard *Matador* operation as off and rolling stock held for that could be released."[30]

The release of the rolling stock points to an issue long misunderstood: Percival's role in this fumbling. Percival went on record after the war as follows. He first anticipated *Matador* would be ordered on 6 December;

discussed it with Brooke-Popham on the evening of 7 December, noting with implied disapproval the C-in-C would not move until the political issue was clear; realized on the morning of 8 December it was too late and dealt with that as fast as possible; but was then unpleasantly surprised to hear 11th Indian Division was so disrupted by the change of orders, because it waited for so long with troops and equipment concentrated at assembly points in the vehicles or trains they would use to advance. Percival insisted the division had no business being so concentrated. It should have been ready at short notice to either advance or move into the Jitra position, so the disruption it suffered was its own fault.[31] Percival was certainly right to blame Brooke-Popham for losing the plot but overlooked his own contribution. The Malaya Command war diary records:

6.12.41.–1510hrs.–Order *Matador* standby issued verbally by GOC to 3 Ind. Corps.

6.12.41.–1520hrs.–Order that trains for *Matador* were to standby issued verbally by GOC to Comd. 3 Ind. Corps.

7.12.41.–2135hrs.–GOC spoke Comd. 3 Corps re *Matador*.

7.12.41.–2200hrs.–BGS spoke BGS 3 Corps. GOC now going to Naval Base where decision on *Matador* would be taken. GOC hoped notify Comd. 3 Ind. Corps by 2300hrs.

7.12.41.–2315hrs.–GOC telephoned from GHQ. Decided <u>NOT</u> to order *Matador* tonight. Immediate telegram being sent to HMG asking what action we should take in event of Thailand asking for help. 3 Ind. Corps to be informed and to have *Matador* ready for dawn 8/12 if ordered.[32]

The orders of 6 December were unambiguous: "get ready for *Matador*." The orders of 7 December imply an expectation it would proceed, especially the emphasized "not" at 2315hrs. Heath made his own contribution: at 2330hrs on 7 December informing Movement Control preparations to operate *Matador* should be complete from dawn the coming morning; complaining at 0814hrs on 8 December no news from Thailand was bad news and asking to be allowed to commence SOE demolitions (permission he received an hour later); informing Movement Control at 0925hrs *Matador* "is again a possibility." These were equally unambiguous directions to prepare to advance.[33] Not surprisingly, given how Murray-Lyon emphasized the whole plan, 11th Indian Division responded accordingly. Its history claims that shortly after hearing the enemy was at Singora, on the morning of 8 December, Murray-Lyon urged his superiors to stand the operation down. But at the time it was poised waiting to advance–and had been for nearly two days. The 15th Indian Brigade war diary is terse but clear for 6 December: "*Matador* ordered." That of 2nd East Surreys spells out the experience of the whole force:

> December 7th   At 1600hrs the alarm was sounded. Company Commanders reported to the Commanding Officer, who issued his orders, which had been written and carefully prepared for weeks. The contents of these orders were: The Battalion was part of a force (6th Indian Inf. Bde.) which was to advance into Thailand on orders. The 1/8 Punjab Regiment, with a Battery of 22nd Mountain Regt. were to move forward to Hadyai. After its capture, our Battalion was to move forward through the 1/8 and proceed to Singora … The object was to hold Singora.
>
> 2000hrs. With these objects in heart, the Company Commanders left the Commanding Officer, and saw the Companies loading their vehicles, and all awaited for the final word to move.
>
> December 8th   At 0600hrs the Commanding Officer sent for Company Commanders and informed them that the Japanese had attacked Khota Baru and fighting was in progress, but we were still 'standing by.'
>
> 1500hrs. Orders were received to occupy our Defence Positions on the Jitra Line.[34]

One of the assumptions of all plans to defend the Empire was that if a crisis arose commanders on the spot could respond effectively. Perhaps the thinking was that contradictions and complications which could not be resolved in peacetime could be cut through when hostilities cleared away the fog of politics. Brooke-Popham's dithering exposed that as false from the start, but his supposedly clearer-headed subordinates only made matters worse. If 11th Indian Division was the force on which the main battle would turn, then the GOC Malaya Command had no excuse for not knowing exactly where it was, how it was disposed, and what it was ready to do. There is no mitigating factor to identify here. An advance that required half its combat force to move forward on a train was tactical folly to begin with—even token Thai resistance would have cut the railway and imposed fatal delay, to an operation as tight as *Matador*. 11th Indian Division now had to dismount, untangle and move back. That would all take time and even worse would be discouraging, given how much emphasis was placed on the advance. At the very least it should have been moving late on the night of 7 December, under orders from headquarters aware of its situation. It took another 14 hours for those orders to come from commanders who did not know what they should have. These considerations were about to play a very negative role in the battle the division now had to fight—and that was not even the end of the bad news.

The most glaring blunder of that crucial 24 hour period after regaining contact with the approaching Japanese fleet was the failure to block the road from Patani. If the Japanese moved down that road they could outflank 11th Indian Division, opening up all northwest Malaya. Brooke-Popham's dithering affected this operation as well. The only place the road could reliably be blocked, The Ledge, was about 40 km north of the border, but nearly twice that distance from Patani. By 0930hrs on 8 December commanders in Singapore were told Japanese forces were spotted in Patani. But Percival only lost patience and finally took it upon himself to order the advance at 1320hrs. And this force was also already compromised. First, for some unaccountable reason Heath delegated responsibility for it to Murray-Lyon, who already had his hands full and could not control such a distant force. Co-ordinating widely separated battles was a job for a corps. Second, an even worse blunder was made arranging the battlegroup designated for the operation. The Ledge was a stretch of the road carved precariously along the edge of a steep hill for several winding kilometres; it could easily be blasted away to carry half the hillside with it and wipe out that stretch of road, imposing many weeks delay at least. The rest of the road was not nearly so easy to hold, especially against tanks. The battlegroup was named Krohcol because it would start from the town of Kroh, on the Malayan side of the border. But half its force, one infantry battalion and one artillery battery, was in Penang on garrison duty and would only move up when so ordered. That order only came on the afternoon of 8 December, so of course they did not arrive in time to join the initial advance. Krohcol essentially came down to one battalion, 3/16 Punjabi, with some artillery and engineer support, ready to move when the order finally came–10 hours after the Japanese landing began, four after the British knew of it for certain.[35]

Krohcol advanced across the border at 1500hrs but promptly halted when its lead scout was killed by a sniper and the column engaged by 50 or so Thai police. By the time it decided to stop for the night it advanced only three kilometres. The next day, over "difficult ground," ie. wet roads, but against "little opposition" other than a clash between the reserve company and a police patrol, this battlegroup led by some 800 infantrymen managed another five kilometres. Meanwhile the rest of the force, led by 5/14 Punjabi, finally arrived at Kroh. At 0730hrs the next morning, 10 December, 3/16 Punjabi mounted the trucks that brought up the rest of the force and drove to the 33 kilometre marker. That brought them within six kilometres of The Ledge, so they debussed to advance to contact. Shortly after 1800hrs A Company made contact with the real enemy, led by tanks. The first one was hit by a round from an anti-tank rifle and fell back, but the race was over. In the last training exercise before war broke out two and a half hours were allotted to reach the target. It took 51 hours of the real thing for the defenders to fail, leaving the Japanese on The Ledge.[36]

3/16 Punjabi and its supporting gunners grappled with Japanese tanks and infantry all the next day, but the damage was done. It was compounded by confusion started by the force commander, Lt.-Col. H.D. Moorhead of 3/16 Punjabi. Moorhead asked for permission to retreat because "there are too many slit eyes around here," but gave the impression he was fighting on The Ledge itself. Murray-Lyon agreed, assuming Moorhead could still damage The Ledge and fall back to protect his own flank. Unfortunately Krohcol never reached it, enabling the Japanese to bring forward two battalions supported by at least one tank company. They attacked at 0830hrs on 12 December. By 1505hrs Malaya Command heard that Moorhead, having been attacked by "overwhelming numbers," had decided to fall back to Kroh, "which he considers to be his last ditch. There he proposes to hold out to the last man." 5/14 Punjabi was duly engaged while 3/16 Punjabi regrouped; by dusk the enemy were pressing the frontier. On 14 December the whole force fought off more attacks but late that evening gave up Kroh and retreated south, relieved by 12th Indian Brigade.[37]

This was another major setback for the defenders, on three grounds. First, failure to blow The Ledge allowed the Japanese to press into Malaya by the interior road. This compromised the main position at Jitra by threatening its flank. Second, failure by everybody from Brooke-Popham to Murray-Lyon to make sure the force was ready to go exposed yet again how the defenders could not cope with the tempo of the battle thrust upon them. Heath admitted to being stunned at how fast the Japanese moved south from Patani along difficult wet roads.[38] Finally, the feeble performance of the force, especially against the Thai police, raised another fundamental issue. Another assumption on which much was based was that if push came to shove the ground troops would fight well. If all else failed ministers and generals would be rescued by the "poor bloody infantry." Moorhead's mission was so important he should have used his overwhelming advantage in numbers to sweep the Thais aside and press on. Instead, unnerved by the absence of half his force and uncertain who was opposing him, he used set-piece assaults to minimize casualties. This took so much time he lost the race, making it all pointless. Nor did his infantry show any particular ability to fight off Japanese tanks and infantry, instead leaning heavily on their artillery support. 3/16 Punjabi were not so much shattered as scattered, by aggressive Japanese infiltration in close country. The Japanese now had two strong forces converging on the Perak River, forcing the defenders to divide their forces if they wanted to stand north of it. If the chain of command could not radically improve its sluggish performance the army would have to continue fighting on bad terms. And if the infantry could not fight more effectively in close country, then it would lose badly and quickly. And all those problems had already unfolded where it mattered most: at Jitra.

Murray-Lyon had much to contend with. His flank on the Kroh road was shaky. A steady tropical downpour hampered his men's efforts to complete their positions and compounded their frustration at being put on the defensive. The collapse of his air support left him naked and blind, all to face the onrush of an enemy coming faster and harder than expected. In spite of all that, one analyst could still reasonably describe what happened at Jitra as "... the biggest disgrace to British Indian armies since Chillianwala in the Second Sikh War of 1848."[39] Jitra was without a doubt the most incompetently fought battle by a British Empire division in the Second World War, and the most decisive of the Malayan campaign. The Japanese boldly exploited the predictable confusion of battle, especially at night, to make their own luck. The defenders could not cope with that confusion, the tactics of the enemy and the tempo of his attack.

The first serious failure came from the division's officers. They let their own disappointment over *Matador* affect the mood of the troops. News of the loss of the capital ships and the heavy defeats suffered by the RAF drove morale even lower, as did the explosions at Alor Star airbase. Japanese air attacks on the ground forces did no great physical damage but made them feel vulnerable. One gunner remembered the Japanese flying so low the troops could see the faces of the pilots, making him think "We were in deep trouble and we knew it." Drenching rain kept filling trenches and fighting positions, soaking hard working troops.[40] Inexcusably, its officers allowed 11th Indian Division to fall into a funk of self-pity before being seriously engaged.

Advancing to screen the debarking at Singora was the Saeki Detachment, consisting of 5th Division's reconnaissance battalion, a tank company and some engineers–500 troops in all. Joined by Tsuji, they were ambushed by an 11th Indian Division screening force on the Thai side of the border, shortly before midnight on 8 December. After a brief scrap the screening force fell back as planned. This small clash gave the Japanese the impression their enemy was feeble, plus a valuable intelligence success when they discovered a map of the Jitra position and outposts in an abandoned armoured car. The British for their part were impressed by how fast and efficiently Japanese infantry responded to the ambush. Worse, division headquarters did not pay enough attention to the fact the Japanese had medium tanks right up front.[41] Tsuji persuaded Yamashita to allow the vanguard to press on before the lead infantry regiment was ready to support it. The defenders blew up bridges to delay the Japanese, but Saeki's men regained contact shortly after crossing the border early on 10 December and drove off another delaying force. Tsuji was so unimpressed he sneeringly concluded "We now understood the fighting capacity of the enemy. The only things we had to fear were the quantity of munitions he had and the thoroughness of his demolitions." There and then the "driving charge" pressed forward. Five hundred men with two dozen tanks and some light guns charged south, nearly a full day ahead of the main force, towards three brigades with nearly 15,000 troops, supported by more than 50 field and 36 anti-tank guns, occupying a defensive position worked on for months.[42] In the end more weight was needed to complete the job. But the audacious charge of the Saeki Detachment scored three crucial successes that unhinged the whole defence.

Murray-Lyon made this possible by letting the enemy defeat his forces in detail. By 10 December he had three brigades to deploy, Heath having sent up 28th Indian Brigade from corps reserve. The plan was to rely on two companies of 1/14 Punjabi to delay the enemy, but unit commanders told Murray-Lyon the main defences would not be ready for another two days. To gain the necessary time Murray-Lyon increased the outpost force to two full battalions. 1/14 Punjabi deployed at Changlun, 12 km north of the main position, supported by a battery of light guns and a section of anti-tank guns, while 2/1 Gurkhas dug in behind a causeway over a stream just north of Asun, five kilometres above the line of defences. That line was held by 6th Indian Brigade on the left, covering the area from the coast to just west of the road junction at Jitra, 15th Indian Brigade on the right, holding from the junction to the jungle hills on the eastern flank, and 28th Indian Brigade in reserve. But one of its battalions had to cover the airbase at Alor Star, while both forward brigades had no reserve after the outpost force was increased. Two converging roads had to be covered, forcing the defenders to divide their anti-tank guns. To prevent Japanese spies from mapping the position some areas were not wired before war broke out, and gaps still remained as the enemy approached. There was not enough infantry to cover the blind spot: the two copses of vegetation near the main road and between 1st Leicesters on the left and 2/9 Jats on the right. So they were held only by a minefield and two anti-tank guns, covered by the fire of nearby platoons.[43] Trying to hold such a long line, with only two battalions in reserve, forced Murray-Lyon to bank on three assumptions: outpost forces would buy time well and fall back in good order; the enemy would attack on his left in the open paddies; the main force would pin them down there, allowing the artillery to win the battle by driving them off.

At first all went well, as desultory fighting broke out on the morning of 11 December and 1/14 Punjabi fell back in the afternoon. But they only damaged an important bridge, allowing enemy tanks to advance quickly. Unaware of this, still worried the main position was not ready, Murray-Lyon changed his mind and ordered them to stage another delaying action north of Asun. They marched back towards the selected position in rain so torrential visibility was almost nil. At 1630hrs the Japanese tank column drove head-on into the Punjabis, their anti-tank guns still being towed along the road. The battalion was literally overrun, scattered into the bush or sent down the road in headlong retreat. The Japanese pressed on, smashing into the Gurkhas at the Asun causeway. A heavy fight erupted when engineers tried to blow it up. The infantry pressed boldly into swamps on the flanks and forced the Gurkhas back, allowing the tanks to resume the advance. They then combined with the infantry to overrun Gurkha headquarters, scattering the whole unit by nightfall. More than half the two battalions were simply lost, most later rounded up and taken prisoner, because they were caught off guard by tanks on the road, or could not cope with infantry pushing through tough country to get between and behind their positions.[44] Murray-Lyon's gamble blew up in his face because the Japanese were better at improvising on the move. They made their own luck by moving forward alert and ready for anything, just as 11th Indian Division asked for it by moving ponderously despite knowing the enemy had tanks in the vicinity. The main position was not yet engaged, but the moment of decision was already at hand. The battle rested on whether the British could force the Japanese into a set-piece slogging match, or cope with whatever the enemy tried to unhinge their positions and ignite a battle of maneuver.

The third key victory scored by the Saeki Detachment was seizing the two copses of vegetation near the main road, including an important observation post used as the principal spotting point for supporting artillery. Impressed by the weight of such artillery brought down against their attack on Asun, Tsuji and Saeki worried they might now suffer for outrunning the main forces if the defenders mounted a heavy counterattack. But a report brought back by Second Lieutenant Oto from a reconnaissance patrol convinced them the safest thing to do was continue to attack. Oto found some unwired gaps between the strongpoints and indications that not all positions were occupied; a rapid advance before dawn could penetrate between the defences. Oto had in fact found the lightly held area near the two copses of vegetation. He led his company into the attack at 0300hrs.[45] That set off a fight which unfolded exactly as the Japanese desired: a rolling melee spilling out between and around the prepared defensive positions.

Confusion in battle and the disruption of plans is so commonplace it must be expected as a given. What matters is how one responds. The reckless attack on a much larger dug-in force succeeded because early morning darkness, fire support from tanks, and failure to hold the copses properly allowed a follow-up company to take that vital ground. Using its cover, the Japanese overran the one platoon of 2/9 Jats close enough to protect the artillery observation post. This severely disrupted the provision of fire support. The small Japanese vanguard carved out a wedge astride the main road, right in the very heart of the whole defensive line. The battle was then decided because the Japanese correctly identified the decisive point, this fight around the main road, and concentrated effectively to win it–whereas 11th Indian Division frittered away its strength by one piecemeal move after another. Intense fighting all morning provoked Tsuji to rush back to summon help. He met 41st Regiment and directed it to march to the sound of the guns. Its artillery engaged first, then its lead infantry battalion arrived and waded into the fight around 1330hrs. This relieved the hard pressed Japanese vanguard and threw fresh troops in against 2/9 Jats, just as the heaviest counterattack the defenders were able to mount began.[46]

Murray-Lyon on the other hand responded to the attack by deciding the battle was already lost and trying to disengage altogether. Influenced by reports of trouble from Krohcol, concerned by the disappearance of his two outpost battalions and the resulting dearth of reserves, especially affected by the threat posed by enemy medium tanks, at 0830hrs he asked for permission to break contact and retreat at least to Gurun, some 50 km south. This amounted to abandoning the only prepared defensive position, and the only defence plan still in play, before the main force was even fully engaged. This was a difficult decision for Percival to make. On the one hand the airbases near Alor Star were already being abandoned and the Jitra position was only adopted to protect them. The information available at the time suggested, wrongly, that the whole right flank of the defence line was under serious pressure–stragglers from the outpost battalions were being confused as enemy moving to attack. The division might well be pinned down in a battle that, if lost, would open up the whole northwest. Murray-Lyon was also the man on the spot. On the other hand such a drastic retreat without mounting a determined defence would send a dire signal to both troops and civilians. It also meant giving the initiative to the enemy. Percival ordered Murray-Lyon to fight it out.[47]

Unfortunately, 11th Indian Division could not fight at Jitra any kind of battle other than the one for which it somewhat reluctantly prepared: keeping unimaginative enemy frontal assaults at bay in the rice paddies by employing superior firepower from intact positions. What Murray-Lyon heard about the situation by mid-morning was enough to suggest only a battalion strength counterattack could check a threat which could rip his whole linear defence open along the road. But rather than hit back immediately by throwing all companies near the enemy wedge into the fight, and sending in a full battalion of the reserve, he kept trying to preserve all his positions and the "integrity" of his "line." Nearly half the infantry of 6th Indian Brigade was siphoned off one company at a time to cover the extreme right flank, plus bridges to the south. A mid-morning counterattack by two 1/8 Punjabi companies sent in from reserve ran into a platoon dispatched by 2/9 Jats on the same mission. The two forces engaged each other. The reserves took so long Japanese reinforcements arrived first, while the Leicesters, much closer, followed orders and sat still, fighting off all who approached them.[48] Murray-Lyon's failure to get a grip when it mattered most comes through clearly from his own statements. At 1240hrs Malaya Command were informed:

"Picture was somewhat brighter than painted in previous report. There had been considerable infiltration; in particular 100 Japs were into the tactical gap on the right. Five or six tanks were in vicinity of Prisoners of War cage. Comd 11 Div thinks that he can clear up Japs who are themselves in a difficult position."

But when the two Punjabi companies moved forward to do just that their mood was so grim Murray-Lyon remarked "I haven't seen that look on men's faces since March 1918," referring to one of the worst defeats the British Army suffered on the Western Front.[49] In mid-afternoon he ordered the Leicesters to pivot on their left and pull back on the right, just like a door opening inwards, in order to restore contact with the Jats and Gurkhas, now grappling with enemy penetration into the rubber. Having been penetrated the line would be restored, reshaped as a right angle. The Leicesters would counterattack next day to drive the enemy back. It would have been better to order them to right wheel and counterattack immediately, but that meant giving up "the line" to pitch into a full scale brawl. The division simply was not ready to fight that way.[50]

Considering that Murray-Lyon had officers scouting a defensive position at Gurun even before he was engaged at Jitra, it is fair to say he was never confident about fighting it out there.[51] The Japanese were impressed by the strength of the Jitra line after they took it, especially by the firepower of the defending artillery. But they also noticed how reluctant enemy infantry were to come to grips when they could not rely on it. The Japanese could improvise effectively at a moments notice, for instance finding the anti-tank ditch across the main road and using it as cover to charge D Company of 2/9 Jats. But 11th Indian Division seemed unable to march to the sound of the guns. Minor probes kept whole companies fixed in their positions, out of the decisive fight.[52] The reference to "the tactical gap on the right" can only indicate higher command was aware of that danger spot near the road junction. But the afternoon battle of 12 December suggests the division never considered how to fight it out at Jitra if the enemy managed to penetrate in between positions, rather than try to charge through them. By 1737hrs Murray-Lyon was telling his superiors "he still has some cards left in his hand and things are never as bad as they seem." Minutes later he was caught up in a panic as transport units stampeded, spooked by close range artillery and machine gun fire on the road. Murray-Lyon started preparing a full retreat then and there, only later appealing to Percival that his troops were exhausted and under great pressure from fresh forces in superior numbers. That meant disengaging with the enemy entangled in the midst of friendly positions and retreating at night down one road, under enemy fire, with much of the force still uncommitted on the left. But waiting till daylight risked fresh infiltration and heavy air attack, and by now the division staff were convinced the troops were too tired and shaken to wait. Percival agreed at 2030hrs and the move began.[53] What ensued was a rout.

The disruption of communications caused by Japanese penetration was the main cause of the rout. 11th Indian Division relied on dispatch riders to pass messages and transmit orders. Radio sets were notoriously unreliable in wet weather, phone lines were often cut, riders intercepted by enemy infiltrators. In such a fast moving situation it was difficult to keep in timely contact with subunits on the battlefield, let alone III Indian Corps and Malaya Command. When the retreat began at least three companies were out of touch and left behind. 6th Indian Brigade had little trouble but the 15th came apart. When the main body of 2/9 Jats reached Tanjong Pau camp at 0400hrs on 13 December it was ambushed by Japanese machine guns: "In the melee which ensued in the darkness the battalion became disintegrated among the buildings, drains and slit trenches of the camp and a sauve qui peut ensued." 1st Leicesters and other units lost men, vehicles and guns on the wrong side of rivers, when bridges were blown prematurely or enemy infiltrators forced them off the road. At 0900hrs 2nd East Surrey were ordered to take up a defensive position at the bridge at Alor Star to cover the retreat; they noted "The road was now almost packed with troops and vehicles moving south, with apparently no control." Murray-Lyon fainted from fatigue, but by 0930hrs was back on his feet and at the same bridge. Suddenly three Japanese on motorcycles roared impudently across; the leader drove through before the division commander and his staff shot the other two.[54] This summed up the mess. Murray-Lyon delayed blowing bridges, hoping to organize an early counterattack, but the Japanese followed up hard, forcing the division to break clean. As stragglers poured in, they were collected and driven all the way back to Gurun. 2nd East Surreys war diary called it "a pitiful sight." Nothing went right for the defenders. Relying on the weight of an armoured train to finish demolishing a bridge, instead it leapt the gaps blown in the span and ploughed on. Not until the early hours of 14 December could some semblance of control be pulled together in front of Gurun, much of Kedah having now been lost. 15th Indian Brigade was down to perhaps 400 men. The division was "a shadow of its former self" having lost half its fighting strength, more than two dozen guns, and great quantities of ammunition and supplies.[55]

Jitra was the most important battle Malaya Command ever fought. What it lost there were three things it could never recover: time, the initiative, and confidence. The battle reflected the ground campaign at large. The defenders relied on forcing the Japanese to fight on their terms: set-piece battles resting on superior firepower. Things would not move fast enough, nor generate enough confusion, to disrupt communications or require much improvisation. The Japanese sought instead to provoke fluid encounter battles, which would keep the defenders on the move and offset their larger numbers on the ground. Control of the air helped, as did the aggressive use of tanks. They unnerved an army led by officers who absorbed scare stories from Europe about fighting an enemy stronger in both. But the key factors were bold and effective use of first rate light infantry by one side, against cumbersome movements ending up in piecemeal counterattacks by the other. 11th Indian Division later assumed it was engaged by men specially trained in infiltration; it was partly right, because Yamashita's whole army was trained in this patently obvious tactic.[56] It is hard to imagine the British attacking a division on the strength of an oral report by a subaltern in the middle of the night, but all too predictable they would send in a platoon to "restore the situation" at the decisive point in the battle. 11th Indian Division was not so much overrun as dispersed; 75% of the at least 3000 casualties it suffered at Jitra wound up prisoners of war, while stragglers drifted back to friendly units for many days after. Murray-Lyon noted very early the Japanese tendency to "walk round any flank through any country." But his diagnosis "this makes adequate reserves necessary for protracted defence and calls for the utmost staunchness by all" suggests no intention to do anything other than fight it out around fixed positions. The division history summed up the crucial blow at Jitra very well: the enemy followed the recipe of a famous Confederate cavalry commander in the American Civil War, Nathan Bedford Forrest, who said "Wal, I guess I jes skeers em and keeps em skeered."[57]

It is true the strategy to defend the airbases and engage the enemy as far from Singapore as possible forced 11th Indian Division to fight at Jitra. It is also true the belated retreat led to a rout. But these things were part of a larger pattern, one exposed by the crucial battles of the first week. The attackers were ready to fight boldly and at maximum tempo. Good command decisions made it possible to prevail at Kota Bharu, to win control of the air, to find and sink the only menace faced at sea, and to win the initiative in the main battle on ludicrous terms. Less than 1500 Japanese infantry supported by a tank company routed a division, because it never came close to throwing its full strength into the fight. The Japanese must have read about Forrest, because they successfully applied another of his maxims: "hit em firstest with the mostest." They were able to concentrate whatever they had on hand to hit as hard as possible, where and when it mattered. The British on the other hand failed to engage in real strength, where and when they really needed to. Another old maxim of generalship is that ground can be regained, but time is lost forever. The contradictions between grand strategy and theatre defence forced Malaya Command to try to do what it could not, not in this terrain against this enemy: fight to hold ground rather than to inflict pain. The result was a comprehensive defeat, the first crippling blow. This gave the Japanese the initiative–and thus the chance to fight the campaign on their terms.

8

The "Driving Charge"

The second crippling blow was inflicted by Japanese success in pressing their "driving charge." Yamashita's army kept the initiative, preventing the defenders from pinning the advance down long enough to regroup. It took Twenty-Fifth Army only a fortnight after Jitra to reach the only position north of Kuala Lumpur at which the defenders could hope to make a prolonged stand. And they did it using barely half their infantry. The Japanese were willing to take the calculated risk. Their campaign strategy was more coherent. That combination gave their fighting units the chance to exploit superior tactics and combat power to good effect.

The calculated risk was whether to wait for the second echelon of the army, which included the entire Imperial Guards Division and most of the tank units, or press on to the Perak River with the forces already on hand. The infantry amounted only to two regiments of 5th Division and the regiment-sized Takumi Detachment of the 18th. This vanguard still comprised little more than 20,000 troops all told. That was not as many as those already engaged, let alone those available to reinforce the battle rapidly if Percival so chose. The Japanese spelt out their own situation:

> ... all the staff planners had a vague but concerted agreement as to a need of finishing the operation with a minimum loss of time by resorting to blitzkrieg type tactics. However it was only after the Army main force had crossed River Perak that the staff planners did keenly and seriously realize that need. Until that crossing, it was not clear even in their minds whether the emphasis of battle leadership should be on the combat results or the minimization of the operational period.

A combination of things swayed the staff: news the British were sending strong reinforcements to the Far East; the rapid pacification of Thailand; the speed with which control of the air was won; the scale of the rout at Jitra and "passiveness" of the enemy; the threat of delays caused by demolitions. Twenty-Fifth Army headquarters opted to press on, feeding its second echelon into the fight as it arrived, to emphasize "not so much the battle results per se or the annihilation of the enemy as the shortening of the entire campaign itself or the quickest possible occupation of Singapore." It was thus left to the vanguard to accomplish the first mission of the entire army: cross the Perak River, to open the route to central Malaya.[1]

The Japanese were less ambivalent about how to do this on the ground. Tactical lessons drawn from the first battles were sharply focused:

> A night assault is effective against the British Army who is not well trained for combat actions at night and inexperienced in close combat. On the other hand, its firepower is excellent. When it could depend on that power, it demonstrated a capability to resist tenaciously. It was our night assault that enabled us to break through both the three-line position at the border and the well-built Jitra position. We must try to move into the enemy's flanks by passing through jungles or marshy areas. Our casualties during this battle were inflicted by artillery shells. They came from the positions inside rubber forests difficult to be spotted either from air or on ground ... An offensive against such positions, therefore, should be made by either taking a roundabout route of attack through jungles, marshy area and others, or advancing our troops during brief pauses of enemy's shellings while undertaking repair works of the destroyed structure, or launching a bold charge in order to quickly penetrate artillery positions.[2]

Over the next fortnight the Japanese used such tactics to push the defenders out of Kedah and Kelantan by a three pronged advance. They were delayed more often by the need to repair demolished bridges and bring up fresh troops than by any serious defensive stand. The advance was usually led by a battlegroup ready to fight as a combined arms team. A simple but brilliant improvisation was the decision to mount forward reconnaissance units on bicycles, to speed up the advance without adding an extra supply burden. Sometimes the defenders were fooled into thinking the noise made by the steel rims of the bicycles rolling along the road was being made by tanks. Tanks were nearly always available up front, along with motorized infantry, light artillery and engineers, in a vanguard light and fast enough to keep up the pressure but strong and balanced enough to deal with anything short of quite determined resistance. When contact was made, the Japanese either put the tanks up front to blast through in a filleting attack, or pinned down the enemy by engaging him frontally, then sent following forces to find a route between or around the enemy positions. One force would make a short flanking march and attack from the side relatively nearby, another would make a deeper encircling march and try to isolate the whole battlefield by cutting the road as much as 10 km behind the defensive position. This pattern became fairly consistent, applied from company to division level depending on the strength of the defences. The idea remained constant: to keep the defenders on the run.[3]

Controlling the air certainly helped the Japanese apply these tactics to good effect. The 3rd Air Group rushed crews into Thailand, Kota Bharu and Alor Star within a week, allowing them to increase the tempo of their operations. RAF Far East tried to get back into the fight, but were again driven off by stronger forces. The day the retreat unravelled at Jitra, one solitary Buffalo was available to help 11th Indian Division. That same day, 13 December, Brooke-Popham sent a long telegram to the COS reporting that Pulford's force was reduced to 127 serviceable aircraft facing more than 300 enemy machines, and pointing out rather plaintively "Additional fighters with trained crews and heavy bombers are required as soon as possible." The defenders tried and failed to stem the flow by attacking bases in Thailand at night. On 15 December the Japanese seized the island airbase of Victoria Point, off the coast of southern Burma. This cut the route by which the all important single-engined fighters could fly in to reinforce RAF Far East. Now they had to be shipped in. In the largest single air battle of the campaign on 22 December an Australian force of 12 Buffaloes was reduced to three serviceable aircraft. The next day Pulford disbanded Norgroup and largely abandoned the battle in the north, to conserve his force to protect reinforcement convoys. That allowed the Japanese to unload at their ports, build up at their bases, and move along the roads without any serious interference from the air.[4]

They were helped even more by a gift from the defenders: usable runways and large quantities of ready to use supplies, including petrol, ammunition and bombs, left behind at abandoned airbases and in army supply dumps. Tsuji called this bounty "Churchill supplies" and there is no doubt it helped keep the advance going without pause. Their airpower allowed the Japanese to maintain the pressure on the defending ground forces. Making those forces do more moving and working at night drained their energy. The Japanese air units only began to emphasize direct support of ground operations from 23 December, but even before then they made their mark on the battle. The 11th Indian Division history tried a light note when describing the problem, but revealed the relentless pressure:

Over at 8 and away at 6 were the Trade Union hours of the Jap air force. The Indian troops called the first sortie the post rice flight, and the Brit troops greeted any aircraft which on rare occasions appeared out of union hours as black legs.[5]

Another important windfall from air supremacy was the easy capture of Penang. The Japanese decided to take the island to prevent the British from using it to threaten their flank as they advanced south towards Kuala Lumpur.

Heavy air attacks to soften up the defences were mounted on the mainland on 10 December and then on the island from 11 December. A large crowd gathered in the streets of central Georgetown to watch what they expected to be a repeat spectacle of bombing the mainland, but they turned out to be the target this time. The Japanese bombing and strafing inflicted close to 2000 casualties and devastated the town centre, provoking mass panic and a collapse of law and order. Sixteen Buffaloes went up on 13 December to defend the area, but made little impression on the much larger enemy force and lost five of their number. Only two companies of regular infantry plus a Volunteer battalion were left on the island. Heath decided it could not be held and the troops would be more use on the mainland. But the evacuation, first proposed on the 12th, was expanded to include all European civilians who wanted to leave, but very few locals. The Europeans scuttled out in secret. This created a backlash when Duff Cooper broadcast a radio talk on 17 December reassuring the populace "everyone" was evacuated from Penang. Governor Thomas had to pacify influential members of the Asian communities, understandably irked by this insensitivity. That prompted him to make a fuss over the whole question of evacuating civilians and the treatment of different races. He insisted all who wanted to leave be treated equally. Because Thomas knew full well before the evacuation started that only Europeans would be pulled out, but said nothing at the time, his behaviour badly strained relations with the military, on an issue likely to become acute.[6] The authorities were being overwhelmed by Japanese pressure, something underlined by two more failures in Penang. The evacuation was so hasty and disorganized the military left without destroying the radio station and demolishing all potentially useful boats. The Japanese soon had Radio Penang back on the air, beaming propaganda at Singapore which only reminded everyone how rapidly the situation was deteriorating. The boats were a more serious matter. Many were hidden by local fishermen. This allowed the Japanese to seize a flotilla, including barges and motor boats, that greatly increased their capability to launch amphibious assaults along the west coast. Belatedly Penang Fortress realized the danger and on 18 December asked Malaya Command to send an SOE party to destroy the boats the next day. The Japanese beat them to it, taking the island and its prizes unopposed.[7] The small distraction to their air effort was more than offset by the psychological effect of losing the island, the added disarray in the chain of command, and the new amphibious threat the defenders faced.

Every time the defenders made any attempt to collect their thoughts Japanese attacks provoked a fresh crisis. The position near Gurun was inherently strong. Kedah Peak rose some 1200 metres above a narrow defile between the coast and the jungle-covered central mountain range. It had to be approached along the trunk road through a very open area of swamp and paddy, offering good fields of fire and easily observed from the high ground. But no serious preparations were made to fight here, so a defensive position now had to be improvised. Murray-Lyon was again in a tight spot. Much of his infantry was still missing. He was afraid positions in open country would be vulnerable to air attack, and be dangerous to retreat through if that became necessary. So he opted to dig in east rather than north of the peak, closer to the village. But this area was rubber plantation, which gave the enemy more cover for a close assault if he made it past the paddy country. In any case Murray-Lyon did not even want to fight at Gurun and told Heath so, when the Corps Commander came up to see the situation for himself on the afternoon of 14 December. He was worried about both his own force and the threat to his flank from the enemy advance on the interior road. Heath reported later that day to Percival that the division was in no shape to fight. He urged the GOC to authorize a full retreat back to the Perak River. Percival's reply that evening was clear enough:

> 3 Ind. Corps will continue to cover Penang and will NOT withdraw further than the line of R. Muda without reference to HQ Malaya Command. All possible stores should be withdrawn from Depots North of R. Perak as soon as possible ... 11 Div if unable to hold Gurun position to fall back to a) R. Merbon position b) R. Muda position.[8]

In this atmosphere of not if but when and where to retreat, the Japanese again struck at just the right time to do maximum damage. At 0130hrs on 15 December they attacked straight down the road. Several hours of confused fighting against infantry, tanks and mortars left 1/8 Punjabi, the outpost battalion, under serious pressure. When at dawn their supporting artillery fell short and hit their own area, they fell back into the jungle to rejoin the main position. That created a gap the Japanese aggressively pushed through. At 0630hrs their infantry penetrated right through the rubber into 6th Indian Brigade headquarters, literally wiping it out. Brigadier Lay escaped, having "left to seek reinforcements," but the position was too confused to be restored. Once again a Japanese vanguard barely larger than a battalion, with some tank support, pushed into the midst of the defensive position in darkness and ignited a melee, forcing the whole division to disengage.[9]

This retreat was more orderly and less aggressively pursued, but the damage was done. The Japanese found the going on the interior road harder, because 12th Indian Brigade took advantage of its orders–to delay rather than hold–to fight a different kind of battle. But pressure on both roads intimidated

ιto concluding they could not stand on either. Brooke-Popham
⌐ the authority to "give ground if necessary to repel the Japanese
ιt his discretion, the day Gurun was lost. The short stretch of road
⌐ Taiping and Kuala Kangsar was the junction between the trunk and
ⴑr roads. After retreating from Gurun, Murray-Lyon, Heath and Percival
⌐ised on extricating the 11th Indian Division, moving it south of that area so
⌐ could not be cut off. Heath was already looking south of Ipoh for a position
at which the division could make an effective stand.[10]

Percival and Heath agreed to give up Kelantan altogether on 14 December,
directing 9th Indian Division to block the railway at Kuala Lipis and other
suitable points. Takumi Detachment shifted its weight to a steady but slow
advance along the east coast, threatening Kuantan. Ando Detachment pushed
12th Indian Brigade back towards Kuala Kangsar. The role assigned 11th Indian
Division on 20 December summed up the whole dilemma:

> ... present object is to impose maximum delay on enemy pending arrival of
> reinforcements. It is important therefore that NO reptd NO ground should
> be given up unless forced to do so by enemy action subject to condition that
> 11 Div must be kept in the field as a fighting formation.[11]

That forced Murray-Lyon to choose, every time his division was engaged,
how deeply to commit it to battle. But there was in fact no real choice. Every
time the division turned to fight, it was already looking over its shoulder to
the next possible position. By keeping the pressure on the Japanese pushed
them onto that treadmill. The remnants of two brigades were consolidated
into a reconstituted 15th Indian Brigade on 20 December, as the division
prepared to fight behind the Perak River. But that river flowed diagonally
southwest, from the central mountain range to the coast. Murray-Lyon feared
the enemy would infiltrate upriver and get behind any defensive position–the
very plan the Japanese adopted. The Japanese closed up to the river just before
Christmas, reinforced by lead elements of the fresh Imperial Guards Division.
They failed to prevent the demolition of the main trunk road bridge, but
were not seriously opposed in crossing. Heath had already decided to make
his defensive stand back at Kampar. 15th Indian Brigade fell back to work on
that position, leaving 12th and 28th Indian Brigades to delay the enemy until
it was ready.[12]

By Boxing Day the Japanese were approaching two important objectives:
Kuantan on the east coast, and the position at Kampar, on the main axis of
advance. It was an impressive performance, advancing more than 300 km
and seizing the initiative even before their full strength was in the fight. This

allowed them to threaten areas the defenders simply could not afford to lose if they hoped to hold Singapore. It happened so quickly Malaya Command now had little choice but to stand and fight. The challenge now increased as the second echelon of Twenty-Fifth Army came forward, ready to escalate the attack. Murray-Lyon paid the price for this failure to pin down the enemy in northern Malaya. He was replaced on 24 December by Paris. His division history summed the situation up well:

> The Divisional sign was a wheel with 11 spokes. It was intended to symbolize the wheels of the 11th Div revolving towards Singora, but those wheels never advanced. That sudden change of orders on the 8th December stopped them, and then the damn things started going backwards.[13]

The "driving charge" paid strategic dividends. By advancing to the edge of central Malaya within three weeks, the Japanese inflicted the second crippling blow.

9

Strategy by Default

The operating premise of imperial defence in the Far East was that if it was ever necessary to respond to a crisis the system could do so before fatal damage was done. That was expressed by Churchill's policy to rely on sending strong reinforcements to save Singapore and Malaya after they were attacked–and by assuming the forces deployed would be strong enough, and handled well enough, to do the job. This required the chain of command from London to Singapore to rapidly devise a new strategy that was realistic at all levels. But the British could not rework their strategy effectively at any level, which compromised the defence at every level. The army was forced to keep working towards a now obsolete grand strategy. That pushed it to pursue a suicidal theatre strategy. Both compromised the forces engaging the enemy, constituting a third crippling blow.

In retrospect, because we know when Singapore fell the problem posed by time and space is clear. There were only two things Churchill and the COS could have done to save Singapore after war broke out. First, immediately make its defence the first priority in grand strategy. That meant reversing the decision to concentrate on Germany first. Second, send truly powerful reinforcements, all combat experienced formations, to the Far East immediately. Nothing less than six squadrons of first class fighter aircraft plus two infantry divisions and one armoured brigade could even have hoped to stop the Japanese by now. They would have had to arrive in Malaya before mid-January, then adapt to the climate and terrain overnight. The Japanese would have regrouped and counterattacked, supported by powerful units of the Combined Fleet. The Eastern Fleet would have needed five capital ships plus aircraft carrier and land-based air support just to make them pause. Absolutely none of the above could have happened. The grand strategy to concentrate on Germany first was too deeply entrenched in coalition politics and in practice, by forces already deployed in the European war. Even if the priority had been changed, it was impossible to move so many forces that far that fast. Those engaged in battle could not quickly disengage. Those in the U.K. were that much farther away. And the shipping simply was not available. Once the Japanese seized the initiative, nothing done in London could have saved Singapore. Nevertheless it is fair to say the most important error was made by the command authority with the greatest responsibility: the central direction of the war. Having compromised Singapore before the war by failing to establish its defence plans on a sound basis, they now undermined its defence again by failing to adjust those plans to changing circumstances. Churchill and the COS were also knocked off balance by the tempo and ferocity of the Japanese advance. Their duty was to reconsider theatre defence in order to realign it with changes in grand strategy, for a now global war. They did not do so.

The Japanese attack on the Western Powers made an already difficult task much harder for London. The explosion of war in the Far East could not then or ever be handled on its own merits. The war was now global and strategic problems in one theatre always affected, and were affected by, problems elsewhere. But this is precisely why it was so important to reconsider the strategy to defend the Far East. On the most fundamental level Churchill's instincts were again sound. His first response to the news of the attack on the Americans was to arrange a summit meeting with Roosevelt. The Prime Minister feared the emotional uproar set off in the United States by the attack on Hawaii might undermine the agreement to concentrate on Germany first and threaten the flow of supplies to the British, in favour of rapidly building up American forces. His initial reaction to the bad news from the Far East was also proportionate. The Soviets successfully halted the German offensive and launched a counteroffensive in front of Moscow. The Eighth Army finally forced Axis forces in Libya to retreat. Above all else, the United States, with its vast war-making potential, was now at last an active ally. All this "far outweighed" the difficulties in Malaya. In this now global war the Axis powers signed their death warrant by provoking the titans, the Soviet Union and the U.S.A., to ally against them. Churchill and the COS set sail for Washington on HMS *Duke of York* concentrating very much on the big picture of global war, as they should have.[1] The margins of time and space now favoured the Allies in making grand strategy for global war. But the opposite was true for the Far East. The Japanese "driving charge" shrank the margins much faster than the central direction of the war could respond.

Churchill wrote down a confident starting position on 12 December. The Allies must hold a line he called the "Malay Barrier": Burma through Malaya/Singapore, then Java, down to northern Australia. This would secure the line of communications between the European theatre, India, and Australia. 18th Division, at sea en route to Egypt, was diverted to the Far East. But the policy would be to send only "minimum essential" reinforcements that would not prejudice the offensive to clear North Africa and the central Mediterranean. Churchill and his delegation settled down to debating grand strategy, confidently expecting Singapore to hold out the six months required to arrange a strategic counteroffensive.[2] They arrived in Washington on 22 December. The fortunes of war in the Mediterranean and Far East moved faster.

Eighth Army's success in Libya took too long, cost too much, and strained its own logistics. This jeopardized the campaign on which so much was based: clearing North Africa. It also provoked a German response that helped the global war effort by drawing submarines from the Atlantic and a full air corps from Russia–but those same forces hit hard in the Mediterranean. By mid-December the Mediterranean Fleet lost most of its light striking forces in Malta, one aircraft carrier and one battleship sunk and two battleships damaged. This made it more urgent than ever to advance in Libya, before the Germans could reinforce there. But by 16 December Brooke, now CIGS, warned the C-in-C Middle East, now General Claude Auchinleck, that defeats in the Far East would force the COS to respond, to prevent a disaster.[3] Allied forces in Luzon fell back towards Bataan while Percival's army fell back in Malaya. By Christmas Day Brooke persuaded the COS to reverse immediate priorities. Offensive action in Africa would continue if possible, but minimum essential reinforcement of the Far East now became the first charge. On New Year's Day the COS spelt out the grand strategy by which the British now proposed to hold in the Far East:

> Security of Singapore and of sea communications in the Indian Ocean is second only to the security of the United Kingdom and the sea communications thereto. The defeat of Germany must remain our primary object. Consequently for the present we should NOT rpt NOT diver more of our resources than are necessary to hold the Japanese. Crusader [the offensive in Libya] should be exploited to the greatest possible extent subject to the conditions that it must NOT rpt NOT prevent the despatch of essential reinforcements to the Far East.[4]

Unfortunately the British Empire's armies were not efficient enough to advance in Africa and hold in Malaya at the same time–especially while the bulk of their combat forces remained in the U.K. The Prime Minister hoped to solve the problem by sending reinforcements from the U.K., on the understanding they would be replaced by American forces. The Japanese moved so fast they ruined that plan. The defeats of 1940, and the agreement to concentrate on Germany first, could not now be undone. This canon of coalition strategy was a promise to the Soviets, and a bargain with the Americans, which the central direction of the war saw as touching directly on the security of the U.K. itself. They were not prepared to reconsider before two things were certain: the Soviets would survive; powerful American forces were ready to engage the

Germans.[5] This reduced efforts to reconcile campaigns in the Mediterranean and the Far East to scrambling improvisation. And the COS were already well aware their directive was hollow.

As early as 13 December Layton warned the Admiralty the Japanese advance would make the naval base untenable and suggested the fleet might have to retreat to Ceylon, in order to protect the lines of communication in the Indian Ocean. The next day the Admiralty left it to his discretion. They did urge him to at least try to hold Java, but all they could offer for reinforcement was the plan to concentrate older capital ships in the Indian Ocean, as soon as possible. Recent losses suggested April was the earliest that might happen. The Defence Committee approved this stipulation, as well as immediate reinforcements for the Far East, on 20 December–but then directed the COS to advise Singapore authorities to evacuate civilians from Singapore. The New Year's Day telegram clarified naval priorities:

> The concentration of the necessary Naval forces in the Indian Ocean to secure our communications must take second place only to the security of the sea routes to the United Kingdom. Instructions will be issued separately by the Admiralty.

On 5 January Layton shifted Eastern Fleet headquarters to Java. For the navy the Indian Ocean, not Singapore, had become the last barrier.[6] It would build up a battlefleet there as fast as possible, but not at the expense of the European war. Singapore would have to hold without one.

It was too important to commit the Americans to "Germany first," and not possible to send really strong forces east without undermining the European campaigns–even had the shipping been available. From the second day of their campaign the authorities in Singapore made very clear how difficult their position was, how strong Japanese pressure was, how important it was to send strong reinforcements quickly, especially fighter squadrons, to give them any chance to accomplish their mission. They also spelt that mission out repeatedly, leaving no room for misunderstanding: to hold the naval base in Singapore ready for use by the main fleet.[7] That compelled the central direction of the war to answer two pressing questions. First, would the reinforcements available be enough to accomplish this mission? Second, did the mission still make sense–was Singapore being defended by the strategy that best fit the grand strategy they now adopted?

The reinforcements arranged by late December were mostly ground and air forces either already at sea or nearer to hand in India and Australia: two brigades of 17th Indian Division, the entire 18th Division, reinforcement drafts of Indian and Australian troops, 58 Blenheim and 52 Hudson bombers, 99 Hurricane fighters, plus miscellaneous personnel and equipment. They would all arrive in January, the first wave on the 3rd of the month. In absolute terms this looked impressive. Five brigades was half Malaya Command's Order of Battle of Malaya the day war broke out. The decision to divert the renowned Hurricanes provoked high hopes Japanese control of the air could be at least neutralized. But how did this program stand up to closer examination? Time was of the essence. By the time these moves were confirmed the Japanese were threatening the whole position. Their advance to the Straits of Malacca forced all convoys to sail the longer southern route to Singapore. They were already approaching central Malaya. Should they seize the airbases in that area, they could cut Singapore off altogether. The second problem was quality. Kirby described these reinforcements well: "the equivalent of a physically unfit British division, two almost untrained Indian brigades, a number of partially trained Indian and Australian reinforcements and aircraft which could but be a wasting asset."[8]

The British division had been at sea since late November and would need time to find its legs. The Indian brigades were given up because they were so raw. If Malaya Command lost too heavily in battle before these formations arrived they would do no more than replenish it with warm bodies. The Buffalo squadrons were expected to be worn away by attrition by the time the Hurricanes arrived. But these aircraft were not the latest model. They were also modified to cope with the desert they were en route to. Fixing that would take time. Finally, most of their pilots had no combat experience. Serious Australian pressure forced the British to agree on 6 January to send experienced Australian divisions back from the Middle East. This kind of reinforcement threatened to make a real difference. But Singapore was told on 8 January these divisions, plus a British armoured brigade, could only arrive in theatre from the end of February.[9] Neither London nor Singapore could change time and space, so the battle had to be fought with what was available. This was an important departure from all prewar plans to defend Singapore. There was no promise for any rescue by a strategic counteroffensive, even after 180 days. The army–possibly assisted by the Hurricanes–must hold by itself.

The root problem was clear. Prompted by news of the defeats at Jitra and Gurun, Churchill spelt it out:

After naval disasters to British and American sea power in Pacific and Indian Oceans we have no means of preventing continuous landings by Japanese in great strength in Siam and the Malay Peninsula. It is therefore impossible to defend, other than by delaying action, anything north of the defensive line in Johore, and this line can itself only be defended as part of the final defence of Singapore Island fortress and the naval base. The C-in-C should now be told to confine himself to defence of Johore and Singapore, and that nothing must compete with maximum defence of Singapore. This should not preclude his employing delaying tactics and demolitions on the way south and making an orderly retreat.[10]

But such a strategy meant changing the mission, because retreating to Johore would allow the Japanese to isolate Singapore there and then. This would make it so difficult to hold the naval base that it meant changing imperial policy. Therefore such a decision could only come from London.

Percival made sure London knew what he was doing, which was the exact opposite of what Churchill suggested: fighting a major battle to keep the Japanese as far north as possible for as long as possible, well north of Johore. He also made sure they were informed of his main problem: because he could not send reinforcements without uncovering the east coast or Singapore, 11th Indian Division was being worn down. Malaya Command's strategy was confirmed by both GHQ Far East and the new War Council established in Singapore by Duff Cooper, then sent to the COS.[11] They confirmed it on 22 December:

> HMG fully agree your conception that vital issue is to ensure security of Singapore Naval Base. They emphasize that NO rpt. NO other consideration must compete with this. They approve your plan to employ delaying tactics and your policy to continue opposition on mainland to cover arrival of our reinforcements and the execution of maximum demolitions. It is for you to judge when and to what line you are forced to fall back, having regard to the danger of expending your forces unduly before the arrival of reinforcements.

Brooke persuaded the Prime Minister to trust the judgement of the men on the spot; this apparently led Churchill to simply drop the idea of a strategic retreat to Johore.[12] But this was caused by miscommunication despite information. Brooke mistook passive query for active recommendation. Both Percival and Brooke-Popham were implicitly asking whether the original strategy still stood or whether larger developments made a change desirable–they were not making recommendations, which perhaps they should have. Hard pressed as they were, London and Singapore unknowingly left the key decision to each other.

The Prime Minister's reluctance to press with his usual vigour was surely influenced by the strong Australian reaction to the Japanese onslaught. Within a week Bennett warned Canberra the situation was already critical.

The Australian government pressed for a more concerted Allied effort to meet the Japanese attack. A blunt Christmas Day telegram from V.G. Bowden, its representative in Singapore, prodded it into action. Bowden said Singapore would fall "within weeks" unless drastic measures were taken. Prime Minister John Curtin made this public declaration on 27 December:

> Without any inhibitions of any kind, I make it quite clear that Australia looks to America, free of any pangs as to our traditional links with the United Kingdom. We know the problems that the United Kingdom faces. We know the constant threat of invasion. We know the dangers of dispersal of strength. But we know too that Australia can go, and Britain can still hold on. We are therefore determined that Australia shall not go, and we shall exert all our energies toward the shaping of a plan, with the United States as its keystone, which will give to our country some confidence of being able to hold out until the tide of battle swings against the enemy.

The Australians saw their forward defence in the "near north" falling apart. Churchill's 1939 promise to implement the "Singapore strategy" in extremis now blew up in his face. Curtin's declaration stung him to the quick.[13] The defence of Singapore was a problem of imperial defence. If the British failed to solve it the Empire, and therefore their power, could not escape unscathed. The Australian demand for the return of I Australian Corps drove that point home. In such circumstances, London saw little choice. To keep the Empire together, Malaya Command must fight to hold the naval base.

That responsibility fell on two commanders who disagreed how to shoulder it: Percival and Heath. Each perceived the problem from the vantage point of his own job. London's failure to make a categorical choice provoked a divergence between the two that became dangerous. Neither found a way to reconcile two contradictory imperatives. Heath wanted to break contact after Jitra and Kota Bharu, but hoped to find a good position on which to stand and fight in Perak. The debacle at Gurun prompted him to appeal for reinforcements from the south, to prevent 11th Indian Division being defeated in detail. Percival refused, arguing "We don't want to dissipate forces from down here." Heath then concluded the best course would be a strategic retreat, all the way to the state of Johore. There his forces could be concentrated with the Australians in the south, along a shorter line where the peninsula narrows below its central bulge. This would shorten the coastline along which they might be outflanked, bring his two divisions together, provide them some rest. Percival insisted the mission to hold the naval base required the army to fight as hard as possible, as far north as possible, for as long as possible. The two met in Ipoh on 18 December but could not agree. Heath looked downwards.

He wanted to place his corps in a better tactical position, lest it be defeated in detail. Percival looked upwards. He believed a strategic retreat would leave his army isolated and thus doomed. Most analysts accept Percival's complaint the two then worked against each other: Heath in principle followed orders to stand and fight, but in practice looked over his shoulder so much he triggered premature retreats.[14] But it was not quite that stark.

Percival's orders put Heath's corps between a rock and hard place: "to keep on fighting the enemy in northern Malaya subject to condition that 3 Ind Corps must remain a fighting formation but not to uncover Singapore Fortress." One reader noted in the margin "what does this mean?" It meant 8th Australian Division and the Singapore Fortress garrison would not be sent north to fight, so Heath and Percival must find the right balance between imposing delay while not allowing the corps to be destroyed. With their difference in focus and priority, tension was unavoidable. Nevertheless, Heath tried harder to fight in the north than Percival later acknowledged, while Percival was more willing to give ground than he later admitted. Heath wanted to retreat in long steps to prepared positions where a strong fight might be made and break clean after each battle, delaying the enemy with small rearguards and demolitions. Percival wanted the main forces to contest every bend in the road, and retreat only "as the situation developed."[15]

Heath decided to make a serious stand near Kampar, a naturally strong position in central Perak dominating the trunk road. Fall-back positions were already being scouted, but Heath insisted this was the strongest defensive position north of Kuala Lumpur.[16] Percival remained unwilling to transfer any of 9th Indian Division's units. He ordered Barstow to delay the Japanese advance along the railway with a small rearguard, holding his main force ready to deny the coastal airbase and lateral road at Kuantan.[17] But on the main axis of advance Percival did not object very violently to Heath's intentions. On 16 December he agreed to retreat to the Perak River "as a first step." He also wanted "the Slim River line," south of Kampar, "to be reconnoitred." Preparing to meet Heath at Ipoh, the GOC "rather thought of having a look at the country on the way up."[18]

On the same day Percival met Heath in Ipoh, 18 December, before the COS confirmed Percival's strategy, Brooke-Popham directed Malaya Command as follows:

... consider recce and construction of defensive positions in Johore. Forward positions must be prepared first but he had in mind:

a) Something on the general line area Mersing-Batu Pahat. This would allow our use of the aerodromes at Kluang and Kahang which he wished to retain but land tactical considerations must come first and it might be found that no suitable position could be found. If this were so, one of the aerodromes might have to go.

b) A "Torres Vedras" line, probably Kota Tinggi position on right and an equivalent position on left.

c) Should the NORTH shore of SINGAPORE Island be prepared for defence? No defence work there now.

BGS [Torrance] said that GOC had already been considering this problem. We had a partially prepared position on the Johore R[iver]. at Kota Tinggi. General Percival was now considering forward positions and no doubt would deal with Johore on his return.[19]

The tempo and power of the Japanese advance forced Malaya Command to make a fighting withdrawal. Yet the mission to hold the naval base severely restricted Percival's room to give ground. Percival settled on a strategy resting on two considerations. One was how his army could stop the Japanese advance, by forcing the enemy into deliberate assaults. The other was the inherent logic of his logistic situation, regardless what his mission was.

Far East Command also directed Malaya Command to investigate "operational and administrative problems associated with protracted defence of Singapore." Percival's 23 December reply summed up the problem:

Importance of Singapore Itself:

Our main food resources, both civil and military, main ammunition holdings and administrative installations are in Singapore. Although we still have the use of Port Swettenham, Singapore will be the main port of entry for reinforcements and material. Harbour and rail facilities are therefore of high importance, although it is preferable that the Naval Base–with its high degree of AA protection–should be used for landing military reinforcements and stores. In order to reduce the scale of air attack which can be developed against Singapore, the enemy should be forced to operate from aerodromes as distant from Singapore as possible.

This was a reasonable point. Only through Singapore could the fighting power required to hold Malaya be marshaled. That alone forced the defenders to fight some kind of defence as far north as possible. But the order to hold the naval base intact was still what really tied Malaya Command's hands. They were being asked to survive, not just to die well and take many Japanese with them. Percival acknowledged there were defensible "lines" in Johore that still offered some hope to keep the enemy far enough away to use Singapore, with difficulty–but noted they were nowhere near prepared for a defensive stand.

This was of course due to the decisions to rely on the air plan and forward defence. The conclusion was predictable. Retreating too fast would uncover the base and kill the mission. Standing fast with no retreat would be "taking a serious risk." The army must therefore "withdraw gradually with the object of gaining time for arrival of reinforcements." III Indian Corps must fight as hard as it could, but must retreat before what Percival still wrongly saw as a "methodical advance" by the enemy. Meanwhile, 9th Indian Division must be ready to "conform" if the Japanese reached the lateral road north of Kuala Lumpur. And defensive positions covering airbases in Johore, and even "on North shore of Singapore Island," must now be prepared. In truth Percival was now making it up as he went along. Everything depended on whether or not III Indian Corps could hold the enemy at Kampar, or any other northern position, for any appreciable time. Having by now lost something "like half of Malaya," when the essential reinforcements finally did arrive their role was "to be determined later, depending on situation immediately prior to their arrival."[20]

There is more evidence that Malaya Command was now making strategy by the seat of its pants. On 14 December, Percival advised Heath to "Use Independent Coy. to strike at enemy's communications moving either by sea against Western flank or by land against Eastern flank." The further the Japanese advanced the greater chance there should be to disrupt their supply lines. The Independent Company, some 300 strong, was organized and trained for just such a mission. Unfortunately this was never done. Heath's staff decided instead to deploy this specialist force to help guard the flank of the main force–yet pressed ever harder for operations to distract the enemy by harassing his supply lines, while complaining it had no forces available to do the job. Instead of pointing out the obvious Malaya Command hastily organized an ad hoc unit under Major Rose of 2nd Argylls to raid Japanese rear areas. Who was floundering more: the corps staff that wasted a specialist unit on a line role, or the army staff that meekly replaced it by throwing in a scratch force to play a suddenly vital role? On 19 December Heath's staff suggested:

The time had come to act offensively against the Japanese, so as to keep as many troops as possible guarding aerodromes and other vital points, etc. Means which he suggested should be investigated were: dropping dummy parachutes at dusk; by seaborne expeditions up the West Coast, and landings at places such as Alor Star [more than 20 km inland]; organization of the Chinese miners in North Perak into guerrilla bands. BGS considered this should be quite possible, and that if rewards of money were offered for each Japanese rifle or head, etc., results would be very satisfactory. He was trying to consider further ideas of this sort and was asking everybody to forward any recommendations. He was handing a paper on these lines to GOC on his way through Kuala Lumpur tonight.

In reply, Torrance took credit for instigating this burst of staff creativity, instead of demanding to know why the Independent Company was being wasted.[21]

Heath soon realized such operations required expert coordination and on 28 December agreed Col. Warren, already in practice playing the role, should take charge. And Roseforce did score a minor success, killing a Japanese officer in a roadside ambush. It is also fair to note that in wartime headquarters will always face sudden problems with no easy solutions. Nevertheless this kind of unforced error only emphasized how badly the tempo of the enemy advance disrupted Malaya Command. It was too late to moan about prewar obstruction of efforts to organize special forces. But the need to disrupt Japanese lines of communication was so pressing Warren should have been called on right away, and the Independent Company should not have been wasted. Malaya Command's naivete about how to conduct irregular operations spoke volumes about the political context in which this army now fought.[22]

RAF Far East reinforced this instinct to "muddle through." Directed to consider the same problems involved in a "protracted defence of Singapore," the air staff answer on 21 December also put the aim clearly: "to hold Singapore until reinforcements arrive, to enable us to hit back." Their appreciation was also more dire. The enemy had the initiative, the chance to cut the reinforcement route, and there was precious little they could do about it. Preserving their strength to contest "the final assault on the Fortress" risked losing all chance of reinforcement. But throwing the strikng force into an all-out assault on the enemy could only be done "at the risk of losing the bulk of it." They recommended dispersing bomber squadrons to Sumatra, using them "sparingly on favourable targets at night" and using the fighters to protect Singapore and reinforcement convoys. Meanwhile the army must hold the line. Far East and Malaya Commands agreed: "the course we must adopt must be the one best calculated to gain time for the arrival of reinforcements," which meant "to hold the enemy as far north of Singapore as possible, provided that this does not lead to the destruction of our field forces"–ground and air.[23] The high command had to take a calculated risk after Gurun. They could choose between falling back to concentrate their forces, striking back to derail the enemy, or trying to delay him without committing their full forces. They chose the strategy which at least promised a more prolonged demise.

On 26 December, just before he left Singapore, Brooke-Popham challenged this strategic consensus. Replying to a COS query about how any setback in Malaya would affect Allied strategy in the rest of the region, Brooke-Popham rudely blurted out the taboo: given how strong Japanese airpower was, should reinforcements still carry on for Singapore? Or should they instead be diverted to Java or Sumatra, from where they might at least deny its bases to the enemy? Brooke-Popham argued that any Japanese move into Johore would rule out any counteroffensive; it would no longer be possible to do more than deny Singapore. It might be better to throw the striking force into a determined attack on Japanese airbases. Given the superiority of their fighters, this seemed the only way to protect the convoys.[24] The very next day, 27 December, Pownall took over Far East Command and soon sent a more congenial appreciation: the mission to hold the naval base, plus the logistical importance of Singapore, made it necessary to keep the enemy at bay in Malaya; the best the forces on hand could do was fight to delay, while trying to conserve their strength. Pownall insisted two more steps must be taken immediately. Over and above scheduled reinforcements another experienced division must be sent to Malaya. And arrangements for coordinating the defence of American, Dutch and British positions were too cumbersome and must be replaced . Only a single command empowered to take rapid action in the theatre as a whole could pull Allied forces together, before the enemy defeated them in detail.[25]

The COS reply on New Year's Day confirmed Pownall's strategy and reinforcements already being arranged. They were ultimately more than Pownall demanded; but the crucial force, I Australian Corps, could not arrive before a decisive battle in Malaya must be fought. A change of command was already in hand. The summit conference in Washington decided to create a unified Allied command to pull together the defence of Southeast Asia. This was the particular concern of General George C. Marshall, Chief of Staff US Army, who wanted to establish unified command in overseas theaters as Allied practice. Churchill waved aside the qualms of his advisers to accept Marshall's proposal to appoint General Wavell Supreme Commander of the American-British-Dutch-Australian [ABDA] Command. Wavell was given at least nominal command of all Allied forces operating from Burma to northern Australia to the Philippines.[26] Unavoidably such big changes took time and generated confusion. Layton decided to shift his headquarters four days before the new Supreme Commander arrived on 7 January, not having been told the change was imminent. Pownall asked to liaise with Wavell. In reply the COS abruptly terminated Far East Command, named him Chief of Staff to Wavell, and subordinated Malaya Command and RAF Far East to ABDA Command.

One decision of great practical consequence was taken right away: it was left to Wavell to decide what to do with reinforcements sent to his command. But for the forces already there, this shuffling caused more uncertainty at the very time the enemy relentlessly pressed his advantage.[27] There was no real adjustment in strategy to respond to the Japanese "driving charge." The defence fought on by default.

10

The Poor Bloody Infantry

The bungled attempt at Jitra to make the ground fit the doctrine set the tone for Malaya Command's fighting retreat. The army tried to fight by defending fixed positions, to force set-piece battles stressing firepower over mobility. But its defensive tactics failed. Quite simply, it was outfought on the battlefield. The reasons were familiar: inadequate prewar preparations plus failure to adapt effectively to circumstances. When III Indian Corps used tactics that hurt the Japanese, this threatened to undo theatre strategy. When they employed tactics conforming to that strategy, this played into the enemy's hands in battle. The system placed the final burden on the "poor bloody infantry" but then compromised their efforts to shoulder it. No one found a solution. This fourth and final blow proved fatal.

There was one important exception to the tactical dead end: the delaying action fought by 12th Indian Brigade. This fight ran along the interior road from Kroh to Kuala Kangsar, then along the trunk road to Kampar. C Company 2nd Argylls first made contact with the enemy north of Grik on 14 December. The brigade conducted a fighting retreat for more than two weeks, guarding the flank of 11th Indian Division. It used to good effect the tactics of "fighting for the road, off the road" it practiced before the war. It was ready to fight at the high tempo required to handle this enemy. The enemy was expected to infiltrate defensive positions. They were set up to smoke him out, not stop him. Armoured cars provided a base of fire on the road, a pivot around which to maneuver. Three to five man "Tiger patrols" harassed Japanese efforts to infiltrate, outflank and encircle. Strong forces were deployed on the flanks, somewhat behind the forward position. When the enemy attacked the forward position on its flank, he was counterattacked from two directions and sandwiched. On two occasions 2nd Aryglls and 5/2 Punjabis caught the enemy in such a sandwich and inflicted heavy casualties. They then disengaged and moved in good order back to the next delaying position. This fighting retreat cost the Japanese time and men. Unfortunately, this had as much to do with the situation as with effective training and tactics. The brigade did not face a serious tank attack, and was authorized to retreat at its own discretion. Its orders were to screen, not stand.[1] This luxury was denied the rest of III Indian Corps. The mission to hold the naval base meant they must keep the enemy at bay. That ruled out any switch in tactics from holding ground to killing the enemy. And the other Indian formations could not have made such a switch anyway. They had not prepared for any such challenge, and could not now adjust on the move under pressure.

At Jitra, Kota Bharu, and Gurun, the task was to stand and fight, to stop the enemy cold. Even when higher command realized there would be further retreat, at Kuantan, Kampar and Slim River, the orders were to fight a major battle, buy appreciable time, hurt the enemy, then break clean, regroup, and do it again. Heath and Percival relied on successful fights at these defensive positions, either because geography gave them no choice–as at Jitra, Kota Bharu, and Kuantan–or because it gave what looked like a good choice–as at Gurun, Kampar and Slim River. The defenders wanted to draw the attackers onto ground where their own strengths could come into play. Malaya Command needed to slow the battle down, to force the Japanese to make set-piece assaults they could cope with. The Japanese relied on experienced light infantry which used a simple and flexible battle doctrine and enjoyed strong support arms–both of which were tailored to local conditions. They found ways to adapt and overcome. The defenders, cumbersome in contact, inflexible in doctrine, especially weak at improvising on the spot, could not. It was far too late to change how the army fought and it did not fight well enough.

On the evening of 15 December, Heath complained to Percival that the enemy attacked with "fanatical fury," disregarding heavy losses to keep charging across the padi fields. The GOC replied:

> We have got to think out some new tactics for dealing with these Japanese–static positions are no good. Something on the lines of a perimeter camp in which you have people, with mobile forces inside to go out and "biff" the enemy where necessary.[2]

But despite stating "static positions are no good," neither Percival nor Heath intended to shift from positional to mobile defence. Given Percival's decision to reject a strategic retreat, three considerations shaped their efforts. First, enemy tactics were accurately assessed. Second, the high command lost confidence in line units ability to adapt to battle conditions and tried to micromanage tactics. Finally, the only real change was to adjust from one form of positional defence to another.

The problem was identified: very few positions, especially if defended by linear deployment, could not be penetrated by enemy infiltration through close country and/or outflanked, especially the latter. The enemy's aggression, skill and willingness to move off the roads when in contact made the battle tactics by which Malaya Command tried to defend the country nearly useless, especially after the retreat below Penang extended the threat along the coast.[3] Percival said the main reason he relieved Murray-Lyon in favour of Paris was to counter an apparent enemy superiority in "bush warfare" tactics. 11th Indian Division was exhorted by higher headquarters to make sure all positions had ample supplies, to allow units to fight on if cut off by the enemy; stop units concentrating vehicles near the forward area; be aware any position could be outflanked and it was better to cover multiple approaches by fighting patrols than by dividing the main force into too many small detachments; harass enemy lines of communications by patrols. None of this was nonsense and it was only natural for higher command to want to circulate advice.[4] But it was also tactical common sense. It all should have been part of a battle doctrine already absorbed and practiced by the army, making it familiar and flexible enough for units to apply on the spot. This is what the Japanese did. Such direction came from a higher command which did not think its army could think for itself. The starkest example was III Indian Corps Operation Instruction No. 7, issued on 23 December. It offered both detailed advice on how to conduct small unit delaying actions, including the reminder road blocks must be "closely covered by fire," and instructions on how to hold the main position around Kampar:

> Your main position should be regarded as a secure base from which troops should sally forth and carry out hostile activity of every conceivable nature. Night operations of even quite small parties are likely to produce a demoralizing effect on the enemy.

Only formations such as 12th Indian Brigade that trained more realistically before the war were now able to adapt to the battle at hand. Both Percival and Heath insisted "we must endeavour to not only imitate enemy methods of ruse and guile but improve upon them."[5] But it was too late to retrain their own force in its own tactics, let alone instantly copy those of the enemy.

There was nevertheless an important shift in battle tactics after Gurun: linear defence became defence at a position laid out in depth along a defile, a shift from horizontal to vertical. The new approach was spelt out by GHQ Far East in its appreciation of 18 December:

> Our experience to date has shown that linear defence is no use since the

enemy has invariably outflanked us and also infiltrated in thick country. It is considered, therefore, that we must choose ground upon which to fight where: a) there is a formidable obstacle with few communications leading to it b) the main communications pass through a restricted area in this obstacle which can be easily blocked c) the position is sited for all round defence and provisioned for a prolonged defence which will not be easily prejudiced by any infantry infiltration round the flanks.

The Kampar area was nominated as the best place to carry out the plan "fortification of and withdrawal to a position where we intend to stop the enemy." Malaya Command accepted this, with an important stipulation. Percival argued that while enemy tanks were a problem, and positions with strong anti-tank obstacles were useful, infiltration and outflanking by infantry was the real threat against which the main positions must be designed.[6] The plan came together from 20 December. Only the main axes of advance could be defended. They would be defended in depth at positions that formed natural defiles, which gave cover against tanks and aircraft and channelled an attacker. Fixed defences, including anti-tank obstacles, mines, booby traps, barbed wire, and improvised road blocks would stiffen the positions. Nevertheless the defence must be aggressive. Ambushes must be sprung whenever possible. There would be no retreat unless and until expressly ordered. When contact was made the enemy would be pinned along his main axis of advance by a holding force, but strong forces must be deployed on the flank–not to screen, but to mount early and vigorous counterattacks. Contact, pin, hit back, maul the enemy as long and hard as possible, then break and fall back to the next prepared position, to repeat. As the enemy approached Kampar, supplies were being stocked for a 10 day stand.[7]

Percival intended to regain control of the battle, to slow down the tempo and buy time for his army to reorganize by a controlled retreat. Had such a plan and the tactics to implement it been worked out on the ground before the war, III Indian Corps could at least have made the battle of northern Malaya a longer, more costly fight. Now it must regroup on the move, under pressure– worse, this provoked still more discord between commanders. Without reinforcements, without much support from engineers, who were underused, or civilian labour, often scarce or unwilling, the tired troops of 11th Indian Division had to fight and dig at the same time. Percival's directives, circulated on 20 and 25 December, were of course very similar to what Simson pressed for before the outbreak of war.[8] III Indian Corps staff seemed unmoved. A much exercised Simson caught up with Heath late on 22 December and found the Corps Commander's own views much changed. Heath now felt he would not stop the enemy north of Kuala Lumpur. He wanted to make much greater use of fixed defences. Indeed, he wanted the positions Percival discussed prepared immediately, to allow his infantry to conduct a controlled retreat to Johore–and gave Simson verbal orders to convey these views urgently to Percival.[9] But despite how narrow the differences between the three men on strategy and tactics were, this only made matters worse.

Heath flatly refused to sign Simson's message, even after Simson told him how he had already been stymied by not having written orders regarding defences. Simson caught up with Percival in Singapore very late on 26 December, and pressed him for several hours to authorize his engineers to work on the network of positions all now agreed was required. Simson also urged the GOC to authorize work on defences on the north shore of Singapore island. Percival flatly refused to endorse either request, according to Simson for only one reason: building defences so far in the rear would destroy the morale of both troops and civilians. But Percival's actions raise a question mark. The 20 December directive discussed the need to take preliminary steps to prepare defences in both Johore and the northern coast of Singapore, as GHQ Far East suggested. The GOC permitted Simson to put his case to Simmons, the Fortress Commander–who also demurred, again supposedly due to concern for morale. But on 28 December Percival ordered Simmons to draft plans to demolish the causeway. The next day the GOC informed Heath, Bennett and Simmons the Public Works Department was directed to build fixed defences, at positions to be selected by their staffs. Simson was not even informed! This passed the whole now urgent task to untrained and unprepared civilians, leaving Simson's army engineers dangling in the wind. Simson himself believed concerns about tactics were a powerful motive. Excepting Heath, senior commanders still seemed to feel that if the troops saw fixed defences as the basis of their tactics they would sit tight behind cover and refuse to counterattack, especially across open country. There is only incomplete evidence on this point, and it does indicate widespread concern for morale. Simson may well again have done his case more harm than good by being obnoxious.[10] Whatever the case, two things are clear. A tactical doctrine that under the circumstances was at least plausible was quickly sketched out by higher commanders. But they could not pull it or themselves together coherently–and doubted their fighting units could make it work on the ground anyway.

On 27 December Brooke-Popham signed off with a report that complained "enemy's novel tactics tended to throw our troops off their balance." Even granting the disparity in experience this should have been nonsense: there was nothing novel about enemy tactics at all. But to the men on the ground there was. Percival acknowledged this in a directive issued on

6 January, admitting he "did not anticipate to the full" enemy tactics, which rarely used "normal attacks by formed bodies."[11] The Japanese did in fact strike in numbers whenever they could, but their emphasis on maintaining contact rather than building up deliberate assaults caught most of Malaya Command off balance–and it was too cumbersome to adjust. The strategy to keep the enemy at bay was being defeated because the defenders were being outfought. On 29 December 22nd Indian Brigade patrols made contact with Takumi Detachment troops advancing towards Kuantan. That same day 12th Indian Brigade broke contact with some difficulty–pressed for the first time by a serious tank attack–crossed the bridge over the Kampar River at Dipang and ended its long fighting retreat, handing over to 28th Indian Brigade and the Kampar defences. Percival and Heath earlier that day confirmed their plans. At Kuantan, to delay losing the airfield as long as possible, they would give up the coast defences north of the river but defend its south bank. At Kampar they would fight, with rested and dug-in battalions. Paris reported that evening the enemy was approaching Kampar in strength, one division with tanks, and "he expects a merry battle tomorrow."[12]

Serious probes of the positions at Kuantan and Kampar began early on 30 December. That same day Percival made his most determined attempt to pull the separate battles together into a coherent campaign strategy. The threat was worse than ever: an advance down the trunk road plus further assaults from the sea, by a force [over]estimated at three full divisions plus reserves of equal size, now nearing the airfields of central Malaya. From those airfields enemy airpower could cut Singapore off. The mission now met the plan:

> To achieve our object of protecting the Naval Base it was necessary to fight the main battle on the mainland and it was hoped to be able to deploy all the reinforcements due to arrive in January for that purpose. Therefore the longer we could delay the enemy in Central Malaya the better.

III Indian Corps would not fight the "main battle." But it must delay and hurt the enemy, to allow Malaya Command to fall back in good order to positions on which it could concentrate, with reinforcements, to make that stand. Percival finally made it specific. To protect approaching convoys, and prevent the enemy from getting in between its two divisions, the Corps must hold north of Kuala Lumpur for a fortnight. Kuantan airbase must be denied until at least 10 January. Kualu Kubu, the junction of the trunk road with the lateral road to Kuantan, must be held until 14 January. But no formations could allow themselves to be shattered.[13]

This was a tall order. A still fighting fit III Indian Corps would be essential to give Malaya Command any chance to fight a "main battle" in January. But rapid defeat at either Kuantan or Kampar, or heavy losses, would compromise the whole strategy. While the enemy was not as strong as estimated he did enjoy command of the air, and was now using it to harass the defensive positions. Worse, Percival's order to fight major battles north of Kuala Lumpur, without reinforcements, left two of Heath's brigades so vulnerable it compromised the whole plan before battle was joined. 12th Indian Brigade, badly needing rest, was instead assigned as the only available reserve for two potentially vital tasks: backstop the position at Kampar; reinforce the Volunteer units watching the west coast, if they were attacked from the sea. If it had to try both at the same time, something must give. 22nd Indian Brigade was caught between two tugs of war: conflicting orders to deny Kuantan yet keep itself viable, and ground that put it between a rock and a hard place.[14] The only hope for Percival's plan was the foundation on which it had to rest: tactics. The "poor bloody infantry" must fight the enemy to at least a temporary halt.

The battles at Kuantan and Kampar were among the most intense of the campaign. Kuantan aggravated the discord between Percival and Heath when it became another failure to impose any significant delay or loss on an enemy force no larger than the defenders. Kampar had even greater impact. 11th Indian Division put up a resolute fight but was pushed out of the most favourable position in which it ever faced the enemy, faster and to less effect than Percival counted on. Heath complained the need to give the infantry enough rest was not fully grasped and bemoaned "the lack of tactical sense on the part of many junior officers and in some cases even unit commanders."[15] The harsh reality was that even when it did find a place that suited its tactics this army could not cope with this enemy, at any level.

22nd Indian Brigade fought at Kuantan with determination but without clear direction. The insoluble problem was the combination of two incompatible factors: the mission and the geography. The latter involved the relative positions of the airbase, river, ferry and road. Even after regaining his third battalion on 23 December, Brig. Painter had nowhere near enough troops to protect the long stretches of beaches north and south of the town. The airbase was only 15 km inland, seven kilometres south of the river, just off the road, and 10 km west of the only river crossing: a single, hand-operated one-way ferry. Painter always considered the whole position, dictated by the arbitrary location of the airbase, "thoroughly unsound."[16] When the enemy advanced from the north along the coast instead of attacking from the sea, that only made matters worse. This flanked the beach defences north of the town held by 2/18th Royal Garwhal Rifles [2/18 Royal Garwhalis]. Fighting north of the Kuantan River now posed two risks. First, if the fight was lost the bottleneck caused by the single ferry crossing would jeopardize any retreat. Second, enemy infantry could march upriver, ford, and move in from the west. But standing south of the river meant letting the enemy come within easy range of the airbase, and did not remove the danger of being outflanked upriver. Finally, if the brigade was ordered to retreat it could only move along the one lateral road–sure to be a prime enemy target. Painter tried to clarify his battle by trumpeting standing orders to defend the airbase "to the last round and the last man, with no question of withdrawal." But these orders were replaced on 22 December by 9th Indian Division, directing the brigade to "deny Kuantan aerodrome to the enemy as long as possible." This was yet another vague and general instruction: "The date of withdrawal from Kuantan will depend upon events elsewhere in Malaya and will be fixed in consultation with this HQ."[17] This indication there would be no fight to the finish at Kuantan compromised its defence. Painter needed clarity, to cope with the awkward ground on which he was forced to fight. Percival needed flexibility, to deny the airbase as long as possible. This decision to pursue inherently conflicting aims in a fast-moving situation challenged Malaya Command to make tough choices at high tempo. It was not up to the challenge.

Percival, Heath and Barstow all agreed 22nd Indian Brigade must shift its weight south of the river, from where it could contest the airbase but ultimately retreat. They all share responsibility for undermining the defence. On 27 December Barstow met Painter, who spelt out very clearly the tactical dilemma these new orders posed, insisting the only way to mount an effective defence was to fight north of the river. Barstow "emphasized that safety of force must not be jeopardized." That surely indicated the brigade was more important than the airbase. But he then muddied the waters again: "Considered however in view of plans made, and that it was [Painter] who had to fight this battle, that he should fight it out on the East side [north of the river and ferry]. Warned him however that every single vehicle had to be got across to West side." The stricture included guns. Precisely how 22nd Indian Brigade could ferry its verhicles and weapons across the river under fire Barstow did not say. For the next five days all four men argued about how to deny the airbase yet preserve the brigade. Painter kept receiving mixed signals about how long to deny the airbase: Heath called for two or three days, Barstow five, Percival until 10 January.[18] The enemy struck in the midst of this confusion.

An aggressive advance by Takumi Detachment forced 2/18 Royal Garwhalis to fight their way back across the river. By midday 31 December Painter felt he could no longer fight north of the ferry at all, but Japanese infiltration complicated everything. 2/18 Royal Garwhalis escaped utter destruction because a spirited defence of the ferry crossing, plus some bad bombing by Japanese aircraft, kept it open long enough for much of the unit to cross–but two companies, plus a company of 2/12 Frontier Force, remained north of the river. Painter regrouped, leaving 5/11 Sikhs deployed along the river, concentrating the rest of his force around the airbase itself. But he also reported to Barstow his position was becoming untenable, so he intended to disengage and retreat west. Japanese efforts to take or outflank the ferry set off a confused fight along the river that in fact prevented any such full retreat– but Barstow's answer sums up the predicament command decisions inflicted on the brigade in the first place:

> 22 Bde should stand as long as possible in denial of aerodrome without jeopardizing his force. That proposed move [that night] was deprecated unless these conditions were fulfilled, that a denial for five days would materially assist general situation Malaya.

That last point referred to reinforcement convoys, an issue only spelt out to Painter for the first time earlier that day.[19] 22nd Indian Brigade duly tried to regroup its stragglers and deny the airbase, but this allowed Japanese infantry to ford the Kuantan River farther west and outflank the position–just what Painter warned would happen. By evening 2 January circumstances on the west coast finally forced higher headquarters to direct Painter to retreat–but he had already decided to do so, the next day.[20] Unfortunately the Japanese moved so fast the brigade had to fight its way out.

The retreat began at 1400hrs on 3 January. 5/11 Sikhs thinned their positions along the river and fell back through the other units without incident. 2/18 Royal Garwhalis began moving out after dusk. This left a gap in the defences. Just as brigade headquarters prepared to move out, around 2000hrs, a strong enemy attack came in through the gap. The rearguard, 2/12 Frontier Force, was heavily engaged in close quarter fighting. Its commanding officer, Lt.-Col. A.E. Cumming, was bayoneted twice, killed both his assailants, led the defence, and was wounded again breaking through Japanese roadblocks. Cumming was later awarded the Victoria Cross. Painter considered trying to rescue his trapped subunits, but in the early hours of 4 January opted to follow orders to preserve his formation and broke contact. Some stragglers did return later, but the battle cost 22nd Indian Brigade more than a third of its infantry.[21] The return was inadequate. The airbase fell to the enemy a week before Percival's target. The convoy arrived in Singapore the day the retreat began, bringing in a raw Indian brigade nothing like as fit to fight in Malaya as the brigade cut up in its defence. The Japanese would not have been able to press the base into use quickly enough to harm this convoy anyway. So why force Painter to fight there at all once the Japanese arrived?

The answer was the connection between the defensive positions and the larger mission. Percival wanted to screen two convoys, one at hand, the other still two weeks out, as much as possible. But the defence of Kuantan was always compromised by the arbitrary location of the airbase and the vulnerability of the road. Once Painter was asked to fight any kind of battle there, his superiors should either have authorized him to fight according to tactical imperatives, or accepted the risk his brigade could be destroyed, if the larger mission was deemed that important. Painter tried to force the issue but was overruled. Barstow went back and forth. Heath steered the brigade towards retreat but shied away from forcing the issue with Percival. And Percival ordered 22nd Indian Brigade to do the impossible, instead of facing the fact his strategic imperative of delay could only be pursued by accepting the tactical risk of destruction. Percival later blamed Heath, with some cause. On 29 January Heath insisted the airbase could be denied "equally well" by defending south of the river; Painter's bluntly opposite view did not reach Percival.[22] But there was also a larger factor.

Making a categorical decision at any level of command threatened to narrow options at all other levels. The entire chain of command, not just Percival, tried to keep their own choices open. This pressed the burden of uncertainty, indeed contradiction, down to the battlefield itself. It should already have been clear to Percival that his formations needed crystal clear orders to cope with this enemy. The ground around Kuantan only reinforced this point. Once they arrived on the battlefield, the Japanese moved unhesitatingly off the roads and into the bush. As long as they took Kuantan, their local supply problem would be solved. But the defenders were hampered by the bottleneck at the ferry, and had to keep the road clear. To both fight and retreat, especially over 150 km to central Malaya, they could not lose their vehicles and guns. Had Painter stayed any longer he could not have disengaged at all. Percival had every reason to conclude he could not have the delay he wanted, with no undue cost, against this enemy. The better choice by this time would have been to preserve his brigade.

If at Kuantan the strategic tail wagged the tactical dog, at Kampar it was the opposite. Heath made his stand here because of the ground. It is still possible to drive south from Ipoh along the old Road Number One and immediately appreciate the problem facing the Japanese. To the east, dense jungle comes to the edge of the road and the ground rises steeply. To the west, a broad flat plain stretches all the way to the coast. In 1941 patches of rubber plantation were strung along the railway, which converged with the road at the town of Kampar. The rest of the plain was open tin-mining ground and large swamps. Gunong Bujang Melaka mountain dominates the whole area, rising over 1200 metres just east of the trunk road; Kampar town is on its southwestern slope. If the Japanese moved east they must cross the difficult broken ground of the central mountain range. If they moved west they would be engaged by artillery enjoying magnificent fields of fire. If they advanced along the road they must overrun defenders well dug in on high ground, protected on one flank by the mountain, on the other by the open plain. This at last was ground that suited the tactics to rely on strong defile positions and firepower. From Dipang a loop road circled the mountain to the east. 28th Indian Brigade took over the outpost positions and deployed along this road, to block any outflanking move and stand poised to counterattack, if the enemy challenged the main defences. Two brigades of seven depleted battalions were reorganized into 15th Indian Brigade with five battalions. It deployed in depth along the trunk road. The amalgamated British Battalion held the main defences, dug in on three parallel ridge spurs connecting the trunk road to the mountain, a kilometre north of town. 1/14, 3/16 and 2/16 Punjabi deployed in an arc west of the road and south of the town, between road and railway. The amalgamated Jat/Punjabi Battalion went into reserve and practiced counterattacks. 15th Indian Brigade worked hard on the defences and was harassed by enemy air, but was also out of combat long enough to be reasonably fresh. All in all eight battalions, dug in on ground of their own choosing and well supported by two regiments of field artillery, barred the way.[23]

The plan was to stand for ten days. The battle lasted only four days, for two reasons. One is very familiar. The Japanese were able to exploit larger weaknesses in the III Indian Corps strategic position to unhinge the defences at Kampar. The other needs more attention. They also outfought the defenders in a set-piece battle. It is the combination that explains Kampar and points to its significance. Facing difficult conditions, the Japanese found a way to fight their way through—at a price in casualties, but not in time. III Indian Corps had an awkward strategic but good tactical position, yet could not make Kampar more than a speed bump. Even in the best conditions available, battle tactics and fighting power could not bail Malaya Command out of its predicament.

Paris drafted a battle plan to alter the tactics used by 11th Indian Division and restore its self-confidence. He was refreshingly candid. The main battle for the army as a whole was yet to come—"Further concentration is, of course, an essential before we can really fight"–but to make it possible the division must mount an orderly fighting retreat. Paris wanted "an offensive withdrawal" with "a sting in the tail." The enemy must be made to feel the stress he had so far inflicted on the division, "sniped, shot up, attacked with Armd. Cars and 'Tiger' patrols and generally harried day and night." Paris emphasized two things: the defensive positions would be held; but this would be done by an aggressive defence, "prepared position will be regarded as a base for offensive operations." This envisaged using Kampar to spring a trap. Once the Japanese main line of advance was clear, the brigade being attacked would pin it down. The other brigade would then counterattack in force. The new division commander called them to arms:

> The present situation has GOT TO CEASE–and the Japanese have got to become frightened of us. I decline to believe that British and Indian troops are incapable of bringing about this desirable state of affairs. ... it is up to us to establish local and personal ascendancy over the enemy immediately opposed to us ..."[24]

Paris wanted to use the favourable ground at Kampar to synthesize the "firepower in a defile" tactics with the "fight to inflict pain" approach used by 12th Indian Brigade. In principle there was nothing very wrong with what he proposed. Unfortunately, three factors prevented the battle unfolding as he hoped: his own units did not fight as envisaged; the strategic situation undermined the whole position; and the enemy took advantage of both things. The Japanese expected the defenders to contest defiles along the trunk road between Kampar and Kuala Lumpur and planned accordingly. Yamashita adjusted his strategy: a deep flanking move, this time from the sea, a narrower flanking move along the coast, and a bold advance straight down the main road. He now had four full regiments to commit to the fight. 41st and 42nd advanced towards Kampar. 4th Guards advanced down the Perak River and along coastal tracks. And the 11th assembled a flotilla of 60 miscellaneous small vessels, some from Penang, to stage amphibious assaults along the west coast, at points where they could move quickly inland along roads and tracks to get behind the defenders on the trunk road. All four forces were on the move when the advance guard narrowly failed to prevent the demolition of the bridge at Dipang, on the evening of 29 December.[25] One patrol forced the outpost company of 28th Indian Brigade to fall back on its main position the next evening; other patrols skirmished with 15th Indian Brigade patrols further west. But any expectation the Japanese had of another walkover was rudely dispelled by very heavy and effective artillery fire. This seriously disrupted probes for weaknesses in the defences on the last two days of 1941. Tsuji sent medium tanks in to help, mortars were brought forward, but for the first time 5th Division was forced to mount a deliberate assault. 41st Regiment concentrated to attack the positions straddling the trunk road, but nearly the entire 42nd Regiment launched a flanking move well to the west, pushing through the swamps to find cover from artillery fire. Tsuji realized on New Year's Eve his forces at last faced a real test.[26] But their strategy, tactics and resolve all combined to pull the Japanese through.

The focal point of the battle was a tough two day close quarter fight for the three ridges held by the British Battalion, especially Thompsons Ridge up front. The British faced frequent severe mortar fire, plus two strong attacks with the bayonet in the early mornings of 1 and 2 January. Both gave them trouble on the right flank, where the ridges ran into the jungle and mountain. D Company ejected the first by a quick counterattack. The second proved more menacing. The Japanese overran the right front platoon. Heavy fighting continued all morning, pinning the British platoons down. Friendly artillery fire suppressed enemy mortars and broke up flanking moves, but could not help this close quarter fight. This forced Morrison, at 1100hrs, to request the brigade reserve to counterattack.[27]

By this time the Japanese were also in an awkward position. 42nd Regiment was bogged down plodding through swamps and in no position to intervene. No serious pressure was being put on the flank and rear of the main defences. 41st Regiment used the ground well to get in amongst the forward positions, but was now fully committed. Japanese aircraft were active but not doing much harm to the defenders, who were well concealed. Now would have been an ideal time for Paris to spring his trap. 28th Indian Brigade should have mounted a strong attack against the bridge at Dipang and the Jat/ Punjab Battalion in brigade reserve should have counterattacked, to catch 41st Regiment in a pincer. Sadly, this was never on the cards. Notwithstanding Paris' initial plan, 28th Indian Brigade fell back along the loop road on New Year's Day for no very good reason, not being under any real pressure. As for the brigade reserve, it made more piecemeal counterattacks, instead of concentrating for a really strong blow. One company was sent up the day before to backstop the British Battalion. That company was now ordered in to attack. It failed miserably. A second company was then brought forward to try. It could not attack until 1700hrs. Capt. J. Graham led a dramatic bayonet charge which ejected the enemy from Thompson's Ridge. But in the process the company lost two-thirds of its men, including Graham, and time ran out when darkness allowed the Japanese to regroup.[28]

What went wrong? Paris, facing broader threats, lost his nerve–but never made sure his units were ready to execute his bold plan, had he ordered them to. Japanese probes west of the main position distracted him and 28th Indian Brigade, which edged back to be ready to meet any threat to the rear, rather than stay poised to counterattack. Piecemeal company attacks reflected the same concern, as the brigade reserve tried to conserve its strength to face any flank attack. But there was little real justification for this. The three battalions holding the southwestern arc faced no serious pressure on these two days.[29] This reluctance to make a really powerful attack if it meant leaving little in reserve–even when there was good reason to hope a real punch might be decisive–was a habit British commanders simply could not shake. To execute his boldest plan, Paris had to find the nerve to risk an entirely different battle at Kampar: a full scale melee. Such a fight might well have allowed him to annihilate 41st Regiment in a pincer movement, but could also have become a brawl from which he could not disengage. The inherent tactical caution of this army, the tendency to use companies when battalions were needed, made a melee unlikely. The strategic situation, and the mission, ruled it out completely. Paris had orders not to let his division be destroyed. On New Year's Eve Heath and Percival agreed to give him discretion as to how long to fight at Kampar. Percival only insisted Heath hold the area north of Kuala Lumpur until 14 January. Heath had already selected one more main defensive position, at Tanjong Malim, and two delaying positions above it. Paris knew this, and by afternoon 2 January also knew Japanese forces had landed on the west coast and were advancing inland, threatening his line of retreat. Even before Capt. Graham's charge, he was already planning not an all-out brawl but a strategic retreat.[30]

The fighting at Kampar was inextricably connected to the threat from the sea. The British Battalion could not take much more punishment, and Paris had no confidence the division could safely fight on south of the town without being either cut off or cut up, or both. The retreat began at 2130hrs on 2 January. The British Battalion had to fight its way out, hard pressed in hand to hand fighting: "The inference was that our withdrawal just, and only just, anticipated a big Japanese attack."[31] This was correct. The enemy entered Kampar at midnight, hot on the heels of the retreating defenders. The Japanese paid for this victory. 5th Division was already tired, and this slogging match forced it to cede the mission to mount further amphibious assaults to the Imperial Guards, and pull 41st Regiment out to rest and regroup. They acknowledged resistance was fierce, gained little from their air support, the tanks did not break through here, and they could not silence the defenders artillery. That artillery pushed 42nd Regiment so far away it took it out of the fight. On the other hand, the assaults on the British Battalion made skillful use of ground, were pressed with great resolve, and ultimately would have pushed the defenders out of Kampar–unless Paris fought it out. Even when finally forced to, the Japanese defeated the defenders on their own ground and terms. This, coupled with their ability to attack the west coast, saw them through. The bold also make their own luck. The losses at Kampar did not slow down the "driving charge." The 42nd Regiment came out of the swamp just in time to take the lead and press the retreating 11th Indian Division hard.[32]

Percival put the best "spin"on Kampar in his postwar memoirs, insisting the battle proved that his Indian troops, when well led from good positions and with adequate rest, could stand up to the Japanese. The position was only abandoned because of the threat from the coast. But in his postwar despatch, Percival acknowledged 11th Indian Divison could not have held Kampar much longer anyway, given the intensity of enemy pressure. Heath, however, put his finger on the real dilemmas of Kampar:

At Kampar, where it had been the full intention to offer the enemy a robust defence on ground of careful choosing, units were given to understand that localities were to offer a last man and cartridge defence and the tails of the men went up amazingly high. But there, as elsewhere, the Divisional Commander could not afford, in view of the situation and his definite instructions, to allow his Division to be wiped off the map.[33]

The troops were indeed aroused. Some responded emotionally:

A welcome feeling of exhilaration elevated me as we held our ground against the stubborn Japanese advances. The words of patriotic songs flowed through my mind. 'Britons, never, never, never shall be slaves.' These words accompanied the incessant roar of our howitzers as they blasted the life from the Japanese and let them know who were the masters. Morale was now so high that I actually expected that we might, perhaps, push forward, and I was not alone in that thought … Our morale had taken another dent from the order to withdraw. We had retreated again just when we had begun to believe that the tide was turning in our favour.[34]

Even the sober language of a battalion war diary captured the expectation: "The main road was held by the British Bn. and with a four Bn. front, extra allotments of amn. and a good fd. of fire, it was hoped we should be able to make a stand."[35] But the division retreated despite the fact only one battalion was ever fully engaged. Whether the army could not implement more effective battle tactics, or its commanders dared not let it try, the result was the same. They retreated yet again. Worse, Percival and Heath now faced another daunting challenge.

The estimated arrival date of the crucial second convoy was still more than ten days away. There was only one more decent defensive position north of the junction with the lateral road. It was not yet prepared. All III Indian Corps brigades were committed, and tired. The enemy was converging, on the area Percival was so keen to deny, from three directions: the trunk road, the west coast, and the lateral road. Malaya Command again had to grapple with a fluid, fast-moving situation requiring careful co-ordination between different headquarters and clear priorities. The Corps objective was clear: hold the area north of Kuala Lumpur until 14 January. It was also clear the army must now prepare a fighting retreat to Johore. Beyond that, grave questions pressed for answers. What should 9th Indian Division do? How could the enemy be delayed on the trunk road long enough to dig in at Tanjong Malim? How strong was the threat on the west coast, and what could be done to contain it? These problems could only be solved together, but Percival and Heath both identified the most pressing: the landings on the west coast, which unhinged Kampar and threatened the whole strategy of a controlled retreat.

The west coast was the "Achilles Heel" of the plan to fight a corps battle north of Kuala Lumpur. Both sides had to improvise at sea. While the Japanese organized their motley collection of assault craft and barges, the defenders formed the Perak Flotilla, five small gunboats, to patrol the coast, escort friendly raiding forces, and intercept enemy shipping. Six fast Eureka patrol boats were sent up from Singapore to assist. Unfortunately the fleet, such as it was, was forced into action with very little air cover. On 23 December RAF Far East told III Indian Corps to request assistance a day in advance. The only support they could offer on a daily basis were two Buffalo fighters stripped down for photo reconnaissance, there was no fighter cover to spare for the "fleet," and any call to bomb enemy vessels had to be answered from Singapore. The enemy on the other hand now enjoyed ample air cover. By 2 January enemy bombers sank the flagship and four of the patrol boats, forcing the flotilla to restrict further operations to nighttime. Enemy dominance forced Pulford to divert the flying boat service from Burma to Singapore, to the long detour of the southern approach; friendly bombers were authorized to "destroy any craft found within 20 miles of coast" north of Port Dickson. The Japanese put the roads on the coastal plain under daily pressure from the air.[36] Under this air umbrella, their makeshift amphibious fleet threatened the whole coast.

This was one challenge too many for the forces Percival sent to fight north of Johore. The Japanese sent a battalion of the Imperial Guards down the Perak River and on 30 December sailed their flotilla from Lumut, to invade the river mouth with a strong battlegroup from 11th Regiment. This ignited a battle on the coastal flank that resembled the campaign at large: the more confusing it became, the better that was for the Japanese. From Kuala Selangor south the terrain was quite flat and open. There were three good access roads to the trunk road between Kuala Selangor and Port Swettenham, all of which could be used to outflank Kuala Lumpur, not to mention more between Port Swettenham and Port Dickson. Once the Japanese secured a beachhead anywhere below Utan Melintang, they would be hard to contain.[37]

The best way to stop any invasion was to defeat it on the water. But the defenders, blown off the water, weak in the air, overstretched on the ground, were again forced into the kind of fight in which they were most overmatched: an encounter battle fought at high tempo. The opening battle set the tone. The Independent Company, still being misused to watch the coast, tracked the Japanese flotilla, waiting for it to land. On New Year's Day at 1000hrs it engaged a tug towing five launches, grounded on a sandbar off the mouth of the Perak River:

> It was impossible to reach them by fire from the shore with the weapons available, and air action was requested by [radio] from 11 Div. 11 Div replied at 1030hrs that two Blenheims were on the way. These, however, never put in an appearance. No. 1 Pl[atoon] motor launch commanded by 2/Lt. Holland engaged the enemy at close range in an exciting fight at 1130hrs. The enemy was ready for our men and had mortars and machine guns in position on the sand bank. After a great fight, with the motor launch circling the grounded enemy at speed, our troops were forced to withdraw with 3 casualties out of the five aboard, two of whom subsequently died of wounds received in this action. At 1300hrs 4 of the launches were refloated and the last launch was away Southwards by 1400hrs. Air action or the loan of some artillery would have blown these launches out of the river, and it is a pity that no suitable action was taken.

The Blenheims did finally attack the enemy force at dusk, and drove it south to Utan Melintang to regroup and await orders. But such spirited but small scale attacks could not stop the Japanese concentrating in force early on 2 January, when the Guards battalion arrived at Telok Anson. This threat forced Paris to order 12th Indian Brigade to relieve the Independent Company and contain the advance. It could only delay the Japanese, who advanced in two directions: east towards the trunk road, south along a coastal track.[38]

This set the pattern for the whole battle along the coast: sometimes vigorous defensive action by forces on the spot could not be supported strongly enough, or quickly enough, to stop the enemy. Brig. R.G. Moir, Commander Lines of Communication, was responsible for the defence of the

Selangor and Negri Sembilan coast. To cover some 300 km, with more than half a dozen good access roads, he had three Volunteer Forces battalions, a Volunteer armoured car squadron and anti-tank battery, one regular artillery battery, and two companies of partly trained regulars from 2nd Battalion the Malay Regiment [2nd Malay]; the Perak Battalion of Volunteers disbanded before this battle began.[39] This pressure forced Heath to respond. However, his Corps was now pulled this way and that by the need to watch both flanks of 11th Indian Division, sort out what to do with the 9th, and regroup on the trunk road. Heath could not establish any priority, or concentrate strong forces, fast enough to gain a firm grip on any of his "fronts."[40] 11th Indian Division retreated fast enough to escape the threat from Telok Anson, but by 5 January the Japanese were threatening to cross the Selangor River. This would place them right in the midst of the network of roads from which they could cut the trunk road, between Tanjong Malim and Kuala Lumpur. The intrepid Independent Company did its best to delay the enemy near the important bridge at Batang Berjuntai. Their action explains why this flank could not be stabilized by half-measures:

> On a signal from HQ both platoons opened fire with a crash on the unsuspecting enemy and caused great havoc amongst their ranks. The reaction of the Japanese was typical of their skill and training in this type of warfare. Troops on either side of the ambush instantly plunged into the jungle towards the flanks of our troops, and a confused battle started almost immediately on both flanks. Owing to the strength of the enemy it soon became obvious that if the Company was to escape annihilation a withdrawal would have to be made ....

If regular infantry could not stop the Japanese in a prepared position, it was unreasonable to expect Moir's improvised forces to do so in an encounter battle. Heath had no choice but to send 15th Indian Brigade to stabilize the coastal flank.[41]

This decision was made on 5 January, when Percival, Heath and Bennett met at Segamat. The coastal battle swayed their discussion. The main reason the Japanese did not break through was they did not have enough amphibious lift or infantry on hand to do so. This might not have been crystal clear to the three generals at the time but they did believe, correctly, that the enemy could keep the pressure on. With 11th Indian Division under pressure once again, III Indian Corps was running out of fighting room faster than the target date was approaching. The high command now had to decide, quickly, how to prepare the "main battle." That meant extricating III Indian Corps as smoothly as possible. The crux remained the connection between Malaya Command's mission and its tactical situation. The boldest possibility involved 9th Indian Division.

For about a week Heath, Barstow, and their staffs pondered an idea that would have changed the campaign one way or the other–had it been adopted. The proposal was for 9th Indian Division to counterattack the Japanese on their left flank as they pursued 11th Indian Division. The plan was never spelt out very clearly, but the general idea ran as follows. 11th Indian Division would maintain contact with the enemy, bait him on, buy time for the 9th to concentrate east of the crucial junction at Kuala Kubu. As the enemy moved through that area, the 11th would stand and fight, the 9th would strike hard from the east. This was the Kampar choice writ large. Such a counterattack would have provoked a large encounter battle on the relatively open ground north and west of Kuala Lumpur. Nobody went so far as to hope for a strategic reversal, given the enemy's control of the air and the open ground in Selangor. But they did hope the enemy could be hit hard enough to force him to retreat and regroup. This would allow III Indian Corps to fall back in good order to northern Johore. But if the attack failed the Corps could be caught in the kind of battle Percival did not want to risk: a fight that could end in its effective destruction. The plan was problematic at best. The losses suffered around Kuantan made it less appealing. To make it work Percival, Heath and their subordinates would have to throw caution to the winds on two levels. First, they would have to accept the risk to Percival's campaign strategy and therefore Malaya Command's mission. Second, they would have to shrug off their ingrained habit to make piecemeal attacks–this was an all or nothing venture from Corps to battalion. Even had the Corps found the nerve to try this, only 12th Indian Brigade really had the skill needed to drive home such a counteroffensive. The attack would face an enemy superior in armour and air support, which mattered in this terrain. Once again Percival had to choose between courses that were all calculated risks. Once again he chose the course that at least postponed the moment of truth: the retreat would continue.[42]

Percival decided to abandon Kuala Lumpur. Malaya Command would stand and fight its "main battle" south of the open country, and multiple roads, of Selangor and Negri Sembilan. The battle would be fought along the general "line" Muar-Segamat-Mersing in northern Johore, where the peninsula narrowed and offered more favourable terrain for defence. But to gain time to evacuate the very large stockpiles of military supplies around Kuala Lumpur, destroy facilities useful to the enemy, and deny the airbases long enough to cover the incoming convoy, Heath must still deny the area Kuala Lumpur-Port Swettenham until 14 January. 9th Indian Division would cover the eastern approaches to the trunk road until forced to retreat through

Kuala Kubu. Now it was 15th Indian Brigade's turn to do double duty: backing up on the trunk road, helping contain the west coast threat. 12th and 28th Indian Brigade would delay the main enemy advance. A brief action would be fought at Slim River, then a longer one at Tanjong Malim, to keep the enemy north of Kuala Kubu until 10 January.[43]

Percival had at least one good reason to opt for this plan. The inbound convoy was carrying the first batch of Hurricane fighters, on whom so much depended and for whom hopes were so high.Only in retrospect is it fair to note the Japanese did not press the convoys as hard as Percival feared, and the Hurricanes were not the saviour so many desired. And after all Percival's mission was unchanged: hold the naval base. But the risk was very real. Keeping most of 9th Indian Division out of the fight left the whole burden on three very tired brigades, fighting on two fronts. Fresh enemy regiments were pressing on both the trunk road and the coastal roads, and their "driving charge" was now being effectively supported from the air. 12th and 28th Indian Brigades had nearly three full days to prepare the Slim River delaying position. But this work was disrupted by enemy air attacks and itself further tired the troops. The division struggled to prepare defences at Slim River and Tanjong Malim and fight at the same time.[44]

III Indian Corps' struggle to keep the enemy at bay without being shattered in the process exploded on the morning of 7 January, at Slim River. In a battle second only to Jitra in both significance and incompetence, 12th and 28th Indian Brigades were routed in six hours. Slim River was not as naturally strong as either Kampar or Tanjong Malim, but it had possibilities. Stewart, now commanding 12th Indian Brigade, was point man at Slim River. But Percival, Heath and Paris all approved the position and toured it the week before the fight. The only senior officer connected to this battle but not open to criticism was Simson. The Chief Engineer identified the trunk road north of the village of Trolak, about seven kilometres north of Slim River railway station, as a defile that could be turned into a good delaying position, where an enemy tank attack could be punished. Simson took the initiative to select sites where anti-tank equipment could be dumped, sped up the supply of materiel to 11th Indian Division, and pressed Heath to follow up.[45] After that almost everything went wrong for the defenders, in a battle that classically illustrated the "fog of war."

North of Trolak the road formed the narrowest of defiles, the jungle crowding up to it, on both sides, for many kilometres. The old trunk road and the railway ran closely together, forming a narrow corridor down to Slim village, next to the railway station. Between Trolak and the station two rubber estates bordered the western edge of the corridor, stretching five kilometres to the west; on the eastern edge, patches of rubber broke up the dense jungle. Slim River itself was a good anti-tank obstacle. But at the station road and railway parted, the road veering east for eight kilometres until again turning south. That forced the defenders to cover two bridges, and the road and railway did not converge again until Tanjong Malim, 15 km south. Heath agreed the narrow defile could be turned into a killing ground for tanks.[46] Yet nearly every possible tactical mistake that could be made was made. Why?

The answers include fatigue, misreading the threat, sloppy deployment, but especially tempo. The division should not have been surprised by the manner and ferocity of the Japanese attack–but it was, and could not respond effectively. 12th Indian Brigade was assigned to the position north of Trolak late on 3 January–despite the fact it had been in action for nearly three weeks, lost 25% of its infantry, and was truly worn out. 28th Indian Brigade moved into the Slim area to back it up. The plan was to delay and retreat in leapfrog style, for three days at Trolak, another day at Slim.[47] 4/19 Hyderabad easily repelled an enemy probe on 5 January. The next day Paris and Stewart concluded the enemy was trying to outflank the position by moving through the jungle, well to the west. That prompted them to make fateful decisions. Paris decided to accelerate the retreat, to pull 12th Indian Brigade back late on 7 January. Because it was now in position, he decided to rest 28th Indian Brigade. Paris ordered a skeptical Brig. Selby to give his men a full nights sleep and only move into position the next morning. Paris and Stewart then decided there was little scope to employ artillery in this area. Only one field regiment stayed up front to support the division, and only one of its batteries went into firing positions. The other two parked off the road in the Cluny Estate, guns in tow. Paris sent forward only two anti-tank batteries, six guns in all. More than half his field and three quarters of his anti-tank guns went back to Tanjong Malim.[48]

These were all dubious decisions, because they ignored or downplayed things that should have been clear at the time. The enemy was advancing without pause. 11th Indian Division could not afford to lose control of the road. Most of its men were so tired their speed of mind and foot was well below par. The whole basis for defending north of Trolak was to bait the enemy into making a tank-led attack, as he had at Jitra. If the enemy came through the jungle the division could at least retreat along the road, without much risk. But if he broke through on the road it could be scattered, on the wrong side of the river. More anti-tank guns and equipment should have been sent forward. This was an ideal spot to bring down preregistered artillery fire on the narrow road defile once tanks were engaged, if not use the guns in a direct fire anti-tank role. Paris and Stewart overlooked these options, then made the position weaker still. Shortly before the war the trunk road north of Trolak was straightened out. The loops of the old road were being reclaimed by the jungle, but still usable. The two rubber estates between Trolak and Slim, and the Cluny Estate between Slim and the road bridge, were crisscrossed by estate roads and tracks. This gave Japanese tanks opportunities to bypass road blocks on the trunk road. Stewart nevertheless decided to leave the loops and estate roads unmined. He wanted his armoured cars to support the forward battalions, and his trucks to pull the infantry out when the time came to retreat. The division had 1400 anti-tank mines in its depot, and a good number of concrete cylinders to use as roadblocks. It sent only 24 mines to 12th Indian Brigade. The brigade built only two roadblocks, neglecting even to chain the cylinders together to make them more effective. The lead battalion, 4/19 Hyderabad, had only one anti-tank gun, a few cylinders, no mines at all, and no experience fighting tanks.[49]

The initial Japanese plan would have suited Paris and Stewart very well: to use a whole regiment to mount a two pronged deliberate attack, along the road and by a wide flank march to the west, striking in at Trolak. But Major Shimada, commanding a company of medium tanks, persuaded Col. Ando to change the plan. They formed a battlegroup with 30 tanks, a battalion of motorized infantry, two platoons of engineers and a battery of light artillery. Led by the tanks, this force would strike hard straight down the trunk road in the early hours of 7 January; another infantry battalion would outflank the defenders on their left, converging around Slim River. The tanks would break through the defences, the infantry would sweep them up. Japanese tactical intelligence was excellent. They knew who opposed them, roughly where they were digging in, and that there were road loops. They rightly expected the cover and confusion of darkness to help conceal their advance and disrupt the defenders. This would be a classic "filleting attack."[50] Stewart knew all about this tactic, had indeed trained the Argylls in his own version of it before the war. Where the Scots relied on artillery bombardment to blast the narrow road defile ahead of the advancing infantry, the Japanese substituted tanks. The ground above Trolak was a decent place to meet this kind of attack. Unfortunately the decisions made by Paris and Stewart turned it into a death trap for their own division. They made bad decisions because they prepared to fight the wrong battle.

Stewart deployed his brigade in depth along the rail and road corridor. 4/19 Hyderabad would delay the enemy, then fall back through 5/2 Punjabi. Both these battalions deployed right on and around the railway and road. They were backstopped by 2nd Argylls, who spread wide to either flank of the corridor along an estate road. The position looked like an upside down letter T. Stewart expected the enemy to outflank the Punjabis, so he deployed the Argylls to be ready to "sandwich" them. Finally, to avoid air attack he moved his brigade headquarters to an estate road in the middle of the rubber, well west of Trolak–even though there were few working radios or field telephones on hand.[51] This was asking for trouble. If he lost control of the road Stewart would face a crisis. His job was only to delay, so his infantry had to be able to retreat; off the road and without vehicles this would be difficult. If he lost touch with his units, it could become impossible. The division should have known all this. Not only did the ground all but shout it out, they were taught at Jitra what a tank blitz could do. And Stewart suffered one bruising encounter with tanks just north of Dipang, while retreating on Kampar. By now his own battalion was less fit, somewhat disrupted by absorbing a new commanding officer and 100 reinforcements the day before the battle. The Hyderabadis were in even worse shape. To top it all off, late on 6 January a Chinese refugee told Stewart's staff that a column of "iron landships" was moving over the repaired bridge at Sungkai, 12 km north. Nevertheless Paris and Stewart made a grave mistake: they assumed the enemy would play it safe and move deliberately.[52] After a solid month of fighting Yamahsita's army this was folly; the price was severe.

The first Japanese mortar rounds hit the Hyderabadis around 0330hrs; the tanks came on minutes later. In less than an hour the Japanese vanguard removed the cylinder block without opposition, knocked out the single anti-tank gun, exploited the darkness to outflank the defenders on a road loop, and scattered the Hyderabadis in disarray. They hit the stronger 5/2 Punjabi positions at 0430hrs and the real fight began. Two tanks were stopped by mines. The Punjabis rained Molotov cocktails and grenades down on the others, which temporarily stalled the column. This made them a sitting duck target for a preregistered artillery bombardment, but no such was laid on. The eight supporting guns of 350th Field Battery instead provided general harassing fire around the whole battalion area. Japanese tanks soon found another road loop, and by 0530hrs were engaging the reserve Punjabi company. In another fierce fight three more tanks were knocked out by mines, anti-tank guns and anti-tank rifles–but the intrepid Japanese tankers moved onto yet another road loop. By 0630hrs both Indian battalions were scattered into the jungle and the Japanese column drove straight for the last battalion in position: 2nd Argylls.[53]

Throughout these early hours Stewart did not know what was going on. Around 0515hrs the commanding officer of 5/2 Punjabis reported his unit was being heavily engaged by tanks. Stewart ordered him to fight on. Shortly after that brigade headquarters lost line communications with all units except D Company 2nd Argylls, a short distance away. This fatally obstructed all subsequent efforts by the chain of command to intervene. Stewart warned the Argylls to build road blocks. He then sent an officer to 28th Indian Brigade headquarters at Slim. Arriving as the Japanese approached the Argylls, this officer told Selby "things going badly in front." On his own initiative Selby ordered his battalions into position, then set out to consult Stewart. Around the same time Stewart reported to division headquarters, all the way back at Tanjong Malim, "some sort of breakthrough, send staff officer." Division then lost contact, prompting Paris to send Harrison to find out what was going on. The Japanese moved much faster than any of them.[54]

Five Japanese tanks drove into two hastily improvised Argyll roadblocks. They overran the only anti-tank gun in position, which had just retreated from the Punjabi defences, and swept the first one aside. The second was in front of a short but important bridge at Trolak. The bridge was wired for demolition. The tanks and infantry charged forward, Second Lt. Watanabe dismounting from the second tank to cut the demolition wires with his sword. They captured the bridge intact. The Argyll armoured cars then bravely engaged the tanks. They destroyed the cars, broke clean through the defences, and scattered the Scottish infantry into the jungle and rubber, shortly after 0700hrs. The tanks pressed on, leaving the fight to their supporting infantry.[55] The defenders now made two crucial mistakes. There was a check position two kilometres south of the bridge, at a bend in the road crowded by jungle. It was a good place for guns to engage enemy tanks at pointblank range. This was a desperate tactic but so was the situation. Around 0600hrs Stewart ordered the reserve battalion, 5/14 Punjabi, to move into the check position. But they were not told enemy tanks were on the move, so they set out from Slim village without their anti-tank rifles. The 350th Field Battery was nearby, carrying on its harassing fire. As will be seen, there is reason to feel they might have stopped the Japanese tanks there and then had they "marched to the sound of the guns." But when he heard enemy tanks were breaking through the Argylls, the battery commander ordered his men to hitch up their guns and retreat. This meant the Japanese vanguard, now 15 tanks, was advancing towards units not ready to stop it.[56]

Nothing but the most desperate response could have stopped the Japanese now. Unfortunately, when Selby reached Stewart's out of the way headquarters at 0720hrs he was told that despite enemy penetration 12th Indian Brigade felt it could fight on. The Japanese tank vanguard was now well ahead of its infantry, but Stewart either did not think they would press on regardless or did not appreciate the damage tanks could do to a rear area not prepared for them. He focused on the melee between his scattered companies and the following infantry. It took Selby a full hour to regain touch with his units; he reached the headquarters of 2/2 Gurkhas, at Slim River station, at 0820hrs.[57] It was far too late. At 0735hrs the leading Japanese tanks, moving in three troops of five, literally ran into 5/14 Punjabi marching north along the road. They tore its two leading companies to pieces and scattered the rest into the adjacent rubber. Ten minutes later the tanks ran into the three anti-tank guns attached to 28th Indian Brigade, sent up to reinforce the Argylls. They were overrun before they could unhitch from their tractors. At 0800hrs the rampaging tanks drove by Slim village. Thanks to Selby 2/9 Gurkhas were in position, but they had no anti-tank weapons so could not stop the column. 2/1 Gurkhas, Selby's third unit, were marching east along the road, also without any anti-tank weapons, to their position halfway between Slim village and the road bridge. For the second time in the campaign this unit met Japanese tanks, this time in literally catastrophic fashion. At 0805hrs Major W.J. Winkfield was leading the battalion in column of route:

> Sudden sense of unease behind me; men looking back and hurrying. Sent Wylie back to correct distances. Then gun fired just behind me and something grazed my leg. Looked to see tank bearing down on me. Dived into ditch. After tanks passed found Bn. had vanished except for a few casualties.

The tanks shot up the rubber for ten minutes, then moved on. In their wake Winkfield could only rally a dozen men out of over 500.[58] The Japanese next shot up a field ambulance unit, which of course could not shoot back. The two remaining batteries of the 137th Field Regiment parked nearby in the rubber could have, but must not have had any idea what was happening. That is the only reasonable way to explain what happened now, because these gunners were close enough to the road to be detected by the tanks. Not long before they must have allowed their retreating comrades from 350th Field Battery to drive right by without communicating, and as late as 0820hrs were still eating breakfast, their guns hitched to tractors. Battalion headquarters was down the road, closer to the designated Gurkha position, but the commanding officer was already dead, caught by the Japanese while driving to his unit. The Japanese now shot the gunners up, knocking out three guns and a number of vehicles, then drove on. The battery officers decided the battle must be lost, spiked the guns and dispersed into the jungle. This was another very unfortunate decision. No Japanese infantry was in sight. The Japanese were in fact now widely separated in at least two groups. The remaining 25 pounder guns could have been most useful had they deployed to cover the road. And dispersal was hardly in the best tradition of the Royal Artillery. It can only reflect fatigue, shock, and loss of leaders. The next gunners to encounter the tanks put up a fight. Four 40mm guns of 16th Light Anti-Aircraft Battery Hong Kong and Singapore Royal Artillery [HKSRA], guarding the road bridge, fired on the tanks at point blank range as they approached at 0840hrs. Sadly the gunners had no armour-piercing rounds and could not pierce the tanks frontal armour. The tanks accelerated towards the bridge. Watanabe used his machine gun this time to disperse the sappers and sever the wires; meanwhile the gunners, having had enough, ran into the rubber. The bridge was captured intact.[59]

In just over five hours 30 Japanese tanks advanced 35 km right through two brigades. Their infantry was still fighting towards Slim River station when the tanks pushed forward on their own. The tanks only accelerated beyond fast walking speed when they reached Slim River bridge. Units scattered into rubber or jungle were shot up by following tanks and hard pressed by infantry. Two battalions were annihilated without firing a shot, three dispersed to the point of collapse; the only two still intact and in position were helpless against tanks. The enemy now controlled the road. The rampage finally stopped when the tankers met a Royal Artillery regiment worthy of the name. The 155th Lanarkshire Yeomanry Field Regiment Royal Artillery [155th Field Regiment], in harbour south of the road bridge, was alerted at 0900hrs. It moved forward with resolve, its commanding officer killed when he literally drove into enemy fire. About four kilometres south of the bridge the road narrows into a severe defile through a patch of jungle. The first gun was destroyed before it could deploy, but the second 4.5" howitzer destroyed the lead tank at point blank range, in that defile. The gunners then damaged the second tank and settled in to fight it out on the road over open sights. Spent, the Japanese waited for reinforcements. The advance ground to a halt; by early afternoon the Japanese turned around to clean up the scattered remnants of 11th Indian Division, to clear the path for a full scale advance.[60]

At Slim River 30 Japanese tanks, supported by no more than 1000 infantry, engineers and gunners, destroyed the fighting power of two brigades in a morning. The only men who had any chance to prevent this in the crucial hours between 0515, when the first reports of serious fighting filtered back, and 0800, when the bold Japanese tankers drove past Slim village, were Stewart, Selby, Harrison, and the commanding officers of three artillery batteries. Tracking their actions explains the disaster. Stewart was so far off to the flank he could not find out what was going on until it was too late. Selby did what he could but had to rely on Stewart, and lost crucial time seeking him out. One of his battalions was destroyed and the road lost before he returned. Harrison met the retreating 350th Field Battery south of the road bridge and was told they were ordered all the way back to Tanjong Malim, due to a "minor breakthrough." Despite being division chief of staff he did not ask why the guns assigned to support the forward position would be sent right out of the battle area because of a "minor breakthrough," nor stop them. Crossing the bridge, he drove straight into the Japanese tanks, assuming them to be friendly armoured cars. Failing this test in vehicle recognition nearly cost him his life and did cost him his staff car. Harrison played hide and seek with the tanks before finally bicycling into 28th Indian Brigade headquarters at 1040hrs, where all he could do was report the destruction of an artillery regiment and an infantry battalion, virtually before his eyes. The failure of all three batteries of 137th Field Regiment to engage has already been described.[61]

Stewart and Selby tried to rally their units, but without any effective anti-tank weapons they could not regain the road. This forced them, that evening, to direct what men they did find to retreat in much harder going, across the river, along the railway, through the jungle. Heavy equipment and vehicles had to be destroyed. D Company, deployed on the left flank, was the only Argyll company to retreat relatively intact. The next day only 1200 all ranks of 11th Indian Division regrouped at Tanjong Malim. The Argylls were down to less than 100, 2/1 Gurkhas to a mere two dozen. While stragglers trickled in for days, many more never made it through the jungle, dying or being captured. The Japanese probably lost less than 150 casualties and killed more than three times that many. Most damaging, they ultimately took more than 3000 prisoners from this battle.[62]

Battle is the wrong word. Slim River was a fiasco. Slim River was also the end of Percival's strategy. That same day Wavell arrived in Singapore to inspect his new command. The next day he went up country to see the situation for himself. The new Supreme Commander met Heath, Paris, Stewart and Selby. They all made a very poor impression on him, not surprising given how drained they were by now. After being briefed by Stewart, Wavell said "Well, I have never listened to a more garbled account of an operation."[63] And the tactical situation could not have seemed much worse. III Indian Corps would now be very lucky to maintain some sort of defence on the trunk road. There was a real chance 9th Indian Division could be cut off by any further Japanese advance, which, coupled with the collapse of 11th Indian Division, now ruled out any counterattack. The threat from the west coast remained ominous at best. Wavell concluded III Indian Corps was too spent to continue its fighting retreat, especially in the unfavourable terrain of central Malaya. He returned to Singapore on 9 January and issued new orders. III Indian Corps would break contact and give up central Malaya. Covered by demolitions and small rearguards, it would make a strategic retreat to northern Johore. The battle to keep the enemy at bay from Singapore was over.[64]

Under the circumstances Wavell had no choice. Heath's force could not fight on without relief. III Indian Corps broke clear, but suffered further losses in confused fighting near the west coast. Kuala Lumpur fell uncontested to the enemy on 11 January. This may only have been a few days earlier than Percival hoped, but when all relevant factors are added up one can only conclude the price was too high. At Slim River the Japanese captured a month's worth of supplies for two brigades, along with 50 Bren Carriers and dozens of very useful trucks. More supplies of all kinds were lost because there was not enough time to destroy the large depots around Kuala Lumpur. These windfalls, plus the failure to wreak any serious havoc with Japanese supply lines, and the capture of the port at Kuantan and airbases in central Malaya, all eased what was now a difficult supply problem for Yamashita's army—enough for it to continue its advance.[65] The decisive issue was whether they had won the race; this rested on a crucial question. Did the defenders still have enough time, space and fighting power to keep the Japanese away from Singapore long enough to allow it to be reinforced strongly enough to defeat them in turn?

The answer was no. Fighting up north for a month without concentrating their forces cost Malaya Command the fighting power of three infantry brigades and RAF Far East the bulk of its fighter force. Malaya Command had just received 45th Indian Brigade, before the end of the month expected 44th Indian Brigade and the entire 18th Division, and within days would receive the first batch of Hurricane fighters. But the three shattered brigades were all at least oriented to the theatre, far more ready to fight than those coming in. The shattering of 12th Indian Brigade was particularly costly because it was the one formation which demonstrated any ability to cope with Japanese tactics—before Slim River. As for the fighters, their pilots also needed time to adjust to the theatre and the enemy, and would be heavily outnumbered. Resting it all on their shoulders could never have worked. The reinforcements Malaya Command really needed, the tough battle experienced Australian infantry divisions and British armoured brigade, had only just begun to assemble in Egypt when Wavell arrived in Singapore. There was no avoiding the bottom line. Malaya Command must now fight its "main battle" with less fighting power, for a longer time and in less space, than it had when the war began. Barring an act of Providence or catastrophic Japanese mistake, the British Empire could now not prevent the fall of Singapore.

Defeat would always have been difficult to prevent; disaster should have been avoidable. This bottom line can not be attributed to any one cause. It was the product of a military system for imperial defence that could not cope, at any time or any level, with the demands placed upon it. The plans by which the British Empire set out to defend Singapore all contained fatal flaws that made each unlikely to succeed, and all compromised each other. Force Z could not stop the enemy because it was never seriously intended to. But the promise that it could forced Far East Command to fight to hold its base. The air plan could not work because the necessary forces were not on hand. But the need to protect it forced Malaya Command to compromise its strategy, then when it failed left the army without air cover. *Matador* could never work because it was strategic and tactical nonsense in the conditions in which it had to be executed–but the focus on it compromised the alternate plan to fight in a prepared position. Once past that position, there was no further plan. The Japanese calculated risk to prosecute a "driving charge" tore into this vacuum, and into the ponderous chain of command that tried to fill it. The tempo the enemy forced on the British chain of command ruined all its efforts to find a viable defence strategy. There were only two ways the defenders could try to resolve the problem, because there are only two links on a chain with only one connection: the ends. The central direction of the war could have changed its policy, allowed Percival to change campaign strategy and accepted the political risks. It refused to do so. That left the fate of Singapore in the hands of the bottom link: the fighting units, especially the "poor bloody infantry."

All bore down in the end on the men at the sharp end. Decisions in imperial defence policy and grand strategy put them in a compromising position and kept them there. Failure to evaluate the enemy soberly made his onslaught all the more shocking when they faced it. The manner by which the Empire prepared for war in Malaya reflected its deepest dilemmas: there were always more military challenges to face than resources to face them, and political fault lines that made categorical choices too intimidating. Because it could not meet all needs, but would not relinquish any commitments, it always had to improvise. Because it did not know where its forces would have to fight, they trained to fight anywhere in general but nowhere in particular. In the end Percival's strategy failed because his army was nowhere near good enough to make it work. The Japanese were bold, tough, professional, and worked their advantages well. But they were far from perfect, made mistakes and took risks that could have been exploited. The reason they were now poised to humiliate the British Empire went beyond circumstances and personalities. This was ultimately a clash of imperial military systems. And the fatal weakness was tempo. One British officer commented: "We couldn't fight off the main roads in the paddy fields. We didn't expect the Japs to come so fast through the paddy and rubber. It was the speed which surprised us."[66] The Japanese attacked Malaya at maximum tempo, from high command to rifle company, with plans and tactics connected to each other, to grand strategy, and to the ground. The defenders could not match the tempo, or the connections, at any level. Now they faced the consequences.

1 Floating dock, Sembawang naval base, Singapore.

2 Marco Polo bridge, northern China, 1937.

3 HMS *Ladybird* after Japanese attack, December 1937.

4 Top Sembawang naval base construction, September 1941.

5 Above Air Chief Marshal Sir Robert Brooke-Popham and staff.

6 Left Maj.-Gen. Sir William Dobbie.

7 Maj.-Gen. L. V. Bond reviews AIF in Malaya, ANZAC Day 1941.

8 Air Marshal Sir J.T. Babington.

9 Field Marshal Sir John Dill.

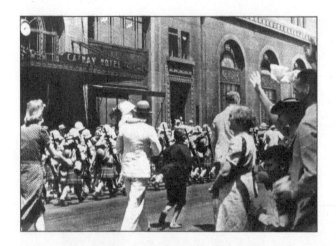

10 TOP Seaforth Highlanders evacuate Shanghai, 25 March 1940.

11 CENTRE European civilians evacuated from Penang, December 1941.

12 BOTTOM Asian civilian refugees, Malaya.

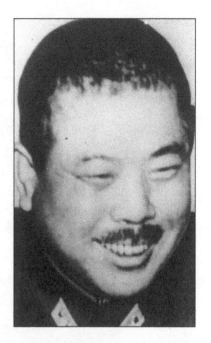

13 Lieutenant-General Arthur
Percival (back right) with Air Vice-
Marshal C.W.H. Pulford (front).

14 Lieutenant-General Yamashita
Tomoyuki.

15 Fifteen-inch coastal gun, Singapore.

16 TOP Wavell (left) inspects Singapore coastal guns, November 1941.

17 CENTRE Maj.-Generals Bennett and DM Murray-Lyon.

18 BOTTOM Indian mountain gunners training amongst rubber trees.

19 Top Argyll and Sutherland
Highlanders training in close
country.

20 Above Labourers in
Singapore making gas masks.

21 Right Japanese 'knee-
mortar' grenade launcher,
Type 89.

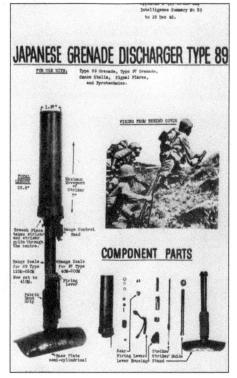

22 Top Japanese collapsable assault boat, Model 95 A.

23 Centre Two Model 95 boats combined to form a 27-foot landing craft.

24 Bottom Japanese medium machine-gun crew in the field.

25 Japanese troops
with 'infantry gun'
in the field.

26 New Zealand
squadron celebrates
a rare aerial 'kill'.

27 Japanese infantry board
landing craft off Kota Bharu,
8 December 1941.

28 TOP Japanese medium
tank being floated across
river, China.

29 CENTRE HMS *Prince of
Wales* leaves Singapore, 8
December 1941.

30 BOTTOM Japanese
'infantry guns' moving
through jungle, Malaya.

31 Admiral Sir W Tennant.

32 RIGHT Stocks of petrol captured by the Japanese, Malaya, December 1941.

33 BELOW Force Z survivors being rescued, 10 December 1941.

34 Japanese tanks advancing along road, Malaya.

35 LEFT Old road loops near 12th Indian Brigade position, Trolak.

36 BELOW Captured British vehicles, Malaya, January 1942.

37 Top General Sir Henry Pownall
and Field Marshal Earl Wavell.

38 Centre Civilians in one of the
few public air-raid shelters
in Singapore.

39 Bottom Japanese infantry
storm into Johore Bharu, for
once too late.

40 TOP Percival and party arrive at Bukit Timah for surrender negotiations.

41 CENTRE Yamashita and Percival discuss surender.

42 BOTTOM Japanese victory parade, Fullerton Square Singapore, 17 February 1942.

The Main Battle Mirage

9 January 1942 was a busy day for the man now responsible for the defence of Singapore. General Archibald P. Wavell, just settling into his new appointment as Allied Supreme Commander Southwest Pacific, toured the northern shore of the island, met with senior subordinates, reflected on what he saw and heard since arriving in Malaya two days before. Singapore was the key position. It was the only hub through which Wavell could absorb reinforcements strong enough to prevent the Japanese from destroying his command, the central position he must hold to link the battles for the "Malay Barrier." And Singapore was already in peril. Japanese naval forces dominated the area. Japanese air forces were now moving into central Malaya, directly threatening the reinforcement life-line from India. Malaya Command was in retreat, badly cut up by the fight to keep that life-line open. And the reinforcements Wavell really needed, the battle hardened formations coming from North Africa, could not arrive before the enemy would attack again.

Yet Wavell was not intimidated. He explained why in a telegram to his successor as C-in-C India. Wavell made five points. First, III Indian Corps suffered a "bad start" because it was compromised by bad plans–the need to defend poorly placed airbases, contradictory plans to advance and defend. Solution: "moral obvious." Second, it suffered two major defeats because it was caught off guard by tank attacks down main roads: "which should never have occurred with proper dispositions against obvious threat." Third, the Japanese trained well to fight in the terrain at hand, but as to their tactics: "Effective counter to these tactics can easily be devised once they are realized." Enemy air superiority was more menacing: "If Japanese had also used their air superiority effectively we might have had complete disaster." Luckily "air bombing was spasmodic, scattered and completely ineffective and fighters were not used on ground targets or retreating troops." The only problem for which Wavell did not have a ready answer was the dilution of Indian units by "milking," the not subtle note on which he ended this optimistic appraisal.[1] Wavell did not think all was lost, because he concluded the Japanese advance owed more to mistakes by the defenders than to Japanese combat power. The new Supreme Commander meant to change that.

Earlier that day Wavell informed the COS of his first command decision:

"Decision taken to withdraw 3 Ind. Corps into Johore and to fight decisive battle in NW Johore with force to be known as WESTFORCE, under command GOC 8 Aust. Div."[2] Wavell swept through Singapore like a tropical storm his first week in command, overruling subordinates, changing plans, asking questions, making calculations. He worked to pull the defence forces together as fast as possible, to stop the Japanese advance. Whether called "main battle" or "decisive battle" the stakes were clear. Malaya Command must now retreat to northern Johore, where the ground offered the chance to concentrate forces. But the Japanese would surely attack as soon as possible, in full strength. This was the penultimate "line" of defence. Any further retreat would allow the enemy to attack Singapore itself. To hold the "Malay Barrier" Wavell must hold Singapore–before the strategic rescue promised by all prewar plans.

The Japanese gave the new Supreme Commander exactly a week after the debacle at Slim River to grip the defence. They bumped into the forward positions on the trunk road, now manned by Australian infantry, on the afternoon of 14 January. Wavell's plan was set, his forces reorganized. Led by the Australians, a regrouped Malaya Command would fight the Japanese to a standstill on the trunk road. This would force them to build up for a more deliberate advance. That would buy time for I Australian Corps to arrive late next month, after which ABDA Command could counterattack. Briefing the COS the day the battle started, Wavell warned them it would be a "near run thing." Success depended on several things. First the Australians must stop the Japanese dead in their tracks. Then the convoys already closing on Singapore must arrive unscathed. Finally, the forces they were carrying must immediately join the "main battle." The next day Wavell spelt it out: provided his first wave of reinforcements arrived intact, he could hold Singapore.[3]

Wavell's optimism was short lived. On 19 January he ordered Percival to "work out plans for prolonging resistance on Singapore Island should Johore battle be lost."[4] That fight was in fact being lost even as he gave that order. Wavell's appreciation was fatally flawed. The Japanese were stronger, and his own forces weaker, than he supposed. By this time there was only one way to stop the Japanese cold in Malaya: catastrophic Japanese errors. Pretending otherwise was walking into a mirage. Wavell made the mirage worse by misreading and mishandling the situation–but did after all inherit it. Percival brought the mirage closer. His hard fight in the north, to allow his army to wage a "main battle" once reinforced, cost so much there was no net gain. But the imperial military system ultimately created this mirage.

Four questions need to be answered to explain this "main battle" mirage and its consequences. First, how did the two sides prepare for battle in northern

Johore? Second, how did they fight? Third, how was this fight connected to broader strategic problems? Finally, how in the end did Malaya Command manage to retreat to Singapore island–and to what end? The argument is stark. The "main battle" of the campaign had already been lost. By trying to fight the battle for Johore as that "main battle," British Empire forces turned local defeat into wider disaster.

11

Stand and Fight

One word underpinned the fight for Johore: reinforcements. The defenders hoped to give theirs time to orient before throwing them into battle. But the Japanese "driving charge" ruined their plans yet again. The 45th Indian Brigade arrived first, on 3 January. It was at best "semi-trained" for desert warfare, diverted, one hour after embarking on 21 December, from Iraq to Malaya. All three of Brig. H.C. Duncan's battalions were products of the heavily milked Indian Army expansions. They were short on experienced British officers, and manned largely by very young troops with no battle experience. Malaya Command sent the brigade to Malacca where there were empty barracks and space to train–but also close at hand if the need arose: "You must, however, be prepared to take part in active operations very shortly after arrival."[1] The sudden collapse at Slim River pulled the brigade into the field even before all its elements cleared Singapore. One unit, the 5th Battalion 18th Regiment Royal Garwhali Rifles [5/18 Royal Garwhalis], started training on 5 January in Malacca, went on stand by to move north on the 6th, moved up as reserve for III Indian Corps on the 7th, and spent the next week falling back in reserve. It moved into position as brigade reserve near Muar at almost the same time the Japanese vanguard bumped into the Australians on the main road. The other two battalions, 7th Battalion 6th Regiment Rajputana Rifles [7/6 Rajputs] and 4th Battalion 9th Jat Regiment [4/9 Jats], moved into their battle position from 11 January.[2]

Sending a raw brigade up front so quickly was hardly wise, but given the tempo of the Japanese advance Malaya Command saw little choice. The fixed defences on the east coast were strong, but Japanese forces were on the move in the South China Sea, and Percival did not want to weaken them; he also felt moving brigades back and forth across the lateral road in Johore would snarl his transport. The trunk road was the main axis of advance so he would not send raw units there. The only other option was to have the brigade take over the defences of Singapore and send its garrison into the fight. Percival rejected this, for both 45th Indian and the 53rd Brigade group, which arrived on 13 January. He still feared a sudden descent on the island by either sea or airborne invasion, and did not want to redeploy battalions familiar with it. Wavell, less concerned, "authorized" Percival to detach a battalion to help the hard pressed forces up country; Percival reluctantly sent 2nd Loyals to help III Indian Corps. Otherwise he chose to risk sending in the new arrivals when the enemy forced his hand.[3] The 53rd Brigade group, three infantry battalions, one anti-tank and two anti-aircraft artillery regiments–the advance force of the 18th Division–was not in much better shape than the Indians. Its soldiers were older and better trained, but had no combat experience as units, no training for Malayan conditions, and been at sea more or less constantly for 11 weeks. The moment they docked equipment had to be hastily unloaded under driving rain, with enemy bombers overhead. Before it had time to sort itself out the brigade was ordered to detach one battalion to support the Australians on the east coast, then another to move into reserve on the trunk road.[4] Percival gained the sheer numbers to restore his Order of Battle, but could only hope they learnt very quickly on the job how to cope with both Malaya and the enemy.

The reinforcements everyone really counted on, the Hurricane fighters, faced the same predicament. Fifty-one arrived in crates, with 24 pilots, some with combat experience, in the same convoy that brought in 53rd Brigade. The situation they faced was grim. Pulford warned London as early as 4 January he must soon shift much of his bomber force to Sumatra, as airfields fell into enemy hands. That same problem made it "optimistic" to count on further convoys arriving safely until he was properly reinforced–Catch 22? This provoked a somber reply from the Air Ministry on 15 January. Allied forces were hard pressed everywhere. A flow of 50 Hurricanes a month for both Burma and Singapore was now underway "but for immediate future a hand to mouth policy is inevitable" for all types.[5] The nearest additional help was a batch of 48 Hurricanes scheduled to be flown off HMS *Indomitable* into Singapore at the end of January. The enemy would attack before then, so the burden fell by default on Pulford's tired Buffalo squadrons, plus the new fighters just received. RAF Far East worked feverishly to prepare the Hurricanes for battle, but while the desire to acclimatize the pilots could be ignored the shortage of tool kits to remove modifications made for desert operations could not. Malaya Command correctly assumed the airbases at Kahang and Kluang, in central Johore, would be a major enemy objective. From there, barely 100 km from Singapore, the Japanese could overwhelm the naval base by heavy air attack alone. Heath shared Percival's anxiety for the new fighters to be "brought into service promptly and in any case before we lost the Johore chain of aerodromes." 232 Squadron went into battle on 20 January, but the enemy moved even faster.[6] All this forced Percival's army into its "main battle" before it gained effective reinforcements.

The Japanese reinforcement situation was also complicated, but more positive. Yamashita's main formation, the powerful 5th Division, was so tired out by its exertions that only one regiment pressed the retreating III Indian Corps through central Malaya. Yamashita rested the bulk of the division for two days after it captured Kuala Lumpur on 11 January. He could afford to do this because the defenders were in headlong retreat and his advance brought another tremendous windfall: the airbases at Kuantan and Kuala Lumpur and large stocks of useful "Churchill supplies," especially in the Federal Capital. In the first two weeks of January the fourth regiment of 5th Division and 5th Guards Regiment both arrived from Thailand, while a second regiment of 18th Division moved south from Kota Bharu. A third regiment of that division, led by Mutaguchi himself, embarked in transports, poised to assault the east coast of Johore. They were covered by a powerful naval escort, reinforced by the aircraft carrier *Ryujo*. Convoys arriving in Singora and Kota Bharu brought more engineer, artillery and other supporting elements. That gave Twenty-Fifth Army eight infantry regiments on hand plus one approaching for its assault on northern Johore. By contrast Wavell and Percival committed only five brigades to its defence, with one moving up in reserve. Kuantan airbase was ready for use by 10 January, Kuala Lumpur by the 15th. With more than 260 combat aircraft forward deployed in Malaya, at least 100 of them single-engined fighters, the Japanese were poised to hit hard. Once their toughest division caught its breath they would in fact be stronger than ever.[7]

These reinforcements shaped the Japanese plan for this "second phase" of the campaign. Yamashita wanted to unhinge the main defences by amphibious assaults from the west coast, but many of his operations staff, impressed by Slim River, wanted to continue making filleting attacks on the trunk road. But all agreed there must be no pause in the "driving charge," so they compromised to make sure the defenders would not be left undisturbed. The Imperial Guards Division would attack along the west coast, detaching a battalion to make a flank assault from the sea. It would advance below the main defences on the trunk road, threatening their flank and rear. Meanwhile a combined arms battlegroup would advance to contact against those main defences. The main body of 5th Division would then take over the fight on the trunk road, assisted by Takumi Detachment from 18th Division. That division's 55th Regiment would resume the advance along the east coast towards Endau, which would also be attacked from the sea by Mutaguchi's force. Before that attack the army and navy air groups would concentrate their forces to destroy what was left of RAF Far East in an all out assault on Singapore. This ambitious plan, making full use of all available ground, air and naval forces, would smash the defenders on the mainland. This would make the final conquest of Singapore a parade. Yamashita adopted the plan because his booty, his reinforcements and the advance of his air support allowed him to accept the calculated risk of keeping the pressure on without pausing to sort out his logistics.[8] Given how desperate the defenders were to buy time for reinforcements, it was, again, the right decision to make.

This time however not everything went according to plan. To cover Malaya Command's retreat and the incoming convoys RAF Far East stepped up night attacks on Japanese held airbases and fought hard to defend Singapore. Pinprick raids on the island resumed on 29 December, but the full attack only began on 11 January. Japanese naval and army air units worked over the airbases, naval base, port facilities, and railway line, attacking in great strength, on occasion over 100 aircraft. Pulford's force of Buffalo fighters was indeed worn down, and bomber squadrons were shifted to Sumatra. But it took the Japanese a full ten days before they were satisfied with their control of the air, which had consequences.[9] By largely ignoring the ground battle just when III Indian Corps retreated in disarray the Japanese missed a perfect target. 5/11 Sikhs war diary caught such a moment vividly on 13 January:

> For some reason no enemy air was over that afternoon. They missed a wonderful opportunity. For some 30 miles [50km] the rd was tight packed with a mass of motor transport, sometimes there being three vehicles abreast. All MT discipline seemed to have gone by the board.[10]

Just as serious, the hard air battle plus an intelligence error compromised the plan to assault the east coast from the sea. Worried by such resistance and impressed by the defences on the east coast, the Japanese decided to postpone Mutaguchi's attack after one of their pilots wrongly reported seeing a battleship at the Sembawang naval base. By the time the ground battle for Johore heated up his force was diverted to Singora and would not arrive in time to assist. This meant that for Yamashita's army to maintain the all important "driving charge" it must engage fresh troops now preparing to stop it, on a narrower front in northwestern Johore, before it could enjoy help from either a diversion on the east coast or unimpeded direct air support.[11]

Unfortunately, the defenders mishandled their own preparations. Battleships aside the Japanese assembled a pretty accurate picture of what preparations were being made to stop them. They identified the centre of gravity of the defence: the area between Gemas and Segamat, on the trunk road.[12] At Tampin in Selangor the trunk road forked. One arm ran due south to Malacca on the coast; the main artery bent east in an arc that ended only at Yong Peng in Johore, where it straightened again to run southeast to Singapore. Once the defenders retreated past Tampin the Gemas-Segamat area was the next obvious place to stand. At Gemas the railway from Kota Bharu joined the trunk railway, and for the next 50 km the trunk road and railway ran closely parallel, diverging again at Labis. The stretch between Gemas and Segamat, mainly rubber plantation, formed a narrow corridor. To the east lay a large tract of dense jungle and coastal swamp that stretched to Endau. To the west lay heavily wooded ground around Mt. Ophir, stretching down to near the west coast. The Muar River ran south through the area, bending southwest at Lenga to run to the west coast. The river, Mt. Ophir, the narrow corridor, the large jungle, and the east coast defences gave the defenders a chance to concentrate on better ground. But one journalist captured the possibilities and problems of this "Johore Line": "really a certain area in north Johore where, if we had enough properly trained and equipped fighting men, we could have exploited the terrain to sufficient advantage to check the Japanese advance."[13]

Malaya Command had to man this "line" by redeploying on the move. It was too sluggish to do this, but the problem was aggravated by discord between commanders. Percival's original strategy was predictable. III Indian Corps would fall back to the "Johore Line" and dig in to defend the main axis of advance; 8th Australian Division would stand fast in the east. This would preserve untangled supply lines running from each force back to Singapore and leave the difficult job of coordinating the defence on either side of Mt. Ophir to the experienced corps headquarters. But it also meant leaving tired formations to carry on bearing the brunt of the fighting.[14] Bennett challenged this plan even before Slim River. Bennett met Percival on 4 January to discuss how Malaya Command should fight in Johore. Bennett wanted Percival to either allow the Australians to "exercise operational control over all troops in the Johore area ..." or at least redeploy 8th Australian Division to the west to confront the main advance. Bennett by now had lost all confidence in III Indian Corps and Heath and feared they would collapse, isolating his brigades on the east coast. This started an argument which Wavell's intervention made worse. An angry exchange between Bennett and Heath at the meeting in Segamat on 5 January put Percival in an awkward position. Bennett was scathing about Heath, telling Australia "in my opinion withdrawals due to lack of fighting spirit in commanders especially corps commander." There was clearly no way Bennett could be placed under Heath's command. Bennett had also been on the ground in Johore for months, and had fresh acclimatized infantry. But Percival did not believe Bennett and his smaller staff could control large forces as well as Heath's corps staff, was reluctant to weaken the east coast defences, and afraid reshuffling formations would snarl the roads. The three men scouted the area along the trunk road and at least agreed the main defensive position would be in the area suggested by Bennett, in the corridor between

Gemas and Segamat.[15] That provoked a debate about tactics.

Percival's memorandum of 6 January urging his army to adopt the enemy's tactics and wage "guerrilla war" in the bush ran directly contrary to what Heath wanted to do in Johore. Heath preferred to stand and fight in more open country, where his infantry firepower and strong artillery could be more effective. Bennett on the other hand promoted tactics of extremely aggressive defence based on springing powerful ambushes, followed by strong counterattacks on the enemy flank. The Australians had been scouting ambush positions for a good three weeks and had several in mind near Gemas. Bennett hoped to stage an ambush big enough to gouge an enemy regiment. The key problem was the ground. The Muar River formed a natural defensive line, crossed by one rail and two road bridges in the heart of the intended defensive position: an isosceles triangle with points at Gemas, Segamat, and Jementah. Placing the main defences behind the river would allow the infantry to block the axes of advance at three choke points and dig in under cover of dense vegetation along the river. All three commanders decided to defend west of the river, in front of it, in order to combine Bennett's desire to spring ambushes with Heath's desire to defend open country. This deepened the main position and made the ambush extremely important to the whole plan.[16]

Rightly expecting the Japanese to attack with their whole army before he could be reinforced, Percival now ordered "There will be no withdrawal south of the line Mersing-Batu Anam [between Segamat and Gemas]-Muar." The mission was unchanged, so the objective remained constant:

> Malaya Command will … [with other services] continue to ensure the security of the Singapore Naval Base. The broad policy is to continue opposition to the enemy on the mainland to cover the arrival of reinforcements.

Percival's rationale was also clear. Without the only lateral road in Johore, from Jemaluang to Batu Pahat, the defenders would lose the ability to redeploy and the airbases at Kluang and Kahang. Not expecting 18th Division to be on hand and ready to fight before the end of the first week in February, Malaya Command must keep the Japanese north of that road for at least three weeks.[17] However, in order to make fresh troops available for the main battle Percival did decide to stand in the east at Mersing rather than Endau. On the afternoon of 8 January Percival warned Bennett to be ready to make one of his brigades "available for offensive operations in the Segamat area." Percival argued that if the enemy did attack before reinforcements intervened the army must "undertake local offensive action in order to gain time." Heath would then send a brigade east to replace the Australians.[18] This sudden readiness by

Percival to drop his objection to shuffling brigades must have been in response to the debacle at Slim River, if not Bennett's complaints. But whatever signal it sent was offset by confusion about tactics.

III Indian Corps was by now in tactical disarray. That same day, 8 January, Harrison sent a report to Malaya Command on "The Dangers of, and means of countering Japanese infiltration behind the main line on which we intend to stand till we again advance." By now Japanese fieldcraft was more than respected: "… unless we devise adequate countermeasures, our long and thin line will undoubtedly be penetrated by very considerable numbers who will cause great havoc, and who may well loosen our hold on the whole line." Harrison appealed for a coordinated review of the problem by all three services and the civil government, warning "Defence is not just a matter of issuing orders to hold a certain line."[19] Yet that is just how III Indian Corps and Malaya Command continued to treat the problem. Such confusion provoked Wavell to intervene.

When he returned to Singapore late on 8 January, Wavell brusquely dictated new orders to Percival. The crucial change was assigning responsibility to defend the main axis of advance in northwest Johore to Bennett rather than Heath. Percival had already decided to commit one brigade of Australians to the trunk road, but this decision overruled his doubts that Bennett and his staff could coordinate separate battles. The crucial orders were "prepare to fight a defensive battle on the general line Segamat-Mt. Ophir-mouth of the Muar River." The first Australian brigade must be reinforced by the second "as soon as it could be relieved by troops from Singapore island, but this could not be carried out till after the arrival of 53rd Brigade." Heath's freshest units were to deploy in 9th Indian Division, which, together with 45th Indian Brigade, would come under Bennett's command and be "used in the southern portion of the position indicated."[20] On 10 January Percival met Heath and Bennett in Segamat to sketch out this new plan. Bennett, through 8th Australian Division headquarters, would now command Westforce. Comprising 27th Australian Brigade, 45th Indian Brigade, and 9th Indian Division, it would defend the area from Muar to the central corridor. III Indian Corps would take charge of 22nd Australian Brigade at Mersing and the rear area from there to the west coast at Batu Pahat; its other formations would regroup.[21]

The Supreme Commander clearly did at first intend to rapidly concentrate both Australian brigades for the main fight, arguing it was necessary to take a calculated risk and better to do so on the east coast where defences were very strong. He later claimed he urged Percival to move 22nd Australian Brigade right away, but allowed himself to be persuaded to wait after Percival stressed the danger of a Japanese seaborne invasion, because after all "I had only been two days in Malaya and was not fully acquainted with the situation." Wavell's claim "I have always regretted since that I did not insist on the move without replacement" has to be set against his rationale.[22] The new Supreme Commander decided not to overrule the man on the spot on a point of detail, but had no qualms about arbitrarily, without discussion, overruling Percival's entire plan to defend Johore! Wavell made this snap judgement because he concluded from his two day tour that Bennett was the only general on the spot with good ideas about how to fight and the will to apply them. Even if Wavell had been right about Bennett, his treatment of Percival raised one of the perennial dilemmas of high command: is it wise to entrust a plan to a subordinate in whom you clearly have no confidence? The maxim "back him or sack him" applies here.[23] The new command team thus began on the wrong foot and things quickly deteriorated. After the conference at Segamat Percival and Heath annoyed Bennett by conducting a personal reconnaissance of the main defensive zone, something the Australian thought should be left to him. Bennett retaliated by faking car trouble to avoid an evening meeting. Percival concluded he should leave Bennett to deploy his units rather than stir up more trouble. Bennett accepted the temporary need to split his division, but did not press very hard for its reunion as soon as possible, despite saying he "badly needed 22nd Group to help me." Percival, left alone to move cautiously, did so. Wavell met Bennett again on 13 January, approved his detailed plans without a murmur, and did not press Percival to move 22nd Australian Brigade.[24] All this implicated both Wavell and Percival in the most serious mistake: Bennett's dispositions.

Percival was right about a crucial point: Bennett and his headquarters staff were too inexperienced and small to handle two separate battles, even had they worked smoothly together. They did not. Bennett's prickliness and his feud with regular officers made his team anything but. Wavell's failure to press for early concentration of both Bennett's brigades–to place the fresh force in full strength where everyone thought it would matter most– suggested the Supreme Commander did not follow up how his plan was being implemented. That is reinforced by the way Bennett interpreted Wavell's vague instructions to use Indian formations "in the southern portion" of his zone. Bennett decided to concentrate the tired but acclimatized 9th Indian Division in the triangle around the trunk road, to give depth to the fight to be led by 27th Australian Brigade. After some discussion the ambitious ambush plan was scaled down to a more realistic company sized operation, aimed to shred the battlegroup the Japanese used to advance to contact. Bennett planned to draw the Japanese into a series of encounter battles in the triangle. If they came on frontally, strong positions straddling road and rail, supported by concentrated artillery, would make them pay. If they tried to go around, one of his battalions, deployed in echelon, would hit them from their own flank.[25] This plan was not unreasonable. But Bennett became so focused on it he lost sight of its connection to the very long left flank of his position, 40 km along the Muar River to Muar on the coast. The Australian commander treated it as a not very vulnerable flank that could easily be refused, instead of what it was: a very exposed flank that, if lost, would automatically compromise his main defence.

Preparations on this flank were compromised by a mistake that should never have happened. There was no bridge at Muar, only a ferry crossing, and the river mouth is 500 metres wide. Percival agreed to deploy 45th Indian Brigade to this area because it was already approaching it along good roads from the south, whereas one of the retreating Indian brigades would have had to be ferried across. He and Bennett also agreed the brigade should concentrate near the town, screening upriver by "detachments and patrols."[26] This made sense in principle. Even if the enemy crossed inland, the formation could still deny the town area, from which four roads radiated. The road from the northern end of the ferry crossing to Segamat was covered by 9th Indian Division in the triangle. Another road paralleled the river along its south bank but ended at Lenga, separated from the trunk road by 25 kilometres of dense bush. But the other two were critical. The coast road, and a road running southeast until it met the trunk road at Yong Peng, could be used to outflank Bennett's main position. Add this to the fact Malaya Command now overestimated Yamashita's force, giving him two full divisions available to attack in the western area plus two more in reserve,[27] and the conclusion is obvious: Percival should have made sure 45th Indian Brigade was sensibly deployed. Wavell should have done likewise. He depended on this "main battle," the broad plan was his, and he was briefed on deployments. Neither did. Left to his own devices Bennett mishandled both defensive positions. Of three regiments of field and two of anti-tank artillery, 72 and 56 guns respectively, Bennett concentrated nearly everything in front of Segamat. Duncan's brigade received only one battery, 8 guns, of each. Two of his battalions deployed up front, the other in reserve at Bakri, southeast of Muar. Bennett ordered one battalion, 4/9 Jats, to cover a 35 km stretch of the river in order to allow the other, 7/6 Rajputs, to concentrate in Muar. Then he ordered the two forward battalions to each deploy two rifle companies on the northern side of the river.[28]

Even at the time this should have stood out as inept. Percival assumed Bennett would use the river as a natural defensive barrier and concentrate the brigade on the southern bank, putting it between them and the enemy.

This was standard procedure, but here there was a problem. The river loops and twists so many times between Muar and Lenga the brigade would be hard pressed to prevent the enemy from crossing, especially at night–hence the intention to use only a covering screen upriver. But Bennett wanted to employ brawling tactics rather than static defence, which he did not trust the Indians to do unless pushed. This was his way to push. The result was to stretch a raw brigade twice as long as was prudent, with only one-third the usual fire support, and one-third of its infantry on the enemy side of a river–with no bridge crossing and with the enemy in control of the air. If the first contact went well, how could the rest of the brigade cross over to help? If it went badly, how could the forward companies fall back? This was inviting the enemy to chop the brigade to pieces one component at a time. The only plausible explanation is that Bennett assumed the enemy would not hit hard along the coast; neither Percival nor Wavell intervened.[29] Nor could concentrating the artillery in the main position make up for the absence of the other Australian brigade. Bennett's plan, thus Wavell's "main battle" itself, rested on a cavalier assumption. One fresh Australian brigade would be so much tougher than the Indians, and its tactics would work so well, that an enemy whose strength was in fact overestimated, who controlled the air, and who so far had overcome all obstacles, would be stopped in his tracks on one narrow front.

Wavell's plan never had a chance, for two reasons. First, the wish was father to the thought. Bennett needed to pile everything he could into the main position, so he assumed the enemy would oblige him by not hitting hard where he could not cover very well. Wavell's plan to salvage his theatre of war rested on a successful stand in Johore, so he assumed Bennett's pugnacity would produce good results. Second, Wavell and his subordinates were intimidated by the prejudices exposed by trying to work together in an imperial force. They all feared any public rift could ignite serious political friction, between their governments and on the ground. Wavell did not sack Percival, even though he could have appointed Pownall to replace him, because he did not want to suggest to the Australians, and to European and Asian civilians in Singapore, that the British commander in charge was not competent. But he undermined him so obviously it had to affect Percival, Heath and Bennett. Percival could not entrust the battle to Heath because neither Bennett nor Wavell would agree. He did not press Bennett as he should have because that risked provoking both Wavell and the Australians. It thus all came down to Bennett. His prejudice against the Indians, and dogmatic faith in his own troops and tactics, led him to draft a battle plan so flawed it would have been failed by any officer cadet course. Wavell's most serious mistake should not be underestimated. Deciding to put on a brave front in public, instead of dismissing Percival and presenting this as a hard-headed step by a new boss taking a firm grip, was simply unwise. But at least it was only indirectly compromising. Bennett's mistake was fatal. Accepting the imperative to hold north of the lateral road for three weeks meant fighting a "main battle" on the "Johore Line" within days. All three areas, the east coast, the central corridor and the west coast, depended on each other. If the enemy breached any one, the others would be untenable. And Bennett had just deployed a raw brigade with very little support, in ridiculous positions, directly in the path of two fresh regiments of the Imperial Guards Division.

Nevertheless the mood of Malaya Command as the Japanese approached was not all downbeat. This was a natural result of fresh troops, itching for a fight, now getting their chance. And Australian preparations were by no means all unwise. In fact their general attitude was commendable. The east coast position was formidable, especially at Mersing. The vulnerable zone extended from Endau, the northern terminus of an all-weather road ending in Singapore, to the town of Jemaluang. In that zone the road ran through difficult undulating country, alternating rubber with swamp, often making it somewhat like a causeway. At Jemaluang the coastal road meets the lateral road to the west coast, and itself veers inland to run south. 8th Australian Division used the ground well, anticipating Percival's decision to make the main stand at Mersing. Forward elements would deny Endau for as long as possible, as well as the wide navigable river that flowed south from it, giving the enemy the chance to outflank the road; as they fell back they would demolish the road at several defiles. The road runs within 300 metres of the coast at Mersing and the river there is narrower, so it was a logical place for the Japanese to invade. The Australians took to the task with real resolve, especially after war began. More than 20,000 civilian inhabitants were evacuated from the Mersing area, sent at least 30 km away. The town was all but razed to the ground, buildings cleared to provide fields of fire and material for obstacles. "Acres of jungle and rubber" went up in flames for the same reason. The division laid down 400 tons of barbed wire, 4000 anti-personnel and 3000 anti-tank mines. Forward patrols made first contact with Japanese patrols on the morning of 14 January, north of Endau.[30] The Japanese may well have chosen wisely by opting not to invade this position from the sea, but still faced the tough task of pushing through it overland. Mersing was certainly the strongest defended zone of the "Johore Line." Nevertheless, intelligence and air reconnaissance reports kept Malaya Command and RAF Far East focused on the possible seaborne invasion. Yet half Bennett's division had now been transferred. Even if 53rd Brigade was sent in, the battle for the east coast road could now only be fought with one brigade. To underline that point, the same battalion which contacted the enemy first, 2/19 AIF, had already been warned by Bennett it might need to move west at short notice.[31]

27th Australian Brigade had less time to prepare the main position in front of Segamat, but tackled the job with similar resolve. From 3 January on its engineers prepared five major road blocks and extensive demolitions from west of Gemas to Batu Anam.[32] Westforce settled into fighting positions from 10 January. Maxwell deployed his three Australian battalions in depth along the trunk road: 2/29 in reserve, 2/26 astride the corridor near Batu Anam, 2/30 on point, screening Gemas. The 8th Indian Brigade, reinforced by 2nd Loyals, sandwiched in with the Australians to straddle the corridor behind Gemas. 22nd Indian Brigade refused the left flank, covering the road from Segamat to Jementah.[33] 2/30 AIF sent B Company forward 12 km west of Gemas, where a small bridge over the Sungei Gemencheh had been selected as the best ambush site. After the ambush shredded the Japanese vanguard the company would fall back on the main position by a side trail.[34] The enemy would then be drawn into Bennett's prepared zone and fought to a standstill.

The tactical key to the plan was the ambush. The site settled the argument about the scale of the operation because it could only support a company. Every bridge but one between Kuala Lumpur and the ambush site was left intact, to draw the enemy on until he became overconfident. The killing ground was excellent. Thirty metres east of the bridge a steep cutting rose more than 4 metres high right next to the road, running some 40 metres. Disguised by a topping of thick vegetation, it still looks like an innocent row of trees and bushes. Three platoons deployed next to the road, the first along the cutting, laying out a killing zone. One battery of 2/15 Field Regiment registered its guns onto the approach to the bridge, the span, and the killing zone. Everyone was in position nearly three full days before contact. But the plan had weaknesses. Lt.-Col. Frederick "Black Jack" Galleghan, commanding 2/30 AIF, was told the Japanese could detect field headquarters by radio detection finding. So he restricted communications between his forward company, battalion headquarters and supporting artillery to two land-lines laid right next to the road. He also moved his main force some five kilometres behind the ambush site, with the guns some distance behind. Everything depended on communications. B Company had to call in fire support as soon as it triggered the ambush. If the guns did not engage right away the enemy, certain to heavily outnumber the ambush force, might fight his way out of the trap. And if the Japanese were not dealt a crushing blow right here, Bennett's whole plan could misfire.[35] Despite the long retreat, neither Australians nor Indians seemed discouraged. Quite the reverse, "orders that a definite stand would be made at Segamat" acted as a tonic. 22nd Indian Brigade, heartened by Australian reinforcement, a good position, and even anti-aircraft artillery and some air support, recorded "A feeling of confidence, which had been to some extent impaired by continuous withdrawal, now reasserted itself."[36] Despite watching the dispirited 11th Indian Division retreat through its positions, Galleghan insisted his battalion "saw it and went into action with their tails up." He set the tone by example. When signallers laying the land-lines from the ambush site ran out of wire Galleghan stopped an Indian signals truck and requisitioned its supply. When the Indian soldier in charge asked who he should report took his stock, Galleghan replied "Colonel Ned Kelly of Australia."[37] How effective their preparations were remained to be seen, but the Australians certainly intended to let the Japanese know who was now on point.

Unfortunately, the tactical weakness of the ambush plan was only one vulnerable part in the "main battle" plan. More ominous was the need to go into action with only half Bennett's division on point. While Wavell, Percival and Bennett all supposedly wanted to send in 22nd Australian Brigade "as soon as possible," the all important decision was left to Percival. By the time Bennett's force became heavily engaged on 15 January, none of Taylor's units were on the move, and two of the new British battalions were being sent elsewhere. Despite the speed of the Japanese advance, this can indicate only one thing. Whatever Wavell intended, Percival would not abandon his own strategy, to try to be as strong as possible in all areas, in order to take a calculated risk to concentrate on the main axis of advance. Percival had to be accustomed by now to the "driving charge." He must have expected to have to fight before the second Australian brigade could hit the road, if he refused to move it before it could be replaced. That meant relying on Barstow's tired troops to stiffen one Australian brigade enough to hold the enemy fast. This seems cavalier–until measured by the broader approach Malaya Command took to the all important "main battle."

This broader approach stood out in two ways: the battle plan for the "Johore Line" and efforts to harass enemy lines of supply. When he first considered how to defend northern Johore Heath envisaged making a stand with six brigades. Bennett now had to make do with four. Kirby later agreed that Wavell ordered Malaya Command to fight the "main battle" there and then, but also argued these were only general instructions that did not leave Percival "tied to static defence or to any particular portion of northern Johore."[38] The last point was not fair. Ordering Percival to fight far enough from Singapore to prevent the Japanese from cutting it off by air attack meant defending as far above the Johore lateral road as possible. The ground further restricted Malaya Command's options, and Wavell did nothing to alter this. On the contrary, after his 13 January visit he drew the bizarre conclusion "the plan I had laid down at my visit four days before was being put into execution," despite the fact the enemy advance "had been more rapid than I had hoped." Wavell still made no effort to set 22nd Australian Brigade in motion, but reported "I felt confident that [Bennett] and his Australians would handle the enemy roughly." Orders from ABDA Command to theatre air forces five days later left no doubt about Percival's task and Wavell's rationale:

> Japanese ultimate objective in the N.W. theatre is capture of Singapore. Immediate object is to prevent arrival of reinforcements in Malaya. Consequently particular immediate object of the Allied Powers is to throw reinforcements into Southern Malaya and to check Jap advance until sufficient reinforcements are available to enable a counteroffensive to be staged.[39]

As always, Percival's choices were shaped by the connection between his fight and higher strategy.

Given Wavell's disappointment at how fast the enemy approached, did Malaya Command approach this "main battle" with the sense of urgency he expected? The evidence suggests otherwise. Many units were told they would have at least a weeks rest. 53rd Brigade was promised on 14 January it would have seven days notice to move north, 11th Indian Division told some artillery units to move into reserve for a month to "rest and retrain the reinforcements." This followed a briefing from Percival himself on 12 January "hoping" the division would have three weeks rest in southern Johore, even though he only expected Westforce to hold for a week. Three days earlier HQ Singapore Fortress ordered its two brigades to reconnoiter the northwestern area of the island, to be ready to defend it against "enemy infiltration" or help "reinforcement troops" take over the job. This was the first serious move towards defending the north coast. Percival warned 11th Indian Division staff he doubted Singapore would hold longer than four weeks after Westforce was pushed back.[40] That might not be enough time for 18th Division to reach the mainland, let alone I Australian Corps. Wavell's intent was to concentrate in a determined effort to bring the Japanese advance on the trunk road to a standstill, not just slow it down. Percival pursued this in principle but avoided it in practice.

RAF Far East did not hold back, but to its cost. Pulford lost at least 15 Buffaloes in a week. His fighters were now routinely outnumbered by at least six, sometimes 15 to 1. Less than half the reinforcement bombers arrived. By 18 January Pulford had no more than 74 bombers and 28 fighters left in Malaya, nearly all in Singapore, to carry out Wavell's orders to, in order of priority, scout for further Japanese seaborne invasions, cover incoming reinforcement convoys, and reduce the scale of Japanese attacks on Singapore and Malaya Command.[41] The enemy forced Pulford to stand and fight by stepping up the pressure on Singapore, whereas Percival had time to affect Wavell's plan by "adjusting" it in practice.

One adjustment Malaya Command made much too late was taking steps to harass Japanese supply lines. Four problems prevented the defenders from conducting the very operations that could seriously have disrupted the Japanese. First was the prewar refusal by both Thomas and Percival to help prepare irregular forces to operate behind enemy lines. Second was the bitter prewar political division between communist and nationalist factions in the Chinese community. Third was Malaya Command's misuse of the Independent Company. And fourth was the belated response by both III Indian Corps and Malaya Command to efforts by Warren and his assistant, Major Spencer Chapman, to organize irregular operations. Given how few Japanese were engaged north of Ipoh and how heavily they relied on captured supplies, valuable time was wasted here. The light did not shine through clearly until Chapman returned from an aggressive personal reconnaissance around the Perak River just as the Japanese crossed it, from 24 to 28 December:

> … it became obvious to Advanced Command that there were great opportunities for parties to operate behind the enemy lines, particularly against communications. It was evident that the men would not be able to cover long distances and that they would have to be equipped to exist independently for long periods.[42]

The main obstacle was familiar: political sensitivities. The civil government was reluctant to accept irregular operations, especially involving Asians, because this signal it expected much of the country to be lost would alarm public opinion. For the same reason they objected to evacuating people or food stocks or declaring martial law; often enough the Japanese advanced too fast for action to be taken. The authorities obviously believed the Asian population would erupt in blind panic if enemy pressure became too great. Malaya Command did nothing to prepare irregular operations until after defeat at Jitra forced it to reconsider. Because they preferred to avoid possibly awkward political consequences, the authorities in Singapore only reluctantly turned to the men in the shadows after the enemy gave them no choice.

The most serious consequence of this caution was summed up by the OM itself: "It was naturally immensely more difficult and less satisfactory to improvise at this stage what O.M. had hoped to do in an orderly manner beforehand." Even now they faced three problems, all political. First, it was deemed necessary to organize "left behind parties"–we will refer to them as groups–on racial lines, rather than mingling European and Asian, almost entirely Chinese, personnel. Because these groups had different characteristics it was decided they would deploy and operate differently, which further complicated matters. Second, the most militarily promising group, the communists, were the most awkward politically. This was complicated by ongoing friction between communist and Chinese nationalist factions. Finally, the late date at which this campaign was pulled together forced the OM and Malaya Command to scramble at short notice to train and equip the groups.[43] Under the circumstances what they accomplished was not bad, but also too little too late.

After first Heath and then Percival became convinced they needed such operations they authorized OM to organize a systematic effort to harass Japanese supply lines by sabotage, ambush and subversion. An obvious source of recruits were Volunteer units driven from the states they knew so well. But because it had been taboo to even consider the possibility this would happen, these men had to be reoriented on the spot when the Japanese advance forced Malaya Command to disband Lines of Communication Command on 13 January. The great majority of the FMSVF, the Asian rank and file, were allowed to return to their families, lost to the war effort. The Europeans were regrouped in Singapore as a depot unit, to be drawn on for replacements.[44] But OM worked hard from late December to recruit them, as well as displaced long-time residents, including planters, miners, and government officers in field departments such as Irrigation, Forestry and Survey. Their independence, and familiarity with the bush, could be better exploited behind enemy lines than in volunteer infantry units. Warren undertook to recruit the men, send them to Singapore for training, identify base sites, and then send them into the bush, in groups ranging from four to eight men. The limiting factors were training facilities and time at No. 101 STS in Singapore, equipment, and the speed of the enemy advance. The campaign was well conceived. Training emphasized sabotage and self sufficiency–groups were to operate for three months–and sites were selected where good jungle cover came near important communications routes. But time and politics proved serious impediments. Training was hasty and minimal; some men went in without any. They were also hampered by the fact they stood out like a sore thumb among the local population. That forced them to avoid locals rather than seek their help, which meant relying on their own food supplies and local knowledge. Four European groups went into the bush north of Johore by 14 January. None had any Chinese assistance, although one met a communist group setting up near Tampin and agreed to "operate separately but to render what assistance they could to each other when necessary." This was better than nothing but hardly an optimal pooling of resources. The first group, led by Chapman himself, went in on 8 January, but were forced to disperse when coolies they hired to carry their gear absconded with their food. The other groups had to bring their own supplies to the campsite and set it up themselves. That meant they were not expected to be operating for at least 10 days–too late to interfere with Japanese preparations for the "main battle."[45]

Greater emphasis was placed on training Chinese groups. The fifth European group to go in did have a communist recruit attached for "intelligence purposes." This sort of pooling of resources was more sensible militarily, but hampered by hesitations by both parties. The Malayan Communist Party (MCP), almost entirely Chinese, offered its services to the war effort "in any capacity" after the Japanese attacked. The approach came through the police Special Branch, specifically through Lt.-Col. John Dalley. It took Dalley until 19 December to persuade the government to agree, leading to a meeting that same night between Special Branch, the OM–represented by Chapman–the SIS and the Party Secretary. That late date represented a waste of precious time, for two reasons. First, the communist recruits later sent to No. 101 STS turned out to be just what the OM wanted, indeed became its mainstay:

> These men, particularly the first lots, included the finest men whom the school had to handle. They were all young–mostly 17 to 20 years old–physcially fit, intelligent, and inspired with an almost fanatical eagerness to fight the Japanese and proved themselves worthy of the Communist traditions. They had a most stimulating influence on No. 101 STS.

The second reason can only be described as incredible:

> British offical [as in government and police] relations with the Malayan Communist Party appear to have settled down for some years on a mutually satisfactory basis, thanks to two main causes: the tolerance by Malayan Police of the Communists' activities as long as they were kept within reasonable bounds by law and order, and the fact that the Chief Secretary of the Party in Singapore was in Police pay.[46]

The Chief Secretary was Lai Tak. Given the fact he was a double agent, it is only fair to wonder why Singapore authorities approached this offer of help from the most dedicated anti-Japanese community in the country with such caution. Dalley's meeting was kept secret. Instinctive reluctance to trust the communists was only part of the problem. The presence of the Kuomintang (KMT) was another. Four officers were sent from Chungking to "observe" the campaign in Malaya and "offer their experience in guerrilla fighting ... as specialists in instructing Malayan Chinese to assist in the campaign." But the OM, persuaded probably by Dalley that the communists were a better partner, did not want such help, doubting it would be effective, fearing it would antagonize the communists. The four nevertheless arrived at No. 101 STS on 12 January to be themselves trained, only to be visited soon after by a Chinese general en route to ABDA Command. Lt.-Gen. Cheng Kai-Min complained about how much time was being spent training the communists, how little his own recruits. In order to protect their operations in China the OM reluctantly agreed to take on such men. But none arrived before 21 January, too late to help the "main battle."[47]

While this did not prevent the deployment of communist groups, it underlined how politically fragile the whole effort was. Communist secrecy did not help either. Lai Tak insisted all communications go through him, probably to preserve his own cover. That provoked "many delays at a time when delays were serious." No. 101 STS nevertheless trained 165 communist personnel from 21 December to 30 January. Two groups went in before the "main battle" began. Two Chinese-speaking officials, R.N. Broome of the Chinese Protectorate and John Davis of the FMS Police, helped select supply dump sites. They saw the groups through the front lines, and helped them settle in. The first, 15 men, went in 35 km north of Kuala Lumpur on 5 January. The second, 30 men, went in on 11 January, five kilometres north of Tampin. Each group was trained to act as a nucleus. Each man was expected to train more groups of five to 10 local men per leader, all operating from the supply dump. Because they could mingle in the local population there was no need to store food or miscellaneous supplies, which made it easier to equip them.[48] This was just the kind of irregular force that might have done real damage to the enemy. After all, Japanese supply lines now ran all the way to southern Thailand. But it should have been prepared before the war began. The campaign behind the lines to weaken enemy pressure on the field army was now at last taking shape. But the "main battle" would be decided first– and Malaya Command knew this when the first groups went in.

By the way they prepared to fight this "main battle," Wavell, Percival and Bennett set it up to turn local defeat into broader disaster. The broad outline was Wavell's. It was diluted by Percival, who pushed the plan to something between what Wavell wanted and Malaya Command intended. Wavell wanted to stop the Japanese advance then and there. That required a determined stand, risking an open road to Singapore if the enemy prevailed–a calculated risk. Percival preferred to take no such risk and deploy his formations so they could retreat yet again if necessary, covering all routes. The Japanese made the point moot by engaging so quickly, but neglecting to press for both Australian brigades to be concentrating where Wavell wanted them can not be ignored. Wavell did not trust Percival but did not prevent him from diluting the plan. Percival did not rate Bennett, but did not prevent him from making his own unworkable plan. Bennett was in charge of the key battle but had only half his own fresh force where it was supposed to be, and no confidence in the troops sent to support it. And along the Muar River he had already set up the fight that would undo the whole army. By late afternoon 15 January, half the fighting strength of the two forward battalions of 45th Indian Brigade was deployed on the enemy side of the river. The Japanese closed up to the ferry crossing and began bombing and shelling the town.[49]

12

From Defeat to Disaster

The tone of the "main battle" was set right where the defenders wanted: at the ambush set by 2/30 AIF on the trunk road. But it was set by the enemy. Japanese scouts bicycled carelessly through the ambush zone, while B Company waited for the main body to appear. But when the parade of cyclists continued without letup Capt. Duffy blew the bridge at 1620hrs. The spectacular explosion blew mangled Japanese into the air and set off a grim close quarter fight. The Japanese could not climb the disguised cutting before Australians tossed grenades down onto the road, and poured rifle and Bren gun fire into them at point blank range. The soldiers trapped in the ambush zone paid a terrible price, but luck plus skill prevented the Mukaide Detachment from being annihilated. The scouts found and cut the telephone wire laid by the side of the road to connect B Company to its supporting artillery. Galleghan and the gunners were so far back they could not be sure just by listening whether the bridge had been detonated or not. As a result, the 25 pounders waiting to pulverize the enemy on the other side of the bridge sat silent.Those Japanese raced to ford the stream and outflank the ambush. Meanwhile the scouts doubled back to the sound of the guns and engaged B Company, forcing it to fight its way back to the main position. It separated and took losses before regaining the battalion the next morning. Japanese engineers, using lumber from the nearby sawmill, improvised a bridge and had vehicles moving across the stream in barely six hours, medium tanks by dawn. There is no doubt the Japanese took a hard blow from this ambush. The Detachment's parent 9th Infantry Brigade, fresh into the fight, admitted it "suffered 70 dead and 57 wounded" while "pushing on precipitously through the jungle" into an ambush. But the Australian objective was "to destroy with one blow not only the forward elements, but also a large portion of the main force moving against us from Tampin." This ambush barely slowed the advance guard down, let alone hurt the main force. Australian claims ranging to over 1000 fatalities inflicted on the enemy must be rejected; the Japanese insist there were only two companies engaged in the ambush. The hard fact is that without the supporting artillery B Company's firepower alone was not enough to prevent the Japanese from extricating themselves with bearable loss. The speed, aggression and skill of the Japanese vanguard served notice to the 8th Australian Division they were in for a fight.[1]

On the other hand the Japanese found themselves in one as well, with an enemy they "found to be skilled fighters." The Mukaide Detachment pressed on to attack 2/30 AIF, just west of Gemas, at 0900hrs on 15 January. This set off a real brawl at close quarters, lasting some six hours. Australian anti-tank gunners and mortars stopped the leading Japanese tanks but suffered in return. The Australians came under heavy air and mortar attack and concluded the enemy were forming up for a full scale assault. Galleghan decided to knock them off balance by counterattacking, but had to wait until the tanks were dealt with, and could only spare a company. D Company finally advanced at 1245hrs. It ran straight into the Japanese advance and was thrown back. 2/30 AIF was undone when half its supporting artillery withdrew on its own. Wrongly believing he faced a full brigade with tank and artillery support, Galleghan secured permission to break contact early and regroup east of the river. The retreat ended successfully around 1800hrs, when 2/30 AIF fell back into the main defensive area. It took up positions on the right flank of what became a line straddling the road-rail corridor where the two ran next to each other. 2/26 AIF was on the left, 1/13 Frontier Force Rifles in the middle. Galleghan overestimated his opponent, but his battalion made its own impression. Taking note of the stubborn resistance, Twenty-fifth Army ordered the full 9th Brigade forward into the fight. This set off a five day battle through the position Heath and Tsuji agreed was one of the best the defence had yet found.[2]

Bennett sent a telegram that night summing up how he saw the situation: 2/30 AIF blooded the enemy and withdrew in good order, his Australian units were doing well, he intended to concentrate his whole division as soon as possible. His reserve unit, 2/29 AIF, should be available to intervene the next day, 2/19 AIF to move in from the east coast the day after that, the rest of 22nd Australian Brigade in 10 days. Nevertheless, "situation most difficult owing to absence air support and fatigued Indian troops in formation. Anticipate strong pressure other positions front." This became an apology for the battle Westforce fought on the main position: it was naked from the air, undermined from within by tired Indian units, and undone by strategic threats elsewhere.[3] This is not inaccurate, but neither is it the whole story. The terrain forced 5th Division to either attack prepared positions along the corridor or struggle through bad ground with open flanks. It prevailed not just because it enjoyed strong armoured and air support, plus help from elsewhere, but also because it fought more effectively. Having drawn the Japanese onto ground of his own choosing, Bennett now failed to fight the rolling brawl he planned on paper. Instead he fell into the familiar pattern of fighting from fixed linear positions, held by battalions aligned vertically astride the corridor. Units fought separate actions, watching their neighbour being attacked while they sat and worried about their own flanks.

After the first hard day of fighting, the two Australian battalions were only pressed once more before the whole battle began to unravel on the night of the 18th. A serious fight that afternoon summed it all up: "The two AIF bns were not seriously engaged; the main enemy infantry effort appeared to be directed against the F[rontier]F[orce] Regt in the centre position astride the road." 2/26 AIF observed the fight with interest:

1200-1700: Considerable activity, both artillery and infantry on our right. It appears as though unit on our right [1/13 Frontier Force] are being heavily engaged.

1700-1830: Firing on our right flank greatly intensified. It is apparent that a major attack is developing on our right. Artillery on both sides engaged in intense duel. Enemy mortars opened up in front of our position app. 320 degrees from Bn HQ. Artillery fire unable to silence mortars as exact position is not known. Slight activity on our front by snipers and patrols.

2000: CO and Adjutant left for Bde (Segamat) for orders. Intensive fire all along area north of railway line. Enemy have advanced and are penetrating FFR position.

2200: CO and Adjutant arrived at Bde where orders issued for withdrawal to position south of Segamat. Report received that Batu Anam is in enemy hands and FFR had been pushed back.

Small probes pinned down the two Australian units while the "line" was breached. Unverified reports of Japanese advances on the flanks prompted Maxwell to plan a full retreat across the Segamat River. Maxwell and Lay "agreed that 27 Aust Bde should withdraw immediately, leaving the FFR to extricate itself at first light."[4] But the failure to pull the fight together came from the top. Bennett summoned Westforce commanders that evening:

Bennett arrived late looking rather flustered. He stormed into the meeting talking wildly about the lack of fighting spirit, the incompetence of senior British commanders and their withdrawal complex. After about 20 minutes of this tirade he suddenly stopped, glared around at the puzzled faces and abruptly left the room, departing as quickly as he had come. No withdrawal plans had been discussed.[5]

Percival and Bennett agreed that evening it would be prudent to withdraw behind the Segamat River. They now began to fear the main force might be isolated by a developing Japanese thrust from the west coast. But that meant giving up Wavell's plan–especially when it set off a retreat just as unstoppable as any Heath conducted in the north. The original intent to stand north of Labis, to preserve the narrow corridor, quickly gave way on 19 January. By 21 January the force retreated all the way to Yong Peng, where it had to split to screen road and railway when the two diverged. Yong Peng, the crossroads where the road from Muar met the trunk road, was barely 18 km north of the true last ditch: the lateral road that ran through Ayer Hitam. 27th Australian Brigade and 9th Indian Division gave up the best defensive position still available north of Singapore after only five days.[6] This had something to do with lack of air support, although RAF Far East tried so hard to help its efforts impressed both enemy and friendly infantry.[7] It certainly had much to do with what happened at Muar, as we shall see. But it also had a lot to do with the battle itself.

This result was in no way down to the troops. Most were indignant at retreating yet again, especially a unit such as 2/26 AIF which saw so little action in what was billed as the big show. That was the point. Only two of the nine battalions in the triangle were really engaged. When it mattered, they were directed to fight in cumbersome set-piece fashion, holding a line each to his own sector. Bennett blamed this on having to send his reserves to deal with other threats. But neither on the 15th when 2/30 AIF was pressed, nor on the 18th and 19th when 1/13 Frontier Force was attacked, did anyone try to attack an enemy flank. Bennett's plan was undermined by problems elsewhere, but was also never likely to materialize anyway.[8] Some quality fighting, especially by 2/30 AIF, was simply wasted by a high command that threw away good ground, and a decent plan, because it could not cope with the tempo of battle the enemy forced on it.

This was especially unfortunate because the stiff initial resistance affected the whole Japanese battle plan. Twenty-Fifth Army decided in light of the tough fighting near Gemas "the main strength of the enemy field army would have to be destroyed on the mainland" once and for all, to prevent serious delay in taking Singapore. The fight on the trunk road also settled the debate about attacking Mersing: "it was obvious that if any landing was attempted at Mersing we would have to be prepared for losses not less than those we suffered at Kota Bharu." The army decided it must now concentrate without undue risk. Mutaguchi and the seaborne elements of 18th Division were diverted to Singora, to move south by road as fast as possible.. To compensate, two battalions of 55th Regiment were ordered to advance along the east coast, to pin down the defenders there.[9] This decision paid off when patrol contact north of Endau on 14 January reinforced expectations the east coast would soon be attacked from the sea. This persuaded Percival to jettison Wavell's plan to send the entire 22nd Australian Brigade into the "main battle": "Endau, Segamat and Muar heavily bombed. Am relieving Australian battalion at Jemaluang 17 Jan but NOT repeat NOT rest of that Brigade in view activity that front."[10]

This summed up an insoluble dilemma. The east coast position was strong but apparently threatened, so weakening it seemed unwise. But the Japanese were attacking everywhere at once, forcing Malaya Command to identify the most dangerous thrust and concentrate against it. Unfortunately Percival made matters worse: "Am concentrating 53 Inf Bde Gp in area Yong Peng-Ayer Hitam-Batu Pahat commencing 16 Jan as this area is key to whole position."[11] This latter appreciation was fair. This second triangle, covering the trunk, lateral and west coast roads, was ground he must hold in order to fight the "main battle" north of the lateral road. But risks could not be avoided, because the road to Singapore through Jemaluang must also be defended. Percival decided, before the enemy gave him no choice, not to risk the raw British brigade to hold strong east coast defences by itself–therefore not to send the entire 22nd Australian Brigade, a formidable force, to support the main position. Instead he gambled the new formation could secure the vital supply lines Westforce needed to fight its battle. This decision backfired when the Japanese made the crucial breakthrough right in its face. This forced Percival to weaken 22nd Australian Brigade anyway, by sending 2/19 AIF west. That prompted Heath and Taylor to agree on 18 January Eastforce was no longer strong enough to hold Mersing. Detachments at Mersing would force the enemy to fight his way across the Mersing River, covering the main position now moving back to the junction at Jemaluang.[12] In retrospect this decision looks pessimistic. The battle which ensued indicated the Japanese were wise not to relax the pressure, because the rest of 22nd Australian Brigade gave them a very hard time.

Percival later singled out the ambush near Gemencheh as an example of what could be done by fresh troops in a strong position.[13] His point would have been better made by describing the fight north of Jemaluang. Not everything went well. Long spells of torrential rain complicated the defence of lower, swampier areas. The road between Kota Tinggi and Jemaluang was so badly flooded supplies had to come the long way around from Kluang along the lateral road. Worse, some defences were compromised. The boom at the mouth of the navigable Endau River was swept away and minefields were flooded. One episode was particularly frustrating:

> ... a company of the 20th encountered a party of 100 Japanese cycling down the road. When fired upon the Japanese made for the cover afforded by the side of the road and were forced into a minefield prepared for their benefit. However, the whole mine field had been flooded by nearly a weeks rain which had rendered the majority of the mines useless.[14]

Nevertheless Eastforce held its own north of Jemaluang, forcing the enemy to fight on its terms, then handling itself very well. The forward detachments at Endau withdrew without trouble on 16 January, covered by navy launches manned by Malay volunteers. The next night engineers thoroughly destroyed much of the road north of Mersing using 2000 lbs. of explosives, forcing the enemy into mangrove and wet paddies. Japanese air attacks did little damage–"2/18 Bn had 1 man killed and 1 scratched by air action"–due to well executed deceptions:

> ... faking was resorted to, dummy positions were constructed in likely areas– dummy roads were smashed through the undergrowth by carrier. We had the satisfaction of seeing dummy positions (when use was made of clothes apparently hanging out to dry in the areas) bombed with no effect on us.[15]

And when the Japanese attacked the real positions along the Mersing River, they were lured onto the undestroyed bridge and cut up by mortar, machine gun and especially artillery fire. That included the company forced into the swamped minefield, "effectively dealt with" by that combination. Repeated crossing attempts failed, some repelled by "Fish Fizzles," a home-made depth charge. The Japanese were stopped at Mersing. This had much to do with the energetic preparations made earlier by the Australians, including levelling the town and evacuating civilians. This allowed them to shape a battle area which their key weapon, the artillery of 2/10 Field Regt., dominated to a degree not achieved since Kampar:

> There was a very good reason why our arty fire was so effective. The whole of the area round Mersing had been surveyed, pegged and sub-divided into 100 yard squares. The area so divided covered the whole range of our guns from any point in a 360 degree traverse. One in particular on Gibbetts Hill covered a couple of miles of the Endau River and the area north of the Mersing River. From this position the officer in charge of the OP [observation post] allowed the enemy to erect and camouflage arty and machine gun positions only giving our gunners the word to fire as soon as his preparations were complete.[16]

The staunch defence of Mersing was undone by the fact the battle could not be fought in isolation. 2/19 AIF moved west early on 18 January. 5th Norfolk bounced back and forth but definitively went west the same day, while the Dogra and Jat companies had to protect the lateral road and the airbase at Kahang. That left only two Australian battalions to stand and fight, with no reserve. 22nd Australian Brigade wrongly concluded it was facing superior numbers, another Japanese gain in return for keeping up the pressure. Taylor duly persuaded Heath on 21 January that he could no longer hold Mersing and Jemaluang, and prepared to fall back to hold the latter. On this front the defenders retreated on their own terms, making the Japanese earn the ground.[17] Unfortunately this did not rescue the main battle–mainly because the situation on the west coast was the opposite in every respect.

The Japanese reaped a dividend from their bold decision to press the "driving charge" on every front when they found the fatal weak spot around Muar. The Imperial Guards Division exploited a poorly prepared defence to trigger an encounter battle it fought boldly. Maintaining a relentless tempo, the Japanese maneuvered with skill and fought with ferocity, first dividing the defenders then defeating them in detail. Percival, Bennett and their subordinates threw away some truly inspired fighting by the troops, especially the Australians, by playing into enemy hands. They were always one step behind, sent reinforcements in piecemeal and never pulled the fight together.

Bennett played into Japanese hands by forcing 45th Indian Brigade to deploy those rifle companies on the enemy side of the river. The entire 5th Guards Regiment ran into them near Simpang Mati on the morning of 15 January and rolled over them like they were a speed bump: "After destroying about 600 on the 15, the team started, before night came, preparations for the crossing of the River Muar in the southeastern sector of Mati." The Japanese came on hard, aiming to "bounce" the river, infiltrate and get behind the defensive positions. 5th Guards crossed upriver in the early hours of 16 January, in the area marking the boundary between the sectors of the two Indian battalions. This, plus the abrupt disappearance of the isolated companies, and the distraction of a gathering opposite the town, left 45th Indian Brigade unaware how quickly and heavily it was already penetrated. The gathering constituted two battalions of 4th Guards Regiment, preparing their own crossing; the third was at sea, moving towards Batu Pahat.[18]

The ensuing battle lasted a full week. Six Japanese battalions engaged 11 from Malaya Command: two Australian, four Indian, five British. In the end Malaya Command lost nearly one third of the infantry committed to Wavell's "main battle." And mutual confidence between commanders and contingents took another severe knock. The battle area resembled two overlapping triangles. The smaller one ran 14 km from Muar to Parit Jawa on the coast, and Muar inland to Bakri; the larger one stretched 50 km from Muar to Batu Pahat on the coast, and Muar inland to Bukit Pelandok. The tempo was relentless, the situation never clear, but the key feature was: roads. Roads defined the triangles and the battle. The sides were the roads running from Muar to Bukit Pelandok and Muar to Batu Pahat. The bases were short roads running from Parit Jawa to Bakri and Batu Pahat to Bukit Pelandok. Those two last junctions were the prize. From them the Japanese could cut off the main force of Westforce on the trunk road, or even advance on Singapore. They had to be defended. Nishimura counted on this. His task was to threaten the main position on the trunk road. If his division broke through on its own so much the better. The intensely competitive division commander planned to do just that by annihilating 45th Indian Brigade. What followed was a textbook example of two things: how to fight a battle "for the road off the road" and the overriding importance of what modern military parlance calls C^{3}I: command, control, communications and intelligence.

For higher command to control the battle effectively, it needed to know what the situation on the ground was. For this it relied on accurate appreciations from the men on the spot and efficient communications up and down the chain of command. None of these conditions were met for Malaya Command on the west coast. In particular, Duncan did not realize how strong the enemy force attacking him was, how deep it penetrated, and how badly it hurt his brigade, until it was almost too late to do anything about it–and his appreciation influenced Bennett and Percival long enough to compromise anything they could do to help. Duncan's optimism is curious because he lost touch with more than half his brigade on the very first morning.

One Japanese attempt to cross near the ferry in the early afternoon on 16 January was repelled by Australian gunners of 65Bty. 2/15 Field Regt., firing over open sights. But the bulk of the Imperial Guards had already crossed upriver. They advanced so quickly Duncan's two battalions around Muar were cut off from each other, and from 4/9 Jats still strung out upriver, before brigade headquarters could respond. Heavy fighting went on all day around Muar. By late afternoon 5/18 Royal Garhwalis and 7/6 Rajputs were each defeated, their commanding officers killed, and both units forced to retreat, the former to Bakri, the latter towards Parit Jawa.[19] Within a day 45th Indian Brigade was on the point of being routed. Yet as late as 1715hrs. Duncan's staff resisted battalion calls for retreat, insisting reinforcements were en route and when they arrived "we would be taking the offensive." Considering there is no way the brigadier could then have had any accurate idea of the situation this was bizarre. Unfortunately Duncan influenced Bennett, who concluded the problem around Muar was a local setback inflicted by a force of 200 or so. This was enough to prompt him next morning, 17 January, to order 2/29 AIF to "restore the situation," but not enough to ring alarm bells already in the back of Percival's mind. The GOC was worried enough to notify Wavell on 15 January he would take steps to secure the area between Yong Peng and Batu Pahat–but worried in general, not yet about Muar.[20]

The west coast battle was decided that day, 17 January. While Bennett and Percival moved deliberately, Nishimura threw his entire force into an onslaught to blow the roads south of Muar wide open. Three fights erupted: along the road through Bakri, around Batu Pahat, and around Bukit Pelandok. They were intimately connected to each other, but are best explained one at a time. 45th Indian Brigade spent the day trying to regroup in front of Bakri. The enemy got in the way. At 0900hrs Duncan "insisted that the enemy were only in small numbers" and planned his counterattack, to be launched when 2/29 AIF arrived. Meanwhile the brigade would deploy in an arc facing west to cover Bakri, blocking the roads from Muar and Parit Jawa. Unfortunately 7/6 Rajputs were so battered only stragglers regained the brigade area. This opened a gap along the coast road. Worse, 4/9 Jats remained well to the north, despite hearing the enemy were threatening Bakri, because they were distracted by a mistaken report the Japanese were probing upriver towards Lenga–the dead end. The battalion, still nearly intact, came no further south than Bukit Pasir, 10 km northwest of Bakri, before pulling into a perimeter for the night. This left the brigade dispersed and its arc in front of Bakri full of holes, already being vigorously probed by the enemy.[21] When 2/29 AIF arrived around 1500hrs Duncan briefed its commanding officer, Lt.-Col. J.C. Robertson. They agreed first to plug the holes, then prepare "a general advance on Muar." 2/29 AIF would take over in front of Bakri. 5/18 Royal Garwhalis would slide south to Parit Jawa, rallying Rajput stragglers, then advance at 0200hrs. The Australians would advance at daylight. Before any of that could happen the Japanese came on. The Garwhalis took the real blow. When their lead company drove toward the designated start line west of Parit Jawa at 1940hrs, "As men were debussing enemy opened fire on column from right and left of road with LMG's and rifles and from Bakri direction with mortars." A confused fight erupted in the bush, ending badly at 2300hrs: "A false alarm, due probably to fatigue and nerves, caused many of the troops to move to the right into thicker cover." After that the battalion scattered. That left 2/29 AIF nearly alone in front of Bakri, still separated from the Jats to the north. Instead of a "general advance," the Australian battalion and what was left of Duncan's brigade now faced imminent attack by a stronger force.[22]

Nishimura seized the initiative. Five of his six battalions drove towards the base of the small triangle. The entire 5th Guards Regiment headed for Bakri, while the two 4th Guards battalions moved on Parit Jawa. 5th Guards cut off the Jats and engaged the Australians; 4th Guards pushed along the coast road. Division headquarters then directed 4th Guards to split yet again. One battalion would continue along the coast road towards Batu Pahat, the other would turn inland at Parit Jawa. Together with 5th Guards it would launch a converging assault on Bakri. Nishimura's commanders deftly combined firepower and mobility. They pushed strong forces behind and between key road junctions before the defenders could seal them off, pre-empting Duncan's counterattack. And they did it without regard for their own supply lines. This suggested the Japanese appreciated how sensitive their enemy was to any threat to his lines of communication, and how sluggish he was when it came to making any "general advance." Granted, the Guards could count on strong air and tank support.[23] But this willingness to take calculated risks won them a crucial advantage of position by dawn on 18 January. They were already moving in force into the larger triangle, and could now move from more than one direction against any position the defenders tried to hold. This turned out to be decisive in the grim fight that now erupted.

In that fight the Australians gave the Japanese all they could handle, but were undone by the cardinal fact: the higher up the chain of command, the worse the mismatch. Bennett and Percival did not ignore developments on the west coast, but both remained reluctant to give up the main position in front of Segamat. On the 17th Percival became concerned about the threat to Yong Peng, warning Wavell at midday "A critical situation is developing owing to capture of Muar by the enemy."[24] Yet that afternoon he and Bennett agreed a few shuffles should contain the threat. 2/19 AIF would now go in to help hold the enemy at Bakri. A 53rd Brigade battalion would replace it at Jemaluang. The rest of that brigade would cover two junctions on the trunk road, while 15th Indian Brigade moved up to Batu Pahat. With these moves underway, Westforce sent this optimistic situation report to Malaya Command at 2145hrs:

> The situation in [Muar area] has improved today. Bakri and Parit Jawa are held by us in force and reinforcements have been sent to the 45 Ind Inf Bde. The Rajput Rifles have suffered severe casualties but parties of men are now drifting back. It is reported that 100 enemy have crossed the road at Parit Turi.

This was dangerously wrong. At that moment the Garwhalis were being cut up at Parit Jawa. The return of Rajput stragglers was just that, a gathering of demoralized troops with few officers. Malaya Command should by now have known that if one Japanese rifle company had already penetrated so far there were bound to be more. This report can only reflect the assumption that with 2/29 AIF on the scene all would be well, an assumption bolstered by Duncan. On the strength of this Percival reassured Wavell "situation has improved during day," explained the steps being taken, and stated "if this comes off situation will be eased."[25] Westforce would fight on.

It was in fact already too late to pre-empt the Japanese attack that began at dawn on 18 January. But neither can it be said Bennett and Percival did all they could. Duncan's optimism, plus the complacency of Bennett's staff, only compounded a problem caused by deploying unwisely in the first place. Percival understood the need to backstop the brigade, but did not appreciate the speed or weight of the Japanese advance. By this time he had no business taking chances with the former at least, whatever information he received. Shuffling companies and battalions was no way to check any strong enemy concentration, let alone regain the initiative. The movement of 2/19 AIF was a case in point. Held in limbo from the 15th, by the time it embussed from Jemaluang it was already 0400hrs. But it moved into positions near the Bakri crossroads from 1030hrs. This swift move from coast to coast suggests what might have been done had Malaya Command moved the full brigade before, rather than after, the enemy forced the pace.[26] Percival and Bennett tried instead to cover everywhere with at least some force. They hoped this would stop the enemy from making a decisive breakthrough anywhere, giving the main force time to pin him down. The units on the west coast now paid the price.

Five tanks of the Gotanda Medium Tank Company led the attack, charging straight down the road from Muar towards Bakri. This sparked what became the most famous single action of the campaign. The tanks ran into two Australian anti-tank guns deployed on the side of the road at the bottom of a reverse slope, supporting 2/29 AIF. At this point a steep cutting made the road a defile, keeping the tanks on the road. The front gun waited until the tanks were almost on top of it, then fired. The armour-piercing shells blasted right through the thin armour, and the tanks advanced slowly in between the two Australian guns. Both guns then engaged them at point-blank range with high explosive shells, knocking them all out. Three more tanks soon followed and engaged the guns in a harrowing duel. An Australian Army photographer caught the whole action on camera; the Gotanda Company was wiped out. The Guards took up the challenge and pressed on hard; they scored an important success by killing Robertson shortly after 1100hrs, catching him on the road. Even as 2/19 AIF moved into position the Japanese launched a full scale attack on the arc covering Bakri.[27]

The arrival of the fresh Australian battalion persuaded Duncan to stand and fight. He sent patrols to order 4/9 Jats to fall back on the brigade, and directed Lt.-Col. C.G. W. Anderson, commanding 2/19 AIF, to rally the stragglers of his other battalions and strengthen the arc. Anderson found 400 odd surviving Rajputs and Garwhalis, deployed them between his battalion and 2/29 AIF, and placed his own companies on high ground covering estate roads coming into Bakri from the west. But there was little fight left in the Indians. The Japanese soon wedged between the two Australian battalions and sent probes round both flanks. 4/9 Jats received the order to withdraw at 1330hrs, moved ponderously against light opposition, then decided after dark to sit tight inside a perimeter and wait till after midnight to move into Bakri. But a night move proved too difficult, so they stopped again to wait for daylight. This gave the Japanese time to infiltrate in strength. The Jats diary describes what happened next:

> The adv was resumed at 0800hrs ... The Bn passed thru the AIF posn [2/29 AIF] astride the rd Bakri-Muar (100 MS) at about 1200hrs. Heavy automatic fire was heard in the direction of Bakri. Bn adv along the E side of the rd but came into a heavy automatic fire ambush. The enemy fire posns were concealed in swamp on the E side and jungle on the west. It was impossible for the Bn to deploy and equally impossible to bring covering fire to bear from the rear. As the fwd elements of the Bn were halted and suffering heavy casualties OC A Coy decided to withdraw the rear half of the Bn in order to adv along a known track through the swamp in order to outflank the enemy. While reorg the remnants of the Bn the enemy brought down very heavy and very accurate arty concentrations.[28]

This barrage killed the commanding officer and dispersed the unit, less than 200 regrouping later that day with the Australians. Tsuji summarized the battle for Bakri:

> Because the violence of the frontal attack completely absorbed the attention of the enemy, the Ogaki Battalion [2nd Battalion 4th Guards Regiment] was able to penetrate through the jungle across their line of retreat.[29]

The converging Japanese attacks did just what Nishimura wanted, pinning the Australian rifle companies down around Bakri while other units outflanked them on both sides. 2/19 AIF demonstrated what could be done by a well led unit that trained hard to fight in close country. It delivered the kind of counterattack the Japanese had not suffered since fighting 12th Indian Brigade north of Ipoh. When he saw his carriers being driven off high ground overlooking battalion headquarters, Anderson threw two full companies into a hammer and anvil attack to pin the Japanese from the front and flank, then crush them from the rear. The Australians moved fast enough to catch and hit hard enough to destroy a Japanese company. But this impressive success was only local, and kept the Australians focused on the fight in front of Bakri. Even as it finished Anderson heard the Japanese were already attacking his transport and support elements on the road to Parit Sulong, behind brigade headquarters. In fact a full battalion was already behind the arc, aiming to cut it off.[30] And the Japanese now brought an important asset to bear: airpower

On 18 January 3rd Air Brigade threw its full weight in support of the Guards advance. At 1000hrs the next day, just as Anderson's counterattack was going well, a Japanese bomber scored a direct hit on 45th Indian Brigade headquarters. Duncan suffered "slight abrasions on the nose" but was shocked badly enough to provoke his brigade major to ask Anderson to assume command. The signals section and most of the staff were killed; this included Major Julius, redoubtable commander of 65 Bty., which had done good work since contesting the Muar River crossing. The fight raged on all afternoon.[31] After nightfall Anderson concentrated the force in a tighter arc around Bakri. But 2/29 AIF and 4/9 Jats were both down to the equivalent of two effective companies, and the remaining Indian troops were spent. Duncan stood fast to delay the enemy and rebuild the brigade by bringing in stragglers and 4/9 Jats. This backfired when he lost more than he gained, including a second commanding officer of 2/29 AIF in one day. Late on 19 January Anderson finally received orders from Westforce to "withdraw on Yong Peng."[32] It was too late.

The only thing Anderson could do to cover the road to Parit Sulong behind him was deploy transport and support elements there, adding a platoon of riflemen to watch the important bridge over the Simpang Kiri River at Parit Sulong. After Parit Jawa was lost this road was the lifeline, the only withdrawal route. It ran more than 30 km to the crossroads just west of Bukit Pelandok, where it met the secondary road from Batu Pahat running through to Yong Peng. For much of this stretch it was closely crowded by jungle and rubber, interspersed by open swamp patches. One such area made it a virtual causeway approaching Parit Sulong. A large force with vehicles, guns, and wounded men could not escape intact other than by moving along this road. 6th Norfolks relieved Anderson's platoon at Parit Sulong bridge on the evening of 18 January, freeing it to bolster the support elements guarding the road. It arrived at 0300hrs on 19 January. Four hours later disaster struck: "200-

300 enemy observed moving in NE direction across EAST side of perimeter." Battle raged until 1630hrs when enemy pressure scattered the force into the bush in three groups. More than 12 hours before Anderson's retreat began, a full enemy battalion seized control of his escape road. Together with the forces pressing from the west, they aimed to squeeze the Indian/Australian force in a vice and wipe it out.[33]

Early on 20 January Anderson prepared his battlegroup for a fighting retreat. Not trusting the Indians to break through at night to rescue his support elements, not being able to spare Australians, he did not know what happened east of Bakri or just what he would face there. All he knew was that enemy ground forces were on both sides of him, and he would face tanks from the west and heavy pressure from the air. Radio contact with Westforce was intermittent; he could only hope friendly infantry still held the bridge at Parit Sulong. The many wounded, including Duncan, were loaded onto trucks and the column moved out at 07000hrs. 2/19 AIF led the way in diamond formation. Behind it on either flank moved two Indian groups, one from 4/9 Jats, the other from the Rajputs and Garwhalis. 65 Bty. and the vehicles advanced on the road between the Indians, while B Company 2/29 AIF and the anti-tank guns formed the rearguard. Anderson planned to move along the road until they reached the edge of the large open swamp patch near Parit Sulong. The force would take cover until dark, then rush for the bridge.[34]

For the next 50 hours Anderson's battlegroup fought for its life along the road to Parit Sulong. The fighting was the most intense battle of the entire campaign, reaching a level of ferocity that stands comparison with any other action on this scale in the Pacific War. The 4th Guards battalion advancing on the coast road cut across country to seize the defile at Bukit Pelandok, in order to isolate the battle area. This screened the other battalion, allowing it to concentrate in full strength to block the road. 5th Guards, supported by a now somewhat depleted tank regiment, pressed on from Bakri, sending one battalion across country to outflank from the left; 3rd Air Brigade took to the air and piled on the pressure. This was another demonstration of how to handle an encounter battle: spread forces out to bring about a fight on the best possible terms, then concentrate them at the right time and place to win it—all at relentless tempo, without regard for supply lines, "fighting for the road off the road." But while Nishimura could and did outmaneuver Percival and Bennett, his men still had to destroy Anderson's force. The battlegroup was outgunned, and most Indian troops, with few surviving officers, were by now of little use.[35] But the Australians were first rate troops who now faced a clear cut challenge: break through or die. They had one other asset: Anderson.

After advancing barely two kilometres, the battlegroup ran into the first

Japanese roadblock. Japanese infantry covered it from a position on top of a cutting, with no less than six light machine guns. When B Company was pinned by fire from these guns, Anderson sent A Company to encircle and attack them from the rear. He then personally led a storming party to overrun them, putting one out of action with grenades, another with his pistol; the rest were taken by grenade and bayonet. This led to a brawl at the position from which Anderson now found his support elements had disappeared. The Australians noted "it was a very grim and determined stand made by this enemy body, who fought to the death." Meanwhile the rearguard fought to keep the enemy at bay, supported by 65 Bty. Shortly after noon the column, having advanced at walking pace in a tighter box formation, ran into a gauntlet of no less than six road blocks. These were made from toppled vehicles and downed trees and covered by machine guns, mortars, and snipers. All afternoon Anderson was everywhere. He organized one attack after another to clear the road, while striving to keep his rearguard in hand as it endured artillery fire and repeated attacks. One threatened to cave in a Jat company. This provoked Duncan, who bravely rejoined the battle to rally his men and was killed for his pains. By 1730hrs the battlegroup was compressed into an area barely 750 metres long, and its situation was becoming desperate. Anderson responded by bringing all its mortars and the firepower of two companies down on the main roadblocks, and throwing his reserve company into an all-out attack. 2/19 AIF's diary describes it best:

> This action brought into distinction the superlative initiative of Australian Troops—every man was fighting mad. Mortar shells were directed on to targets by infantrymen a few yards from the target (voice relayed back), gunners were fighting with rifles, bayonets and axes (range too short for 25 pdrs. except to Jap rear areas West). A gun crew pushed its 25 pdr. round a cutting and blew out the first road blocks (vehicles) at 75 yds range. Carriers pushed within 5 yds of Jap MG's and blew them out. Two carriers almost cut the walls of a 4 inch walled concrete house to pieces with Vickers. House contained 3 Jap MG's and about 60 men. Men went forward under heavy MG fire and chopped road blocks to pieces with axes. About 1830hrs the Japs had had enough and cleared out, leaving hundreds of casualties.

The claim about Japanese casualties is exaggerated but the fight was clearly savage. Unfortunately the battlegroup could not pause to lick its wounds. It had to press on so it could move in darkness through the open swamp, where there was no cover from the air.[36]

The battlegroup soon made contact with the 2/19 AIF platoon scattered the day before by the attack on the support elements. The news was bad: more enemy infantry were ahead. Anderson knew that if the enemy held the bridge at Parit Sulong his force was in dire straits. The vehicles, thus the wounded and the guns, would not be able to break through to friendly positions. But attempts to contact Westforce by radio failed, and staying put in the open was too dangerous. Two volunteer dispatch riders rode ahead to scout the bridge, and the advance resumed. They returned an hour later, reporting they were challenged in a foreign language, but not fired on, by four sentries near the bridge. At 0400hrs Anderson sent another patrol to scout the bridge, then ordered 2/19 AIF to advance and take it at dawn. The scouts were fired on at the bridge and reported this to Anderson at 0615hrs, about a kilometre from the objective. Two English-speaking Malays now assured Anderson the bridge was held by the Johore Military Forces and offered to lead him forward. Anderson decided to rush the bridge without further ado. As 2/19 AIF charged forward rapid fire broke out from the left flank, followed by a Japanese company attacking with fixed bayonets. The Japanese were around them on three sides. The battlegroup would have to break through by itself.[37]

This attack was repelled but the rearguard soon came under heavier attack led by tanks. This fight raged on all day. Radio contact was reestablished with Westforce, which promised efforts were being made to relieve the force; firing to the southeast confirmed this. The Jats tried to clear the riverbank between the village and the bridge, but could not destroy enemy machine gun positions that kept firing on the road. Pressed from all sides, Anderson could only spare A Company to attack the bridge. They fought hard, supported by mortars, and seized the western end of the span, but could not destroy well built houses on the other side of the river from which enemy machine guns swept the bridge. By noon the battlegroup was compressed into a triangle no more than a kilometre long from its apex at the bridge, its vehicles trapped by wide deep drains on either side of the road. It was running short of ammunition and supplies, and the casualty toll was rising. Calls for air support brought attacks on enemy columns down the road towards Muar, but Japanese air attacks, plus tank and artillery fire, increased as the day wore on. The result was not surprising: "Gradually the rear was forced in, as the perimeter had to contract owing to casualties and defections of the Indian trps." The battlegroup was trapped and being destroyed.[38]

That evening the most seriously wounded were loaded into two ambulances and driven onto the bridge, where the Japanese were asked to let them pass. Giving a sign of worse to come, they not only refused but insisted the vehicles stay put, using them as hostages in no man's land. They also demanded Anderson surrender immediately, and escalated their attacks. Tanks penetrated the perimeter and were engaged by 25 pounders plus hunting parties equipped with grenades and anti-tank rifles, in a fight that raged all evening. The ambulances returned at midnight after a wounded officer released the handbrakes. They rolled back off the bridge and were quietly pushed back to safety. Bennett sent messages assuring Anderson "all Australia was proud of you." The sentiments got through, but relief forces did not. Contact with an alarmed Westforce headquarters dwindled as the battlegroup's radio batteries weakened, until Anderson made one last appeal: "After an extremely anxious hour or so when all we heard was crackling static we eventually managed to pick up a faint signal requesting an airdrop of food, ammunition and morphia. After that all transmission ceased." Anderson also asked for an air attack on enemy strongpoints on the far side of the river, to support a final desperate attack to clear the bridge after dawn.[39]

RAF Far East did what it could, ordering 224 Group at 0445hrs: "2 Albacore 36 Sqdn and one Shark ex Tengah to provide close support by offensive action for operations commencing 0800 or soonest 22/1 in area Yong Peng-Muar Road. Sembawang to provide 4 and Kallang 2 Buffaloes for fighter escort. If successful repeat on return." The determination to help resonates through this order—but so does the weakness of the means. The antiquated biplanes pressed bravely on, returning to make a vivid report at 1245hrs:

Two Albacores dropped 8 containers at 0750hrs 22 Jan in area 676915. 3 containers seen on road North of bridge about 675918 but NO movement to collect them seen. 6 to 10 lorries seen stationary NE side of road between bridge 676915 and Parit Sulong facing South. Trucks and possible AFV's seen on road between Parit Sulong and MS 95. Firing taking place SW from bridge 676915. Area surrounding bridge devastated. Offensive air action area Yong Peng will be delayed owing to lack of fighters at present.

The fighters, as so often, were busy protecting an incoming convoy[40]—which task, it will be remembered, was a major reason Wavell laid on his "main battle." Three containers full of medical and other supplies did reach the Australians. Another attack was launched, actually reaching the bridge. But without stronger fire support and more ammunition it was beaten back by machine gun fire. By 0900hrs Anderson concluded the bridge could not be taken and the enemy would soon overrun his force. He made the painful decision to abandon the most seriously wounded, leave the vehicles, guns and equipment, break the force into company groups and escape across country towards friendly lines. Most, including many walking wounded, got clear from the battle area relatively easily, although all then had to run a tough gauntlet through difficult country and enemy air and ground patrols—and not all made it through. Anderson led out a company that regained friendly lines on the road to Yong Peng around midnight on 23 January. The 2/19 AIF war diary claimed with understandable pride "the force went out as a force."[41] But the price was severe.

The Australian units suffered nearly 75% casualties. 45th Indian Brigade was destroyed, with all its senior officers killed, wounded or captured. In all only 500 Australians and 400 Indians returned, out of more than 4500 committed to battle.[42] And this was not the worst. This fight hurt the Japanese, something Tsuji acknowledged in his lyrical style:

> The confused enemy, upon realizing [the road to Parit Sulong was blocked], reversed their main effort against the [5th Guards Regiment] attacking their front, and counterattacked the Ogaki Battalion [2nd Battalion 4th Guards Regiment] in their rear. This unit, while holding the enemy at bay, gradually withdrew, the casualties including its battalion commander ... Between 16 and 23 January a desperate fight had occurred. When the Gotanda Medium Tank Company lost all its tanks, the surviving officers and men had attacked on foot, reaching the enemy artillery position and the Parit Sulong Bridge, where the last of them met a heroic death after holding up the enemy for some time ... The force which made the flank attack through the jungle was the Ogaki Battalion, and it was a strategical situation such as held one in breathless suspense ... After an investigation of achievements a troop citation was awarded the Ogaki Battalion and the Gotanda Company, and these became the revered sacrifices of the whole Army.

But beyond the resolution and self-sacrifice there was another dimension: "For many of those thrown into such hazardous circumstances it was a war of extermination." This was indeed one battle in which the Japanese "received as good as they gave."[43] Angered by the price of their own boldness, the Imperial Guards discarded the thin veneer of discipline Yamashita tried to maintain in his command. After the fight was over, the Japanese rounded up 110 Australian and 40 Indian soldiers too badly wounded to escape. Most were brutally abused all day. An Australian survivor, Ben Hackney, witnessed a senior Japanese officer giving orders to junior officers before leaving the scene. That night the prisoners were wired or roped together, then led off to be butchered. Some were dowsed in petrol and set alight, some beaten to death, others beheaded. The remainder were machine-gunned at dawn. This disgusting atrocity did not of course become known to the rest of Malaya Command before the campaign was lost, but one thing was already clear to all. This enemy was ferocious in every sense of the word.[44]

The Australian troops clearly matched or bettered the Imperial Guards in every aspect of this battle: skill, resolution, leadership. The attempt to salvage the west coast flank failed in spite of their efforts. It failed mainly because the Japanese higher command outgeneralled its counterparts. They made decisions that allowed the Guards battalions to reap larger strategic rewards, beyond killing the trapped force, from their bold advances and hard fighting. 45th Indian Brigade disintegrated when most of its senior officers went down, but was so spread out by Bennett the defenders were asking for it. The enemy moved so fast neither Bennett nor Percival could have prevented a defeat, and Duncan certainly made things worse by being too optimistic. But even so Percival's responses might have been enough to prevent utter disaster. Why did they not?

Two efficient AIF battalions reached Bakri early enough to extract 45th Indian Brigade before the road could be strongly blocked–had 4/9 Jats not been so far north and taken so long to come in. Percival later credited Anderson's retreat with saving Westforce, by soaking up Japanese airpower and buying time for the main force to retreat to Yong Peng.[45] But Westforce would not have had to retreat in the first place had the Muar front not caved in. And the effort to relieve the force at Bakri was so badly handled it led to larger consequences that outweighed any distraction. Percival sent four battalions to screen the trunk road and keep the road to Anderson open. He rightly identified the junction at Bukit Pelandok as the pivotal point. Only two Japanese battalions advanced into this area and they dispersed their efforts widely, from the bridge at Parit Sulong, to Bukit Pelandok, to the lateral road east of Batu Pahat. There is no way they could also have broken through to Yong Peng before the main force got there. But this small force managed simultaneously to isolate Anderson's force, help destroy it, seize and hold Bukit Pelandok, and threaten Batu Pahat. One reason was of course Japanese skill. But the defenders mishandled this battle so badly the only adjective that fits is inept. The key problem, once again, was tempo.

Imperial Guards headquarters made the first important decision after hearing on 19 January that elements of 5th Guards had cut the road to Parit Sulong. The 4th Guards planned attack on Batu Pahat was postponed, leaving the battalion already landed by sea to fend for itself. The battalion advancing along the coast road wheeled left and cut across country. Together with 5th Guards elements it moved to block Anderson's retreat and isolate him by seizing the Bukit Pelandok junction.[46] Marching to the guns in this bold fashion caught the defenders unprepared. This gave a force not quite two battalions strong the chance to punch above its weight.

Percival's decision to send 53rd Brigade to backstop Westforce set the ball rolling. As noted, on the decisive day, 17 January, both commanders decided the fight for Muar should continue. Percival decided to spread 53rd Brigade out, one battalion each to cover Batu Pahat, Bukit Pelandok, and Ayer Hitam, to act as a safety net. Bennett's headquarters finally sounded an alarm at 1800hrs on 18 January, warning Malaya Command that as the coast road was open it was "essential develop Bukit Payong area immediately." Percival, having just been informed by intelligence that the enemy force in the area was in fact the entire Imperial Guards Division, now not only agreed Westforce must retreat but also decided more must be done to protect the lines of communication from the coast. To allow Bennett to concentrate on the trunk road, and on the grounds that blocking the coast and screening the trunk road now required close coordination, Percival transferred command of all forces west of the trunk road to III Indian Corps. This made sense on paper, but unfortunately the only semi-reliable means of communication with those forces was now through radio at Westforce headquarters. Percival explained these decisions to Wavell, arguing this thrust from the Muar area was "definitely the main one." But barely half an hour later Duncan described the situation as "fairly reasonable." Percival updated Wavell at 2320hrs, reporting the fight would continue near Muar and the roads would be "held at all costs." III Indian Corps had already assigned 15th Indian Brigade to cover Batu Pahat. This allowed 53rd Brigade to concentrate further inland–including taking over the bridge at Parit Sulong.[47] But the defenders, even if their high command did not yet realize it, were already losing the race to "get there firstest with the mostest."

While the Guards marched boldly to the guns, Percival, Bennett and Heath met at Yong Peng on 19 January to pull the battle together. They now agreed to withdraw to Labis, order the forces at Bakri to retreat, and confirm Heath's decision to concentrate 53rd Brigade from Parit Sulong to Yong Peng. This might have been enough–two days earlier. 45th Indian Brigade was already shattered and the arc at Bakri was outflanked. Previous decisions had already dispersed 53rd Brigade. This forced Percival to order the nearest uncommitted units, 3/16 Punjabi and 2nd Loyals, to join it; but the former was regrouping, and one company of the latter was still in Singapore. The high command was looking at the right area, but their mental map of the battle was obsolete. They still envisaged parallel retreats into the receptive arms of III Indian Corps units dug in to screen the lateral road. But Guards units were not only behind the Bakri force but already in amongst the covering forces behind them. Half an hour into the conference Brig. Duke arrived to report 53rd Brigade was already in contact.[48]

The high command lost its last chance to avoid strategic disaster there and then. The crucial point was Bukit Pelandok; it connected the fights at Bakri, Batu Pahat, and on the trunk road. There was only one battalion there, fresh off the boat. And it was already under attack. Yet Percival decided sending in these two battalions to help–one tired and depleted, the other widely scattered–would be enough. But he ordered 53rd Brigade not just to hold the junction but also to extract the forces retreating from Bakri. Percival explained these decisions to Wavell that evening: "Difficult to estimate the strength of these parties but probably NOT great ..." Indeed, they can not have exceeded two companies. But they must have moved very fast indeed, and were boldly attacking high ground from two directions. Percival's next words make his decisions harder to understand: "... though I think Japs are making their main effort here and are concentrating in Muar area." He expected "this will make us more concentrated to meet the Muar threat" but was now getting worried, saying "Should appreciate a talk with you tomorrow 20 Jan if you can spare the time."[49] Over four days the Japanese attacked from Muar to Bukit Pelandok with five battalions and Malaya Command reinforced 45th Indian Brigade over four days by committing five in response. Yet now the GOC was getting ready to ask his boss to call off the whole "main battle." Once again the Japanese wrong footed Malaya Command by keeping the tempo high. Once again they would be rewarded for taking that calculated risk.

These decisions left the "main battle" in the hands of 53rd Brigade. This was Percival's calculated risk. It was as fatal as the deployment at Muar. The brigade was too new to the country, too widely dispersed, too haphazardly reinforced, and too badly led to accomplish its mission. The first problem was timing. The brigade described its troops as "healthy but soft," not ready to fight in this terrain:

> On disembarkation it immediately became obvious that tps would not be given necessary time in which to shake down, test and train with their new equipment and generally put themselves into the picture. Efforts to give instruction in local tactical methods were begun but never reached lower ranks.

Indeed. The brigade disembarked into a "hectic turmoil unloading ship, attempting to sort out equipment, drawing rations, special scales of clothing, mortar amn., anti-malarial clothing, returning winter clothing [!], blankets, etc, sun helmets, surplus baggage (officers had brought up to 4 cwt. each) [!] ..." As this turmoil unfolded Duke was ordered on 14 January to send 5th Norfolks to Jemaluang. The next day he was ordered to send another battalion to Yong Peng. Two companies of 6th Norfolks went north on 16 January, while brigade headquarters reported to 11th Indian Division at Ayer

Hitam. There it was ordered to cover the whole area from Batu Pahat to the trunk road, "an immense front," with only two battalions. Worse, while settling in on 18 January "It was decided to destroy br[idge] on the rd between [Batu Pahat] and [Bukit Pelandok] ...." This decision was premature. At that point no enemy tanks were anywhere near the bridge. All it did was cut the direct link between Duke's two positions that was only 15 km long, forcing any movement between the two to go through Yong Peng and Ayer Hitam, more than four times the distance. This is what forced Percival to shuffle units around on 19 January. 2nd Battalion The Cambridgeshire Regiment [2nd Cambs] was already at Batu Pahat so it was transferred to 15th Indian Brigade; in return Duke received the Loyals and Punjabis. Meanwhile 5th Norfolks went back and forth from Jemaluang to the trunk road, changing destinations seven times in five days, until finally settling in very late on 19 January as reserve, in Ayer Hitam. All this left a raw brigade headquarters facing a fight that turned out to be the pivot of the "main battle" with only one of its own battalions under command. There were only two artillery batteries on hand and it was also short of carriers.[50] Finally, it was attacked before the arrival of the two battalions it did not know, but which at least knew Malaya.

All this helps explain the key fact of Bukit Pelandok: a smaller Japanese force decisively outfought 53rd Brigade. It started with the ground. Duke personally deployed 6th Norfolks in the crucial area. The main features were a causeway through a marsh, dominated at both ends by high ground, and two defiles. The defiles were bordered on the north or right flank of the road by jungle which climbed into a line of hills running parallel to the road, and by high ground at the eastern end. The longer defile was overlooked by hills on both sides. On the right flank Bukit Belah overlooks the junction itself. The shorter defile is three kilometres west of this junction, dominated by high ground known as Bukit Payong. The bridge at Parit Sulong is 11 km west of the junction. The Japanese approached from the west. But 53rd Brigade identified the causeway at the eastern end of the position as "the most dangerous point" and deployed accordingly. This was unwise. Even today a personal inspection indicates right away the correct point: the hills overlooking the road junction, especially Bukit Belah and another hill next to it on the north side. They are easier to approach under cover from the direction the Japanese were coming, and anyone holding them can deny the whole area. Duke's force did not have good maps and did not know the country, but this does not excuse such an elementary blunder. The importance of the causeway was that if it was lost any retreat to Yong Peng would have to be off the road across country; the implication speaks for itself.[51]

6th Norfolks started deploying on 16 January. To offset their inexperience, the brigade kept the position tight to the road. Duke put two companies on the hills astride the long defile, one company behind it, and one company at the eastern end of the causeway. The two forward companies each detached a platoon, one to relieve the 2/19 AIF platoon at Parit Sulong and hold the bridge, the other, mounted, to patrol the road between there and the main position. As 3/16 Punjabi companies arrived they were deployed on a ridge at the western end of the causeway. Duke directed his companies to patrol around their own positions, but not to venture into the jungle: "with the tps in the condition in which they were, active patrolling in the jungle and marshes was not practicable." Given the ground, and his orders to extract the force from Bakri, it is hard to see how he could have prepared more poorly. The platoon holding Parit Sulong, the link to Anderson, was too weak to hold off even a company without support—but too far forward to receive any in a hurry, especially as the guns were too far back to help. It was connected only to the equally small force patrolling the road. Bukit Payong, the high ground closest to Anderson, was left open. The bush was left unpatrolled. The vital hills were held by two companies not in touch with each other and depleted by patrols too close to give much warning of a sudden attack, yet too far to help if one materialized. Duke's whole force leaned back towards Yong Peng, not forward towards Anderson. The brigade complained "The actual orders and role of these isolated [platoons] seem to have been vague. They seriously reduced the fighting value of their coys and were of little value isolated at Parit Sulong."[52] But they were not supposed to be "isolated at Parit Sulong." The mission was to extract the Bakri force; it could only come one way. Holding a getaway route would not help if it could not make it there. If the enemy seized even one hill overlooking the defiles the cat would be amongst the pigeons.

The enemy did just that. Whether they came from Bakri or the coast road, Japanese infantry cut across country after going through the junction. At 1330hrs on 19 January, while the Bakri force fought hard to hold its arc, they attacked both forward companies on the hills at Bukit Pelandok. The enemy attacked before either company received any warning from its patrols. The Japanese used jungle cover to get above C Company on the left flank and drove it off the hill with mortar and machine gun fire. D Company on the right flank stood fast, but its Forward Observation Officer lost touch, then went back to brigade headquarters to report it was driven off as well. Not sure where his own troops were, Duke pulled back to regroup. He decided to counterattack on both sides of the road in leap-frog style, but wait for the cover of night to approach the objective. At dawn on 20 January one company of 3/16 Punjabi would storm the hill just to the right of the road, Bukit Belah. Another Punjabi company would then secure the adjacent hill. They would both support B Company 6th Norfolks, which would retake the hill on the left flank. Unfortunately, the enemy did not sit still overnight either–and D Company still held the objective the Punjabis now stormed.[53]

Moorhead led the assault himself. He was guided by the same artillery officer who reported D Company driven off. Confused by first light, the two friendly forces exchanged fire. Moorhead cleared that up, but minutes later, as they reached the crest, Japanese infantry stormed Bukit Belah from the other side. The two sides exchanged machine gun fire and grenades. Moorhead was killed, the Punjabi company nearly destroyed, and the Norfolks now truly driven off the hill. Meanwhile B Company 3/16 Punjabi took the adjacent hill, but then sat tight all day. B Company 6th Norfolks advanced to retake the hill left of the road, but came under harassing fire from both sides of the defile. Evidently the Japanese did not fight private battles on single hills. The company commander withdrew. Faced with the collapse of his counterattack, Duke turned to his newest reinforcements: B Company 2nd Loyals, just arrived straight from Singapore. He ordered it to take the hill on the left by attacking through the bush on its left. It duly marched into the jungle and disappeared. That settled matters: "As the attempt to regain the defile by direct attack had failed and both Bns were now very weak and disorganized, it was decided to reorganize and hold ground." Duke pulled back between the defile and the causeway.[54] This was despite the fact the enemy did not advance after seizing the defile, not even to take the hill next to Bukit Belah. There was in fact only one Guards battalion in the area, and it separated to seize both the defile and the Parit Sulong bridge. Duke did not know Anderson's force was then fighting the battle of the roadblocks. Nor did he know the Japanese seized the Parit Sulong bridge unopposed at 1600hrs.[55] But he did know Anderson's force was now cut off–and he knew why.

The Australian postmortem warned against rushing to judgement. But it also commented "It is felt that the leadership on this occasion was lacking in enterprise and dash."[56] 2nd Loyals were not reluctant, but in their years in garrison in Singapore had not made any serious effort to train in close country. 3/16 Punjabi was in fact the amalgamation of survivors of that unit with those of 2/16 Punjabi, after their ordeals in the north. The unit was so fragile Moorhead voluntarily resumed command to pull it together. When he went down it floundered. 6th Norfolks were the achilles heel. Consider the detachments assigned to guard the road and bridge at Parit Sulong:

The two plts of 6 Norfolk sent to Parit Sulong area appear to have decided during the morning of the 20th to rejoin their unit by jungle routes on the assumption that they were cut off from their unit. They apparently were told this by some RAMC officer.

The Norfolks abandoned the lifeline hours before the enemy appeared.[57] Failure to press home the attack on the left cost the B Company commander his job. The more resolute D Company commander was abandoned to fend for himself on Bukit Belah. Where did this weakness stem from? The answer comes from the officer commanding headquarters company. When enemy bombers attacked battalion positions on 18 January, he was ordered by the commanding officer to relocate forthwith, without proper reconnaissance. Next day, 19 January, after the Japanese attack:

> On my return to Bn HQ I found that for all practical purposes the 2nd i/c appeared to have assumed command of the Bn and the Bde Cmdr in his numerous visits dealt almost entirely with the 2nd i/c; the CO appeared to be very much shaken. At dusk I was ordered by the CO to place all available men in a circle around HQ at intervals of a few yards and with fixed bayonets; all ranks were ordered to remain alert throughout the night. Personally I spent the night walking round the perimeter (about 400 yards diameter) waking the men who were already weary and in need of rest.

The next night he had to talk the battalion commander out of repeating this performance, but Duke did not make the obvious decision until the morning of 22 January: "... the CO was sent back to B Ech for a rest, under the Bde Comdr's orders."[58]

Duke believed the brigade was not fit to fight any but the most carefully orchestrated battle. Before his counterattacks Duke warned Percival and Bennett he intended to do no more than hold the defile–despite the fact the fighting there surely signalled a clear threat to the Parit Sulong bridge. Percival and Bennett received reports on the disruption of the brigade, but neither understood just how much this influenced Duke.[59] As a result they made decisions which made matters worse. The next morning, 21 January, Percival transferred Anderson's force and 53rd Brigade back to Bennett's command. He felt that now that the main force was falling back on Yong Peng the rescue operation on the road to Bakri was directly connected to it and should be coordinated by the same headquarters–which also had radio contact with all formations. The GOC met Heath, Bennett and Key at Yong Peng shortly after noon. Bennett presented a plan for 53rd Brigade to retake the defiles by another counterattack led by 2nd Loyals, "to assist the AIF Bns and 45 Ind Bde to rejoin." Percival endorsed the plan, then turned to his priority: how to carry on the "main battle." The mission was clear: "... it was still the intention to fight the enemy North of the line Jemaluang-Kluang-Ayer

Hitam-Batu Pahat"–the lateral road and its airbases. The challenge would be to switch from Phase I to Phase II. Phase I would be extracting Anderson and bringing Westforce back to Paloh and Yong Peng, to screen the lateral road. Phase II would be reorganizing Malaya Command to hold that new line. Percival himself noted "the change from Phase I to Phase II will depend on how today's battle in the [Bukit Pelandok] area goes."[60] Higher authority pressed Percival to carry on this "main battle." That trapped him between a rock and a hard place, because his plan was already surpassed by events on the ground. Anderson's force was already trapped at Parit Sulong, 53rd Brigade had already missed the last slim chance to rescue it, and command decisions were central to both outcomes.

After Slim River, Heath persuaded Percival that Key was the only man who could rebuild 11th Indian Division.[61] As the battle unfolded Key spotted the importance of Bukit Pelandok. After 53rd Brigade came under his command he immediately went to inspect it there. He found 6th Norfolks "very nervous and poorly deployed" and became concerned about the brigade's combat readiness. Key's obvious lack of confidence only made Duke defensive. Controversy surrounds what happened next. The 53rd Brigade says Key pressed Duke to focus on the "main task" to protect Yong Peng at the expense of extracting Anderson's force. The 11th Indian Division tells a different story. Key pressed Duke to extract the force, but was misinformed by the brigade about its situation on 20 January; once Key realized the truth that evening, he ordered a dawn counterattack to retake the defiles. Duke's emissary protested, so Key postponed the attack but insisted it proceed as soon as possible. When Key heard the next morning the brigade was returned to Bennett all he could do was send a staff officer to suggest Westforce would want an immediate attack, and urge Duke to advance at 1400hrs. By the time Bennett could confirm the order it was too late. The Australian record paints yet another picture. Bennett pressed for a counterattack to extract Anderson's force. Key objected on the grounds an attack would not clear the route as far as Parit Sulong, would increase the risk of enemy infiltration, and would therefore jeopardize the brigade's "primary role": screen the trunk road. Bennett referred the dispute to Percival, who ruled in his favour. Through the disagreements, three things are clear. First, neither Key nor Duke had any confidence the brigade could pull off another counterattack after the first failure. Second, the Australians noticed this, and saw it as writing off Anderson's force. Third, by the time Bennett took charge it was too late to attack on 21 January. Percival could only advise Wavell the enemy's "main effort" was being met by the counterattack to extract Anderson, and hope for the best.[62]

After 20 January 53rd Brigade did not really try to retake the defile, let alone rescue Anderson. By the time Duke's force was ready it was impossible to rescue the trapped column. B Company 2nd Loyals in fact reached its objective, but lost touch with brigade headquarters and was driven back into the jungle by friendly artillery. Thinking them lost, brigade headquarters concluded its infantry could only try a tightly controlled set-piece assault with deliberate preparations, especially for artillery support. Bennett's GSO1, Col. J.H. Thyer, came to pass on the order to attack at midday on 21 January.He found Duke and his staff inspecting the objective from open ground, in full view of it. When Thyer remonstrated, they said there were probably no enemy on the hill. When he then suggested storming it instead of laying on a set-piece attack they did not answer. The whole operation was postponed until 1700hrs, to allow the infantry to assemble and the artillery to register the target. More delays in bringing in the rest of the Loyals pushed it back again to dawn; but the artillery insisted it must then register again first. Hearing this, Westforce offered artillery support. Duke replied he did not need it. When the artillery resumed at dawn, it was too far off target. By the time everyone was finally ready at 0900hrs on 22 January, a heavy enemy air attack caught the infantry on the start line and cut them up. Duke did not know Anderson was giving up at that moment. He did know all surprise was now lost:

> The chances of holding [the defiles] once recaptured seemed small. In the event of failure to recapture or hold it, the situation would be very serious as the main task of preventing the enemy penetration to the main line of comm at [Yong Peng] would be endangered with three weak and disorganized units.

Duke now pulled back to screen the causeway. Fate then taunted him when B Company 2nd Loyals struggled back into his position at 1000hrs, having cut its way through the jungle. Brigade headquarters was unfazed: "Coy Comd had shown great perseverance but in fact the deployment of British tps wide of a rd in these jungles was impracticable." Unfortunately it did not prove so for the enemy.[63]

Percival later focused on the last aborted attack when he argued it was impossible to rescue Anderson's force. Duke was excused: "just arrived from England where training had probably been on more deliberate lines."[64] The strength of enemy airpower was another consideration. There is no doubt it was more effective than in any ground engagement to date. Japanese bombers knocked out Duncan's headquarters, interfered with Bennett's communications, spooked 6th Norfolks, stopped Duke's last attack. Japanese fighters kept Pulford's flyers busy, which covered the amphibious assaults on the west coast. Japanese reconnaissance flights were an important force multiplier, giving the defenders no rest and providing information that allowed the infantry battalions to move fast and take chances. On the other hand Anderson's force faced the same problem, yet fought with resolution and some sense of fieldcraft.[65] 53rd Brigade was simply not ready to handle an independent action in an unprepared position. Higher command put it there nonetheless; Australian units would surely have tried harder to relieve Anderson's force? Now the whole army faced the consequences. Having eliminated Anderson's force, the Imperial Guards now occupied the central position. From there they could attack Batu Pahat from three directions, Yong Peng from two, or outflank both by driving towards Ayer Hitam. Phase I of Percival's transition had failed. Could Phase II still be salvaged?

The answer was no. One reason was a struggle embedded in the "main battle": the tug of war over command and control. Bennett did the most damage. From the start he fought a parallel battle to keep the authority Wavell gave him, to control the main force and operations along the trunk road. The fiery Australian could not handle the frustration caused by the collapse of all his plans. And unfortunately his immaturity was not confined to private venting sessions in a diary. Bennett sent this telegram to Australia on 19 January:

> Whole situation most serious. Mersing-Gemas-Muar fronts each held by 2 Australian Battalions with very FLIMSY support by Indian troops who have not stood firm and by new English units inexperienced in local conditions. Even Malaya Command expressed doubt as to their reliability.

This was not entirely unfair. Bennett's division was broken into three separate forces instead of being concentrated and 53rd Brigade was weak. But Bennett was as responsible as Percival for splitting up his division and what followed was nonsense:

> We cannot plug up Segamat holes and are finding it difficult to hold present positions against overwhelming numbers. So far our companies have to meet attacks by whole battalions, and face always a situation that cannot continue for long.[66]

Only Anderson's force was outnumbered during the "main battle." In fact the enemy was tougher than Bennett expected, while he and his division were not as good as he thought. When Percival on 17 January first suggested directing Heath and Key to watch the Muar flank, Bennett "told him I anticipated that plot but objected strongly to it as I could not trust them." The next evening Bennett launched his tirade against 9th Indian Division and "senior British commanders." The 19 January meeting at Yong Peng dealt with truly pressing matters: ordering the Bakri force to retreat and concentrating 53rd Brigade to extract it. For the record Bennett "drew attention to the fact that Tommy gun ammunition is being expended unnecessarily and suggested that this should be checked." Privately, Bennett complained about the decision to bring Heath back into the battle: "They want to filch my res. bde. too. Protested. Later moves mooted when comd. question raised. Corps wants the lot and he will get it."[67]

When it became clear Anderson's force was in grave danger, Bennett exploded in protest to the Malaya Command Liaison officer at his headquarters:

[Bennett] complained bitterly at the failure to allow the 2/19 and 2/29 to withdraw earlier. He stated that his G Staff had telephoned at about 1300hrs [19 January] stating that they were in touch, and asking permission to give the order. NO decision was given, and enquiries made later in the afternoon were met with a denial that the original request had ever been made. He maintained that two bns might be lost through indolence or inefficiency of staff, and that he intended to make a full report. He added that if the two bns were lost "All Australia would know the reason."

This threat to stir up political trouble was both the last thing a multinational army in the middle of a battle needed and part of a pattern too pronounced to excuse as harmless release of steam. The Australians were going to suffer a heavy defeat, his plan was falling apart, and he needed someone to blame. Bennett denounced Taylor, handling a model defence on the east coast, as "very unreliable" for moving one company without checking with him first. When Thyer tried to prod 53rd Brigade Bennett concluded "Thyer queer. He messed up time of attack by foolish interference." But after ordering Anderson to give up the breakout, a "very very sad and upset" Bennett denounced 53rd Brigade, rightly noting "they did not want to attack."[68] This all might have been more convincing–had Bennett not himself written Anderson off from the start.

After Percival agreed Anderson must retreat, Bennett sent another telegram. Despite the challenge this now posed–"Enemy parties on road behind them and now threaten to cut communications north of Batu Pahat"–Bennett's own priority lay elsewhere: "Yong Peng is key point notwithstanding for my own communication and this is now threatened unless British units covering it do better than in past." The next morning, as Anderson's retreat began, Bennett told 27th Australian Brigade:

2/29 and 2/19 are cut off and have suffered very heavy casualties. An attempt is being made to extricate them but I fear that it will not succeed. The possibility of the landing at Batu Pahat followed by a drive on Ayer Hitam and Kluang leads me to consider the position critical. However, we can only hope that it will be possible to extricate our Bns in the area.

In his diary he noted, "If Yong Peng or Ayer Hitam goes we will have a long walk and a good swim." Bennett reiterated the point that evening: "Relief is impracticable ... My own front now very thin as troops have been taken to Yong Peng area to try to hold communications open," and again very early on 21 January: "Their position is desperate and no assistance can be given." That same day 27th Australian Brigade settled in to defend Yong Peng, less than 15 km from Bukit Pelandok, unmolested except by air attack. It remained "content to rest and await results of the proposed counter-attack by the 2 Loyals ..." While 53rd Brigade procrastinated, "Westforce as a whole was able to enjoy a reasonably quiet night." Yet Bennett had already warned Australia about Duke's next attack: "... complete link up is improbable if not impossible." The excuses were repeated:

> At outset of battle [sic] I had 2 Australian battalions each at Endau–Gemas–Bakri near Muar road distances being 180 and 105 miles respectively. Indian troops poor morale and lacking fighting qualities. Our equipment ample and efficient our only lack is numbers.[69]

By "our" Bennett meant his 8th Australian Division. The last point was a dig at the decision not to send his third brigade to Malaya. Apart from that, and damning his subordinates, Bennett saved recriminations for his British colleagues. Candid admissions stayed in house. As stragglers from Anderson's force began to regain friendly areas, Bennett privately complained "too many Indians." Bennett summarized why he did not intervene in a telegram recommending Anderson for a well deserved Victoria Cross:

> British troops abandoned their attack which was pre-DOOMED to failure as it lacked enthusiasm. Could not afford allow Australian attack as whole position here depended on them all others being unreliable.[70]

Percival was trapped between Wavell, who had no confidence in him, and Bennett, in whom he understandably lost confidence. Every effort the GOC made to grip the battle risked running aground on three rocks: being undone by the enemy; provoking Wavell by discarding his plan; or being undermined by Bennett. The Japanese were the biggest rock. They left him neither time to breathe nor margin to err. Percival did not mishandle the battle on the trunk road. But his heart was never in Wavell's plan, and his actions suggest he hoped all along to ease the army back towards what he regarded as a safer course of action. That especially meant reducing Bennett's personal role. The enemy advance just allowed the GOC to do what he wanted anyway. But when the west coast flank suddenly erupted, he had to throw the raw British brigade and tired Indian battalions straight into a fight no less dangerous than any he feared on the east coast. The three rocks made Percival twist and turn to no real advantage. Handing control of the western area to Heath overstretched III Indian Corps headquarters, forcing it to direct operations from Mersing to Batu Pahat for three crucial days–the three days in which defeat became disaster.

Percival tried two ways to escape the trap. First, he raised the issue of campaign strategy with Wavell. Percival did not condemn his mission to deny the naval base and did not deny this required the army to fight north of the lateral road. He did worry about the consequences of fighting this "main battle" according to Wavell's plan, with Bennett on point. Only one explanation fits the circumstances and actions. Despite running out of time and space, the GOC still wanted to preserve the army as a whole, rather than risk a defeat so shattering it disintegrated long before I Australian Corps could arrive. Percival felt that a still fighting army driven back to the island left more options open than trying and failing to stop the Japanese dead in their tracks. This raised the question of how to defend the island, if it finally came to that.

It has long been thought serious planning to defend Singapore island did not begin until after Wavell's "main battle" played out. In fact Malaya Command headquarters produced its first draft outline on a map, dividing the island into sectors and identifying company defensive positions, on 18 January. That same evening Percival concluded the attack from Muar jeopardized the whole army. To him the issue was clear: should the battle continue, or should the army fall back yet again? Percival raised this question with Wavell before asking on 19 January to meet him in Singapore. Wavell knew full well how little time and space was left to keep the enemy away from the island, how intimate the connection was between its defence and his "main battle." But he was also caught in a tight squeeze, pressed between a relentless enemy and an aroused Prime Minister. Wavell visited Singapore on 20 January to make sure Percival struck the right balance. He made two things clear. The previous day he ordered "you must make it clear to everyone that the battle is to be fought out in Johore without thought of retreat"; Percival said Wavell now repeated this in person: "continue the fight in Johore and to try to hold the Japanese there until reinforcements arrived." But Wavell also discussed plans to defend the island, at a level of detail that indicates he knew the army must soon retreat to it. Two days later Percival noted "Your letter 21 Jan. Concur with your lay-out and personalities which agree with my outline plan. We must see who we get in before we finally settle the personalities." This referred to the outline plans for island defence. These plans could only be finalized once approaching convoys arrived and the outcome of the mainland battle was clear. Wavell and Percival quietly made a deal. Percival could plan his retreat and last-stand island defence. But he must do it in strictest secrecy, because the army must meanwhile delay that outcome by fighting out the "main battle" without looking over its shoulder. Until he was permitted to reconsider theatre strategy, Wavell saw no choice but to insist Percival continue the fight.[71]

Both men knew that decision raised the real possibility Malaya Command might be destroyed on the mainland. To prevent this Percival turned to his second escape option. He used defeat in the west to reorient his army to the plan he preferred in the first place. Percival sketched out his design at the Yong Peng meeting on 21 January. Malaya Command would realign itself into three formations. Eastforce would cover the area from Kahang to Jemaluang, carrying on its delaying action near Mersing. Heath would delegate responsibility to Taylor. Its line of communication ran to Singapore along the road from Jemaluang. Westforce, under Bennett, would cover the area from east of Kluang to west of Ayer Hitam; it would hold forward at Paloh and Yong Peng. Its lines of communication ran along the railway and trunk road. 11th Indian Division would deny the west coast, hold Batu Pahat, and maintain contact with Westforce along the lateral road. Its line of communication was the west coast road. Percival expected this realignment to be complete by 24 January. While the objective was to continue the fight north of the lateral road, Percival sent two signals undermining this. First, 53rd Brigade would revert to 11th Indian Division after it fell back on Yong Peng. Second, if Westforce retreated it, and thus Bennett, would come under Heath's command. Heath would direct subsequent operations on the mainland.[72]

This of course anticipated there would be such operations. It also approximated the plan by which Percival wanted to defend Johore in the first place, apart from Bennett directing operations in the centre. Bennett would be constrained. Heath's more experienced and larger staff would play a larger role. The army could deploy with untangled north-south lines of communication. This was a recipe for an organized fighting retreat, which of course is why Wavell rejected it in the first place. But by now the army would be lucky to regroup and make such a deployment, so he let it pass. Heath on the other hand saw this as a chance to regain control of the battle, Bennett as a sign he was about to be marginalized. Both were driven by profound lack of confidence in the other. Bennett no longer trusted any British or Indian formation. Heath feared Bennett would mishandle the defence of the trunk road and pressed for joint control. Percival decided his orders would stand, which satisfied neither subordinate.[73]

The Imperial Guards advance now escalated the threat around Batu Pahat. They seemed poised to isolate it and cut the road to Ayer Hitam. This would blow open the west coast, threaten the trunk road, and abort Phase II. Bennett sent 2/26 AIF to cover the western approaches to Ayer Hitam on 22 January. He saw this as guarding his left flank. Heath and Key knew 5th Norfolks and 2nd Cambs had already engaged enemy patrols on the lateral road and rightly feared they were losing control of the artery. They insisted the Australian battalion push forward to secure the route to Batu Pahat. Bennett refused, believing Key would lose the battle and thus leave his force exposed. While 2/26 AIF dug in unmolested around Ayer Hitam, an enemy force cut the road several kilometres west of it late that afternoon. This was the poisoned harvest sown by Muar and Bukit Pelandok. Percival's commanders lost confidence in each other and their units. Bennett especially looked out for number one.[74] Percival's team ceased to act as one. This ruined his plan to fight for the lateral road before it even began. Full fledged disaster now stared Malaya Command in the face. It was already taking shape around Batu Pahat.

Batu Pahat is the western anchor of the lateral road. It lies 10 km inland on the south bank of the Simpang Kanan River, then crossed at the town by a ferry. The river is narrow but remains navigable for small boats quite far inland, running parallel north of the road towards Ayer Hitam. The road to Bukit Pelandok is less than 15 km long. A good road connects the town to a hilltop lighthouse on the coast, also on the south bank. A line of hills peaking in Bukit Banang rises just south of this road. They overlook the road to the lighthouse, the town, and the coast road. A usable airstrip lay 14 km south of town; the ground in between was mixed jungle, rubber, and quarry. The coast road running south meets a branch road at Pontian Kechil that links it to the trunk road, just north of Johore Bahru. All this made Batu Pahat essential to hold but easy to assault.[75] 1st Battalion 4th Guards Regiment, the division reconnaissance unit, set off in boats from Malacca on 15 January to do just that, to provide a distraction for the main attack on Muar. It landed near the lighthouse at 0800hrs on 16 January then advanced inland, moving south of the hills. They concealed it from the scratch forces watching the area, a cavalry squadron plus the intrepid Independent Company. Their landing was duly reported. But the Japanese force avoided battle and crossed the coast road, establishing itself south of the town in good cover in the formerly Japanese owned plantation near the airstrip. It then set about to make a nuisance of itself.[76]

This force was strong enough to pose a real threat. It could deny the coast road, the lateral road, the airstrip, even harass the town. When other elements of the division approached from the north, it could form a pincer movement that would threaten any force trying to hold the area. Malaya Command needed to crush it before it could become really dangerous. As soon as he heard of the landing, Percival ordered the British Battalion out of its much needed rest at Kluang and back into the field. It arrived at 1230hrs. This was so prompt it makes it hard to believe the Japanese could not have been found by a really energetic advance to contact. Unfortunately neither unit on the spot could report anything more definite than that a small enemy force invaded and moved south. The British Battalion played it safe, sending one company charging down to the lighthouse while the remainder deployed in town, along the river road, and astride the coast road just south of town. This allowed the Japanese force to well and truly conceal itself.[77]

Overnight a fatal misperception settled in, from battalion to army headquarters. Reports of initial contact with an enemy force some 60 strong– it was in fact ten times that size–produced a reassuring report to Malaya Command. The town and coast road were thoroughly swept but no enemy found. The new commander of 15th Indian Brigade, Brig. B.S. Challen, personally went to the lighthouse and "No enemy were encountered and he is therefore sitting in comfort." Local civilians later told the British Battalion the enemy were southwest, below Bukit Banang. This was not quite accurate. They were in fact southeast, inland from the road. But it surely should have provoked some curiosity. Instead "the CO collected a large haul of duck eggs." Percival decided the situation was "in hand" so he handed the area over to 53rd Brigade, allowing the British Battalion to resume their rest. 2nd Cambs moved in from midday and by dusk the handover was complete. The raw unit also deployed in a tight arc covering the town, no more than five kilometres out. The enemy sat undisturbed. Percival reassured Wavell that evening all was quiet, albeit "Japs who landed there yesterday have NOT been found."[78] This turned out to be another 17 January non-decision that came back to haunt the defenders.

2nd Cambs sent out patrols the next morning. One bumped into the enemy and lost two men. But the hidden force remained undetected, although enemy aircraft operated over the area all day; this sparked incorrect reports of another Japanese landing. These reports, plus Bennett's concerns about the coast road, prompted Percival that evening to direct 15th Indian Brigade to assume command at Batu Pahat, and to send help. But help amounted to returning the British Battalion. Key, that same day, promised it seven to ten days rest. Sure enough hours later the battalion was back on the road, which must have done wonders for morale![79] Over the next two days 15th Indian Brigade settled into a tight perimeter around the town. This lethargy coincided with the Imperial Guards decision to redirect their advance, which forced their hidden battalion to hold on alone as it ran out of supplies. The artillery did "quite a lot of shooting" at targets near the airstrip, but the infantry settled for not very aggressive patrolling. The road to Bukit Pelandok was ignored. Almost the entire length of the lateral road to Ayer Hitam was left to 5th Norfolks to patrol from there, which their carrier platoon did–in daylight. The brigade was finally aroused late on 20 January when it heard about the debacle at Bakri.[80] Too late. By their lack of aggression the defenders not only threw away their last chance to hunt down the force behind them, they also left a gaping hole the enemy could exploit to trap them in return.

This neglect made the battle which finally erupted around Batu Pahat on 21 January the very type at which the Japanese excelled: an encounter battle. At the Yong Peng meeting that afternoon Percival took pains to direct Key to make sure the position at Batu Pahat was strong and well stocked. He intended to hold it as long as possible even if it became cut off, to deny the coastal road to the enemy.[81] This made some sense–but was too late. Once again the defenders fell behind the tempo of battle on the ground. The margin this time was tight. But because the Japanese were much better in this kind of fight, it was enough.

Earlier that morning the British Battalion took the initiative to arrange with 2nd Cambs "for an offensive sweep to be made round the hill where it was known the Japanese party was lying up." This was, finally, a serious attempt to deal with this force, involving four companies in a converging advance to contact. The decision followed a report which finally made the brigade realize what it might be up against:

A local school master, vouched for by [T.S. Carey, Malayan Civil Service senior official in the area], visited Minyak Beku each day and reported on movements of Japanese as learnt from locals. His history was that there were 500 lying up in the wooded hilly country near the coast.

This could have been determined two days earlier by more energetic patrolling, or by being more receptive to local sources. When the action began, nothing went right. The main force, two British Battalion companies, was held up by

Japanese machine gun fire from concealed ground. Their other company tried to march to the sound of the guns but gave up due to "thick country," reversed course, carried on to the rendezvous point, and found itself alone. This was because the 2nd Cambs company bumped into an enemy force holding a village and was deterred from trying to outflank it by swampy ground on both sides of the track. The advance was called off in late afternoon: "except for more or less localising the area where the Japanese were, the result of the sweep was negative." This was polite spin to conceal the fact an entire battalion spent the day thrashing around in the bush to no purpose. The brigade now realized its position was serious, facing a strong enemy force in the rear plus imminent threats to front and flank. Worse, the high command now intervened. Heath and Key brought direct orders from Wavell: "Batu Pahat must be held and the road to Ayer Hitam kept open." If that road was cut, the brigade could be completely isolated. A 2nd Cambs patrol sent along the road returned that evening to report the enemy was now blocking it, barely beyond the perimeter.[82]

Even while the actions at Parit Sulong and Bukit Pelandok raged on, an Imperial Guards force that can not have exceeded two companies cut across country and onto the lateral road. When 5th Norfolks realized shortly before dusk on 21 January that enemy parties were in the area, they responded energetically but ineffectively: "It was therefore decided to spread the battalion out along the road towards Batu Pahat the companies being about a mile apart from one another." This was no way for a single battalion to keep open a road the enemy could easily deny by using small parties concealed in close country to fire on it. Sure enough the Norfolks bumped into such parties, forcing them to wait for daylight to try again. Meanwhile Challen sent two companies to sweep the route from the other direction. This made some sense. The only way to keep such an artery open was to advance to contact, then move off the road to destroy all enemy forces trying to deny it. But after finding abandoned roadblocks, and capturing 60 bicycles and equipment left behind by the force that built them, the companies were ordered back to Batu Pahat in the morning, after things became difficult there. The road was left to 5th Norfolks. They established themselves near the halfway point, again spread out at intervals back to Yong Peng, and assigned carriers to patrol to Batu Pahat. The predictable soon happened. The road having been declared open, trucks moving along it were ambushed at 1600hrs. A carrier platoon sent to help was blocked by an enemy force with six to eight machine guns plus mortars. Before the carriers could engage Challen ordered them back to Batu Pahat, where the defenders had run out of time.[83]

The enemy air force made many sorties that morning to drop supplies to their isolated battalion. Challen correctly deduced it must be running low on ammunition. But instead of trying to destroy it, he puled everyone back into the perimeter. The reluctant hunter now saw himself as the hunted. That afternoon Challen warned Malaya Command he faced an imminent pincer attack. This warning provoked the dispute with Bennett about covering the road to Ayer Hitam.[84] The next morning, 23 January, Nishimura's staff detected a great opportunity to make a decisive breakthrough. Their main force was now concentrated on both roads between Batu Pahat and the trunk road, while the battalion south of the town remained fighting fit. By shifting its main axis of advance, the division could repeat the maneuver of using a detachment to isolate the focal point and concentrating to crush the defenders there:

> Konoye Division decided at about 1200hrs on the 23rd to employ its main force for the pursuit of the enemy along the coastal road. The main force started to attack the enemy in Batu Pahat while the rest confronted another in Yong Peng.[85]

Their ability to shift direction without slowing down again allowed the Japanese to hit the defenders at the right time in the right place. Key accepted Challen's warning, but while higher command debated the battle unfolded. The newest roadblocks prevented 15th Indian Brigade from restoring contact on the lateral road with 5th Norfolks, and headquarters lost radio contact with division. A few hours after the Japanese command decision:

> ... the Brigade decided that the Ayer Hitam Road was blocked, as there were indications of the enemy working South on both his flanks, as there were reliable reports of enemy operations on the road to the South and as he was out of touch with Division, he would withdraw South and issued orders accordingly.

Challen wanted to withdraw to more defensible ground south of Senggarang, where dense jungle narrowed the coastal plain. 15th Indian Brigade moved out that evening. But the gods of war had other ideas:

> Soon after dark, when the Cambridgeshires had already started their withdrawal from the town, the W/T set came to life and a message from Division was received ordering that Batu Pahat should still be held ... As a result of this change there was great confusion and congestion of the MT and the Cambridgeshires lost several men in street fighting when they had to go back into the town, into which the Japanese had followed them.[86]

Percival countermanded Challen's retreat as soon as he heard about it. Malaya Command did not know how strong the force behind 15th Indian Brigade was, but supposed it was not too strong to be pushed aside by a relieving force from the south. Meanwhile it was reinforcing the brigade and believed it well stocked enough to hang on in town. This was another example of placing local tactical considerations behind broader imperatives: the direct order from Wavell to fight on in Johore. Percival and Heath knew the only way to do this was to hold the lateral road. Losing any junction on that road meant compromising the whole line. So 15th Indian Brigade must stand fast.[87] But this strategic imperative prevented it from breaking clear when that was still possible. Worse, the Imperial Guards victories now gave them control of the area west of the trunk road. That meant the main axis of advance was compromised as well. The "main battle" thus ended with a decision that lost the next one before it even began.

Wavell's decisions backfired. Defeat in northern Johore turned into strategic disaster for his entire theatre. By imposing his plan on it, Wavell opened Malaya Command to a blow that left it too weak to fight on as a coherent field army. This was not because inefficient units could not make sensible command decisions work on the ground. Nor was it because good fighting units were undermined by bad command decisions and staff work. It was due to both, because the problem was systemic. But it started with Wavell's intervention and unravelled from there. The Japanese were aggressive, efficient and lucky. But the defenders gave them the opportunity. Percival, for once, did not do his level best to carry out instructions. This had to be because he feared what that would lead to. His tinkering did not make things any better but Percival's original design for battle in northern Johore would have resulted in less damage.[88] Malaya Command could not have saved Singapore. And one can only speculate. But Heath surely would not have placed 45th Indian Brigade in such a dire position, and as a result there should not have been immediate collapse on the left flank. Because there was, the arrival of 53rd Brigade was immediately cancelled out by the destruction of 45th Indian Brigade. The fact both brigades fought so poorly made matters worse, as did Bennett's obvious lack of confidence in Indian and British units. Because of all that Westforce did not even try to fight the rolling brawl in front of Segamat that it planned on paper. This wasted all preparations for that battle, the centrepiece of Wavell's whole plan, by allowing the Japanese to concentrate against one battalion at a time. The defeat at Batu Pahat then compromised the fall back plan before it could begin. This general collapse pushed already strained confidence between the different contingents in this imperial army to the breaking point.

The consequences did not stop there. The Japanese demonstrated, even on the east coast, that the defenders could not stop them cold. The quality problem was the most worrying. The British Empire forces could no longer ignore the truth: when it came to all but the most set-piece battles, they were badly outmatched.[89] One result was especially ominous: the most effective fighting force in the order of battle, the one formation that could still trouble the enemy, was badly worn down without inflicting equivalent damage in return. At the tactical level the combat units of 8th Australian Division outfought the Japanese. The Australians defended the east coast with a skill that left Japanese staff officers very relieved they did not assault from the sea, or mount more than a holding action.[90] When Australian companies were engaged on the trunk road they made the enemy pay a price and broke off battle on their own terms. The actions around Bakri were outstanding examples of how battalions could defend effectively in the mixed terrain in which so much of this campaign was fought. 2/19 AIF's counterattack gave the Japanese a dose of their own medicine. And the fighting retreat to Parit Sulong speaks for itself. 8th Australian Division proved very tough indeed, for which Bennett deserves some credit. But it was no tougher than its enemy. And its efforts were undone by two things. One was the overall strategic situation. The Australians could not stop the enemy by themselves. But RAF Far East could not prevent the enemy from threatening both coasts, putting pressure on Singapore, and supporting ground operations with real effect. The rest of the army either badly needed to regroup or was too raw to be fit to fight. The other problem was that the division was badly mishandled. Bennett had a point. Instead of Percival's plan to divide the division in two so the army could guard the east coast but also slow the enemy down on the trunk road, or Wavell's plan to concentrate it to stop the enemy on that road, it was parceled out piecemeal into three components. Each was strong enough to hurt the enemy but not enough to make a larger difference, not even at Parit Sulong. And on the main road, it became painfully clear that above the level of unit tactics this army simply could not fight effectively. Malaya Command had some good battalions. But when it came to operating in larger formations it remained addicted to the set-piece, and could not cope with Japanese skill and speed.

This was the Achilles heel of Wavell's plan. The fact Yamashita's army could afford to take calculated risks, because it enjoyed command of the air and sea, was not decisive in this battle. Quality was. The Japanese were good enough to overcome problems of C^{3}I this battle produced, to operate effectively on any level at great speed. Malaya Command could not handle such problems, could not function effectively above battalion level, could not operate beyond first gear. One can not imagine Percival even considering leaving a battalion on its own behind enemy defences for a week. Japanese infantry companies on the roads behind Bakri and Batu Pahat risked being cut off from lines of communication and supply. Yet this did not faze them. Infiltration always seemed to be a one way street. Yes, the Imperial Guards were more battle ready than 45th Indian Brigade. But what mattered more was how the two high commands conceived this battle. To the defenders the battle area was two dimensional. It was a fight to stop the enemy by holding him north of a line of territory running from coast to coast. Each position had to be held whether it was tactically defensible or not. But this army was not good at using ground. Too often it still tried to make the ground fit the tactics, to drag the enemy into a set-piece. Bennett saw the need to avoid this, but failed disastrously to do so. To the attackers, this was a chance to destroy the enemy army. It, not ground, was the prime objective. They saw the battle area as a three dimensional zone of operations, in which bold penetrations could prod the enemy out of prepared positions and force him to brawl. This was not unlike Bennett's defence plan for the trunk road, but there was one vital difference. The Japanese could make it happen on the ground.

One Australian staff officer considered Wavell's plan "absolutely crazy," saying "Wavell chose a defence line from the map which neither he nor Percival had inspected."[91] This is not unfair. The Japanese were good enough to respond on the run and fight effectively as an army, not just a collection of battalions. Wavell gambled his army could do the same. He was wrong. The disparity was as if Yamashita had three moves to every two by Percival. Even a free hand to fight according to tactical considerations would no longer have mattered. Malaya Command could not fight other than on fixed lines, with a "front" and a "rear." Wavell's interventions were erratic, but even worse they were unwise, because the "main battle" was lost before he arrived. By ordering Malaya Command to stop them cold, he gave the Japanese the chance to break its back. This turned defeat into disaster for three reasons. Malaya Command was defeated so quickly it would now be forced to fight for Singapore long before serious reinforcements could arrive. It was defeated so badly it now had little chance to make that last battle much of a fight. Finally, as Wavell realized, the island was now likely to fall much earlier than he could afford.

Wavell misunderstood the fighting power of the forces engaged in Malaya. Yet again, however, circumstances and personalities were not the whole story. Wavell was the latest defender of Singapore pressed by broader imperatives of imperial defence into plans that could not work at the operational level.

The "main battle" became a disaster because what really mattered was not the fact but the manner of defeat. The manner of this defeat set Singapore up for a quick and easy fall. If that happened ABDA Command would be very hard pressed to hold the "Malay Barrier." If they failed, the Allies would face a longer and harder war. Even if they won that war the British Empire would face a crisis, because losing the Malay Barrier would shatter it in the Far East, isolate Australia and New Zealand, and leave India open to attack. The price for trying to brazen it out might now prove more than the Empire could bear.

13

The Price of Empire

Tempo had as much influence at the summit as on the ground. The central direction of the war could not catch up to the Japanese advance. This brought them to a moment of truth: where did the defence of Singapore now fit into imperial defence and grand strategy? If the campaign should continue, how and to what purpose? In the end they found answers coherent in principle, but already obsolete in practice. The reason was familiar. The politics of imperial defence drove them to keep trying to make the situation fit the plan.

Churchill and the COS spent the week between Slim River and the attack on Johore sorting out the details of agreements reached in Washington. Three immediate challenges faced them. First, they needed to make new plans for coalition warfare, based on British grand strategy. Second, they needed to strike an effective balance between stopping the Japanese and clearing North Africa. Third, they must maintain Australian confidence in British war direction. These were all interdependent. The problem in the Far East jeopardized the advance in North Africa, because both relied on the same inadequate pools of shipping and combat ready forces. Failure in either theatre would undermine any plans made in Washington for global grand strategy. Success in both rested on securing maximum support from both the Americans and the Dominions.

The trip to Washington succeeded, but with strings attached. The discussions made a direct connection between how the coalition would wage global war and how it would tackle immediate problems. ABDA Command became the springboard to a broader agreement. Marshall suggested on 11 January the situation in ABDA Command was now the most pressing danger; Dill agreed. The discussion helped the military chiefs settle the arrangements by which they would allocate coalition resources. The COS persuaded the Prime Minister to support the principle resources should go wherever the strategic needs were greatest. This "emergency" basis could be wholly favourable to the British Empire as it was already heavily engaged overseas, whereas American mobilization was only now beginning to accelerate. They also put across the point "allocations could hardly be decided except by the military staffs sitting together." But on 13 January, when the British and American staffs met to do this, Marshall split the difference. The Americans agreed priority should be determined by operational requirements and allocations should be made from a "common pool." But Marshall insisted there be only one Combined Chiefs of Staff (CCS), sitting in Washington. It would have the broadest mandate to direct grand strategy–under the executive supervision of the President and Prime Minister–and full control over shipping.[1]

Churchill took the agreements back to London and endorsed them to his War Cabinet on 17 January. His personal partnership with President Roosevelt was established as the apex of the coalition. The two most important objectives in British national war policy were achieved. The Americans confirmed the agreement to concentrate on "Germany first," and accepted the principle to combine American and British Empire war-making power in a "common pool." Their war production plans were enormously expanded. The Prime Minister argued: "these Agreements were, in his view, wholly favourable to us. In practice as we were already fully engaged in the war, our resources would not be drawn upon." But this raised an obvious problem: how long would the Americans remain willing to throw their ultimately enormous power into a grand strategy determined by the British? The American rejection of a parallel CCS in London, the worst British setback of the conference, underlined the danger. As the relative strength of the two partners changed, as the centre of decision-making shifted to Washington, could the British maintain their voice as an equal partner? Churchill's reassurance only indicated how uncertain this was: 'In assessing the value of these instruments, regard had to be given to the personalities behind them."[2]

American intervention made the difference between victory and failure in global war. Above all else the Allies must win. But the nature of the new coalition would have a massive influence on something only slightly less vital: the role of the British Empire in winning the war, and thus its postwar prospects. Through cultivating Roosevelt and Marshall, Churchill hoped to exploit the leverage of greater British experience, and the magnetic pull of campaigns already underway. He now refined his ultimate objective: persuade the Americans to help the British Empire fight global war without asking too high a price in return. This required concessions. A single CCS was one. Accepting ABDA Command under Wavell was another. Overarching considerations of national war policy dominated the agenda. It could not be otherwise, no matter what happened in the Far East; this was global war. Yet Churchill and his colleagues were also determined to make sure the Empire remained a cohesive great power, led by the British. In the Far East, this raised the bar too high.

Two things remained constant. The British needed to secure as much support from their Dominions as possible. Yet they wanted to keep as much control over the direction of the war as they could. The more the Japanese advanced, the more worried the Australians became about their own security. This plus the conference in Washington provoked them to push harder for a voice in coalition decisions. This was a problem the British could not ignore, especially after the exchange between Churchill and Curtin in late December. If the Australians pushed their way into the inner circle, or even worse turned to the Americans for patronage, the British would lose influence over the direction of the war–and the Empire would face an uncertain future. The "Singapore strategy" after all relied on a compliant Australia. Now the British faced the consequences of its failure.

On 2 January Churchill and the COS met Casey, now Australian Minister in Washington. Arguments over the Mediterranean campaign, the exchange with Curtin over Singapore, and the decision to form a unified Allied command next to Australia without first consulting it had all soured relations. The Australians wanted the earliest possible concentration of Allied naval forces against the Japanese and a greater voice in directing the war–including a representative in the British War Cabinet. Churchill confessed any concentration against the Japanese relied entirely on the Americans. Australian complaints were only reinforced by the decision to return their I Corps from the Middle East, plus alarming reports from Malaya and Singapore. Now they heard the British tell them only the Americans could help.[3]

Churchill sent a telegram to Curtin on 13 January–just as 8th Australian Division prepared for battle. Churchill suggested it would do well, noting the Japanese had not yet fought more than a handful of "white battalions ... the rest being Indian soldiers." This self-incriminating reassurance was expanded by describing the reinforcements en route, especially the two Australian divisions, to "the new theatre of so much direct interest to Australia." This was a sacrifice by the British, "we shall have to do our best to replace them from home," and ships were also scarce. But it all gave reason to hope Wavell could hold Singapore and counterattack after they arrived, as he planned. Churchill implied it was time to stop crying over spilt milk: "I do not see how anyone could expect Malaya to be defended once the Japanese obtained command of the sea and whilst we are fighting for our lives against Germany and Italy." Perhaps mindful of his personal role in all that, Churchill tried to soften the point by hinting at his own frustration:

> The only vital point is Singapore Fortress and its essential hinterland. Personally my anxiety has been lest in fighting rearguard action down the Peninsula to gain time we should dissipate the force required for the prolonged defence of Singapore. Out of the equivalent of 4 divisions available for that

purpose, one has been lost and another mauled to gain a month or six weeks time. Some may think it would have been better to have come back quicker with less loss.

Having dropped his earlier discussions with the COS about how to defend Singapore, the point was now moot. Churchill asked Curtin to accept the new situation: Wavell was on the spot, and reported it better to fight on to hold "the essential hinterland" than withdraw to the "Island Fortress," and thus lose the naval base.[4]

This presented the Australians with a *fait accompli*. Establishing Wavell as an Allied commander gave him a different status, one London could use to put breathing room between itself and the defeat unfolding in his area. The mine on which it did not want to tread was whether or not Singapore could still be held. On 8 January the COS sent Wavell a clear hint: "We contemplate that the two Australian divisions from Middle East may be required in Netherlands East Indies"–which could only mean Singapore would already be lost–"but decision where to employ rests with you."[5] This was risky. Wavell could have decided Singapore was doomed, so the Allies should change their whole strategy. And if he had the Americans might have agreed–but not the Australians. Churchill and the COS were reassured by Wavell's quick action to take charge of the battle in Malaya and his new strategy. Wavell, a very experienced imperial commander, understood the imperative of imperial defence: pursue a strategy aiming to deliver the best military outcome in return for the least political friction. On 12 January he told the COS he intended to use I Australian Corps plus 8th Australian and 18th Divisions in Malaya. He wanted:

> ... if circumstances allow, to have complete Australian formation for counter-offensive in Malaya and to use Indian troops at present in Malaya to garrison Netherlands East Indies. This will avoid splitting up Australian troops.

The COS certainly knew their man. This pushed the right buttons: keep the Australians together, hold Singapore, give them the main role. Naturally Wavell pointed out the enemy might have other plans, which meant "we may have to use reinforcements as they arrive at points of greatest danger." Nevertheless, "I propose, however, to aim at target." That phrase might usefully summarize the entire British approach to the defence of Singapore over two decades![6]

Churchill was right about the Washington conference. The need to maintain American confidence was overriding. The agreements reached there were a blueprint for victory. The Red Army, geography, enemy mistakes, and their own grand strategy gave the Allies time to generate the power to win the war. But meanwhile there was a problem no amount of talking could conceal: the Americans were not yet ready for war. Allied plans rested on a promise of power yet to come. This dilemma pressed the British Empire harder, because it was already fully engaged. Just as the forces in North Africa finally began to drive the enemy back, everything else sagged. The RN reeled from the strain of the Battle of the Atlantic, heavy losses in the Mediterranean, and new troubles in the Far East. The RAF was stretched to the limit by the stalled bomber offensive from home, the need to protect the metropolis, plus the strain of reinforcing the Middle and Far East at the same time. The situation in Malaya was grave. The US Pacific Fleet was for the moment out of the fight. General Douglas MacArthur's forces in the Philippines thus faced a siege without promise of relief. MacArthur abandoned Manila and on 7 January, the same day as Slim River, pulled his troops back to the peninsula of Bataan to fight it out. The Japanese dominated the air and sea and had the initiative all over Southeast Asia. The defence of Singapore rested, as always, on broader considerations. They now translated into how to get the necessary reinforcements to Singapore in time to save it, without undoing the offensive in North Africa.[7]

Within the month everything went sour. The "main battle" defeat in Johore ruled out any chance the I Australian Corps could save Singapore. Auchinleck spared no effort to get the corps moving, but it took time to dispatch such a large force. The Australian high command also insisted it be fully balanced, with logistic tail and replacement pool in place, before departing. While this would enable it to step off the ship straight into the fight, it also postponed that date. By 15 January Auchinleck reported the vanguard would not depart before 5 February, and thus could not reach Singapore before the end of that month.[8] Meanwhile he had his own problems. The tank battles to relieve Tobruk were so costly they raised serious questions about whether British Empire ground forces could handle German armour. Respect for German fighting power, plus the need to relieve tired forces, slowed the advance across Libya. Just before fighting began in Johore, intelligence reports of German reinforcements raised the stakes. Clearing North Africa could ease the strains on shipping, the navy, the air force, and the Soviets. But German ground forces were more effective in combat, moved faster, and decided to strike back, not sit tight. They counterattacked on 21 January, compromising Auchinleck's offensive and thus British grand strategy.[9]

All this prompted Churchill to look into the situation in Malaya. The Prime Minister reacted strongly to a press report in Singapore on 15 January that boasted air supremacy would be gained in three days. Rightly connecting this to the arrival of the Hurricanes two days before, Churchill scolded Wavell for the security breach–then asked direct questions about "your idea of what would happen in event of your being forced to withdraw into the island." Churchill stated "It has always seemed to me that the vital need is to prolong defence of the island to last possible minute, but, of course, I hope it will not come to this." This made it clear the Prime Minister still did not understand the authorized defence plan for Malaya and Singapore. The mission was to hold the naval base. The COS did not change this mission after Layton moved naval headquarters to Batavia on 4 January, even though they had no plans to use the base. In fact the opposite was true. The Eastern Fleet would now be reconstituted in the Indian Ocean, absorbing the scratch British naval forces left to ABDA Command. But this could not be done until the Mediterranean situation was stable.[10] Yet the strategy remained to keep the enemy far enough to the north to allow the navy to use the base. The policy was to defend the island itself only against the least likely threat, a direct attack from the sea. Churchill and the COS sparred over this the year before. They opted to let sleeping dogs lie when his interest lapsed, rather than spell out details. That now cost them when this question to Wavell set off an explosion.

Much depended on what Churchill meant by "prolong defence of the island to last possible minute." If meant literally, the army could fight just to deny its facilities to the enemy, on the island itself if it chose. The mission would become to kill as many Japanese as possible for as long as possible; the defenders could destroy the base themselves. If on the other hand it was not meant literally, if the bases must be preserved–or if the island itself must not fall, however damaged it became–then there remained no choice but to fight on as far north as possible. Churchill's language rang the alarm to Wavell. The Prime Minister referred to Singapore as "the fortress" in nearly every telegram or minute he wrote. For whatever reason, a dangerous misunderstanding had arisen. The Army designated Singapore a Fortress with a capital F, by which it merely meant the island was an independent administrative and operational area, whose headquarters reported directly to Malaya Command. This was to allow that headquarters to focus on the detailed problems of defending this unique position. The Prime Minster had vast experience as a scholar, soldier and statesman. But he had never been to Singapore. And he either decided not to ask or was kept in the dark the year before. So he saw it as a fortress with a small f. This to him had only one possible definition, the traditional strategic one: "*a completely encircled* strong place," a position prepared to defend itself against attack from any direction, to withstand a long siege. Singapore was no such position.[11]

Wavell responded the next day, 16 January. He had already asked Percival to report on plans and preparations to defend the island, but warned the Prime Minister:

> Until quite recently all plans based on repulsing seaborne attacks on Island and holding land attack in Johore or further north, and little or nothing was done to construct defences on north side of island to prevent crossing Johore Straits ...[12]

Churchill's reaction indicates–hard as it may be to believe or explain–that only now did he finally clearly understand the defence problem in Singapore. Churchill later wrote "My immediate reaction was to repair the neglect so far as time allowed. But I was also angered." That put it mildly. The minute the Prime Minister sent to the COS on 19 January is a seminal document. It expressed the consternation of a leader suddenly realizing utter disaster now stared him in the face, in part because things he might have done had not been done. And it precisely captured the gap the system could never fill: how to reconcile local tactical imperatives with broader imperial ones:

> It never occurred to me for a moment, nor to Sir John Dill, with whom I discussed the matter on the outward voyage, that the gorge of the fortress of Singapore, with its splendid moat half a mile to a mile wide, was not entirely fortified against an attack from the northward. What is the use of having an island for a fortress if it is not to be made into a citadel? To construct a line of detached works with searchlights and cross-fire combined with immense wiring and obstruction of the swamp areas, and to provide the proper ammunition to enable the fortress guns to dominate enemy batteries planted in Johore, was an elementary peace-time provision which it is incredible did not exist in a fortress which has been twenty years building.

This charge would have provoked Hankey to his own explosion, given Churchill's role in the 1920s in stifling the naval base! And it also indicated the Prime Minister simply did not understand how much technological advances in airpower changed this problem; from at least 1936 it was generally understood coastal artillery would be supremely vulnerable to any enemy who controlled the air over Singapore. Perhaps to deflect such criticism, Churchill turned to his own record:

> If this was so, how much more should the necessary field works have been constructed during the two and a half years of the present war? How is it that not one of you pointed this out to me at any time when these matters have been under discussion? More especially should this have been done because

in my various minutes extending over the last two years I have repeatedly
shown that I relied upon this defence of Singapore Island against a formal
siege, and have never relied upon the Kra Isthmus plan ...

Churchill indeed made his views clear the year before, but received only a
broad explanation why it was necessary to defend the mainland as a whole.
Then both parties dropped the matter, rather than raise the taboo: whether
Singapore could really be held at all, after June 1940. Both gambled, probably
because they implicitly agreed it was better to avoid the question of how a
battle for the island itself must end. Churchill now lashed out about tactical
neglect. This was unfair, because the driving force was the imperial political
imperative. If the Japanese attacked Singapore itself, the "Singapore strategy,"
the promise to Australia and the Empire, was ruined anyway. The Prime
Minister's closing tirade zeroed in on that main concern:

> Seaward batteries and a naval base do not constitute a fortress, which is
> a completely encircled strong place. Merely to have seaward batteries and
> no forts or fixed defences to protect their rear is not to be excused on any
> ground. By such neglect the whole security of the fortress has been at the
> mercy of ten thousand men breaking across the straits in small boats. I warn
> you this will be one of the greatest scandals that could possibly be exposed.[13]

Had it always been made clear Singapore must be defended to the bitter
end, even if that meant the naval base was destroyed by enemy artillery fire,
this might have been fair. But it was never so specified. Singapore must remain
intact, so the navy could sail in and take charge of the war. Even after 1937
the air force was to keep the enemy at bay long enough for help to arrive. The
"period before relief" never after 1937 envisaged the defence of Singapore
itself, save for one contingency: direct attack from the sea. Churchill's scenario
envisaged a strategically logical retrogression from forward defence to close
siege. But the latter could only deny, not hold, the naval base. Imperial defence
policy for Singapore was never related closely enough to strategic realities
to make sure policy on paper matched circumstances on the ground. It was
instead designed to conceal the fact there was no match. Now at last the Prime
Minister understood this and his own inability to change it. That same day
he told the COS he took full responsibility for grand strategy, but demanded
to know why Japanese amphibious attacks on the west coast could not be
stopped and why so little was done to prepare a tactical defence of Singapore
island. His explosion prompted the COS to send Wavell telegrams on both
counts, and order him to prepare "the utmost possible defence of the island."

This was the first time London gave any such order.[14]

This crossed the 19 January telegram from Wavell, reporting the fight in Johore would continue but plans to defend the island would now be made; it reached Churchill early on 21 January. The explanation was blunt:

> Number of troops required to hold island effectively probably are great or greater than number required to defend Johore ... I must warn you, however, that I doubt whether island can be held for long once Johore is lost. Fortress guns sited for use against ships and have mostly ammunition for that purpose only, many can only fire seawards. Part of garrison has already been sent into Johore and many troops remaining are of doubtful value. I am sorry to give you depressing picture, but I do not want you to have false picture of island fortress. Singapore defences were constructed entirely to meet seaward attack. I still hope Johore may be held till next convoy arrives.

A blunt confession followed: after the arrival of the rest of 18th Division, "subsequent reinforcements will probably have to be used for defence of Java and Sumatra ..." This sent a clear signal. Wavell now expected defeat–early and therefore disastrous defeat. This topped a week in which the Prime Minister heard there was no guarantee the navy could safely bring the convoys to Singapore, no guarantee the air force could check the Japanese onslaught, and the enemy was now attacking southern Burma, whose commander reported "I cannot guarantee safety of Burma with forces now available." All this provoked Churchill to convene the Defence Committee that evening, to discuss the taboo: should the fight for Singapore continue, and to what purpose?[15]

The issue went through the COS first. They discussed a minute from the Prime Minister which broke the taboo. Wavell believed the battle for Johore was almost lost. After that, the only way to hold Singapore for even a few more weeks was to commit the reinforcements en route–and then very likely lose them anyway. Now, at last:

> ... the question arises whether we should not at once blow the docks and batteries and workshops to pieces and concentrate everything on the defence of Burma and keeping open the Burma Road. It appears to me this question should be squarely faced now and put bluntly to General Wavell ...

The Prime Minister accepted the loss of Singapore would be a tremendous shock to India and argued only a strong defence of Burma could offset this. Burma now seemed more important, also because it was the strategic connection to China. The dilemma was clear:

We may, by muddling things and hesitating to take an ugly decision, lose both Singapore and the Burma Road. Obviously the decision depends on how long the defence of Singapore Island can be maintained. If it is only for a few weeks, it is certainly not worth losing all our reinforcements and aircraft.

The issue was what to do with approaching reinforcements, which Churchill admitted could still be "doomed or diverted." They amounted to 44th Indian Brigade plus Indian replacement troops, 2/4 AIF–a machine gun battalion–plus Australian replacement troops, the balance of 18th Division, and the Hurricanes to be flown off the carrier. These were large forces, arranged by fate in a neat imperial triangle. Redirecting them required a "decisive change of policy." The COS and the Defence Committee discussed whether to send such an order to Wavell. They agreed Burma was a higher priority in the long run but Singapore was the immediate priority. Churchill "leaned upon my friends and counsellors." Prompted by Brooke, they pulled back from the ugly decision and instead "leaned upon" Wavell, agreeing to wait on events and leave it to him as the man on the spot.[16]

This non-decision sent more than 25,000 Indian, Australian and British personnel towards a battle the central direction of the war now accepted was already lost. Percival received a telegram pressing him about the water supply, evacuating civilians, and destroying facilities useful to the enemy; the Rear Admiral Malaya, E.J. Spooner, received one reminding him to evacuate expert shore personnel before it was too late. These were preparations for defeat, not relief.[17] There are arguments to justify this non-decision. The central direction of the war had a duty to do all it could to support those ordered to fight on; the British government had a duty to defend its colony and protectorates, and had promised the Dominions it would do so. These must be weighed against its other duty: to win the war as fast as possible with the least possible loss. Churchill himself noted "There is no doubt what a purely military decision should have been."[18] But at the summit there is no such thing as a "purely military decision," by which he meant diverting reinforcements. Broader considerations were decisive. They were the prestige of the British Empire and the reputation of the British as an ally. That boiled down to four things: expressing defiance to the enemy; projecting resolution to Asians, both within and outside the Empire; impressing the Americans; reassuring the Dominions.

Churchill now rated Burma over Singapore not just because he knew the latter was lost but also because he needed to hold Burma to protect India and satisfy the Americans. If India was even attacked the Empire would be pushed to the edge of the abyss, whatever the outcome of the war. And in Washington Churchill realized how important China was in American grand strategy. On

23 January the Prime Minister told Wavell that Marshall insisted on including Burma in ABDA Command because he believed the lifeline to China must be kept open in order to win the war. But on the other hand a British "scuttle" from Singapore, while the Americans fought it out in Bataan, would produce an effect "terrible to imagine."[19] Meanwhile the Australians delivered the sharpest possible warning on just that note.

In addition to Bennett's telegrams, Bowden sent a steady flow of reports to Australia. Most described civil and military authorities in Singapore in ever more negative terms. They went to the Minister for External Affairs, Dr. H.V. Evatt. Evatt was the most nationalist member of Curtin's Cabinet, suspicious of the British, increasingly frustrated by Australia's lack of influence in Allied policy, ambitious for power, truculent by nature. On 18 January Evatt pressed Bowden to provide details on support for the AIF, to help his "great struggle to see that the Japanese war is given its proper place in the scheme of defence reinforcement and supply." Two days before, the Australian Chiefs of Staff warned that if Malaya fell Australia itself would be vulnerable to attack. Then came the news about setbacks in Johore.[20] In that context, the Australian government received a report from Sir Earle Page, its representative in London, about the Defence Committee discussion on 21 January. Page said they discussed evacuating Singapore; he argued this would do irreparable harm to Allied prestige and unity and never be accepted by Australia. There is some confusion about this; some sources, including Churchill, say Page was not there. But there is no confusion about one key fact: the Australians saw this issue very differently. The Australian Cabinet and Chiefs of Staff met on 23 January. They noted the loss of Anderson's force and a report from Bowden calling the situation "desperate and possibly irretrievable." This plus Japanese threats to the Solomon Islands persuaded them to press Churchill yet again about Malaya. Page's report arrived as they prepared a telegram. Curtin was away in Western Australia. Evatt took it upon himself to amend a paragraph. Churchill received the following:

> ... After all the assurances we have been given, the evacuation of Singapore would be regarded here and elsewhere as an inexcusable betrayal. Singapore is a central fortress in the system of the Empire and local defence ... we understood that it was to be made impregnable, and in any event it was to be capable of holding out for a prolonged period until the arrival of the main fleet ... On the faith of the proposed flow of reinforcements, we have acted and carried out our part of the bargain. We expect you not to frustrate the whole purpose by evacuation.

Churchill's November 1939 promise to hold Singapore prompted the Australian decision to send forces to Europe. Now they called that in. The Australian public feared Japan would attack Australia itself; this forced the government to issue an ultimatum: "Even in an emergency diversion of reinforcements should be to the NEI and not Burma. Anything else would be deeply resented ..." Such was the damage caused by the gamble on the "Singapore strategy." India, and thus Burma, was the British priority. Australia was the Australian priority–and its forward defence was the Malay Barrier, especially Singapore. If they wanted to keep the imperial partnership, the British must fight it out in Singapore.[21]

Churchill took exception to this ultimatum. He had an ugly argument with Page in Cabinet on 26 January about who was looking out for number one. In his memoirs the Prime Minister called the telegram "serious and unusual," the accusation "not in accordance with the truth or military facts." But the Australians clearly hit a nerve. One bullet was dodged when the Americans agreed to restrict the central direction of the war, in practice, to the two main partners. But the British had to accept Page as Australian Representative to their War Cabinet. It was very clear the Australians had little confidence left in British plans or assurances. That gave the British no choice. Churchill insisted in his memoirs that this Australian warning did not compel his government to send in the reinforcements and fight it out in Singapore. Raymond Callahan rightly notes this was "one of the least convincing statements" in all six volumes. Churchill's 23 January telegram to Wavell about Burma may have been a hint to the Supreme Commander to use his Allied status to make a decision the British government dare not.[22] If so it fell on deaf ears. The "ugly decision" was never taken because neither government in this awkward imperial partnership dared do so.

The Australian and British governments were trapped–by themselves. By describing Singapore as the lynchpin of imperial defence in Asia, they inflated it into a bastion public opinion saw as both bulwark and symbol of imperial power. Losing it would be bad enough; abandoning it would shatter the Empire in Asia even if the Allies won the war. Rather than admit their pledge could not be honoured, and argue it was now better to fight to hold what might be saved, the British government hid behind its field commander and let events run their course. The Australian government was in an even worse position. If they accepted the argument it was too late to save Singapore, therefore better to consider broader strategic imperatives, they knew public opinion would see this as letting down the Australians already fighting there and leaving Australia open to invasion. They preferred to call in obsolete promises from the British and deflect all blame to them–a decision David Horner labelled "strategic analysis versus politics and emotion."[23] No one wanted to take political responsibility by openly renouncing, even in compelling circumstances, the promises to public opinion about imperial defence. Both governments preferred to argue they did all they could and challenge anyone to prove otherwise.

Churchill did just that in the last week of January by arranging a Vote of Confidence in the House of Commons. The Washington agreements provided an excuse. Frustration with the war provided a reason. Critics sniped at Churchill's role in directing the war, recent decisions in grand strategy, and defeats in the field. But an underlying sense of salvation, prompted by American entry into the war, provided a safety net. Churchill took advantage. He attacked his critics, taking full responsibility for grand strategy and thus the general war situation, warning in thinly veiled terms Singapore would soon be lost, but insisting the government was pursing the right policy–and as long as he was Prime Minister he would direct the war his way. The government was sustained by a vote of 464 to 1 on 29 January. Churchill understood that sooner or later only victories could keep him in office. But he also correctly concluded that as far as the Far East was concerned this amounted to trusting him to do his best. This was a relatively easy escape. But there was one price: fight on for Singapore.[24]

The trap closed remorselessly as January ended. In Bataan, MacArthur's forces roughly handled several Japanese attacks, then fell back in good order to fight out a siege rapidly becoming an inspiration to the Allied cause. This helped the British militarily, but hurt them politically by making the defence of Malaya look weak by comparison. On the 27th the Australian government passed on Bennett's complaints about the Indian Army. That same day Wavell authorized Percival to retreat to Singapore island. On 29 January Wavell reported this decision and noted "We have rather anxious period ahead." The enemy was on the move again in Burma, and assembling three large naval expeditionary forces. ABDA Command had no naval striking force to engage them. Airpower would be decisive, especially over Singapore. Wavell asked for help:

> Considerable pressure being exerted by Australia for diversion reinforcements ABDA area to defend Australia. You will realize that with above picture essential at present to assemble maximum strength this area to resist Japanese advance.[25]

That same day the Australian Chiefs of Staff advised their government to expect the worst. They could no longer assume any part of the Malay Barrier, let alone Singapore, would hold out–and the US Pacific Fleet might not gain control of the Pacific for quite a while. Australia must now plan for the maximum scale of attack. The next day Spooner closed the naval base. Wavell sent all but a "token force" of fighters out of Singapore to Sumatra. Finally, on 31 January, as the army retreated onto the island, Churchill rebuffed Bennett's complaints, arguing it was imperative to rush reinforcements into battle and the Japanese were unlikely to invade Australia—but admitted only the Americans could now stop them from doing so. Churchill had to promise Curtin his troops would "receive all possible support." The reinforcements came in after all.[26] The jaws snapped shut. Singapore would fight it out.

These bitter weeks at least finally exposed the taboo about defending Singapore. On 20 January, the same day he first suggested holding the Burma Road should now be a higher strategic priority than holding Singapore, Churchill put it squarely to Wavell. Allied commander or not, on issues as important to the Empire as Singapore the Prime Minister would continue to send "personal suggestions" or "ask questions." Then the veil dropped:

> … I want to make it absolutely clear that I expect every inch of ground to be defended, every scrap of material or defences to be blown to pieces to prevent its capture by the enemy, and no question of surrender to be entertained until after protracted fighting among the ruins of Singapore city.[27]

This was categorical. Singapore must be defended not just to hurt the enemy, but even more to preserve the reputation of the Empire. This can also be seen as cynical. On the one hand, wider consequences of defeat might indeed be mitigated if a long siege pinned down the enemy. On the other hand, such an objective could have been considered a long time before, had either government been willing to reconsider the mission to hold the naval base. Even now, when circumstances demanded it, they refrained from doing so. Instead they left it to events on the ground to force the pace. What mattered, at the summit of imperial defence, was that the policy was not changed. It was instead overwhelmed. This left room for the argument "we did our best." It was, always, the politics of empire that drove its defence.

Percival reminded Brooke of that complication when he replied on 22 January to the order to deny facilities to the enemy:

> There is already doubt in minds of Asiatic population as to our ability, or even intention, to hold Singapore. Any conspicuous measures of destruction or even preparations for destruction taken now would be calculated to cause a landslide in public morale, which could never be stopped.[28]

Percival implied his superiors were now asking him to do what no British government was ever willing to do: place military considerations above concerns about undermining British prestige in Asian colonies. He was not quite right. Because of that, it is better to see British policy as consistent rather than cynical. It was consistent with the strategic illusion on which plans to defend Singapore were based. The plans were never militarily realistic. Their purpose was always political: to provide a plausible argument that Singapore could and would be defended. Churchill did not depart from that tradition by ordering a fight to the death. He completed it. The worst outcome would not be losing Singapore–it would be suffering a political disaster. A "scuttle" meant breaking a promise, being humiliated, losing not just a battle but a reputation. That guaranteed political disaster, with lasting international and imperial repercussions. A humiliating defeat would do the same–but might still be avoided. Defiance and defeat only after fierce resistance could yet pre-empt political disaster. Criticism could be subsumed by resolution. For that, London and Canberra gambled yet again. Unfortunately, what they wanted could only be achieved on the ground. And there it was already too late.

14

End of a Mission, Death of an Army

Yamashita's mission was to capture Singapore as fast and cheaply as possible. His strategy was to destroy Malaya Command on the mainland. The "driving charge" put the Japanese in a position to do that by the last week of January. That last week is generally described as more of the same. Malaya Command fell back steadily, suffering more than necessary yet again, compromising any last defence of the island still further. This needs to be amended. The Japanese could have annihilated Malaya Command in southern Johore, and they did not. Because of that, they had to fight for the island after all. There were several reasons: discord between high commands; less than optimal use of airpower; some effective fighting by the defenders. But the real problem was that the pace of its "driving charge" finally stretched Twenty-Fifth Army to the limit.

This did not give Malaya Command any last chance to hold Singapore. It did give it a chance to make that last battle a serious fight, one that could help ABDA Command by pinning Japanese forces down in a long costly siege. But Malaya Command now lost that chance in southern Johore. Reasons included final defeat in the air, further discord between commanders and some egregious blunders on the ground. But the cardinal fact was that Malaya Command, as an army, was already dead. This was the price of Wavell's "main battle." Just when the enemy finally slipped a notch the defenders could no longer take advantage. They ran out of time, space, and especially capability. A field army functions as such when the separate actions of its units can be coordinated beyond their own local battlefield, by a higher command, to produce a broader strategic effect. Malaya Command was killed by its own strategy, fighting to hold the naval base. It died in northern Johore, when that strategy forced it to fight a "main battle" beyond its means. That left a collection of units no longer able to exploit success for any larger effect, nor prevent defeat from having wider consequences. Malaya Command's mission changed to something that finally made strategic sense–just when it became too weak to accomplish it.

Yamashita's headquarters moved to Gemas on 19 January. The breakthrough on the west coast gave Twenty-Fifth Army a chance to make their attack on Singapore a walk-over. Their plans for taking southern Johore would not have surprised Percival. The Imperial Guards Division would cut off and destroy the force in Batu Pahat, charge down the west coast road, and advance on Johore Bahru along the road from Pontian Kechil. 5th Division would throw its full strength into parallel advances along the trunk road and the railway. Meanwhile, two battalions of 18th Division would keep up the pressure in the Mersing area, other elements would help capture airbases, and Mutaguchi's force would rush south from Singora. The airbases at Kluang and Kahang were indeed major objectives, to be captured as fast as possible. 3rd Air Group would support ground operations. With four separate axes of advance and a very promising position west of the trunk road, Yamashita's staff saw good reason to expect a major breakthrough somewhere. Given the tempo at which their infantry could operate, that should allow them to trap Percival's army by getting between it and Johore Bahru. 3rd Air Group directed its reconnaissance unit to "watch the Johore Bridge and to prevent the enemy from entering Singapore island."[1] This all made sense. The roads and railway converged at Johore Bahru and the causeway was a perfect bottleneck target, the only way Malaya Command could get its guns, vehicles and heavy equipment back to Singapore. But there was a problem: the strains of the advance now finally began to tell.

The first strain was unavoidable: demolitions. The Japanese could not prevent the destruction of dozens of bridges and causeways in Johore. Each demolition further stretched the hard-pressed engineer units. This delayed the advance of supplies, reinforcements, and especially tanks. The latter were also forced to regroup after heavy losses around Gemas and Bakri. Yet the pressure could not be relaxed. So the infantry advanced on southern Johore without, for once, the support of its armoured fist. The next problem was also unavoidable: logistics. Japanese supply lines now ran hundreds of kilometres north to Kota Bharu and Singora. Keeping the "driving charge" moving meant both supplying the army and moving up the air forces.[2] That now threatened to overtax Japanese capabilities. These challenges provoked two problems: rifts between commands, and some dislocation in strategy.

It started at the top. Southern Army carried out on schedule a plan to transfer more than a third of the air units supporting Yamashita to other operations. Yamashita reacted defiantly, "All right, in that case we shall not rely upon the co-operation of the Air Force [sic]. The Army will now capture Singapore singlehanded." Tsuji called this decision "ploughing the land but forgetting the seed."[3] Japanese airpower remained formidable, but could have been decisive. Indeed, the Japanese had a chance to concentrate their assets in a co-ordinated onslaught that must have overwhelmed Singapore then and there. But to do that they needed to combine all their forces to concentrate on the decisive point. That point was now the retreat routes back to Singapore plus the reinforcement route into it. Instead the different arms set their own priorities and nobody tried to pull them together. 3rd Air Group worked hard to control the air, bomb Singapore, and provide reconnaissance and close support to ground operations—but did nothing to interfere with convoy traffic to Singapore, made few attacks on vehicle columns retreating along the roads, and, incredibly, did not attack the causeway. Yamashita's headquarters did not complain. Southern Fleet focused on broader operations in the South China Sea, instead of trying to close convoy routes to Singapore. 22nd Naval Air Flotilla could not move into Malaya because the army air formation had priority to deploy at captured airbases, so it could not reach the convoy routes. Therefore it confined itself to supporting naval operations and bombing Singapore.[4] These operations all contributed. And the Japanese were hard pressed to move air units forward fast enough to keep pace with the advance on the ground. But the fact remains: they missed a chance to sever an artery.

The defenders influenced this dislocation by committing their new fighters to battle. The Hurricane contingent was organized into No. 232 Squadron and went into action on 20 January. Maltby later admitted "too much had been expected of this handful of Hurricanes." But they did at least force the enemy to fight them for the rest of January. The new aircraft made an immediate impact, shooting down eight unescorted bombers raiding Singapore. This raised even higher hopes among the defenders, but the Japanese took up the challenge head on. The Hurricane II could outclimb and outpace the Zero above 20,000 feet, but was slower at lower altitude, and could not turn with it at any height. Only a few of the pilots had combat experience, whereas all the Japanese did. That all made "dogfighting" inadvisable. Despite being so warned, the new unit found out the hard way the next day when they came up against large numbers of escorting fighters, tried to mix it up, and lost five of their number, including the commanding officer. The squadron fought on. Its strafing runs turned the tables to some extent on Japanese ground forces, forcing transport to be cautious on the roads; that added to Japanese supply problems. But it struggled to make an impact on the heavily escorted bomber forces, and was soon worn down. By 30 January, the day Wavell transferred all but one fighter squadron to Sumatra, 17 Hurricanes, one-third of the contingent, were destroyed. Conceding defeat, the batch being flown in from HMS *Indomitable* was diverted to Sumatra.[5]

Southern Army aggravated things by declaring Singapore would be conquered ahead of schedule. Terauchi's staff wanted the airbases at Kluang and Kahang pressed into service quickly, to help the imminent assault on

Sumatra. This threatened to saddle Yamashita's army with a second task before it completed the first. An improvised small boat supply run from Thailand brought Kuantan airbase on line quickly enough to help operations in Johore. The same could not be done for Kluang and Kahang, which 3rd Air Group needed to strengthen its attacks on Singapore. All these problems forced Twenty-Fifth Army headquarters to make adjustments. To speed the advance of 18th Division's elements from Singora, where they landed on 22 January, Tsuji combed the other divisions for transport. The capture of large numbers of British vehicles made this possible. But it also slowed down the advance in Johore, yet could not bring down this major reinforcement in time to join the battle on the mainland. Specialist units were assigned to seize and repair the airbases, but while the squadrons could rapidly fly in, their supplies and support could not. The army was outrunning its logistics. That prompted Yamashita to request a major convoy operation to bring support units, ammunition and supplies for his forward air forces directly to Endau. On 24 January two cargo ships—one named the *Canberra Maru*—left Singora, escorted by 10 destroyers and two cruisers. They reached Endau at 0730hrs on 26 January and were spotted 15 minutes later by two Hudsons scouting for just such an operation.[6]

The defenders had to contest what they mistakenly thought was another amphibious invasion. Ideally this called for a co-ordinated air and naval attack with everything they had. They had the will but not the means. News of the landing did not reach RAF Far East until 0920hrs. That made it too late to co-ordinate a combined attack, because without air superiority the navy could only attack at night. In order to attack before the landing could be completed, the air force had to go in alone. The small striking force included the two squadrons, Nos. 36 and 100, which had been in Singapore the longest and had the best trained aircrews in RAF Far East. Unfortunately they flew aircraft rightly described as "flying coffins," especially the slow and obsolete Vildebeeste. Pulford had to throw his whole force into a daylight attack. But many units had sortied the night before. The staff then decided to rearm the strike planes with torpedoes rather than bombs. Worse, the slow speed of the obsolete bombers made it difficult to co-ordinate their approach with fighter escort. This all caused delays that divided the strike force into two separate waves and gave the enemy plenty of time to prepare.[7]

The first wave attacked at 1635hrs, 21 bombers in all, escorted by 23 fighters. But 12 of the bombers were Vildebeestes and 15 fighters were Buffaloes. They faced two covering fighter squadrons. Heavy cloud cover helped the bombers press home their attack, but they did no real damage. Another wave of three Albacores and nine Vildebeestes, escorted by 12 fighters, attacked an aroused Japanese force at 1900hrs. By the time the raids ended the torpedo bomber force was shattered; 13 aircraft were shot down. The Japanese lost two fighters. Pulford drew the only possible conclusion: "Vildebeestes and Albacores are not to be employed in daylight raids in future." The navy fared no better. Just as the first wave attacked at Endau, the old destroyers HMS *Thanet* and HMAS *Vampire* sailed from the naval base to try a night attack. The ships had only three torpedoes each. Early on 27 January they were intercepted by the Japanese covering force, four modern destroyers backed up by a light cruiser. *Thanet* was sunk despite a smoke screen provided by *Vampire*. The Australian warship broke contact and returned safely to Singapore. This was the closest the navy and air force ever came to taking the lead to defend Singapore. They pressed their attacks with impressive courage. Unfortunately that bravery, and the skill and experience of the torpedo bomber pilots, was wasted when they were forced into such a desperate fight with such outmatched weapons. The Japanese rightly concluded the sky and sea around Singapore now lay open for the taking.[8]

The final retreat to the island made a siege battle possible. But the conduct of that retreat guaranteed the siege would be short and therefore a strategic disaster. Two problems predominated. First, the starting position was untenable. Second, mutual confidence within the army all but vanished. From the start everyone fought with one eye on the enemy, the other looking over their shoulder to the island. Malaya Command retreated along four routes. On two of them, its units outfought the enemy. Local successes helped make it possible to reach the island. But local defeats made the price too high.

A command decision by Wavell shaped this battle as well: the decision to fight as if some part of Johore could still be held, even though he knew it could not. Percival had to pursue the same strategy, even though he knew fighting on in Johore might finish off his army. But he also prepared for a final retreat. Such preparations percolated down the chain of command, starting with a confidential letter to senior commanders on 20 January. The effect was predictable. The army looked back to retreat, not forward to fight. In that context, Malaya Command regrouped to hold the lateral road. But only hours after ordering 15th Indian Brigade to stand fast at Batu Pahat on 23 January, Percival scrapped his plan for Westforce to fight on north of that road. Wrongly believing the Japanese had one full division on the east coast and two on the west, the GOC ordered Bennett to retreat to Ayer Hitam and Kluang, after which he would take orders from Heath. Percival also appointed Paris to take over planning the defence of the island, and ordered all formations to send officers to reconnoiter positions in Johore Bahru and Singapore. Paris, ordered on 19 January to scout a "final line in Johore," suggested a position just north of Johore Bahru. But next morning Heath "decided to fall back on to the island if the line at Batu Pahat-Kluang fell."[9]

The problem for the men on the spot was, as ever, the connection between mission and situation. Heath and Percival now agreed the two no longer contradicted each other. If the lateral road and airbases were lost the naval base could not be held. Kirby later criticized them for staying at Batu Pahat, arguing the coast road could have been denied further south. South of Senggarang the area between the coast and trunk roads was mainly swampy and the Imperial Guards in fact did not attempt to move through it. But both commanders agreed there was no place to stand between the lateral road and Singapore. Dobbie's perimeter defence line was nothing more than a few pillbox positions on the road above Kota Tinggi. Percival's aim remained constant: to deny the airbases, to keep alive his mission to hold the naval base. By now that meant to cover the arrival of the rest of 18th Division. To the GOC, "It was clear that the crisis of the campaign had arrived."[10] But by the evening of 24 January Percival notified Wavell: "I want to be able to hold line of rd. Kluang-Batu Pahat for another 24 hrs at least as posns further south are NOT rpt NOT good." Percival was in fact now asking Wavell to allow him to launch a general retreat. Shortly before sending this telegram his staff drafted Operation Instruction No. 36, clearly assuming the Supreme Commander would concur:

> In the event of the forces now operating in Johore being forced back into Singapore Island, the following will be the outline plan for withdrawing the Force across the Causeway ... The ground around Johore Bahru is unsuitable for defence ... The forces available are insufficient to hold an extensive bridgehead ... A small bridgehead will be held covering the approaches to the Causeway. The withdrawal through this bridgehead will be carried out rapidly as soon as our forces have reached points to be selected in advance by Comd 3 Ind Corps, well in advance of the bridgehead. The order for this withdrawal will be given by Comd 3 Ind Corps.[11]

Nothing better expresses the impact the mission had on Percival than his judgement that only now had the "crisis" arrived. For his army, that moment came in the week after Jitra, when it was ordered to fight according to the mission assigned rather than the ground. Percival's "crisis" was the point at which the mission became impossible, rather than when the tactical position became untenable. That point was the Johore lateral road, before which the GOC dutifully saw a "slender" hope "our strategy might be successful." Wavell answered "you have not much ground behind you" but praised the army for "determined ... necessary and well timed" resistance.[12] The Supreme

Commander was not yet ready to authorize a final retreat; that meant taking responsibility for declaring Singapore indefensible. He and Percival were as keen as their superiors to let events on the ground assume that responsibility. But a fighting retreat is the most difficult operation a field army can attempt. To succeed it needs crystal clear orders, and all its commanders must work as one from start to finish. Neither condition applied to Malaya Command.

On the morning of 25 January 15th Indian Brigade finally found the Japanese battalion south of it. Key now agreed it must withdraw. But Heath and Percival insisted on waiting until they all met at Bennett's headquarters that afternoon to decide. After hearing Key's report, Percival agreed to order the brigade to retreat to Senggarang. Westforce would retreat as well, to prevent being outflanked. It would then stand for at least two days. But after that "Subsequent withdrawals to take place to positions, to be laid down in advance, which would in turn be held for a minimum fixed period and longer if possible." Eastforce and 11th Indian Division would conform, "under orders to be issued by 3 Ind Corps." Percival later insisted the only matter discussed was "the immediate policy for the conduct of operations," which Heath would coordinate. But Heath, Bennett and Key were all aware of Percival's earlier orders, and all knew the outline plan for the defence of the island was completed the day before. What they heard, understandably, was Percival delegating authority to Heath to direct a general retreat that could have only one terminus: Singapore. Percival did not want this to be explicit before Wavell authorized it, hence the order to Bennett to stand for two days–enough time to effect the change. After the fact he complained Heath exceeded his authority by issuing maps outlining a retreat ending in Singapore, including times and dates each formation would hold each position until reaching the island. But Percival did give Heath such authority–and most units interpreted the orders they now received the same way: retreat to Singapore.[13]

Percival identified the crux of the matter:

> The loss of the Batu Pahat force, however, forced upon us the necessity of withdrawing into the Singapore Fortress area and of concentrating upon its defence. We had then failed in our object of protecting the Naval Base. Our task thereafter was to hold the Singapore Fortress area.[14]

Both Percival and Wavell knew by 20 January this change in mission was now unavoidable. But neither could act openly until given permission, because this meant changing agreed policy for imperial defence. Once the retreat began the mission changed instantly, in practice. The new mission was clear, and given the circumstances even made strategic sense. Defend Singapore island as long as possible, and hurt the enemy as much as possible. The army, at last, was free to fight its own battle. But now it must retreat safely first, even before being authorized to do so. Sending such mixed signals was confusing, ate up time, fostered the tendency to look over the shoulder. These were liberties Malaya Command could not take against this enemy.

The general retreat was compromised right where it became necessary: Batu Pahat. Nishimura sent most of his division across country to outflank Batu Pahat on 24 January; the rest made a holding attack on the town. The same day Percival sent 5th Norfolks to join 15th Indian Brigade, and 53rd Brigade to deny the west coast road, specifically ordering it to link up with Challen. Because the road from Ayer Hitam was cut, both had to detour all the way down the trunk road, then back up. This gave Key five battalions to deny Batu Pahat.[15] But he never had a chance, for three reasons. First, the Japanese already had a better position; second, they moved faster; third, his units now tried not to deny the coast road but rather to avoid being trapped on it. After Challen finally realized on the morning of 25 January how strong the force behind him was, he ordered his units to retreat. But it took nine hours before they could disengage. 53rd Brigade was now reduced to two understrength battalions, 3/16 Punjabi and 6th Norfolks. Duke set up headquarters at Benut at 0830hrs. That afternoon he received orders which indicated to him the high command was now planning the final retreat to Singapore. He noted his own headquarters had "no means of exit to the south." This must explain why, despite the order to link up with Challen's brigade south of Batu Pahat, Duke directed his units to secure Rengit and Senggarang–several kilometres south of the rendezvous. 5th Guards Regiment swung wide to the flank and drove on Rengit. 4th Guards pressed Batu Pahat and, joined by its hidden battalion, made a shorter flanking move on Senggarang. The Norfolks ran into an ambush that split them in two. The rest of the brigade ran into enemy patrols near Rengit. Duke's infantry held Rengit, but two strong Japanese forces were now in between them and Challen's force. 15th Indian Brigade now had to fight its way out.[16]

15th Indian Brigade moved south at 0200hrs. At 0500hrs they ran into a strong Japanese position, covering a bridge from nearby houses. There were in fact now seven roadblocks between Senggarang and Rengit, along a 12 km stretch of road running through swamps and plantations. 2nd Cambs tried two frontal assaults, one at very close quarters, and brought 25 pounders up to point blank range. To no avail. Key visited Duke at 1000hrs and told him to break through and relieve Challen's force. But Duke, fearing more enemy attacks on his own flank, kept most of his infantry in position. As it happened the enemy made two strong attacks around Rengit that afternoon.

Duke organized a battlegroup of seven armoured cars, five carriers, 100 reinforcement troops from 6th Norfolks, plus a few gunners and engineers, to extract 15th Indian Brigade. They were to drive to Rengit, then dismount, sweep north and clear the road. Instead the whole force stayed in the vehicles and drove straight into the enemy, where "the whole affair developed into an MT charge." The only vehicle to run the gauntlet was the carrier carrying the commander, Major C.F.W. Banham, commanding officer 135th Field Regt. He literally rammed through the last block around 1400hrs. Such grit was not enough to clear a gauntlet now held by at least a battalion. Late that afternoon Challen ordered his men to destroy their guns, vehicles and heavy equipment, leave the badly wounded at the aid station, and move out across country on foot.[17]

This launched a retreat the British Battalion called "one long nightmare." Struggling through deep swamps, harassed by enemy patrols, the force made less than two kilometres an hour. At 0100hrs on 27 January it decided to split in two; one group led by the British Battalion made for the coast, the other moved inland. Both made it to safety more or less intact, although not without difficulty. Challen was taken prisoner while trying to rally 2nd Cambs. 1500 or so men holed up near the coast, close enough to hear Japanese driving along the road. Volunteers took small boats and reached friendly positions further south. Alerted, the RN organized its most successful action of the campaign. From 28 through 31 January, two river gunboats and some patrol craft evacuated, at night, almost the entire group. The other group straggled into Benut, still held by 53rd Brigade, from the late afternoon of 27 January; 2700 made it back. While most troops thus escaped to fight another day, this battle to deny the west coast road was over before it began because the defenders did not want to fight it. They complained about hard going across country and tired troops. Neither problem stopped the Imperial Guards from forcing the issue.[18] This defeat cost Malaya Command more guns, vehicles, supplies, its plan to hold the lateral road, and yet more cohesion.

The last two losses were the most important. They are best explained through a disagreement years later between Percival and Kirby. Percival believed Heath's order to begin a general retreat, according to a strict timetable, undid 15th Indian Brigade. This timetable forced Challen to press on at full speed rather than clear the road by deliberate attacks. Kirby disagreed, insisting by the time Challen set out the enemy was too strong to push aside by any tactics. There is evidence to support both views. The Imperial Guards were strongly concentrated by that time, their blocks well placed and tenaciously defended. On the other hand before Challen and his staff moved out Key told them the retreat would begin from Rengit on the evening of 27 January. Challen was orchestrating an all out attack by two full battalions when Banham broke through to give him pertinent advice. Not only would it be very difficult to clear the road to Rengit, it was now rumoured that a full retreat to Singapore was imminent. When Challen heeded this advice and ordered the dispersal, this forced his brigade to move out before it could regroup. When his force struggled to make time through the swamps, fear 53rd Brigade would soon fall back influenced the decision to split up. Both Percival and Kirby were in fact right. Challen gave up trying to break through with his brigade intact because of the timetable he faced. But only a determined and coordinated assault by both brigades on both ends of the gauntlet might have done the trick. What mattered most was that Challen and Banham believed the rumour. Duke's half-hearted attempts to keep the route open suggest they had good reason and were not alone. The Japanese correctly concluded this defeat would force Percival to give up Johore.[19]

Percival and Heath later agreed they tried to hold Batu Pahat at least one day too long. And all senior commanders agreed there was no choice but to start a general retreat once the west coast road was compromised. Percival told Wavell on 27 January:

> Very critical situation has developed. Enemy has cut off and overrun a majority of forces on West Coast road and has reached Benut. Unless we can stop him it will be difficult to get own [columns] on other roads back in time especially as they are both being pressed. In any case it looks as if we should NOT rptd NOT be able to hold JOHORE for more than another three or four days.

Wavell now at last granted Percival discretion to withdraw to Singapore island, but it was too late to avoid the danger Percival identified: "We are going to be a bit thin on the Island unless we can get all remaining trps back."[20] That was now the problem. The high command was giving up on Johore and the word was spreading. Nobody wanted to be left behind. But that lapse in discipline made it harder to get everyone back safely, because it fostered a save yourself first mentality.

That mentality undermined a more successful action on the east coast. 22nd Australian Brigade remained in good shape at Mersing but knew it would soon be ordered to retreat. On 23 January its engineers blew the Mersing bridge and prepared more demolitions on the road south to Jemaluang. Meanwhile 2/18 AIF planned a battalion ambush between Mersing and Jemaluang. Japanese probes around Mersing were easily rebuffed. This prompted Yamashita to order a battlegroup led by Col. Saeki, hero of Jitra, to advance east along the lateral road to help 55th Regiment take Kahang and Mersing. The defence forces at both Kluang and Kahang airbases were unreliable and 2/17 Dogra was needed to cover the area south of Jemaluang, so both bases were demolished and evacuated on the afternoon of 25 January. That day Westforce retreated from Kluang, opening the flank. Fortunately for Taylor very thorough demolitions slowed the Japanese advance from both directions, but it was definitely time to move.[21] The next day 2/18 AIF took up forward positions north of Jemaluang. Its commanding officer, Lt-Col. A.L. Varley, met Taylor to finalize plans. The two Australian battalions would retreat leapfrog style south of Jemaluang, after 2/18 AIF staged its ambush. Both men took note of the landing at Endau, expecting to face stronger enemy ground forces as a result. Taylor also stipulated the ambush force must be ready to retreat immediately after springing the trap, to conform with Heath's orders for the general retreat.[22]

The battalion plan was pretty good. Noticing how much the enemy disliked being fired on by Australian artillery, Varley set up a killing box seven kilometres north of Jemaluang. Jungle and high ground made this stretch of the road a defile running through two rubber plantations. D Company deployed at the northern end, 500 metres west of the homestead of Nithsdale Estate on the main road, along a track at the base of Gibraltar Hill. B Company deployed at the southern end, the same distance east of the road. This formed a box through which the Japanese would be allowed to advance until they ran into A Company, deployed on high ground astride the road in the Joo Lye Estate, some two kilometres south of the homestead. C Company lay in reserve. Once the trap was sprung, the battalion mortars plus two batteries of field artillery would pound the area between the forward companies for seven minutes; then they would fire a rolling barrage, advancing 100 yards every two minutes. D Company would advance behind it, pushing the enemy towards B Company; they would trap the enemy in the barrage. There were unfortunately two problems. First, the plan assumed the trap would be sprung in daylight; this was reinforced by an air reconnaissance report an enemy battalion was advancing from Endau towards Mersing on the afternoon of 26 January–and thus could not reach the trap before dawn. The artillery fire plan was based on a good observation post in the A Company area using daylight to exploit the guns to full effect, to avoid hitting friendly infantry sweeping in. Second, Taylor leaned backwards and was not committed to following through.[23]

A few minutes into 27 January 2/18 AIF learned the old lesson that in war the enemy does what he wants rather than what you want. D Company observed infantry moving past the homestead and along the road in column, much earlier than expected. These troops were from the 55th Regiment, already fighting around Mersing for a week. Soon Japanese scouts bumped into and started to probe A Company, the backstop. Once Varley was convinced a large force was in the trap he ordered the guns to begin firing, at 0315 hrs. When D Company's commander finally called in half an hour later, Varley launched the sweep. The result was a slow advance in rubber country so black the B Company commander remarked "We moved forward by each man holding the bayonet scabbard of the man in front and so dark was it that most of the time I was unable to see any sign of the man whose bayonet I was holding." D Company ran into the main enemy force shortly before dawn. This provoked an intense close quarter struggle. An intrepid patrol by his intelligence sergeant finally gave Varley an accurate picture of who was where. At 0745hrs he brought artillery fire down on the Japanese with devastating effect, then prepared to send A Company forward to mop up the enemy. But before it could advance Taylor ordered him not to commit any more troops. He did not want the battalion so engaged it compromised the order to retreat by stages "into Singapore," confirmed that morning. Varley tried to dodge this order, first retreating, then recalling his reserve companies to stand fast until the ambush companies could "fight their way out." B Company was preparing to attack to help D Company when it received the order to pull out. The battalion soon did so, leaving D Company to try to fight back to safety. It was badly cut up, suffering most of the battalion's 98 casualties.[24]

This ambush hurt the Japanese more. The supporting artillery fired more than 900 rounds in one hour. Japanese losses must have been severe. 55th Regiment all but stood still, leaving Saeki to take Jemaluang from the west late on 28 January, more than a day after the Australians left it. Eastforce faced no further enemy pressure as it retreated south to Kota Tinggi, to cover the final retreat to Singapore. Unfortunately this did not earn Malaya Command any larger relief, because to the Japanese this remained no more than a holding action. But on the other side, Taylor's order sent an ominous signal. His formation did not meet anything it could not handle. However, bad news from the west coast, the retreat in the centre, the landing at Endau and Heath's general retreat all obviously infected brigade headquarters with the growing fear of being left behind. Varley clearly objected to being ordered out, B Company's commander said Taylor's order was to "abandon any troops entangled with the Japs," and 8th Australian Division headquarters "adversely commented on" the order when it heard of it.[25] If the most efficient formation in Malaya Command was no longer willing to take any risk to finish a fight, even when it had an advantage, this did not bode well for the army.

The problem lay not so much at the top with Percival, or on the ground with the troops, but more in between. The senior officers of Malaya Command lost confidence in each other at the worst possible time: as the army tried to prevent a retreat from becoming a rout. The problem was most complicated, the outcome most serious, in the centre. Westforce faced a very difficult task: to conduct a parallel retreat in which each force relied on the other to protect its flank. This called for close coordination and steady nerves. The troops did enough to deserve a happy ending. They did not get one because their commanders were no longer up to the challenge.

Bennett deployed 27th Australian Brigade on the trunk road, where he saw the greatest danger. The Japanese did at first concentrate there and pressed hard. The first sharp encounter was just north of Ayer Hitam on 25 January. 2/30 AIF took up a defensive position three kilometres north of the crossroads, anchored on two hills straddling the road. A Company 2nd Loyals set up on the hill to the left. A Company 2/30 AIF set up on the hill to the right, backed up by the Loyals HQ Company. The ground to the north is flat and open, providing excellent fields of fire. The hill on the right was thick with long grass, providing good cover. A large swampy area to its right was refused by a platoon guarding the right flank of the hill; it sent a standing patrol with automatic weapons to guard a knoll off to its right front. The fight raged all day in drenching rain, as the Japanese probed both flanks. One heavy attack on the right hill was enfiladed and repelled by the fire of the standing patrol. A subsequent attack forced the patrol back, but was then itself caught in a crossfire from the hill and the covering platoon on the right. There was one weak point and the Japanese eventually exploited it, using jungle cover to push the Loyals off their hill at dusk, then bringing machine gun fire to bear on the road. But the force, well covered by its forward position on the right, broke contact after dark, moved across country, rendezvoused with transport south of the village, and broke clear. This was a successful battalion action. The Australians made good use of artillery, mortars and automatic weapons to exploit well chosen ground. They hurt the enemy enough to force him to shift his main effort to the railroad. Had Galleghan been ordered to hang on, however, he would soon have been in trouble. The Japanese were denying the road junction by artillery fire from late morning. The battle peaked just as Percival decided to authorize the general retreat. And the Loyals were now so worn down they were sent back to Singapore to regroup once the retreat began.[26] This sums up the final retreat down the trunk road. Set free to fight a delaying action, 27th Australian Brigade could fight to hurt the enemy rather than hold ground. But it was also caught between enemy pressure and a larger battle quickly falling apart, so it had to keep dropping back.

Two other notable actions took place further south. On 28 January the brigade deployed in Namazie Estate, 30 km south of Ayer Hitam. The ground to the left of the trunk road was dense jungle; to the right the undulating estate ground was easier to penetrate. 2nd Gordons, sent up from Singapore to replace the Loyals, dug in astride the road. 2/26 AIF covered the estate to the right. The jungle closed in on the road just south of the position. It was obvious the Japanese would try a right flanking move through the estate, to block the road where it defiled. 2/30 AIF set up in echelon on the right to prevent this. The battle heated up in the early afternoon. The Japanese indeed probed the right but 2/26 AIF held steady. Galleghan fed three companies forward to counter their pressure. Late in the afternoon two companies launched a well executed bayonet assault covered by machine gun fire, retaking high ground from an enemy force gathering to attack. The brigade had to retreat before it could prepare an ambush Maxwell wanted to try in the defile, but its aggressive defence allowed it to do so after dark without being pursued.[27] The next day the brigade deployed at road milestone 31, near Ayer Bemban. 2/26 AIF took the point, blocking the road where it defiled between rubber and swampy jungle. The enemy attacked at 0800hrs, but this was excellent ground. All four rifle companies occupied high ground giving them good cover and clear fields of fire. The Japanese suffered accordingly, punished by medium machine guns finally able to engage at long range and by two artillery batteries. In the late afternoon an enemy force gathering on the road was spotted, shelled, then dispersed by a rapid company assault with the bayonet. The enemy retaliated by air dropping tear gas but then broke off at dusk; the brigade retreated overnight according to plan.[28] Such actions resembled the defensive tactics Bennett wanted to use in front of Segamat, especially the aggressive defence at the Namazie Estate. The Japanese maintained the pressure on the trunk road, but the Australians made them pay for it.

One other unit action in the Westforce retreat deserves a glance. Retreating south to Kluang along the railroad and secondary roads, 9th Indian Division was pressured by the enemy near Paloh on 23 January. Elements of 22nd Indian Brigade were cut off. Barstow decided to counterattack to extract them. Painter ordered his two weakened battalions to advance along the railway to engage the enemy at Niyor. His strongest unit, 5/11 Sikhs, with a battery of field artillery in support, would advance along a track left of the railway, then right wheel along another track to assault Niyor from the flank. Nothing went as planned. There were no good maps, no reliable intelligence about the enemy, and a Japanese advance to contact prevented the holding force from advancing at all. 5/11 Sikhs having moved out at 1430hrs, Painter ordered them to cut their advance short and take the enemy in the flank. But without good maps Lt.-Col. J.H.D. Parkin decided to advance to Niyor, then double back and take the enemy from the rear. When they ran into a road block just outside Niyor, the Sikhs set up a perimeter for the night. A spirited battle erupted in undulating ground after daybreak on 25 January, the Sikhs getting the better of it. As Parkin prepared a battalion assault, he was ordered to retreat to Kluang. Parkin decided to launch a quick company assault. He wanted to make the enemy think the advance continued and secure high ground to screen his retreat. Covered by mortar fire A Company charged uphill with fixed bayonets, screaming "Sat Siri Akal!" They caught a tightly bunched enemy force assembling for its own assault and routed it. The Sikhs destroyed at least an enemy company and forced the Japanese to break contact. So screened, the brigade reassembled that evening without further pressure and joined the general retreat.[29] Unfortunately this local success was thrown away when the high command mishandled that retreat–and the same brigade paid the ultimate price.

On the first full day of that retreat, 26 January, Bennett noted in his diary "Situation most difficult–Troops weary. Comds anxious."[30] This was exactly the problem. The troops were certainly tired, not least of retreating, especially on foot in the dark, and of being harassed from the air. But some key commanders were worse than tired. They were now afraid the retreat might become a rout and their force might be left behind. The excuses were the temper of the troops and the vulnerability of certain positions. The cause was their growing lack of confidence in each other. The outcome was pressure for more rapid retreats. The result was disaster for 22nd Indian Brigade, and 27th Australian Brigade escaped the same fate in spite, not because of, its commander.

Maxwell buckled on this final retreat. Bennett "lectured him" on 24 January for complaining his men were tired. Over the next week Bennett scolded Maxwell for a daily litany of complaints about tired troops, threats from the flank, dipping morale. Finally on 29 January Bennett lost patience with his brigade commander, telling him "roundly and frankly" that complaining his men were tired made a bad impression when comparing their two weeks of battle to the seven weeks endured by Indian units. There was of course serious pressure in such a fighting retreat, and Maxwell did hear plenty of complaints. Every day the 2/26 AIF war diary complained about constant retreating, fatigue, enemy air pressure and the absence of friendly air support, noting "general despondency, "physical exhaustion," and "many crack ups and general lowering of morale." Even Galleghan argued his men were not fit to stage an ambush below the Namazie Estate and retreated early to avoid being cut off at the defile. Nevertheless, the performance of the troops suggested they were still full of fight if given the right leadership. Maxwell let their venting and his own anxiety sway him. He set his headquarters so far to the rear that Galleghan took charge on the battlefield. A "windy and worried" Maxwell feared his brigade would be left behind as the retreat approached Singapore. Bennett again drew the right conclusion. In civilian life Maxwell was a medical doctor, always looking after the welfare of his patients. Now "his men were to some extent his patients."[31]

Maxwell's decline did not compromise his own brigade, but did reflect the decline of the army–and indirectly compromised 9th Indian Division. Japanese pressure was of course a major factor. The full 5th Division pressed Westforce hard. Two regiments advanced on each axis, with strong air support. Nevertheless the ensuing disaster was an avoidable error. The cause was the degeneration of the army into separate groups focusing on their own fight. That left them all vulnerable if something went wrong. Something of course did. The parallel retreat called for close coordination between 9th Indian Division and the Australians. There were tracks and estate roads connecting the two axes which the enemy could use to outflank either formation if they did not synchronize their defensive stands to guard each other, especially north of Layang Layang. This was complicated by the fact the secondary road running parallel to the railway ended there. That meant the Indians had to send their vehicles, guns and equipment to the trunk road from there, leaving the infantry to retreat along the railway on foot. Worse, between Rengam and Layang Layang, a 16 km stretch, a veritable maze of estate roads ran along the right flank of the railway. Barstow had to make sure his brigades covered each other through this area. Bennett had no confidence in the division but felt this was the less dangerous task to assign it. On the other hand it had to rely on the Australian headquarters to keep all three brigades in step with each other. Each disappointed the other.

The program for the retreat was drawn from orders Heath gave on the afternoon of 26 January, issued overnight by Westforce as Operation Instruction No. 4. This order was often identified as the root of disaster, because it required 9th Indian Division to hold a position well north of Layang Layang until 1600hrs on 28 January, to protect the flank of 27th Australian Brigade by denying tracks running to the trunk road. It was a confusing order, drafted by a tired staff: the main body specified rail mile 440, south of Layang Layang, whereas an appendix had it as rail mile 437. The plot supposedly thickens because Galleghan retreated early from the Namazie position, either on his own or prompted by Maxwell, probably with Bennett's approval. But the real problem lay elsewhere. Westforce felt the priority was to give 9th Indian Division a good head start for each bound of the retreat because it had to secure a vulnerable right flank. That suggested 27th Australian Brigade should conform to the Indians. But Barstow saw his task as to cover the right flank of the Australians.[32] The key factor was the attitudes of the headquarters involved.

Barstow personally discussed the retreat with Bennett or Maxwell every day. He was certainly aware of Maxwell's growing concern and knew very well what a low opinion Bennett had of his division. This made him determined to make sure it did all that was asked of it. The problem really began when Barstow, shortly after meeting Bennett early on 27 January, issued verbal orders to his brigades. That day all the division's artillery, vehicles and heavy equipment would cross over to the trunk road, then fall back towards Singapore. To screen that, as well as cover the flank of the Australians until they moved south of the connecting tracks, 22nd Indian Brigade would hold astride the railway above mile marker 437 until late afternoon 28 January. After this the division would withdraw leapfrog style, the brigades working the movements out between themselves. Painter complained "the sectors on the map bore no relation to possible defensive positions on the ground, the first position which could be held with any reasonable chance of success being just south of Layang Layang." Barstow replied "the orders of General Gordon Bennett were implicit, and that the sectors as marked must be held." Barstow did direct "22 bde to give particular attention to right flank" but made it clear the division must conform to Australian movements.[33]

Barstow's determination to please Bennett proved fatal. It put his division in a very bad tactical position–one it was no longer cohesive enough to cope with. Painter had good reason to complain. The ground to the right was mainly palm oil plantation. It was more dense than rubber but liberally crossed by tracks, perfect cover for infiltration. If the enemy did outflank, the only way to protect the brigade was to deploy 8th Indian Brigade as close behind as possible. Barstow scouted the ground himself and ordered 8th Indian Brigade to hold high ground south of a stream, just south of Layang Layang. That afternoon Parkin, concerned about the position his battalion was ordered to hold, found the same ground while looking for a better one. There he met Lay, presumably inspecting the ground the division commander wanted him to secure. Lay "could not say what position his brigade was going to occupy." Now agitated, Parkin asked to move to another position, or at least send one of his own companies to secure the high ground. Painter refused. That night Lay not only pulled his brigade back some eight kilometres behind 22nd Indian Brigade, he also failed to stop the premature demolition of the railway bridge. Predictably the Japanese found and advanced along the estate tracks on the right; the Sikhs heard vehicles moving most of the night. By daylight on 28 January 22nd Indian Brigade found itself cut off. The demolition cut its communications by destroying the telegraph wire; the signals vehicles departed the day before and there were no portable radios. Patrols bumped into enemy forces advancing on the brigade from the rear. Painter drew the obvious conclusion and decided to retreat. He opted to move across country, to outflank certain enemy blocks on the railway, and try to regain the next defensive position south of Layang Layang.[34]

9th Indian Division is largely responsible for allowing 22nd Indian Brigade to be forced into the bush. At this stage nobody should have been taking any chances with the Japanese. Maxwell's whinging did foster a jittery mood in general, but Barstow still surely should have been less cringing to Bennett. He also should have paid closer attention to his brigadiers, especially Lay. And Painter should have made certain his rear was secure, even by himself if necessary, after accepting orders putting his formation in such poor ground. But the fog of war was also at work, with so many conflicting dangers pressing the same men. That made it more important for headquarters to work together. Yet while this may explain how the brigade became isolated, its destruction is another matter. Bluntly, the army abandoned it.

8th Indian Brigade has the most to answer for. At 0730hrs it reported to Barstow "Posn confused and appeared to be JAP-self-JAP-5 Sikh." Two hours later it admitted the bridge was blown prematurely and "suspect that enemy will now during 28 Jan infiltrate between the two bdes. Situation NOT clear." At 1000hrs Barstow reported to Westforce "Undoubtedly bit of a shimozzle going on in difficult palm oil area North of Layang Layang" and went to see for himself.[35] When he reached 8th Indian Brigade Barstow found 2nd Baluchis had not only failed to occupy the ridge but were now, according to Lay, themselves cut off. Barstow ordered an immediate attack, to restore contact with the missing brigade. Lay demurred, not entirely without cause. His brigade was worn down, and now without any artillery support. But Barstow insisted, then went ahead with his admin officer, Col. W.A. Trott, and his Australian liaison officer, Lt.-Col. C.J.A. Moses. Barstow told them he would have to replace Lay. They found the Baluchis resting undisturbed, more than two kilometres south of the ridge. The party pressed on, crossed the partly wrecked bridge, and ran into a Japanese ambush. Moses and Trott went one way, Barstow another. Barstow was never heard from again. His death removed the only person outside 22nd Indian Brigade willing to go to real lengths to retrieve it. When the news filtered back up the chain of command, Westforce, Heath and Percival all sincerely believed the brigade could not be cut off by very strong forces and should be able to fight its way out. This complacency should have been dispelled. Moses witnessed the 2nd Baluchis attack ordered by Barstow and saw it "beaten off with many casualties. Japs holding it strongly and sitting waiting for 22 Bde." But his later report to Westforce headquarters focused on Barstow's disappearance. Nor did 9th Indian Division headquarters sound any alarm. That afternoon Percival agreed to accelerate the final retreat to Singapore by one day, to the morning of 31 January. That evening 8th Indian Brigade retreated accordingly, some 11 km. Meanwhile 22nd Indian Brigade struggled through very difficult country, further hampered by dwindling supplies, skirmishes with the enemy and having to carry its wounded.[36]

The next morning, 29 January, division headquarters told Lay it was of "utmost importance" to move forward to extract the missing brigade "if tactical situation allows." On the other hand "you are required to deny the line Sedenak to the enemy till night 30/31 Jan in accordance with previous instructions." To Lay the order to secure the line well south overrode the suggestion to move north; in any case the suggestion was dropped that afternoon. Not until 22nd Indian Brigade's intelligence officer reached division headquarters very late that night, having gone ahead with a small party, did the news of just how grave the position was finally filter up the chain of command. By that time Westforce was falling back to the last positions it would hold before the road and railway converged at Kulai, after which the plan was to drive all the way back to Singapore in one bound. This left 22nd Indian Brigade exhausting itself in the bush to reach a position already abandoned. The weakness of the air force now hit home. Enemy aircraft forced the brigade to take cover frequently but RAF Far East could not meet a request to locate it with reconnaissance aircraft. It was already stretched covering an incoming convoy and the evacuation of 15th Indian Brigade. Malaya Command did not know its lost formation was no more than 15 km from the nearest friendly position. Bennett and Heath both later tried to delay the retreat by some hours to buy more time, while Percival arranged for boats to evacuate any who made it to the Straits of Johore. But that speaks for itself: the brigade was on its own.[37]

22nd Indian Brigade did its best, but there is a big difference between advancing to contact and trying to escape and evade, when moving large numbers across country. 5/11 Sikhs were the only reliable unit left, and they were worn down by a gruelling four days of retreat. Local civilians tried to help by guiding the force, but neither party really understood each other and the efforts went to naught. The Japanese tried both to destroy and, when they realized it was Indian, to subvert the force. Neither effort worked until the troops lost confidence in their leaders. The mortal blow was a decision to leave the wounded at a plantation dispensary. After this even the Sikhs fell apart as a unit. On 1 February, more than a day after the general retreat finished,

Painter surrendered the 400 men left under command in a plantation about 25 km northeast of Johore Bahru. Less than 80 made it back to Singapore, mostly Sikhs still led by Parkin.[38]

This cost Malaya Command an entire brigade, a formation worn down by combat but also experienced and still fit to fight. There were anxious moments in the last two days of January as everyone else converged on the causeway. This produced more bickering between formations afraid of being left behind. While Heath, Key, Maxwell, Thyer, and Taylor were all involved, Bennett again took the cake. From the start he complained about Heath's plans for final retreat, insisting they would lead to disaster. But when the crunch came, Bennett stepped aside. On 28 January, a day his entire command was pressed near to breaking point, Bennett spent the afternoon with his friend the Sultan of Johore, announcing he would escape from Singapore when the time came. On the afternoon of 30 January, as his command prepared for its final dash, Bennett drove over to Singapore, leaving the last crucial movement in the hands of a staff he did not even trust.[39] Some credit must be given to arrangements made from 24 January to mount a final rearguard.[40] But the reason there was no *coup de grace* was the Japanese failed to deliver one. Malaya Command made one contribution: beating the enemy up on the trunk and east coast roads. That was more than offset by defeat on the west coast and the disintegration of 22nd Indian Brigade, which finished 9th Indian Division as a formation. What ultimately checked the Japanese were overstretched supply lines and foolish misuse of airpower. Yet while the "driving charge" failed to annihilate Malaya Command on the mainland, it certainly shattered it as an army. The force that crossed the causeway on the morning of 31 January was more an exhausted horse being corralled than a fighting mad rat being cornered.

It did not necessarily look that way at the time. Left largely alone by the enemy, the army made its last dangerous motor transport retreat across the causeway hindered only by more acrimony within its high command. The outer rearguard, commanded by Taylor, held a semi-circle screening the link from five kilometres out. It fell back in the early hours of the morning, handing over to the inner rearguard holding the final perimeter of some 250 metres–under orders to fight to the death if necessary. This inspiring task went to the most deserving unit in Malaya Command: 2nd Argylls. The battalion had been somewhat rebuilt by volunteers, recouping its own detachments, and absorbing 210 Royal Marine survivors from Force Z. It carried out its mission with the sense of occasion that builds regimental traditions. When 2nd Gordons, last of the outer rearguard, crossed over, an Argyll piper played their regimental march, Cock o' The North. Finally at 0730hrs the Argylls themselves came across in open order, two pipers defiantly blaring A Hundred Pipers and the regimental quick march Hielan' Laddie. Stewart crossed last, then gave the order to blow the demolitions. Sappers blew a 20 metre gap in the fixed link at 0815hrs. The battle for Malaya was over. Singapore was now besieged.[41]

Stewart's flair in retreat was also the stuff of legends such as built empires. But the defeat that forced him to do it was the kind that shattered them. Heath later said "except for the withdrawal of the 22nd Indian Brigade the plan was well executed." This was nonsense. Thanks to the enemy falling short and some battalions standing tall, large numbers of men and much equipment made it back to the island. The price however was too high. Percival knew this: "The heavy losses of men and equipment on the mainland during the last week of January necessitated considerable modifications in [the plan to defend Singapore island]." 15th Indian Brigade had no equipment. 53rd Brigade was much reduced. 9th Indian Division was disbanded, its remaining units absorbed by 11th Indian Division. And the tough 8th Australian Division lost more than a third of its fighting power. The second wave of reinforcements arrived while the final retreat took place: 44th Indian Brigade and replacement troops, 2/4 AIF and replacement troops, the bulk of 18th Division. Percival now realized what this amounted to. Even though the Indians arrived on 21-22 January, he retained them in Singapore rather than throw them into the fight.[42] Malaya Command once again no more than made up its numbers. It was in fact far weaker than when the campaign started, in three crucial ways.

First, its strategic position was now hopeless. Heath and Percival were right to conclude there was no way to stand below the lateral road and more to lose by trying, but the tactical advantage provided by retreating behind the Straits of Johore was more than offset by the larger strategic position. The Japanese so dominated the surrounding air and sea space that Wavell redirected I Australian Corps towards Sumatra and Java even before the retreat finished. Singapore would not be relieved.[43] Now it must be defended against an enemy army a kilometre away, a contingency not planned for before the war because it was not seen to be manageable. Second, Malaya Command was more makeshift than ever. Full strength units were raw and just arrived, neither acclimatized nor fit to fight. Veteran units were worn down or lacked equipment. The raw replacement drafts could not replace the combat power lost on the mainland. Percival now had no real reserve. Finally, most important, the field army was dead. Malaya Command was now a collection of units with little confidence left in their high command or each other. Some were still full of fight. Others were broken. What they found on Singapore island made this worse. The army believed what everyone else believed. Their job was to protect the naval base. They were buying time for "Fortress Singapore" to finalize its supposedly formidable defences, then they would dig in behind its ramparts and defy the enemy to dig them out. The navy abandoned the base and started to demolish its facilities literally before the eyes of the retreating troops. Worst of all, there were no ramparts. Units directed to the coastal sectors they were now assigned to defend found practically nothing waiting for them. They would have to do it all themselves. The base was gone. There was no fortress. There would be no rescue.[44]

After the decision to take a calculated risk with the defence of the Far East in order to concentrate on the war in Europe, the already poor odds of holding Singapore became a serious longshot. When the US Pacific Fleet was neutralized at Pearl Harbor, the question changed: Singapore would fall, but how long would it take, and what would it cost? The Japanese provided much of the answer. They had their problems, but the safety net was there. Their decision to mount a "driving charge," their dominance in the air and at sea, and their efficiency on the ground, at all levels, gave them the best chance to exploit the opening fate and British policy provided. Yamashita was given 100 days to take Singapore. After 55 he stood poised to invade it. Percival summed it up: "There was never any time to recover if things went wrong." The *coup de grace* was not delivered on the mainland, but that was the only real Japanese failure. For a cost of 4500 casualties, the equivalent of a regiment, the Japanese inflicted four times that many on Malaya Command, destroyed Force Z, broke RAF Far East. Twenty-Fifth Army fought more than 90 battles, repaired more than 250 bridges and causeways, captured more than 300 guns, 50 carriers, large quantities of supplies of all kinds, and some 3600 vehicles and 800 items of rolling stock.[45] It was an impressive performance. But it worked so well because Malaya was defended so badly.

From the very beginning the "Singapore strategy" was a gamble. The military system for imperial defence rested in the Far East on one central assumption: if necessary the Empire could hastily improvise an effective defence to hold the naval base until its main forces were free to relieve it. Much was done. Large numbers of aircraft and ground troops were sent to Malaya. The Empire's forces wore the same uniforms, used the same equipment, organized and fought along compatible lines. Nevertheless, the central assumption was disastrously wrong. The navy was sidelined from the start. The air force never recovered from a disastrous starting position. That left it all to the army. The army's chances rested on another key assumption: an imperial army required to be prepared to fight in any terrain or climate could quickly adapt, pull together and fight effectively wherever it found itself. The battle for Malaya demonstrated how wrong that was. Hastily assembled in piecemeal fashion, forced to fight according to the mission rather than the ground, resorting time and again to generic methods that were all it knew rather than adjusting to local conditions, Malaya Command was dismantled in Malaya. But the cardinal point is this: the same system produced both ponderous set-piece tactics on the ground and rigid implausible policy at the summit.

The British and Australian governments placed the defenders of Singapore in dire straits because they dared not challenge the imperative that underpinned imperial defence: stick to the policy that claimed it would produce the most desirable strategic result in return for the minimum political friction. Churchill pulled back twice in 1940 from pursuing the logical consequence of events, once with the Australians, once with the COS. In the end his policy was to rely on the Americans, reassure the Australians, rock no boats, rely on the assumption the armed forces could contain this enemy before they did unbearable damage. That assumption was so wrong, the policy which it justified turned defeat towards disaster. Personalities did matter–all the more so in a multinational force. In this difficult situation their margin of error was too slim to give any real chance to recover. Brooke-Popham decided to let the plan move forward as designed, rather than insist it was bound to fail. Wavell followed the script for imperial defence to the letter. Because it was so wrong and he made such poor decisions about personnel, defeat became disaster. Percival took the instrument he was given and directed it according to his orders and the methods it knew. By the time the retreat to Johore made his disagreement with Heath moot, it was too late. Bennett, reflecting in his diary just after leaving the mainland, best captured what happened in Malaya:

> This retreat seems fantastic. Fancy 550 miles in 55 days–chased by a Jap army on stolen bikes without artillery. It was a war of patrols. All that happened was that they patrolled outside our resistance and sat on a road behind us. Thinking we were cut off, we retreated ... Never felt so sad and upset. Words fail me. Why? This should not have been. The whole thing is fantastic. I thought I could hold Johore–but I assumed that British troops would have held their piece.[46]

Even if there was something to that, why was it reasonable to expect raw troops just off the boat to fight well in alien country? That points again to grand strategy, or perhaps simply to circumstances. But what really comes through is the discord that so compromised Malaya Command. This was the unforced error. Governments did not want to drink political poison. They asked the "poor bloody infantry" to bail them out. When they could not, contingents fell to blaming each other. Thyer described "a gradual build up of a psychology during the withdrawal, and commencing at the Thailand

Border, which vitiated the principle of co-operation and the full sense of responsibilities to subordinate commands." Malaya Command never really became a true army, a fighting team operating as such. This was Percival's task, but singling him out comes close to blaming the stage magician for not doing real magic. The system turned military defeat into disaster. Now all it could do was ask Percival's army to carry out a new mission: die for the Empire. Die well and take a long time doing so. Buy time for defence elsewhere and restore a reputation fast being torn to pieces. But the defeat it suffered on the mainland left it too weak and divided to do either. Its death would now shake rather than buttress the Empire. Churchill saw this when he at last realized how wrong he was about the vital connection between policy, intelligence and operations. And as usual he expressed it better than anyone else:

> I had put my faith in the enemy being compelled to use artillery on a very large scale in order to pulverise our strong points at Singapore, and in the almost prohibitive difficulties and long delays which would impede such an artillery concentration and the gathering of ammunition along Malayan communications. Now, suddenly, all this vanished away and I saw before me the hideous spectacle of the almost naked island and of the wearied, if not exhausted, troops retreating upon it.[47]

SECTION FIVE

A Matter of Time

On 19 January 1942 the Financial Secretary of the Straits Settlements told Malaya Command he was custodian of a very large quantity of currency notes that must be destroyed in any "emergency"; as the job would take three days, Mr. Weissberg asked for advance warning before any "emergency." Singapore Chinese merchants were ahead of the government–they stopped accepting the ubiquitous "chit" from Europeans and demanded cash in hand at least a week earlier. These practical men of commerce broke the taboo by accepting the obvious: the island would soon be invested.[1] Singapore island was bound to be quite a different battlefield from those contested on the mainland. For the first time since the opening day of the war the Japanese would have to attack a position they could not go around, across open water. The island consisted largely of plantation, jungle and mangrove, but was flat, with very little high ground. Good roads radiated out from town in every direction. In addition to the four airbases, and the naval base in the centre of the north coast, the only real urban area in Malaya sprawled along the central area of the south coast. The peacetime population of perhaps three quarters of a million was now swollen by refugees to possibly a full million. The great majority were Chinese, the remainder Malay, Indian and Eurasian. Both sides planned for a fight they had hoped to avoid–for the Japanese, to take the island by storm; for the British, to hold out on an island never meant to withstand a close siege and not in any way suited to do so.

The retreat onto the island finally forced Singapore's defenders to accept the fact they were trapped. There was no escape and they could expect no further help. It stood to reason that to have any hope to hold out the defenders must tap every possible resource, remove any lingering obstruction. The more perceptive could have drawn this conclusion a month earlier. One study suggested "Whether the island could fight off a siege would depend on the effectiveness of its civil defence. Under the circumstances, only total mobilization of all resources and manpower could stave off the approaching catastrophe."[2] But for Singapore in 1942 it does not fit the facts. The final battle did expose the failure to mobilize Malaya for total war. But what if the British had thrust aside all qualms, overcome all obstacles and fully mobilized the country? That would not have stopped this enemy from isolating Singapore.

And once isolated, the island must fall. Nor could a popular rally to the barricades have changed the outcome. Great Power armies could be slowed but not stopped by such resistance, a fact demonstrated more than once since Paris in 1871. Nevertheless, the siege of Singapore should not be written off as mere anti-climax. This last fight was short but sharp. It produced myths that still cloud our understanding of why imperial defence failed in the Far East. It should be seen as a microcosm of the campaign.

This microcosm can be brought out by examining three points. First, the effort to coordinate military and civil operations and mobilize all resources was less successful than it could have been. But there were more reasons than usually cited and it mattered less than often argued. Second, preparations for battle reflected the whole campaign. The Japanese enjoyed advantages of position, morale and firepower. They needed to solve problems posed by logistics, a tight timetable and barely adequate numbers. The defenders remained numerous, still had firepower and some will to fight. But they had no real support, and a weak tactical position forced them to adopt an impractical plan. Finally, the Japanese paid a price for taking a calculated risk, but reaped the greater reward of rapid victory–whereas the defenders broke under relentless pressure and unravelled from within. Wavell wanted Malaya Command to fight on for at least two months.[3] The defenders could not manage more than two weeks. Their surrender finally shattered the wishful thinking the British Empire in Asia could be defended by pretense and improvisation. This was fitting, because that wishful thinking turned defeat into disaster.

15

Siege

Malaya Command assumed direct responsibility for the defence of Singapore island on 30 January 1942. That same day the navy handed over the base at Sembawang, while the air force retained only one fighter squadron. This left the army in control, but Percival now had to combine Command, Corps and Fortress headquarters to execute a new plan, dividing the island into separate areas of responsibility. Sorting out civil-military relations proved an even greater challenge. The politics of Malaya always complicated its defence. With the army forced back to the metropolis this complication became acute. While civil-military friction did not in the end decide the battle, it did help explain why things ended as they did.

The problem started at the very top and is often described as a feud between Shenton Thomas and Duff Cooper. While they did clash, there was more to it. In theory there was an instrument by which the different authorities defending Singapore could pull together: the Far East War Council. There, nearly every morning, the Governor and his Secretary for Defence met with the Minister Resident, the military commanders if available, and Bowden. Unfortunately they failed to make the Council an effective instrument, for three reasons: the rift between Cooper and Thomas, chronic friction between civil and military authorities, and the local government's attitude to problems of mobilization. But there was an underlying problem: the British government failed to set clear imperatives.

The British government must be faulted for allowing relations between Cooper and Thomas to become a problem. Appointing Cooper Minister Resident but leaving Thomas the constitutional executive made it all but certain they would clash over what to do and how to do it. Cooper had great influence but no clear powers. The disagreement over the evacuation of Penang started the rift. Thomas was widely criticized on the grounds the civil government was obstructing the war effort because it would not set aside cautious procedures by which it took executive action in peacetime. But Thomas had at least one friend, Brooke-Popham, who worked with him to contain Cooper. The issue came to a head shortly after Brooke-Popham left, when Cooper on his own initiative appointed Simson Director-General of Civil Defence, with full powers to requisition resources to bolster civil defences in Johore and Singapore. Thomas fought back, revoking Simson's authority in Johore and refusing to replace officials Simson insisted were inefficient. When Wavell arrived a few days later, his appointment made Cooper's post redundant–but allowed Cooper to put his case to the new Supreme Commander. Wavell had to decide whether or not to replace Thomas, perhaps by appointing a Military Governor in Singapore.[1]

Wavell decided not to do either, perhaps a blessing considering his choice for Military Governor would have been Bennett! But he did sack the official Cooper and Simson identified as the most obstructive: Stanley Jones, the Colonial Secretary. Thomas appeared to take this clear warning to heart by making a resounding public proclamation to his officials on 15 January, ordering them to set aside "red tape" procedure, take responsibility, act boldly and directly. This attempt to imitate the Prime Minister's "action this day" approach did not impress the Straits Times, which dismissed it as too little too late to produce the necessary response from a hidebound civil service. The newspaper turned out to be right when Thomas made little real effort to force his people to throw caution to the winds.[2] By the time the siege began, mistrust between the military, civil service and population was widespread.

On paper all government departments had plans to deal with problems they expected to face in war, ranging from air raid protection through stockpiling and rationing, fire fighting, law and order, even traffic control. These plans did not stand up well to the test of war, because too many officials were more concerned about process than results. The Governor set the pace. He was patriotic and conscientious, but painfully aware of the delicate political balance on which the administration of these fragile colonies rested. That made him reluctant to depart from the civil service instinct to disturb the status quo as little as possible. New arrangements were made to expand protection against air raids and provide more labour for defence works. When neither produced any improvement criticism from European residents only made matters worse.[3] The frustration boiled over into a clash of personalities–but London's indecision and the question of how to deal with the great majority of the population were the real problems.

The consequences of indecision came out most clearly over the order to deny resources to the enemy. The directive sent to Singapore in December took as its example the Soviet strategy of "scorched earth": to destroy by any possible means all resources and equipment the advancing enemy might seize and use. This went beyond destroying military stores. In any case the armed forces failed so miserably to do even that their "Churchill supplies" reduced the Japanese logistics problem from dangerous to difficult. And the Far East War Council diluted the directive in practice, preventing the destruction of food stocks, essential services and Asian owned businesses. Hoping to avoid another Penang style fiasco, London sent pointed reminders as the enemy advanced. The COS put Percival on the spot on 20 January by asking him to personally guarantee no useful booty would be left to the enemy in Singapore. On 2 February he replied. Malaya Command was ordered to hold Singapore to the last, but also to make sure "in the last resort complete scorched earth policy is carried out." This could only be guaranteed if started now, before the battle interfered. But that would both remove equipment needed for the defence and "undermine the morale of both troops and public as to prejudice seriously our ability to hold Singapore." This was a question of higher policy only London could settle. The British government sent a comprehensive directive to the government of Burma on how to apply an effective "scorched earth" policy: carefully plan in advance, rigorously apply in practice, persuade the public such measures are a necessary last resort, selectively destroy those things most useful to the enemy, but be ruthless with things slated for destruction. But Percival received only a feeble reply on 6 February. Yes, fighting to the finish came first, but all possible preparations must now be made to deny vital resources to the enemy, especially naval facilities and coastal artillery. As far as the COS were concerned "we think that preparations for these most important demolitions can be made forthwith, since the sites are in forbidden areas."[4]

Percival won this debate but his victory was hollow. London's assumption preparations could be kept secret was of course naive,[5] but more important it sidestepped Percival's key point: the impact of drastic measures on the Asian population. This was the cardinal issue in mobilization. The army, local government and European civilians widely agreed taking drastic measures to defend the country would disrupt and therefore alarm the Asian population. This could provoke serious unrest and jeopardize the prestige on which British control ultimately rested. This raised the question of what mattered more. Was it to preserve the impression the British were in control and all would be well, even by neglecting steps that could strengthen the defence against Japanese attack? Or was it to do whatever could be done to bolster that defence, even if it meant admitting the British were in trouble? Only the British government could make that call. It did not do so. That left Singapore authorities to follow their own inclinations. This produced serious friction, wasted effort and lasting bitterness.

Thomas remained inclined not to rock the boat but resented the roasting he received from prominent Asian civilians over the Penang evacuation. This made him loath to pressure either his own officials or Asian leaders. Special Branch took it upon itself to bring the squabbling Chinese factions together, with little help from the Governor. This was important because the Chinese were by far the most promising reservoir of anti-Japanese support, especially in Singapore. But the Chinese Protectorate would not set aside its reluctance to galvanize Chinese assistance for fear this would strengthen the MCP. This no longer made sense. They were a distant threat–the Japanese were hammering on the door. This attitude only antagonized Chinese leaders. When Simson took on the extra post, in addition to his job as Chief Engineer Malaya Command, things only got worse. F.D Bisseker, a prominent businessman and member of the legislature, was appointed his deputy. There was bad blood between him and the civil service because he frequently criticized government policies in the legislature. Thomas blamed Bisseker for leading what the Governor termed the "scuttle" from Penang. Jones flatly refused to help because Bisseker was involved; Thomas tolerated this. Meanwhile Japanese air attacks escalated. The government decision before the war not to provide extensive air raid shelters now backfired, especially when the population increased. When the government belatedly decided to build shelters wholesale after all, on 7 February, the general reaction was scorn.[6]

The problem became acute on the most obvious point: how could the Chinese be mobilized to assist the war effort? Every British military officer and civilian official in Singapore understood the importance of the Chinese. In Malaya and Singapore they were the urban working class. They alone could provide the numbers needed to perform essential services of the war economy. The Malay and Indian populations were more rural, less involved in occupations directly useful to the war effort, correctly seen as generally less inclined to be anti-Japanese. In addition to the sabotage groups organized by the OM, Special Branch efforts led to the organization in January of a force of Chinese irregular volunteers. The military labelled it Dalforce after its prime organizer, Lt.-Col. Dalley. It attracted 4000 recruits but by this time Malaya Command could offer little more than "elementary" training and "firearms of sorts." Nevertheless this force prepared for battle with real resolve. This provoked criticism that the army neglected a vital pool of manpower by doing so little to develop the standing Volunteer forces, then resorting to such hasty expedients. Percival insisted they could never attract the authorized quota of Chinese for the Volunteer battalions. Chinese leaders replied this was because the real policy was a racially driven determination to keep any military role for their community to a bare minimum.[7] Whatever the truth, there is no doubt the authorities in Singapore struggled to overcome qualms about relying on the Chinese population even though they knew they had no choice. Nowhere was this more obvious than on the issue of manual labour.

This problem had a more direct impact on the defence of Singapore, and caused more acrimony, than all other mobilization issues combined. After Percival decided to take matters into his own hands and increase pay rates to attract more men, the WO and the local government both undermined his initiative by not supporting it. The agreement to give priority to airbase construction and repair absorbed scarce labour until the last days of January. Problems in organization made matters worse. Even after Simson's new appointment Malaya Command retained a Directorate of Labour that competed with the new office for an inadequate supply. The navy jealously guarded its large pool of more than 10,000 workers doing who knew what. Heavier Japanese air attacks caused damage that provoked demands for labour to do everything under the sun, at once–just as the army desperately called for workers to build more field defences.[8] Under the circumstances it would have taken a first rate organization which knew exactly how best to tap into the local population to come close to meeting the demand. No such existed and the main reason was attitude.

The problem that most exercised the authorities was the tendency of local labourers not just to run for cover when attacked by Japanese bombers but then fail to return to work. There were often practical explanations for this. Chinese workers needed the same things other workers needed: leaders in whom they had confidence, arrangements for shelter they could trust, decent food and lodging or transport, enough pay to provide for their family. Some senior military and civilian personnel realized the only way to secure enough labourers and keep them on the job was to work through prominent Chinese leaders who would do the actual organizing. But they could not overcome the tendency to assume Asian labourers were unreliable under fire because they were Asian, not because they were scared of being bombed and saw nothing being done to protect them. Simson and Bisseker resorted to improvising, working especially with a prominent young Chinese businessman named Lim Bo Seng. Simson credited Lim with working tirelessly and investing a great deal of his own money to provide as many labourers as possible. Lim, Tan Kah Kee and other prominent Chinese working through the Chinese Mobilization Council also arranged for volunteers to bolster fire fighting and medical services, improve air raid protection facilities, help maintain law and order and rally support for the war in the Chinese community. The Chinese community as a whole behaved very much as nearly every community under fire in the Second World War behaved. It displayed the gamut of human reactions, ranging from great heroism to rank cowardice and profiteering, but in general endured stoically and responded to whatever lead it received.[9]

Sadly, too little of this impressed itself on the army or government at the time. In fact this demonstration of self-sufficiency by the Chinese made some officials nervous. Despite the very real affection most had for the country, the European community on the whole could not set aside the prejudice Asian civilians were unreliable under fire. This prevented them from seeing the real reason many organizations started to buckle when enemy pressure became intense. Asian police officers, railway workers, volunteers and labourers were not stupid. When they concluded those directing them had no real idea what to do, not a few took matters into their own hands. When Singapore came under siege the problem became severe. There were never enough men to work on defences far from finished and now under direct enemy fire. The port facilities were attacked so heavily the Singapore Harbour Board labour force all but melted away. Percival and many others assumed this was because it was Asian. Another British officer sensibly if condescendingly noted even European labour "will not stand up to it unless shelter is available when bombs are actually falling"! Whatever the cause, this forced Malaya Command to send combat troops to work on the docks, in addition to working on their own defences. Services in Singapore continued to function, but the siege quickly pushed them towards the breaking point.[10]

There were exceptions in all communities, but most people in Singapore under siege wanted to do all they could to fend off the enemy. Unfortunately, most of those willing to take any initiative did not have enough authority to change the situation; most of those who did were reluctant to try. Simson later argued it took three years to prepare a civilian population for total war. That might have been true in a homogenous country whose people shared a common sense of identity and an instinctive attachment to their land. Neither condition prevailed in Malaya and Singapore. Even the Chinese were more inclined to focus on loyalty to China's war than loyalty to Malaya; Lim Bo Seng was a KMT officer who saw himself as fighting China's war in Singapore. Not much more could have been done, barring a sea change in British attitudes, to mobilize a mixed Asian colonial population. Politics again drove defence. The British preferred to defend the country without trying to harness its full potential; by December 1941 it was too late to reconsider. European civilians, shattered by defeat on the mainland, did more turning on the army in recrimination than rallying to its side. The most visible sign of crisis was the death toll inflicted by Japanese attacks. By the time the siege began it was at least 150 civilians a day, too many to clear quickly from the streets. This all made Singapore feel more like a burden than a refuge to the army.[11] More truly alone than ever, Malaya Command prepared to fight its last and most difficult battle.

After the war Yamashita admitted he hoped not to have to attack across the Straits of Johore and fight for Singapore. Anticipating "serious resistance"

Twenty-Fifth Army prepared accordingly. Three problems needed to be solved. First, the timetable remained tight; two infantry companies were already withdrawn to be rebuilt for the next offensive, scheduled to begin that month in Sumatra. Such further commitments ruled out starving Singapore to death by methodical siege, but made economy of force as important as ever. Second, supply lines were very strained, but the army needed more firepower to deliver the *coup de grace* and could not pause to sort out its logistics. Yamashita decided to proceed even though only one battalion of 3rd Guards Regiment arrived to join the fight; the other two were in Saigon waiting for transport. Finally, this final battle plan was not inherited from higher headquarters but drafted by Twenty-Fifth Army itself. This aggravated friction with Southern Army and Nishimura, both of whom chafed at some provisions.[12] Yamashita and his staff tackled these problems the same way they overran Malaya: accepting intelligent calculated risks, making professional preparations, aligning the strategic aim with the tactical problem.

The Japanese objective was unchanged: conquer Singapore as quickly and cheaply as possible. This was now refined to a target date: 11 February, a national holiday known as Kigensetsu, anniversary of the accession of the semi-legendary Emperor Jinnu. A pause was unavoidable because the army could not simply bounce across the Straits of Johore, 700 metres wide at the narrowest point. Combat units needed to be reinforced and redeployed, air units moved forward, heavy artillery brought into position, essential equipment such as assault boats, rafts and ammunition brought in. But the pause must be as brief as possible, because the "driving charge" must continue. In addition to tightly stretched supply lines there were two tactical concerns, both threatening to produce heavy casualties. The army must establish a beachhead on the island by amphibious assault, then force a final surrender before Malaya Command could retreat into the city to fight it out street by street.[13]

Japanese intelligence remained generally good. The Japanese knew 18th Division had just reached Singapore and were aware of the scale and location of the island's coastal artillery. They identified two "switch lines" being prepared to block the approaches to the town from west and east and took careful measure of the terrain and field defences on the north coast. Tsuji insisted the Japanese were surprised but delighted by how hastily improvised these last defences were; he criticized failure to prepare stronger ones as shocking neglect, for which however he wrongly singled out Governor Thomas. The two regiments of medium artillery were now reinforced for this last fight by 2nd Independent Heavy Artillery Regiment, equipped with 5.9" guns, directly under Army control. This gave Yamashita 168 medium and heavy guns.

They joined the air forces in an escalating bombardment designed to pave the way for the amphibious crossing. The key targets were airbases, coastal and field artillery, field defences and petrol stocks. The Japanese expected to face mines and other underwater obstacles and were concerned the British might prepare traps by draining pools of petrol into the Straits and igniting them. The bombardment began on 4 February, supported by an observation balloon hoisted over Johore Bahru. There were however two errors in Japanese intelligence, both of which later caused difficulty. They estimated Percival's force as no more than 30,000 combat troops, only half his true strength, nearly all of whom they believed to be British and Australian–also way off. And the relatively feeble response from the defenders artillery persuaded them the enemy guns had been suppressed–an error that later forced them to cope with an unwelcome surprise.[14]

There was no way to outflank the island's defences. They must be stormed. Yamashita's final plans were something of a compromise, but not on the crux of the matter: the army would establish a beachhead by throwing its main force into an all-out night assault across the narrow stretch of the Straits of Johore west of the causeway, on the northwest and west coast of the island. The attack would be carried out by 5th and 18th Divisions; 16 battalions would cross the first night, in three waves. It would be preceded by a day long bombardment by all supporting artillery. It would be protected by deceptions to convince the enemy the main attack would be made east of the causeway. These included careful movement by night into staging areas, forcible eviction of all civilians from the Johore coast, and a feint attack by the Imperial Guards Division on Pulau Ubin. Yamashita personally went over the plan with all his battalion commanders. His army now fielded 27 infantry battalions, supported by tanks, artillery, specialist amphibious, engineer and anti-epidemic medical units, and some 140 aircraft forward deployed.[15]

The Japanese saw this for what it was: a river crossing–over tidal salt water to be sure, but a river nonetheless. They were equipped for and experienced at such operations. The plan focused on solving the two tactical problems. The assault posed two dangers: the open water was a killing zone in which troops in canvas-sided assault boats would be very vulnerable, while the coast was dominated by a belt of mangrove swamp, sometimes hundreds of metres wide. The first danger would be met by rushing across in concentrated force, to overwhelm the defenders at the point of attack. To meet the second, junior officers were directed to lead their assault platoons straight into the darkest patches of mangrove. The Japanese had a pretty good picture of the coastal defences. They were based on denying likely landing points and penetration routes by concentrating infantry companies at defended localities. In the chosen area these strongpoints were widely separated in close country. The Japanese decided to penetrate between them. That meant struggling through difficult country, but also promised better cover. The plan aimed to provoke confusion if not chaos, which should work to the advantage of the attackers as their following waves came across. The second problem was to finish the enemy off before the fight could drift into the city. Yamashita planned to accomplish that by seizing the high ground around Bukit Timah, which would give him control of the vital supply dumps, a chokehold on the reservoirs, and provide a dominant observation post from which to direct pulverizing fire on the city. This would be done by 11 February; Percival was expected to surrender when he lost the crucial high ground.[16]

On the whole this was a good plan, especially for the initial assault. When difficult swamp terrain delayed the assembly of his assault force, Yamashita made two sensible adjustments. First he cut the attack front in half. Now it ran from Lim Chu Kang at the northwestern corner of the island to the Berih River, some 10 km long. That put two of his divisions against one Australian brigade. Second he delayed the operation for a day, pushing it back to the night of 8/9 February. Moreover, the swamps on their side also helped conceal the Japanese. Plantation roads allowed the engineers to bring boats and equipment down to the assembly areas. These were along the banks of two rivers, the Skudai and the Melayu, which ran into the Straits at an angle that concealed their course upriver from the Australians on the other side. This allowed the Japanese to assemble their assault forces right in front of the target area, while air cover kept prying eyes away. On the other hand Nishimura's jealousy forced Yamashita to make a less wise adjustment. The original idea was that after their feint the Imperial Guards would cross on the second and third days behind the main force, coming in in reserve. This would also minimize the strain on the supply of assault boats. That second fiddle role annoyed Nishimura so much that to placate him Yamashita agreed the Guards could launch their own assault on the second night. They would attack just west of the causeway, then advance south towards the high ground. This would form a converging attack, meeting the main thrust from the west around Bukit Timah. That could spread the defences, but would also severely tax the amphibious engineers. This was a bit riskier than necessary, while Yamashita's hope Percival would simply surrender once he lost Bukit Timah was a little wishful. If he did not, the Japanese would have to make a possibly costly general assault on the city.[17]

Yamashita knew he would take Singapore. A large expeditionary force was preparing to move against nearby Sumatra even as he prepared his own battle. Had he needed help to overwhelm Singapore he would have had it.

But his challenge was to win without help, ahead of schedule and without a high price. That meant storming the island yet avoiding heavy losses. The concentrated assault was the best choice he could have made, while longer delay would have helped Malaya Command more than his own army. The real risk was the supply situation. 3rd Air Group now had squadrons at Kluang, but admitted it was only "almost possible to meet the requirements of the operations." Churchill's vision of this siege belonged to an era when duelling heavy artillery settled a siege. Airpower made that obsolete. But the Prime Minister did sense one valid point. Bringing in enough firepower and ammunition to overwhelm the island's defences would strain Japanese supply lines severely if they did not pause to build up stocks. Yamashita's staff calculated the artillery ammunition on hand as 10.5 standard loads. They needed 1.5 for the prior bombardment, 4 for the assault, 2.5 for the advance to Bukit Timah. That left less than a quarter for reserve.[18]

The Guards launched their feint on 7 February. The bombardment damaged many of Singapore's petrol storage tanks, sending huge columns of black smoke billowing high into the sky, hanging like a shroud over the island. Yamashita moved into the Sultan of Johore's residence, the Istana Bukit Serene, which boasts a five storey tower providing direct observation over the coast his main force prepared to assault. From there he could encourage his men and intervene if necessary. Labouring mightily, his engineers dragged assault boats and barges to the assembly points. Meanwhile the army artillery pounded the island, especially the Australian positions just across the water.[19] The battle now hinged on a space not more than 600 metres wide: the final approach to the island and the first 300 metres inland. If the assault forces made it through without crippling losses, they could establish a beachhead too strong to repel. The end would then be quick.

Percival also saw that 600 metre strip as the area where the battle would be decided. Wavell saw it this way:

> Much depended on the ability of the garrison of Singapore Island to make a prolonged resistance. General Percival had the 18th British Division practically intact, the 8th Australian Division of two brigades at good strength after arrival of reinforcements, and the equivalent of some four or five brigades of mixed British and Indian infantry, besides local forces. In view of the size of the island ... this force was obviously weak in numbers, but the enemy could not employ large forces, and I considered that an active defence should enable the island to be held for some time, for some months I hoped.

Wavell not only hoped he planned–planned to build up in Java and Sumatra while the Japanese bogged down in a three month siege of Singapore. Percival planned accordingly. This gave him no choice between keeping most of his army inland in reserve or deploying it on the coast to repel any landing outright. The island was too small, the army too weak and disorganized. Only a successful coastal stand could buy any real time. The plan itself shrank down to meet the Japanese at the 600 metre belt.[20]

Percival's most important decision was to appreciate where the main enemy assault would come. His entire defence plan was shaped by inaccurate intelligence. Malaya Command decided Yamashita had five divisions available with another moving forward. The real figures were less than three divisions with no reserves at hand. Japanese preparations to invade Sumatra were seen as threats to Singapore. This all persuaded Percival to make each sector of the island coastline as strong as possible, hoping each force could either repel an invasion or pin it down long enough for the army to counterattack. The most likely approach was across the narrow Straits of Johore, but would the attack come east or west of the causeway? The ground to the east was easier to penetrate, with better road access to the city. It could be approached by a force coming straight down the Johore River, a threat Percival identified during his first posting in Singapore before the war. And Malaya Command did not know the Japanese could move their vehicle-carrying boats by road, so they concluded it was more likely the enemy would bring them to the more accessible Johore River. The ground west of the causeway was harder to penetrate but farther from the coastal defence guns, and the Straits were narrower. Wavell suggested the Japanese main attack would come there and urged Percival to deploy his strongest force to face it. Both agreed 18th Division was that force. But Percival inclined to think the attack would come in the northeast. Wavell did not insist.[21]

The final retreat to Singapore provoked Bowden to doubt the British were ever serious about trying to hold it. When Spooner told him the naval base would be demolished when the army reached the island the Australian concluded that would leave Singapore with nothing more than "sentimental value," for which the British would not fight. That was wrong, but Bowden was not the only doubter. The most prominent skeptic was Churchill himself. On 1 February the Prime Minister asked for a report on the losses of men and equipment on the mainland. The next day, provoked by Wavell's decision to withdraw all but one squadron from Singapore, he asked him to explain this move "which appears, at first sight, to indicate despair of defending Singapore."[22]

Percival took up the challenge to convince all and sundry the fight would continue. Malaya Command issued this proclamation on 1 February:

The battle of Malaya has come to an end and the battle of Singapore has started ... Our task is to hold this fortress until help can come–as assuredly it will come. This we are determined to do. In carrying out this task we want the help of every man and woman in the fortress. There is work for all to do. Any enemy who sets foot in our fortress must be dealt with immediately. The enemy within our gates must be ruthlessly weeded out. There must be no more loose talk and rumour-mongering. Our duty is clear. With firm resolve and fixed determination we shall win through.

This was little more than bravado but it tells us more about the situation than about Percival, whose personal resolve was unswerving. Help was not coming, could not come, and he knew it. But if he said so frankly, then asked his troops and a million civilians to sacrifice themselves for the Empire, the defence would collapse then and there. The real challenge was to translate these strong words into action on the ground. This did not find Percival at his best. At an unfortunate press conference on 5 February the GOC, never the most charismatic figure, gave many the impression there was no drive from the top.[23]

Wavell replied to the Prime Minister on 3 February, explaining the fighters had to go to Sumatra because the bases on Singapore were now in range of Japanese artillery. ABDA Command believed the Japanese were stretching their airpower very thin and if the Allies could build up their own they might knock them off balance. The next day Wavell indicated reinforcements would now be sent to Dutch ports, because Singapore was cut off. Any attempt to get through would have to be "a special operation." Churchill argued the toss, suggesting a more determined fight for Singapore would keep Japanese airpower more effectively distracted from Sumatra. This ignored the cardinal point, the fact Singapore was now under direct ground fire. But Wavell took the hint, asking the COS on 8 February to tell him the "general outline of allied plan for defeat of Japan," assuring them his own staff were already working on counteroffensive plans. Pownall accepted the fact the Japanese would go all out to take Singapore, for the very reason Churchill remained determined to hold it: Singapore was "a big political objective." In that context it did not pay to look defeatist. Bennett chafed at what he saw as "usual British negative attitude." But his own suggestion on 4 February was as flawed as Churchill's, with less excuse: "Consider best policy is strong counter offensive as soon as reinforcements of aircraft and quality troops can be arranged." And how were such reinforcements to run the gauntlet now thrown around Singapore?[24]

Percival's first order regarding the defence of Singapore against attack from the north was issued on 23 December. The basis of the tactical plan went back to the first reconnaissance order, issued on 9 January. It emerged in full outline on 23 January when Malaya Command issued orders for "Protracted Defence of Singapore Island." The objective was to deny Singapore Fortress. The strategy was to repel invasion at the coastline, or pin it down long enough to allow other forces to counterattack it into the sea. The tactics were spelt out clearly, just as the Japanese appreciated them:

> The Northern and Western shores of the island are too intersected with creeks and mangroves for any recognized form of beach defence. The general plan in each area will therefore include small defended localities to cover known approaches, such as rivers, creeks and roads to the coast or tracks along which vehicles can travel. These localities will be supported by mobile reserves in suitable assembly areas, from which they can operate against enemy parties seeking to infiltrate near these communications or in the intervening country.[25]

Given the terrain this made tactical sense. The trick, as always, was to make it happen in practice. There were two inherent weaknesses in the plan: the foremost line of defence and the counterattack.

Mixing it up with Japanese infantry in close country was asking for trouble. That made it all the more important to hold at the water's edge. The best way to do that was to hammer the enemy very hard where he was most vulnerable: crossing the water. That, as always, left the decisive role to the artillery. Malaya Command decided that to fight a three month defensive battle it must ration artillery fire, to conserve ammunition. It imposed a daily quota of rounds per gun, not to be passed on day to day. The quota went down from as many as 30 to as few as 10 rounds, but there was a nuance not properly explained. The quota only applied to harassing fire before the invasion started. Once the enemy invaded it would automatically lapse. Many instead saw the restriction as further evidence of weakness at the top. Percival's decision to spread his field artillery out, so all coastal sectors could call for at least moderate support, was riskier. This meant no one sector would be able to bring down overwhelming fire now or never. Unfortunately that was just what the tactical situation would demand, because the Japanese were bound to concentrate on one area.[26]

All brigades were ordered to fight in place, to the death, if their area was invaded. Once the main invasion was identified the army would counterattack to repel the enemy. Prepared counterattacks require liaison between the unit in place and the units coming in, plus reconnaissance by the latter. The only such reconnaissance laid on was by the formation that became command reserve: 12th Indian Brigade, or what was left of it. It was scheduled to practice with 22nd Australian Brigade–on 9 February. Percival drew a distinction between counterattacks. Only the reserve force close to hand, the area reserve, could deliver an immediate counterattack; he directed each area to hold one battalion ready. The command reserve would launch any "general"counterattack. But the size and terrain of the island made it impractical to launch any such attack in larger than brigade strength. In fact neither would be strong enough to repel the kind of attack the Japanese were planning. And Percival's argument about the general counterattack is not convincing. There is more than enough room on the island for a larger movement. On the other hand a brigade sized reserve was all he could organize, because he wanted to hold all coastal sectors in strength. This looks like making a virtue out of necessity. The only kind of counterattack that made any sense once the Japanese got past the coast defences was a general advance: Malaya Command had to be ready to strip other coastal sectors, to send at least a division marching to the guns. But the switch lines made it look more likely there would be yet another retreat. And in fact all the GOC intended was to rebuild his command reserve by gathering detachments from sectors not yet attacked. Percival's subordinates drew their own conclusion about his plan.[27]

Malaya Command cobbled together its plan to hold the island in as much haste as the Japanese planned to take it. The first obstacle was fallout from the disaster in Johore. The defence plan divided the island into four areas: Southern Area, covering the city and south coast from the Jurong River to Changi; Northern Area, stretching from Changi to a point just east of the causeway and covering the naval base; Western Area, running from the causeway around to the Jurong River; and a Reserve Area in the centre, covering the high ground, reservoirs and large supply dumps. In the original plan Percival wanted to use 53rd Brigade as command reserve until the remainder of 18th Division arrived. Then he intended to send III Indian Corps into reserve and deploy the fresh British formation on the coast. But the disbanding of 9th Indian Division ruled this out. 18th Division had to move right into the front line. 11th Indian Division absorbed 8th Indian Brigade but stayed in the front line. Percival assigned III Indian Corps to command Northern Area. Heath had only the depleted 15th Indian Brigade for an area reserve. Malaya Command's central reserve was reduced from at least two full brigades to the reforming 12th Indian Brigade, barely 1200 strong. 2nd Argylls were somewhat revived, but the other two battalions were so diluted with raw replacements they were not fit to fight. The "main battle" defeat in Johore cost Percival the reserves his plan needed to make any sense at all.[28] Now the only real chance he had to influence the battle was to send the army marching to the guns.

The disaster in Johore also possibly persuaded Percival not to take

Wavell's suggestion to disband III Indian Corps headquarters and send Heath out of Singapore. Once Malaya Command took direct control, it no longer needed a corps headquarters between it and the different areas. But one suspects the GOC remained unsure how to handle the large but now badly disrupted Indian contingent.[29] Dalforce would have been best used broken into small detachments to provide local expertise to assist regular formations, especially the fresh 18th Division. The original idea was not far from that: to place Dalforce detachments in areas the enemy might try to infiltrate, watching the flank of the nearest regular unit. Some volunteers were assigned to regular brigades. But the rest were assigned to cover areas such as a swampy patch on the north coast just west of the Kranji River, between the positions taken up by the two Australian brigades. This took too many away from direct liaison with regular brigades and left too few to survive any serious attack. Spoiling raids to disrupt Japanese preparations were an obvious tactic. The Independent Company was ordered to launch such raids– but also to guard oil refineries on the small island of Pulau Bukom, south of Singapore. The poorly trained SSVF covered the city itself. But the rest of the south coast was held by two regular formations, 1st and 2nd Malaya Brigades, the heart of the Singapore garrison. Their Southern Area sectors were already well protected by the fixed defences–coastal artillery and a chain of machine gun pillboxes, stretching from Changi to the Jurong River. Percival distrusted intelligence assurances the Japanese forces at sea were aiming for Sumatra, not Singapore. Nevertheless, leaving five battalions of regular infantry to guard a coast already protected by defences designed to repel attack from the sea was double-locking the back door. Given how thinly stretched the battalions on the north coast were, and how small the vital command reserve was, this made little sense.[30]

The general understanding in the ranks was that the fighting retreat on the mainland was akin to a huge skirmishers patrol. They had to do the dangerous work of falling back through the countryside fighting all the way, but once they made it to the fortress all would be well. The gates would slam shut behind them. The walls would be stout. The guns would keep the enemy at bay while they rested. Then they would man the ramparts. This of course turned out to be fantasy. Units of the garrison and the Fortress Engineers worked on island defences from 1939–on the south coast. The CRE Fortress logged more than 1100 messages in the two months before the siege began. Many complained of problems with labour, obstruction from the civil government, shortage of transport. But only one came from a brigade asking for help for coast defences–on the south coast.[31]

Late January was too late to erect serious defences on the north coast, but we can not just dismiss this as moot. This had a serious effect on the most important defence preparation: to rebuild the army as an army. This was already going to be a real challenge. Once the army took stock of the situation its reaction made it impossible. Four factors did the damage: air and artillery defences, the fate of the naval base, the state of the field defences and the condition of the combat units. Malaya Command remained a collection of battalions with very little mutual confidence left. Once again the more serious crisis came higher up the chain of command. But this time the price was terminal, especially for the Australians.

The erosion of confidence was revealed by a discussion on what should have been a detail handled by the local command: the tactical defence of the island. Simson drafted detailed instructions about field defences, but when Malaya Command moved too slowly for his liking he passed his ideas on to Cooper. Cooper passed them to Churchill and the COS, who sent them back to Wavell and Percival! The general idea was to build well concealed and strongly entrenched company positions, covered by wire entanglements, which could put up an all round defence and dominate landing points and routes of penetration by fire. Such areas should also be blocked by wire, mines, booby traps "or any other means possible." Simson especially intended that to include pools of flaming petrol in the water, a technique prepared for coastal defence in the U.K. Other pointers included warnings about night attack, Japanese mobility and "unlikely landing places," and internal threats from the "fifth column." These ideas were already taking root in Malaya Command, but this begs the question: if his superiors thought Percival needed such detailed advice, why leave him in charge?[32]

The issue flared up on 9 January when Wavell visited the northern coast with Percival and asked why there were no field defences. This meeting is controversial. One story has Percival saying he feared building defences would be bad for morale. A furious Wavell pointed out morale would suffer even more when the Japanese poured across an undefended causeway. There is scant direct evidence for this exchange and it seems unlikely Percival would not mention the mission to hold the naval base as a motive. But he and Thomas did repeatedly express concern about undermining confidence in the army and population and Percival later rightly complained it was hard to build defences when work had to be done in secret–Wavell's standing order before the final retreat began. Whatever the case Wavell certainly ordered work to start and Malaya Command did lurch forward that same day.[33] But when Paris took charge two weeks later "not a trench had been dug (except for a few by 2 MIB) [2nd Malaya Brigade, near Changi] not a coil of wire had been deployed" and he had no field engineers. When the combat units took over a week later,

Paris presented them layouts for artillery and anti-tank positions, "a start" of anti-tank ditches near the causeway and "in front of the Jurong position"–the western switch line–work underway to plant flame obstacles and depth charges in major creeks and "positions mainly dug, partially cleared and wired." He admitted more progress was made in Northern than Western Area. Stocks included 10 Beach Electric Lights, 2500 anti-tank mines plus another 15,000 "in a few days," and more than 1000 booby traps. The navy provided 24 boats of various types for patrolling, a "large quantity" of explosives for demolition work and a plan to wreck the naval base. But Paris had only a patchwork labour force made up of detachments from 44th Indian Brigade, a pioneer battalion, some 400 Chinese labourers and "a certain number" of construction machines. Very few battalion officers scouted their areas before the army arrived. That added up to a not surprising result: the combat troops decided the work done on the ground was nowhere near enough.[34]

The virtual withdrawal of the air force further discouraged the troops. Eight Hurricanes and six Buffaloes were left to cover Singapore as the seige began, to be maintained by drawing on squadrons now in Sumatra. The Buffaloes were soon worn down but the heavily outnumbered Hurricane squadron fought on. This became harder when Japanese artillery fire forced Pulford to abandon all airbases except the civil station at Kallang, near the city, from 4 February. Two days later Kallang came under fire, making sorties even more adventurous. Churchill's pressure only complicated things. Wavell rescinded permission for Pulford to shift his headquarters to Sumatra. RAF Far East would stay in Singapore; more Hurricanes would fly in from Sumatra to help. But enemy pressure was too strong. No new fighters came in. Those on hand could not prevent the sinking of the *Empress of Asia* on 5 February, taking much of 18th Division's equipment with her. The only reason more ships were not lost was the Japanese did not try harder to get them. Bombers, including US Army Air Force B17s, continued to raid the mainland, but the troops could not see this so they were not encouraged. What they saw was the Japanese pummelling Singapore. All its relatively lavish anti-aircraft defences–six regiments, with some 140 guns of various calibres–could do was force them to bomb from higher altitude. All available reconnaissance aircraft were employed tracking the Japanese fleet, whose approach kept Percival anxious about the south coast. That left Malaya Command only one stripped-down Buffalo to call on for reconnaissance over Johore. Its last report was made on 4 February. On 7 February at 1238hrs Malay Command asked for a flight over all roads in southern Johore. Reports of sounds of Japanese movements were coming in thick and fast–many of them deceptive measures–and the army needed eyes. Two minutes later the last Buffalo was reported destroyed on the ground.[35]

It is tempting to see that as an epitaph for the air defence of Singapore, but there is a better one. On 1 February an officer in London wrote a paper entitled Some Consequences Resulting From the Failure to Prepare a Plan to Reinforce the RAF in the Far East. It tracked the main bomber reinforcement ordered to the Far East: 52 Hudsons from the U.K. By that date, only 11 had reached Singapore. Some 266 Hurricanes were ordered to the area. Only 99 arrived and not all went into action before Singapore surrendered. The anonymous critic put his finger on the problem: no one ever thought through let alone prepared the myriad technical arrangements needed to move aircraft, crews and ground support such a long distance. The easy assumption reared its head again: when the need arose they would get through somehow.[36] This amateur error condemned Pulford's command to fight against odds too great. Their defeat was more serious because the army was already rattled by defeats in Europe blamed on being naked in the air. The Australians, angered by such defeats in Greece and Crete, made an issue of it up to the highest level. This magnified Japanese superiority, making it seem even more dangerous. Japanese control of the air ruled out any Dunkirk style evacuation of the army or relief from outside. Only the desperate pretended otherwise.

Malaya Command's effort to preserve its artillery also sent mixed signals. How hard should the guns try to disrupt Japanese preparations? What role could the big guns of the coastal defences play? This added up to a central question: should Malaya Command go after the enemy, or wait to be attacked? The defenders boasted 226 guns of all calibres, ranging from old 18pdr. guns used in a direct fire beach defence role to the mighty 15" monster guns of the Fixed Defences. From early January Fixed Defences started to do what it could to bring the coastal guns to bear on targets to the north. The limiting factors were terrain, equipment and the tactical situation. The guns could not be moved and there were only so many good positions available for observation posts. No general artillery plan could be made until the field army arrived on the island. The only guns that could fire on Johore Bahru and the causeway were two of the three 15" guns of the Johore Battery near Changi; the other had an older mounting that restricted its arc of fire. The guns of the Buona Vista battery were blocked by Bukit Timah hill and the other batteries were out of range. Many batteries were protected from air attack by concrete overhead cover. Most now removed it in order to expand their arc of fire, but that of course made them more vulnerable. By such steps four of the 15" guns, all six 9.2" guns and most of the eighteen 6" guns were able to register on at least some targets to the north. But these improvisations could not match the comprehensive preparations to repel attack from the sea. That mission remained operative. Malaya Command duly brought the two Fire Commands into an artillery plan and authorized formation commanders to call for support from the big guns. But they were enjoined not to request such support if field artillery could provide it, so as not to strain the barrels of the coastal guns–and calls for 15" fire had to be made direct to Commander Fixed Defences. He would bear in mind the need to be ready to meet any seaborne attack when considering fire missions. Ammunition was the biggest limiting factor. The armour-piercing rounds held in the magazines were designed to sink ships but were not much use against ground troops; on impact they would bury deep into the ground with a bowel-draining concussion, but probably not harm anyone not right next to them. The high explosive shrapnel spreading rounds that could maim infantrymen were in short supply. The two Fire Commands held only 50 such rounds for each 6" gun, 25 for each 9.2" gun, none at all for the monster guns. A query to the RN turned up one 15" round at the naval base, duly sent to the Johore Battery. Fixed Defences requested a large supply for all calibres, but it was too late. In any case, while the coastal guns could help they were never designed to repel attack from the north.[37]

The artillery plan took that into account by assigning the primary role to the field guns of the nine artillery regiments. 9th Indian Division's gunners were split up. 5th Field Regt. eventually went to Western Area. 8th Australian Division had only its own two field regiments for support, with some 60 guns. Yet the Australians opted out of the overall fire plan, making their own arrangements for observation and counterbattery fire. Northern Area's five field regiments had over 90 guns. 18th Division's artillery commander complained after inspecting the division sector on 31 January "It was apparent that no artillery reconnaissance in which guns would be firing North had been carried out at all." The division lost its anti-tank guns on the *Empress of Asia*.[38] Every unit complained about not having enough good positions and being reined in when the Japanese bombardment started. The most annoying restriction was the order not to fire on Johore Bahru, especially on the tower of an administrative building overlooking the causeway–still standing–that the Japanese adopted as an observation post. This stemmed partly from the policy to conserve ammunition but also partly from the desire not to antagonize either the Sultan or his population, a point pressed hard by Bennett. That restriction was finally lifted on 5 February and at times the Japanese felt themselves to be taking a pounding. But in fact Malaya Command and III Indian Corps kept a tight leash on the artillery duel. They had good reasons: not just to conserve ammunition but also to keep good firing positions concealed for as long as possible. Given how small the island was, the advantage the Japanese had from air observation, and especially the vital role the guns must play to break up any invasion this was fair. Artillery was the most important weapon the defenders had left. Their plan depended on it. Malaya Command opted to let the enemy come rather than seek him out on the mainland.[39]

The handover of the naval base added to the confusion. Spooner reported an evacuation but what really happened was a scuttle. Just how this happened remains unclear. Spooner made it clear by 27 January at the latest that he would hand the base over to the army when they retreated to the island. Yet when the navy left on 30 January the necessary demolitions were far from complete and no arrangements were made for the army to draw on the huge stocks still held on the base. Naval sources later insisted the army ordered them out within six hours and gave the impression they would take responsibility for demolitions. Army sources insisted the navy left without trying to sort any such details out. The large floating dock was sunk, the small floating dock removed to the commercial harbour, the power station, graving dock and pumping machinery were damaged, naval engineers marked what to salvage and what to demolish. But large stocks of materiel, weapons and ammunition remained intact, gates were left unguarded, work was left unfinished on the table. The two services fell out over this fiasco so badly neither buckled down to repair it. When Spooner heard looters were helping themselves he urged Malaya Command to post a guard before the rum could be pillaged. The AIF complained vehicles leaving the base were interfering with their efforts to dig in near the causeway. The naval liaison officer with III Indian Corps went to the base one night to investigate a fire raging near the Stores Basin. When he found the infantry deployed to guard the area, the battalion commander insisted the fire was the navy's responsibility because his men had no idea what was where in the large facility. The same problem impeded efforts by army units to requisition stores themselves, but red tape snarled all efforts to transfer materiel officially. When a salvage party went to the base on the night of 6 February they found row upon row of "some of the most modern and up to date precision plant" left intact. They had to work at night without light, because the base was now under enemy artillery fire. For two months the army was told again and again the reason it fought was to protect that base. Whose fault it was mattered less than the fact stories of how the base was evacuated spread rapidly across the island, losing nothing in the telling.[40]

The circumstances were grim, the challenge formidable—nevertheless the harsh verdict of the ranks was not unfair. No one pulled Malaya Command together as a field army working to a co-ordinated plan. Improvisation was indeed the order of the day. There were not enough anti-boat obstacles, so engineers set petrol traps in the mouths of rivers and creeks. Simson claimed

Malaya Command headquarters obstructed this plan but the unit war diaries do not go that far—engineer companies went ahead on their own as best they could. These traps had to be sprung at the right moment, which meant lighting up the area on command. Sudden illumination was a key beach defence tactic, to catch the enemy on the water. But there were not enough Beach Electric Lights, so the engineers decided to use automobile headlights instead. However the Governor balked at requisitioning private vehicles! By the time he relented it was too late to cover all areas. Simson also claimed he stockpiled large quantities of stores in Western Area, but Malaya Command transferred them to Northern Area and only returned them days before the invasion began. There is no independent confirmation of this, but engineers in both Western and Northern Areas complained about being short of materiel, even after raiding the naval base. Percival did not ignore problems of detail; at least twice he toured positions in the very area later invaded. But on the whole Malaya Command did not provide enough support to the combat units as they prepared for battle.[41]

The experienced 11th Indian Division staff delivered a bleak verdict: "The vaunted fortress … was no fortress. It was an undefended tropical island, its coast indented with creeks and belted with mangrove swamps. The enemy had proved that he knew how to exploit those swamps. Our troops had shown that they were at sea in them." The division was no longer fit to fight. It spent the first days of February absorbing the depleted 8th Indian Brigade and sending the even weaker 15th Indian Brigade into area reserve. 28th Indian Brigade, rebuilt after Slim River, deployed from east of the causeway to the naval base. 8th Indian Brigade backed it up. When it became clear the troops were at least heartened by the sense their long retreat was finally over, division ordered the sappers wiring the naval base to work in secret so their preparations would not spoil this mood![42] 18th Division was only reunited under its GOC Maj.-General M.B. Beckwith-Smith after its last elements arrived on 5 February. 53rd Brigade had to be rearmed from stocks—one reason there was nothing left for Dalforce. The division deployed all three brigades along the coast from the naval base to Tampines, next to Changi. Beckwith-Smith faithfully passed on Percival's orders: "The object of the defence was to break up any enemy attempt to land before they reached the shore." Companies worked on defences, all complaining how little had yet been done. In another fine example of co-operation 5th Norfolks had to borrow a naval officer's plan of the naval base, because the maps issued to the army blacked the area out! Enemy artillery fire became heavy from 4 February, forcing work to continue only at night. That slowed the work and tired the troops. Nevertheless the division soon began to feel ready to fight. That was perhaps an understandable reaction to being on the ground at last–but there was more to it. The division prepared only to defend its own sector. It saw a familiar tactical problem: hold the line: "It seemed as though a situation comparable to trench warfare was developing."[43]

Western Area covered nearly 40 km of coastline. 44th Indian Brigade was assigned to cover slightly more than half, an awkward sector in the southwest corner forcing it to face three directions. There was a dual 6" gun battery of Faber Fire Command at Pasir Laba near the mouth of the Berih River, the northern edge of the brigade sector. There were no field defences, nor had any reconnaissance been carried out. On the other hand this was the swampiest sector of the island, making it less likely to be invaded. Brig. Ballentine put all three battalions on the coast, supported by a field regiment and one company of 2/4 AIF. 8th Australian Division staff saw the brigade as a reserve available to counterattack if the attack came further north; but Ballentine noticed something about island defence preparations: "no recces or plans had been made and executed by any higher formation [for counterattack]. Ground west of the Jurong [River] was unknown to Army reserves."[44]

The other two sectors of Western Area were very different. 22nd Australian Brigade covered the central sector, stretching 15 km from the Choa Chu Kang Road to the Kranji River, facing west and north. The Kranji River caused a problem. 27th Australian Brigade covered the remaining sector, some 4 kilometres from the river to the causeway. Extending its sector to ease Taylor's burden seemed advisable, but meant splitting the formation on two sides of the wide estuary. Western Area could not afford to give Taylor an extra battalion because it needed to retain one in reserve. 8th Australian Division decided it was best to concentrate Maxwell's brigade in a shorter sector. 2/29 AIF was designated area reserve and trained accordingly, but also had to cover the banks of the Kranji River, to guard against infiltration. The division organized a Special Reserve Battalion, from administrative and miscellaneous troops, to augment its reserve. Bennett accepted Taylor's suggestion to organize a fourth rifle platoon for each line company, from second echelon and headquarters personnel. Another company of 2/4 AIF was assigned to support 22nd Australian Brigade, along with the large Dalforce contingent. But these improvisations could not conceal a dangerous fact: 22nd Australian Brigade was holding a front of close country three times too long for its strength.[45]

Taylor's troops were "disgusted" to find how little work was done to prepare their sector. Their supporting engineer companies were stretched to the limit preparing petrol traps, boom defences, working on roads and gathering stores, so the infantry shouldered the heaviest burden. Here as elsewhere some fighting positions were built as breastworks, because the water table was too high to dig very deep. Ominously, the Straits narrowed to less than 700 metres near the dividing line between the 2/18 and 2/20 AIF sectors. Here also the men were forced to work at night and complained about restrictions on their own artillery. Maxwell's brigade had a much better tactical position in a smaller area, but stragglers from 22nd Indian Brigade reported the gap blown in the causeway was easily fordable at low tide. Once it was repaired, vehicles and heavy equipment could drive across at will. This made it important to deny the artery by direct fire for as long as possible. 2/26 and 2/30 AIF deployed up front to do just that, but faced the same frustrations preparing defence works as everyone else outside Southern Area.[46]

The most important preparation for battle was to rebuild the infantry battalions. Headquarters and support elements were combed for officers, but that of course left those bodies short. 18th Division was in the best condition, although 53rd Brigade had to draw on the replacement pool to rebuild its units. On the other hand its other brigades were as yet unblooded. The Indian component was in rougher shape. The more experienced the unit the more patchwork it now was. 4/19 Hyderabadi and 5/2 Punjabi drew from the 7000 reinforcements who arrived in late January. Stewart felt the Punjabis were no longer "of any use at all," the Hyderabadis "not much better." So much for the command reserve. 15th Indian Brigade took a week to replenish its lost weapons and equipment. Only three of Heath's battalions remained in their original form and even these were heavily diluted by drawing on the recent reinforcements. These men arrived without full stocks of personal weapons and gear and no better trained or ready for combat than 44th and 45th Indian Brigades. The Indian contingent was strong only in numbers.[47]

Sadly, the Australians were little better off. One of the most bitter controversies of the entire campaign surrounds the 1800 odd replacement troops who arrived from Australia on 24 January. Despite the heavy casualties 8th Australian Division suffered in Johore—more than 1200 all told—there were more than enough men in its General Base Depot to replenish its units. The problem was quality: these men were nowhere near ready for battle. Stories that they were sweepings from big city prisons were nonsense, but the truth was almost as bad. The dire need for trained infantrymen in Malaya arose much faster than the system could effectively respond. To cut corners the AIF sent troops overseas with only basic training. Training depots in the theatre to which they were assigned would make them battle ready. This system was running well in the Middle East by late 1941, but 8th Australian Division had not seen action so had not set up a similar facility. When the Australian War Cabinet and COS agreed on 23 December 1941 to send these men Bennett's depot was full. But the pace of the Japanese "driving charge" forced Bennett to use them immediately. There were two alternatives, but both relied on Australian authorities deciding in December the situation in Malaya was too perilous to take chances. One was to draw on the large pool of well trained replacements in the Middle East, no farther away than Australia. The other was to allow more trained militiamen from the Australian Military Forces to volunteer for overseas service in the AIF. No one pursued the Middle East option and the militia were quickly restricted from volunteering after war broke out in Asia, so as not to deplete home defences by a sudden outrush. Sending the untrained men was administratively easier. Given the warnings sent by both Bowden and Bennett, this was indeed a scandal. Now 8th Australian Division paid the price. Many of these men had never seen a Bren gun or anti-tank rifle, some had not even handled a rifle, very few knew any fieldcraft, some had only been in the army a few weeks. One officer called them "not only almost useless but actually a positive menace to anyone near them and to any commander who expected his orders to be carried out." Every infantry battalion received some. 2/20 AIF received 90, but the badly battered 2/19 AIF had to take in over 600 and 2/29 AIF more than 500. These two units were unfit to fight–compounded for 2/19 AIF when Anderson was hospitalized by dysentery on 7 February–and the whole division was affected. 8th Australian Division was a shadow of the formation that fought so well in Johore.[48]

Lack of confidence within Australian division headquarters and between the Australian brigadiers and their superiors turned Western Area into the weakest link in the defences of Singapore. The problem started with Bennett. Despite his pugnacious pose, Bennett behaved so erratically his own subordinates resorted to working behind his back. That sowed confusion and cross-purposes. The most fiery controversy arose over the "switch line," called the Kranji-Jurong Line after the two rivers it was supposed to connect in a defensive barrier. The position was tactically appealing, especially to block tanks. It was much shorter than the long coastline to the north and west. 35th (Fortress) Coy RE started marking it out as early as 12 December and actually began building an anti-tank ditch on 15 January, working with a local contractor. But the decision to defend the coast relegated it to a backstop given no great priority. 8th Australian Division staff found "work proceeding in a leisurely peace-time manner," hampered by the labourers tendency to disappear whenever enemy aircraft appeared. On 2 February Taylor told Bennett the position should be surveyed, to provide the option of falling back to a shorter more defensible front. Thyer argued the Japanese were bound to punch through the thin crust of coastal defences and push inland, in which case the only chance to stop them would be to fall back on a well-prepared position on good ground. Bennett flatly refused even to consider developing a stop line. He insisted the division must stand and fight and derided what he termed the retreat mentality. Fortress Engineers gave the Australians "all available earth work machines" to help complete the anti-tank ditch. But instead of appealing to Percival, Thyer went ahead on his own to try to expand the anti-tank ditch into a comprehensive second line of defence. When Maxwell put the case to Thyer the next day he was told "plan for complete defensive position being finalized." On 5 February division staff directed their artillery to survey the position, to be ready to support it. But Thyer kept the work so quiet Ballentine never heard it was being done. This was unwise, considering his brigade would also be expected to fall back on the line. Bennett's attitude was absurd, but by going behind his back Thyer put the division between two plans rather than linking the two.[49]

Thyer's initiative was an implied vote of no confidence. Maxwell made a similar vote more explicit. 27th Australian Brigade had the best tactical position in Singapore. Its front was narrow, its companies deployed in depth. On 3 February it reported the men were now "very fit and completely rested." But Maxwell concluded there was no point fighting on at all. Bennett had to lecture him again on 1 February about "wet nursing soldiers," yet left him in command. When the two met on 6 February Maxwell persuaded Bennett to relieve Lt.-Col. A.H. Boyes from command of 2/26 AIF in favour of Major R.F. Oakes. Boyes was a regular. Oakes was from 2/19 AIF, Maxwell's old unit. Casualties forced the division to do some shuffling, but 2/26 AIF did well on the mainland and there was no clear reason to shift Boyes. Division staff soon assigned him to command X Battalion, another scratch unit being formed from depot personnel–hardly a vote of no confidence. Maxwell kept his brigade headquarters close to division headquarters and well back from his battalion positions, so he needed someone he could rely on to act on his behalf up front. Maxwell then asked Bennett how long he thought the battle would last; the GOC replied ten days.[50]

Taylor had no more confidence in the defence plan than his colleagues and less in Bennett. Taylor and his battalion commanders decided the enemy was bound to penetrate any coastal defences they could mount in such a long stretch of close country. Taylor agreed the enemy would be vulnerable on the water but assumed they would come in such strength the rifle platoon positions would soon be surrounded. He felt the only ground the brigade might be able to hold was a shorter line between the Berih River and Ama Keng, a village just north of Tengah airbase. Assuming platoons would try to fall back on company positions if being surrounded, Taylor arranged to have companies fall back on a battalion rendezvous if necessary–and for battalions to retreat to the Ama Keng position if it came to that. Taylor later argued he was only preparing to control what his troops would do in battle anyway. But his orders were verbal–and he never informed either 8th Australian Division or Malaya Command his rifle platoons were not going to fight it out on the coast. A fighting retreat at night in close country, with enemy infantry all around, is one of the most difficult operations of war a unit can attempt, more difficult by far for a brigade than a platoon. To pull it off you need tough veterans plus timely and effective support. 2/19 AIF had so many raw replacement troops it was combat ineffective; 2/18 AIF was also heavily diluted. Taylor never told the artillery assigned to his support about his plan change, so they did not prepare to support the Ama Keng line. Taylor did not want Bennett or Percival to know what he intended, so they could not countermand it. He doubted Percival would launch a counterattack that might justify any sacrificial stand on the coast and believed Bennett would overrule any decision he made. He was undoubtedly right in both cases. But by adopting his own plan Taylor made it even less likely they could do anything to help in the vital first hours of any invasion and more likely their overall plan would be compromised before they realized it.[51]

The 8th Australian Division was in fact in disarray. After an early effort to persuade Percival to send more infantry to his sector, Bennett distanced himself from the whole problem. He moaned about the loss of Johore and thought about becoming Military Governor, or even GOC Malaya Command. Meanwhile he did not know what his brigadiers intended and did not find out. Communications were crucial to a battle in which the first twelve hours would be decisive. The whole army relied on landlines, but they could be cut by bombardment. The Australians mistrusted radios but dispatch riders were too slow. Taylor resorted to arranging signals from flare pistols so his battalions could call for fire support that way if all else failed. As for intelligence, as early as 2 February division headquarters directed brigades to send patrols to discover what the enemy was doing. But it had to repeat the order with emphasis on 5 February and the first patrol did not cross until late the following night. Late on 7 February 22nd Australian Brigade reported its patrol spotted three large concentrations of enemy infantry near the opposite coast. The news was passed on to Malaya Command the next day–hours after the Japanese began the all out bombardment to cover their main invasion, now only hours away.[52]

The rest of the army was in little better shape when it came to C³I. Taylor was not the only brigadier to wonder how Malaya Command would mount a major counterattack when it made no effort to prepare one. One might also ask why Percival did not make sure the switch lines were in order if after all he planned to fall back on them. Heath later suggested the defenders thought the Japanese could not send more than one brigade across the water in one night. This was a force he thought they could handle, now that the army finally had a killing zone where it could bring the range and firepower of its artillery and machine guns fully to bear. But it would only take half an hour to cross through this zone. Everything had to go as planned for the defenders to exploit any advantage.[53]

By 8 February this was impossible, especially after Taylor's changes. When the Imperial Guards made their feint attack on Pulau Ubin they chased away a standing patrol from 54th Brigade. This clash plus reports of Japanese movements at sea confirmed Percival's own inclination. On the morning of 8 February he told Wavell the enemy was concentrating east of the causeway. Percival's intelligence staff, impressed by the Australian patrols, disagreed. The crescendo of artillery fire now falling on Western Area might have been taken as a warning to listen to them. But Percival and his operations staff stuck to their appreciation. Malaya Command was now in a situation where caution no longer made sense. Its orders were to fight to the death. Yet headquarters began the siege by warning combat units not to make "warlike noises" in their area, so as not to alarm the civil population. Surely being cut off and bombarded was already alarming enough? Malaya Command worked frenetically in the first week of February to prepare Singapore for invasion. But it was much activity for too little achievement. There was drive at the top, but no ruthlessness.[54] That broke, beyond repair, the chain of confidence that binds an army together.

Churchill wanted glorious defiance to restore British prestige. Wavell wanted a long bloody fight to pin the enemy down. But the defenders began the siege of Singapore with only a remote chance to achieve either goal—and even that depended on the enemy making mistakes. Instead Malaya Command finished itself off when its leadership buckled under the strain. Malaya Command advised area commanders early on 3 February to adopt this strategy:

Experience has shown that the Japanese soldier will not stand up to bayonet charges. This therefore is the best way to defeat him. All ranks must be imbued with the spirit of the attack. It is no good waiting for the Japanese to attack first. The endeavour of every soldier must be to locate the enemy and, having located him, to close with him. The soldier should, if exposed, cover his advance with fire, either from Tommy gun, rifle or light automatic, until he is able to attack with the bayonet. If every soldier is determined to kill at least one Japanese the enemy will not have a chance.[55]

Trying to inspire hard-pressed men by gratuitous lectures on section tactics only made army headquarters look ridiculous, not resolute. On the other hand, this message was consistent with a longer and larger story–if you aim it up rather than down the chain of command. This was the last British strategy for the defence of Singapore, in a chain stretching back more than twenty years. It suffered from the same fundamental weakness as the first. It looked resolute on paper but could not be implemented in practice. Unlike all previous strategies however, this one also amounted to a confession. Singapore was indefensible. Bayonets could not stop air or seapower. The only thing still to be settled was the scale of the disaster.

16

Invasion

Soon after dawn on 8 February 1942 Japanese artillery opened up on Singapore island. They were joined by aircraft spotting for targets, bombing and strafing. A few guns blasted Northern Area to distract the defenders, but the bombardment concentrated on the western part of the island. 2/18 AIF held the central zone of the 22nd Australian Brigade sector. It tracked the bombardment. The volume reached as high as 80 rounds in ten minutes in one company position. The whole area was saturated by a barrage some veterans said was more intense than anything they experienced on the Western Front in the Great War. The brigade had eight rifle companies in coastal positions and four close behind in local reserve. Most suffered relatively few casualties. The men were well dug in and many shells were absorbed by wet swampy ground. On the other hand the barrage prevented two companies from moving after dusk into their forward positions on the coast, knocked out at least one Beach Electric Light, cut nearly every landline connecting forward companies and artillery observers to headquarters and supporting units, damaged 8th Australian Division headquarters and knocked out quite a few vehicles. The Japanese expected the bombardment to give away their intentions but decided they must take the risk, to blast through the defences and cover the dangerous water crossing. Malaya Command only received the Australian patrol report in midafternoon: there was no evidence the Australians were about to be attacked. Bennett met Percival and neither considered invasion imminent. Neither at first did Taylor, at his headquarters near Tengah airbase. But by 1800hrs Taylor agreed with his battalion commanders–the enemy was coming.[1]

The Japanese 5th and 18th Divisions assembled in their jumping off areas, hidden in the bends of the Skudai and Melayu Rivers. Yamashita sent the message "Am watching you all from the Sultan's Tower." Yet not everything went smoothly. The first assault wave of each division comprised two battalions supported by engineer and mortar detachments. Each would cross in two wings, right and left. They moved to the boats that evening. Each division used 50 small motor landing craft and 100 Type 95 canvas-sided boats powered by outboard motor. When the engineers miscalculated the tide some infantry struggled in deep water to board their boats. The 18th

Division right wing made a dangerous move south hugging the coast opposite the enemy for seven kilometres before reaching its crossing point, north of the Berih River estuary. But the Australians did not detect any of this. The moon, down to a quarter, did not rise until 0130hrs. No beach light lit up. The barrage drowned out all other noise. 2nd Lt. Ochi and his 5th Division platoon were on the far left flank of the invasion, closest to Yamashita. When the tide neared its apex the left wing came out from the Skudai River and charged across the Straits towards Lim Chu Kang, held by 2/20 AIF. Four hundred metres from the Singapore shore a red flare lit up their target area and they came under fire: "As shots whistled around them, their boat nosed left, seeking out a darker spot to land, although that meant sailing into dense mangrove."[2]

Such decisions helped the Japanese overrun Singapore in a week. But while they fought hard for that victory, they did not take Singapore island. Malaya Command lost it. Once the attack began the battle was in the hands of the junior officers and troops. But no matter how hard they fought they could not win unless their higher command prepared well and intervened effectively as the battle unfolded. The troops of 22nd Australian Brigade had only one fleeting advantage. If the Japanese crossed the water in numbers, they would be there to stay. Some units could still fight and the defenders still had ample ammunition. But Malaya Command could not coordinate operations effectively, at any level. When Ochi and his machine gunners made it into the mangrove, along with thousands of their comrades, that was that.

The last battle was the campaign in microcosm. This army was left alone to fight a battle it could not win. The challenge was to prevent humiliation. The defenders instead brought it on themselves. Mainland mistakes were repeated. While more than half the army sat idle, the remainder fought and lost the decisive engagements. The enemy ran ahead of his supplies and split his forces in two. This left him open to a roundhouse punch to the head, but all Malaya Command could do was try to poke a finger in his eye. When the enemy broke the finger that left only one strategy by which the army might still avoid military humiliation. The Prime Minister expected it to. The enemy feared it would. In fact Malaya Command neither would nor could– but it was only an instrument. The problem was systemic, grounded in the politics of imperial defence. The only thing Malaya Command successfully accomplished as an army on Singapore island was to surrender.

The first Japanese objective was Tengah airbase, which they wanted within 12 hours. They did not quite manage that, but the first 18 hours were decisive. During that time they carved out a beachhead into which poured the infantry of 5th and 18th Divisions, a force too strong to repel. In this confusing encounter the fog of war was thick indeed. To lift it we need to ask four questions. How did the Japanese get across so easily? How did they get inland? What did 22nd Australian Brigade do? And how did the higher command respond?

Four things helped the Japanese cross the water: speed, concentration, darkness and confusion. Both sides knew the narrowness of the Straits gave the Japanese the chance to race through this dangerous killing zone. To counter this 22nd Australian Brigade had five 75mm guns on the coast in a beach defence role, four platoons of 2/4 AIF with 16 medium machine guns to support the rifle platoons, and 30 guns of 2/15 Field Regt. Four Beach Electric Lights would light up the water to locate direct fire targets for the machine guns; the artillery preregistered four targets in front of each battalion. No part of this plan worked as hoped. The beach defence guns attracted so much fire three were destroyed before the invasion began. The light in the 2/18 AIF sector was knocked out by artillery fire and none of the others lit up. Taylor thought the enemy would immediately destroy the lights and had delegated control to battalions. None ordered the crews to light up, probably because no one in authority could contact them quickly enough. The battle began between 2200 and 2300 hrs, all along the brigade front. Some Japanese made the crossing in 20 minutes; few took longer than 30. The machine guns were only going to engage when they were halfway across, which reduced the time still further. The lights would not have survived, but a quick location of targets would have helped the machine gunners do more damage. As it was they produced most of the fire the Japanese did take when they were most exposed. When one barge caught fire machine gunners in the 2/20 AIF area used the light to shoot up the Japanese first wave. Ochi saw two nearby boats sunk and his own was hit. Machine gunners in the 2/18 AIF sector near Sarimbun, deployed on a rise that became an island at high tide, nearly wiped out the first Japanese company landing in front of them. One small Japanese force strayed into the estuary of the Berih River and was actually repelled. On the other hand none of the flares all three battalions sent up attracted any effective artillery support while the enemy was crossing. And in any case the brigade front was so long the available guns could only cover one third of even the registered targets at one time, so there were bound to be gaps. The Japanese went straight for the dark gaps between positions firing on them, ran the gauntlet and pushed into the mangrove. The great majority of their force had still to cross but now their first wave mixed it up with the Australian infantry, covering that reinforcement.[3] This first Japanese success was the most important, because it destroyed Percival's optimum strategy. The killing zone was lost. Now the ground did not favour the defenders.

Once into the bush and rubber the Japanese set off the kind of light infantry brawl at which they excelled. They exploited sheer numbers and the fog of battle to push infantry inland fast enough to defeat the Australian effort to pin them down. The sacrificial aggressiveness of the first wave covered the quick turn around of the engineers. The following waves assembled directly opposite their target area, reducing the crossing time. Two more crossed before dawn. The infantry bypassed defended positions, following junior officers using compasses strapped to their wrists. The more confusion they sowed the better and in much of this area vegetation was so dense night visibility was almost nil. They aimed for two recognizable landmarks: the village of Ama Keng and the Lim Chu Kang Road. The gaps between the Australian positions were large enough for the Japanese to push strong forces between them and onto the road. Two particularly damaging penetrations came along streams dividing battalion sectors: along the Murai between the 2/19 and 2/18 AIF areas and along the Karang between 2/18 and 2/20 AIF, barely three kilometres to the road. Taylor did not have enough infantry to deny the coast. But trying to do so also left his units without enough infantry to prevent infiltration, either by denying all routes or by counterattacking before the Japanese reached the road. Platoons fought on their own. Some put up very stiff resistance indeed; one Japanese engineer officer remembered "the fight after the landing was extremely severe." But sheer weight and bad ground soon told. Within two hours nearly every platoon engaged was either trying to fall back on the company rendezvous or being wiped out. As early as 0130 hrs 2/18 AIF retreated towards Taylor's brigade stop line hinging on Ama Keng; 2/19 AIF started a similar move at dawn.[4]

Taylor expected his coastal defences to be penetrated but hoped his battalions could reorganize between the Berih River and Ama Keng, a much shorter line. If so they might still keep the enemy west of Tengah airbase, buying Malaya Command time to respond. But the strong fight they put up near the coast lasted long enough for enemy infantry to get between them and the brigade fall-back position. Taylor lost all chance to control the battle before it started, when the landlines were knocked out. No battalion radios were reliable and no one saw any signal flares. One battery received a desperate appeal to "bring fire down everywhere," but without better information the gunners could only engage the predicted targets. No higher headquarters could effectively assist what remained a platoon battle in the dark.[5] The result was not surprising. While trying to fight their way back Taylor's units were badly dispersed. 2/19 AIF was scattered by an enemy force that seized high ground dominating its line of retreat. Only A Company made it through intact, but it held the southernmost position of the brigade sector and was not heavily engaged. 2/18 AIF, supported by the engineers of 2/10 Field Coy, fought a tough close quarter battle to deny the Lim Chu Kang road. It retreated towards the Ama Keng rendezvous. Then around 0600hrs Taylor changed the plot. He did not know where 2/19 AIF was and the small numbers of infantry that did reach his perimeter were now hard pressed. So he retreated to reform the brigade two kilometres south, just in front of the airbase. This made it harder for those groups still trying to work past enemy blocking parties. 2/20 AIF, the least diluted battalion, fought a bitter action all night. Most of its machine gunners, starting with 10,000 rounds, ran out of ammunition. D Company never made it to the battalion perimeter. It was forced to retreat across the Kranji River and badly dispersed along the way. The rest fought on until at 0900hrs Assheton decided to fall back to the brigade rendezvous. Unfortunately strong enemy forces now blocked the road. Assheton was killed, after which the battalion was badly scattered. By 0930hrs 22nd Australian Brigade still held Tengah, but less than 400 men were in its new position.[6]

Taylor's brigade was hit too hard and fast, too compromised by a bad position and too diluted with new men to fall back intact to any stop line. Once the Japanese crossed the water everything really depended on whether the rest of the army could intervene in time. Malaya Command's plan assumed 22nd Australian Brigade would stand and fight. It might have been better for Taylor to try this. The Japanese were hurt more by close quarter fighting around company positions on the coast than they were crossing the water. And his own battalions were really scattered when they tried to retreat. But Taylor believed such a sacrifice would be pointless, because Percival would not exploit it to counterattack strongly enough to repel the enemy. He felt the GOC would instead organize yet another stop line while the Japanese destroyed his brigade. This begs the question of whether Taylor's companies could kill enough Japanese to jeopardize Yamashita's fighting power–but Taylor did not want to try. Even an unsuccessful fighting retreat might bring back enough of his brigade to keep fighting, to whatever purpose. 22nd Australian Brigade reported it was being attacked all along its front around 2300hrs. Bennett passed the report to Malaya Command and half an hour later spoke with Taylor. But neither he nor Percival now moved fast enough.[7]

For the rest of the crucial first day 8th Australian Division and Malaya Command never had an accurate picture of the situation. Nevertheless their reactions underline two cardinal points. The high command, apart from Bennett, never intended to do anything other than fall back step by step, to conduct a conventional linear defence. But the army was too weak and unprepared to do this effectively and too badly divided to recover. Before midnight Bennett ordered 2/29 AIF to reinforce Taylor. Before dawn he directed the Special Reserve Battalion to do the same thing. At 0535 hrs on 9 February Thyer told Malaya Command that 22nd Australian Brigade had pulled back from the coast but was battling it out west of Tengah airbase, where Bennett wanted to form a blocking position. He also asked for help from the command reserve. Then at 0700hrs Bennett personally ordered divisional artillery to fire with everything they had at the western edge of the brigade area, nearer the coast. And at 0830hrs Percival released his command reserve, 12th Indian Brigade.[8] It was not enough. The high command could not catch up to the tempo of battle.

Neither Australian reserve unit reached Taylor until after dawn, too late to help extract his brigade. Then at 0930hrs Bennett ordered Taylor to counterattack with 2/29 AIF, to retake the Ama Keng area. Bennett realized the sooner the counterattack the more chance to hit the enemy before he was too well established. On the other hand Bennett must have known 2/29 AIF was too diluted to press any such attack and must have realized how strong the enemy force was to have already dispersed a whole brigade. The order smacked of desperation. In any case it was aborted by a Japanese advance that prompted Taylor to retreat again. By early afternoon Taylor's remnants moved east of Tengah to form yet another blocking line, straddling the Choa Chu Kang Road around Bulim village. Meanwhile Bennett made no effort to tell 44th Indian Brigade what was going on. Ballentine only found out the Australians were retreating when Taylor's brigade major informed him in person. Percival's only intervention was to order the coastal battery at Pasir Laba to stay and fight even though its guns were already knocked out. Nobody prepared a net of military police checkpoints to control the rear area, standard practice for any linear defence. As a result hundreds of Taylor's infantrymen who did get past the Japanese, many without weapons or equipment, wound up all the way back at the General Base Depot, nearly halfway across the island–some brought there by belatedly deployed military police. When Bennett found out Taylor was retreating he denounced him for disobeying orders but soon agreed to regroup around Bulim. But behind his back Thyer was already warning both Taylor and Ballentine to prepare to fall back to the Kranji-Jurong Line.[9]

By nightfall a makeshift stop line took shape around Bulim. The intention was to move what was left of 22nd Australian Brigade and the Australian reserve units, along with 12th and 44th Indian Brigades, back to the Kranji-Jurong Line in the morning. Percival later argued that he "followed the teaching current at the time," which laid down that a commander only released his general reserve when satisfied there was no major threat developing "on other parts of the front"–and that the all important general counterattack would be made by this reserve. But what Singapore needed was a commander who read the battle, not the textbook. Percival indeed held on to 12th Indian Brigade until after dawn. But he knew how weak the brigade now was. 5/2 Punjabi were too weak to take the field so only the Argylls and Hyderabadis moved forward, in a formation Paris insisted was unfit to attack. Percival knew the longer it took the more likely the Japanese would build up too much force to repel. He also received enough information to conclude Taylor either could or would not stand fast on the coast. But the only other order he gave was for 15th Indian Brigade to take over as command reserve. Everyone else stood fast. Percival still expected the enemy to mount another attack at least as strong further east. He told Wavell what he really intended:

Advance stopped temporarily by use of command reserve, but situation is undoubtedly serious in view of the very extended coast line which we have to watch. Have made plan for concentrating forces to cover Singapore if this becomes necessary.[10]

Unfortunately Western Area could neither stop the Japanese nor fall back in good order. The Australian high command was paralyzed. Bennett wanted to counterattack, desirable in theory but impossible in practice. His staff and Taylor wanted to retreat, but Bennett prevented them from preparing any fall-back position–and now it was too late. 22nd Australian Brigade moved into the Bulim position with barely a quarter of its strength under command. Little wonder, given this was the third brigade line adopted in one day. More of its infantry were back at the depot than in the line, but instead of returning them to their units many were redirected into another improvised unit; hundreds more remained missing. Taylor "forgot for a time" the two reserve units were now under his command awaiting orders; division scrambled to coordinate the movements of three converging brigades. Because of this confusion it took more than half the night to sort out the new line. Ballentine's brigade was hardly engaged; his concern was to establish contact with the units to his left and right, in proper 1917 style. Such pawn shuffling cost Malaya Command and 8th Australian Division a chance either to hit back or at least pull their own defence together. After moving onto Tengah airbase the Japanese did not put any real pressure on the forces lining up around Bulim. The reason should have been obvious. They were fully occupied bringing the rest of their main force across the water, including tanks and guns, many of which were floated across on rafts. That job was complicated by the need to send boats to the Imperial Guards, for their attack that night.[11] But while Percival left his army strung out along the coast, waiting for the main enemy force to invade, it was already concentrating on the island, preparing to advance in strength. The only thing blocking it was a motley force preparing to fall back to a line it could not hold, because Bennett insisted it would not be needed. By the end of the first day the issue was decided. The battle for the island would be short.

The next enemy move provoked more discord which made it shorter still. As soon as 2/29 AIF moved west Maxwell complained his left flank was wide open. The noise of battle plus the arrival of stragglers from Taylor's brigade further unsettled him. At 1100hrs on the 9th he asked for permission to pull his left battalion, 2/26 AIF, back from the coast and turn it left, to block any threat to his rear from the west. Bennett refused, but did allow Maxwell to order 2/26 AIF to refuse the left flank. What happened next long remained unclear, because Maxwell took matters into his own hands, took pains to conceal that at the time, then later tried to cover up by rewriting the brigade war diary and misleading Key and the official historians. Around noon Maxwell again requested permission to "change his front," this time by pulling both battalions back to face west, lined up along the trunk road. Bennett did not agree, nor did Thyer. Kappe's postmortem is the only record that agrees with Maxwell the request was granted, on condition the brigade did not move until after it destroyed large petrol storage tanks in its sector. Maxwell later suggested it was Major C.B. Dawkins, division GSO 2, who granted permission. Dawkins died in battle two days later, leaving Maxwell as Kappe's only source. Earlier that morning Malaya Command asked AIF headquarters to explain naval reports the army was planning to retreat from the Kranji area. Dawkins claimed "no orders had been issued to withdraw from Kranji and no such orders were going to be issued." While Malaya Command did order the brigade to destroy the oil tanks and the large magazine in the Kranji area, it did not do so before 1300hrs and did not authorize any retreat. Dawkins was yet another regular officer Bennett neither liked nor trusted, making it unlikely he would authorize what Bennett most opposed: retreat. Maxwell called a conference at his headquarters at 1330hrs. At that meeting he sent Galleghan to hospital to have an ear problem treated. Galleghan was the senior battalion commander, widely expected to command the brigade before Bennett's surprise decision to promote Maxwell. They did not get along. That same morning Oakes took over 2/26 AIF. Maxwell told his commanders the brigade's orders were to destroy the oil tanks that evening, then pull back from the coast and left wheel to face west. Maxwell delegated full control to Oakes, authorizing him to co-ordinate the movement of both battalions and even change the plan if he felt it necessary.[12]

27th Australian Brigade enjoyed a strong position. 2/30 AIF held rising ground overlooking the causeway, with good fields of fire for machine and anti-tank guns and good observation for artillery. 2/26 AIF, covering its left flank, had to worry about the Kranji River on its left, but had a narrow frontage in a very swampy area. It was dominated by scattered patches of higher ground, all well scouted by the battalion. There was only one good penetration route: a road from Kranji pier on the coast to the trunk road two kilometres south. The unit deployed in depth along the road, two companies on the coast, two more echeloned in reserve. Battalion headquarters was deployed on rising ground just south of the road junction—now the site of the Kranji Commonwealth War Cemetery—which gave good observation for supporting fire. Each battalion had a battery of 2/10 Field Regt. and machine gunners from 2/4 AIF in support.[13]

Another punishing barrage hit the brigade sector most of the day. Nearly all landlines were knocked out and 20 Bty., supporting 2/26 AIF, took a battering that badly wounded its commander and destroyed several vehicles. On the other hand the Imperial Guards Division rushed into an attack neither properly organized nor skilfully executed. The division planned an assault by an infantry group of four battalions heading straight for 2/26 AIF, covered by a flank guard of one battalion attacking just west of the causeway, followed by the reserve: two battalions and a tank regiment. Not all boats being sent over from the main invasion arrived on time, but Nishimura sent the infantry group ahead on its own, at first one battalion at a time.[14] This piecemeal crossing gave the Australians the chance to defeat them. Unfortunately Maxwell's prior decisions ruined that chance.

The crossing began around 2100hrs. The infantry group frontally assaulted 2/26 AIF at the Kranji pier and spilled over onto either flank. They ran into a very tight defence and were punished by Australian machine guns. Fighting at close quarters, the Australians kept the Japanese bogged down in the swamps and off the road. The whole battle area was lit up by blazing petrol leaking into drains and ditches, covering everyone with clingy black soot. An Australian remembered "no difficulty was experienced in holding the enemy at this front." The Australians could have really pulverized such a clumsy assault had their supporting fire been poised. 20 Bty. was instead "not in a position to assist." That might have been due to its earlier suffering, but more likely it was already moving to new positions to support the line the brigade would fall back on. The battalion had to call on 60 Bty., which could only answer after "considerable delay" and only bear on Kranji pier. Nevertheless when that fire came it caught another piecemeal Japanese crossing and hit it hard. But the battalion relied principally on its mortars. They did not have the firepower to flay the enemy on the water. The retreat was delayed when the engineer platoon wiring the petrol tanks lost their equipment to a direct hit. Lt. Watchorn of 2/12 Field Coy RAE then showed great initiative. At 0400hrs he drained the tanks and set fire to the stream of petrol that flowed into nearby mangrove. This ignited a firestorm that swept into the Mandai Kechil stream, on the left flank of the 2/30 AIF sector. This inferno tore into at least a company of Guards, incinerating them. Corporal Tsuchikane, caught in the midst of such action, felt it was "a picture of hell–*Abikyokan*–Buddhism's worst of all hells." This setback was so dramatic it prompted some Guardsmen to report the invasion was being annihilated. Nishimura demanded Yamashita call off the attack, which would surely have resulted in nearly all those already on the island being killed or captured. Yamashita, a stronger character, insisted on obtaining a more reliable report. Tsuji was disgusted with Nishimura and called this attack the "only real mistake" in the whole campaign. They got away with it because Oakes went ahead with the preplanned retreat–indeed expanded it, as Maxwell had authorized. When Watchorn reported success 2/26 AIF broke contact without difficulty at 0430; 2/30 AIF moved out at almost the same time. By dawn they were settling into a new position in an arc east of the trunk road, facing mainly west. 2/26 AIF overlooked the junction of trunk road and Choa Chu Kang Road at Bukit Panjang, but 2/30 AIF straddled the Mandai Road a good two kilometres east of the trunk road. This retreat broke off a battle the brigade might have won, conceded the causeway and opened a gap between the Australians and 11th Indian Division to the east.[15]

The Imperial Guards survived their poor attack and pushed onto high ground south and east of the causeway to threaten the flank and rear of 11th Indian Division. Key did not discover the Australians were gone until 0650hrs, when 28th Indian Brigade told him an Australian patrol gave one of their patrols a slip of paper at 0430 indicating the new position 2/30 AIF was taking up. He could have found out a bit earlier, because at 0510hrs Thyer told Malaya Command the 2/30 AIF "has been obliged to withdraw." But he would not have found out early enough to take remedial action, because Maxwell made sure no one outside the brigade knew it intended to retreat. 27th Australian Brigade reported the initial landing but for the rest of the night higher command believed its situation was stable. Dawkins made the first external report of intense fighting at 0500hrs. Nor did Maxwell know Oakes retreated south to Mandai Road, farther away from the Indians. Oakes did this because he knew Maxwell's main concern was to prevent the Japanese from pushing between the two Australian brigades. But why not worry as much about the enemy force attacking in the north? By ignoring this threat Maxwell and Oakes not only allowed the Guards to penetrate between them and the Indians, they also left the trunk road open north of Bukit Panjang. That gave the Guards the chance to charge that road and attack the vital Bukit Timah area.[16] What explains this folly?

The answer is Maxwell. Maxwell and Oakes only spoke once during the battle. This gave Maxwell "plausible deniability." When Maxwell set up the retreat he did not anticipate his brigade would be attacked. When the plan was triggered he did not know the situation had changed because he left it all to Oakes, to cover his tracks. Maxwell later admitted his decision to delegate control was a mistake, one he made because "I am a doctor in civil life and did not know enough of soldiering." This was part of a tactical confession: use the mistake, retreating too far, to conceal the sin: retreating on his own authority. Key was forced to commit his reserve, 8th Indian Brigade, to try to regain the ground west of the naval base. The Guards took it first. Key told Harrison that Maxwell would have been arrested if he was a British officer. This would have been justified. Maxwell deliberately disobeyed a direct order. By doing so he wilfully abandoned an important tactical position, ignoring the safety of the Indian formation to his right. This cost the army its only good chance to maul a badly executed Japanese attack. Maxwell was indeed "finished as a commander," but the most important thing his actions indicated is that the army no longer functioned at the operational level.[17]

Yamashita advanced his headquarters to Tengah airbase shortly after dawn on 10 February, after hearing the Guards attack was safe after all. The flare-up with Nishimura did leave a dangerous legacy. Yamashita wanted the Guards to do just what Maxwell and Oakes made possible: drive south on Bukit Timah, to converge with the rest of the army. But Tsuji exploded and impulsively told the division to do whatever it liked–the rest of the army would win the battle without them. This provoked the Guards to advance southeast, probing for a gap to get between Heath's forces and Singapore and strike the fatal blow. Twenty-Fifth Army nevertheless remained in good shape. Thirty-six hours into the battle the great bulk of its infantry was on the island and its main strength was concentrated. Japanese reconnaissance reported no strong fortifications barring their path. Yamashita prepared to attack Bukit Timah with his main force that night.[18]

Percival's response to this first day of battle surfaced in his signal to Wavell: "Have made plan for concentrating forces to cover Singapore if this becomes necessary." Very early on 10 February Malaya Command issued Operation Instruction No. 40, drafted by Percival himself. Western Area, assisted by 12th and 15th Indian Brigades, would hold the Kranji-Jurong Line. But "Should it be impossible to hold the enemy on the line mentioned GOC Malaya intends to withdraw to an inner posn on which the final battle for Singapore will be fought." The final position would be a semi-circle perimeter covering the city, including Bukit Timah hill and the reservoirs. Nearly the entire length of this perimeter was ground not suited for positional defence. Its only supposed virtues were that it screened the city and supply dumps and provided the army with yet another continuous line. The original plan was to repel the invasion outright. The second plan was to evict him by a counterattack–but this order indicates Percival never meant that seriously. The GOC would not commit more formations to the battle in the west because he did not want to open up the north coast. But if that battle was lost he now intended to give up the rest of that coast anyway and fall back to a weak last-ditch position! Once again Percival chose to accept defeat rather than throw in all his strength, even though this no longer made military sense. Percival passed this on as a warning order, but his dismay when not everyone read it as such must be set against two considerations. First, Taylor was not the only officer expecting Percival to retreat and looking over his shoulder. Second, the order insisted formations scout designated areas and make other preparations as soon as possible.[19]

The order started down the chain of command after dawn on 10 February. Bennett's headquarters read it as a warning order, as did Maxwell. Ballentine saw it as a warning order but later admitted it made him anticipate a final retreat and issuing it was asking for trouble. That came when Taylor misread it completely. At 0900hrs a liaison officer from division headquarters gave him the typewritten order designating a sector along Reformatory Road as the final brigade area. He also said some stragglers regrouped at the depot would be returned near that area. Taylor concluded 22nd Australian Brigade was to retreat forthwith to that perimeter. Taylor ordered his commanders to start the retreat, then went to scout the area and report to Bennett.[20]

This set off a two day battle over the crucial high ground and supply dumps in the Bukit Timah area. Yamashita and his staff decided their enemy looked so disorganized it was better to risk a quick assault to take Bukit Timah by storm than wait for the rest of their tanks and guns to cross to the island. 5th and 18th Divisions prepared to attack after dusk. On the other side, at least some senior officers expected "an organized counterattack on the grand scale." Instead Percival resorted to more stop-gaps. He ordered Lt.-Col. L.C. Thomas, commanding 9th Northumberland Fusiliers, to assemble a battlegroup from 18th Division: two battalions from separate brigades plus the reconnaissance battalion and some anti-tank guns. Tomforce moved west onto Bukit Timah Road that afternoon. Despite the fact there was no sign of another invasion Percival refused to pull an intact brigade, a cohesive formation, off the northern coast. The reconnaissance battalion had no real role after losing its vehicles on the *Empress of Asia* and was dismounted as infantry. Tomforce was not sent to help evict the Japanese by a counterattack, something it did not practice. It was sent to help hold the Bukit Timah area, ground it did not know. Percival surely knew how makeshift this reinforcement was.[21] His caution provoked Wavell, who arrived that morning for his last visit to Singapore.

Wavell and Percival went to see the situation for themselves, visiting Bennett, Heath and Key. At some point after that first visit Taylor reported to division headquarters. Bennett tore a strip off him for misreading the warning order and insisted his brigade stand fast. But Bennett then called Torrance at 1345hrs and sang a very different tune. The Australian insisted his units could not attack before Tomforce arrived to take the lead, but did not spell out the full extent of Taylor's retreat. He then "asked that situation be represented to GOC as he considered that plan given in Comd Op Instr No. 40 might have to be rushed through." Percival must have been surprised to hear Bennett call for the final retreat; he and Wavell returned to Bennett's headquarters seeking an explanation. There they discovered Taylor's premature retreat, which Bennett presented as a *fait accompli*. Percival realized Bennett no longer believed his division could contain the Japanese. This did not persuade Wavell. He ordered Percival to mount the strongest possible counterattack as soon as possible, to at least retake the lost line. Percival did what he could, but had no clear idea of the condition of the units involved. First he confirmed an earlier decision to transfer 27th Australian Brigade to Key's command, to help him stabilize the northern flank. Then he ordered Bennett to concentrate all available forces in Western Area for a counterattack to regain the Kranji-Jurong Line. That amounted to 22nd Australian plus 12th and 15th Indian Brigades. 44th Indian Brigade and Tomforce would stay in reserve, to cover Reformatory and Bukit Timah Roads.[22]

Wavell's effort to put some fire into the defence was too little too late. The crucial point was to counterattack immediately and these were the only forces close enough to do so—but speed must be matched by strength and they simply were not up to the challenge. First, the counterattack force amounted to little more than a brigade in total and even that misled. Taylor's formation was a brigade in name only. Some personnel returned from the depot, but Japanese air attacks harassed the retreat towards the final perimeter, causing further dispersion. Taylor had no more than four companies in the line. The Special Reserve Battalion consisted mainly of support personnel with no infantry training; its commander barely kept them in the field when they were heavily bombed from the air. 2/29 AIF, now also missing one company, was put under command of 12th Indian Brigade. This was not enough given that

4/19 Hyderabadis were ineffective and 2nd Aryglls at half strength. 15th Indian Brigade was barely half strength in numbers but of all formations involved it was in the best condition! Second, the units involved were on the move in some confusion most of the day. Taylor's retreat sparked a general withdrawal by one unit after another when they discovered a suddenly exposed flank. Few moved back without further dispersion. At least one unit, 6/1 Punjabi, turned its retreat into a semi-flight that disorganized 44th Indian Brigade well into the evening. Percival's ill-advised warning order thus provoked a premature retreat with a stark consequence. Western Area gave up the Kranji-Jurong Line, such as it was, without a real fight. This aborted the strategy to defend the switch line. The army simply no longer had the ability to maneuver as an army.[23]

Bennett demonstrated this by how he executed Wavell's order. He changed the plan produced by his staff, ordering the advance to begin before the units involved could be brought into any sort of alignment. Bennett made no effort to find out where any formations were, what condition they were in, or provide any reconnaissance. He simply chose objectives arbitrarily on a map and told Taylor and the staff to "get on with it." This prompted Taylor to complain "it looked like murder." Not surprisingly the whole operation never came close to pulling together. Some formations were in fact already on the line indicated as their first objective, prompting Malaya Command to conclude the first phase was a success. Others went into tight perimeters when they realized they could not reach their first objective in the dark. That left dangerous gaps in close country. 12th Indian Brigade pulled in to screen the t-junction at Bukit Panjang. Stewart in particular expected the enemy to strike first.[24] They did not disappoint.

Shortly after dusk Yamashita launched a simultaneous attack astride two roads, the Jurong and Choa Chu Kang, by 18th and 5th Divisions. This sparked a brawl in the dark at close quarters over the whole area west of Reformatory Road and north of Bukit Timah village. The Japanese advance shattered the counterattack. The strongest blow hit 12th Indian Brigade: a filleting attack led by more than 50 tanks, straight along the Choa Chu Kang Road. The Japanese pushed aside the anti-tank defences, disintegrated 4/19 Hyderabadis, dispersed 2/29 AIF and drove 2nd Argylls into the Dairy Farm area. The Argylls fought their last battle in the area between the trunk road and the main water pipeline from the mainland. Stewart wanted to counterattack at dawn, but his battalion was badly dispersed. Less than 50 men mustered under command the following evening. Japanese tanks drove through Bukit Timah village shortly after midnight but then stopped, probably to wait for infantry to catch up. At that point only a few anti-tank and field guns and elements of

Tomforce blocked the road in front of them. The Japanese advance prompted 15th Indian Brigade to cancel its own, but the Jat Battalion did not receive the recall order. It was left isolated until Singapore surrendered. The rest of the brigade retreated across country towards Reformatory Road, but less than half made it through. 22nd Australian Brigade retreated when units realized the enemy was infiltrating between them. The Japanese attacked Taylor's headquarters at dawn. A mixed force led by the brigade major drove them back, but enemy pressure soon forced the defenders back to Reformatory Road. The gunners of the nearby Buona Vista battery destroyed their 15" guns at 0600hrs. Along the road, between Ulu Pandan and Bukit Timah, Australian, Indian and British units, now all mixed together, faced heavy pressure. And by daylight Japanese infantry controlled the whole area around Bukit Timah hill and probed towards the reservoirs.[25]

Higher command did not think the enemy force on the trunk road was very strong but realized they must retake Bukit Timah hill right away. Without it, and the dumps and reservoirs it commanded, Singapore could not fight on for longer than days. But once again Malaya Command learned the hard way time matters even more than ground. Percival still had more than 30 infantry battalions and 200 guns on the island–but the only troops close enough to attack the vital ground in time were Tomforce, in reserve several kilometres east of the village. Bennett's headquarters first ordered it to help 12th Indian Brigade deal with penetrations, but then at 0430hrs ordered Thomas to counterattack at dawn. Eschewing half measures for once, the order was to "mop them up" by attacking in full strength. Tomforce would retake Bukit Timah village, then clear the area all the way to Bukit Panjang. Thomas planned an extended line sweep astride the road, starting from the Racecourse. The reconnaissance battalion would advance along the road and retake the village. 1st Battalion 5thRegiment Sherwood Foresters [1/5 Sherwood Foresters] would sweep on the left while 4th Battalion Royal Norfolk Regiment [4th Norfolks] did likewise on the right, including the hill and pipeline area. Malaya Command was confident enough to note it did not want to destroy the supply depot at the Racecourse because the counterattack would "restore the situation." An hour later the fighting came close enough to force it to close the joint army-air force operational headquarters at Sime Road, less than three kilometres east of the pipeline, and move back to Fort Canning.[26]

Tsuji climbed Bukit Timah hill to survey the battle area just in time to get a bird's eye view of British infantry in extended line advancing, with fixed bayonets, towards the railway. He was impressed. When the defenders fired a heavy artillery barrage on the whole area he even began to regret falling out with the Guards. But the Japanese brought up tanks, guns and mortars and played their trump card: powerful close air support. This plus stout resistance along the railway embankment stopped the British advance. Elements from the aborted counterattack were caught up in the melee. Some joined the fight but others fell back; Paris told Thomas his brigade was shattered, then went back to report. Despite strong artillery support the attack was never going to succeed. The Japanese were forward in numbers and the tactics simply did not fit the ground. Extended line abreast made sense in the open country of Northwest Europe but quickly snarled in the bush around Bukit Timah hill. When the advance stalled Percival personally pressed Thomas to continue. Tomforce demonstrated the ability to learn quickly by reorganizing to advance in greater depth on a narrower front, especially towards Bukit Timah hill on the right. Unfortunately the enemy was now too strong to push back. Japanese pressure forced Thomas to retreat in late afternoon towards the Chinese High School.[27]

This turned out to be the only serious counterattack Malaya Command made on Singapore island. Percival tried to reinforce it by ordering 27th Australian Brigade to attack Bukit Panjang from the north, to press the Japanese between converging pincers. Had this come off Tsuji might have had real cause to be anxious. But there was never any chance it would. There was no co-operation between the brigade and 11th Indian Division. Higher command thought the Australians were denying the trunk road north of Bukit Panjang and the Indians controlled the high ground south of the causeway. Neither assumption was correct. Key and the Australian commanders blamed each other for not moving forward. Even after Percival ordered Maxwell to report to Key on the evening of 10 February Maxwell made no effort to co-operate. Earlier that afternoon, influenced by Percival's final perimeter warning order, he told his units any further retreat would be southeast along the pipeline towards a rendezvous point near the Racecourse. 2/26 AIF was close enough to Bukit Panjang to be sideswiped by the Japanese tank breakthrough at the junction, but sat still. Percival's attack order released the Australians from Key's control but did not arrive until 0730hrs on 11 February. By then Tomforce was on the move and Maxwell was again out of touch with his units, because his headquarters remained too far away. At 1000hrs 2/26 AIF started to retreat. The rearguard company finally received the attack order from a dispatch rider at 1130hrs, but it could not attack alone and the order indicated the enemy already held the rendezvous point. It moved east instead, winding up at the depot. The rest of the battalion skirmished along the way with a large enemy force and was dispersed. The attack order was rescinded before noon and soon after 2/30 AIF retreated east, winding up on Thomson

Road. By abandoning his brigade Maxwell allowed it to be scattered. This undermined both the northern flank and the counterattack.[28]

On the other hand the heavy artillery support punished the Japanese 18th Division threatening Bukit Timah from the southwest. Behind such cover Taylor finally pulled his reduced brigade back into some sort of order. The units between Ulu Pandan and Bukit Timah Roads formed all round defence positions that stood up to enemy pressure all day, until the Tomforce retreat made their line untenable. By nightfall on 11 February two things were clear: the counterattack had failed and Percival's final perimeter was already breached on a wide front, from Ulu Pandan to the reservoir area. During the day Malaya Command sent in more reinforcements: another 18th Division battlegroup and 2nd Gordons. They arrived in time to help establish a new line that night several kilometres east, astride Ulu Pandan and Bukit Timah Roads. But this was just another stop gap. The final perimeter could not be long delayed.[29]

That morning Yamashita sent Percival a letter demanding surrender. Percival ignored it.[30] Militarily this was bravado. Percival's army still outnumbered its enemy. But that was far outweighed by the fact it faced an effective field army which also enjoyed full control of the air and sea. Percival could not harness his strength–Yamashita could. The Japanese had already overrun more than a third of the island, including one of the two main magazines and most of the vital supply and ration dumps, sat on the dominating hill with a perfect view over the city, and were moving fast into the reservoir area. They could reinforce and resupply without interference. Malaya Command did not counterattack more effectively because it could not. The defence plan failed when the Japanese breached the island in strength. Percival did not help by sending units forward piecemeal, but even this was not decisive. The defence fell apart because Malaya Command could no longer operate as an army even had it tried. It was too late for operations "on the grand scale." All it could do now was delay the unavoidable.

17

Surrender

Even before Percival ordered his final retreat on 12 February he saw his most dangerous military problem. In principle he could still draw the Japanese into the city, to force them into a bloody slogging match. But in practice his army could no longer put up any such fight. Instead the GOC now struggled to prevent it from disintegrating. If it did there would be a rout, ending in a brutal massacre inside the city. Percival was trapped in one last tug of war. The army lost confidence in its higher command. On the other hand the order to fight on remained uncompromising. The last days of a beaten army trapped in a dying city are never orderly, or free from controversy and recrimination. The fall of Singapore proved no exception.

The gap between what the Empire required and what could still be done was exposed, unwittingly, by Churchill. Reports of the battle prompted him to telegraph Wavell on 10 February to make clear "the way we view the situation in Singapore." The message was blunt: the British Empire must not be humiliated in Asia. With supposedly 100,000 troops on the island, half of them British or Australian, "defenders must greatly outnumber Japanese forces who have crossed the Straits and in a well-contested battle should destroy them." Therefore:

> There must at this stage be no thought of saving the troops or sparing the population. The battle must be fought to the bitter end at all costs. The 18th Division has a chance to make its name in history. Commanders and senior officers should die with their troops. The honour of the British Empire and the British Army is at stake. I rely on you to show no mercy to weakness in any form. With the Russians fighting as they are and the Americans so stubborn at Luzon, the whole reputation of our country and our race is involved. It is expected that every unit will be brought into close contact with the enemy and fight it out.

Wavell, fresh from his last visit to Singapore, passed this on in an Order of the Day. He added his own flavour, pointing out "the Chinese, with almost a complete lack of modern equipment, have held back the Japanese for 4 and a half years. It will be disgraceful if we yield our boasted Fortress of Singapore to inferior enemy forces." But the real disgrace was Wavell's weakness, passing on such tendentious emotional blackmail. "Our race" pointedly excluded the Indians. The Russians were fighting on their own soil in favourable conditions. The largely Filipino forces held a naturally strong defensive position in their own country, against second rate Japanese forces. Wavell had already diverted 7th Armoured Brigade to Burma and left Singapore "without much confidence in any prolonged resistance." If he did not realize Malaya Command could no longer fight a "well-contested battle" then he had no business being in command. Even if he thought Churchill really might put a colonial population through a fight to the death in the city, Wavell already focused on Sumatra and assumed Singapore could do nothing more to help. Wavell had two duties: make sure his forces did all they could, but also make sure his superiors clearly understood what they could still do. But when Churchill made the issue racial honour and imperial prestige Wavell dared not tell him the truth: the army was too big to lose yet too weak to endure. He would not confront Churchill until events made the issue moot–but asking the "poor bloody infantry" to bail them all out was not so hard: "I look to you and to your men to fight to the end to prove that the fighting spirit that won our Empire still exists to enable us to defend it."[1]

Percival's own Order of the Day on 11 February was little better:

> In some units the troops have not shown the fighting spirt which is to be expected of men of the British Empire. It will be a lasting disgrace if we are defeated by an army of clever gangsters, many times inferior in numbers to our own. The spirit of aggression and determination to stick it out must be inculcated in all ranks. There must be no further thought of withdrawal without orders. There are too many fighting men moving about in back areas. Every available man who is not doing other essential work must be used to stop the invader.

By clever gangsters Percival meant an enemy who used "unconventional" tactics, ignoring his own lines of communication, operating with so little transport, attacking without much fire support.[2] That kind of orthodoxy was one reason Malaya Command found itself in such bad shape in the first place. But Percival's fear his army was losing the will to fight was more important. The enduring controversy revolves around this. Most finger pointing was exaggerated or misread cause and effect. But in the smoke there was fire. Malaya Command did start to disintegrate on Singapore island; the main cause beyond enemy pressure was the general collapse of confidence; and higher command was overwhelmed by it all.

In late afternoon 11 February Heath called Torrance to discuss the northwest flank. The conversation ended because "A lot of stragglers were reported coming South on the Serangoon rd past HQ 3 Corps. Corps Commander would see what all this was about."[3] George Seabridge, editor of the Straits Times, was one of many who concluded the army disintegrated that day. Most European residents and quite a few British officers pointed fingers at the Australians. In extreme form the charge read as follows. The Australians gave up the coast without a fight, deserted en masse and streamed into the city, seeking to escape. When they found there was no escape many lost all discipline and became a mob. Their behaviour destroyed the defence of the island. The extreme response came from the Australian official history. Some incidents did occur, notably the boarding by force of the Empire Star by some 200 Australian troops "and others," but they involved only a few hundred bewildered young replacements. The combat units did not suffer serious desertion; the division fought effectively to the end. Many Australians argued the defence fell apart because Indian units broke under pressure. On the other hand the extreme accusation against 8th Australian Division does not stand up either.[4] So what happened? The root problem was surely the army's growing conviction it was trapped in a battle it could neither win nor escape. This called for exceptional leadership at all levels. Instead the high command fell apart, on personal and national lines. Diversity became the achilles heel.

On Singapore island the Indian Army component began haemorrhaging to death, one unit at a time. The causes were inexperience, fatigue, bad leadership and subversion. The least damaged battalion, 2/17 Dogras, was wasted guarding a coastal defence battery on the mainland. Only three of the remaining 14 Indian units were neither inexperienced nor heavily diluted by replacements Harrison called "immature boys." The Jat Battalion found "the new men knew no field drill and had to be led rather like sheep." From the beginning of the campaign Major Fujiwara's F-Kikan tried to subvert Indian troops, especially officers, urging them to join the Japanese struggle to "liberate" Asia from Western imperialism. Prewar problems with Indian battalions gave the British reason to worry about such tactics. Fujiwara's efforts did not enjoy much success on the mainland. But he did recruit a number of Indian prisoners of war to be the nucleus of an Indian force. The first leader was Capt. Mohan Singh from 1/14 Punjabi, recruited after being captured near Jitra. On the island the Indian Army was less experienced and in dire peril. Fujiwara went all out against this tempting target, committing three "pacification teams" of his Indian recruits, controlled by a Japanese propaganda unit.[5]

Defeat in battle did the real damage. The most devastating blow came on 11 February when the Indian military hospital at Tyersall was destroyed by air attack. Hundreds of wounded troops were incinerated. But Fujiwara was right: the best time to subvert troops is when they feel trapped or abandoned. 4/19 Hyderabadis melted away by mass desertion before the Japanese attack on the evening of 10 February. 6/1 Punjabi's hasty retreat past the Kranji-Jurong Line was caused by Taylor's mistake, but Ballentine admitted "panic on the part of very young troops" disrupted the brigade for hours. Australian accounts of Indian troops panicking on the retreat to Reformatory Road and during the fighting along it are too numerous and consistent to dismiss. 1/15 Punjabi gave up a position south of the causeway for no reason on the night of 10 February. 1/8 Punjabi retreated without orders the night of 11 February when it was mortared. Key personally rallied the unit, but the next day three of its companies disappeared. F-Kikan induced them to desert. Several units saw a large Indian force resting with Japanese troops at MacRitchie Reservoir that same day. Fujiwara's unit scored an identical success on 14 February, dissolving 2/10 Baluch. 11th Indian Division noted with relish the deserters were spotted and shelled by their own artillery the next day. That same afternoon the Sikh Battalion dispersed under bombardment; only the company controlled by the commanding officer stood fast. The claim of the division history that as Singapore surrendered "at this hour every post of the 11th Indian Division was intact and every man at his post" is demonstrably false. Numerous war diaries and eyewitnesses agree there were large numbers of Indian troops wandering leaderless in the city in the last days of the battle. Indian gunners manning coastal artillery at Labrador fought well until enemy fire became too punishing late on the afternoon of 13 February. They ran for cover and refused to return to duty. Coastal defence batteries on Blakang Mati withstood heavy punishment for days. But after being ordered to destroy their guns on 14 February, Indian gunners from several batteries took off their uniforms, hoisted a white flag and told a British officer "the British Raj was coming to an end and that further resistance was useless." He concluded the men had decided the battle was lost and the best thing to do was wait it out. Key and Heath tried to stop this general decline. On the other hand Paris gave up on his command after it was pushed off Choa Chu Kang Road. 11th Indian Division and 44th Indian Brigade fought as formations to the end, but the weight of evidence became too great to ignore. The Indian Army was buckling and even steady units would not be able to fight on much longer.[6]

The collapse of 8th Australian Division as a formation was more dramatic and damaging but has been badly misunderstood. The most wounding accusation was that the Australians were "known as daffodils–beautiful to look at but yellow all through."[7] There were individual examples of cowardice, but for the most part this is slander. The Australians certainly did not desert en masse without a fight. The Japanese lost half their battle dead in the entire campaign on Singapore island and did most of their fighting on the island against the Australians. But many British officers and civilians remembered it differently. Numerous personal and official eyewitness accounts agree large numbers of Australian troops appeared in the city in the last days of the battle for no reason. Some broke into homes and looted; many were drunk. Some declared the battle was over and refused to return, others tried to hijack boats at gunpoint.[8] Australian records captured the bare facts. 14,972 AIF personnel were counted in Changi in captivity on 17 February, two days after Percival surrendered. Thirty-nine left Singapore as authorized evacuees on 13 February. After that the numbers can only be approximate, but the scale makes the point. Close to 2000 were in hospital on the final day of battle; add on medical, administrative and support personnel and the total might rise to 3000. Bennett had his entire division back under command on 12 February. That left a raw total of 12,000 available for the final battle, for which all non-combat personnel who could be spared had already been combed into the improvised reserve units. The highest claim, made by the Thyer/Kappe postmortem, is that at most two-thirds of those "fit to fight" stayed in position to the end. Bennett himself reported some 5000 in the final perimeter, 2000 from the infantry battalions. The Japanese did not take anything close to 7000 Australian prisoners before the final surrender.[9] Where were they?

Wavell endorsed the mass desertion charge. Soon after Singapore surrendered he returned to India as C-in-C. There he oversaw the debriefing of military and civilian escapees from the island. He appointed one of them, Major H.P. Thomas, to compile a report on the campaign and fall of Singapore, drawn from more than 60 such interviews. Wavell sent the report to Brooke with a covering note: "I have read, I think, all the principal reports which compose the evidence, and a good many others, and I consider this summary fair and accurate." It included two appendices. Appendix A was a commentary on the official report Bennett made after his controversial escape from Singapore. These comments clearly implied the Australians did not fight on the coast and the counterattacks around Bukit Timah failed because "Beyond any doubt morale and discipline at this time had gone to pieces." Appendix B listed trenchant criticisms of Shenton Thomas, but also claimed "For the fall of Singapore itself, the Australians are held responsible, while their presence in the town in disproportionately large numbers during the last days, coupled with the escape of large numbers on ships and in boats, has aroused great indignation."[10] It is true there was great indignation. But the rest of the sentence fatally misleads when not placed in proper context.

That context is the difference between straggling and desertion, how widespread they were and why the former became the latter. The AIF defined the difference in July 1940:

> Desertion is being AWL [absent without leave] in furtherance of an intention
> to quit the Defence Forces not to return or with the intention of escaping
> some particular important military duty ... the only difference between
> desertion and AWL is a difference of intention. In the case of desertion the
> intention is not to return at all or not until some important military duty such
> as embarkation is over whereas in the case of AWL the intention is to return
> but after a period.[11]

In Singapore in February 1942, substitute "cut off by enemy action but
trying to return" for AWL. Substitute "trying to escape the island or hide
in the city until the army surrendered" for desertion. The problem started
with straggling. Straggling was sparked by heavy fighting, nearly always in
reaction to circumstances on the spot. The experience of 15th Indian Brigade
was typical:

> The country consisted of small hills, partly open and partly covered with scrub
> or rubber. The Brigade was fired on by mortars and LMG's from both flanks
> and from the rear and also machine-gunned from the air ... The Brigade was
> badly split up owing to various parties making for isolated patches of cover.

But for the first three days the Australians did nearly all the fighting. Galleghan
put it bluntly: "had there been a well-organised system of stragglers posts
from the beginning of the fighting on the island there would have been much
less trouble." Because there was no such system, when the Japanese invasion
scattered Taylor's brigade the division was caught completely off guard.
Serious efforts to organize military police patrols and set up collecting posts
did not begin until late on 9 February. By then hundreds of men had already
made their own way back to the General Base Depot. Because the headquarters
of both 2/19 and 2/20 AIF were knocked out, staff officers redirected these
men into improvised units instead of returning them to the brigade. The next
day Taylor's premature retreat to Reformatory Road scattered his units again.
Taylor's brigade and attached units suffered 625 battle casualties from 8
through 10 February. But less than 500 fought on Reformatory Road the next
morning and the brigade never boasted more than 900 for the remainder of
the battle. The brigade was dispersed by massive enemy pressure, darkness,
dense bush, five retreats in two days and mishandling by higher headquarters.
Maxwell made matters worse by allowing his brigade to be dispersed.[12] The
first report of large numbers of Australian stragglers in town, made on 9
February, turned out to be exaggerated. But when Brig. Newbigging, Percival's

chief administrative officer, toured sentry posts in the city at 0415hrs on 11 February he "proceeded in fear of his life." That day the Malaya Command war diary logged report after report of troops causing trouble in the city, the majority concerning Australians. Malaya Command only finally began to establish a systematic network of collecting posts and checkpoints in the city that afternoon. It was too late.[13] The situation was much too complicated to baldly state that before a certain time troops away from units were stragglers, after it they became deserters. But the mood of the troops did respond to the course of the battle. Straggling did begin to turn into desertion.

Even as 8th Australian Division Provost Company tried to contain the problem, its war diary identified the causes. It first used the word "panic" to describe the situation just behind the battle area on 9 February. It first used the word "stragglers" on 11 February, but reported that up to that point most troops wanted food, rest and above all direction, especially back to their unit. Then things changed dramatically:

12. [February] Many soldiers of all units finding their way into Singapore saying they needed a sleep and a meal, and giving panicky accounts of the front line actions. Under the circumstances as much food as possible was provided by us, after having being [sic] collected by members of this unit from the wharves, under shell fire and aerial bombing. Soldiers are becoming very sullen, and they are so numerous that it is very difficult to collect and return them to Assembly Area.

13. [February] Conditions as on the previous day. Enemy air activity increasing. Some AIF soldiers very reluctant to return to the line, saying "there is no organisation there." British and Indian troops wandering aimlessly about. Representations made to APM Malaya Command to provide directional information for British troops, but with no result.

14. [February] More and more soldiers in Singapore, morale very low. All imaginable excuses being made to avoid returning to the line. Arms and equipment being discarded all over Singapore. Wharves crowded with soldiers viewing chances of getting off in boats.

15. [February] Enemy air and artillery action on Singapore greatly increased. Water mains severed, electricity cut off, and town very badly battered. Soldiers everywhere. Daily requests to Malaya Command to collect and direct British soldiers, but nothing done. AIF soldiers collected by this unit and transported to Botanical Gardens, but morale shocking. A lot of men hid themselves to prevent and avoid return to the line. Very heavy air raids and shelling about 1600hrs. Fires in several parts of the town, vehicles on fire along the whole length of streets, general pandemonium and confusion. Rumour that "cease fire" would be at 1600hrs caused troops to throw away arms and

ammunition, and all guns in Singapore to stop firing. Rumour proved false. Great activity in getting troops out of town and to take up arms again to hold the line until 2030hrs, when "cease fire" really became operative.

Bennett and Callaghan both later admitted there were so many Australians in the city after 12 February that the division no longer functioned as such. So did the far more thorough postmortem conducted by Thyer and Kappe. This report correctly insisted that whenever Australian troops received decent leadership they fought well even in difficult conditions–such as the remnants of 2/19 and 2/20 AIF, led for two days by Major R.O. Merrett. But it also discussed more than a few examples of companies buckling under the strain and agreed with the military police: the Australian division fell apart because the men lost confidence in their leaders–"there is no organisation there."[14]

The troops were not stupid and insisted on being led by officers who appeared to know what to do. When the battle dissolved in confusion because higher command could not put dispersed units back together, some gave up in disgust or resignation. The army and city were swamped by rumours: the AIF would be evacuated; the Americans were invading Malaya. The Australian problem started not with attitude but circumstances. While Percival waited for the main battle, they fought it. But the situation deteriorated because their own higher command failed utterly to respond. It failed because it no longer functioned. The Australian official historian drafted a section to rebut the confessions in the Thyer/Kappe report by smearing its authors. Thyer confessed to the deepest personal bias against Bennett. Wigmore argued the report was an overdone attack on Bennett by men who blamed him for their defeat, written when their spirits were at their lowest ebb and their desire for revenge got the better of them. He suggested the feud ruined working relations after, not before, the final surrender. This must be set against the evidence depicting a dysfunctional division headquarters. Even his draft called attention to stories of command failure and morale collapse, which may be why Wigmore did not print it.[15]

The Taylor-Bennett relationship fell apart completely. Taylor was so exhausted he sent himself to hospital on the morning of 12 February. On the way he reported to Bennett, who lost control:

He then went on to say that the 22nd Bde had run away from the enemy when he landed on the island, that we had let down the remainder of the force, that both I and the Bde were a disgrace to Australia and the AIF, and that he would relieve me of my command.

When Bennett did so, one officer concluded Bennett punished Taylor for leaving him in an impossible position when Wavell ordered the counterattack. The collapse of the Australian high command affected the entire army. When Percival ordered Maxwell to report to Key on 10 February Maxwell procrastinated. He was told the Indians blamed him for opening their flank and would be hostile. That foot dragging compromised 11th Indian Division. Percival's GSO 1 remembered Maxwell asking the GOC in person, before the invasion, to surrender rather than waste lives in a hopeless fight. Maxwell only admitted talking to Percival about evacuating nurses, but Thyer remembered Maxwell complaining that as a doctor his job was to save lives. Bennett said Maxwell and the division medical officer urged him to use his influence to "have the whole show called off" after the final retreat began. One of Bennett's brigadiers was exhausted, the other was a defeatist. Both lost control of their formations. But Bennett did the most damage. He had no confidence in either brigadier but left both in command until it no longer mattered. He bickered so much with his staff his headquarters was all but paralyzed. Bennett never recovered from failure in Johore and never committed himself to the fight on the island. Instead he spent more and more time planning his escape, from the island and from blame.[16] The Japanese scattered 8th Australian Division, but its own higher command finished it off.

Nevertheless, the most important evidence the Australian military police recorded was that the straggling/desertion crisis eventually affected the whole army. Some British officers agreed. Ballentine remembered:

> In adverse conditions in thick country it was so easy for men to slink rearwards and seek a passage home. There were no battle police to round up would-be deserters. When I say this I am alluding to all formations with whom I was in contact.

Stewart insisted the problem of "a number" of troops turning up in town "applies equally to British troops." Straggling was routine and desertion not uncommon in armies defeated in battle. Percival personally witnessed it in France in 1918 and around Dunkirk in 1940. It happened again in Greece and Crete in 1941; on Crete, the rearguard spent most of its time fending off deserters who tried to rush for safety. In Greece, Crete, Hong Kong and Dieppe, multinational British Empire forces blamed each other for defeat in what became international controversies. What made Singapore different was that all the worst factors were present. The army was so large and defeated so completely. Imperial fault lines included the Indians. Everyone knew this was the last battle and realized there would be no escape for the great majority.

Combat units were dispersed time and again in battles on the mainland, but that was in an empty countryside. When it happened on Singapore island the stragglers wound up in the city, in full view of the population. More troops fought to the end than gave up and many civilians did not panic. But when the city became the rear area of a battle the army was losing order finally did break down. Indian stragglers seemed mainly bewildered. Australians on the other hand were belligerent, many even defiant. One such group told Key "we're fed up with this place. If you don't get out of the way we'll shoot you."[17]

When disaster finally stared everyone in the face, many resorted instinctively to pointing fingers at "the others." For a multi-national army, defending a multi-ethnic population, blaming "the others" was a luxury none could afford. Gossip and rumour poisoned the mood of the city then and still influences the argument now. Much of it came from people who did not see enough, or did not have enough professional knowledge, to draw conclusions about the army as a whole. Prejudice provided proof. This was illustrated by a wartime book by a journalist who escaped Singapore, contrasting "peculiar" Australian behaviour with the bravery of a "considerable number" of British troops who refused to surrender, fixed bayonets and wound up being massacred–the story, passed on by "reliable sources," was a fairy tale. The Australians insisted large numbers of British troops wore the distinctive Australian style slouch hats, leaving the Aussies to take the blame when they broke and rampaged. Only two British units adopted this headgear when they ran out of their own, 2nd Loyals and 1/5 Sherwood Foresters. Heavy fighting produced stragglers from both, as well as at least two other British units: 4th Battalion The Suffolk Regiment [4th Suffolks] and the British Battalion. But Australian evidence of Australian desertion makes it ridiculous to suggest nearly all stragglers were in fact disguised Brits–just as British evidence makes it ridiculous to suggest no Brits were involved.[18]

The basis of this argument is what really matters. British officers and influential British civilians vividly remembered every incident of Australian behaviour they saw and did not like or understand. What stood out for many was an image of the big cocky Australians turning out to be "daffodils." This happened for the same reason Australian soldiers clearly remembered any snobbery they experienced from British civilians in Malaya, and Australians later remembered every assurance London gave about the "Singapore strategy" as a patronizing lie. Such inherent friction was part and parcel of trying to defend a far-flung Empire, whose collective baggage held many past grievances, popular prejudices and stereotypes. It was smoked out in Singapore by unbearable pressure. Bennett led Australian finger-pointing at the Indians, supposedly calling them "black rats." Heath spoke for many British officers when he said he finally realized in Singapore the Australians talked tougher than they fought. These were not just spleens vented by angry losers after the fact. This disparate collection never became a real team. On Singapore what cohesion they had rapidly evaporated. The straggler/deserter problem became a crisis because Japanese pressure exposed Malaya Command for what it was: a collection of units with little faith in each other or their chain of command. Malaya Command lost control of the army when it could not prevent different national components from degenerating into separate contingents blaming each other for their fate. A British officer put it succinctly: "... when armies fall apart it is invariably from the top downwards."[19]

Bennett cast the most dramatic vote of no confidence. After Percival ordered the retreat to the final perimeter, he ordered the AIF to concentrate in its own final all around defensive position. This turned the Australian position into an ellipse around AIF headquarters at Tanglin Barracks, with only one side facing the enemy. But he then went beyond a sensible effort to pull his division back together. Bennett refused Maxwell's urging to surrender the AIF, but in every other respect took it out of the common fight. His last telegram to Australia on 14 February reported "AIF now concentrating in Tanglin area two miles from city proper ... can rely on troops to hold to last as usual. All other fronts weak ... If enemy enter city behind us will take suitable action to avoid unnecessary sacrifice." By that Bennett meant he would not retreat into the city to fight it out, but keep the AIF together in place until Percival surrendered the army or was overrun. To conserve ammunition, he ordered artillery and machine gunners to fire only on targets attacking AIF positions. Bennett ordered the AIF to turn its back on the rest of the army. These orders were confirmed even after the Australians captured maps indicating the main Japanese attack was targeting the sector just south of the Australian perimeter. Australian gunners were forbidden, at least twice, to fire on Japanese infantry advancing across their front in enfilade to attack their neighbours.[20]

18th Division had a different experience, but this too was due to circumstances. It was not vulnerable to subversion. Most of the division was fresh and fit. There were no crippling feuds between senior commanders. It did no fighting on the island before Tomforce advanced on Bukit Timah. Nevertheless it did not escape the general decline. Its problem was not dysfunctional but rather inexperienced leaders. When five tanks attacked 1/5 Sherwood Foresters near the Chinese High School on 12 February the battalion scattered; that afternoon its commanding officer reported only 20 men back in position. On 13 February a detached company of 5th Battalion Bedfordshire and Hertfordshire Regiment [5th Beds and Herts] abandoned its position "without orders or necessity" after the officer commanding was killed by heavy shelling. That same night the Japanese used firecrackers to bait 54th Brigade headquarters to reveal its positions, a tactic they used often during the campaign. This unit, commanded by senior officers, reacted with "several hours" of "pandemonium" firing. The next night the brigade reported two of its battalions were "spent." On the final day the third, the reassembled 1/5 Sherwood Foresters, abandoned their positions after hearing a white flag was spotted. Even one of the division's finer moments indicated why the army was now compromised. The second detached battlegroup, commanded by Brig. T.H. Massey-Beresford from 55th Brigade, went west to help hold the reservoirs on 11 February. Massey-Beresford considered this futile, because it left too few troops to hold the northern coast but sent too few to restore the position at Bukit Timah. But after receiving the exhortatory Orders of the Day he proposed to lead Masseyforce "on a front of 1000 yards astride [the trunk road] headed by himself with the Union Jack." He hoped such boldness would at least revive morale if not stop the enemy. This inspired his officers, whose "unhappy faces lit up with cheerful smiles at the prospect of death with honour." But tactically it was a ludicrous proposal to repeat the Tomforce attack. When Heath rejected it however, he claimed it would only repeat a previous Australian failure.[21]

Malaya Command suffered from one final self-inflicted threat on Singapore island: the notorious "fifth column." In the Spanish Civil War Franco's forces took Madrid by attacking it from outside with four columns, supposedly assisted by an organized network of sympathizers among the population within. This spectre bothered the army throughout the campaign. The reason was only slightly exaggerated by a British resident serving as a junior officer with 2nd Loyals: "Never was an army defending a country more foreign to that country than was the British Army in Malaya in 1941-42." Language was a problem. So was acclimatization, or the lack of it. Driving them both was attitude. Heath stated the civil population was not a governing military factor because it did not develop "an effective hostile attitude." But it did become an unsettling factor when a large majority of the rank and file decided that was how many Asians felt. The stories started right away: lights were shone out to sea to guide the Japanese to the beaches at Kota Bharu! Soon every winking light was sinister, every accurate Japanese bombing raid was treachery, every pile of lumber near a bridge was collaboration, all Japanese scouts wore native dress. Individuals recorded the full spectrum of behaviour by Asians of all communities: active collaboration with the Japanese; a straightforward desire to stay out of the way and survive; enthusiastic support, at personal risk, for the Allies. But a consensus did emerge, expressed crudely by an officer who spent most of January trekking through the countryside trying to rejoin a friendly force: "Chinese and Tamils were friendly and could be relied upon. All Malays should be avoided or shot."[22]

Such attitudes caused the summary execution of some civilians in Malaya by jittery units. 18th Division spent hours every day on Singapore island patrolling for fifth columnists it assumed must be snooping around its positions. Even the experienced III Indian Corps claimed "within 48 hours of establishing Corps HQ the local laundry had hung out their washing in the shape of an enormous arrow pointing straight at our building." Asian attitudes varied from region to region, but there was no organized fifth column. Fujiwara did woo Indian sympathies and the Japanese did exploit espionage assets, especially the large body of freely available information gathered by expatriate Japanese before the war. But the Japanese decided not to make a serious effort to organize Malay collaboration during the campaign. They felt it would be a distraction costing more than it produced. Most incidents were not what they seemed. Japanese infantry did routinely don native dress, sometimes because their own was tattered, sometimes as a *ruse de guerre*. But lumber was piled near bridges by the Public Works Department, to help Malaya Command. Japanese airmen flying at speed were not likely to see arrows made of laundry; headquarters gave themselves away by locating in prominent buildings surrounded by vehicles. Many Malays who told stragglers to move on did so because they were afraid. Many who guided Japanese patrols did so under duress.[23]

British authorities assumed the Malay population as a whole was "loyal," or at least non-political. Malay nationalism was not menacing before the war, but the Malays were not nearly as satisfied with the status quo as officialdom believed. There were in fact collaborators, more anti-British than pro-Japanese. But the real problem was that the Malays "failed" as a community to rally to the cause and staunchly oppose the Japanese, as the Chinese did. This shocked the British, to the core. They did not believe the Malays could make mass political decisions, so they jumped to the patronizing conclusion there must be a fifth column. Military intelligence and the police both concluded this fear was greatly overdone:

> ... the amount of genuine fifth column activity in the Colony was astonishingly small. Hundreds of hysterical reports were received and investigated, in the weeks preceding the capitulation. The Detective Branch reduced these to approximately 100 cases worthy of investigation; and final investigation produced a handful of cases in which there might have been evidence of enemy influence.

But such sober analysis did not soothe the army, which decided it was not defending a friendly population. That made its job harder. It also underlined how fragile this part of the Empire was in the first place. Even the level-headed and experienced Inspector-General of the Straits Settlements Police could offer only a tepid endorsement: "Generally the Malay, whatever his behaviour, behaved better than was expected of him during the attack."[24]

Malaya Command fought on despite losing Bukit Timah. That forced Yamashita to finish it off. This was a risky proposition that gave Twenty-Fifth Army anxious moments as the end approached, too slowly for their liking. Malaya Command was trapped in a semi-circle extending barely five kilometres beyond the commercial harbour. Yamashita faced his nightmare: going into the narrow city streets to kill a larger force cornered like a rat. He would have been relieved to know this was never going to happen. The British government did not in the end have the nerve to order Malaya Command to die fighting–and the army could not carry out the order anyway. For the last time Malaya Command missed a chance to make its enemy pay a real price for victory because it could not seize an opportunity. Strategic co-operation was no longer possible. Communications now all but collapsed, which paralyzed higher command. That destroyed what faith the army had left in it, and in the contingents they fought alongside. In extremis the troops turned to the structure that formed the backbone of British Empire armies: their own battalion. Bennett's decision to pull the AIF into its own laager was only the most extreme action in a pattern that spread throughout the army. Staunch units stood and fought, but the battle degenerated into local fights not connected to a general defence. The issue was already decided, but as usual it proved as difficult to end a campaign as to start one–and much depended on how hostilities ended.

Percival's final retreat did force the Japanese to resort to brute force. There was no way to outflank this perimeter on land and no time to do so by water. Yamashita ordered his army to advance in full strength. The aim was to destroy Percival's army and shatter its rear area before it could fall back to fight in the streets. The Imperial Guardsadvanced southeast, but Heath's forces retreated to their final perimeter before the Japanese could get behind them. This deflected the Guards towards Paya Lebar, probing for a gap. 5th Division, reinforced by nearly all remaining tank units, attacked astride the trunk road, sparking heavy fighting south of the reservoirs. 18th Division attacked along the south coast, driving towards the harbour. Launching three fairly widely separated attacks against a larger force was risky in principle, made more so by what was now Yamashita's biggest headache. To their consternation the

Japanese found themselves facing artillery fire that increased as the defenders retreated. Some of this came from the powerful coastal guns and all of it caused them real problems. Heavy bombardment kept the Guards from repairing the causeway breach until 12 February. This plus heavy shelling in the Bukit Timah and Reformatory Road areas forced 18th Division to set its advance back an entire day. Worst of all, the shelling made it harder to bring up supplies, especially ammunition. Yamashita's staff feared they might yet face a counterattack "on the grand scale" while they struggled to concentrate their power.[25]

The Japanese did not know Malaya Command could no longer do any such thing. In for a penny, in for a pound–they met the challenge by counterbattery fire and playing their trump card. Control of the air finally became decisive in the land battle here on Singapore island. Japanese aircraft now concentrated on the defenders artillery. Because the guns were now in and around the city itself, at positions such as the Botanical Gardens, Government House and the Padang, this increased the punishment it was already suffering. Heavy air attacks devastated Orchard Road, the warehouses along the Singapore River, the city centre and the docks and warehouses in Keppel Harbour. Pulling out all the stops, the Japanese ordered their artillery to "fire at Singapore streets in order to create panic among citizens."[26]

Japanese airmen could intervene effectively because they had such a concentrated target and no longer faced any opposition besides anti-aircraft fire. 232 Squadron was overwhelmed by superior force and ABDA Command now faced another threat: the Japanese force closing on Sumatra. Japanese air attacks chewed up Allied airpower faster than it could be reinforced. On 10 February Wavell ordered the squadron and all remaining RAF personnel to evacuate Singapore, so ABDA Command could concentrate airpower to defend Sumatra. Late on 13 February Pulford joined the last official evacuation, in a flotilla of the remaining seaworthy craft led by Spooner himself. This air force withdrawal made strategic sense, but only drove home Singapore's isolation. Pulford's farewell to Percival caught the mood: "I suppose you and I will be held responsible for this, but God knows we did our best with what little we had been given."[27]

Yet another controversy surrounds the question of evacuation, especially of civilians. It is easy to see where the bitterness came from. Even for those who made it last-minute evacuation was a nightmare, while those who stayed behind endured the living hell of occupation by the Japanese. This trauma cast the main issue: why were more civilians not evacuated from Singapore before the Japanese cut it off? The evacuation of civilians had no direct affect on whether Singapore fell quickly or not. But it did reflect central problems in its defence: race, responsibility, personalities, priorities and the politics of imperial defence.

Before the war one school of thought felt compulsory evacuation of civilians, especially families of servicemen and officials, would send a signal the British were ready to clear the decks and fight. But another felt it would provoke a crisis in the colonies by signalling to the Asian populations the Europeans were ready to abandon them. Shenton Thomas certainly belonged to the latter. No compulsory evacuation order was issued for Malaya or Singapore. The Penang evacuation and ensuing controversy hardened opinions. There were in principle two ways to settle the question. One was to leave the population to fend for itself. But Japanese cruelty in China and Hong Kong made that unthinkable. The other was to order civilians to evacuate battle areas, as a military necessity. This was not possible either and the main reason was the politics of race. The small European community could be evacuated, to Australia, India or even the U.K. itself. On the other hand many in and out of government did not believe until very late in the day this would be necessary. Many also felt they should "set an example" by staying put. Shenton Thomas was not the only one who saw this consideration as the foundation of the British Empire in the Far East, as important as military power itself. As for the Asians, Malays would not want to be evacuated. Many Indians and especially Chinese would, but this raised a painful question: where could so many go? It is commonplace to point to the Cooper-Thomas feud as the problem. This rift did affect evacuation efforts.[28] But the root of the problem ran deeper. The central direction of the war did not square up to this responsibility.

The COS agreed it would be militarily prudent to evacuate as many civilians who did no essential war work as possible. But when the British government sent directives to Cooper and Thomas on 22 and 23 December they authorized and encouraged them to evacuate civilians, but did not order them to make it compulsory. They also declared it was "most important to avoid racial discrimination." This was passing the buck. Many families left to choose for themselves would stay together until defeat seemed imminent—then it would be too late to get away. But the really delicate problem was the Chinese. Many thousands would want to go. Some were prominent leaders in anti-Japanese activities, certain to be on a Japanese target list. There was not enough shipping to send them all to the U.K., which would not want them all anyway. India, Australia and the Dutch East Indies also refused to accept more than small numbers. Nobody wanted to grasp the nettle and either demand refuge for as many Chinese as could get out or order the Europeans out regardless of any backlash it caused in Singapore. That allowed Thomas to sidestep the whole issue. Passages were available on ships leaving Singapore throughout the campaign, but the government made no effort to publicize this or encourage evacuation. When the COS raised the issue again on 21 January, as a question not an order, Percival reported 5200 European women and children had been evacuated but another 4800 remained in Singapore. Most now wanted to go.[29] The vicious circle took hold: by the time the government did not have to encourage let alone order evacuation, it could no longer arrange it.

Air attacks forced the P & O Company, the agent of passage, to relocate offices, which caused many delays. The government insisted on maintaining passport controls, to make sure refugees did not embark for barred destinations. That caused more delays and provoked much anger. The invasion of the island plunged the dockside into chaos. The Governor ordered the Harbour Board technical staff to evacuate on the grounds they did essential war work. The police received conflicting orders regarding whether to stay on the job or try to escape. Civilians crowded into the port seeking escape. Many abandoned cars, which created gridlock. Those who reached the docks were trapped between enemy air attacks and the disintegration of administration and order. The final official evacuation arranged by Spooner on 13 February was the worst. Because only five hours notice was given, many never received word. Those who did boarded a motley flotilla of 40 vessels bound for Java, accompanied by military personnel selected to escape—and not a few deserters. Few made it past the Japanese fleet advancing on Sumatra. Spooner and Pulford were among those who died, after being cast away on a deserted malarial island. Some 10,000 women and children were evacuated from Singapore during the campaign, including 3000 Asians. But hundreds of European women and children remained, with thousands of others of all races who would have escaped if they could. This fiasco was not militarily decisive.[30] But it highlighted the vicious circle that was. Those responsible for imperial defence would not make command decisions about its most sensitive issues. Those left in Singapore to muddle through could not do so.

It was not unique in a city under siege for law and order to collapse when its defences began to crumble. In Singapore that was spurred on by the trauma of evacuation and separation. Essential services finally buckled, as many workers and volunteers gave up and went to ground. Fires went unchecked, looting increased. Liquor stocks were deliberately destroyed. The Governor and Lady Thomas were forced into the Singapore Club in the Fullerton Building after Government House was heavily attacked. Every hospital was filled beyond capacity and many other buildings were pressed into service, including St. Andrew's Cathedral and the Cathay Cinema.[31] This atmosphere affected the army, just as its decline panicked the population. It pointed very visibly to the end. Instead of trying to take advantage of Japanese problems, Percival could only try to prevent his command from disintegrating because of its own.

When Malaya Command ordered the general retreat on 12 February it signalled the end was nigh, because the final perimeter was already untenable. Some units had to deploy in residential areas just outside the city. From Bukit Timah hill the enemy could overlook the whole final perimeter. The supply position was worse. Many warehouses full of civilian rations were destroyed by Japanese bombing. The military lost so many supplies around Bukit Timah that for the first time stocks of nearly everything were dangerously low. The worst threat was the water supply. By 13 February Malaya Command controlled only the southern shore of one of the two reservoirs, MacRitchie, and the pumping station feeding water from it. Percival hinted to Wavell that if he lost that foothold, or the distribution system broke down, he must capitulate.[32]

Another dramatic signal was the order to destroy the coastal artillery. Changi Fire Command did so on 12 February, the gunners moving into the perimeter as infantry. Faber Fire Command's batteries at Labrador and on Blakang Mati fought on until the 14th when they were either knocked out or ordered to spike.[33] These were tangible blows. This fight was now a test of endurance between tired infantry in which the Japanese most feared the defenders artillery, especially the "drum cans" fired by the coastal guns. Henry Frei titled his study based on ordinary Japanese soldiers memories of the battle The Guns of February. But their high command could provide a convincing incentive: victory lay within their grasp. Malaya Command could offer no such hope and found it harder and harder to communicate with let alone control units. Many now fought on their own without higher direction. One order that reached virtually every unit sent a signal few misread: send a dozen selected personnel to army headquarters for a "special mission." This was the evacuation led by Spooner and the secret did not remain so for long.[34]

This all led to the last tactical irony of the campaign. When Malaya Command finally forced the Japanese to frontally assault a linear defence, it could no longer co-ordinate a set-piece battle. The Japanese were only slowed down by their own supply problems, the weight of Malaya Command's artillery, and some stubborn defending by individual battalions. Because they could maneuver, co-ordinate units and combine arms, they made headway. The Japanese main assault, a two regiment push south of the reservoirs by 5th Division, forced 18th Division into battle just as it tried to shuffle into line. Beckwith-Smith tried to pin the enemy down in a positional battle in mixed terrain: reservoir catchment scrub mingled with residential gardens and detached colonial houses. The Japanese disrupted this by, predictably, infiltrating between units at night. 18th Division tried to build a stable line by committing every unit. That restricted it to local counterattacks, which helped the enemy. Massey-Beresford decided to establish a stop-line running from Farrer Road along Adam Road, then towards Broadcast Hill. The heaviest fighting soon developed along that arc. Three days of infantry brawling punctuated by heavy shelling on both sides pushed the British back on Mount Pleasant. There was heavy fighting around the Chinese Cemetery [Bukit Brown], but 1st Cambs stood fast in a terrific fight around Adam Park, holding Percival's own residence. By the evening of the 14th the division's fighting power was declining so quickly only the weight of supporting artillery kept any line intact. Japanese tenacity was the main reason but the division's inexperience was also a factor, summed up unintentionally by Massey-Beresford: "I have been unable to get away from the reflection that this wooded country without prepared positions and with limited troops is INDEFENSIBLE especially in the face of the expert infiltration tactics of the enemy."[35]

The Japanese 18th Division, tough coal miners from Kyushu, attacked along the south coast. The division was harder hit by the first four days of fighting on the island, but Yamashita's staff deliberately provoked it by designating 5th Division to break into the city and giving it most of the supporting armour. Here the defenders held better ground. Pasir Panjang ridge ran parallel to the south coast for five kilometres, from Reformatory to Alexandra Roads. There were strongpoints along the ridge, designed to repel attack from the sea but giving good observation over approaches from the west. Some pillboxes along the coast road could also bear west. Artillery support included two 6" guns at Labrador, which could bear on targets as far west as Pasir Panjang village. Two roads sandwiched the ridge lengthwise: the coast road along the south and Ayer Rajah Road along the north. 44th Indian Brigade held the area above Ayer Rajah Road. 1st Malaya Brigade held from there to the coast. The ridge itself was held by Malaya Command's only regular infantry unit native to the country it defended: 1st Battalion The Malay Regiment [1st Malay].[36]

1st Malay was an experiment that now vindicated its champions. The long years of British ascendancy in Malaya, dating from 1874, generated a stereotype in British perceptions of the Malays: a complacent even idle people, who would not make "good soldier material." Ideas of inherently "martial races" were common in the Empire at the time, especially in India; in Malaya they were reinforced by the sense it was just as well for political stability and British ascendancy that this image be true. Some Malaya Command officers disagreed and in 1932 persuaded the WO to raise a trial company. When it was deemed successful 1st Malays were raised in 1936, manned by Malays recruited from all over the country. The battalion was a regular unit of the British Army. At first all officers and senior nco's were British, but by 1941 there were nine Malay junior officers and many nco's. The commanding officer, Lt.-Col. J.R.G. Andre, spoke Malay and had been with the unit for some years. The second battalion was raised in 1940, but still short a full rifle company when war broke out. Apart from two brief company detachments on the mainland the regiment stayed in Singapore as part of the garrison. Both battalions remained unaffected by seeing Australian and Indian stragglers moving through them as they redeployed. By evening 12 February 1st Malaya Brigade held the sector from just north of Ayer Rajah Road to the sea. 1st Malay held the ridge itself, three rifle companies forward and one in reserve.[37]

The three main tactical features were the junction of Reformatory and Pasir Panjang Roads; the westernmost hill on the ridge, just west of Reformatory Road, on which a mosque now sits; and the northern slope of the ridge, which provided excellent fields of fire over Ayer Rajah Road and ground to the north. The first two were held by companies of 1st Malay, the last by attached Australian carriers supported by elements of 2nd Malay. On the morning of 13 February heavy shelling forced the Malays off the hill west of the road. From that foothold the Japanese infiltrated along the heavily wooded ridge. Fighting escalated all afternoon, particularly around the road junction. The 1st Malay company holding the village stood fast, supported by machine gun pillboxes and the 6" guns at Labrador. But after the carriers on the northern slope left or were driven off their positions, the Japanese brought down enfilade fire north of Ayer Rajah Road and on Pasir Panjang village. When the coastal guns were neutralized in late afternoon the whole area became untenable. Brig. G.G.R. Williams ordered the brigade to retreat after dark to the Alexandra Road area and regroup. Andre personally evacuated all pillboxes, leaving one company on a dominant hilltop to block Japanese infiltration overnight.[38]

1st Malay fought stubbornly in a positional defence, but this was a brigade battle. Williams complained he received almost no direction from Southern Area; his battalions complained they received too little from him. Elrington of 2nd Loyals and Williams both assumed the Australian carriers on the northern slope gave up their vital position for no good reason. Battalions pulled in on themselves. There was no reserve. Gaps opened up in the retreat and no higher authority made any effort to pull the sector together. 2nd Loyals retreated to their own base at Gillman Barracks but lost contact with 1st Malays on the left and British and Indian units on the right, despite the fact the gaps were no more than a few hundred metres. Andre lost touch with the company he left at the crucial position: the hilltop near the Opium Factory. It dominated the

Buona Vista Road, which bisects the ridge, and overlooked the whole area. The retreat placed Alexandra Hospital in the front line, on the dividing line between brigade sectors. It stood barely 400 metres from 2nd Loyals but they left it to the unit in whose sector it lay. The remnants of 15th Indian Brigade actually waited overnight at the hospital while senior officers searched for orders. But when the British Battalion left before dawn nobody evacuated any patients or staff. Williams actually ordered his brigade to retreat all the way back to the Singapore River for a final stand. Simmons countermanded the order, but none of the front-line units received it anyway.[39]

The Japanese infiltrated through woods overnight and attacked the next morning, pushing hard along the ridge and Ayer Rajah Road. 2nd Loyals defended their own homes. The battle raged all day, infantry fighting at close quarters on wooded slopes and around barracks blocks. The heavy bombardment unleashed by both sides prevented either from breaking the other, but also kept the Loyals isolated from their neighbours. 1st Malay resisted Japanese attacks near Buona Vista village, including at least one using civilians forced to run ahead as human shields. Worse followed on the hilltop near the Opium Factory. Japanese infiltration cut off C Company, helped by burning oil flowing through wide drains behind and below the Malays. C Company beat back Japanese assaults with steady Bren gun fire, but both sides suffered heavily. By late afternoon only one officer survived, 2nd Lt. Adnan Saidi. The Japanese overran the position and gave no quarter; only four Malays escaped the enemy and the drains. The Japanese massacred the remainder, reportedly torturing Adnan to death. Late in the afternoon the battalion retreated to a knoll on the edge of Keppel Golf Course, overlooking the junction of the coast road and Alexandra Road. They were supported by a British Battalion platoon and some anti-aircraft gunners. When the Japanese came straight down the road they ran into an ambush from this knoll that cut one company to pieces. Both sides then slumped in exhaustion overnight.[40] But this kind of punishment had already provoked the Japanese to commit the most ominous atrocity yet.

Shortly before 1430 hrs on 14 February, retreating Indian troops took advantage of a rise in the ground and the cover of large buildings to fire on the Japanese as they advanced astride the railway. Unfortunately, this was the grounds of Alexandra Hospital. Minutes later a Japanese company in full battle gear charged into the hospital. Their quarry was gone but when the staff tried to surrender Japanese infantry rampaged through the overcrowded military hospital in a killing frenzy; one patient on the operating table was bayoneted to death. At least 50 people were massacred before the blood lust abated; within the hour more than 200 survivors were rounded up. Most were marched across Ayer Rajah Road and crammed into small servants quarters behind a nurses residence. The next day the Japanese started taking them out in pairs and murdering them by bayonet. When "friendly fire" hit the building at 1430hrs the survivors bolted. Most were cut down by machine gun fire but at least five escaped. The main motive for this massacre was to avenge heavy losses suffered from punishing artillery fire, which pounded the whole area through these last actions. Japanese front line infantry were in fact being driven close to a breaking point by the strain of battle.[41]

The IJA routinely brutalized its own soldiers and showed almost no respect for internationally accepted rules of war after 1931. It saw this as total war between races and empires with irreconcilable cultural differences over who would set what rules for Asia. And it fought accordingly, a law unto itself. Heavy punishment in battle often provoked Japanese soldiers to run amok, as at Parit Sulong and Alexandra. Nothing can excuse these disgusting atrocities, but culture and circumstances explains them. Yamashita was something of an exception among Japanese general officers in trying to maintain discipline for its own sake, but no one fighting the Japanese in 1942 could safely assume they would not put a city and its defenders to the sword if forced to take it by storm. Percival did not know about Alexandra but knew what happened in Nanking.[42] He recognized his final challenge: to capitulate while his army could still surrender as an organized force–and while Yamashita could still rein his army in enough to accept capitulation with discipline and control.

Four considerations affected the capitulation of Singapore: the strategic situation in the region; the supply situation in Singapore; the fighting power of both armies; and the fate of the civil population. The first step was Wavell's signal to Churchill on 11 February. The Supreme Commander followed up two days later by "warning of serious change in situation which may shortly arise necessitating complete reorientation of plans." This referred to "unexpectedly rapid advance of enemy on Singapore," allowing the enemy to threaten both Sumatra and Java before I Australian Corps could intervene. This long message was Wavell's first warning the whole Malay Barrier, ie. his command, would be overrun. He suggested diverting the Australians to whatever last ditch position might still be salvaged: Burma or Australia itself. The next morning Wavell zeroed in: Percival would soon be forced to surrender; Japanese forces were invading Sumatra by air and sea; it was time to reconsider grand strategy. Wavell's first signal crossed a telegram from Churchill promising Roosevelt the large British Empire force in Singapore would fight to the "bitter end." But his second prompted the Prime Minister and COS to discuss the question on 13 February. Churchill finally accepted the fact Malaya Command could no longer fight long enough to assist the

Allies elsewhere no matter what he said. Therefore he agreed with Brooke: forcing the civil population to endure the "horrors of street fighting" could now only produce "needless slaughter." On 14 February Shenton Thomas chimed in: Singapore was on the brink of total collapse. Churchill handed the baton to Wavell that evening: "You are of course sole judge of the moment when no further result can be gained at Singapore and should instruct Percival accordingly."[43]

Percival knew by the weekend he would have to surrender–but spent most of it seeking a reason not to. All he found was the least humiliating reason to capitulate. Heath started the search, persuading Percival to summon commanders to state their views at Fort Canning on the afternoon of 13 February. Heath insisted the army was nearly spent, the city was being destroyed, so he "did not see any use in continuing the struggle." Bennett said the city was "crowded with battle stragglers," implying they should surrender before the army fell apart. Percival replied their orders were to fight on and he wanted to counterattack. Heath, Bennett, Key, Simmons and Beckwith-Smith all replied they could not counterattack because they had no reserve and their troops were all exhausted. Percival complained: "There are other things to consider. I have my honour to consider and there is also the question of what posterity will think of us if we surrender this large army and valuable fortress." Heath replied "You need not bother about your honour. You lost that a long time ago in the north." Percival argued he could not ignore larger strategic issues outside Singapore and refused to surrender, but agreed to send a full report to Wavell. The writing was so clearly on the wall the meeting then discussed the final evacuation that night. Heath's charge was outrageous but Percival could not ignore the obvious. His commanders were not just venting frustrations. They had no confidence left in either the army or him.[44]

Earlier that same day the Municipal Engineer gave Simson an ominous report: the water supply would collapse, perhaps within 24 hours. The problem was not the supply itself. The Japanese did not turn off the flow after they took the island reservoirs; a brave civilian engineer manned the pumping station at Woodleigh even after it became part of the front line. The problem was distribution. Nearly the entire pipeline grid was above ground. Simson received all the help he asked for but Japanese bombing and shelling now outpaced all efforts his engineers made to protect and repair the pipes. Dozens and dozens of breaks and leaks spilled precious water, reducing the pressure so much that on the 14th Simson agreed the system would soon collapse and reported this to Percival. There was more: the loss of the massive supply dumps around Bukit Timah, plus the fact Alexandra magazine was now under fire and difficult to use, reduced supplies of many types of ammunition to critical levels. Later that morning the Governor urged Percival to surrender before the water ran out and sent his report to London. Percival toured the defences, met Key and reviewed the situation with his most aggressive general. Key argued the water situation, the collapse of units on the western front and the dire threat to the civilian population all made it pointless to fight on. Percival suggested "a simultaneous advance on all fronts as a dying gesture." Key said this could only end in a massacre of the army followed by pillage of the city when the Japanese stormed in with blood boiling. He urged Percival to surrender "while Japanese soldiery could be controlled by their commander."[45]

Such pressure prompted Percival to call another conference at Fort Canning on the morning of 15 February. Simson confirmed the latest reports on the supply situations. Within a day the army would run out of ammunition for 25pdrs–the mainstay of its artillery–petrol, and water. Heath claimed "there would be a serious situation" if Indian troops ran out of water. When Percival suggested counterattacking to retake the supplies near Bukit Timah, everyone else agreed it could not be done. Bennett mentioned stragglers again, insisting most were Indian. Percival finally agreed to capitulate. Someone suggested destroying heavy weapons and other equipment, before the Japanese could demand them in return for agreeing to cease fire. Percival decided it was too dangerous to destroy weapons before settling a ceasefire but ordered the destruction of technical equipment, codes and documents. During the discussion Wavell's telegram arrived, authorizing surrender. This removed Percival's last objection.[46] But now the tricky part began.

The situation was too chaotic to expect the battle to be terminated without problems arising. But the confusion that now engulfed Malaya Command was not just a consequence of surrender–it reflected the most basic cause. The hardest time to maintain discipline, on both sides, is when a battle is ending. Arranging to cease fire while battle rages between two badly frayed armies requires close coordination within and between them. It was important to make sure nobody gave up too soon and left themselves open to attack, or fought on after the agreed time and provoked the enemy to resume battle. Percival agreed to send a delegation to invite Yamashita to enter the city to parley. Heath pointed out it would take time for both sides to inform all forward units when to cease fire and what to do then. He suggested 2000hrs, to allow time to spread the word. This prompted "objections" on the grounds it would be dark by then, which increased the chance of confusion and mistakes, and it was crucial to end hostilities that night. Percival agreed and ordered the delegation to propose 1600hrs. But by the time they set out it was already 1130hrs. Brig. Newbigging, Colonial Secretary Hugh Fraser, and Heath's GSO 2, Major Cyril Wild, fluent in Japanese, drove in a staff car flying a white flag until they reached the forward position at the junction of Adam and Bukit Timah Roads. They then walked into enemy territory and were taken to the nearest company headquarters, where they handed over a letter from Percival replying to Yamashita's letter on the 11th. An hour later Col. Sugita met the party bearing Yamashita's reply. This brushed aside the invitation to visit Percival–who after all was surrendering to whom!– and invited him to visit Japanese headquarters as soon as possible to discuss surrender. Newbigging wrote in 1600hrs as the time for the meeting. But Wild noticed a troubling clause: the Japanese insisted all Allied units cease fire and stand fast while discussions took place but did not offer to do the same in return. Sugita refused to discuss this, then ordered Wild to fly a large Japanese flag from the top of the Cathay Building as soon as Percival agreed to meet Yamashita, so the Japanese could prepare for the meeting. Wild persuaded Sugita to agree the flag need only be flown for ten minutes, but returned to friendly lines with great misgivings.[47]

Wild had reason to be worried: this was cutting it too close. By the time the delegation returned to Fort Canning it was already 1500hrs. Heath's headquarters was in the Cathay Building, only minutes away, but Wild saw a serious misunderstanding unfolding. Percival now expected the army to fight on until he reached a final agreement with Yamashita. But the order that went out after the morning conference, which every formation in the army prepared to obey, was to cease fire at 1600hrs. Even if Percival was at that moment meeting Yamashita, there could not yet be a final agreement. Yet even after Wild briefed Heath, raised the flag, returned to Malaya Command and warned Percival about the conflicting orders, Percival set off for his meeting before the contradiction could be sorted out with all formations. This was asking for trouble. Were units to allow troops to try to escape or not? Should weapons now be destroyed to prevent the enemy from capturing them? Should units stand fast or retreat to a rendezvous point? The sight of the Japanese flag could prompt them to cease fire before it was safe to do so. But Yamashita might conclude Percival was playing false if he came to parley while fighting continued. Many troops saw the staff car with a white flag. The news was bound to spread quickly and certain to be misunderstood by some. If some units downed arms while others fought on, the whole process could collapse.[48]

After the morning conference Bennett ordered the AIF to stand fast and forbade the men to escape. Australian headquarters feared mass dispersal in a *sauve qui peut* could lead to slaughter if the enemy became frustrated trying to round up large numbers of stragglers wandering around a battlefield. They rightly decided it was safer to keep units together. At 1600hrs Malaya

Command ordered the Australians to destroy their artillery. Bennett refused to do so until a ceasefire was confirmed. From their positions Australian troops saw British units on the right "breaking up," some passing through their lines. But as the Australian provost company noted, so many AIF personnel ignored Bennett's orders their own position became chaotic. At 1800hrs Malaya Command told the AIF Percival had capitulated and the ceasefire would take effect at 2030hrs. Most units received orders no later than 2000hrs. Bennett confirmed the veto on escape but division headquarters now passed on orders to comply with Japanese demands by handing over weapons and equipment. At least some units did so. Others refused in disgust. All ceased fire at the appointed time without serious incident.[49] But the last problem the Australians faced came, as so often, not from the enemy but from their own commander.

The division war diary recorded for 1900hrs "Gen G Bennett, Maj Moses, Lt Walker not seen at HQ after this hour." On 11 February Bennett ordered a small select party to prepare to escape. When the time came, without warning his own staff let alone Percival, Bennett led this party away into the night. Bennett's decision remains controversial. His motives were typical of the man. He assumed he had experience fighting the Japanese that must be preserved to help defend Australia–and could not bear the thought of rotting in a prison camp while regular force rivals took charge of the Australian Army! Why not admire this as the brave act of a true fighter? Because Bennett had responsibilities he could not simply walk away from as if he were a private soldier. It was for Canberra, not Bennett, to decide if he could help the nation more by escaping than by staying with his men to lead them through the ordeal of captivity. Bennett decided for them and abandoned his own men. Malaya Command, fractious within, hard-pressed from without, could not afford anything less than exceptional high command from all contingents. Bennett fell well short of what the army required–and disgracefully below what his men deserved.[50]

The experience of units melting away in confusion right next to others battling on was repeated all over Singapore that afternoon. Newbigging's party drove with their white flag through an area held by 18th Division. Seeing that flag "proved disastrous" for 54th Brigade, provoking 1/5 Foresters to abandon their positions, sparking a rumour the army had already surrendered. When a Malaya Command staff officer arrived at brigade headquarters at 1545hrs to order it to fight on until Percival and Yamashita settled the issue he was told "this was now impossible." The brigade was scattered on both sides of the trunk road. It ceased fire at 1630hrs, then sat tight and listened to heavy fighting less than two kilometres away. 55th Brigade stopped firing at 1600hrs. All it could ask its "tired mixed elements" to do was hang on to Lornie and

Braddell Roads "by the skin of their teeth." On the other hand heavy fighting continued around Mount Pleasant Road and Adam Park, barely 600 metres from where Percival crossed into enemy territory. 4th Suffolks and 1st Cambs battled on because Beckwith-Smith threw caution to the winds and committed his entire division artillery to deliver a "crescendo" of fire support between 1400 and 1500hrs. After that the ammunition position became "extremely grave" and the troops "fatigued beyond measure." 9th Northumberland Fusiliers summed up the day for all: "Except for messages from coys to Bn HQ reporting the situation on our own front, nothing certain was known by us of the state of affairs elsewhere, although countless rumours flew around."[51]

Harrison went to Fort Canning just in time to catch Torrance and Percival on their way to parley and confirmed the order to fight until ordered otherwise. 11th Indian Division flatly refused to hand over any guns and fired off all remaining ammunition. Things were more confusing in the eastern sector. Outright desertion increased all day until the rumour of a ceasefire at 1600hrs prompted some units to abandon their positions en masse. Coastal gunners now fighting as infantry stood their ground. Under direct orders from a brigadier one gunner officer shot two officers from a deserting unit who refused to rally their men, killing one. But such summary action came too little too late to stop the line south of Paya Lebar from disintegrating before the ceasefire took effect. At least one anti-tank battery accepted orders not to destroy any more guns and bring those not yet spiked back to the SSVF depot. On the western front the battle for Gillman Barracks raged on under heavy artillery fire from both sides until late afternoon. But just to the north the British Battalion sat tight, suffering nothing more than mortar fire and confusing orders. Some troops were furious when told they must surrender. But by mid-afternoon Malaya Command was truly finished, because too much of it now believed the fight was over. The news surrender talks were underway destroyed too much of its will to fight for it to last another night.[52]

Yamashita was almost as keen to secure capitulation as Percival now was to offer it. But the situation confronting the two commanders has long been distorted by remarks Yamashita made after the war:

My attack on Singapore was a bluff–a bluff that worked. I had 30,000 men and was outnumbered more than three to one. I knew if I had to fight long for Singapore I would be beaten. That is why the surrender had to be at once. I was very frightened all the time that the British would discover our numerical weakness and lack of supplies and force me into disastrous street fighting.

This statement was used to criticize Percival on the grounds he did not need to surrender–even snatched defeat from the jaws of victory.[53] Given the condition of Percival's army and the state of his supplies that is ludicrous. Yamashita did not know just how far gone Malaya Command was. But he did know it was trapped. The Japanese had a firm grip on the entire region. Had Yamashita needed help to finish off Singapore he would have had it quickly, from strong air and naval forces concentrated to invade Sumatra. They would have bombarded the city into total physical collapse in short order, especially with no coastal guns left to oppose them. So what exactly did Yamashita mean and why did he say this?

Two problems provoked this concern: the Japanese were surprised by how big Percival's army was and even more surprised it still had so much artillery firepower. This surprise turned into real concern when ammunition supplies, especially for field artillery, fell to dangerously low levels. Army headquarters put it cautiously: "Therefore, the Army studied the preservation of ammunition and the progress of battle hereafter." Front-line troops put it vividly: "Anger welled up in Arai as he cursed the British artillery. The British infantry appeared on the verge of surrendering, yet their artillery keeps pounding us; they all deserved to be shot." Twenty-Fifth Army staff simply did not expect to be still fighting after a week on the island. By now some 5th and 18th Division rifle companies had very little ammunition left; one machine gunner estimated he was down to 20 seconds worth. More than half the artillery ammunition set aside in reserve was used up. Yet still the enemy fired back, so intensely Suzuki and Sugita did not think they could be about to surrender. Fujiwara met 5th Division officers who feared the whole advance was about to stall. Yamashita personally visited forward units running short of ammunition to apologize and urge them to "go forward relying only on the bayonets."[54] Yet while this concern was genuine, it did not literally mean fear "I would be beaten."

The Japanese were caught off guard by fierce resistance in three places: the Mount Pleasant area, Adam Park, and around Gillman Barracks. 18th Division guns fired 150 rounds per gun per day the last three days, a rate of fire that made the "guns of February" the root of Japanese concern. Yamashita and his staff did not know this firepower was a wasting asset, made possible by rationing counterbattery fire before the invasion, used in sheer desperation and about to run out. But they did know they could summon air and naval support to protect the infantry if they had to pause and regroup. Their own directly attached air groups had already dropped 773 tons of bombs on Singapore in 1018 sorties since the siege began and now had a squadron setting up on Tengah airbase itself. Yamashita also knew the defenders could not fight through such covering fire even if they did retain surprising punch in defence. They had no air support and the Japanese saw with their own eyes how close the city was to death: "Singapore city was a scene of chaotic confusion with a cloud of pit-black smoke enclosing the metropolis. Aerial bombing, artillery fire, and the oil tank explosions had created a hells port." Yamashita knew airpower could soon suppress the guns in that crowded trap. He also believed his troops would respond to calls to advance boldly one more time. They vindicated him:

> Very soon they would be in Singapore! At the latest their ammo would be gone early next morning. Machine-gunners without bullets–ha! What clowns they were! But there was no other way than forge ahead. If only to see Singapore–even if only with one eye left! Chikatan, chikatan, chikatan, their steam engine pushed on.

Finally, army headquarters knew there was enough ammunition and tank support–the Guards in particular remained in good shape–to launch one last general advance overnight. All three divisions planned big attacks that evening. Even if this did not destroy the enemy, it would keep them at bay while the Japanese regrouped.[55]

Yamashita did not lie. But he did exaggerate for effect and made this statement in his own terms. The "driving charge" was always a calculated risk. What really bothered Yamashita and his staff was the prospect it might now "fail" to deliver the only result which mattered to them. If supply problems forced them to break contact before the enemy surrendered, or if they were pulled into street fighting with infantry numbers dwindling and supplies running low, they would have to ask for help. They would get it. Singapore was top priority in Japanese grand strategy at that moment. But this would jeopardize grand strategy by upsetting the carefully balanced timetable and economy of force on which the offensive to overrun Southeast Asia was based. When Sugita said reinforcements were "too far distant to be of any use" he meant in finishing Singapore off there and then.[56] This was not frivolous. Asking for help meant changing the plan. That meant losing face. Losing face meant destroying your career. Nor was this theoretical. Even as Yamashita tried to finish off Singapore his colleague Homma had to seek help to destroy Allied forces in Luzon. Homma's target of 53 days was never realistic, his army was weaker than Yamashita's and his enemy defended much stronger ground. None of that mattered. When the General Staff sent in stronger ground and air forces to help overrun Bataan, delaying operations elsewhere, Homma's career was over. Even Yamashita's success made him vulnerable; rivals, especially Tojo, now looked for any excuse to take him down. Yamashita needed success that very night. Japan did not. It had Singapore in its grasp.

Yamashita's headquarters were now at the Ford Motor Factory next to Bukit Timah hill, then the only building of any size in the area. Yamashita showed a good grasp of how important appearances were in wars between empires by choreographing the whole event, using the Japanese press. They took photographs and shot film soon seen all over the world: Percival and party walking uphill carrying a Union Jack next to a white flag, as Yamashita insisted; a gaunt-looking Percival sitting down across a table from his energetic host; Percival and party standing next to their conquerors for a souvenir photo. The talks began at 1715hrs and lasted just over an hour. Percival tried to stall, haggling over details. Yamashita did not get everything he wanted; Japanese internees and prisoners of war were already in India, many guns and equipment were already destroyed. But finally Yamashita put his foot down and demanded to know whether Percival surrendered or not, threatening to launch a general advance within the hour if he refused. Percival submitted. Yamashita agreed to allow Malaya Command to use 1000 armed men to keep order until the city was handed over, to protect civilians and to freeze his army in position that night. Ceasefire took effect at 2030hrs.[57]

Confusion reigned along the perimeter as the news spread and the guns fell silent. Many defending troops first realized what happened when they heard nearby Japanese shouting "Banzai!" 2nd Loyals fired on one such party, probably the last shots fired in defence of Singapore. Men of the Malay Regiment took off their uniforms and melted into the civilian population, as some had already done when cut off by the enemy. Survivors from Dalforce did likewise. Many small parties, such as Bennett's group, tried to beg, buy or steal boats to escape. Japanese troops toasted their victory, but those up front were too worn out to cheer as if they were "in a raucous locality in downtown Tokyo" and settled for "a muffled soft Banzai ... one as only could be uttered on the very front." Most troops on both sides simply sat down to rest. Yamashita later said he came off more ferociously than intended because he could not find the words in English to offer Percival some consolation. But the pose certainly worked because Percival and party left the meeting convinced they only narrowly headed off a catastrophe. They were right. Yamashita told Percival they must agree to ceasefire by 2030hrs or it would be too late to call all units off from the attacks they were preparing to launch. As it was some Japanese units only heard the news as they moved forward. Wild saw, probably by design, a Japanese map outlining the attack 5th Division was going to mount that night. While this attack was only meant to push the British completely off the slopes around Mount Pleasant, Wild felt it would have broken right through into the city. 18th Division records suggest he was right. And the Imperial Guards planning an attack from the east would have walked through the disintegrating defences and carried them into the heart of the city.[58]

Percival later dismissed any suggestion mass desertion forced him to surrender before his army melted away. He also denied surrendering to prevent a wholesale massacre of civilians. His own explanation never wavered from the one he gave his men: without the "sinews of war," water and ammunition, they had to surrender. This is not convincing. Percival knew well enough the only order his army could now carry out as an organization was to capitulate. But he could not put this on record, not just for personal reasons. That would reveal that in this first big test the basis of imperial defence in Asia failed: the Empire's armies did not stand united. His war was over but the Empire's was not and it needed unity more than ever. His final signal to Wavell, a superior who did nothing to help and much to hinder him, was in that spirit: he surrendered because his army had nothing left to fight with, but all ranks did everything they could "and are grateful for your help."[59]

The reluctance to admit civilians were a factor is more puzzling. It would not have been dishonourable. Percival's superiors finally authorized his surrender when their arithmetic indicated any strategic gain from killing more Japanese would be outweighed by political disaster when fighting ended with a bloodbath in the city. If Singapore was going to fall anyway, Asian civilians would see any decision to fight it out in their streets not as a necessary choice of grand strategy but as callous indifference to their survival. No European empire in Asia could rebound from that and every British decision maker knew that. Percival demanded protection for civilians for the same reason Yamashita froze his troops in place that night. Even the next morning Yamashita moved cautiously: "After the advance of the entire army to Singapore each unit was halted on the outskirts of the city in consideration of possible outbreaks of disorders and inauspicious events." Yamashita never allowed his main combat forces to enter the city. He took control by sending in military police backed up by carefully selected infantry companies.[60] He did not trust his army to enter the city without going on a rampage, to celebrate victory and vent anger. Singapore now faced a cruel occupation. But by surrendering before it could be taken by storm, its defenders at least spared it catastrophe.

Epilogue

The Worst Disaster?

The surrender of Singapore did not determine the outcome of the Pacific War. For the Japanese, who lost the war, it became a secondary event, one to which they devote comparatively little attention. American accounts rarely did more than mention it in passing. For the British Empire on the other hand, the defence and fall of Singapore provoked immediate and lasting controversy. The Empire has all but disappeared now. But for the modern states which fought the campaign, this defeat remains central to their memory of the war against Japan. These reactions make one thing clear: the manner of this defeat was its worst consequence. To explain, we must review both the subsequent course of the war and efforts to understand and explain the campaign.

Japanese Military Police moved into Singapore city to take control early on the morning of 16 February 1942. They were reinforced by two battalions, made up from detachments from all three divisions. Lt. Onishi entered Raffles College, where Yamashita soon set up headquarters. There he met defeated Allied soldiers who amazed him by their attitude: "They showed no feeling of shame, or of humility; they seemed to take it more like a sports event; they had lost one match." Onishi did not speak English and mistook fatigue for indifference, but did have one insight: "But for the Japanese who had given their life for this match, for whom the felling of the citadel of white colonial supremacy had meant everything, it created a strange impression."[1] The Japanese now discovered that attacking the Western Powers gave them problems they had no idea how to solve.

The campaign to expel the Western Powers from Southeast Asia was not one of them. Over the next ten weeks, the Japanese overran Sumatra and Java, completed the conquest of Borneo, seized the important base of Rabaul between New Guinea and the Solomons, landed on northern New Guinea, crushed Allied naval and air forces in the Java Sea, pushed Allied forces back in Burma, defeated Allied forces in Bataan and besieged the fortress island of Corregidor. Roosevelt ordered MacArthur to escape; after a harrowing journey he made it to Australia. The Combined Fleet, staging from Singapore, sortied deep into the Indian Ocean. It narrowly missed destroying the heavily outgunned Eastern Fleet, drove it temporarily back to East Africa and worked over the naval and air bases on Ceylon. Japanese airpower attacked eastern

India and northern Australia. Japanese victories provoked political crises in both countries. The threat to India provoked enough trouble to tie down an army twice as large as Malaya Command, to suppress a "Quit India" campaign launched by Congress. The Australians lost their entire 8th Division, another brigade in Rabaul and the advance force of 1 Australian Corps. The door to Australia itself looked wide open and Australian public opinion feared the Japanese would move through it. The Australian government insisted home defence must now come first. It rejected British and American requests to divert 7th Australian Division to bolster the defence of Burma.[2] By the beginning of May most Australian forces were back home and relations with the British were badly strained. The Japanese offensive finally ran out of steam after forcing the Allies to surrender in the Philippines and expelling them from Burma. In five months the Japanese overran every British Empire and Allied position between India and Australia. This put them in the central position, in between the three major Western Allies and astride their routes to China. But now they had to decide what to do next and how to harness this area they went to war to exploit.

Within a week the Japanese made it clear they were in Singapore to build an empire of their own, not liberate the locals from other empires. Looters were summarily executed; severed heads were impaled on fences, to spell out the warning. But their approach to the Asian communities at large was more varied. They had no serious plan to invade let alone "liberate" India, but the Japanese hoped their victories would inspire an explosion there that would force the British out of the war. Fujiwara organized on 17 February a mass rally at Farrer Park Racecourse, to persuade the possibly 55,000 Indian soldiers now in Japanese captivity to join Mohan Singh in the INA. Fujiwara and Singh grandly announced the Japanese crusade to liberate Asia from Western imperialism and urged the men to help "free India." The Malays the Japanese at first more or less ignored. But they had other plans for the Chinese, who they saw as irreconcilable.

On 18 February Twenty-Fifth Army headquarters ordered the Military Police to "purge" Malaya and Singapore of "all anti-Japanese elements." This mission was assigned to the army before the war. But before Singapore fell it was too busy to do more than compile a list of groups assumed to be dangerous. Interrogations plus the study of captured British records in Ipoh did little more than refine that list; any individual belonging to one of the target groups was designated "anti-Japanese." The list included Dalforce, the MCP and known contributors to the China Relief Fund; but also "rascals," ex-convicts and Hainanese. When army headquarters insisted the entire community must be screened–the screening in Singapore would be the first of three stages in the purge—the Military Police replied they needed 10 days, and help from the infantry units sent into the city, to do the job. But units from the Imperial Guards and 18th Divisions were already scheduled to move on to Borneo, Burma and Sumatra, so headquarters insisted it must be done in three. On 19 February Yamashita ordered "Overseas Chinese" between ages 18 to 50 to assemble two days later at five central locations, to be "screened." There they would be interviewed and sent through three checkpoints. Local informers wearing hoods would help the Japanese decide who to condemn. The Military Police knew informers would use this chance to settle personal scores and realized such hasty screening could only be arbitrary. And of course the whole operation was barbaric in principle. But it did at least reflect a policy. Rather than tie down overstretched infantry to guard the vital Southern Resources Area the Japanese would brutalize their most devoted enemy, to intimidate them into accepting Japanese imperium.[3] On the other hand they had no idea let alone policy about what to do with the huge numbers of Western soldiers and civilians who surrendered to them. In Singapore alone the Japanese found themselves holding nearly 3000 civilians and more than 40,000 British, Australian, New Zealand and Dutch troops. The troops were disarmed and collected in the city. The civilians, led by the Governor, gathered on the Padang on 17 February and roasted in the sun. After a symbolic victory parade in central Singapore that morning, the Japanese forced their European captives to march along Beach Road to the Changi area. They wanted Asian civilians to see their former masters humbled; but public reaction to the long hot march was largely sympathetic, if low key. Over the next weeks the Japanese turned Changi into a large prisoner of war and internment zone for Westerners—while they decided what to do with them.[4] Anyone trying to figure out Japanese policy from this first week could conclude they wanted only to use the Indians, would not even try to appease the Chinese, took the native race for granted, and had no idea how to force the Allies to accept their defeat as final.

The *sook ching* or "purification by elimination" ran for nearly a week in Singapore. The whole operation, pressed by senior officers from Yamashita's headquarters, was indeed an arbitrary brutal effort to cow the Chinese by sheer terror. At one screening point at Jalan Besar stadium:

... the men were lined up and paraded before a high-ranking officer. As they passed him he flicked one index finger. If it was his left it meant the person must be detained; a flick of the right finger was a sign to go home. The fate of many thousands of people hung on the whim of a single person, on the wagging of a finger.

Chinese were beheaded or shot in several locations outside the city, including the beaches at Blakang Mati and Changi. The Japanese later admitted to killing at least 6000. Singapore Chinese claims after the war ranged up to 50,000. An accurate figure might be near the 25,000 Sugita supposedly admitted to a Japanese reporter.[5] Such brutality certainly kept Singapore quiet. But it did not prevent the MCP from launching armed resistance on the mainland, where there was more room for such activity. The irregular groups organized by the OM formed the nucleus. They grew into an army that with Allied help harassed the occupying power for the rest of the war. The more area the Japanese conquered, the more overstretched they became. They could not replace control by force of arms with control by acquiescence–and as the war dragged on made less effort to do so.

The selfishness of Japanese policy cost Yamashita his job and ruined Fujiwara's mission. Before the Japanese government decided how to treat its new subjects Yamashita publicly described Malays as "citizens" of the new Japanese empire. Tojo pounced, exiling him to command an army group in Manchuria. The government refused Yamashita's request to visit home en route to his new post. The Japanese public celebrated the conquest of Singapore and lionized their new "Tiger of Malaya," but the government strictly controlled what it was allowed to know about the war. The question of how Japan should treat the area it conquered was not open for discussion. Fujiwara discovered why: Japanese policy was to pillage it for the resources Japan needed to win its larger wars. When Fujiwara found out about the *sook ching* he complained such behaviour was bound to be counterproductive. If Japan's crusade to liberate Asia turned out to be merely a screen to disguise its own imperialism then all efforts to recruit Asian allies would fail. Fujiwara was naive: Tokyo still agreed on very little, but on a cardinal point was nearly unanimous. The crusade to liberate Asia was for public consumption. Races other than the Chinese could be treated moderately–provided they accepted their status as helots for the new Sparta and followed orders.[6]

The Japanese made it even more obvious how shallow their war policy was when it came to grand strategy. Beyond failing to devise a realistic plan to force the Allies to accept the loss of Southeast Asia, they made a more serious error: to mistake temporary advantage for basic military superiority. The policy was to establish a defended perimeter along a vast arc ranging from the northern Pacific to the Burma-India border. Ground and air forces would hold strongpoints along this "military frontier," supported by the mobile striking power of the Combined Fleet. Sooner or later the Allies, especially the Americans, would tire of trying to break through this perimeter and sue for peace. Meanwhile the Japanese would harness the resources of Southeast

Asia and use them to finish off China. But this was a wish, not a plan. It relied on the Allies behaving as the Japanese desired, not on giving them no choice by breaking them. And strategic loopholes threatened it from the start. The US Pacific Fleet was only hurt, not destroyed, so command of the sea remained insecure. MacArthur's escape established a connection that could turn Australia into a bastion from which the Americans could counterattack the Southern Resources Area. The IJA could not carry on into India, so the Japanese could only hope a rebellion would do their work for them. And the Allies had one hidden advantage: they were reading much Japanese signal traffic. The Japanese made these loopholes worse by allowing their victories to go to their heads. They concluded they could take strategic and tactical liberties with the Allies. Predictably, they argued about what to do next. Calls to invade Australia did not attract much support, but the Naval Staff decided it would be wise to isolate it by seizing New Guinea, the Solomons, Fiji, Samoa and New Caledonia. Yamamoto disagreed. He wanted to concentrate on finishing off the US Pacific Fleet in a decisive battle. The IJA supported him, because Naval Staff plans called for a big increase in the defensive perimeter, which would pin down more troops. The Americans complicated matters by making a dramatic air attack on Tokyo, launched from the deck of the USS *Hornet*. This shocked the Japanese into realizing the war had only just begun and they too could be hit. They settled the debate by making an imbecilic choice: isolate Australia and go after the American fleet at the same time.

Japanese hubris was checked before their grand offensive even finished, in the first week of May. In the Battle of the Coral Sea American naval units forced the Japanese to abandon a seaborne invasion of Port Moresby, on the southern coast of New Guinea–from which they could have cut the line of communication between Australia and the U.S.A. Exactly a month later Yamamoto lost his decisive battle when the US Pacific Fleet sunk four of his fleet carriers–two-thirds of his striking force–at the Battle of Midway, drowning their irreplaceable veteran air crews. These defeats left them open to counterattack. They responded by stubbornly pressing the drive to isolate Australia, attacking overland towards Port Moresby and advancing through the Solomon Islands. In New Guinea they ran into tougher Allied troops, including Australian veterans recalled from the Middle East, who used better tactics and good ground to fight them to a standstill on the Kokoda Trail. The Americans counterattacked in August, seizing a Japanese airbase on the Solomon island of Guadalcanal. These clashes expanded to become grinding campaigns of attrition on the ground, at sea and in the air, which by 1943 were chewing up the whole Japanese war machine. Japanese forces in Burma had less trouble repelling a poorly executed British/Indian counterattack. But the need to maintain a large army there, plus occupation commitments all over Southeast Asia, strained Japanese manpower.

The Japanese gave up Guadalcanal in February 1943. Over the next year the mobilization of American military power imposed itself on the Pacific War. The US Pacific Fleet took the offensive in the central Pacific and battered the Combined Fleet. American and Australian forces made costly but steady progress in New Guinea and the Solomons. This counteroffensive exposed the basic folly of Japanese war policy. The whole Japanese grand strategy relied on extracting resources from Southeast Asia, bringing them to Japan, then projecting them as military power in China and the Pacific. American submarines tore into supply lines the IJN barely tried to protect, because it concentrated on fleet engagements. The Japanese defended zone began to buckle under the strain. The only way the Japanese could extract what they needed was to force prisoners of war and Asian civilians, in huge numbers, into slave labour building railways, working mines, doing whatever the Japanese needed to fuel their war effort. This exposed the Japanese occupation as the empire building it was and turned Asian opinion against the Japanese–if not always towards the Allies. In desperation the General Staff decided to invade India in March 1944, to try to knock the British and Indians out of the war. Mutaguchi, who commanded 18th Division in the Malayan campaign, was in command. Despite warnings to the contrary in New Guinea and the Solomons, the Japanese decided they could rely on the same feeble performance by British and Indian forces, take the same risks with supply lines and use the same tactics that worked in Malaya. But the British and Indians learned some lessons from studying the experience of Malaya and their own early experience in Burma–and now enjoyed much stronger air support. Lt.-Gen. William Slim's Fourteenth Army stood and fought in strongholds around Imphal and Kohima, resupplying by air. Mutaguchi's army, including elements of the INA, was not strong enough to reduce the strongholds and did not have enough supplies to bypass them. In June it reeled back in defeat. In the second half of the year the Allies attacked on every front except China. Matching the Japanese in resolution, bettering them in tactics and overwhelming them in firepower, they steadily tore the Japanese Empire apart. The only time the Combined Fleet returned to Singapore was in autumn 1944, when survivors of heavy defeats at the hands of the US Pacific Fleet resorted to using the base to regroup because they could not run the gauntlet back to Japan. By now Japanese forces in Malaya and Singapore were all but cut off from the homeland. Their final plan to defend the area was to fight to the death after they massacred all remaining prisoners of war–who, with thousands of local civilians, were forced to build the defences the Japanese planned to die in.

Sudden Allied victory in August 1945 spared Singapore and the region this final catastrophe. The threat was real. The Japanese garrison defended Manila to the death in 1945, subjecting that city to a catastrophe second only, on the Allied side, to that suffered by Nanking. But what Singapore endured was bad enough. The last year was particularly terrible. After the Japanese lost control of the sea lanes the distribution of food within the areas they occupied broke down. By summer 1945 mass famine was very close. Rapid defeat in 1942 forced Singapore and Malaya to endure a long occupation–but also allowed them to escape the fate of Manila. The Allies had the means and the will to defeat Japan, and devised a coherent grand strategy to accomplish that goal. But its thrust lines came from the central and southwest Pacific, pressed by the Americans.

The Australian war effort was integrated with the Americans under MacArthur as Supreme Commander Southwest Pacific; his focus was north, through the Philippines towards Japan. British and Indian forces were reduced to a holding role. The only mission the Americans urged on them was to retake Burma, to reopen the supply line to China. The COS quickly embraced this supporting role. The conclusion they drew from the fall of Singapore was that the U.K. could not mount a major offensive against the Japanese before winning the more important war in Europe. Two days after Percival surrendered Wavell suggested the Malay Barrier was now untenable. Brooke took the hint and on 25 February Wavell returned to India to resume command, leaving the Dutch to direct ABDA Command through its death throes.[7] The Australian turn to partnership with the Americans only confirmed the COS decision to do no more than hang on to India. The biggest military result of the fall of Singapore was that it knocked the British onto the sideline in the war against Japan. Far away from the main Allied thrust lines, well down the list of American priorities, Singapore suffered accordingly.

Prime Minister Churchill did not quietly accept this reduction in the British war effort against Japan. He pressed the COS to pursue more aggressive plans to retake Burma. When he deemed it necessary to promise the Americans the British would fight on until Japan surrendered unconditionally, Churchill also committed the British to deploying a Pacific Fleet to carry out that promise. This sparked the most heated argument of the war between Prime Minister and COS. The main cause stemmed directly from the rapid fall of Singapore: the Prime Minister was determined to reconquer the colonies lost in 1942, to restore the prestige and therefore viability of the Empire in Asia. The COS understood the logic, but insisted the Empire simply could not afford to do this until Germany was defeated. The Allies agreed in autumn 1943 to establish a unified Southeast Asia Command (SEAC). But as Supreme Commander they appointed Admiral Lord Louis Mountbatten. Mountbatten was in some ways a good choice; his charisma created the impression of energy in the theatre and improved working relations with the Americans. But the COS intended this to replace, not accelerate, any strategic offensive. The cold hard fact was that the loss of Singapore disrupted the strategic connection between the British and Americans in their war against Japan. Provided the British appeared to be trying to reopen a link to China, the Americans could be appeased. And the Americans understood what drove Churchill: their nickname for SEAC was "Save England's Asian Colonies."[8] The Defence Committee did not agree to deploy a Pacific Fleet until August 1944. Meanwhile the Eastern Fleet was rebuilt and patrolled the Indian Ocean; only in 1944 did it cautiously begin to raid Japanese bases in the East Indies. The British Pacific Fleet did not reach the theatre until spring 1945. The campaign to retake Burma began late in 1944. Fourteenth Army was better equipped, better trained, enjoyed much stronger air support, had as much experience and was better led than its opponent–Slim proved to be the most able general the British Army produced in the Second World War. Nevertheless it had to fight long and hard before finally destroying Japanese forces in Burma and retaking Rangoon, in May 1945. SEAC planned to liberate Malaya and Singapore by invading the west coast of central Malaya and advancing south–operation *Zipper*. Before they could attack the surrender of Japan dropped Singapore back into British hands.

Being on the winning side allowed the British to regain their Empire in Southeast Asia. But losing it dramatically in the first place, taking so long to get it back, and having to rely more on American victories than on their own to do so forced them to pay a price. The defeat in 1942 was most serious as a political failure, so the worst consequences were political. They fell into four categories: India, Malaya and Singapore, Australia, and British influence in general. They were serious, but were not uniform and have been exaggerated.

The surrender of Singapore inflamed nationalism in India, not least because of how many Indians were lost. The question of how and when to leave India was one of the most emotional issues in prewar British politics; Churchill became politically isolated over this, not German rearmament. When Labour defeated the Conservatives and Churchill in the general election in July 1945, the argument turned decisively. The Attlee government was not radical in foreign policy. It did not intend to terminate the Empire. It felt British power, prosperity and influence still rested on remaining the leader of a strong imperial bloc. But nor did it intend to stand still. The fall of Singapore reinforced its intention to withdraw from India–but made that more complicated. Nearly all Indian troops captured in Malaya and Singapore had a tough time. Possibly 40,000 spent some time in the INA, but there were a number of reasons why they joined. Perhaps 60% of the Indian officers had "nationalist feelings." Some joined to liberate India. Others, and many of their men, joined because it was either that or hard labour as prisoners of war–or to stay with their friends, or because they were told the Raj was finished and had no way to tell otherwise, or to get better food. The most common abstract motive was to be part of an organized body ready to help India no matter who won the war. After Mohan Singh fell out with the Japanese, a far more prominent Indian leader took his place: Subhas Chandra Bose, rival of Nehru and Gandhi. The Japanese used the INA to further their own ends, throwing them into the Burma offensive without the training or equipment to succeed. Indian prisoners who did not join or left the INA were spread out all over Southeast Asia as slaves; many did not survive. The Indian troops who reconquered Burma did not think very much of those who joined the INA. British officers had mixed views. Some regarded INA recruits as traitors, others as men who made a pragmatic choice, still others as men who were let down by the British and acted accordingly. The British screened former INA members and put on trial those they regarded as ringleaders who wanted to expel the British from India. But this sparked a furore in India, playing into the hands of Congress.[9] The repercussions of losing a large Indian army in Malaya and Singapore, plus the explosion of civil war and anti-British feeling in Burma, helped convince the Attlee government it must arrange the best possible terms for withdrawal. There is an important connection between surrender in Singapore in 1942 and independence and partition in India in 1947–and Burma in 1948.

The end of the Raj in India did not end the British Empire–but certainly marked the beginning of the end. This was especially true for Southeast Asia. Without the Indian Army there was no strategic reserve for the Empire in Asia. The lesson of 1942 was crystal clear. In any future major war, British forces alone could not hold Malaya and Singapore. But the humiliation of 1942 did not make it impossible for the British to return to Malaya and Singapore. On the contrary, they remained the governing power in Malaya until 1957, in Singapore until 1963, defended both and did not finally withdraw from their bases in Singapore until 1971. And when they left they did so against the wishes of the government in Singapore. On the other hand the consequences of 1942 did affect how they behaved after the war and why they finally left.

Malayans did not contest the British return because they were so glad to be rid of the Japanese, who brought them to the brink of famine and catastrophe. The only group that might have resisted, the MCP, was directed by its international fraternity to sit and wait. There was no other group ready to replace the imperial power, as there was in Vietnam and the Dutch East Indies–where in consequence imperial wars broke out in 1946. But defeat in 1942 and cruel occupation thereafter changed the country and people to which the British returned. In the eyes of Malays, Chinese and Indians alike the British "let us down" and left them to the tender mercy of the Japanese. Everyone agreed the clock could not be turned back to the prewar status quo; but few agreed where the country should go next. The only certainty was that once the Asian communities answered that question the British presence would become untenable. But the Japanese policy of divide and rule further poisoned communal relations, especially between the Chinese and Malays. This made it harder to find that answer. The CO, cut off from the country by the occupation, did not catch this change in mood.[10] When it tried to rationalize the administration of Malaya by creating a unified colony, removing the powers of the Malay sultans in the process, this provoked Malay nationalists to organize at last. 1948 was the pivotal year. First the British gave in to Malay nationalism, scrapping the union in favour of a federation. They left Singapore out because without its large Chinese population the Malays would dominate the federation, which persuaded them to accept it. The British also wanted to retain direct control of the island because it remained the hub of their military presence in the region. The communists replied by launching armed insurrection, which became known as the Emergency. In due course the British correctly decided the only sure way to defeat them was to win the support of the Malay and Chinese communities–and the only way to clinch that was to grant independence on terms both could accept. Independence for Malaya in 1957 helped win the war–but made it necessary to settle the status of Singapore, and the British presence there.[11]

No British official in Singapore in 1939 would have agreed the British would have to consider leaving the island in their lifetime. After 1942 none could ignore the question of how long they could stay before it became counterproductive. The Emergency and attendant political upheavals persuaded the British to focus not on hanging on by whatever means possible but on leaving the region on their own terms. This became part of the larger adjustment which the British made from an Empire they ran by ascendancy to a Commonwealth they tried to lead by influence. In Southeast Asia the goal became to leave behind viable friendly states that could defend themselves, would join the Commonwealth, and align with the West in the Cold War. The challenge was framed by the Emergency: to resist communist subversion and resolve communal differences.

Humiliation in 1942 helped knock enough arrogance out of British thinking to foster this more pragmatic attitude. The British could not in the end bring about their optimal result. Singapore merged with Malaya to help form Malaysia in 1963, but the two parted company on hard terms in 1965. This forced the island to struggle to survive as something no one planned it to be: an independent city-state. Chronic economic troubles at home forced the British government to announce in 1968 it would no longer maintain strong military forces overseas. This made their military withdrawal from Singapore in 1971 look like a scuttle. But this is too harsh. The British decision to accept the fact humiliating defeat in 1942 meant things must change in Southeast Asia allowed them to leave behind a better legacy than either the French or Dutch Empires. They were both forced out by war and left behind new nations mired in turmoil. The race question that so complicated the destinies of Malaya and Singapore did so more in spite than because of the British–and paled in comparison to what Vietnam and Indonesia endured. The teenage Lee Kuan Yew concluded from surviving 1942 and the Japanese occupation that Singapore must always be ready to defend itself, because any distant power it relied on for protection might not be able to help when the time came. But he was also impressed by "British coolness in the face of impending defeat," especially by the elan 2nd Argylls showed retreating onto the island. As Prime Minister of Singapore from 1959 he relied on the British to protect his state during the turbulent years of its journey from self-government to unwanted total independence–and protested vigorously when they decided to leave too early.[12]

The impact of the fall of Singapore on British-Australian relations was just as slippery to pin down. Despite the pronounced turn towards military co-operation with the Americans, Australian forces fought on alongside the British in the European war; Australian and New Zealand divisions played a crucial role in the decisive victory of El Alamein in November 1942. The two governments continued to work together; Australia pressed hard for a British Pacific Fleet. One reason was the fact the Australians learned pretty quickly the Americans were as ready as the British to take them for granted! After the war, Australian and New Zealand forces joined the British to defend Malaya and Singapore during both the Emergency and the subsequent Confrontation when Sukarno tried to undo the formation of Malaysia, shared the treaty commitment to defend Malaya, contributed to the Commonwealth Strategic Reserve deployed to do so, and joined forces with the British and Canadians to contribute the Commonwealth Division to the United Nations war effort in the Korean War. Australian and British planners produced joint plans to defend the Far East and "near north" should the Cold War become another general war. This time the British, having learnt from 1942, nominated Australia as the directing ally to defend Southeast Asia in a global war. And the Pacific

Dominions remained in the innermost loop, with the British, Canadians and Americans: the Western allies who shared signals intelligence after 1945. On the other hand Australia and New Zealand looked to the Americans, not the British, as their main security partner after 1945. The ANZUS treaty signed by the three in 1951 pointedly excluded the British. Australia and New Zealand, but not the U.K., contributed military forces to support the American war in Vietnam, to encourage American commitment to their own security. The British did after all lose something important because of disaster in 1942: Australian trust in their word.

To some extent this was unfair. Australians did not concentrate on why their own governments accepted British reassurances before 1941, even when those reassurances became paper thin. Nor did they critically examine their own role in defending Malaya and Singapore. They focused instead on "the great betrayal," instinctively sure Curtin was right: the British would have let Australia be overrun, so long as the Allies won the war in the end. Australian received wisdom was clear: the British gambled on the security of Australia because they wanted Australian help, but then refused to pay the price when the gamble blew up in their face. Australia was badly scared by 1942, and projected much of its fear and anger onto the British. That anger was inflamed after the war when it became clear how much Allied prisoners of war suffered. Most of the prisoners gathered at Changi were eventually widely dispersed, a great many to slave labour from which they never returned. Nearly 28% of Western prisoners of war held by the Japanese did not survive, compared to 4% of those in German hands. The death toll for a small population such as Australia–nearly 8000 all ranks–still resonates today. Death in a victorious campaign in New Guinea was one thing. Death resulting from British humiliation seemed quite another. This was all to some extent concealed by the Empire's transformation into the Commonwealth– and by the American eclipse of the British as the leading Western power. But it could only be downplayed, not ignored. No postwar Australian government, however pragmatic or friendly, could operate as if this public mood did not exist. Australia could never again send all its strength to help the British in return for nothing more than a promise. The most serious loss the British suffered was what they always prized most: their influence.

Churchill's instinct was correct. Had Singapore fallen only after a long inspiring defence, the British would not have lost as much influence as they did. Their defeat would have been excused as being caught overstretched–as was American defeat in Luzon. Instead the British faced triple humiliation: they lost a huge army after a short and apparently feeble defence, it surrendered the citadel they insisted would not be lost, and worst of all it was thrashed by a non-European foe. At the same time the British failed to make any progress in the war in Europe before the Americans entered the war. Togther this cost them the chance to establish their grand strategy as the plan by which the Allies would win final victory. American mobilization then reduced the British to a junior partner at the top table. The COS were also right in 1940: the minimum the British must preserve was "a footing from which we could eventually retrieve that position." But India was too remote to be that footing. And SEAC did not do enough to restore British prestige by retaking Burma. Roosevelt had to order his navy to accept the British Pacific Fleet as part of the Allied attack on Japan in 1945; they saw it as militarily unnecessary and politically irritating. This all marginalized the British in the postwar occupation of Japan and reorganization of Asia. Before the war the British Empire was the most prominent Western power in the Far East, in both China and Southeast Asia. Disaster in 1942 put an end to that forever.

This outcome needs to be seen in context. The profound forces that generated external and internal challenges to the British Empire as a world power were not created by the Second World War. They were already well underway. Without American solidarity the British could not win a general war in 1918, let alone 1941. The Dominions asserted their voices in the direction of imperial defence from 1917. The British presence in China ultimately rested on Chinese weakness, something the British could not dictate. And national feeling and communist intrigue in Southeast Asia were alive and active before the Japanese moved south. The "Singapore strategy" was an obvious confession that in relative terms British power was on the decline. But it mattered a very great deal indeed how they managed that decline. The Empire did not have to stumble into humiliation and accelerate its own demise. The more their power seemed challenged, the more determined the British became to preserve their influence, especially over the direction of imperial defence. Economic growth and military power could not be maintained by words— influence could be, and might just help the British brazen it out. The Empire they tried to defend after 1918 was too big and brittle, especially in the Far East, to be defended without fundamental changes. But such changes meant sharing power and thus influence. This the British refused to do. The Churchill government was only partly right. Singapore was strategically expendable. The Allies won the war. But it was not politically expendable. That turned defeat into disaster. The most basic reason was the oldest problem in human governance: by trying to keep it all without making sacrifices, the British paid a much higher price when they failed after all.

The fall of Singapore was overdetermined. The argument that a hard pressed government in London did its best but was undone by incompetence on the ground has never been tenable. But neither has the argument that stubborn defenders did all they could only to be let down by distant superiors. The postmortems started when Percival surrendered and in due course smoked out the crux of the matter. The determination to make the situation fit the plan was always liable to end in defeat. It was inherently unwise. It also rested on three dubious assumptions: liberties could be taken with the Japanese; an improvised multi-national force could pull together quickly under pressure to fight effectively as a team; imperial forces designed to fight anywhere in general could learn on the job to fight in Malaya in particular. The combination produced disaster. But the story proved too painful to tell, so it was spun.

First to discuss the fall of Singapore in public and in detail were the Japanese. Their wartime postmortems were meant to help win the war by encouraging the army, impressing Asian civilians and disparaging the Allies. There were trenchant observations, especially about British mistakes, but flowery rhetoric expressed the mistakes that led the Japanese to final defeat and total disaster. Their amphibious invasions succeeded in spite of bad weather and vulnerable craft, but only at a high price and thanks in the end to Brooke-Popham's hesitation and "God's help and miracles." Tactical surprise proved decisive again and again: Jitra, Slim River, Muar. The Japanese multiplied their fighting power by taking risks with supply lines and doing the unexpected; but they only got away with it because their enemy moved too slowly, was too rigid in defence and became intimidated. This proved decisive on Singapore island, where the Japanese lost perhaps 40% of their casualties before landing and their infantry fought to a finish despite being close to exhaustion. Light, fast and highly mobile striking power destroyed a heavier army that relied on firepower. But the Japanese ignored their own statistics: without captured "Churchill supplies" the "driving charge" would have stalled by Kuala Lumpur, and even a victorious campaign wore down Japanese airpower faster than it could be replaced. They concluded their soldiers were better disciplined, tougher, more willing to fight and pay the price than the Allies.[13] This confirmed the rationale justifying the decision to attack the American titan: Japanese discipline and will to win would checkmate Allied manpower and industrial superiority. American naval aviators at Coral Sea and Midway, followed by Australian infantry and American marines in New Guinea and the Solomons, demonstrated just how wrong that was. The victory at Singapore was too easy, because it caught the Allies unprepared and disorganized at every level. The Japanese made a fatal mistake in assuming that would not change.

There was a flurry of public reflection on the Allied side, but it came from public opinion and the press. More authoritative reviews were not published during the war. Two days before he surrendered Percival sent a long analysis of why the Japanese defeated his army; it was circulated, unedited, to the War Cabinet. In the heat of battle three things caught his eye: training, previous war experience, discipline and morale. The Japanese, emphasizing light infantry, developed "a battle technique particularly well adapted" to areas in which they intended to fight. British observers in China badly underestimated the IJA because they did not understand how difficult it was to campaign there; as a result Malaya Command overlooked the old truism "battle remains the best training for war." It also misunderstood sloppy deportment for weak discipline; Japanese discipline and morale, resting on loyalty to the Emperor and an offensive spirit, were excellent. Airpower and tanks helped "but were not determining factors." The deciding factor was the toughness of what were surely picked Japanese troops.[14]

The surrender of Singapore hit a special nerve. Percival's analysis was more accurate and less defeatist than the reaction of many looking on from afar. The War Cabinet reviewed his report and agreed the Japanese were underestimated and "our military performance in Malaya had left much to be desired." But it then peevishly insisted diverting 18th Division was a mistake only in hindsight–one for which Australian pressure was responsible! When Brooke decided on 11 February Singapore was about to fall he noted in his diary: "have during the last ten years had an unpleasant feeling that the British Empire was decaying and that we were on a slippery decline ... We have had a wonderful power of recuperation in the past, I wonder if we shall again bring off a 'come back'?" Pownall felt "helpless," fearing Allied forces had "no punch." Wavell, the scholar, looked for deeper causes. In a letter to Brooke on 17 February he regretted not being more ruthless, saying he should have counterattacked instead of just defending in Johore, and replaced Percival with someone more inspirational. However:

> The trouble goes a long way back, climate, the atmosphere of the country (the whole of Malaya has been asleep for at least 200 years), lack of vigour in our peace-time training, the cumbrousness in our tactics and equipment, and the real difficulty of finding an answer to the very skilful and bold tactics of the Japanese in this jungle fighting. But the real trouble is that for the time being we have lost a good deal of our hardness and fighting spirit.[15]

The search for answers went beyond the sociological into the ridiculous: Japanese forces moved so fast because they were at home in the jungle and moved through its trees like monkeys. The fallacy the Japanese were naturally superior jungle fighters spread widely and took many Allied victories to put to rest. But while it lasted, the pendulum swing from under to overestimating the Japanese distorted perceptions of what happened in Malaya and Singapore. The fact the enemy was Asian was the main reason this defeat proved so hard to take. Everyone expected a rough ride when the Japanese invaded, but they were not supposed to be able to do so much damage so fast. British control of the Empire suddenly seemed so shaky that in June 1942 the Colonial Secretary informed governors:

> I have been considering in light of experience in Malaya whether it is not possible to associate Colonial peoples more closely in defence of their territories, with view both to strengthening existing defence organization and also fostering spirit of resistance among population generally in case of attack.[16]

Such consternation did not last. Confidence in Allied power soon resurfaced. The most notable example came from the eye of the storm. The day after the surrender Nishimura's chief of staff met Key to discuss formalities. Unwittingly, he brought up the crux of the matter. Spreading a map on the table he noted the Japanese were about to overrun all of Southeast Asia. After that "We do not want India. We do not want Australia. It is time for your Empire to compromise. What can you do?" The Japanese did not know how to bring the war to an end–but Key did: "[Key] cupped his hand round Sumatra, Java and the Philippines, swept it northwards and covered Japan. 'What will we do? We will drive you back and occupy your country. That is what we will do.'" It took new Allied armies to redeem Key's promise, but the more systematic approach the Allies took to total war finally vindicated him. That systematic approach soon followed Percival's lead in analyzing why Singapore fell. The day Wavell left ABDA Command Pownall pondered why it failed, in a reflection that combined denial with candour. Prewar public opinion and government policy were too complacent and inert. The Japanese were underestimated. The Australians were parochial and selfish. But at the end of the day:

> Our policy was to avoid war with Japan as long as we could ... With all our other commitments I don't believe that however highly we had rated the Japs as fighters we would have been able to improve the condition of our forces in the Far East. We just hoped it wouldn't happen. And it did ....[17]

Churchill promised the House of Commons in a secret session in April 1942 that when circumstances allowed there would be a full public enquiry into the fall of Singapore. This promise was never kept. The air was already heavy with recriminations. Bennett made it out of Singapore to Australia where he was welcomed by the government, who used his escape as a public relations distraction, but shunned by fellow generals, who regarded it as abandoning his men. Their rancour kept Bennett in Australia for the rest of the war, fuming about his treatment. But in March 1942 he submitted the first insider report–unpublished–on the campaign. It pointed fingers in just about every direction but singled one factor out: "The very low morale displayed by the Indian troops throughout this campaign was the most important influence responsible for the failure to hold Malaya." This report should not be ignored. Mixed in with spite and self-pity were some astute observations. He blamed poor Indian morale on the inherent weakness of "Eastern races" but also on abysmal leadership from British officers. He dismissed charges of a serious fifth column. He pointed out the Japanese did not use their dominance in the air very effectively; the real problem was that it scared an army that could have coped with it had it been better led.[18] By endorsing the report on the loss of Singapore drawn from reports by evacuees, Wavell sent Churchill a litany of criticisms of every aspect of the conduct of the war in Malaya. Perhaps the most damning came from Stewart. He combined sociological platitudes with professional analysis which, coming from a fighting commander whose reputation survived unscathed, carried weight–so much weight that his critiques of tactics and operations in Malaya were written up in several reports and he was debriefed at length by the Australians, who applied his ideas in subsequent training. Besides insisting static defence could never work in jungle terrain and pointing out how much the Japanese disliked Allied artillery, Stewart kept coming back to a central theme: training and tactics were rigid and unrealistic. One size did not fit all. There was a reason British Empire forces were being beaten over and over again, from Norway to Malaya:

> It was the failure of a MENTAL OUTLOOK and of the SYSTEM which was its expression. Leaders faithfully and efficiently served that system in the light of the mentality and the tempo to which they had been trained ... A Nation of Theorists was beaten by a Nation of Action.

Adding this to the finger pointing at the Australians produced an uncomfortable mixture. Churchill severely restricted circulation of these reports, rejecting Attlee's advice to discuss them with the Australians. Reports prepared by Layton, Wavell and Brooke-Popham were also filed. The war continued and the Empire needed to concentrate on the problem at hand. Civilian evacuees spoke about the campaign in public talks, journalists published books, Bennett published Why Singapore Fell. But the rest of those most closely associated with the fall of Singapore remained either unwilling to talk about it–authorities in London and Canberra–or unable to–prisoners of war. Churchill used the pressure of war to push the whole problem onto the backburner, stressing the need to avoid recriminations with the Australians and, as he put it years later, "their beastly general."[19]

After Japan surrendered the issue resurfaced. Surviving prisoners of war brought out not only reconstructed war diaries but also narrative and analytical postmortems, written during the long days in captivity. Some amounted to a few paragraphs written by a commander. Others, such as Harrison's history of 11th Indian Division and the Australian report spearheaded by Kappe, ran to over 100,000 words, reflecting exhaustive work by syndicates of officers. Heath and Percival argued at length over Percival's draft report. Heath persuaded Percival to place more emphasis on broader considerations and less on the army being outfought on the ground. Heath went to his grave wrongly seeing Japanese armour as the "arm of mobility" which trumped him in the north–when it had of course been the infantry. In the end the two never agreed over the strategy for retreating north of Kuala Lumpur; Percival continued to insist his mission to hold the naval base forced him to fight for every inch of ground. Harrison accepted Percival's generous conclusion the government had to take chances in grand strategy in 1940. Kappe condemned the higher command of 8th Australian Division for mishandling operations, especially on Singapore island. Such postmortems covered nearly all aspects of the campaign and later provided valuable material for scholars, starting with the official histories.[20] But they were not published. So the public controversy focused more on the commanders.

Yamashita returned to combat duty in autumn 1944, after Tojo resigned in disgrace over the fall of Saipan. Sent to command the defence of the Philippines, Yamashita conducted a brilliant defensive campaign in northern Luzon but was blamed for the orgy of atrocities in the battle of Manila–fought against his direct order to evacuate the city, by troops from which he was physically isolated. The Americans held him responsible and executed him after a controversial war crimes trial–but the British certainly would have done likewise over Parit Sulong, Alexandra Hospital and the sook ching had he escaped prosecution in Luzon. MacArthur had Percival flown in to be present when Yamashita surrendered and on the deck of the USS Missouri when the Japanese government surrendered unconditionally. But when Percival returned home he found himself cast as the scapegoat. Apart from a brief audience with the King he was cold-shouldered and given only one last duty: to write his report, without any real assistance.[21] In Australia, Percival forced the government's hand by formally reporting Bennett left his post without permission the night Malaya Command surrendered. The Australian government conducted a judicial inquiry into Bennett's escape, which for a time pushed the fall of Singapore back into the headlines. The verdict was that Bennett's action was not unlawful but not in the best tradition of command responsibility. Ironically this did not ruin Bennett in the eyes of survivors from his division. Many of its senior officers shunned him, with an animosity that stood out in the war diaries and the Thyer/Kappe report. But the troops were smarting. They suffered through the war as prisoners. Upon being liberated they discovered other Australian troops were celebrated for victories, whereas their defeat provoked finger-pointing and soul searching at home in 1942. One press comment by Sir Keith Murdoch ascribed defeat to a national lack of discipline and amateurish approach to war. The survivors interpreted criticism of Bennett as more such criticism of their division and championed him in retaliation. Never was support less deserved.[22]

In the end the most important questions were why did Singapore fall so easily and why did it matter so much—and in the end the only place to find the most important answers was where the story started: with the central direction of imperial defence. In January 1946 some of Churchill's wartime speeches were published, including the speech in which he promised a public enquiry into the fall of Singapore. This raised interest in Australia; Prime Minister Chiffley cabled Attlee to ask whether such an enquiry would in fact now be held. Attlee referred the problem to the COS but neither he nor they wanted any enquiry. Attlee spelt it out to the Australians on 31 January:

> Why, if there is to be an enquiry over Singapore, should there not be enquiries into other disasters, such as Tobruk, Crete and Hong Kong? But one cannot accept a position where every serious military reverse becomes the subject of a public enquiry ... The enquiry would be the occasion for much individual mud-slinging and recrimination, with each of the protagonists trying to lay the blame on others ... No Government concerned would be immune from the controversies thus aroused ....

The Secretariat sounded the warning bell before Attlee replied: "Please see Mr. Churchill's Directive of the 28th April 1941. It would make awkward reading if there were an inquiry into the Malayan campaign." The directive was Churchill's diktat to the COS: British policy assumed any Japanese attack would provoke American intervention so there was no need to raise the priority of the Far East—and any change would come from him. Those inside the loop saw the problem from the start: there was no firewall between poor tactical performance in Malaya and the central direction of imperial defence. The JPS did their job, warning in March that any enquiry must expand so far and wide to find the necessary answers it would do more harm than good. The COS did not quite agree: Cunningham feared political pressure might make some sort of enquiry necessary. He had the JPS investigate "the practicability of limiting such an enquiry to the military events directly leading up to the loss of Singapore." The JPS, to their credit, replied "it would not be possible to hold an enquiry into the Malayan campaign from the time of the Japanese landing without consideration of wider questions, the discussion of which it has already been agreed would be undesirable." Any enquiry restricted to the last battle on Singapore island would also "be most undesirable and likely to stimulate public demand for a wider investigation."[23]

When political pressure abated both governments dropped the whole idea. Attlee and the COS decided to meet public hunger for answers by publishing the despatches of the responsible commanders. Percival had a draft ready by August 1946. It supported the decision in 1940 to take chances in the Far East and did not criticize the central direction of the war. Attlee's Military Secretariat advised him the report was "sober, fair and objective" and should be approved–but would also revive demands for a public enquiry, which should be rejected for the reasons already cited. Attlee stuck to the strategy of publishing the despatches, but Percival's provoked so much controversy it was not published until February 1948. Thomas "reacted violently," writing his own long defence of civil administration and civilian behaviour. In the end the CO did not object to publishing Percival's report but did not endorse it. Darvall denied he or anyone else ever gave Percival any assurance the Japanese invasion force would be worn down 40% by air attacks before it reached the coast. Percival accepted some corrections but largely stuck to his guns. He even solicited MacArthur's help to try to prove the Japanese forces that defeated him were much larger than Churchill stated; at one point he argued they used 300,000 men and lost 87,000 killed! The Attlee government agreed to suppress Layton's report because it made too many personal criticisms of individuals, but published Percival, Maltby and Brooke-Popham. The danger was reduced because:

> The texts of the despatches have been carefully revised to eliminate any material which in itself would be likely to lead to controversy and the Dominion Governments concerned have seen any passages likely to be of special interest ... Where necessary changes have been made which met their comments ...[24]

Such editing was more spin than suppression, but the spin was emphatic. The tactic did not, could not, abort controversy. One interesting rejoinder came within a month from Tan Kah Kee. He wrote "on behalf of the Chinese community" as Chairman, Southeast Asia Federation of China Relief Fund Committees, to protest Percival's claim the defence was compromised by Asian unwillingness to stand up to enemy attack and failure to support the war effort. Percival replied his despatch was a military report which stuck to relevant military concerns. The WO backed him up, but the CO distanced itself from the issue, appeasing Tan by lavishing praise on the wartime behaviour of the Chinese community. Percival decided to bring his arguments before a wider public by publishing his memoir, The War in Malaya, in 1949. The book, and the published despatches, did not distress the governments concerned. By accepting the grand strategy decisions made in 1940 and not condemning those made in 1941, they did what Cunningham hinted at in 1946: shift the discussion away from the higher direction of defence and onto the men on the spot.[25]

The British government and COS stuck with the deflection tactic. In June 1947 the British Defence Committee in Southeast Asia, based in Singapore, requested permission to interview participants and study original documents of the 1941-42 campaign, in order to "draw from the information available useful lessons for the future and not to delve unnecessarily into past troubles or mistakes." First on the list of COS objections was "The majority of available documents contain severe and bitter criticism of Australian troops." In September they refused, on the grounds "it is by no means certain the lessons learned ... would compensate for the almost certain deterioration in Commonwealth Relations which would follow." Any such study could only take place "on a very high level"–in London. Churchill did more than anyone else to cement this deflection by the account published in his memoirs, an instant best-seller all over the English-speaking world. Using as a decoy his consternation to discover so late in the day Singapore island was no fortress, Churchill, advised by a syndicate that included Pownall, zeroed in on the conduct of the campaign by the men on the spot.[26]

The story of the defence and fall of Singapore certainly can not be told without investigating the conduct of the campaign. It was there after all that defeat degenerated into disaster. But it must be repeated: there was no firewall, in time, methods or policy. The broad lines spelt out in Attlee's reply to Chiffley raised the very danger Cunningham crudely tried to avoid by proposing to scapegoat the men on the spot. The JPS reply was definitive:

We consider that the main point which arises from our examination is that it is impossible to discuss our policy in the Far East in isolation. Every theatre was inter-dependent for men and materials which, at the time, were in very short supply. To obtain, therefore, a true picture, it would be necessary to review the progress of the war against Germany and Italy and to decide whether the strategy pursued was correct and whether more forces could have been spared for the Far East, review our relations with the Dutch, with the Americans and with the Dominions and India, review the whole question of the preparations which were carried out in the years between the two world wars.

Such a worldwide review could not be carried out without the evidence of the statesmen and military leaders responsible for our policy both before and during the war. This inquiry could not be confined to purely military matters, and would involve a discussion of controversial and delicate political issues.[27]

The list of those issues was long and the JPS pulled no punches. No one would escape scrutiny: "Important witnesses would have to be called, the summoning of whom might be very embarrassing. For example, the presence of Mr. Churchill and Lord Wavell would be essential." Churchill was now a living legend, symbol of British defiance and victory. His stature helped prop up British global prestige, which could be compromised by any condemnation of his leadership. Wavell was Viceroy of India, which the British wanted to retain as an ally after they withdrew. He directed the final defence of Singapore, so any enquiry would either justify or censure and "in view of his present position we consider that any public arguments regarding the correctness of his decisions would be most undesirable."

Grand strategy would be front and centre. The Prime Minister and COS accepted the air plan as a stop-gap but retained the "Singapore strategy": "the main reason for the defence of Malaya was to preserve the facilities of Singapore as a naval base"; that would raise the following questions:

Whether we over-insured in other theatres at the expense of the Far East; whether the decision to rely on airpower was correct in view of existing shortages; whether all possible steps were taken to provide the aircraft necessary; whether until the necessary aircraft could be provided, we made satisfactory interim arrangements for the defence of the Far East.

The most important allies would be involved. Because defence policy for the Far East came to rest on "the extent to which we were able to count on active support from the U.S.A." any enquiry "might involve recriminations between Britain and America." Australian criticisms at the time would surely be revived, "and accusations would be made that the U.K. did not keep the Dominions fully informed of events." Churchill's insistence in 1941 "that Japan would not attack until we were heavily beaten elsewhere and that fear of the U.S.A. was a deterrent to the Japanese" would be undermined by evidence of how badly Japanese intentions and capabilities were misread, despite available signals intelligence: "The methods of our Intelligence Services are and should remain secret. Any inquiry into the Malayan Campaign must include discussion of the methods of gaining information, and this might, as has occurred in the Pearl Harbor inquiry, prove very embarrassing." Reinforcement questions would point to the central direction of the war: "Particular criticism is likely to be directed at the decision to send the PRINCE OF WALES and the REPULSE to the Far East and involve an undesirable examination of personal relationships between the Admiralty, the Chiefs of Staff and the Prime Minister." Theatre commanders warned over and over again how badly they needed reinforcements. Failure to provide them could only be related to overall shortages and priorities in grand strategy. Raising those issues would mean "there is no part of our war strategy or our manpower and production policy, either during or previous to the war, which might not come under examination." London approved both the air plan and MATADOR. That would raise the following points:

> That our plans were inflexible and were based on the presence of forces that were not expected until a much later date;
>
> That operation *Matador* was based on the assumption of a warning period which, in fact, was unlikely to be obtained.

"The main reason for the lack of flexibility in planning" pointed squarely to Churchill and GHQ Far East: "... the misjudgement of the timing of the Japanese attack and the complacent attitude which this engendered." Tactics and training "were generally inadequate" despite the fact effective methods were "worked out by some units before the war"; the evidence would suggest "the higher command failed to adopt them and gave an inadequate lead on tactical doctrine." As for equipment, "the land forces were not properly equipped for the type of warfare that ensued" and the air forces "had aircraft inferior to the Japanese and were not adequately equipped for anti-shipping operations which was to be their main role." There were so many allegations about a collapse in morale that "public discussion of these accusations which could not be completely refuted might well have the most grave repercussions throughout the British Commonwealth, the Far East, and indeed the whole world." When an enquiry reached the last battle, it would reveal "Singapore could not fulfil its purpose as a naval base if Southern Malaya was in the hands of an enemy," so "the Island relied on the defences of the Malay peninsula for its landward defence." Not only could there be no detachment from broader strategy, fault would surely be found with "our command organization for combined Civil and Military defence." The impossible structure Brooke-Popham had to work in as C-in-C Far East would "bring to light the reasons for the many changes and involve discussion of the character and ability of the higher commanders concerned." To top it all off, studying civil-military relations "would almost certainly disclose, in addition to any military faults, facts to discredit the British Colonial administration in Malaya and by implication possibly that in other parts of the Colonial Empire."[28]

This confession identified the problems analyzed by scholars ever since. By endorsing the air plan and MATADOR but insisting Malaya Command hold the naval base, the central direction of the war clung to the "Singapore strategy" after circumstances made it positively dangerous. This compromised the men on the spot. This was not a new confession. The same day 11th Indian Division was shattered at Slim River, senior staff in the WO submitted a brief for Attlee to answer questions in Parliament about the situation in the Far East. They admitted the government accepted the air plan, ordered Percival to hold the naval base, and endorsed his strategy to retreat step by step in the north. Percival never saw that brief, nor the JPS reports in spring 1946–and no wonder. They made it clear there was nothing he could do to prevent defeat– and no cause which helped turn defeat into disaster that could be blamed solely on problems on the spot.[29] In these early postwar years the British Empire was transforming itself. Its future as a great power was at stake. It could not afford to wash this dirty laundry in public because the worst stain was indelible. The military system for defending the British Empire focused on preserving British political authority first and foremost. Its credibility rested not just on British power but also on British judgement. Those who made the main decisions would not compromise this authority even if the only way to preserve it was to pursue dubious strategic plans. They rationalized this by insisting the threat from an Asian power was not serious enough to make this reckless. Disaster in Singapore exposed their judgement as unprofessional– over two decades and nine governments. This story could not be told in full.

The Eastern Fleet, RAF Far East and Malaya Command were outgeneralled and outfought from start to finish. The failure of the "poor bloody infantry" to hold the line and buy their superiors time to improvise was the direct reason defeat became disaster. Defeat was comprehensive but also to a large degree self-inflicted. The list of mistakes and misjudgements is long. How could GHQ Far East assume in autumn 1941 it had all the time it needed to prepare for war? Why did Brooke-Popham dither when he knew The Ledge was vital? How could anyone assume Buffalos flown by inexperienced pilots could match Japanese fighters? Why did Phillips not break radio silence when discovered at sea? The airbase evacuations were disgraceful. Jitra was humiliating. Slim River was a fiasco. Muar was a farce. Percival's decision not to challenge his mission forced him to condemn his army to being defeated piecemeal–and he knew this. A retreat psychosis did set in. Leadership declined alarmingly. Lay's conduct at Gurun and in Johore was malfeasance. 53rd Brigade's performance in Johore was feeble. The way different national contingents in Malaya Command lost confidence in each other because they were different was fatal. But these problems were driven by more profound forces and can not be understood apart from them.

Slim River may serve to illustrate the whole. British reluctance to spend money on defence before the war is the most common cause veterans singled out to explain disaster in Malaya and Singapore. It was not irrelevant to 11th Indian Division's predicament at Slim River. The Empire's armed forces were overstretched and underequipped because public opinion did not want to provide the resources they needed to shoulder the burdens placed on them– and governments did not want to challenge the nation to reconsider. They preferred to try to make bricks without straw. Richmond's warning was not ignored nor misunderstood–but the considered judgement was that it could not be applied. The more the British government insisted all would be well, the deeper the hole it dug for everyone. When the crisis exploded in 1940, it made another judgement call: not to admit the "Singapore strategy" was now obsolete, but brazen on regardless. The "Singapore strategy," air plan and MATADOR compromised the army from the start. The Japanese "driving charge" put it on the spot before the central direction could do anything to respond. This all brought two tired brigades to the wrong position on the wrong day. But British public opinion and government policy were not directly responsible for the fact the Empire's armies were not ready to fight a high tempo war of movement on land. The need to be ready to fight in three different continents, over a wide variety of terrain and climate, was a reason but not an excuse. The British Army was designed to fight set-piece battles at a tempo controlled by senior officers, in which firepower preserved and replaced manpower. Despite mechanization, tactical mobility was not emphasized. Slim River exposed the weakest of the Empire's military assumptions. If even the most innovative and best led brigade in Malaya Command could not respond effectively to changing conditions under pressure, disaster beckoned.

The great wave of defeats that exposed the weaknesses of the British Empire's prewar military system ran from Norway in spring 1940 to Burma in spring 1942. The only major defeat after that, the loss of Tobruk, stemmed from other causes. British Empire armed forces were already changing their way of war. Bolstered by more and better equipment, they produced more effective doctrine, training, tactics and techniques. One principal innovation is relevant to the fall of Singapore. The army adopted the system of battle drill to train for war on the ground. This combined the need to disseminate a coherent doctrine with the need to cultivate the habit of taking the initiative, to apply appropriate tactics to particular situations–problem solving, rather than forcing the situation to fit the plan. Such a sweeping change in behaviour came only after humiliation forced the military to reconsider its way of war.[30]

Disaster at Singapore has too often been attributed to British desperation. This is wrong. The deepest problem was British complacency. The national tradition was to overcome defeat, even debacle, and muddle through in the end. Somehow it would be alright on the day. The British public would not spend the money to provide enough power to guard the Empire in the Far East, as Jellicoe first proposed. But the British government would not admit that made it impossible to devise viable defence plans based on British power alone. If the crunch came, somehow the Empire would muddle through. Malaya Command's miserable performance in battle turned defeat into disaster. But it stemmed from the broader weaknesses of the military system– and judgements made by those who ran it. Wavell pushed the army into a main battle in Johore because his job was to hold the Malay Barrier. Percival fought in the north because his job was to hold the naval base. Churchill and his predecessors clung to the "Singapore strategy" because that was the price to obtain Dominion help for imperial defence elsewhere–and because liberties could be taken with an Asian enemy.

Postwar deflection of blame to the men on the spot and finger-pointing between nationalities put the systemic causes of disaster in the shadow. But they were always there to be seen. When Percival's despatch was published in February 1948, the *Manchester Guardian* came close to the crux. Without a battle fleet, with the air force hopelessly understrength, with the Japanese now on the doorstep, the only rational move in autumn 1941 was to:

> ... scrap the whole faded fabric of the earlier planning. The object of the Army should have been no longer to protect a naval dockyard that had no ships or to protect some scattered airfields that had no aircraft, but to prevent a Japanese invasion army from establishing and maintaining itself in Malaya. The method surely should have been to cut the force in Singapore to the barest minimum, plough up every airfield not in full use and properly defended, and regroup our forces into a compact field army.[31]

This was not done because it could only end in the loss of Singapore. The British government would never admit there was no realistic military strategy to hold Singapore and release the men on the spot to do the best they could. It was not willing to pay the necessary political price–until the Japanese forced it to. Different personalities would not have made a fundamental difference. Had Montgomery been sent to Singapore in spring 1941, he would have insisted on being allowed to fight his own battle his way, as Bond did–and been replaced, as Bond was. Malaya Command was comprehensively defeated because the assumption which justified both the "Singapore strategy" and Churchill's gamble was wrong: the Empire was not cohesive enough to pull together *after* trouble started. Singapore was really lost at the planning table. The politics of imperial defence made it impossible to base its defence on sound military principles.

Yet when all is said and done the most important outcome is the most ironic. The fall of Singapore was part of a world war and can only be seen as such. The Japanese were never going to survive the war they launched in December 1941. They found Singapore easy pickings because a window of opportunity gave them a strategic advantage in 1941. But they could only open that window by starting a war they were bound to lose. Constitutional states can survive and even learn from disasters. Authoritarian ones die from them.[32] Disaster in Singapore helped the British decide to walk away from their empire. The Japanese could only take Singapore by pursuing a national policy that destroyed theirs.

Maps

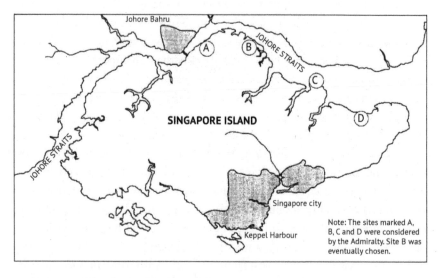

1 Singapore island naval base options.

2 Japanese invasions and advances, 8 December 1941.

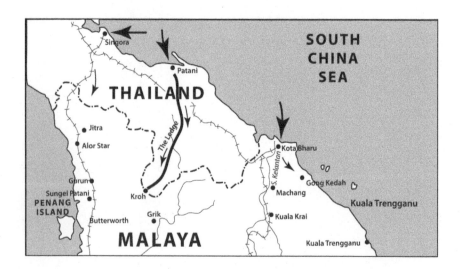

3 Southern Malaya.

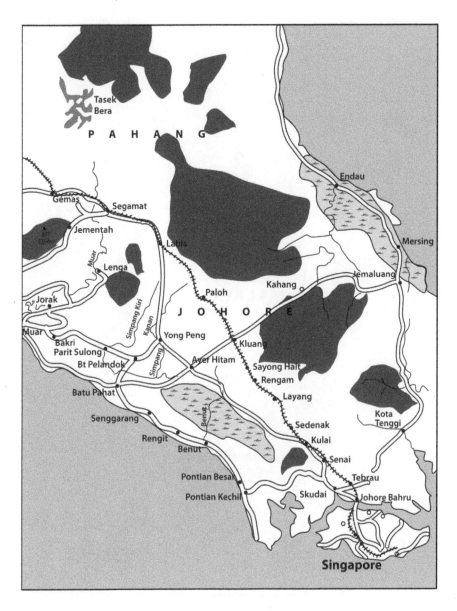

KEY

○   Airfields

╪╪╪   Railway

⎓   Main road

▮   High Ground

▭   Swamp

4 Malaya: topography and land use, 1941.

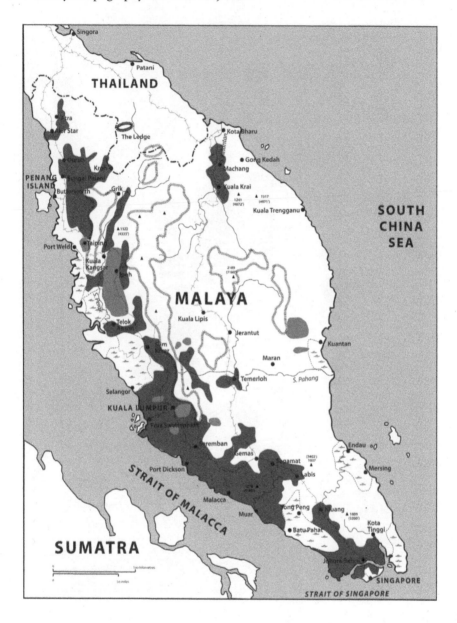

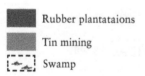

KEY

Rubber plantataions

Tin mining

Swamp

Land above 1,000 metres

Other areas are covered predominantly by jungle.

5 Malaya: location of British Empire forces, 8 December 1941.

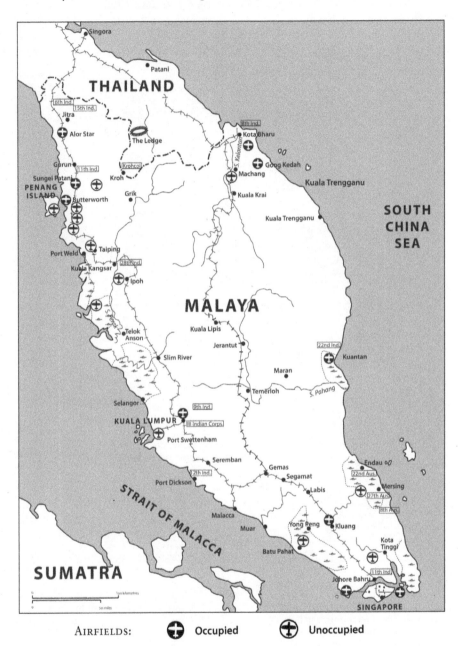

AIRFIELDS: ✠ Occupied   ✛ Unoccupied

MILITARY UNITS

6th Ind.	6th Indian Infantry Brigade	22nd Ind.	22nd Indian Infantry Brigade
8th Ind.	8th Indian Infantry Brigade	28th Ind.	28th Indian Infantry Brigade
9th Ind.	9th Indian Infantry Division	Krohcol	Krohcol battlegroup
11th Ind.	11th Indian Infantry Division	8th Aus.	8th Australian Infantry Division
12th Ind.	12th Indian Infantry Brigade	22nd Aus.	22nd Australian Infantry Brigade
15th Ind.	15th Indian Infantry Brigade	27th Aus.	27th Australian Infantry Brigade

6 (TOP) Singapore defences.
7 (BOTTOM) Japanese attack on Singapore, 8 February 1942.

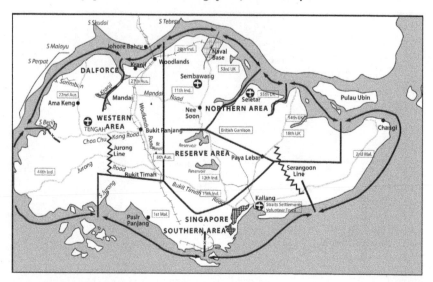

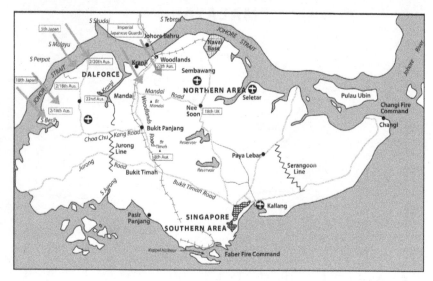

MILITARY UNITS

11th Ind. 11th Indian Infantry Division
12th Ind. 12th Indian Infantry Brigade
15th Ind. 15th Indian Infantry Brigade
28th Ind. 28th Indian Infantry Brigade
44th Ind. 44th Indian Infantry Brigade
1st Mal. 1st Malaya Brigade
2nd Mal. 2nd Malaya Brigade
18th UK 18th British Army Infantry Division
53rd UK 53rd British Army Infantry Brigade
54th UK 54th British Army Infantry Brigade
55th UK 55th British Army Infantry Brigade
Straits Settlements Volunteer Forces Brigade
8th Aus. 8th Australian Infantry Division

22nd Aus. 22nd Australian Infantry Brigade
27th Aus. 27th Australian Infantry Brigade
2/18th Aus. 2/18th Australian Infantry
Battalion
2/19th Aus. 2/19th Australian Infantry
Battalion
2/20th Aus. 2/20th Australian Infantry
Battalion
5th Japan 5th Japanese Army Infantry Division
18th Japan 18th Japanese Army Infantry
Division
Japanese Imperial Guards Division

Appendix One: Note on Sources

Any scholar working on the defence and fall of Singapore must accept a lower standard of evidence than military historians usually find comfortable. The national and racial tints to the controversy that still surrounds the story did some damage, but were not the main problem. The most reliable evidence for historians, their primary sources, are written records made at the time by those involved in the event. These include minutes of meetings, reports and plans, memoranda, telegrams, logs of telephone conversations, war diaries, personal diaries and letters. Generally, with some caveats, the closer to the moment the record was written the more seriously scholars take it. On the British Empire side, no such records were freely available to researchers before 1972. Only a handful of accounts escaped this serious impediment: the "official" histories. The "official" histories were written by scholars given privileged access to government records. But they were not allowed to cite them in the published volumes. Their work was subject to "vetting" by a committee of senior officers reporting to the government of the day. In the British case, Pownall sat on the committee that vetted Kirby's work, which reported to some of the same Cabinet Office officials involved in directing the war! And Kirby and Wigmore worked with two double edged swords. First, they were able to interview at length many of the officers involved in the campaign, but then grappled with serious criticism of their drafts from some of those same officers, especially Bennett and Percival. Second, they were able to pool their efforts–but then had to "adjust" their work to avoid doing too much damage to current relations between the British and Australians. The two volumes which appeared in 1957 were impressive, considering the constraints they faced–but Kirby himself underlined their limitations by publishing his own more critical account in 1971. The official history produced in 1960 in a rare moment of co-operation between India and Pakistan faced a bigger constraint. Bhargava and Sastri were treated like private scholars by the British government, which refused to allow them to consult records describing the higher direction of policy and war. As for memoirs, even the most honest and well connected author was constrained by a personal agenda and limited access to the necessary records. And on top of all this was a problem no memoirist or scholar could avoid. This campaign was unique in the Second World War for one reason: circumstances prevented both sides from preserving many of the most important contemporary records from which the story could be reconstructed.

In 1945 American bombing raids destroyed buildings in which the great bulk of the official records of the Japanese government, army and navy were held. This undermined any study of the Japanese experience in the Second World War, including prewar plans and diplomacy. From the 1960s Japanese scholars eventually produced an "official" history of the war, running to more than 100 volumes, by drawing on surviving records, interviews, and the same sources non-Japanese scholars later turned to: postmortems written by Japanese officers. For the Malayan campaign the following were the most important. From a number of accounts written during the war itself, only one rose above simple propaganda: Outline of the Malayan Campaign, produced by Twenty-Fifth Army in June 1942. It presented the rhetoric of an arrogant empire and the familiar romantic prose, but also produced some hard-headed analysis. Other useful sources were further removed in time, but produced as systematic appraisals of the event by principals involved at the time. Most important were the volumes in the extensive Japanese Monograph series, produced under the auspices of Allied intelligence during the postwar occupation of Japan. These are the only significant sources available in English, but, together with some strong translated Japanese work, they allow us to correct many points in previous accounts of the Japanese side of the story. Too many early scholars accepted uncritically the often serious exaggerations in Tsuji's 1960 memoir as their basis for "the other side of the hill." Critically reading the once-removed primary sources now available reduces that problem.

"Once-removed" primary sources are a daunting challenge for one important dimension of the British Empire side of the story: the campaign itself. By the late-1990s the release of the remaining surviving official records in the U.K. and Australia–those pertaining to special operations and intelligence were the last to emerge–closed most gaps in the primary sources regarding prewar problems. Those that remain are the result of records that did not survive, such as much detail regarding the activities of RAF Far East from 1936 to 1940. The problem becomes serious from 1941, at the level of sources most important for studying any military campaign: war diaries. In principle the system was clear. From an independent engineer company up to and including a theatre command, every unit was required to maintain and submit a diary of all its activities plus all communications going in and out. But in practice the quality of these diaries varied wildly. This in part reflected the British Army tradition of treating units as semi-independent organizations. Some army commanders cracked down on units which treated the diary as an annoyance, to which they assigned a junior officer to do the bare minimum. Others, including Percival, were less strict. Diaries were submitted monthly. The pre-December 1941 diaries of most Malaya Command units survived, with copies sent back to England or Australia. Unfortunately some were bare minimum records: "Trained" was a typical daily entry in such files. But the worst problem came after the war started. Some diaries were lost in battle, for instance at Slim River. Many, especially for January and February 1942, were not submitted to higher headquarters in time or not sent out of Singapore before the siege began. This forced Malaya Command to burn many records on 13 February, before the last evacuation. Its own diary for the month up to that point was taken to Ceylon by an evacuated officer. Despite their inconsistency, the war diaries are by far the most important source for studying how the army and air force prepared for and fought the campaign. Their destruction was much worse than retaining records before 1972 and 1992. It meant studies of the defence and fall of Singapore would always be forced to accept as primary sources records that military historians normally only use to cross-reference with those written at the time: reconstructed diaries and individual postmortems.

Montgomery wrote a lengthy despatch to describe his command of 21st Army Group in the campaign in Northwest Europe in 1944-45. Military historians see this despatch as a necessary but second tier source, coming well behind the war diaries of the army group and formations under its command as primary sources for studying that campaign. Historians studying its counterparts for the Malayan Campaign must make more allowances. Some despatches were written during the war, with memories fresh but not all records to hand: Bennett, Brooke-Popham, Layton, Wavell. Others were written on behalf of senior commanders who did not survive: Brooke-Popham and Layton for Phillips, Maltby for Pulford. The most important was published in February 1948 on the third anniversary of the surrender: Percival. Until the mid-1990s it was the most detailed record that even approached the definition of primary source available to private scholars and it remains important today. In the absence of many contemporary records that did not survive these postmortems must be given more weight than would normally be the case.

This is especially so for the most important category: formation and unit war diaries. Other than those for GHQ Far East and Malaya Command, many were in part or in full the product of long days in Changi and other POW camps. Sometimes a diary itself was rebuilt: for example 2/26 AIF. Sometimes a narrative history took its place: Harrison for 11th Indian Division, others for 18th Division, 44th Indian Brigade, etc. Sometimes both were produced: 8th

Australian Division headquarters and the long analysis produced by Thyer and Kappe. Written after the fact, these records add that drawback, plus the loss of written evidence, to the perennial problems of bias and selectivity. On the other hand they often add summary reflection and second thoughts. As a result it is frequently impossible to establish with final authority such details as exact timings, numbers, even dates, for unit activity, movement and action. But that does not prevent these "once removed" diaries from capturing the atmosphere and perceptions of the time and the thrust of events. Given that many were produced by serious collaboration between quite a few people involved, as close to the event as possible, they are nearly all more substantial than individual accounts or interviews produced even longer after the fact. They remain the closest we will ever come to conventional written primary sources for this campaign.

One final source is a type becoming more popular with military historians: the files of "official" historians given privileged access to contemporary records long before they were opened to the public. That access included personal contact with nearly all surviving principals, who naturally wanted their say in what would be widely seen–disclaimer aside–as the study of record. The longest and most detailed discussion anyone ever had regarding the defence and fall of Singapore was carried on for almost five years by Percival and Kirby. The interviews Kirby and Wigmore conducted with nearly every surviving senior Australian officer produced much that influenced their final volumes, for better or worse. The full extent of the damage Bennett did really only emerges in his exchanges with them. Both historians recognized Kappe's postmortem as an account they simply could not ignore. These records must of course be treated with caution. But no scholar wanting to understand the defence and fall of Singapore can pass them over, because circumstances made them the only systematic cataloguing of the memories of those who directed its defence that we will ever have.

Appendix Two – Orders of Battle

Some of the hardest questions to answer about the defence and fall of Singapore are also the most obvious. How big were the armies involved? How many troops, tanks and guns did they have? How many casualties did they inflict and suffer? The loss of so many primary sources was one source of confusion about numbers. Wartime exaggeration and the fog of war were two more. Incorrect intelligence, which many refused after the war to accept was wrong, was a fourth. Arguments over whether to count volunteer forces and units that did not engage were a fifth. It now appears the Japanese forces were nowhere near as large as Percival insisted they were, but larger than many scholars thought. On the other hand Malaya Command was not as large as scholars first declared it was. This appendix has two sections. Number One is the Order of Battle for both sides at their full strength on paper–a peak never reached on the ground at any one time by either side. Number Two outlines the casualties suffered by both sides.

Section One – Orders of Battle, full strength

JAPAN:

TWENTY-FIFTH ARMY 125,408 all ranks (33,005 in Lines of Communication units)

Army troops:
- two independent heavy artillery regiments plus mortar battalions
- one tank corps (three regiments)
- two independent engineer regiments plus ancillary troops

IMPERIAL GUARDS DIVISION 12,594 all ranks

Divisional troops:
- Guards Artillery Regiment
- 3rd, 4th and 5th Guards Regiments (only one battalion of 3rd Guards deployed in campaign)

5TH DIVISION 15,261 all ranks

Divisional troops:
- 5th Reconnaissance Regiment
- 5th Field Artillery Regiment
- 9th Brigade: 11th and 41st Regiments
- 21st Brigade: 21st and 42nd Regiments

18TH DIVISION 21,775 all ranks

Divisional troops:
- 18th Mountain Artillery Regiment
- 23rd Brigade: 55th and 56th Regiments
- 35th Brigade: 114th and 124th Regiments (brigade headquarters and 124th Regiment operated in Borneo only)

56TH DIVISION
(This division was left in reserve, then reassigned to Fifteenth Army in Burma)

The divisions that fought in Malaya and Singapore were affected by two army-wide reorganizations. From 1938 many formations were converted from a structure of two brigades each comprising two regiments to a triangle structure of three regiments. But the old structure was retained for two of the three formations Yamashita deployed, to allow them to form strong independent detachments to carry out certain missions–such as the assault on Kota Bharu and advance along the east coast. In 1940 the Imperial Guards and 5th Divisions, designated Order-16 formations, were converted from pack horses to full motorization. 18th Division remained an Army Order formation, still relying heavily on pack horses. This complicated Yamashita's supply problems, one reason he left 56th Division at home. In the end Twenty-Fifth Army committed barely enough infantry to carry out its ambitious mission; only nine and two-thirds of its 14 regiments actually fought in Malaya and Singapore. This is the source of the claim Yamashita was heavily outnumbered. But his army was a task force specifically equipped for the campaign it faced. The army tank regiments, boasting 228 medium and light tanks, were reinforced by scout regiments assigned to the three combat divisions, fielding 37 light tanks. The 330mm rockets of the army mortar battalions provided the final increment of firepower needed on Singapore island.

British Empire:

MALAYA COMMAND 130,246 all ranks

Army troops:
- 12th Indian Brigade: 2nd Argylls, 4/19 Hyderabadis, 5/2 Punjabis
- Miri (Borneo) Detachment: 2/15 Punjabi, plus engineer and ancillary troops
- 1 Independent Infantry Company
- 18th Light Tank Squadron
- 85th Anti-Tank Regiment
- six anti-aircraft regiments, plus engineer and ancillary troops
- Volunteer Forces: four battalions Straits Settlements Volunteer Forces, four battalions Federated Malay States Volunteer Forces, one infantry and one engineer battalion Johore Military Forces, Dalforce (16,000+all ranks)

III Indian Corps

Corps troops:
- 28th Indian Brigade: 2/1, 2/2 and 2/9 Gurkha Rifles
- 5/14 Punjabi (later brigaded)
- Indian State Forces: 1st Bahawalpur, 1st Hyderabad, 1st Mysore
- engineer, anti-aircraft and ancillary units

9th Indian Division

Division troops:
- 5th and 88th Field Artillery Regiments
- 8th Indian Brigade: 2/10 Baluch, 1/13 Frontier Force, 3/17 Dogra
- 22nd Indian Brigade: 5th Sikhs, 2/12 Frontier Force, 2/18 Royal Garwhals

11th Indian Division

Division troops:
- 3rd Cavalry, 22nd Mountain, 137th and 155th Field Artillery, 80th Anti-Tank
   Regiments
- 6th Indian Brigade: 2nd East Surreys, 1/8 and 2/16 Punjabis
- 15th Indian Brigade: 1st Leicesters, 2/9 Jats, 1/14 and 3/16 Punjabis

8th Australian Division

Division troops:
- 2/4 AIF (Machine Gun), 2/4 Anti-Tank, 2/10 and 2/15 Field Artillery Regiments
- engineer and ancillary troops
- 22nd Australian Brigade: 2/18, 2/19 and 2/20 AIF
- 27th Australian Brigade: 2/26, 2/29 and 2/30 AIF

18th Division

Division troops:
- 9th Northumberland Fusiliers (Machine Gun)
- 18th Battalion Reconnaissance Corps
- 125th Anti-Tank, 118th, 135th, and 148th Field Artillery Regiments
- 53rd Brigade: 5th and 6th Royal Norfolks, 2nd Cambs
- 54th Brigade: 4th Royal Norfolks, 4th and 5th Suffolks
- 55th Brigade: 5th Beds and Herts, 1/5 Sherwood Foresters, 1st Cambs

Singapore Fortress

Fortress Troops:
- 122nd Field Artillery Regiment
- Indian State Forces: Jind and Kapurthala Infantry

Coastal Defence units:
- 7th and 9th Coast Defence and 16th Defence Regiments RA, Singapore Volunteer
   RA and Malay Training Wing RA (all divided into Faber and Changi Fire
   Commands, under command HQ Fixed Defences)
- 1st Malaya Brigade: 1st and 2nd Malay, 2nd Loyals
- 2nd Malaya Brigade: 1st Manchesters (Machine Gun), 2nd Gordons, 2/17 Dogra

Independent Reinforcement Formations
- 44th Indian Brigade: 6/1, 7/8 and 6/14 Punjabis
- 45th Indian Brigade: 7/6 Rajputs, 4/9 Jats, 5/18 Royal Garwhalis

Section Two–Casualties and Losses

Japanese:

Malayan mainland–
Twenty-Fifth Army total   4565 (1793 killed, 2772 wounded)
Imperial Guards Division   900
5th Division   1987
18th Division   1100

Singapore Island–
Twenty Fifth Army total   5091 (1714 killed, 3378 wounded)
Imperial Guards Division   679
5th Division   1707
18th Division   2646

Grand totals–
Twenty Fifth Army total   9657 (3507 killed, 6150 wounded)
Imperial Guards Division   1579
5th Division   3694
18th Division   3646

British Empire:

Malaya Command total   7500-8000 killed

11,000+ wounded
120,000+ prisoners of war or missing

The many retreats on the mainland left behind large numbers of troops who could only be listed as missing–some of whom returned, some died, some were taken prisoner. Many Asian volunteers and regulars were released by the Japanese shortly after the capitulation. And many wounded men were also taken prisoner, and or succumbed to their wounds. The problem was compounded by the chaos that overwhelmed the army on Singapore island. Many units provided no returns at all. This all made it impossible to determine Malaya Command casualty numbers with any certainty. The numbers can therefore only be informed estimates. It appears that 8th Australian Division lost at least 3000 killed and wounded; two thirds of the former died on Singapore island. 18th Division lost some 2500 killed and wounded. While it is impossible to determine the total casualties suffered by III Indian Corps, they must have accounted for more than 60% of the overall total. War diaries, intelligence reports and personal papers remain the basic source for establishing orders of battle and casualties. The first accurate Japanese Order of Battle came into British hands in 1949: PRO, WO32/15539, Papers relating to Percival Despatch, May 1949. Important published sources include the official histories plus recent detailed summaries in Tohmatsu's article in Gow, Hirama and Chapman, The History of Anglo-Japanese Relations, and Appendix 2 in Warren, Singapore 1942.

Bibliography

Primary Sources – Archival

Australian War Memorial:
AWM52 series   War Diaries, 8th Australian Division and units
AWM54 series   Written Records, 1939-1945 War
AWM55 series   Allied Translator and Interpreter Service Records
AWM67 series   Official History, 1939-1945 War: Records of Gavin Long, General Editor
AWM73 series   Official History, 1939-1945 War: Records of Lionel Wigmore
AWM Miscellaneous series Records, 1939-1945 War

British Library
A.B. Cunningham Papers

Churchill College Archive Centre, Cambridge University, U.K.:
Hickleton Papers (Earl of Halifax)

Imperial War Museum, Dept. of Documents, U.K.:
Heath Papers
Percival Papers
Wards Papers
Wild Papers
Miscellaneous Files (Subject Heading Malaya and Singapore)

India Office Records, British Library:
L/Mil/17 series, Indian Army Records

Liddell Hart Centre for Military Archives, Kings College, London, U.K.:
Brooke Papers
Brooke-Popham Papers
Pownall Papers
Vlieland Papers
Wort Papers

National Archives of Canada:
Department of External Affairs Papers, RG25

Christchurch College Library, Oxford University, U.K.:
Portal Papers

Public Record Office, U.K. (now part of the National Archives, U.K.):
ADM1   Admiralty and Secretariat Files
ADM116   Cases of the Admiralty and Secretariat
ADM167   Board of Admiralty Minutes and Memoranda

ADM181	Navy Estimates
ADM199	War History Cases and Papers, Second World War
ADM205	First Sea Lord Files
AIR23	RAF Overseas Commands, Far East
CAB2	Committee of Imperial Defence Minutes
CAB4	Committee of Imperial Defence Memoranda, B Series
CAB5	Committee of Imperial Defence Memoranda
CAB8	Oversea Defence Committee Minutes
CAB16	Committee of Imperial Defence Ad-Hoc Subcommittee Files
CAB21	Cabinet Office Registered Files
CAB23	Cabinet Minutes, CC series, 1919-1939
CAB24	Cabinet Memoranda, 1919-1939
CAB27	Cabinet Miscellaneous Committee Records
CAB29	International Conferences Minutes and Papers 1916-1939
CAB32	Imperial Conference 1937 Minutes and Memoranda
CAB53	Chiefs of Staff Minutes and Memoranda 1923-1939
CAB63	Lord Hankey Papers
CAB65	War Cabinet Minutes 1939-1945
CAB66	War Cabinet Memoranda, WP and CP series, 1939-1945
CAB69	Defence Committee (Operations) Files 1940-1945
CAB70	Defence Committee (Supply) Files 1940-1945
CAB79	Chiefs of Staff Minutes 1939-1945
CAB80	Chiefs of Staff Memoranda 1939-1945
CAB84	Joint Planning Staff Memoranda 1939-1945
CAB94	Oversea Defence Committee Minutes and Papers 1939-1945
CAB99	Commonwealth and International Conferences 1939-1945
CAB104	Cabinet Office Supplmentary Registered Files
CAB106	Cabinet Office Historical Section Files
CAB119	Joint Planning Staff Files
CAB120	Minister of Defence Secretariat Files 1940-1945
CAB122	Joint Staff Mission Washington Office Records 1940-1945
CAB128	Cabinet Minutes 1945 and on
CO980	Malayan Research Bureau Reports 1943-1944
DEFE5	Chiefs of Staff Memoranda 1945 and on
DO35	Dominions Office Original Correspondence
FO371	Foreign Office General Correspondence, Political
HS1	Special Operations Executive Far East Registered Files
PREM3	Prime Minister's Office Correspondence and Papers 1940-1945
T172	Chancellor of the Exchequer: Miscellaneous Papers
WO32	War Office Registered Files (General Series)
WO33	War Office Committees: Reports and Papers
WO106	Directorate of Military Operations and Intelligence
WO172	War Diaries 1939-1945: GHQ Far East, Malaya Command and units
WO208	Directorate of Military Intelligence
WO268	Quarterly Historical Reports, Far East Land Forces, 1945- 1948

U.S. Army Center for Military History, Japanese Monograph Series:
No. 24   History of the Southern Army 1941-1945
No. 54   Malaya Operations Record November 1941-March 1942
No. 55   Southwest Area Air Operations Record Phase I

No. 102 Submarine Operations December 1941-April 1942
No. 107 Malaya Invasion Naval Operations (Revised Edition)
No. 146 Political Strategy Prior to the Outbreak of War, Part II
No. 147 Political Strategy Prior to the Outbreak of War, Part III
No. 150 Political Strategy Prior to the Outbreak of War, Part IV
No. 152 Political Strategy Prior to the Outbreak of War, Part V

Primary Sources – Miscellaneous

J. Barnes, D. Nicholson (eds.). The Empire at Bay: The Leopold Amery Diaries 1929-1945. London. Hutchinson. 1988.

Cabinet Office, U.K. Principal War Telegrams and Memoranda 1940-1943, vols. 1-7.Nendeln, Lichtenstein. KTO Press. 1976.

Command Paper 2083.Correspondence with the Self-Governing Dominions and India regarding the development of Singapore Naval Base. House of Commons Parliamentary Paper, 25 March 1924.

Major H.S. Flower diary and history of 9th Northumberland Fusiliers, Singapore island, February 1942, unpublished.

W.J. Hudson, H.J.W. Stokes (eds.). Documents on Australian Foreign Policy 1937-49.Vols. IV-V. July 1940-June 1942. Canberra. Australian Government Publishing Service.1980-82.

H. Kenway and H.J.W. Stokes, P.G. Edwards (eds.). Documents on Australian Foreign Policy 1937-49. Vol. III. January-June 1940. Canberra. Australian Government Publishing Service. 1979.

W.F. Kimball (ed.). Churchill and Roosevelt: The Complete Correspondence, vols. 1-3. Princeton.University Press. 1984.

T. Kitching. Life and Death in Changi: The War and Internment Diary of Thomas Kitching 1942-1944 (edited by Goh Eck Kheng). Singapore. Landmark Books. 2002.

W.N. Medlicott et al (eds.). Documents on British Foreign Policy 1919-1939. Second Series. Volume X. Far Eastern Affairs, March-October 1932. London. HMSO.

R.G. Neale (ed.). Documents on Australian Foreign Policy 1937-49. Vols. I-II. 1937-39. Canberra.Australian Government Publishing Service.1975-76.

Nobutaka Ike (ed.). Japan's Decision for War: Records of the 1941 Policy Conferences. Stanford. University Press. 1967.

Lt.-Gen. A.E. Percival.Operations of Malaya Command from 8 December 1941 to 15 February 1942. London Gazette, February 1948.

E. Robertson. The Japanese File: Prewar Japanese Penetration in Southeast Asia. Singapore. Heinemann Asia. 1979.

M. Simpson (ed.). The Somerville Papers.Aldershot.Navy Records Society.1995.

Singapore Command and Staff College Library.The Outline of the Malayan Campaign.Compiled by Twenty-Fifth Army HQ, 30 June 1942.

Department of State.Foreign Relations of the United States, 1937-40. Washington, D.C., USGPO, 1954-59.

N. Tracy (ed.). The Collective Naval Defence of the Empire, 1900-1940. London. The Navy Records Society. 1997.

Memoirs

H.G. Bennett. Why Singapore Fell. Sydney. Angus and Robertson Ltd. 1944.

F. Bloom. Dear Phillip. London. The Bodley Head. 1980.

R. Braddon. The Naked Island. Victoria. Penguin Books Australia.1993(1951).

A. Bryant. The Turn of the Tide. New York. Doubleday. 1957.

F.S. Chapman. The Jungle is Neutral. London. Chatto&Windus. 1963.

W.S. Churchill, W.S. The Second World War.6 vols. Boston.Houghton Mifflin.1948-53.

G. Chippington. Singapore: The Inexcusable Betrayal. United Kingdom. Self Publishing Association Ltd. 1992.

J.B. Crasta. Eaten by the Japanese: The Memoir of an Unknown Indian Prisoner of War. Singapore. SNP Editions Pte.Ltd. 1999.

P.V. Dean. Singapore Samurai. New South Wales. Kangaroo Press. 1998.

Foong C.H. The Price of Peace: True Accounts of the Japanese Occupation. Singapore. Asiapac. 1997.

Fujiwara Iwaichi. F. Kikan. Japanese Army Intelligence Operations in Southeast Asia during World War II. Singapore. Heinemann Asia. 1983.

O.D. Gallagher. Retreat in the East. London. G.G. Harrap. 1942.

C. Huxtable. From the Somme to Singapore: A Medical Officer in Two World Wars. New South Wales. Kangaroo Press. 1995 (1987).

H.L. Ismay. Memoirs. London. Heinemann. 1960.

D.H. James. The Rise and Fall of the Japanese Empire. London. Allen & Unwin Ltd. 1951.

Maj.-Gen. Sir J. Kennedy.The Business of War. London. Hutchinson. 1957.

Lee Kip Lee.Amber Sands: A Boyhood Memoir. Singapore. Federal Publications. 1995.

Lee Kuan Yew. The Singapore Story: Memoirs of Lee Kuan Yew. Singapore. Times Editions Pte.Ltd. 1998.

G. Mant. The Singapore Surrender. Kuala Lumpur. S. Abudl Majeed & Co. 1992(reprint).

J. McEwan. Out of the Depths of Hell: A Soldier's Story of Life and Death in Japanese Hands.Yorkshire. Leo Cooper. 1999.

I. Morrison. Malayan Postscript. London. Faber and Faber Limited. 1942.

P.G. Pancheri. Volunteer! The Story of One Man's War in the East. Singapore. P.G. Pancheri. 1995.

G. Patterson. A Spoonful of Rice with Salt. Durham. The Pentland Press Ltd. 1993.

A.E. Percival. The War in Malaya. London. Eyre &Spottiswoode. 1949.

G. Rocker. Escaped Singapore Heading Homewards. Singapore. Graham Brash. 1990.

D. Russell-Roberts. Spotlight on Singapore. United Kingdom. Times Press and Anthony Gibbs & Phillips Ltd. 1965.

H. Siddhu. The Bamboo Fortress: True Singapore War Stories. Singapore. Native Publications.1991.

I. Simson. Singapore: too little, too late. Some Aspects of the Malayan Disaster in 1942. London. Leo Cooper. 1970.

A. Tedder. With Prejudice. London. Cassell. 1966.

Tsuji Masanobu. Singapore: The Japanese Version. Sydney. Ure Smith. 1960.

T.H. Wade. Prisoner of the Japanese: From Changi to Tokyo. New South Wales. Kangaroo Press. 1994.

A.H.C. Ward et al (eds.). The Memoirs of Tan Kah Kee. Singapore. University

Press. 1994.

J. Wyett. Staff Wallah: At the Fall of Singapore. New South Wales. Allen and
    Unwin. 1996.

Secondary Sources – Official Histories

K.D. Bhargava, K.N.V. Sastri. Campaigns in South-East Asia 1941-42. (Official
    History of the Indian Armed Forces in the Second World War 1939-45).
    India. Combined Inter-Services Historical Section India & Pakistan. 1960.

J.R.M. Butler. Grand Strategy. Vol. II. 1939-May 1941.(History of the Second
    World War, United Kingdom Military Series). London. HMSO. 1957.

N. Gibbs. Grand Strategy. Vol. I. Rearmament Policy.(History of the Second
    World War, United Kingdom Military Series). London. HMSO. 1976.

G.H. Gill. Royal Australian Navy 1939-1942. Canberra. Australian War
    Memorial. 1957.

J.M.A. Gwyer. Grand Strategy. Vol. III. Part I. June 1941-August 1942 (History
    of the Second World War, United Kingdom Military Series). London. HMSO.
    1964.

P. Hasluck. The Government and the People 1939-1941. Canberra. Australian
    War Memorial. 1952.

S.W. Kirby. The War Against Japan. Vol. 1.The Loss of Singapore.(History of the
    Second World War, United Kingdom Military Series). London. HMSO. 1957.

M. Matloff, E.M. Snell. Strategic Planning for Coalition Warfare 1941-42.
    Washington. USGPO. 1953.

S.W. Roskill. The War at Sea 1939-1945. Vol. 1.The Defensive.(History of the
    Second World War, United Kingdom Military Series). London. HMSO. 1954.

L. Wigmore. The Japanese Thrust. (Vol. IV, Series One, Army. Australia in the
    War of 1939-1945). Canberra. Australian War Memorial. 1957.

Secondary Sources – Unit Histories

2/19 Battalion AIF Association.The Grim Glory of the 2/19th Battalion AIF.
    Sydney. 1975.

Lt.-Cmndr. A.C. Bell.History of the Manchester Regiment First and Second
    Battalions 1922-1948.Altrincham, U.K. John Sherratt and Son. 1954.

R.W. Christie (ed.). A History of the 2/29th Battalion–8th Australian Division
    AIF. Victoria. High Country Publishing.1991 (Second Edition).

N. Haron. The Malay Regiment 1933-1955. [unpublished thesis] 1987.

W.R. Magarry. The Battalion Story: 2/26th Infantry Battalion, 8th Australian
    Division, AIF. Queensland. Privately published. 1994.

J. Moffatt, A.H. McCormick. Moon Over Malaya: A Tale of Argylls and
    Marines. Stroud.Tempus. 2002.

M. Moore. Battalion at War, Singapore 1942. Norfolk. Gliddon Books. 1988.

A.W. Penfold, W.C. Bayliss, K.E. Crispin. Galleghan's Greyhounds: The Story of
    the 2/30th Australian Infantry Battalion. Sydney. 2/30th Bn. AIF Association,
    1979 (1949).

D. Ramli. History of the Malay Regiment 1933-1942. Singapore. Donald Moore.

1955.

I.M. Stewart. History of the Argyll and Sutherland Highlanders 2nd Battalion: The Malayan Campaign 1941-42. London. Nelson. 1947.

D. Wall. Singapore and Beyond: The Story of the 2/20 Battalion as told by the Survivors. East Hills.2/20 Battalion Association. 1985.

Secondary Sources – Articles, Biographies, Monographs, Surveys

Akira Iriye. The Origins of the Second World War in Asia and the Pacific. London. Longman. 1987.

R.J. Aldrich. Intelligence and the War Against Japan: Britain, America and the Politics of Secret Service. Cambridge. University Press. 2000.

E.R. Alfred. "The Famous Wrong Way Guns of Singapore. Where are they now?" in The Pointer, 12, 1, 1985.

L. Allen. Singapore 1941-1942. United Kingdom. Frank Cass and Co. Ltd. 1993 (1977).

E.M. Andrews. The Writing on the Wall: The British Commonwealth and Aggression in the East 1931-1935. Sydney. Allen & Unwin. 1987.

S. Arneil. Black Jack: The Life and Times of Brigadier Sir Frederick Galleghan. Melbourne. Macmillan. 1983.

Ban K.C. Absent History: The Untold Story of Special Branch Operations in Singapore 1915-1942.Raffles. Singapore. 2001.

N. Barber. Sinister Twilight: The Fall of Singapore. London. Arrow Books Limited. 1988 (1968).

C. Barnett. The Collapse of British Power. Gloucester. Alan Sutton. 1984 (1972).

C. Barnett. Engage the Enemy More Closely: The Royal Navy in the Second World War. New York. W.W. Norton and Company. 1991.

W.G. Beasley. Japanese Imperialism 1894-1945. Oxford. University Press. 1987.

C. Bell. The Royal Navy, Seapower and Strategy Between the Wars.Stanford University Press. Stanford. 2000.

R.J. Bell. Unequal Relations: Australian-American Relations and the Pacific War. Melbourne. University Press. 1977.

C. Bridge, B. Attard (eds.). Between Empire and Nation: Australia's External Relations 1901-39. Melbourne. Scholarly Press. 1998.

A. Bryant. Turn of the Tide. London. Doubleday. 1957.

K. Caffrey. Out in the Midday Sun: Singapore 1941-1945. London. Deutsch. 1974.

R. Callahan. The Worst Disaster: The Fall of Singapore. London. Associated University Presses. 1977.

R.Cheong. The Singapore Naval Base: A Local History. Singapore. The Pointer Supplement. 1991.

M. Clisby. Guilty or Innocent?The Gordon Bennett Case. Sydney. Allen & Unwin. 1992.

J. Connell. Wavell: Supreme Commander 1941-1943. London. Collins. 1969.

R. Connolly, B. Wilson. Cruel Britannia: Britannia Waives the Rules 1941-42. Singapore Betrayed, Australia Abandoned. New South Wales, Australia. Privately published. 1994.

I. Cowman. "Main Fleet to Singapore? Churchill, the Admiralty and Force Z," in The Journal of Strategic Studies, 17, 2, 1994.

I. Cowman. Dominion or Decline: Anglo-American Naval Relations in the Pacific 1937-1941. Oxford. Berg. 1996.

J. Crawford (ed.). Kia Kaha: New Zealand in the Second World War. Auckland. Oxford University Press. 2002.

C. Cruickshank. SOE in the Far East. Oxford. University Press. 1983.

R. Dallek. Franklin D. Roosevelt and American Foreign Policy 1932-1945. New York. Oxford University Press. 1979.

D. Day. The Great Betrayal: Britain, Australia and the Onset of the Pacific War 1939-42. New York. W.W. Norton. 1989.

J.W. Dower. War Without Mercy: Race and Power in the Pacific War. New York. Pantheon Books. 1986.

R.B. Edgerton.Warriors of the Rising Sun. New York. Norton. 1997.

P. Elphick, M. Smith. Odd Man Out: The Story of the Singapore Traitor. United Kingdom. Coronet Books. 1993.

P. Elphick. Singapore: The Pregnable Fortress. A Study in Deception, Discord and Desertion. London. Hodder & Stoughton. 1995.

P. Elphick. Far Eastern File: The Intelligence War in the Far East, 1930-1945. London. Hodder & Stoughton. 1997.

S. Falk. Seventy Days to Singapore: The Malayan Campaign 1941-1942. London. Robert Hale. 1975.

B.P. Farrell. "Yes Prime Minister: Barbarossa, Whipcord, and the basis of British Grand Strategy, Autumn 1941," in The Journal of Military History, 57, 4, 1993.

B.P. Farrell. The Basis and Making of British Grand Strategy 1940-1943: Was There a Plan? Lewiston, N.Y. The Edwin Mellen Press. 1998.

B.P. Farrell, S. Hunter (eds.). Sixty Years On: The Fall of Singapore Revisited. Singapore. Eastern Universities Press. 2002.

B.P. Farrell (ed.). Leadership and Responsibility in the Second World War: Essays in Honour of Robert Vogel. Montreal. McGill-Queens University Press. 2004.

J.R. Ferris. Men, Money and Diplomacy: the evolution of British Strategic Policy 1919-1926, Ithaca. Cornell University Press. 1989.

J.R. Ferris. "'The Greatest Power on Earth': Great Britain in the 1920s," in The International History Review. XIII, #4, 1991.

J.R. Ferris. "Worthy of Some Better Enemy: The British Estimate of the Imperial Japanese Army 1919-1941 and the Fall of Singapore," in Canadian Journal of History, XXVIII, August, 1993.

D. Fraser. And We Shall Shock Them: The British Army in the Second World War. London. Hodder and Stoughton Ltd. 1983.

H.P. Frei. Japan's Southward Advance and Australia: From the Sixteenth Century to World War II. Melbourne. University Press. 1991.

H.P. Frei. Guns of February. Singapore. University Press. 2004.

D. French. Raising Churchill's Army: The British Army and the War Against Germany 1919-1945. Oxford. University Press. 2000.

M. Gilbert. Winston Churchill. Vol. V. 1922-1939. London. Heinemann. 1976.

M. Gilbert. Winston Churchill. Vol. VI.1939-1941. London.Heinemann. 1983.

A. Gilchrist. Malaya 1941: The Fall of a Fighting Empire. London. Robert Hale. 1992.

R. Gough. Special Operations Singapore 1941-42. Singapore. Heinemann Asia. 1985.

I. Gow, Y. Hirama, J. Chapman (eds.). The History of Anglo-Japanese Relations 1600-2000. Vol. III: The Military Dimension. Basingstoke. Macmillan. 2003.

J. Grey. A Military History of Australia. Melbourne. Cambridge University Press.1999 (1990).

P. Haggie. Britannia at Bay: The Defence of the British Empire Against Japan 1931-1941. Oxford. Clarendon Press. 1981.

T. Hall. The Fall of Singapore. Sydney. Methuen Australia. 1983.

I. Hamill. The Strategic Illusion: The Singapore Strategy and the Defence of Australia and New Zealand 1919-1942. Singapore. University Press. 1981.

M. and S. Harries. Soldiers of the Sun: The Rise and Fall of the Imperial Japanese Army. New York. Random House. 1991.

A.D. Harvey. Collision of Empires: Britain in Three World Wars 1793-1945. London. Phoenix. 1992.

J.B. Hattendorf and R.S. Jordan (eds.). Maritime Strategy and the Balance of Power. London. Macmillan. 1989.

W. Heinrichs. Threshold of War: Franklin D. Roosevelt and American Entry into World War II. Oxford. University Press. 1988.

R. Holmes, A. Kemp. The Bitter End.Chichester.Antony Bird Publications Ltd. 1982.

D.M. Horner. High Command: Australia and Allied Strategy 1939-1945. Sydney. George Allen and Unwin. 1982.

R. Hough. The Hunting of Force Z. London.Collins. 1963.

E.P. Hoyt. Three Military Leaders: Togo, Yamamoto, Yamashita. New York. Kodansha America Inc. 1993.

B.D. Hunt. Sailor-Scholar: Admiral Sir Herbert Richmond 1871-1946. Waterloo. Wilfrid Laurier University Press. 1982.

IenagaSaburo. The Pacific War 1931-1945. New York. Random House.1978 (1968).

L. James. The Rise and Fall of the British Empire. New York. St. Martin's Press. 1994.

Janes Editors.Janes Aircraft of World War II.Janes. Glasgow. 1995.

J. Keegan (ed.). Churchill's Generals. New York. Grove Weidenfeld. 1991.

G. Kennedy, K. Neilson (eds.). Far Flung Lines: Essays on Imperial Defence in Honour of Donald Mackenzie Schurman. London. Frank Cass and Co. 1997.

J. Kennedy. British Civilians and the Japanese War in Malaya and Singapore 1941-45. London. MacMillan Press. 1987.

P. Kennedy. The Realities Behind Diplomacy. London. Routledge.1983 (1981).

A.S. Kenworthy.The Tiger of Malaya: The Story of General Tomoyuki Yamashita and "Death March" General Masaharu Homma. New York. Exposition Press. 1953.

W.F. Kimball. The Juggler: Franklin Roosevelt as Wartime Statesman. Princeton. University Press. 1991.

C. Kinvig. Scapegoat: General Percival of Singapore. London. Brassey's. 1996.

S.W. Kirby. Singapore: The Chain of Disaster. London. Cassell. 1971.

P. Kratoska (ed.). Malaya and Singapore during the Japanese Occupation. Singapore. University Press. 1995.

P. Kratoska. The Japanese Occupation of Malaya: A Social and Economic History. Sydney. Allen & Unwin. 1998.

J. Leasor. Singapore: The Battle that Changed the World. Garden City, N.Y. Doubleday. 1968.

J.C. Lebra. Japanese-Trained Armies in Southeast Asia: Independence and Volunteer Forces in World War II.Hong Kong.Heinemann Educational Books. 1977.

C. Lee. Sunset of the Raj: Fall of Singapore. London. Pentland Press. 1994.

R. Lewin. The Chief: Field Marshal Lord Wavell. London. ?????. 1980.

A.B. Lodge. The Fall of General Gordon Bennett. North Sydney. Allen & Unwin Australia. 1986.

Low N.I. When Singapore was Syonan-To. Kuala Lumpur. Eastern Universities Press. 1973.

P. Lowe. Great Britain and the Origins of the Pacific War in East Asia 1937-1941. Oxford. Clarendon Press. 1977.

C. Mackenzie. Eastern Epic.Vol. 1, September 1939-March 1943.Defence. London. Chatto and Windus. 1951.

G. Mant. Massacre at ParitSulong. New South Wales. Kangaroo Press. 1995.

A.J. Marder. Old Friends, New Enemies: The Royal Navy and the Imperial Japanese Navy. Vol. 1, Strategic Illusions 1936-1941. Oxford. Clarendon Press. 1981.

D. Marquand. Ramsay MacDonald. London. Jonathan Cape. 1977.

J. McCarthy. Australia and Imperial Defence 1918-39: A Study in Air and Sea Power. St. Lucia. University of Queensland Press. 1976.

F. McDonough. Neville Chamberlain, Appeasement, and the British Road to War. New York.Manchester University Press. 1998.

I. McGibbon. Blue Water Rationale: The Naval Defence of New Zealand 1914-1942. Wellington. P.D. Hasselberg. 1981.

W.D. McIntyre. The Rise and Fall of the Singapore Naval Base 1919-1942. London. MacMillan Press Ltd. 1979.

B.J.C. McKercher (ed.). Arms Limitation and Disarmament: Restraints on War 1899-1939. Westport, CT. Praeger. 1992.

W.N. Medlicott. British Foreign Policy Since Versailles. London. Methuen. 1968.

M. Middlebrook, P. Mahoney. Battleship: The loss of the Prince of Wales & the Repulse. London. Penguin. 1979.

B. Montgomery. Shenton of Singapore: Governor and Prisoner of War. Singapore. Times Books International. 1984.

M.H. Murfett. Fool-Proof Relations: The Search for Anglo-American Naval Cooperation During the Chamberlain Years 1937-1940. Singapore. University Press. 1984.

M.H. Murfett. "Living in the Past: A Critical Re-examination of the Singapore Naval Strategy 1918-1941," in War and Society, II, I, 1993.

M.H. Murfett (ed.). The First Sea Lords: From Fisher to Mountbatten. Westport, CT. Praeger. 1995.

M.H. Murfett, J.N. Miksic, B.P. Farrell, Chiang M.S. Between Two Oceans: A Military History of Singapore From First Settlement to Final British Withdrawal. Singapore. Oxford University Press. 1999.

J. Neidpath.The Singapore Naval Base and the Defence of Britain's Eastern Empire 1918-1941. Oxford. Clarendon Press. 1981.

I. Nish. Alliance in Decline: A Study of Anglo-Japanese Relations 1908-1923. London. The Athlone Press. 1972.

D. Omissi. The Sepoy and the Raj: The Indian Army 1860-1940. London. Palgrave Macmillan. 1994.

Ong C.C. "Major General William Dobbie and the Defence of Malaya 1935-1938," in Journal of Southeast Asian Studies, XVII, #2, September 1986.

Ong C.C. The Landward Defence of Singapore 1919-1938. Singapore. Heinemann Asia. 1988.

Ong C.C. Operation Matador: Britain's War Plans against the Japanese 1918-1941. Singapore. Times Academic Press. 1997.

F. Owen. The Fall of Singapore. London. Joseph. 1960.

D.K. Palit. The Campaign in Malaya. Uttar Pradesh. Palit and Dutt.1971 (1959).

H.N. Pandit. NetajiSubhas Chandra Bose. New Delhi. Sterling Publishers. 1988.

R.A.C. Parker. Chamberlain and Appeasement: British Policy and the Coming of the Second World War. London. Macmillan. 1993.

C.N. Parkinson. Britain in the Far East: The Singapore Naval Base. Singapore. Donald Moore. 1955.

T.H. Place. Military Training in the British Army 1940-1944. London. Frank Cass. 2000.

J.D. Potter. The Life and Death of a Japanese General. New York. Signet Books. 1962.

H. Probert. The History of Changi. Singapore. Prison Industries in Changi. 1970.

H. Probert. The Forgotten Air Force: The Royal Air Force in the War against Japan 1941-1945. London. Brassey's. 1995.

E.B. Reynolds. Thailand and Japan's Southern Advance1940-1945. New York. St Martins Press. 1994.

J. Robertson. Australia at War 1939-1945. Melbourne. William Heinemann. 1981.

A.O. Robinson. "The Malayan Campaign in the Light of the Principles of War," in Journal of the Royal United Services Institution, CIX, August and November 1964.

S.W. Roskill. Naval Policy Between the Wars. Vols. 1-2. London. Collins.1968, 1976.

S.W. Roskill. Hankey: Man of Secrets. Vols. 1-2. London. Harper Collins.1972, 1974.

M. Shennan. Out in the Midday Sun: The British in Malaya 1880-1960. London. John Murray. 2000.

C. Shores et al. Bloody Shambles. Vol. 1. The Drift to War to the Fall of Singapore. London. Grub Street. 1992.

M. Smith. The Emperor's Codes: Bletchley Park and the Breaking of Japan's Secret Ciphers. London. Bantam Press. 2000.

J. Smyth. Percival and the Tragedy of Singapore. London. Macdonald. 1971.

C.P. Stacey. Canada and the Age of Conflict.vol. 2. Toronto. Macmillan. 1981.

R. Storry. Japan and the Decline of the West in Asia 1894-1943. London. Longman. 1979.

Lord Strabolgi. Singapore and After: A Study of the Pacific Campaign. London. Hutchinson. 1942.

A. Swinson. Defeat in Malaya: The Fall of Singapore. London. Ballantine Books. 1969.

N. Tarling. Britain, Southeast Asia and the Onset of the Pacific War. Cambridge. University Press. 1996.

C. Thorne. Allies of a Kind: The United States, Britain, and the War Against Japan, 1941-1945. London. Oxford University Press.1996 (1978).

I. Trenowden. Operations Most Secret–SOE: The Malayan Theatre. London. William Kimber. 1978.

C.M. Turnbull. A History of Singapore 1819-1988. Singapore. Oxford University Press. 1989.

H.P. Willmott. Empires in the Balance: Japanese and Allied Pacific Strategies to April 1942. Annapolis. Naval Institute Press. 1982.

J. Uhr. Against the Sun: The AIF in Malaya 1941-42. Sydney. Allen Unwin. 1998.

I. Ward. The Killer They Called a God. Singapore. Media Masters. 1992.

I. Ward. Snaring the Other Tiger. Singapore. Media Masters. 1996.

D.C. Watt.How War Came. London. Heinemann. 1989.

H.L. Wigglesworth. The Japanese Invasion of Kelantan in 1941.Kota Bharu. 1991.

Yap S.R etal.Fortress Singapore: The Battlefield Guide. Singapore. Times Books International.1995 (1992).

Yong C.F., R.B. McKenna. The Kuomintang Movement in British Malaya 1912-1949. Singapore. University Press. 1990.

Yong C.F. Chinese Leadership and Power in Colonial Singapore. Singapore. Times Academic Press. 1992.

List of Photos and Maps

Photos

Abbreviations:

Author: Author's personal collection

IWM: Imperial War Museum

MS: Mainichi Shimbun

1–Floating dock, Sembawang naval base, Singapore (IWM)

2–Marco Polo bridge, northern China, 1937 (IWM)

3–HMS *Ladybird* after Japanese attack, December 1937 (IWM)

4–Sembawang naval base construction, September 1941 (IWM)

5–Air Chief Marshal Sir Robert Brooke-Popham and staff (IWM)

6–Major-General Sir William Dobbie (IWM)

7–Maj.-Gen. L.V. Bond reviews AIF in Malaya, ANZAC Day 1941 (IWM)

8–Air Marshal Sir J.T. Babington (IWM)

9–Field Marshal Sir John Dill (IWM)

10–Seaforth Highlanders evacuate Shanghai, 25 March 1940 (IWM)

11–European civilians evacuated from Penang, December 1941 (IWM)

12–Asian civilian refugees, Malaya (IWM)

13–Lieutenant-General Arthur Percival (back right) with Air Vice-Marshal C.W.H. Pulford (front) (IWM)

14– Lieutenant-General Yamashita Tomoyuki (IWM)

15–Fifteen-inch coastal gun, Singapore (IWM)

16–Wavell inspects Singapore coastal guns, November 1941 (IWM)

17–Maj.-Generals Bennett and D.M. Murray-Lyon (IWM)

18–Indian mountain gunners training amongst rubber trees (IWM)

19–Argyll and Sutherland Highlanders training in close country (IWM)

20–Labourers in Singapore making gas masks (IWM)
21–Japanese "knee mortar" grenade launcher, Type 89 (IWM)
22– Japanese collapsible assault boat, Model 95 A (IWM)
23–Two Model 95 boats combined to form 27' landing craft (IWM)
24–Japanese medium machine gun crew in the field (IWM)
25–Japanese troops with "infantry gun" in the field (IWM)
26–New Zealand squadron celebrates a rare aerial "kill" (IWM)
27–Japanese infantry board landing craft off Kota Bharu, 8 December 1941(MS)
28–Japanese medium tank being floated across river, China (IWM)
29–HMS *Prince of Wales* leaves Singapore, 8 December 1941 (IWM)
30–Japanese 'infantry guns' moving through jungle, Malaya (MS)
31–Admiral Sir W. Tennant (IWM)
32–Stocks of petrol captured by the Japanese, Malaya, December 1941 (MS)
33–Force Z survivors being rescued, 10 December 1941 (IWM)
34– Japanese tanks advancing along road, Malaya (MS)
35–Old road loops near 12th Indian Brigade position, Trolak (Author)
36–Captured British vehicles, Malaya, January 1942 (MS)
37–Field Marshal Earl Wavell and General Sir Henry Pownall (IWM)
38–Civilians in one of the few public air raid shelters in Singapore (IWM)
39–Japanese infantry storm into Johore Bahru, for once too late (IWM)
40–Percival and party arrive at Bukit Timah for surrender negotations (IWM)
41–Yamashita and Percival discuss surrender (IWM)
42–Japanese victory parade, Fullerton Square Singapore, 17 February
    1942 (IWM)

Maps

1 Singapore island naval base options.
2 Japanese invasions and advances, 8 December 1941.
3 Southern Malaya.
4 Malaya: topography and land use, 1941.
5 Malaya: location of British Empire forces, 8 December 1941.
6 Singapore defences.
7 Japanese attack on Singapore, 8 February 1942.

Updated maps based on originals in Coates, John *An Atlas of Australia's Wars*. Melbourne: Oxford University Press, Second Edition, 2006 and Farrell, Brian P. *The Defence and Fall of Singapore* 1940-1942. Stroud: Tempus, First Edition, 2005.

Index